P9-DUH-603

THE DEVELOPMENT OF THE AMERICAN PRESIDENCY

A full understanding of the institution of the American presidency requires us to examine how it developed from the founding to the present. This developmental lens, analyzing how historical turns have shaped the modern institution, allows for a richer, more nuanced understanding. *The Development of the American Presidency* pays great attention to that historical weight but is organized by the topics and concepts relevant to political science, with the constitutional origins and political development of the presidency its central focus. Through comprehensive and in-depth coverage, Richard Ellis looks at how the presidency has evolved in relation to the public, to Congress, to the executive branch, and to the law, showing at every step how different aspects of the presidency have followed distinct trajectories of change. Each chapter promotes active learning, beginning with a narrative account of some illustrative puzzle that brings to life a central concept. A wealth of photos, figures, and tables allow for the visual presentations of concepts.

New to the Third Edition

- Analysis of the 2016 election, including the role of the Electoral College and implications of Trump's nomination for the "party decides" thesis;
- Exploration of Trump's Twitter presidency and the effectiveness of using social media to bypass the Washington press corps;
- In-depth coverage of the development of twentieth-century president–press relations, including a new section on broadcasting the presidency that explores the development of the presidential press conference and presidents' use of radio and television;
- Study of national security policy in the Obama administration, with a special focus on the targeted killing of American citizens and Obama's legacy for presidential war powers;
- Examination of the original understanding and contemporary relevance of impeachment as well as updated discussion of the president's pardon power;
- Discussion of recent developments in the legislative and legal realms, including Trump's first hundred days, the Garland–Gorsuch episode, and abolition of the filibuster for Supreme Court appointments;
- Preliminary assessment of Trump's place in historical time.

Richard J. Ellis is the Mark O. Hatfield Professor of Politics at Willamette University. He has been awarded Oregon Teacher of the Year from the Carnegie Foundation for the Advancement of Teaching, as well as numerous other awards for both scholarship and teaching. He is the author or editor of more than fifteen books, including *Judging Executive Power: Sixteen Supreme Court Cases That Have Shaped the American Presidency*; *Debating the Presidency: Conflicting Perspectives on the American Executive*; and *Presidential Travel: The Journey from George Washington to George W. Bush*.

THE DEVELOPMENT OF THE AMERICAN PRESIDENCY

THIRD EDITION

RICHARD J. ELLIS

Routledge
Taylor & Francis Group

NEW YORK AND LONDON

Published 2018
by Routledge
711 Third Avenue, New York, NY 10017

and by Routledge
2 Park Square, Milton Park, Abingdon, Oxon, OX14 4RN

Routledge is an imprint of the Taylor & Francis Group, an informa business

© 2018 Taylor & Francis

The right of Richard J. Ellis to be identified as author of this work has been
asserted by them in accordance with sections 77 and 78 of the Copyright,
Designs and Patents Act 1988.

All rights reserved. No part of this book may be reprinted or reproduced or
utilised in any form or by any electronic, mechanical, or other means, now
known or hereafter invented, including photocopying and recording, or in
any information storage or retrieval system, without permission in writing
from the publishers.

Trademark notice: Product or corporate names may be trademarks or
registered trademarks, and are used only for identification and explanation
without intent to infringe.

First edition published by Routledge 2012
Second edition published by Routledge 2015

Library of Congress Cataloging in Publication Data
Names: Ellis, Richard (Richard J.), author.
Title: The development of the American presidency/Richard J. Ellis,
Willamette University.
Description: Third Edition. | New York: Routledge, 2018. | "First edition
published by Routledge 2012"–T.p. verso. | "Second edition published by
Routledge 2015"–T.p. verso. | Includes index.
Identifiers: LCCN 2017038454 | ISBN 9781138039230 (hardback) |
ISBN 9781138039247 (paperback) | ISBN 9781315176048 (ebook)
Subjects: LCSH: Presidents–United States.
Classification: LCC JK516.E55 2018 | DDC 352.230973–dc23
LC record available at https://lccn.loc.gov/2017038454

ISBN: 978-1-138-03923-0 (hbk)
ISBN: 978-1-138-03924-7 (pbk)
ISBN: 978-1-315-17604-8 (ebk)

Typeset in Minion and Stone Sans
by Sunrise Setting Ltd, Brixham, UK

Printed in Canada

For Juli

BRIEF CONTENTS

FULL CONTENTS

PREFACE

Every president takes the same constitutionally prescribed oath of office. They all swear to faithfully execute the office of President of the United States and, to the best of their ability, preserve, protect, and defend the Constitution. But every president brings wildly different abilities to the office and vastly different understandings of what counts as faithfully executing the office. Indeed, presidential history seems awash in differences: different experiences, different temperaments, different management styles, different rhetorical strategies, different goals, and different challenges. The immense importance for the nation and the world of what political scientist Fred Greenstein labels "the presidential difference" has been vividly underscored since Donald Trump took the presidential reins from Barack Obama.

"...and will to the best of my ability, which is terrific ability,
by the way. Everyone agrees, I have fantastic ability. So there's
no problem with my ability, believe me...."

Courtesy: Paul Noth for the *New Yorker*.

What use is a book about presidential history if every president is so radically different, every context so exquisitely unique? It's all very well to invoke that familiar adage, "those who forget history are destined to repeat it," but what about that other time-tested aphorism, "generals are always fighting the last war"? How can both proverbs be right when they teach such contrary messages? The former tells us to hoard history's hard-earned experiences; the latter commands us to discard the outdated lessons of the past and to think anew. So which is it? How are we to know whether or when the past is a useful guide to thinking clearly about the present?

When it comes to the study of the presidency, many political scientists would answer this question by distinguishing between traditional and modern presidencies, with the dividing line usually placed at the presidency of Franklin Delano Roosevelt. In this interpretation, there is not a great deal to be gained from close investigation of pre-modern presidents because the demands placed upon them and the resources at their disposal were radically different from the expectations and opportunities for leadership in the modern presidency. Presidents of the late eighteenth, the nineteenth, and the early twentieth centuries are therefore largely of antiquarian interest, best left to historians.

This book adopts a different view. It pays a great deal of attention to presidents of the late eighteenth, the nineteenth, and the early twentieth centuries. This is not because I have any doubt about the immense differences between the presidency of today and the presidency of the early republic. Whereas before there was a lone secretary, for instance, now a staff of hundreds helps the president to manage the bureaucracy, negotiate with Congress, and communicate with the American people. Far from denying such changes, this book is dedicated to tracing how and when they occurred and assessing their significance for the US political system.

The tremendous differences between the nineteenth-century presidency and the twenty-first-century presidency do not, however, mean that comparisons across time are not possible or fruitful. No nineteenth-century president had access to Twitter, for instance, but the responses to the supposedly "unpresidential" tweets of Donald Trump arguably have their closest historical analogue in the reactions to Andrew Johnson's "undignified" rhetoric in his infamous Swing around the Circle in 1866 (see Chapter 3). And today's hyper-partisan media environment is in many ways closer to that of the mid-nineteenth century than the mid-twentieth-century media environment. The presidential N is sufficiently small already that we should be reluctant to cast aside the experiences of three-quarters of the presidents who have held the office.

Still, there is no denying that the dichotomy between traditional and modern presidencies is a useful shorthand for aspects of presidential development. However, it also distorts the past by slighting the changes in presidential roles and responsibilities that have occurred *throughout* American history. Granted, the presidency of the mid-twentieth century looked little like the presidency of the early twentieth century. But so, too, the presidency at the turn of the twentieth century differed dramatically from the presidency of the mid-nineteenth century. We do well to remember that what we label the traditional presidency was once the modern presidency. The past was once present.

By the same token, the present will soon be past. The tradition/modernity dichotomy lulls us into a false sense that meaningful change ceases once the traditional presidency matures into the modern presidency. The presidency today is as unlike the so-called modern presidency of 1960 as the modern presidency was unlike the allegedly traditional presidency of 1900. Unable to deny the import of the changes of the past half-century, some scholars now speak of a post-modern presidency, but there is little agreement about what defines the post-modern presidency or when it began.

To divide the past into traditional and modern presidencies also obscures that different aspects of the presidency have changed at different rates and at different times. In recounting the development of presidential staff, it may make sense to see FDR's presidency as a pivotal turning point in the creation of a modern presidency (see Chapter 7). But if one is mapping the development of presidential communications with the public, recognizably modern patterns and practices took shape many decades earlier (see Chapter 3). In organizing the developmental account topically, this book accents the ways in which different aspects of the presidency have followed distinct trajectories of change.

The problem with the sharp dichotomy between traditional and modern presidencies is not merely that it oversimplifies the complex, messy evolution that has characterized presidential development. After all, any organizing construct must simplify reality in order to make it comprehensible. The more fundamental mistake is the assumption that prior to the emergence of the modern presidency, American presidents were, with a few notable exceptions, passive and inconsequential, more like glorified clerks than political leaders. This is the view advanced in the most influential book ever written on the presidency, Richard Neustadt's 1960 classic *Presidential Power*. I take my bearings instead from another great political scientist, Henry Jones Ford. Writing in 1898, during the presidency of William McKinley, Ford noted that "The agency of the presidential office has been such a master force in shaping public policy that to give a detailed account of it would be equivalent to writing the political history of the United States." My contention is that Ford is a better guide to American history than Neustadt—that presidents have long been a driving (and disruptive) force in American political life.

There is another, related reason to be wary of the tradition/modernity division, with or without the post-modern coda: namely, that it slights important continuities in the presidential office, especially those institutional characteristics and political incentives that are rooted in the Constitution. Whereas Neustadt dismissed the "literary theory of the Constitution" as largely irrelevant to understanding the "probabilities of power" in the modern presidency, I begin from the premise that the institutional relationships established by the Constitution, and political arguments about the Constitution, remain central to understanding the contemporary presidency. That is why so many chapters in this book begin with the decisions and arguments of the framers of the Constitution.

Starting with a careful examination of the constitutional framing and the early history of the presidency is important, too, because it enables us to critically assess many contemporary claims about presidential authority. Too often presidents and their apologists ransack the past with little appreciation for historical context. Chapter 10 begins with a paradigmatic instance: Richard Nixon's 1977 televised interview with David Frost, in which he invoked Lincoln's words—words written in a letter explaining why Lincoln had enlisted black men in the fight against slavery—to justify burglary and other illegal acts. Other chapters in the book interrogate sweeping claims that have recently been made about the commander-in-chief clause (see Chapter 5), the so-called unitary executive (Chapter 8), and the pardon power (Chapter 10). This book is written in the firm conviction that close attention to the full scope of presidential history is vital if we are to inoculate ourselves against extravagant and erroneous readings of the meaning of the Constitution and early presidential precedents.

An understanding of presidential history serves another important civic function of providing a more realistic sense of what presidents can be expected to achieve. A mythologized past often gets in the way of more measured evaluation of the achievements and limitations of our current presidents. For instance, as we will see in Chapter 4, many of those on the left who criticized Barack Obama for failing to be bold like the great FDR had little or no understanding of how Roosevelt actually governed, the compromises he was compelled to make, and the political context that made his achievements possible. Similarly, placing unilateral presidential directives in historical perspective, as we do in Chapter 6, enables us to more soberly evaluate controversies over Obama's executive orders and George W. Bush's signing statements. By teaching about past presidents, in sum, political scientists can help citizens and students more realistically evaluate current presidents (see Chapter 11).

I do not claim to have written the first contemporary textbook to take seriously the origins and development of the American presidency. In 1990, Sid Milkis and Mike Nelson published their pioneering text on the history of the American presidency, which they subtitled "Origins and Development." Currently in its eighth edition, it has superbly educated both teachers and students about the importance of presidential history for more than a quarter-century. If their book has been so successful, why is there a need for another text focused on presidential history?

That is precisely the question I put to Routledge's then acquisition editor Michael Kerns when he first proposed such a book to me. Michael's answer was simple: political scientists typically organize their presidency courses topically—presidential elections (second chapter), the president and the public (third chapter), congressional relations (fourth chapter), and so on—and that made Milkis and Nelson's chronologically organized volume an awkward fit for most classes. And while there were several excellent topically organized texts, they paid scant attention to the Constitution and even less to the first 150 years of presidential development. Teachers and students of the presidency needed a text that was attuned to the full story of the development and origins of the presidency but that organized that story topically rather than chronologically. This is that book.

If Michael deserves credit for the idea, I shoulder responsibility for its execution. Fortunately, I had a lot of help along the way. Michael's encouragement helped to guide me through the early stages of the project's formulation, and development editor Nicole Solano prodded me to bear in mind the differences between a textbook and an academic book. Dylan Sheldon helped me to pare down the text for the second edition, and another outstanding Willamette student, Andrew Wakelee, did the same for this new third edition. In revising this edition, I have also benefitted from the sage counsel and generous support of Michael's successor at Routledge, Jennifer Knerr. I am grateful, too, to the reviewers who were commissioned for this edition—Ryan J. Barilleaux,

Miami University; Terri Bimes, University of California-Berkeley; Jasmine Farrier, University of Louisville; John Woolley, University of California-Santa Barbara; Graham G. Dodds, Concordia University; and Julia Azari, Marquette University—as well as many others for the previous editions. Their incisive and challenging comments helped to spur many an improvement, while their appreciative comments helped to buoy my spirits. Most of all I am thankful to all those who have assigned the book in their classes. They are the ones who truly made this third edition possible.

Richard J. Ellis

CHAPTER 1

ENVISIONING THE PRESIDENCY

No one can definitively say who the first British prime minister was, but every American school boy and girl knows that George Washington was the first president of the United States. Unlike the office of prime minister, which emerged gradually during the eighteenth century, the presidency was invented during a few months in the summer of 1787 by those whom we are fond of calling our "founding fathers." Prior to that moment, there was no American presidency; indeed, the new nation had no national chief executive of any sort.[1]

THE REVOLUTIONARY EXPERIENCE

The colonists' revolt against British rule had engendered not only a deep antipathy to monarchy but a suspicion of all executive power. In the state constitutions written in 1776 and 1777, Americans systematically emasculated their governors. Governors typically served one-year terms, were selected by the legislature, and possessed little power. At the national level, the Articles of Confederation made no provision at all for an executive branch of government, let alone a chief magistrate. Such limited powers as the national government had under the Articles were vested entirely in the Continental Congress. At first, Congress attempted to carry out administrative and executive functions through legislative committees, but dissatisfaction with this arrangement led Congress to set up several executive departments: foreign affairs, finance, war, and marine. The establishment of executive departments improved the day-to-day administration of the nation's affairs, but the executive branch remained an appendage of the legislature. Congress appointed and dismissed department heads, and issued detailed directives whenever it saw fit. Congress was the boss, the executive branch the hired help.

The concentration of power in the federal legislature was at odds with Americans' professed attachment to the separation of powers. Four state constitutions drafted in 1776 and 1777 provided that the legislative, executive, and judiciary departments "shall be separate and distinct, so that neither exercises the powers properly belonging to the other." Many Americans believed that placing all powers in the same branch of government was the very definition of tyranny. So how did revolutionary Americans resolve this conflict between their rhetorical adherence to separation of powers and the institutional reality of legislative supremacy?[2]

This famous painting from 1940 depicts the signing of the Constitution on September 17, 1787. Standing bolt upright on the dais is the man every convention delegate believed would be the first president of the new United States: George Washington. Off to Washington's left, chin in hand, is Pennsylvania's James Wilson, the convention's most vocal and influential champion of a strong presidency. James Madison is seated at the base of the dais, the crumpled papers on his desk a reminder of the invaluable notes he kept of the convention debates. Seated to Madison's right is the 81-year-old Benjamin Franklin, who, despite his centrality in the painting, had little influence on the convention's deliberations. Appearing to whisper in Franklin's ear is Alexander Hamilton.

Courtesy: Getty Images.

Part of the answer is that the federal government under the Articles of Confederation was weak. Having denied the central government the powers to tax or coerce the states, few Americans worried about it becoming tyrannical, even if all its powers were vested in the legislature. But the more important answer is that when revolutionary-era Americans invoked the separation of powers, as historian Gordon Wood has pointed out, they were "primarily thinking of insulating the judiciary and particularly the legislature from executive manipulation." The main threat to liberty, in the eyes of Americans, came from the executive using its influence to corrupt members of the legislature by "appointing them to executive or judicial posts, or by offering them opportunities for profits through the dispensing of government contracts and public money, thereby buying their support for the government." Separation of powers in 1776 was thus invoked primarily as a means of constraining what was perceived to be the most dangerous part of government: the executive.[3]

After 1776, experience at both the state and federal level began to modify Americans' single-minded dread of executive power. Executive power was still to be feared but so too, many Americans were learning, was unchecked legislative power. In *Notes on the State of Virginia*, Thomas Jefferson, having just completed two frustrating years (1779–81) as Virginia's governor, observed that in that state, "all the powers of government, legislative, executive, and judiciary, result to the legislative body." Although the state's constitution paid lip service to the separation of powers, Jefferson noted that in practice the judiciary and executive members were dependent on the legislature "for their subsistence in office, and some of them for their continuance in it." As a result, neither the executive nor the judiciary was capable of resisting legislative encroachment. The legislature, Jefferson lamented, "decided rights" that should have been left to the judiciary, and made a habit of directing the executive branch on every possible detail. It now seemed clear to Jefferson that "173 despots [could] be as oppressive as one."[4]

At the federal level, the absence of separation of powers taught a different lesson. There, the failure to institutionalize independent branches of government drew criticism not for creating a tyrannical government but for fostering a feeble one. Writing to a friend late in the summer of 1787, as the delegates at the federal Constitutional Convention in Philadelphia were nearing the end of their labors, Jefferson expressed his conviction that it was essential "to separate . . . the Executive and Legislative powers," the want of which had "been the source of more evil than we have experienced from any other cause." The problem, in Jefferson's view, was that by becoming absorbed in "executive details," the federal Congress's attention had been diverted from "great to small objects," which made it appear "as if we had no federal head." Even for Jefferson, then, the separation of powers was understood as a means to strengthen, not merely restrain power.[5]

For those Americans who sought to replace the Articles of Confederation with a new federal constitution, the separation of powers played a pivotal rhetorical role. There was no denying that the Articles of Confederation violated the ideal of separation of powers, and few Americans were willing to defend the status quo by repudiating the ideal. Even those who distrusted Alexander Hamilton's vision of a powerful central government did not dispute Hamilton's contention that "confounding legislative and executive powers in a single body," as the Articles of Confederation had done, was "contrary to the most approved and well founded maxims of free government which require that the legislative executive and judicial authorities should be deposited in distinct and separate hands."[6]

As the Constitutional Convention began in May 1787, then, there was broad agreement among the delegates that a separate executive branch was necessary. But the convention's 55 delegates, representing 12 states, had very different ideas about what that branch should look like. They disagreed about basic things, like whether there should be one president or several co-presidents. They differed, too, on whether a chief executive should be required to seek the advice and consent of an executive council, as most state constitutions required the governor to do. They were uncertain whether the president should be selected by the legislature or elected by the people. Nor did they have fixed ideas about how long a president should serve, and whether he should be eligible for reelection. The delegates were equally uncertain about what powers should be vested in the president. Opinions ranged widely about whether the executive should be empowered to veto legislation, appoint judges, or draw up treaties.

THE FRAMERS' DOUBTS AND DISAGREEMENTS

Envisioning what an American presidency should look like and anticipating how it would work was extraordinarily difficult because the republican executive the delegates were trying to create was unlike anything the world had seen before. Europe knew only monarchies, and the Articles of Confederation, as we have already noted, had no chief executive. The myriad state constitutions provided many instructive models, but transposing state experiences onto a national scale was a formidable challenge, particularly when it came to foreign affairs. Although the delegates did their best to draw upon relevant experience, ultimately the creation of the presidency carried them into uncharted waters where they were forced to navigate by hunches, hopes, and fears.[7]

It is important not to succumb to an exaggerated reverence for the wisdom of the founding fathers. In praising their wisdom and prescience, we too often forget that even after their work was completed, they were still largely in the dark about how—or whether—the presidency would work. And in speaking of what "the founders" thought or intended, we are prone to lose sight of the multiplicity of intentions that went into creating the Constitution. A builder has a clear plan he follows in erecting a house, but different "framers" strove to build quite different executives. The presidency was a product of bargaining and compromise, not the reflection of a single design or purpose.[8]

The uncertainty and disagreements that vexed the framers' deliberations over executive power were confessed by Virginia governor Edmund Randolph at his state's ratifying convention. A delegate at the Constitutional Convention, Randolph had refused to sign the document in part because of his concerns about the new presidency. But between the close of the Constitutional Convention on September 17, 1787, and the start of the Virginia ratifying convention on June 2, 1788, Randolph reversed course and decided to support ratification of the Constitution. At the ratifying convention, he tried to explain his flip-flop. "Every gentleman," he said, "who has turned his thoughts to the subject of politics, and has considered the most eligible mode of republican government, agrees that the greatest difficulty arises from the executive—as to the time of his election, mode of his election, [and] quantum of power."[9]

At the Constitutional Convention, it was Randolph who introduced the Virginia Plan, which the delegates used as the starting point for their deliberations. On June 1, 1787, the delegates took up the plan's seventh resolution:

> that a National Executive be instituted; to be chosen by the National Legislature for a term of ____ years, to receive punctually at stated times, a fixed compensation for the services rendered, in which no increase or diminution shall be made so as to affect the Magistracy, existing at the time of increase or diminution, and to be ineligible a second time; and that besides a general authority to execute the National laws, it ought to enjoy the Executive rights vested in Congress by the Confederation.

The convention's starting point did not even stipulate that the executive should consist of a single person, because three of Virginia's seven delegates—Randolph as well as George Mason and John Blair—preferred a three-headed executive.[10]

The person who had done the most thinking about what was needed in a new constitution was Randolph's fellow Virginian, James Madison. His tenure in the Continental Congress during the early 1780s had convinced him of the need for a radical overhaul of American political institutions. Madison was appalled at the weakness of the federal government, which was dependent on the states for raising and provisioning armies. After leaving Congress in 1783 he turned his penetrating intellect and extraordinary diligence to remedying what he described as "the vices of the political system of the United States." He carried out an intense study of the history of confederacies and republics, ancient and modern, a task that was aided by two trunks full of books on history and politics that had been sent to him by Jefferson, who was stationed in Paris as minister to France.

Although Madison had thought long and hard about many of the political problems facing the new nation, he had given next to no thought to the appropriate scope and shape of executive power. Asked in 1785 for his suggestions on a constitution for Kentucky (which at the time was still part of Virginia), Madison confessed his uncertainty about executive power:

> I have made up no final opinion whether the first Magistrate should be chosen by the Legislature or the people at large or whether the power should be vested in one man assisted by a council or in a council of which the President shall be only primus inter pares. There are examples of each in the U. States and probably advantages and disadvantages attending each.

James Madison. Most of the iconic images of the "founding fathers" that we carry around in our heads are from portraits rendered a decade or more after the Constitutional Convention. As a result, we tend to forget how young many of the founding fathers were at the time the Constitution was written. This miniature was painted four years before the convention, in 1783, when James Madison was 32.
Courtesy: Getty Images.

Madison's ideas about the executive were still largely unformed two years later. Writing to George Washington only a few weeks before the opening of the Constitutional Convention, Madison acknowledged that "a national Executive must ... be provided" but admitted that he had "scarcely ventured as yet to form my own opinion either of the manner in which it ought to be constituted or of the authorities with which it ought to be cloathed."[11]

One delegate who did have definite views about executive power was Hamilton, but those views were not widely shared by others at the Constitutional Convention. Hamilton conceded as much on the convention's final day when he reminded his fellow delegates that "no man's ideas were more remote from the plan than his were known to be." The delegates were well aware of how distant Hamilton's own ideas were from the final Constitution because he had presented his vision to the convention three months earlier in a five-hour speech. Hamilton believed that if the delegates were to establish a strong government, they had to relinquish or at least relax republican principles. When it came to executive power, Hamilton believed that "the English model was the only good one." The British system worked, in Hamilton's view, because "the hereditary interest of the King was so interwoven with that of the Nation, and his personal emoluments so great, that he was placed above the danger of being corrupted from abroad—and at the same time was both sufficiently independent and sufficiently controlled to answer the purpose of the institution at home." Because a hereditary monarch was anathema to republicanism, Hamilton proposed instead an elected chief executive who would serve "during good behaviour," that is, for life unless he did something egregiously corrupt.[12]

When he came to write his justly famous *Federalist* essays on the presidency (numbers 68 through 77), Hamilton suppressed his misgivings. The aim of the *Federalist* papers, after all, was to persuade the American people to ratify the new Constitution, not to sow seeds of doubt. Rather than tout "the English model," Hamilton stressed (in *Federalist* No. 69) the many ways in which the American president was totally unlike the king of Great Britain. The burden of Hamilton's ten *Federalist* essays on the presidency was to persuade the American people that the framers had got the question of executive power just right. Privately, however, Hamilton worried that the framers of the Constitution had made the president much too weak.

Other leading supporters of the Constitution also harbored private doubts about this new presidency. Writing from Paris in November 1787, Jefferson inquired of his friend John Adams: "How do you like our new constitution?" The Virginian confessed that he found "things in it which stagger all my dispositions to subscribe to what such an assembly has proposed." No part of the new government disturbed Jefferson more than the presidency, which seemed "a bad edition of a Polish king." Jefferson complained:

> He may be reelected from 4 years to 4 years for life. Reason and experience prove to us that a chief magistrate, so continuable, is an officer for life. When one or two generations shall have proved that this is an officer for life, it becomes on every succession worthy of intrigue, of bribery, of force, and even of foreign interference. ... Once in office, and possessing the military force of the union, without either the aid or check of a council, he would not be easily dethroned, even if the people could be induced to withdraw their votes from him.

Alexander Hamilton was even younger than Madison. At the time of the Constitutional Convention, he was 30. This miniature is one of the few portraits of Hamilton that is not rendered in a heroic style.

Courtesy: The Granger Collection, NYC—All rights reserved.

From Jefferson's point of view, the framers had created an office that could easily become a monarchy in all but name.[13]

Whereas Jefferson worried that the presidency was too powerful, Adams fretted that the president would prove too weak. "You are afraid of the one—I, of the few," Adams wrote back to Jefferson. "You are apprehensive of Monarchy; I, of Aristocracy." Adams would have preferred that more power be given to the president and less to the Senate. Responding to Jefferson's fear that the president would be reelected as long as he lives, Adams was blunt: "So much the better as it appears to me." Turnover in the presidency, Adams feared, would not only weaken the office but make it an object of "foreign Influence." Adams felt a sense of "terror" in contemplating an elected chief executive. "Experiments of this kind have been so often tried, and so universally found productive of Horrors, that there is great Reason to dread them," he told Jefferson.[14]

In short, the founders were anything but sanguine about the presidency. Publicly, in venues such as the *Federalist*, they worked tirelessly to assuage the public's anxieties and fears, but in private they expressed their own apprehensions about the presidency they had created. Some supporters of the Constitution, such as Jefferson and Randolph, feared that it harbored "the foetus of monarchy" and would endanger republican institutions. Others, like Adams and Hamilton, fretted that mixing executive power with republican principles would enfeeble executive power and engender discord and division that could tear apart society. The wildly different diagnoses offered by the Constitution's best and brightest defenders are a testament to the uncertainty that enveloped the making of the presidency.[15]

FOUR VISIONS OF THE PRESIDENCY

The founding generation's uncertainty and sharp disagreements about the presidency have not stopped Americans from believing that the Constitution contains a fixed meaning and reflects a unified vision. Not that Americans have agreed on the content of that meaning or vision. The rival interpretations can be divided into four main camps: (1) those who celebrate the Constitution for creating a powerful presidency; (2) those who criticize the Constitution for creating a too powerful presidency; (3) those who celebrate the Constitution for creating a carefully constrained presidency; and (4) those who criticize the Constitution for creating an overly constrained presidency. These four types, as Table 1.1 shows, are derived from two dimensions: (1) whether the Constitution is seen as a warrant for presidency-centered governance, and (2) whether presidency-centered government is seen as beneficial for the political system.[16]

The Potent Presidency

The argument that the Constitution created a potent presidency starts with the opening sentence of Article II of the Constitution: "The Executive Power shall be vested in a President of the United States of America." Partisans of the potent presidency contrast this sweeping language with the circumscribed wording of Article I: "All legislative Powers *herein granted* shall be vested in a Congress of the United States." Article II's opening sentence, on this reading, is far more than an affirmation that the executive shall consist of a single person with the title of president. Whereas Article I enumerates the special powers given to Congress, the "vesting clause" of Article II is said to endow the president with "inherent executive powers that are unenumerated in the Constitution." Among these are the powers to remove executive officials, to declare neutrality, to conduct foreign relations, and to deploy military force. Congress is therefore not to interfere with the president's exercise of executive powers or his control over the executive branch except where the Constitution explicitly allows for it—as, for instance, in the requirement that the Senate must approve ambassadors or treaties.[17]

TABLE 1.1 Four Visions of the Presidency

	Vision is supportive of strong presidency	Vision is suspicious of strong presidency
Constitution is seen as warrant for strong presidency	The potent presidency	The princely presidency
Constitution is seen as constraint on strong presidency	The progressive presidency	The perverted presidency

Proponents of a constitutionally potent presidency also find a grant of great power in Article II, section 3's command that the executive "shall take Care that the Laws be faithfully executed." Because the president is responsible for ensuring that subordinates faithfully execute the law, the president must be free to remove subordinates at will. Any statutory constraints on the president's power of removal are therefore unconstitutional because they prevent the president from carrying out his constitutional duty to ensure that the laws are faithfully executed.

The potent presidency thesis is premised upon the belief that the legislature was "the branch most feared by the Framers." According to this reading, the Constitution was fundamentally an attempt to check legislative power. In order to achieve this objective, the framers erected a strong and independent executive power that could resist the tendency for power to be sucked into what Madison described as "the Legislative vortex."[18]

A second assumption that underlies this thesis is that the framers, in the words of Terry Eastland, "designed and empowered the presidency so that it would provide the energy that the government under the Articles of Confederation lacked." The Constitution "equips and asks the President to be strong" not only to check legislative power but to create an effective national government. From this perspective, the touchstone text is Hamilton's *Federalist* No. 70, specifically his insistence that "Energy in the executive is a leading character in the definition of good government." According to Hamilton, an energetic executive is not only "essential to the protection of the community against foreign attacks" but is equally vital "to the steady administration of the laws; to the protection of property against those irregular and high-handed combinations which sometimes interrupt the ordinary course of justice; [and] to the security of liberty against the enterprises and assaults of ambition, of faction, and of anarchy."[19]

This interpretation of the framing of Article II has a distinguished pedigree in American history, but in its contemporary form it is rooted in the reaction of conservative Republicans to a "resurgent Congress." As then vice president Dick Cheney explained in a 2003 interview, "For the [past] 35 years ... there's been a constant, steady erosion of the prerogatives and powers of the president of the United States." Cheney could point to a spate of laws passed by Congress in the 1970s that had been designed to rein in the use and abuse of executive power during the Vietnam War and Watergate. These laws included the Case Act of 1972 (regulating executive agreements); the War Powers Resolution of 1973 (requiring congressional consent for the deployment of military forces abroad); the Congressional Budget and Impoundment Control Act of 1974 (restricting executive discretion to refuse to spend appropriated monies); the Hughes–Ryan amendment to the Foreign Assistance Act of 1974 (requiring presidential reporting to Congress of covert actions); the Foreign Intelligence Surveillance Act of 1978 (regulating national security surveillance); and the Ethics in Government Act of 1978 (imposing restrictions on the conduct of government officials and providing for an independent counsel). In the eyes of Cheney and his Republican allies, these statutes were not only misguided but unconstitutional. A weak or hamstrung presidency was inconsistent with the framers' original intent, and therefore defending presidential power required renewed fidelity to the text and purposes of the Constitution.[20]

During the 1980s, officials in the Reagan administration were especially intent on exerting presidential control over the vast federal bureaucracy. Lawyers in the administration developed what came to be known as the "unitary executive" doctrine. According to this teaching, the Constitution vested the executive power in the president and therefore the legislature could not interfere with the president's power to direct the actions of officials in the executive branch.

During the administration of President George W. Bush, particularly after the terrorist attacks of September 11, 2001, the argument of a constitutionally potent presidency was extended further. The president, according to leading figures in the Bush administration, had an inherent constitutional power to prosecute the war on terror and to keep the nation safe. The president, the administration argued, did not need Congress to authorize or sanction his actions because his power was rooted in the commander-in-chief clause of Article II, which states that "The President shall be Commander in Chief of the Army and Navy of the United States, and of the Militia of the several States, when called into the actual Service of the United States." The president, in the most ambitious constitutional readings of the Bush administration, had a "plenary"—that is, absolute— constitutional power to act unilaterally in the war on terror even if it meant not complying with laws passed by Congress.[21]

The hallmark of the potent presidency thesis, in sum, is that the Constitution endows the presidency with all the power necessary to defend the national interest and ensure that the laws are faithfully executed. The framers' teachings, from this perspective, are a source of enduring wisdom, and the greatest danger we face is in failing to heed their good counsel about the need for a strong presidency.

The Princely Presidency

Adherents of the princely presidency thesis adopt a similar reading of the Constitution, but instead of celebrating the Constitution for creating a potent presidency they worry about the adverse impact of the presidency on democratic politics. From this point of view, "the counterpart of the leader as masterful hero is a passive citizenry." Alarms about the presidency being "an impediment to democratic politics" were sounded with particular urgency by Anti-Federalists, who opposed ratification of the Constitution because of what Virginia's Patrick Henry called its "awful squinting ... towards monarchy."[22]

Unlike Hamilton, who in *Federalist* No. 69 accented the many differences between the British monarch and the American president, the Anti-Federalists stressed the ways in which the "powers and prerogatives" of the president resembled those of a monarch "save as to name, the creation of nobility and some immaterial incidents." They pointed to the president's power to receive ambassadors as well as his power, exercised in conjunction with an "aristocratic" Senate, to select ministers to foreign courts and "to make treaties, leagues and alliances with foreign states." Anti-Federalists were especially worried that the president, like the king, was "the principal fountain of all offices and appointments," and they predicted that this would enable the president to influence and "corrupt" the legislature in the same way that the king had corrupted the British Parliament. They noted, too, that the president had been granted the monarchical power to veto laws.

Although two-thirds of Congress could technically override a president's veto, Anti-Federalists thought it unlikely that Congress would ever muster a supermajority. In practice, the qualified veto would become indistinguishable from an absolute veto.[23]

Anti-Federalists worried, too, that the Constitution made the president "the generalissimo of the nation." Like a king, the president was given "the command and control of the army, navy and militia" and had been made "the general conservator of the peace of the union." The Anti-Federalists recognized that the Constitution explicitly vested the power to make war in Congress, but they thought that in practice this was not as different from the British monarchy as it might seem. Even a king, after all, "never thinks it prudent" to make war "without the advice of his parliament from whom he is to derive his support." The real power of war-making, Anti-Federalists predicted, would be in the hands of the executive, just as it was in Britain.

The most incisive Anti-Federalist critics, such as the pamphleteer who wrote under the pseudonym "Cato," saw that the problem with the Constitution lay not only in the powers and prerogatives that were explicitly granted to the president but also, and perhaps more importantly, in the "vague and inexplicit" language of Article II. Article I spelled out the specific powers granted to the Congress, but Article II was suffused with an "inexplicitness" that would, Cato predicted, give the president "possessed of ambition [the] power and time sufficient to ruin his country."

Anti-Federalists scoffed at Hamilton's argument in *Federalist* No. 69 that the powers of the president were not much different from those granted to state governors. The Anti-Federalists noted that governors were directly elected by the people, whereas the president was to be chosen by a small group of electors who might or might not be selected by the people of the state. Moreover, the governors had been "divested of the prerogative of influencing war and peace, making treaties, receiving and sending embassies, and commanding standing armies and navies." The president, Cato concluded, "is not more like a true picture of [a state governor] than an Angel of darkness resembles an Angel of light."

The Constitution, according to critics of the princely presidency, is by design a fundamentally undemocratic charter, and Article II is perhaps its least democratic aspect. Democracy, on this understanding, must be local and participatory to be meaningful. By creating a central government to rule over a vast nation, a government that could not possibly involve people in the act of governance, the Constitution necessarily required and fostered a passive citizenry. On this view, the idea that the president was the representative of the people and accountable to the people was a myth. No one person could possibly represent the vast heterogeneity of the United States, and elections were too crude an instrument to ensure democratic control. At best the president could be "the Guardian of the people," as Gouverneur Morris described him at the Constitutional Convention. The idea of guardianship, however, is fundamentally undemocratic. It posits a hierarchical relationship in which the president looks out for "his people," much as a king looks out for the interests of his subjects. Americans who celebrate the presidency as the instrument or embodiment of democracy, according to these exacting critics, accept a comforting myth that obscures the powerlessness of citizens.[24]

The Perverted Presidency

Throughout American history, critiques of presidential aggrandizement have been voiced most frequently by those who cherish the Constitution rather than find fault with it. From this perspective, the Constitution's checks and balances were designed to restrain the abuse of power, particularly executive power. The problem, in the view of these critics, is that the presidency has been let loose from its constitutional moorings and become a presidency that perverts the founders' constitutional plan.

During the 1830s, this perspective was voiced by adherents of the Whig Party, which formed in reaction to the perceived usurpations of "King Andrew." The fundamental problem, according to Whigs such as Daniel Webster and Henry Clay, was that Andrew Jackson and his followers thought of the president as "above the Constitution." In the eyes of the Whigs, the Constitution and the laws were "the sole source of executive authority." What made Jackson dangerous was that he claimed to derive power directly from the people (see Chapter 3). The Whigs also objected to Jackson's expansive claims of presidential power, which they believed violated the text and spirit of the Constitution. The Whigs argued that the Constitution established a president who was to execute faithfully the legislative will, nothing more (see Chapter 4). In the Whig imagination, in short, Jackson was a power-seeking demagogue who had enabled the presidency to slip its constitutional leash, thereby setting the nation on the path to "executive despotism."[25]

A century later, during the 1930s, the Republican Party took up the cry of constitutional usurpation in opposing President Franklin Delano Roosevelt. In the view of many Republicans, Roosevelt exploited domestic (the Great Depression) and foreign (World War II) crises to subvert the modest presidency envisioned by the framers. They pointed accusingly to the explosion of executive agencies and the growth of the White House staff. They also looked with alarm upon Roosevelt's efforts to reorganize the executive branch so as to bring the bureaucracy under greater presidential control. Even more disturbing was FDR's audacious "Court-packing plan," in which FDR tried to expand the size of the Supreme Court so that he could appoint justices who were more sympathetic to the New Deal (see Chapter 9). After Roosevelt was reelected again in 1940, making him the first president in American history to serve more than two terms, isolationist Republicans who opposed American involvement in World War II warned darkly of the "Roosevelt dictatorship."

In the early 1970s, it was the turn of liberal Democrats to raise the alarm about presidential usurpation. The Vietnam War and Watergate gave pause to liberals who had long considered the president a force for good. A particularly influential statement of this rethinking was Arthur Schlesinger's 1973 book, *The Imperial Presidency.* Schlesinger placed particular emphasis on the war-making power, specifically "the capture by the Presidency of the most vital of national decisions, the decision to go to war." The framers had wisely placed that awesome power in the hands of Congress, but a combination of congressional abdication and presidential usurpation had upset the Constitution's carefully calibrated system of checks and balances. The imperial presidency, in Schlesinger's view, was quite literally a "revolutionary presidency" because it overthrew the Constitution's most fundamental tenets.[26]

Liberal Democrats' concerns about executive usurpation reached their zenith during the administration of George W. Bush. Liberals feared that the open-ended nature of Bush's "war on terror" was being used to justify a host of executive actions that were contrary to the nation's constitutional scheme (see Chapters 5 and 10). A bevy of books written during the Bush years decried "the new imperial presidency" and the "unchecked and unbalanced" presidency. Almost all of these books began from the premise that the Constitution established a system of checks and balances that was being undermined by the high-handed actions of the Bush administration.[27]

During the presidency of Barack Obama, however, it was conservative Republicans who loudly sounded the alarm about unchecked presidential power perverting the framers' carefully calibrated system of checks and balances. Obama's executive orders, as we will see in Chapter 6, were a particular focus of a growing Republican critique of what conservative columnist George Will called "an absurdly president-centric conception of government." Whereas the contemporary liberal critique of the imperial presidency has tended to highlight the dangers of unaccountable presidential power in the national security realm, the conservative critique focuses overwhelmingly on the dangers of unfettered presidential power in domestic politics. Both share the conviction that a president-centric government perverts the wise course charted by the founding fathers.[28]

The Progressive Presidency

If Obama's presidency rekindled long-dormant conservative Republican anxieties about a powerful presidency, it also revived liberal Democratic hopes in a progressive presidency. The vision of a progressive presidency begins from a similar constitutional premise as that of the perverted presidency thesis but reaches far different conclusions. Exponents of the progressive presidency agree that the Constitution is dedicated to thwarting the exercise of executive power. However, they do not see these restrictions on the executive as a cause for celebration, but rather as the cause of the nation's failure to effectively address the many serious problems it faces, including health care, poverty, and the environment. The Constitution, on this reading, produces an intolerable inertia, and only the president possesses the resources and vantage point to break through the institutional roadblocks to collective action.[29]

This vision, which dates from the Progressive Era, helped to justify the twentieth century's impressive expansion of presidential power. Few Americans in the nineteenth century dared to criticize the Constitution. There were exceptions, of course, like the abolitionists who denounced the Constitution, in the words of William Lloyd Garrison, as a "covenant with death and an agreement with hell." Most nineteenth-century critics, however, preferred to follow the safer course of finding fault with some modern perversion of beneficent constitutional principles.

Intellectuals in the Progressive Era, in contrast, exposed the Constitution as a document designed to protect the economic interests of the propertied and the rich. The fanciful myths that had grown up around the wisdom of the founding fathers, according to the likes of Charles Beard and J. Allen Smith, prevented us from seeing the framers as they really were: shrewd, power-seeking politicians who strove to protect and advance the economic interests of the groups they represented. The framers, on the progressive reading, had little or no interest in advancing democracy or popular control. Indeed, according to the progressives, the group the framers feared most was "the propertyless masses" who might decide to use their numbers to confiscate the wealth of the few.[30]

The presidency, in this view, was a crucial cog in the anti-democratic wheel of the Constitution. After all, hadn't Hamilton, in *Federalist* No. 71, openly declared that a leading virtue of the presidency was that it would be able to "withstand the [people's] temporary delusion" and not display a "servile pliancy" to every "prevailing current" of opinion? The president, Hamilton taught, should not show "an unqualified complaisance to every sudden breeze of passion, or to every transient impulse which the people may receive from the arts of men, who flatter their prejudices to betray their interests." The president, in short, was intended to be a bulwark against the egalitarian and democratic forces unleashed by the American Revolution.

Progressives believed, however, that the presidency could be remade as a popular instrument that could break through the institutional roadblocks erected by the framers, a potential that had been demonstrated by the presidencies of Jefferson and especially Jackson. The greatness of the presidency, in the words of Henry Jones Ford, was "the work of the people, breaking through the constitutional form." The people looked to the president for progressive change because neither Congress nor the courts were cut out for the job. By design, the courts were guided by precedent and insulated from public pressures. Congress, though putatively the people's branch, could not be relied upon to reflect the will of the people because legislative decision-making had become distorted by powerful special interests. The powerful pull of parochial concerns and local constituencies prevented Congress from acting in the public interest. Any actions Congress took would likely be gradual and watered down by compromise. Bold, decisive change that challenged established interests and settled understandings must come from the president. Or so the progressives believed.[31]

Among the most influential exponents of the progressive presidency thesis was Woodrow Wilson. In *Constitutional Government in the United States*, published four years before he ran for president, Wilson faulted the framers for failing to understand that government is "not a machine, but a living thing." The trouble with a government of checks and balances was that "no living thing can have its organs offset against each other as checks and live. On the contrary, its life is dependent upon their quick cooperation, their ready response to the commands of instinct or intelligence, their amicable community of purpose." By dividing government against itself in a mechanical system of checks and balances, the framers endangered the health of the body politic.[32]

Fortunately, as Wilson saw it, the organic development of the presidency had saved the nation from the framers' mistake of trying to make "a government out of antagonisms." Despite the mechanistic constitutional structures, the president had developed into "the unifying force" of the nation, becoming "the leader both of his party and of the nation." The nation looked to the president for leadership because the president's voice was "the only national voice." He was the only one who spoke "for the real sentiment and purpose of the country," the only one who spoke "for no special interest." The president, in short, was the only leader who was "the representative of no constituency, but of the whole people."[33]

The progressive vision of the presidency was developed by a host of liberal-left intellectuals writing in the middle of the twentieth century. It informed, for instance, Harold Laski's 1940 treatise *The American Presidency*, which drew an invidious contrast between the cohesiveness and accountability of the British parliamentary system and the divided initiative and fear of strong government that characterized the American constitutional system of checks and balances. The Constitution, Laski wrote, was a "child of the eighteenth century," and its creators were "above all afraid of arbitrary power." To erect a system "upon foundations that are inherently suspicious of leadership as such" may have made sense in an age of monarchy and hereditary rule, but "no democracy in the modern world," Laski explained, could "afford a scheme of government the basis of which is the inherent right of the legislature to paralyze executive power." Only presidential leadership, in Laski's view, could save the nation from the antiquated constitutional system bequeathed by the framers.[34]

The progressive vision of the presidency received its paradigmatic expression in Richard E. Neustadt's celebrated *Presidential Power*, published in 1960. Neustadt began with the wisdom of President Harry Truman. Predicting the frustrations that General Dwight D. Eisenhower would encounter in the White House, Truman reportedly said: "He'll sit here ... and he'll say, 'Do this! Do that!' *And nothing will happen*. Poor Ike—it won't be a bit like the Army." A general could order his subordinates to take certain actions but a president could only plead with and persuade others, even those in the executive branch. The fundamental problem identified by Neustadt was that the Constitution had made the president little more than a "clerk," while the nation's pressing problems meant that "everybody now expects the man inside the White House to do something about everything." The widening gap between public demands and formal powers left the president in an almost impossible leadership situation. The nation's success in navigating the immense challenges of the twentieth century depended on the president's success, which in turn depended on the president's political skills and savvy.[35]

Mid-twentieth-century liberals believed, in sum, that the framers' elaborate system of checks and balances was a luxury that the nation could no longer afford. Those checks were fine for the nineteenth century, when there were few demands on the federal government, but in the twentieth century the framers' design had become a threat to the security and welfare of the American people. Only aggressive and skilled presidential leadership, progressives argued, could make this anachronistic eighteenth-century system work in the modern world. What was needed, in short, was a "modern presidency" for a modern world.

Donald Trump is no liberal, but his vision of presidential power is infused with progressive concerns about "an archaic system" that prevents policymaking in the public interest. Unlike Wilson, Trump does not fault the Constitution directly, but rather takes aim at the "archaic rules" that have taken hold in the legislature that get in the way of the president closing deals that serve the American people. Like mid-twentieth-century liberals, Trump has called for systemic reform, most especially abolishing the Senate's "very outdated filibuster rule," that would make the presidency stronger and the political system more effective.[36]

Partisan Vision?

How seriously should we take these four visions of presidential power? Are they motives for action or merely justifications for partisan and ideological advantage? After all, liberals started to lose faith in the progressive presidency at precisely the historical moment that the Democratic Party seemed to lose its lock on the presidency. And Republican enthusiasm for the constitutionally potent presidency coincided with an era in which they dominated presidential elections—and that enthusiasm notably dimmed once their hold on the presidency appeared to slip. It's not just elected politicians who change arguments and positions depending on which party controls the presidency. Supreme Court justices' support for presidential power have also perceptibly shifted in response to changes in the party that controls the presidency. Antonin Scalia, for instance, an outspoken champion of presidential authority during the Reagan and Bush years, became one of the most exacting critics of presidential authority during Obama's presidency. Indeed, few among us, citizens and even scholars, are immune from viewing debates about the presidency through the lens of the current occupant of the White House. How many of us can honestly say that they think about presidential power in the same way with Donald Trump in the White House?

Trump's presidency has affected the way many Americans envision the office not only because we see the world through partisan and ideological lenses, but also because presidents behave differently and so teach us different lessons about the possibilities and perils of the office. Views of the presidency are not fixed, impervious to experience. None other than James Madison, the so-called father of the Constitution, backed a strong presidency at the Constitutional Convention, but 12 years of Federalist presidents turned him into a vocal skeptic of presidential power. None of this should surprise us. After all, as the Preamble to the Constitution makes clear, political institutions, including the presidency, are a means to other ends—liberty, justice, peace, and security.

Nonetheless, our ideas about the presidency do matter. Shared as well as contested norms, as we shall see throughout this book, powerfully shape the ways that presidents behave. The power presidents wield ultimately derives from the expectations and beliefs that members of Congress, Supreme Court justices, the media, the American people, and presidents themselves have about the presidency's proper role in the political system.

Each of the four visions we have outlined includes important insight and knowledge. None can be dismissed as entirely wrong or entirely right. Nor is it likely that one will ultimately prevail, though our reverence for the Constitution often prevents the progressive and princely presidency visions from getting the full hearing they deserve. Instead, contemporary conflicts over presidential power largely play out along the potent-versus-perverted presidency axis, both sides enlisting the Founders and the Constitution in their quest to strengthen or constrain the presidency.

THEORIES OF POLITICAL DEVELOPMENT

Each of these four visions of the presidency contains an implicit or explicit theory of political development (see Table 1.2). Both the perverted and the progressive

TABLE 1.2 Central Concerns, Key Ideas, and Representative Proponents of the Four Visions

	The Potent Presidency	The Princely Presidency	The Perverted Presidency	The Progressive Presidency
Key Ideas	Unitary executive Unilateral and inherent powers	Elective monarchy Monopolization of public space	The imperial presidency The rhetorical presidency	Modern presidency Presidential power is the power to persuade
Central Concerns	Congressional usurpation of executive power	Passivity of the citizenry Lack of true democracy	Rise of presidential war Demagoguery and lack of deliberation	Inertia of American political system Unrealistic public expectations
Representative Proponents	Alexander Hamilton, Dick Cheney, John Yoo, Terry Eastland	Patrick Henry, "Cato," Bruce Miroff	Henry Clay, Arthur Schlesinger, Louis Fisher, Jeffrey Tulis	Woodrow Wilson, Harold Laski, Richard Neustadt

presidency theses posit disruptive, transformative changes that make the presidency of today fundamentally unlike the presidency envisioned by the framers and enacted by Washington or Jefferson. The potent and princely presidency theses, in contrast, see development less in terms of regime transformation than as a natural or logical evolution of the constitutional regime established by the framers. From the latter two perspectives, the development of the presidency is "prefigured in the regime's political architecture."[37]

Advocates of the potent presidency thesis do not imagine that the framers were omniscient, of course. Nobody believes that Hamilton, brilliant as he was, could foresee the precise contours of American political development. What the potent presidency thesis holds instead is that the building blocks of what we think of as a distinctly modern presidency were part of the original constitutional presidency. As government responsibilities have increased, of course, the president has been expected to do more. But "relative to the tasks that government performs," as David Nichols writes in *The Myth of the Modern Presidency*, "modern Presidents do no more—and no less—than Presidents have done in the past." Government has grown but the presidency has remained fundamentally as it was always intended to be—the republic's preeminent leadership position.[38]

From this vantage point, the development of the American presidency has entailed a process of rediscovering latent powers of the office that had been there all along. Time, on this reading, has gradually stripped away the nineteenth-century Whiggish patina that for too long had obscured the underlying strength and true purpose of the Hamiltonian presidency. As the presidency grew more powerful and more independent of Congress in the twentieth century, it came to more closely resemble the potent institution that Hamilton had intended. The more presidents have relied on their inherent and unilateral constitutional powers, the closer the nation has moved toward realizing the original intent of the framers and recovering the deepest meanings of the Constitution.

Critics of the princely presidency share the view that the key to the contemporary presidency lies in the Constitution's "genetic code." Not that these critics lay all of the ills of the contemporary presidency at the doorstep of Hamilton and his elitist brothers-in-arms at the convention. Political scientist Bruce Miroff, the most penetrating contemporary exponent of this perspective, accents the ways in which twentieth-century changes in the mass media, particularly the emergence of television, enabled presidents to "dominate and diminish the public space" in a way that had not been possible before. But while the monopolization of public space was a twentieth-century development, Miroff sees this not as a perversion or distortion of the Constitution, but as a logical unfolding of the framers' commitment to heroic statesmen and passive, apolitical followers. Modern presidential leadership, Miroff explains, is animated by the Hamiltonian vision of "the energetic ... statesman, the masterful executive who shapes and commands an efficient administrative machine, the armed statesman who is a 'Hercules' to America's enemies, the sponsor of industrial growth who seeks economic rather than civic virtue from the people."[39]

The perverted presidency thesis, in marked contrast, posits a radical break between the past and present. On this view, the disjunction between the old and new is the defining mark of presidential development. Different scholars, of course, point to different pivotal periods. Jeffrey Tulis traces the rise of the "rhetorical presidency" to the first two decades of the twentieth century. Theodore Lowi suggests that the party-centered politics of "the traditional system" was displaced by the "plebiscitary presidency" beginning in 1933. And Schlesinger suggests that the "runaway" imperial presidency jumped its constitutional rails in the 1950s and 1960s. Transformative change need not happen all at once. It is always possible to find precedents for practices that seem novel. Change may be sequential, first one part shifting, then another. But the key point, from this perspective, is that the cumulative effect of these shifts—whether they happen in a very short burst of time or over a longer period—is a profound rupture in political practice and ideas, such that one can properly speak of an entirely new regime.[40]

Presidential development, from this point of view, involves a falling away from original principles and practices. These theories often have about them a touch of the jeremiad, lamenting the degradation of the old constitutional order. Frequently the lamentation is capped with a call for reforms that might bring back a touch of the old virtues. Tulis, for instance, calls for a "neo-Whig theory of the president" in which the president teaches citizens to expect less of the president and allows Congress more space for deliberation, and Lowi proposes a strengthened, more responsible multiparty system. But these normative hopes for the future are divorced from any real theory of presidential development. The history of the presidency, from this point of view, points in only one direction, one that tragically takes us ever further from the original constitutional design.[41]

The progressive presidency thesis, too, charts a developmental course marked by profound transformation, from the traditional to modern presidency. The traditional nineteenth-century president is seen as playing a minor or episodic role in initiating legislation, whereas the modern president routinely sets the national policymaking agenda and musters legislative support for his legislative program. And whereas the traditional presidency had only a personal secretary or two, the modern president heads a massive "presidential branch" tasked with helping him achieve his policy objectives. These transformations in the presidency, from the progressive point of view, are no cause for lament. Rather, they are necessary and salutary adjustments to the demands of modern, activist government.[42]

That does not mean that presidential development is seen as unproblematic. From the progressive point of view, the Constitution's archaic checks and balances remain a powerful and pervasive drag on the power of the modern presidency. The public's expectation that the president should set the legislative agenda and secure support for that agenda is difficult to live up to in a constitutional system of "separated institutions sharing powers." The result is that the public quickly becomes disillusioned with presidents, making it difficult for them to realize the progressive potential of their office. Similarly, a large presidential branch makes it more difficult for presidents to ensure that their preferences are being followed by their many underlings. From the progressive point of view, then, the development of a new modern presidency has been necessary but not sufficient to solve the nation's complex problems. For many progressives, only constitutional reform is capable of delivering the presidential leadership the nation needs.[43]

The progressive explanation for the development of the modern presidency is a functional theory of development—a new, modern presidency emerged because the American political system required a new kind of president in order for the system to cope with modern problems—but it also highlights the contributions of particularly pivotal presidents, most especially Franklin Delano Roosevelt, who is typically made the dividing line separating modern from traditional presidencies. However, earlier presidents are also credited with contributing to or at least foreshadowing the modern presidency: the likes of Woodrow Wilson, Theodore Roosevelt, Abraham Lincoln, and Andrew Jackson frequently receive mention in the progressive pantheon of proto-modern presidents. Like the potent presidency thesis, the progressive presidency theory inclines toward history characterized by "peaks and valleys of presidential leadership." The great, noteworthy presidents are those who built up presidential authority; the forgettable failures are those who weakened the office by ceding power to Congress.[44]

There is truth in each of these theories of development and the visions of the presidency that underlie them. My primary aim in this book is not to argue for one theory or vision over the other. It is instead to trace the development of the presidency, from its creation in 1787 through to the early twenty-first century, allowing readers to reach their own conclusions about the merits and demerits of these rival ways of thinking about the development of the presidency and its place in the constitutional system.

Notes

1 Under the Articles of Confederation, there was an office with the title of "president," but it bore no resemblance to the presidency established by Article II of the Constitution. The office was elected annually by the Continental Congress from among its members and its holder served essentially as an honorary presiding officer.

2 Francis Newton Thorpe, ed., *The Federal and State Constitutions, Colonial Charters, and Other Organic Laws of the States, Territories, and Colonies Now or Heretofore Forming the United States of America*, 7 vols. (Washington: Government Printing Office, 1909), 3817. In *Federalist* No. 47, Madison wrote that "the accumulation of all powers, legislative, executive, and judiciary, in the same hands, whether of one, a few, or many, and whether hereditary, self-appointed, or elective, may justly be pronounced the very definition of tyranny."

3 Gordon S. Wood, *The Creation of the American Republic, 1776–1787* (Chapel Hill: University of North Carolina Press, 1969), 157.

4 Thomas Jefferson, *Notes on the State of Virginia*, ed. William Peden (Chapel Hill: University of North Carolina Press, 1954), 120.

5 Charles C. Thach, Jr., *The Creation of the Presidency, 1775–1789: A Study in Constitutional History* (Baltimore: Johns Hopkins University Press, 1923), 71.

6 Gerhard Casper, *Separating Power: Essays on the Founding Period* (Cambridge, MA: Harvard University Press, 1997), 16–17.

7 On the importance of state constitutions, particularly the New York constitution, on the framers' deliberations, see Thach, *The Creation of the Presidency*.

8 The best critical discussion of original intent is Jack N. Rakove, *Original Meanings: Politics and Ideas in the Making of the Constitution* (New York: Vintage, 1997). Also see Jack N. Rakove, "Mr. Meese, Meet Mr. Madison," *Atlantic Monthly* (December 1986), 77–86.

9   Edmund Randolph, Debate in Virginia Ratifying Convention, June 17, 1788, http://press-pubs.uchicago.edu/founders/documents/a2_1_1s16.html.

10   Richard J. Ellis, ed., *Founding the American Presidency* (Lanham, MD: Rowman & Littlefield, 1999), 31.

11   William T. Hutchinson, et al., eds., *The Papers of James Madison* (Chicago: University of Chicago Press, 1962), 8:352, 9:385.

12   Ellis, *Founding the American Presidency*, 265–68.

13   Lester J. Cappon, ed., *The Adams–Jefferson Letters: The Complete Correspondence between Thomas Jefferson and Abigail and John Adams* (Chapel Hill: University of North Carolina Press, 1959), 212.

14   Cappon, *Adams–Jefferson Letters*, 213–14.

15   Max Farrand, ed., *The Records of the Federal Convention* (New Haven: Yale University Press, 1937), 1:66 (Randolph, June 1, 1787).

16   My formulation of these four types has been influenced by Stephen Skowronek's important essay "The Conservative Insurgency and Presidential Power: A Developmental Perspective on the Unitary Executive," *Harvard Law Review* (2009), 2071–103.

17   John Yoo, Memorandum Opinion for the Deputy Counsel to the President, September 25, 2001 ("The President's Constitutional Authority to Conduct Military Operations against Terrorists and Nations Supporting Them"), www.justice.gov/olc/opinion/president%E2%80%99s-constitutional-authority-conduct-military-operations-against-terrorists-and.

18   The first quotation is from Judge Laurence Silberman's opinion in *In re Sealed Case* 838 F.2d 476. Madison's words are from a speech at the Constitutional Convention on July 17, 1787 (Farrand, *Records of the Federal Convention*, 2:35). Similarly, in *Federalist* No. 48, Madison wrote that "the legislative department is everywhere extending the sphere of its activity, and drawing all power into its impetuous vortex."

19   Terry Eastland, *Energy in the Executive: The Case for the Strong Presidency* (New York: Free Press, 1992), 10.

20   Cheney quoted in Andrew Rudalevige, *The New Imperial Presidency: Renewing Presidential Power after Watergate* (Ann Arbor: University of Michigan Press, 2005), 211. The list of laws is from a draft of an essay by Nancy Kassop, written for Richard J. Ellis and Michael Nelson, eds., *Debating Reform: Conflicting Perspectives on How to Fix the American Political System* (Washington, DC: Congressional Quarterly, 2011). Also see James Sundquist, *The Decline and Resurgence of Congress* (Washington, DC: Brookings Institution Press, 1982).

21   Jeffrey Rosen, "Power of One," *New Republic*, July 24, 2006. John P. MacKenzie, *Absolute Power: How the Unitary Executive Theory Is Undermining the Constitution* (New York: Century Foundation Press, 2008).

22   Bruce Miroff, *Icons of Democracy: American Leaders as Heroes, Aristocrats, Dissenters, and Democrats* (New York: Basic Books, 1993), 1. Bruce Miroff, "Monopolizing the Public Space: The President as a Problem for Democratic Politics," in Thomas Cronin, ed., *Rethinking the Presidency* (Boston: Little, Brown, 1982), 218. Patrick Henry, speech at the Virginia Ratifying Convention, June 5, 1788. All of Patrick Henry's speeches at the Virginia convention are available at www.constitution.org/afp/phenry00.htm.

23   All the quotations in this and the following three paragraphs are from Cato IV and V, published November 8 and 22, 1787. These two essays are frequently reproduced in readers on the presidency. See Ellis, *Founding the American Presidency*, 262–65; and James P. Pfiffner and Roger H. Davidson, *Understanding the Presidency* (New York: Pearson Longman, 2005; third edition), 18–22.

24   Morris, July 19, 1787, in Ellis, *Founding the American Presidency*, 74.

25   Richard Ellis and Aaron Wildavsky, *Dilemmas of Presidential Leadership: From Washington through Lincoln* (New Brunswick, NJ: Transaction Publishers, 1989), 118. Henry Clay,

Register of Debates in Congress, Twenty-Third Congress, First Session, Senate, December 30, 1833, 85.

26 Arthur M. Schlesinger, Jr., *The Imperial Presidency* (Boston: Houghton Mifflin, 1973), viii–ix.

27 Rudalevige, *New Imperial Presidency*. Matthew Crenson and Benjamin Ginsberg, *Presidential Power: Unchecked and Unbalanced* (New York: Norton, 2007). Frederick A.O. Schwarz, Jr. and Aziz Z. Huq, *Unchecked and Unbalanced: Presidential Power in a Time of Terror* (New York: New Press, 2007). Also see Peter M. Shane, *Madison's Nightmare: How Executive Power Threatens American Democracy* (Chicago: University of Chicago Press, 2009); Gene Healy, *The Cult of the Presidency: America's Dangerous Devotion to Executive Power* (Washington, DC: Cato Institute, 2008); and James P. Pfiffner, *Power Play: The Bush Presidency and the Constitution* (Washington, DC: Brookings Institution Press, 2008).

28 George F. Will, "Trump Is Something the Nation Did Not Know It Needed," *Washington Post*, July 28, 2017.

29 See, for instance, Grant McConnell, *The Modern Presidency* (New York: St. Martin's Press, 1967); and William G. Howell and Terry M. Moe, *Relic: How Our Constitution Undermines Effective Government* (New York: Basic Books, 2016).

30 Charles Beard, *The Supreme Court and the Constitution* (New York: Macmillan, 1912), 92.

31 Henry Jones Ford, *The Rise and Growth of American Politics* (New York: Macmillan, 1898), 292–93. Skowronek, "The Conservative Insurgency and Presidential Power," 2087.

32 Woodrow Wilson, *Constitutional Government in the United States* (New York: Columbia University Press, 1908), 56. Also see Daniel D. Stid, *The President as Statesman: Woodrow Wilson and the Constitution* (Lawrence: University Press of Kansas, 1998), esp. ch. 3.

33 Wilson, *Constitutional Government*, 60, 68.

34 Harold J. Laski, *The American Presidency: An Interpretation* (New York: Harper & Brothers, 1940), 155, 158, 163–64.

35 Richard E. Neustadt, *Presidential Power* (New York: John Wiley, 1960), 6, 9.

36 Byron York, "Trump vs. the filibuster," *Washington Examiner*, August 26, 2017, www.washingtonexaminer.com/byron-york-trump-vs-the-filibuster/article/2632675.

37 Jeffrey K. Tulis, "Reflections on the Rhetorical Presidency," in Richard J. Ellis, *Speaking to the People: The Rhetorical Presidency in Historical Perspective* (Amherst: University of Massachusetts Press, 1998), 221. My analysis in this section has been shaped by Tulis's reflections on the different ways to conceptualize the development of the presidency.

38 David K. Nichols, *The Myth of the Modern Presidency* (University Park, PA: Pennsylvania State University Press, 1994), 7. Also see David K. Nichols, "A Marriage Made in Philadelphia: The Constitution and the Rhetorical Presidency," in Ellis, *Speaking to the People*, 16–34.

39 Miroff, "Monopolizing the Public Space," 227. Miroff, *Icons of Democracy*, 48–49. The term "genetic code" is from Tulis, "Reflections on the Rhetorical Presidency," 214.

40 Jeffrey K. Tulis, *The Rhetorical Presidency* (Princeton, NJ: Princeton University Press, 1987), 173. Theodore J. Lowi, *The Personal President: Power Invested, Promise Unfulfilled* (Ithaca: Cornell University Press, 1985), 22. Schlesinger, *Imperial Presidency*, x. Tulis, "Reflections on the Rhetorical Presidency," 221–22. This perspective need not assume that the new patterns entirely erase the old. In developing the idea of the rhetorical presidency, for instance, Tulis posits that political development is "layered," with "later changes altering but not obliterating or elaborating prior political arrangements" (221).

41 Jeffrey K. Tulis, "Revising the Rhetorical Presidency," in Martin J. Medhurst, ed., *Beyond the Rhetorical Presidency* (College Station: Texas A&M University Press, 1996), 5, 11–12. Lowi, *The Personal President*, 195–96.

42   A clear analytic statement differentiating the modern from traditional presidents can be found in Fred I. Greenstein, "Change and Continuity in the Modern Presidency," in Anthony King, ed., *The New American Political System* (Washington, DC: American Enterprise Institute, 1978), 45–46. Also see Fred I. Greenstein, "Introduction: Toward a Modern Presidency," in Greenstein, ed., *Leadership in the Modern Presidency* (Cambridge, MA: Harvard University Press, 1988), 1–6.

43   Neustadt, *Presidential Power*, 26. On the progressive ideas for constitutional reform, see Lloyd N. Cutler, "To Form a Government: On the Defects of Separation of Powers," in Cronin, *Rethinking the Presidency*, 162–75.

44   Nichols, *The Myth of the Modern Presidency*, 7.

PART I

THE PRESIDENT AND THE PEOPLE

CHAPTER 2

SELECTING THE PRESIDENT

Introductory Puzzle: How Did Jefferson Almost Lose to His Vice President?

What a presidential contest: Thomas Jefferson pitted against John Adams, two giants of the American Revolution—the former the author of the Declaration of Independence, the latter the draftsman of the widely admired Massachusetts state constitution. The incumbent Adams was the choice of the Federalist Party, the challenger Jefferson the choice of the Republican Party. The election was a cliffhanger. Only after the South Carolina legislature decided on December 2, 1800, to cast all eight of its electoral votes for the Republican ticket was Jefferson's victory assured. Jefferson received 73 electoral votes to Adams's 65, giving him three more than the 70 needed to win the presidency. The framers' system seemed to have worked splendidly: two distinguished characters with national reputations vying for the presidency and an electoral system that produced a clear winner in a competitive contest.

Or had it? Fast-forward to February 17, 1801, three weeks before the new president was scheduled to be sworn in. The House of Representatives had just finished its 35th round of balloting and was still unable to decide on a winner in the presidential contest. If Jefferson beat Adams in December, why was the House voting in February to determine who should become the next president?

The short answer is that Jefferson had ended up tied in the electoral college with his running mate, Aaron Burr, and the Constitution required that the House of Representatives settle any ties. The longer answer requires us to understand the unusual electoral system that the framers of the Constitution had created.

The Framers' Presidential Selection Plan

Few things vexed the framers more than determining how the president should be selected. Over the last two months of the Constitutional Convention, the delegates devoted approximately ten days to debating the question and voting on alternative schemes. How the president was selected would determine which states would exercise the most power over the nation's most important political office.

Dissatisfaction with the electoral college is as old as the republic. This cartoon from 2004 captures a widely held view that the electoral college is an unnecessarily complex relic of a bygone age. Ironically, the framers of the Constitution initially regarded the electoral college as one of their greatest inventions. Even the Anti-Federalists who opposed the Constitution often praised the electoral college (in the words of the *Federal Farmer*) as a "judicious combination of principles and precautions."

Mike Keefe, *The Denver Post* & InToon.com.

If the president was elected directly by the people, the least populous states would suffer. Delaware, for instance, had one-tenth the number of people of Pennsylvania. Southern states with large slave populations would also be at a disadvantage since slaves could not vote. The main alternative to popular election was selection by the national legislature. However, allowing the legislature to choose the president raised two problems. First, many feared that the president would not be an effective check on the legislative branch if he owed his appointment to the legislature. A second concern was that the president might use his office to corrupt the legislature, buying legislators' support through promises of offices or favors. Most delegates agreed that legislative selection required that the president be given a relatively long term and be made ineligible for reelection. Only a president who had no electoral incentive to accede to legislative demands would stand firm against legislative encroachments on executive power, and only a president who had no prospect of reelection could be trusted not to corrupt the legislature.

The delegates spent much of the latter part of July arguing over these questions and voting on dozens of different electoral plans, including one that would allow the president to serve "during good behavior," which essentially meant for life. Better an elected king, some delegates reasoned, than a president eligible for reelection by the legislature.

Ultimately, though, the delegates ended July as they had begun June: with an executive selected by the national legislature, serving a seven-year term, and ineligible for reelection.

Yet doubts about this scheme still lingered. Many delegates disliked making the executive ineligible for reelection. If the president was doing a good job, why not allow the people to retain him? And if the president was made the "tenant of an unrenewable lease," as James Madison put it, wouldn't it remove a "powerful motive to a faithful & useful administration"? More ominously still, would a chief executive who was denied a legitimate outlet for his political ambitions be tempted to seek violent and unconstitutional means to maintain himself in power? "Shut the Civil road to Glory," Gouverneur Morris warned the convention, "and he may be compelled to seek it by the sword."[1]

When the convention returned to debating presidential selection toward the end of August, these philosophical doubts mixed with state interests to stymie the convention again. It was all very well to agree that the legislature should select the president, but that formulation left out *how* the legislature should select the president. If the president was selected by joint ballot of the two houses of Congress, the larger states would have the advantage. If, on the other hand, each house could veto the vote of the other house, or if the legislature cast votes by state rather than by individual members, then the smaller states would be advantaged. It was this clash of state interests that forced the convention to hand the issue over to the Committee on Postponed Matters, out of which emerged the most original part of the founders' handiwork: the electoral college.

The idea of an electoral college had been introduced several times during the convention. The Committee on Postponed Matters' contribution was to hammer out a compromise over its mechanics that was acceptable to both large and small states. The committee achieved this first by creating a formula for electors—the number of representatives plus the number of senators—that advantaged the more populous states, and second by providing that if no candidate received the votes of a majority of the electors, the election would be decided by the Senate—choosing from among the five top vote-getters—thereby advantaging smaller states. Moreover, the committee's formula meant that the convention's compromise over slavery, by which slaves were counted as three-fifths of a person for apportioning representatives in the House of Representatives, would be preserved in the presidential selection process. How the electors were to be selected—whether by the state legislature or by the people directly—was left up to the state legislatures.

One of the problems that the committee foresaw was that electors would be inclined to select someone from their own state, thereby fragmenting the electoral vote and perpetuating parochialism. To counteract this tendency, the committee proposed that each elector vote for two people, at least one of whom could not be an inhabitant of the elector's state. This voting method led the committee to introduce the office of vice presidency, which would be bestowed upon the person with the second highest number of electoral votes.

The convention debated the committee's proposal for several days, and made only one significant change. Fearful that the Senate was now too powerful, the delegates voted to give the House of Representatives rather than the Senate the power to select the president if no candidate gained the requisite number of votes in the electoral college. However, to preserve the power of small states, each state was given an equal vote.

'ention delegates had reason to be pleased with their invention. During the
debates the electoral college attracted generous praise, even from the Contractors. A satisfied Hamilton observed in *Federalist* No. 68 that the electoral
college was "almost the only part of the system, of any consequence, which has escaped
without severe censure, or which has received the slightest mark of approbation from its
opponents."

Founding Elections

The framers' satisfaction with their handiwork seemed justified by the nation's first
presidential election, in which George Washington secured the vote of each of the 69
electors. The electors' other votes were widely distributed among ten other candidates,
representing six different states. John Adams, who secured the vote of 34 electors, 25
more than his nearest rival, became vice president. So far so good. Or so it seemed.

The System Fails: The Elections of 1796 and 1800

Already, however, problems with the presidential selection process were surfacing. Less
than a year after stoutly defending the electoral college in *Federalist* No. 68, Hamilton
confided to James Wilson his fear that the system might malfunction. Everybody, he told
Wilson, "is aware of that defect in the constitution which renders it possible that the man
intended for Vice President may in fact turn up President. Everybody sees that unanimity
in [John] Adams as Vice President and a few votes insidiously witheld [*sic*] from
Washington might substitute the former to the latter." Such a perverse result was possible
because the Constitution required electors to vote for two people but did not establish
separate ballots for president and vice president.[2]

The problem identified by Hamilton remained largely theoretical so long as the
universally admired Washington was running, particularly since so many Southerners
distrusted Adams. In 1792, Washington received the vote of all 132 electors, while Adams
garnered only 77 votes. However, Washington's decision not to seek a third term in 1796,
combined with the emergence of an organized Republican opposition, strained the
framers' system to the breaking point.

Neither Federalists nor Republicans held a party convention or caucus to select their
nominees in 1796, but it was widely recognized that Vice President Adams would be the
Federalists' presidential candidate and South Carolinian Thomas Pinckney the party's
vice-presidential candidate. Republicans meanwhile rallied around Jefferson for president and New York senator Aaron Burr for vice president.

Hamilton and his confederates worried that Adams's unpopularity in the South
would lose him the election, and saw an opportunity to take advantage of the framers'
peculiar electoral system to elect Pinckney as president instead. With Jefferson and
Adams locked in a tight race, Pinckney's path to victory was clear: electors in Federalist
strongholds in the Northeast must vote for an Adams–Pinckney ticket while one or
more southern states cast their electoral votes for Jefferson and Pinckney. After
receiving assurances that South Carolina would cast all eight of its electoral votes for

Jefferson and Pinckney, Hamilton urged New England's Federalists to vote for Adams and Pinckney.

In the end, South Carolina did cast all eight of its electoral votes for Pinckney and Jefferson, but Hamilton's plan to make Pinckney president was thwarted by 18 electors who voted for Adams but withheld their vote for Pinckney. That was enough to deprive Pinckney not only of the presidency but of the vice presidency as well. Pinckney ended up in third place, his 59 electors nine fewer than Jefferson's 68. Adams became president with 71 electoral votes, one more than the 70 required to win.[3]

If Adams won in 1796 by securing 71 electoral votes, why were Jefferson's 73 electoral votes in 1800 insufficient to win the presidency? In both elections, 70 electoral votes should have been enough to secure victory. Jefferson's problem in 1800 was that Republicans were so loyally united behind their ticket of Jefferson for president and Burr for vice president that nobody remembered that, for Jefferson to win the presidency, at least one elector would have to withhold a vote from Burr. Both Jefferson and Burr secured 73 electoral votes, and under the framers' electoral scheme that meant that the choice between the two would be left up to the House of Representatives.

Because we know that Jefferson won—he prevailed on the 36th ballot—it is easy to underestimate the depth of the crisis. In hindsight, it may seem plain that Burr could not possibly win when not a single elector had intended to make him president. Surely every member of Congress, even Federalists, would see the injustice of making Burr president and relegating Jefferson to the vice presidency. But that was not the way many Federalists saw the situation—and it was the outgoing Federalist-controlled Congress, not the newly elected Republican-controlled Congress, that, under the Constitution, was given the power to choose the next president. The scheme to make Burr president was ultimately foiled less by the pangs of Federalist conscience than by the fortuitous aspect of the framers' voting scheme that gave each state delegation one vote.[4]

Although a majority of representatives in the House were Federalists, they had a greater number of "wasted votes" because their votes were more concentrated in particular states. For instance, all seven of Connecticut's House members and all four of New Hampshire's were Federalists. Republicans, in contrast, had narrow majorities in a number of states, including North Carolina, New York, and New Jersey. As a result, Republicans could count on majorities for Jefferson in half of the 16 states, while the Federalists controlled only six states. However, two states (Vermont and Maryland) were deadlocked and therefore unable to cast a vote for either candidate, leaving Jefferson one state short of a majority.[5]

Amazingly, the framers had made no provision for a situation in which no candidate could secure a majority of House votes. Federalists toyed with two options. First, they pointed to a 1792 statute that required a special election if both the president and vice president were unable to carry out their duties, and that made the president pro tem of the Senate the interim president. Alternatively, some Federalists suggested that they could use their majority in the lame-duck Congress to pass a new statute that would allow them to name an interim president—perhaps somebody like the popular secretary of state, John Marshall—and perhaps even dispense with a special election.[6]

Republicans were furious at the Federalists' audacity, but Federalists had little difficulty in justifying these tactics to themselves and others. To begin with, Federalists put little stock in Republican claims that Jefferson's victory represented the will of the people. The "plain fact," declared one Federalist newspaper, was that "a majority of the freemen of the United States have really elected Mr. Adams, to the Presidency." Only the Constitution's infamous three-fifths clause had enabled Jefferson to defeat Adams. The statutory solution proposed by the Federalists was necessary because the Constitution had failed to provide a solution. Stretching the 1792 statute seemed a small price to pay for rescuing the Constitution.[7]

Moreover, the Federalists' statutory solution to the standoff made arguably more legal sense than the alternative bandied about by Republicans. In the event of a deadlock, Madison proposed that Jefferson and Burr summon the newly elected Congress into session. Madison recognized that such a process was not "strictly regular" but the "irregularity" of his plan, he maintained, violated the Constitution "in form only rather than in substance," whereas the Federalist plans were "substantial violations of the will of the people" and the Constitution. Both sides, in short, were desperately trying to devise extra-constitutional schemes that could resolve the crisis created by the framers' flawed constitutional design.[8]

Jefferson asked President Adams to promise to veto any Federalist effort to appoint an interim president, warning that this "very dangerous experiment" would be met with "resistance by force, and incalculable consequences." These were not idle threats. The Republican governors of Virginia (James Monroe) and Pennsylvania (Thomas McKean) were preparing their state militias to march on Washington, DC, should the Federalist Congress try to appoint an interim president. Jefferson made it clear to his opponents that if they appointed an interim president his party would convene a new constitutional convention, rip up the young Constitution, and write a new one. That prospect, he told Monroe, filled Federalists with "the horrors" because they rightly feared that "the present democratical spirit of America" meant they would "lose some of [their] favourite morsels of the constitution."[9]

The Federalists, however, refused to blink. Adams told Jefferson that the Virginian had it within his power to resolve the crisis. All he needed to do was to reassure Federalists that as president he would "maintain the navy," "do justice to the public creditors," and "not disturb those holding offices." In other words, if Jefferson would promise not to embark on revolutionary policies and would assure his opponents that they would not be cast out of office, the government would "instantly be put into Jefferson's hands." If Jefferson wanted to be president, he needed to deal. By refusing to do so, Adams implied, Jefferson was recklessly creating a constitutional crisis.[10]

The real culprit of the crisis, however, was neither Jefferson nor the Federalists but the framers of the Constitution, who had engineered a system of presidential selection that was ill-equipped to deal with a politics organized around political parties. That the crisis was ultimately averted owed little to the Constitution and a great deal to the statesmanship of a few backed by the threat of violence from the many.

Balloting in the House began on February 11, and tens of thousands of citizens poured into Washington. In the eyes of nervous Federalists, these unruly throngs were composed of "men of the most abandoned and profligate characters." A "noisy, angry crowd" had to be cleared out of the House lobby. "Stories circulated that some Federalist members had received written death threats, while stones had come crashing through the windows of others." House members were said to have been "frequently stopped on their way from the House to their lodgings, and most daringly insulted." Federalists complained that Republicans were playing the "Parisian game," using violent "excitement out-of-doors" to intimidate and coerce.[11]

It was against this ominous backdrop that Delaware's James Bayard played the statesman. A loyal Federalist, Bayard voted for Burr on each of the first 35 ballots. Behind the scenes, however, he pressed his Federalist colleagues to recognize political reality. Unless someone gave way before March 4, Bayard pointed out, the nation would be "without a president, and, consequently without a government." Bayard informed his fellow Federalists that he was unwilling to let that happen. And because Bayard was Delaware's only representative, he and he alone had the power to decide how Delaware cast its vote.[12]

Today Bayard is celebrated for his willingness to put country above party, statesmanship above politics. What we are less prone to recall is the prospect of violence, civil war, and a new constitutional convention that helped to concentrate Bayard's mind. As he explained to President Adams shortly after the deadlock was broken, Delaware was "the smallest State in the Union" and lacked the "resources which could furnish the means of self protection" in the event of military conflict. Delaware would have been caught in the middle, a literal battleground state in the event that Republican militias in Pennsylvania and Virginia faced off against Federalist militias from New England.[13]

The closer one looks, the more one appreciates how narrow was the Constitution's escape. The peaceful resolution of the crisis only looks inevitable with the complacency of hindsight. But in 1800 the Constitution was not yet 13 years old, and it is not difficult to imagine a sequence of events that could have precipitated Republicans calling a new constitutional convention, with new rules for the nation or perhaps even for two nations.

The Twelfth Amendment

Efforts to fix the Constitution's obvious design flaw by requiring electors to cast separate ballots for the president and vice president were initially stymied by the same partisan motives that had wrecked the framers' original plan. Jefferson's fortuitous accession to the vice presidency in the election of 1796 whetted the Federalists' appetite for constitutional reform but prompted Republicans to dig in their heels. And after Burr's near triumph in 1800, the roles were reversed. Now the Republicans pushed for a constitutional amendment while Federalists stubbornly defended the status quo.

The reasons for the two parties' positions are not hard to discern. For the party that could command a majority, the framers' system was vexing. The only way to ensure the party's presidential standard-bearer would not end up in a tie with the party's vice-presidential candidate was to scatter the electors' votes for the vice presidency. But the more votes were siphoned away from the vice-presidential candidate, the more likely it was that the opposition party would be able to secure the vice presidency. For a party in the minority, however, the system presented no dilemma, only an opportunity to have their presidential candidate secure the vice presidency if the majority party miscued, as the Federalists did in 1796.

In 1802 the Republican-controlled House passed a constitutional amendment that would create separate ballots for president and vice president, but the proposal was defeated by a single vote in the Senate. In championing the framers' original design, the Federalists emphasized that the electoral college had involved a compromise between small states and large states: large states were advantaged in the initial election and small states were given more power in the event of a contingent election. By providing for separate votes for president and vice president, Federalists argued that the amendment would make a contingent election less likely, thereby undoing one of the Constitution's "inviolable" compromises.[14]

The rhetoric of small and large states only thinly disguised the underlying partisan concerns that drove support for and opposition to the Twelfth Amendment. In the upcoming election of 1804, the candidate who carried Virginia, Pennsylvania, and New York would secure more than 70 percent of the electoral votes needed to win the presidency, and those states were now solidly Republican. Federalists appeared to be a fading political force, and their only hope was to use the framers' design either to get their leading candidate selected as vice president or, alternatively, to frustrate the Republicans' choice for president by voting for the Republican vice-presidential candidate. Republicans understood this and were determined to change the rules of the game so that the Federalist minority could not thwart the Republican majority.

The Republicans secured—only just—the two-thirds majority they needed in both the House and the Senate to send the amendment to the states. Of the 16 states, 13 voted to ratify the amendment, one more than the three-fourths required by Article V of the Constitution. Only the Federalist strongholds of Massachusetts, Connecticut, and Delaware refused to approve the amendment.[15]

Passage of the Twelfth Amendment, as historian Richard P. McCormick has written, signaled "recognition and approval ... that parties were to operate in the election of the President." Yet ironically, the Twelfth Amendment was enacted only because of the extreme weakness of one of those two parties. Had the Federalist Party been stronger, it would have stymied the very amendment that parties had made necessary. An additional irony is that Republicans favored the Twelfth Amendment not as a way to legitimize political parties but as a way to wipe out the Federalists. As a Republican senator from Georgia explained, the amendment would ensure that "never will there be a Federal President or Vice President again elected to the end of time."[16]

When Caucus Was King

After passage of the Twelfth Amendment, Republicans no longer needed to pay much heed to the machinations of the Federalist opposition, which was fast becoming irrelevant in presidential politics. All that mattered now in presidential elections was deciding who would be the Republican presidential and vice-presidential nominees. Although the framers had rejected the idea of having the legislature select the president, from 1808 until 1824 the president was essentially picked by Republican members of Congress who caucused to agree upon their party's nominee.

Only when the congressional caucus renominated President James Madison in 1812 did Republicans come close to losing their grip on the White House, largely because the Federalists capitalized on divisions within Republican ranks by backing New York Republican Dewitt Clinton, the nephew of Madison's first-term vice president. Federalist opposition to the War of 1812, however, buried the party for good, and in 1816 it did not even formally nominate a presidential candidate to oppose Republican James Monroe. In 1820 Monroe ran completely unopposed and secured every electoral vote but one.

The presidential elections of 1816 and 1820 were devoid of any real drama or meaningful public participation. In 1820 fewer than 1 percent of white males cast a ballot. This was due in part to property and taxpayer restrictions on the right to vote and in part to the lack of competition between candidates. In about half the states, moreover, the state legislatures rather than the people still chose presidential electors.[17]

On the surface, the framers' system seemed to be working much as it had been designed to. Monroe's nearly unanimous reelection seemed a consummation of the framers' desire for a politics without partisan divisions and for a president whose national reputation would transcend the pull of factional and sectional loyalties. Monroe was no Washington, but few could match his résumé. A veteran of the American Revolution, Monroe had also been United States senator, a two-time governor of the nation's most populous state, foreign minister to both Great Britain and France, and both secretary of war and secretary of state. He was exactly the sort of virtuous public servant that the framers hoped the nation would choose as president.

Beneath this veneer of unanimity, however, ran deep divisions. By 1824, it was becoming clear that the Republican Party could no longer contain the nation's diversity of ideas and interests. People across the nation were becoming increasingly restless with the "Virginia dynasty" that had monopolized the presidency for 32 of the nation's first 36 years. People were also becoming increasingly unhappy with "King Caucus," the congressional nominating caucus that enabled a relatively small group of national politicians to handpick the presidential candidate.

The Republican congressional caucus attempted to close ranks around Secretary of the Treasury William Crawford, but the nomination proved to be more curse than blessing. It made Crawford a creature of King Caucus, a Washington insider who was the candidate of the politicians rather than the people. Only about one-quarter of Republican congressmen participated in the caucus, which further undermined the value of the nomination. Outside of Virginia and Crawford's home state of Georgia, there was little inclination to line up behind the congressional Republicans' anointed successor. In the western states, many people preferred Kentucky's Henry Clay, while the Northeast backed Massachusetts' John Quincy Adams. Most popular of all, particularly in the Southwest, was the war hero General Andrew Jackson. The overthrow of King Caucus led to the first competitive presidential race since the adoption of the Twelfth Amendment in 1804.

The 1824 Election: The System Fails Again?

The wide-open character of the 1824 election put the system to its first real test since the near disaster of the 1800 election. In many ways, the 1824 contest was more like what the framers envisioned than were the fiercely partisan races of 1796 and 1800 or the nearly unanimous coronations of 1816 and 1820. The four main rivals were each prominent political figures with national reputations—Adams was secretary of state, Crawford secretary of the treasury, Clay Speaker of the House, and Jackson a United States senator. Parties, moreover, played no real role in structuring the vote choice; each candidate counted himself a Republican. Moreover, as many of the framers anticipated, the electoral vote was sufficiently fragmented that the election was kicked into the House.

The framers understood the House election as part of the compromise between small states and large states. Many convention delegates believed that the House would often decide the winner, and quite a number, particularly those from small states, thought that selection by the House was desirable because it preserved a role for small states and elite judgments in the choice of president. The fallout from the 1824 election would demonstrate just how different the politics of the 1820s were from the politics of the 1780s and 1790s.

In the 1824 election, Jackson was by far the top vote-getter, garnering 43 percent of the popular vote and 38 percent of the electoral vote. He was the only candidate who demonstrated strong national appeal, winning in most of the southern states as well as the mid-Atlantic states of Pennsylvania, New Jersey, and Delaware and the far western states of Indiana and Illinois. Adams was a strong second, with 30 percent of the popular vote and 32 percent of the electoral vote, though the only states he won were in the Northeast. Crawford and Clay were a distant third and fourth, splitting about a quarter of the popular vote and 30 percent of the electoral vote between them. Jackson, in short, was the people's choice. He was not, however, the choice of the House of Representatives.

Under the Twelfth Amendment, the House had to choose the president from the top three electoral vote-getters. That eliminated Clay, who had four fewer electoral votes than Crawford despite receiving more popular votes. As Speaker of the House, however, Clay was well-positioned to influence the final choice. Clay helped to move six states into Adams's column—the three that Clay had carried (Kentucky, Ohio, and Missouri) and three in which Jackson had secured a majority of the electoral votes (Louisiana, Illinois, and Maryland)—thus giving Adams the 13 states he needed to secure the presidency (each state delegation received one vote). Three days later, Adams named Clay secretary of state, producing howls of protest from Jackson's supporters about the "corrupt bargain."

The system had worked exactly as the framers had designed: four widely known politicians vying for the presidency, no candidate with a majority in the electoral college, and the House of Representatives exercising its independent judgment about who would make the best president. But what the framers would have counted as a success felt like a profound injustice to legions of Jackson supporters. King Caucus had been dethroned only to have elite rule resurrected in the form of a corrupt bargain in the House of Representatives.

The claim that the House had thwarted the popular will was bolstered by changes in the way in which presidential electors were selected. In the beginning, states had largely vested the task of selecting electors in state legislatures, and so selection by the House of Representatives was not any more removed from the people than was selection by the electoral college. By the 1824 election, in contrast, a majority of the states selected electors by popular vote. Thus in selecting Adams, who garnered only about two-thirds as many popular votes as Jackson, the House appeared to be directly contravening the will of the people in a way that would not have been the case in 1788 or even 1800.[18]

PLAYING A NEW PARTY GAME

The near disaster of 1800 had precipitated passage of the Twelfth Amendment, but no amendment resulted from the 1824 election, despite widespread feelings that the House had robbed Jackson of the presidency. Not that the idea of an amendment wasn't considered: Jackson was among those who called for an amendment to abolish the electoral college and allow the people to directly elect the president. But whereas the elections of 1800 and 1802 had given Republicans huge majorities in both the Senate and the House, enabling them to secure the two-thirds majority required for a constitutional amendment, the elections of 1824 and 1826 left Congress almost evenly divided between the supporters of Jackson and Adams. Constitutional change was therefore out of the question. Instead, Adams's opponents focused on extra-constitutional changes that could prevent the House from selecting the president in future.[19]

Party Rules

New York senator Martin Van Buren believed that the solution lay in the formation of organized political parties that would give the electorate a choice between rival platforms. Even prior to 1824, Van Buren had been critical of the anti-party sentiments of President Monroe, who believed parties were "the curse of the country." Whereas Monroe celebrated the "cooling down" and even disappearance of partisan attachments during the so-called "Era of Good Feelings," Van Buren regarded politics without parties as a recipe for a politics lacking in principles and fragmented by regional loyalties and personal ties.[20]

Van Buren pressed for a national nominating convention that would bring together all the supporters of General Jackson. It was imperative, Van Buren insisted, that the anti-Adams forces not be split between contending factions, as they had been in 1824. Van Buren's ultimate objective was to create a new party that would recreate the old Jeffersonian coalition of "the planters of the South and the plain Republicans of the North."[21]

Van Buren thought that the framers had been right to worry about presidential elections being hijacked by sectional prejudices and local attachments, but he believed they had been wrong to think that political parties were part of the problem. "Party attachments," Van Buren countered, "furnished a complete antidote for sectional prejudices." National parties contesting presidential elections would not only knit together the nation's diverse regions but also give the people the opportunity to choose between competing policies and principles. Parties, in Van Buren's view, thus served to foster both national unity and popular control of government.

Despite his best efforts, Van Buren was unable to persuade Jackson's supporters to hold a national convention in 1828, largely because they feared that a convention fight over the vice presidency might fracture the coalition and damage Jackson's chances against President Adams. Instead, Jackson's allies opted to leave the nomination to the states—relying on party conventions in states controlled by Adams's supporters and on state legislatures in states controlled by Jackson's supporters. In all but one state, the anti-administration coalition endorsed the ticket of Jackson for president and South Carolina's John C. Calhoun for vice president; the only exception was Georgia, which preferred its native son Crawford for vice president. Even without a national convention, then, Van Buren and his allies managed to unite the opposition around a single presidential candidate and avoid the multi-candidate field that had enabled Adams to win in 1824. Yet, as historian Richard McCormick reminds us, in 1828 "a party did not select Jackson to run for President, rather Jackson's candidacy gave rise to the formation of a coalition in support of his election." Van Buren's vision of a party-centered presidential selection process had not yet been realized.[22]

In 1828 the coalitions organized around Jackson and Adams did not even have consistent names. In Pennsylvania, Jackson's supporters were known as the Jackson Democratic party; in other states they were the Jackson Republican party; and in still others they were simply the Jackson party. Those who supported Adams typically identified themselves either as the Adams party, the Administration party, or the Adams Republican party. It would be several years before Jackson supporters consistently described themselves as Democrats and those on the other side called themselves Whigs.[23]

Party names may have been in doubt in 1828 but the result of the election never was. Jackson trounced Adams, winning nearly 70 percent of the electoral vote. Adams did well in all the states that his father had carried in 1800, but the United States was no longer the same country it had been in 1800. Whereas Pennsylvania was the westernmost state above the Mason–Dixon Line in 1800, by 1828 the nation had added Ohio, Indiana, and Illinois, all states that Jackson carried. South of the Mason–Dixon, the nation had added Mississippi, Alabama, and Louisiana, and Jackson carried each of these states too. Moreover, many of the northeastern states that were the Adamses' electoral base had seen relatively slow population growth; winning Connecticut, Rhode Island, Vermont, New Hampshire, and Massachusetts netted John Adams 39 of the 70 electoral votes needed to win in 1800, whereas in 1828 those same states brought John Quincy Adams only 42 of the 131 electoral votes required to win. In contrast, Kentucky, Tennessee, and Georgia, which were worth only 11 electoral votes when Jefferson won them in 1800, yielded more than three times that many electoral votes for Jackson in 1828.

Another sign of change: in 1828, well over 1 million Americans voted in the presidential election, three times the number who had participated just four years earlier and more than ten times the number who voted in 1820. Presidential elections were, at long last, becoming contests that invited mass public participation. Prior to this point, gubernatorial elections and even elections for the local sheriff often attracted more voters than the presidential contest. By 1828 only two states (South Carolina and Delaware) still permitted electors to be selected by the state legislature. Parties, moreover, were rapidly evolving into organizations capable of mobilizing voters rather than merely organizing divisions among elites.[24]

In 1831, for the first time in the nation's history, parties organized national nominating conventions to pick presidential and vice-presidential nominees. In September 1831 the Anti-Masonic Party nominated William Wirt for president, and three months later the National Republicans selected Senator Henry Clay as their presidential nominee and adopted a proto-platform that detailed their objections to President Jackson and his policies. Six months later, in June 1832, the Jacksonians held a nominating convention of their own. Fittingly, the convention selected Martin Van Buren to be Jackson's vice president. The Jackson–Van Buren ticket went on to soundly defeat the opposition, winning more than three-quarters of the electoral votes.[25]

However, 1832 was no rerun of 1804. Although Jackson won a lopsided victory in the electoral college that rivaled Jefferson's margin of victory in 1804, the electoral college landslide disguised the closeness of the 1832 race in key states. In New York, New Jersey, and Ohio, Jackson's margin of victory ranged between 1 and 4 percent.[26]

The profound difference between presidential elections in the Age of Jefferson and the Age of Jackson is illustrated by the even sharper contrast between the 1808 and 1836 elections. On the surface, the two elections may not look so different. Just as the 1808 election was won by Jefferson's handpicked successor, secretary of state James Madison, so the 1836 election was won by Jackson's handpicked successor, vice president Van Buren. But the similarities end there. Federalist strength in 1808 was limited to New England, and very few states in the nation had a closely contested presidential contest. In 1836, in contrast, there was for the first time a competitive presidential race in almost every state. In both 1828 and 1832, the average vote differential between the presidential contenders had been 36 percentage points; in 1836 the average margin dropped to only 11 points. And whereas almost half the states in 1832 had been decided by at least a two-to-one margin, in 1836 only one state (New Hampshire) was carried by a margin that large.[27]

Madison's victory in 1808 had highlighted the absence of partisan competition and the public's minimal role in deciding who would be president. Van Buren's victory, in contrast, augured an entirely new system of presidential selection, one built around intense party competition and mass political mobilization. The new party system, to be sure, was still not fully formed. The Whigs' opposition to Van Buren was so disjointed that they were unable to hold a national nominating convention or agree upon a single candidate. Instead the Whigs launched three candidates, each with a different sectional appeal: Massachusetts senator Daniel Webster, Tennessee senator Hugh Lawson White, and General William Henry Harrison of Ohio. The Whigs' strategy was not to win the electoral college vote, but rather to draw enough votes away from Van Buren to throw the contest into the House of Representatives. The strategy failed: Van Buren received a tad over 50 percent of the popular vote and, more important, secured 58 percent of the votes in the electoral college.

Four years later, the Whigs finally figured out how to play this new party game. In December 1839, they held a national nominating convention, and on the fifth ballot settled on the popular war hero William Henry Harrison as their standard-bearer. For their vice president they agreed upon a former Democratic senator from Virginia, John Tyler. Although Harrison was no country bumpkin—being instead a college graduate whose father had signed the Declaration of Independence—the Whigs cast him as a rustic man of the people who lived in a log cabin and drank hard cider. Meanwhile, they tagged his opponent Van Buren as a foppish aristocrat with a taste for fancy clothes and foreign wines. Jackson had been styled "Old Hickory" and now the Whigs had their "Old Tippecanoe." And Tyler too.

In 1840, both Democrats and Whigs used campaign slogans, candidate nicknames, torchlight parades, and mass meetings to mobilize their supporters. And they were astoundingly successful. Turnout rocketed to an unprecedented 80 percent of eligible adult males. The election, moreover, was no aberration. Instead it fixed a pattern that endured for the rest of the century. Between 1840 and 1896, turnout in presidential elections averaged 77 percent and never dropped below 70 percent. And elections were generally very close. The average margin of victory in the popular vote during the last six decades of the nineteenth century was roughly 5 percent.

By 1840, the nation had left behind the system of presidential selection envisioned and executed by the framers. Gone was the system of genteel elites carefully selecting from the nation's most distinguished characters. Gone too, or at least nearly eclipsed, was the vision of a president above party. Mass-based national political parties now controlled the nomination process and mobilized millions of voters in the general election. The president was openly acknowledged to be not only the head of state but also the leader of his party.

Although the framers would hardly have recognized the party-based presidential campaigns and elections of the mid-nineteenth century, this new system was a logical, if unintended, development of the system the framers designed. For it was the winner-take-all nature of the presidential contest that, more than any other factor, spurred the emergence of mass-based national political parties. The rivalry between Jefferson and Adams in 1796 and 1800 had initiated the transformation, but the collapse of the Federalist opposition outside of a handful of northeastern states arrested the development of parties and depressed voter participation. It was "the revival of the contest for the presidency after 1824," as historian Richard P. McCormick points out, that "had the immediate effect of stimulating the formation of a new party system." Organized parties developed earliest in those states in which the presidential election was most closely contested, which generally meant the states that lacked a sectional favorite. When Adams faced off against Jackson in 1828, the mid-Atlantic states were the site of the most intense partisan organization. The 1832 matchup between Jackson and Clay stimulated partisan organization throughout the northern states, and when Jackson was no longer on the Democratic ticket in 1836, replaced by the New Yorker Van Buren, parties mobilized across the South and Southwest.[28]

If the contest for the presidency, contrary to the framers' plan, spurred the development of mass-based political parties, those parties, ironically, enabled the framers' system of presidential selection to succeed. Without organized political parties capable of concentrating votes on a few candidates, elections resembling the 1824 contest would have become commonplace. In a crowded field, with multiple candidates appealing to different sections of the country, the electoral college would have routinely failed to deliver a winner, and the House of Representatives would have selected the president. The framers might have thought such a contingency election acceptable, just as they thought it acceptable for state legislatures to choose presidential electors, but in a democratic age

the framers' design would have become intolerable. The political parties s
mers' electoral design by making the prospect of a House election much mc
fact, no presidential election since 1824 has failed to yield an electoral col

Of course, that does not mean that the electoral college has worked flawlessly ᴗ.
has been without its critics. Throughout American history there have been repeated calls
to abolish the electoral college. Those calls, however, have focused less on the problem of
the contingent House election than on the problem of the winner of the popular vote not
winning the electoral college vote—an event that would occur twice in 12 years in the late
nineteenth century: first in 1876 and then again in 1888.

The Electoral College Misfires: 1876 and 1888

How is it that in little more than a decade the electoral college twice produced a different
winner than the popular vote, something that had never occurred before and would not
happen again until the election of 2000? Even in 1800 and 1824, when the election was
decided by the House of Representatives, the top popular vote-getter also secured the
most electoral votes. Between 1828 and 1872, the electoral college invariably worked to
amplify the margin of victory: the winner averaged barely above 50 percent of the popular
vote but received 71 percent of the electoral college vote. Was it just bad luck that a system
that had worked so reliably to magnify the margin of victory suddenly produced two
presidents who failed to gain a plurality of the popular vote?

The first and most obvious reason why the electoral college misfired twice in 12 years is
the closeness of the elections during this period. In the four elections between 1876 and
1888, an average of only 1 percent in the popular vote separated the two major party
presidential candidates. During the preceding half-century, only one election had been as
close: the 1844 election in which James Polk bested Henry Clay by 1.5 percentage points.
However, the closeness of the elections is not a sufficient explanation. As Table 2.1 shows,

TABLE 2.1 Top Twelve Closest Presidential Elections, 1824–2016

Popular Vote Winner	Year	Popular Vote Margin	Electoral College Winner	Electoral Vote Margin
James Garfield (R)	1880	0.1	James Garfield (R)	59
John Kennedy (D)	1960	0.2	John Kennedy (D)	84
Al Gore (D)	2000	0.5	George W. Bush (R)	5
Grover Cleveland (D)	1884	0.6	Grover Cleveland (D)	37
Richard Nixon (R)	1968	0.7	Richard Nixon (R)	110
Grover Cleveland (D)	1888	0.8	Benjamin Harrison (R)	65
James Polk (D)	1844	1.5	James Polk (D)	65
Jimmy Carter (D)	1976	2.1	Jimmy Carter (D)	57
Hillary Clinton (D)	2016	2.1	Donald Trump (R)	77
George W. Bush (R)	2004	2.5	George W. Bush (R)	35
Grover Cleveland (D)	1892	3.0	Grover Cleveland (D)	132
Samuel Tilden (D)	1876	3.0	Rutherford Hayes (R)	1

there were three extremely close presidential elections in the late twentieth century—1960, 1968, 1976—in which the electoral college did not miscue. Moreover, the popular vote margin in 1876 was not all that small. The 3 percentage points that separated Samuel Tilden and Rutherford Hayes were actually greater than the 2.5 percent popular vote margin that separated President George W. Bush from John Kerry in 2004.

Understanding why the popular vote winner twice lost the electoral college between 1876 and 1888 requires us to cast our minds back to the Civil War and the titanic struggle over the expansion of slavery that precipitated the war. In 1848, with the Southerner Zachary Taylor as its standard-bearer, the Whig Party carried a majority of the southern states. Eight years later, however, after the passage of the Kansas–Nebraska Act, which repealed the Missouri Compromise prohibiting slavery above the 36th parallel, the Whig Party collapsed, no longer able to hold together northern "Conscience Whigs" and southern "Cotton Whigs." The Whig Party was replaced by the anti-slavery Republican Party, which was made up of northern anti-slavery Whigs such as Abraham Lincoln and northern anti-slavery Democrats. The cross-sectional parties of the 1830s and 1840s, which competed on almost equal footing in the great majority of states, were replaced in the 1850s by parties with a pronounced sectional bias.

After the Civil War, the parties retained their strong sectional cast. The Republican Party remained predominantly a party of the North while the Democratic Party dominated in the southern states. However, the political balance between the two major parties tended to be far more even in northern than in southern states, which meant that the Democratic Party had far more "wasted votes" than the Republican Party. In 1888, Cleveland won the popular vote by 100,000 votes yet lost the electoral college vote decisively because he won by massive margins in the seven Confederate states that seceded before Lincoln took office: Alabama, Florida, Georgia, Louisiana, Mississippi, South Carolina, and Texas. In those seven states, Cleveland triumphed by 42 percentage points on average and picked up 440,000 more votes than the Republican nominee Benjamin Harrison. In contrast, only one state (Vermont) went for Harrison by a similarly lopsided margin.

The 1888 election illustrates the powerful impact that the electoral college had on nineteenth-century political development. Because each state's electoral votes were apportioned on a winner-take-all basis and because the Deep South was overwhelmingly Democratic, neither party had an incentive to cater to these voters in the presidential election. Republicans could win, as Garfield did in 1880, Harrison did in 1888, and William McKinley did in 1896, without carrying a single southern state. Republicans could thus "wave the bloody shirt" with impunity. In contrast, the Democratic Party was compelled to tamp down sectional feelings and to forge a cross-sectional message that would enable them to attract northern voters. Each of their presidential and vice-presidential nominees in the latter half of the nineteenth century hailed from northern battleground states, particularly New York, Indiana, Ohio, and Illinois. Not until 1912, nearly a half-century after the Civil War, would the Democrats nominate a Southerner as either president or vice president: the Virginia-born Woodrow Wilson. But Wilson had been governor of New Jersey and president of Princeton University, and had never run for or held office in the South.[29]

In forcing the two parties to focus on winning the support of the median voter in large, highly competitive states such as Ohio, New York, and Illinois, the electoral college arguably served the nation well by moderating sectional conflicts.[30] If the president had been popularly elected, the Democratic Party in the late nineteenth century would have placed greater emphasis on turning out its southern base. But if the electoral college can be credited with providing Democrats an incentive to neglect the Deep South in presidential elections, it must be faulted for creating the same incentive for the Republican Party. The winner-take-all character of the electoral college meant that Republicans had less incentive to mobilize black voters in the South than they would have had under a system of popular election in which every vote would be equally important, no matter the state in which it was cast. If the president had been elected by popular vote, the Republican Party would thus have been less likely to allow southern states to systematically disenfranchise African Americans, as they did after 1876.

The election of 1876 pitted New York Democrat Samuel Tilden against Ohio Republican Rutherford Hayes. Voter turnout was nearly 82 percent, the highest in the history of American presidential elections. Tilden received about 1.5 million more votes than the Democratic nominee of four years earlier, boosting the Democratic popular vote from 2.8 million to 4.3 million. Republicans, in contrast, only increased their vote totals by about 400,000, climbing from about 3.6 million votes in 1872 to 4 million in 1876.

When Hayes retired on election night, he was certain he had lost. Tilden had already secured 184 electoral votes, one short of the number needed to win, and it seemed all but certain that he had also won Florida and probably Louisiana and South Carolina. The following day, Hayes told reporters it was clear that "Democrats have carried the country and elected Tilden." While Hayes seemed resigned to defeat, his fellow Republicans were determined to use their control of canvassing boards, governorships, and federal troops to secure victory.[31]

In Florida, the canvassing board, made up of two Republicans and one Democrat, voted along party lines to throw out votes in several precincts that had voted Democratic. The board tossed out every vote in Key West—a precinct that Tilden had carried by 401 to 59—on the grounds that election inspectors had not counted the votes until the day after the election and had done so in private. The board also scrubbed away a Democratic vote advantage of 350 in two precincts in which election inspectors had left the ballot boxes unattended while they took a dinner break. By the time the board had finished, it had manufactured a 926-vote victory for Hayes. In Louisiana, the canvassing board—composed entirely of Republicans even though state law required its membership be divided among the state's parties—threw out a sufficient number of votes in Democratic precincts to erase Tilden's 6,000-vote lead and gift Hayes a 5,000-vote victory.[32]

Republicans believed these actions were justified because Democrats had used violence and intimidation to prevent African Americans from voting. Republicans were also convinced that Democratic vote totals in the South had been boosted by widespread fraud. In South Carolina, for instance, which had no registration laws, white turnout exceeded the state's adult white population. There were reports of hundreds and perhaps thousands of Georgians crossing over into South Carolina to vote.[33]

Democrats accused the Republican canvassing boards of trying to steal the election, and counted on the Democratic-controlled Congress to rescue Tilden. Four years earlier, when Louisiana's "notoriously biased and corrupt" canvassing board had given the state's eight electoral votes to Republican Ulysses S. Grant, the Republican-controlled Congress had refused to count Louisiana's votes because the board's decision had been so "obviously rigged." With Congress now under Democratic control, Democrats hoped that Congress would again invalidate Louisiana's electoral votes, and perhaps Florida's as well. If Congress refused to count the electoral votes of even one of these states, the presidential choice would go to the House, where Tilden would certainly win. Indeed, disqualification of even a single Hayes elector would also send the election into the House.[34]

The critical question was who would decide which votes should count. The Twelfth Amendment had fixed some of the electoral college's problems but it had not altered the Constitution's ambiguous command that "the President of the Senate shall, in the presence of the Senate and the House of Representatives, open all the certificates and the votes shall then be voted." The vice president had died the year before the election—so the responsibility to "open all the certificates" fell to the Senate's president pro tem, Michigan Republican Thomas Ferry. Hayes's allies insisted that Ferry could decide whether to count the disputed electoral votes. Democrats countered that Ferry's power was limited to opening the certificates and did not extend to deciding which electoral votes should be counted. The framers' complex electoral scheme and their failure to spell out clear procedures for resolving disputes and deadlocks had once again precipitated a constitutional crisis.[35]

In an attempt to defuse the crisis, Congress established a 15-person commission to decide how or whether the disputed electoral votes should be counted. The commission was composed of five members from the House, five from the Senate, and five from the Supreme Court. The Senate chose three Republicans and two Democrats, while the House selected three Democrats and two Republicans. Four justices were named to the commission, two of whom were affiliated with the Republicans and two of whom were Democrats. The four justices were empowered to choose the fifth justice, whom both sides presumed would be David Davis, considered by nearly everybody to be "a genuine political independent."[36]

The selection of Davis was "the sine qua non of any agreement between Republicans and Democrats" since it was assumed—correctly, it turned out—that the other 14 members would vote along party lines in determining how to count the votes. It had come to this, then: the selection of the president of the United States was to be left in the hands of one wise old man. Admittedly, that was better than the Republican-controlled Senate's preferred plan, which was to pick six justices—three reliable Republicans, two Democrats, and Davis—and then draw lots to eliminate one of them. Democrats understandably regarded this plan to "raffle" off the presidency unacceptable, particularly since the scheme stacked the odds against them.[37]

The agreed-upon plan to trust in Davis, however, hit a snag when he was appointed by the Illinois state legislature to serve in the United States Senate. Davis's senatorial appointment was supported by a coalition of Democrats and independents, but it was engineered by Tilden's unscrupulous private secretary William T. Pelton, who hoped to make Davis feel indebted to Tilden and the Democrats. Pelton's devious plan, of which Tilden knew nothing, boomeranged when Davis accepted the Senate seat and then declined to serve on the commission since his independence would be compromised. As a result, the Democrats had to settle for Justice Joseph Bradley, a well-respected and pragmatic judge but also a loyal Republican.

Bradley sided with the Republicans on every decision. All 20 disputed electoral votes were awarded to Hayes, each by an eight-to-seven decision. The Democratic-controlled House used delaying tactics to drag out the vote-counting process in a bid to gain concessions from the Republicans. Southern Democrats, in particular, sought assurances that Hayes would withdraw federal troops from Louisiana, Florida, and South Carolina and reestablish "home rule"—that is, rule by southern whites. Not until four in the morning on Friday March 2, 1877, were the final electoral votes counted and Hayes declared the winner. The following Monday, Hayes took the oath of office to become the 19th president of the United States, and shortly thereafter he ordered that federal troops be withdrawn from southern states.[38]

Running (not Standing) for President

Thankfully, the 1876 election was an aberration. The nation would not witness its like again until the 2000 election, which would also be decided by Supreme Court justices voting along partisan lines. In important ways, however, the Hayes–Tilden contest was a typical nineteenth-century contest, with both presidential candidates and their political parties campaigning much as they had for the past 40 years.

The norm in the nineteenth century was, as James Polk expressed it upon accepting his party's nomination in 1844, that "the office of president of the United States should neither be sought nor declined." Hayes had echoed these sentiments on the day he was notified of his nomination, assuring well-wishers that "the honor had come to him unsought, and that it was one which could not be declined." Presidential candidates, according to this nineteenth-century ideal, were to stand for office rather than to run or stump for it.[39]

The norm against a presidential nominee campaigning for the office dated to the founding period but had, remarkably, survived the emergence of mass-based political parties and the adoption of universal white male suffrage. Even as presidential campaigns had become absorbing partisan spectacles, complete with brass bands, torchlight parades, marching companies, and emotional orations, presidential candidates remained sidelined, compelled to conceal their ambitions behind a mask of disinterest.

Both Hayes and Tilden went to extraordinary lengths to avoid the appearance of electioneering. As Ohio's governor, Hayes did make a couple of public appearances during the campaign, most notably in Philadelphia for the Centennial Exhibition, at which he shook thousands of hands. But in the few short speeches he gave in the months before the election, Hayes avoided saying anything that might be construed as partisan or political. After his nomination, Tilden was even more cautious about appearing in public, preferring to wait in the governor's mansion for "the call of the people."[40]

GRAND DEMONSTRATION OF THE DEMOCRACY IN NEW YORK CITY, October 5, 1868.—[See Page 632.]

A massive night-time parade in New York City in support of the Democratic Party and its presidential nominee Horatio Seymour in October 1868. The large banner reads "Reduce Taxation before Taxation Reduces Us."

Courtesy: Library of Congress, Prints and Photographs Division, LC-USZ62–119286.

Tilden and Hayes followed the accepted practice of leaving the job of promoting their candidacies to legions of party orators, who fanned out across the country to inspire and mobilize the faithful. Reflecting the decentralized character of nineteenth-century political parties, each state party organization had nearly free rein in how they conducted the presidential campaign. The national party committee did attempt to coordinate the campaign, sending speakers where they could be of service and funneling money into crucial battleground states, but neither Tilden nor Hayes was actively involved in shaping the national party's strategy or message. Hayes rarely even communicated with Republican national chairman Zachariah Chandler and refused to "interfere" when his allies complained about the way the erratic Chandler was conducting the campaign. Tilden was a master political tactician, yet left the details of his campaign to Democratic national chairman Abraham S. Hewitt.[41] Although both candidates convincingly played the part of reluctant suitor, some observers tired of the performance. The *Nation*, for instance, mocked Hayes for saying nothing more than that "ours was a republican form of government and this was the hundredth year of the national existence." Adherence to "the strictest requirements of the code," the *Nation* editorialized, prevented voters from hearing candidates explain their views on the vital issues that faced the nation. The demand that presidential candidates "take the stump on their own behalf" reflected a growing feeling among reformers that presidential elections should be about the candidates at least as much as they should be about the parties.[42]

In at least one respect, the election of 1876 did display signs of an emerging candidate-centered campaign. During the previous four decades, presidential nominees had written public letters in which they formally accepted their party's nomination. These letters were generally brief and often did not go much beyond some obligatory words of thanks and an endorsement of the party's platform. They aptly symbolized the subordination of the candidate to the party. In 1876, however, the acceptance letter was seized upon by both candidates as an opportunity to elaborate their political views, albeit in ways that closely followed the party's platform. Neither letter, however, was geared to move or motivate voters. When a Democratic newspaper editor complained to Tilden that his 4,500-word letter was "able but too long for people to read," the nominee snapped that "it was not intended for *people* to read."[43]

As Tilden's response suggests, presidential candidates in the late nineteenth century were beginning to be buffeted by conflicting expectations. On the one hand, they were not supposed to solicit votes; on the other, they were increasingly expected to communicate their views to voters. People wanted their presidential candidates to be dignified, but they also wanted to be able to judge for themselves a candidate's suitability for the nation's highest office.

James Garfield, the Republican nominee in 1880, struggled to carve out a role that would satisfy these contradictory expectations. Invited to New York to soothe a party rift, he initially resisted for fear that such a trip would appear undignified, but ultimately relented. He encountered enthusiastic crowds at virtually every stop but assiduously avoided politics in his brief remarks. The immense crowds that Garfield drew induced many Republicans to call for the candidate to abandon "the foolish custom which seals a presidential candidate's lips," but President Hayes and other leading Republicans urged him to follow the traditional code and "sit cross legged and look wise until after the election." In the face of the conflicting advice, Garfield hit upon an innovative arrangement that would later be dubbed the "front-porch" campaign. By remaining on his Ohio farm, he placated the traditionalists who believed candidates should await the people's call, but by greeting swarms of visitors at his home he "played the good democrat, addressing the people as equals in his own home."[44]

In 1884, Republican nominee James Blaine decided on a bolder course. He traveled around the country, making about 400 speeches in which he pressed his party's case for high tariffs to protect American industry. Blaine made no apologies for these popular appeals: "I am a profound believer in a popular government," he explained, "and I know no reason why I should not face the American people." Republicans praised his "bold and brilliant" efforts while Democrats predictably charged him with "vote-begging." Blaine's opponent, Grover Cleveland, opted for a more "dignified" pose, remaining at the governor's office in Albany, just as Tilden had done in 1876.[45]

Condemnation of Blaine's campaigning—combined with Blaine's defeat—encouraged Benjamin Harrison, the Republican nominee in 1888, to emulate Garfield's successful front-porch strategy of eight years earlier. Unlike Garfield, however, who had carefully avoided discussing issues, Harrison spoke often about the virtues of the protective tariff as well as the need for increased veterans' pensions and civil service reform. Harrison's front-porch campaign was also much better organized and more carefully scripted than Garfield's. As historian Gil Troy recounts, "a committee arranged the visits and reviewed proposed introductory speeches [and] two to three times a day, at the appointed hour, Harrison would stride from his house in Indianapolis to nearby University Park, listen to the greetings, and respond." Harrison spoke to more than 100 delegations totaling some 300,000 people, going in the course of a few months from a relatively unknown ex-senator from Indiana to the principal spokesman for the Republican Party. Some wondered if this behavior was entirely proper. *Harper's Weekly*, for instance, pronounced the candidate's continuous rounds of handshaking and speech-making to be "wholly unnecessary torture for a Presidential candidate" and worried that it put at "risk ... his health, his election, and his reputation." Except that it seemed to work: Harrison unseated President Cleveland, who not only refused to stump but also forbade his cabinet members from doing so.[46]

The Republicans reprised their successful front-porch campaign tactic in the election of 1896, which pitted William McKinley against William Jennings Bryan. From his home in Canton, Ohio, McKinley delivered 300 or so speeches to approximately 750,000 people who made the pilgrimage to his front door. While McKinley's campaign built upon the successful campaigns of Garfield and Harrison, Bryan opened an entirely new chapter in presidential campaigns by taking his case directly to the American people, speaking to an estimated 5 million Americans in 600 speeches across 27 states. Neither Bryan nor McKinley shied away from issues, the former focusing almost exclusively on "free silver" while the latter emphasized the virtues of the protective tariff. By 1896, the nominee was fully expected to be the principal spokesman and central figure of the campaign.[47]

To be sure, Bryan's stumping did bring partisan censure. Republican John Hay, who in 1884 had praised Blaine's speaking tour as "bold" and "brilliant," now condemned Bryan for "begging for the Presidency as a tramp might beg for a pie." Republicans, though, seemed more disturbed by Bryan's policies and his emotional appeals than they were by the act of stumping itself. Indeed, a number of worried Republicans, including national committee chairman Mark Hanna, urged McKinley to join Bryan on the stump. McKinley rejected their pleas, explaining that he "might just as well put up a trapeze on [his] front lawn and compete with some professional athlete as go out speaking against Bryan." McKinley would play to his strengths and speak from his front porch, but political strategy rather than custom kept him there.[48]

The rematch between Bryan and McKinley in 1900 revealed that the norms governing candidate behavior had changed for challengers much more than they had for incumbents. While Bryan campaigned in essentially the same way he had in 1896, President McKinley dramatically altered his campaign. There would be no front-porch campaign this time. "The proprieties," McKinley believed, "demand that the President should refrain from making a political canvass on his own behalf." Just like President Harrison in 1892 and President Cleveland in 1888, President McKinley left the campaigning to his surrogates. Unlike his predecessors, however, McKinley had a dynamo for a surrogate: vice-presidential nominee Theodore Roosevelt. Roosevelt initially vowed not to campaign from "the rear end of a railway train" like a "second-class Bryan," but he proved to be a first-rate Bryan, delivering approximately 675 speeches to an estimated 3 million people, besting Bryan who gave around 550 speeches to 2.5 million people.[49]

The power of "the proprieties," as McKinley called them, was strikingly evident in the 1904 election when Roosevelt, now president following McKinley's assassination in 1901, faced off against Democrat Alton Parker. Although Roosevelt had never been shy about using the bully pulpit during his first term, he fell almost completely silent after his nomination. The strain on him was terrible. "I could cut [Parker] into ribbons if I could get at him in the open," Roosevelt told his son. "But of course a President can't go on the stump and can't indulge in personalities, and so I have to sit still and abide by the result." Not that Roosevelt was entirely passive; behind the scenes he was furiously ghost-writing speeches for others to deliver and "bombarding" the chairman of the Republican Party National Committee, George Cortelyou, with advice.[50]

If convention kept Roosevelt from stumping, it forced an unwilling Judge Parker to campaign more actively. Parker had wanted to preserve a "judicious silence" during the campaign because he regarded stumping as "undignified" and thought "personalities" were beside the point. His hopes of conducting a low-key, front-porch campaign were undermined, however, by withering criticisms from supporters and opponents alike. Republicans assailed Parker as the "Mummy," and Democrats urged their candidate to take his case to the country. Parker relented, and in the week leading up to election day he spoke to large crowds in New York, New Jersey, and Connecticut. Parker's stumping signaled the demise of the front-porch campaign. Originally created as a way for presidential candidates to campaign with dignity, the front-porch campaign now appeared to be an archaic effort to avoid the people.[51]

The 1908 campaign began with both candidates, William Howard Taft and William Jennings Bryan, seemingly intent on conducting a front-porch campaign reminiscent of McKinley's 1896 campaign. By the end of summer, though, Bryan had reverted to his old ways. Concerned by Bryan's popularity as well as by the paucity of people visiting his Cincinnati front stoop, Taft decided that he, too, needed to take to the stump. The *Washington Times* assured both candidates: "It is not undignified, it is not improper. The people want to see and listen to the men asking for their votes." A poor public speaker, Taft could not hope to match Bryan's eloquence, but he came close in quantity, delivering 400 speeches during an 18,000-mile tour of the country. For the first time in the nation's history, both major party presidential nominees crisscrossed the nation in search of votes. Moreover, Taft became the first victorious presidential candidate to mount a full-scale speaking tour, and thereby helped to erase the association between stumping and defeat that had grown up after the losing campaigns of Blaine and Bryan.[52]

When Taft ran for reelection in 1912, he immediately reached for the protective cover of the norm that forbade an incumbent president from actively campaigning for office. Invoking "the dignity of his office," Taft fell nearly silent after his acceptance speech, except during the week leading up to the election when he wrote "a few dignified letters for publication." If Taft was happy to be relieved of the obligation to stump for office, the Progressive Party nominee Theodore Roosevelt was "dee-lighted" to be free of the conventions that had kept him off the campaign trail in 1904. Roosevelt immediately took to the hustings, denouncing Taft all across the country until a would-be assassin's bullet in mid-October slowed the Bull Moose.[53]

Woodrow Wilson, the Democratic Party candidate in the historic 1912 election, disdained the emotionalism of the "extended stumping tours" that he associated with Bryan and Roosevelt. Respectful of the "old-fashioned" proprieties, Wilson emphasized that people "look for dignity in high office." He initially refused to mount a demeaning "rear-platform" campaign of the sort that Taft and Bryan had engaged in in 1908. "I don't mind talking, but I do mind being dragged over half a continent," he explained to a friend. The telegraph, he pointed out, was a far more effective means of communicating his message than trying to traverse the nation by train. Wilson's position was untenable, however, and he was soon compelled to hit the campaign trail.[54]

As president, however, Wilson was determined not to stump for his reelection in 1916. He regarded campaigning as not only beneath the presidency but also "a great interruption to the rational consideration of public questions." Wilson's Republican opponent, Charles Evans Hughes, showed no such hesitation. Upon accepting the nomination of the Republican Party, Hughes resigned his position on the Supreme Court and promptly set out on a punishing "14,000 mile and thirty nine day Western trek," shaking the hands of many thousands of "plain people," exploring "copper shafts with miners and trad[ing] quips with cowboys," and giving hundreds of speeches attacking the Wilson administration.[55]

Hughes' aggressive campaigning and Wilson's passivity spread anxiety in the Democratic ranks, particularly after Republicans swept the September state elections in Maine, one of many states in which Hughes had campaigned. Both sides were well aware of the old political adage "As Maine goes so goes the Union." Forced to respond, Wilson consented to some strategic traveling "before non-partisan organizations," though he insisted that he would not turn these trips into "a speech-making campaign." In early October, for instance, he journeyed to Omaha, Nebraska to celebrate the state's semi-centennial, making 14 stops along the way in the critical state of Ohio. He adhered to his promise not to make "rear-platform speeches," but he did manage to shake plenty of hands. In fact, when Wilson returned home from another ostensibly "nonpolitical" trip to the Midwest later in the month he was forced to wear "a leather finger protector due to injury from too many handshakes." Compared to his Republican opponent, President Wilson was certainly a model of traditional restraint, but his campaigning—which included seven campaign speeches delivered at his estate in Shadow Lawn as well as several political speeches in New York State during the closing week of the campaign— was far more active than that of any previous incumbent.[56]

The idea that campaigning by rail was beneath the dignity of presidential candidates continued to resonate in the early twentieth century. Warren Harding, the Republican nominee in 1920, vowed to emulate McKinley and stick to his front porch because it was the "method of campaigning" that best conformed to his "conception of the dignity of the office." However, like Parker in 1904 and Taft in 1908, Harding was forced out onto the stump, both to combat opposition charges that he was violating his "clear duty" to meet the people and to appease local Republican politicos who demanded that the candidate visit their state. Harding's Democratic opponent, James Cox, showed none of the same hankering for older traditions. Cox was "perpetually in motion," traveling 22,000 miles and speaking to over 2 million people during his unsuccessful campaign. Cox, observed one magazine editor, "is everything: manager, producer, director, leading man and caption man." If the mid-nineteenth-century presidential candidate had a cameo or at best a small supporting role in the campaign, by the early decades of the twentieth century the candidate was clearly the star of the political show.[57]

How actively presidential candidates campaigned was now down to political strategy and personal inclination; traditional "proprieties" about presidential dignity mattered little or not at all, as can be seen from Herbert Hoover's contrasting behavior in the 1928 and 1932 elections. In 1928, confident of his commanding lead and uncomfortable with public speaking, Hoover campaigned as little as possible, delivering seven carefully crafted speeches but little else. In 1932, in contrast, after the Republicans' defeat in the Maine elections, President Hoover threw himself into "the rough and tumble" of partisan campaigning, traveling all across the Midwest, excoriating the Democratic challenger Franklin Roosevelt for lying, evasiveness, and even profiteering. For the first time in the nation's history, the incumbent president campaigned as actively as the challenger, trading partisan barbs before partisan crowds across the nation.[58]

The arrival of the modern president as campaigner was confirmed in the 1936 election. Roosevelt made a series of supposedly "nonpolitical" trips during the summer that enabled him to appear as "President of the whole people." As Roosevelt's aide Samuel Rosenman explained, such trips—whether to a drought-stricken area of the Midwest or a northeastern state working on flood control—were "the most effective political trips a President can make." Unlike Hoover, who in 1932 was forced onto the stump only after losses in Maine, Roosevelt planned from the outset to undertake an explicitly political stumping tour in October. During the five weeks leading up to the election, Roosevelt delivered explicitly political speeches all across the nation. In auditoriums as well as from the rear platform of a train, the president aggressively defended New Deal programs and assailed the Republicans.[59]

Roosevelt was reelected in a landslide that buried not only his opponent, Alf Landon, but also the traditional proscription against presidential stumping. Future incumbents would, of course, continue to capitalize on the president's nonpolitical duties during a campaign. "Campaigning by governing" would remain a favorite presidential technique, particularly during times of international crisis or war. Presidents on the stump would still often try to take the "high road," leaving the harsher partisan or personal attacks to the vice president or the national party chairman. But the question of whether it was dignified for a president to travel the country and solicit the people's vote had been settled.[60]

To be sure, the technology for communicating to voters that was available to Roosevelt and Landon in 1936 is worlds apart from the technology that is available to presidential candidates today. Radio and the rear platform of a train gave way in the 1950s to television and the tarmac. In the first decade of the twenty-first century, the internet sparked another revolution in the way presidential nominees and voters communicate. Yet in many ways, what the American people expect of a presidential candidate remains fundamentally the same today as it was in 1936. People expect their presidential candidates to travel around the country, to speak to American voters, and to ask for their vote. They expect nominees to show that they have the ambition to be president—that they have the "fire in the belly." Candidates for the presidency are expected to run, not stand, for office.

The Rise of the Presidential Primary and the Slow Decline of the National Nominating Convention

If by 1936 the rules of engagement for presidential nominees had become relatively clear, the rules governing candidate behavior *prior to the nomination* had become decidedly less straightforward than they had been a half-century earlier. From the 1830s through the first decade of the twentieth century, the nomination process had been remarkably stable. Party nominees were selected by national nominating conventions, which were made up of delegates selected from every state. The selection of these delegates began with meetings at the precinct and county levels and culminated in a state convention. Although the process was open to all loyal party members, state party notables largely controlled the selection of national convention delegates and determined how the delegates would vote. There were no elections, and public opinion did not directly affect the party's selection of its nominee.

Party leaders in the nineteenth century typically sought out one of two types of candidates. First, parties might seek to nominate a candidate who was "politically neutral but personally illustrious," which in the nineteenth century usually meant war heroes and generals. Generals William Henry Harrison (1840), Zachary Taylor (1848), Winfield Scott (1852), George McClellan (1864), Ulysses S. Grant (1868, 1872), and Winfield Scott Hancock (1880) are prime examples. This was a particularly common strategy when a party felt that it could not command a majority of the electorate in the general election. The second, more common strategy was to nominate a reliable partisan servant who was acceptable to diverse segments of the party coalition. Often this meant picking a politician who was not closely aligned with any faction within the party.[61]

The selection of Lincoln as the Republican presidential nominee in 1860 was a classic example of this second pattern. In 1860, the two most prominent Republicans were the ex-Whig William Seward and the ex-Democrat Salmon Chase. Both had their fervent backers but both also faced strong opposition from within the party. Lincoln, in contrast, was little known outside of Illinois. Whereas both Seward and Chase had been governor and senator of major states—New York and Ohio respectively—Lincoln's only national position was a single term in the House of Representatives in the late 1840s. Lincoln was well aware that his name was "new in the field" and that he was "not the FIRST choice of a very great many." His policy, he told a supporter, was "to give no offense to others— leaving them in a mood to come to us, if they shall be compelled to give up their first love." The nineteenth-century nomination system privileged candidates who were the first choice of few but acceptable to many.[62]

Nineteenth-century nominating conventions were genuine decision-making bodies. Sometimes the party coalesced around a candidate before the convention, as with Republican William McKinley in 1896, but often multiple ballots were required to settle on a nominee. The leader on the first ballot often was not the ultimate victor. In 1860, for instance, Republican convention delegates were split between five major candidates on the first ballot. Seward had three-quarters of the votes necessary to secure the nomination while no other candidate had more than half of the requisite votes. Seward, however, was unacceptable to many in the party, and on the third ballot the convention chose Lincoln instead. In 1880 it took the Republicans 36 ballots to decide on James Garfield, a candidate who had no votes on the first ballot. Indeed, Garfield did not pick up a single vote until the 33rd ballot.

Democratic conventions were often even longer and more contentious, in large part because of a party rule, adopted in 1836, that required the nominee to receive the votes of at least two-thirds of the delegates. In 1852 it took the Democrats 49 ballots to agree on New Hampshire's Franklin Pierce, who did not gain his first vote until the 35th ballot. In 1912, Woodrow Wilson was nominated on the 46th ballot. The most protracted convention of all took place in 1924, when the Democrats required 17 days and 103 ballots to nominate former West Virginia congressman John W. Davis.

The two-thirds rule almost cost Franklin Roosevelt the Democratic nomination in 1932. Roosevelt was the clear frontrunner and received nearly 60 percent of the votes on the first ballot. Many Democrats, however, distrusted Roosevelt and preferred Al Smith, who had been the party's nominee in 1928. After three ballots, Roosevelt failed to lift his vote total above 60 percent, raising the prospect of a deadlocked convention. "The last thing a candidate wanted," explain the authors of an important study of national party conventions, "was to come close to nomination on the first ballot and to make no more progress on the next two or three. When that did happen, the candidacy would generally collapse and some other candidate would make a run." Smith hoped that, having stalled Roosevelt, he could create a stampede toward Cleveland mayor Newton Baker, who had received no votes on the first three ballots. Roosevelt's men, however, were able to make enough backroom promises to key party figures to secure FDR victory on the fourth ballot. Four years later, President Roosevelt used his commanding position within the party to repeal the two-thirds rule.[63]

Roosevelt won his party's nomination in 1932 in roughly the same way that candidates had been securing party nominations for almost a century: through "an insider strategy of negotiation with party leaders." To be sure, FDR dramatically departed from precedent when he flew to Chicago to accept the nomination, becoming the first presidential candidate in American history to accept his party's nomination at the convention. But apart from that innovation, the 1932 nominating convention more closely resembled the conventions of the nineteenth century than those of the twenty-first century, in which delegates merely ratify a choice that has already been reached by the voters.[64]

The staying power of the nineteenth-century national nominating convention was particularly remarkable in light of the sweeping criticisms directed at nominating conventions in the opening decades of the twentieth century. Progressives assailed the convention system as undemocratic, echoing reformers' complaints against King Caucus a century before. Nominating conventions, reformers complained, were controlled by corrupt party bosses and yielded candidates who did not reflect the preferences of the parties' rank-and-file members. The solution, Progressive reformers insisted, was to give voters a direct say in selecting the parties' nominees through primary elections.[65]

A handful of states experimented with direct primaries in the first decade of the twentieth century, but not until 1912 would primaries play a significant part in presidential nominations. A dozen states, including the delegate-rich states of California, Illinois, Massachusetts, New Jersey, Ohio, and Pennsylvania, held primaries in 1912 to select all or most of their convention delegates.[66]

On the Republican side, former president Theodore Roosevelt used primaries to challenge incumbent William Howard Taft. Roosevelt won 9 of 12 primary contests and amassed 1,164,765 votes, about 400,000 more than Taft, who won only one primary. Roosevelt was attempting something that no presidential candidate had ever tried before: to gain the nomination by going over the heads of party insiders. Taft was initially inclined to campaign the old-fashioned way by lining up support from party notables, but, faced with the prospect of a humiliating defeat in his home state of Ohio, he felt compelled to join in the campaigning. Taft's campaigning, however, could not stave off the drubbing he received from Roosevelt, who collected 55 percent of the Ohio primary vote, compared with less than 40 percent for Taft.[67]

PROMINENT CANDIDATES FOR THE REPUBLICAN PRESIDENTIAL NOMINATION AT CHICAGO.—[FROM PHOTOGRAPHS BY BRADY.]

Prior to the 1860 Republican national nominating convention, few would have bet on Abraham Lincoln emerging as the party's presidential nominee. William Henry Seward, who appears at the center of the gallery of prominent candidates, was widely considered the front-runner. To Seward's right are (from the top, going clockwise) Edward Bates, Salmon Chase, Abraham Lincoln, John Fremont, and William Pennington. To Seward's left (from the top, going counter-clockwise) are Nathaniel Banks, John McLean, John Bell, Cassius Clay, and Simon Cameron.

Courtesy: The Granger Collection, NYC—All rights reserved.

After Roosevelt's stunning victory in Ohio, many of the former president's backers felt certain that he would be nominated at the convention. Even Roosevelt confessed that he was now "reasonably sure" he would be the Republican nominee. However, Roosevelt and his allies misjudged the political situation. Although the nation had just witnessed its "first primary campaign," the route to the nomination remained firmly under the control of party leaders. Three-quarters of the states held no primaries and Taft's people controlled the majority of these state delegations. Even more important, Taft's supporters controlled the party's national committee, which was empowered to decide how to award more than 250 contested delegates. The committee awarded 93 percent of these disputed delegates to the president, thereby ensuring that Taft would win the nomination despite his anemic showing in the primaries.[68]

The primary contest on the Democratic side had equally little effect on the party's selection of a nominee. New Jersey governor Woodrow Wilson won the Democratic nomination not because of his success in the primary elections but because, as historian Lewis Gould points out, he had "latent second- and third-choice backing that none of his rivals could duplicate." Indeed, Wilson was thrashed in a number of the primary contests by Speaker of the House Champ Clark, who defeated Wilson in Illinois by a nearly three-to-one margin and in California by a two-to-one margin. Wilson won his share of primaries too—in Wisconsin, Ohio, and New Jersey, for instance—but both of the leading contenders relied primarily on the tried-and-true inside game of amassing delegates. Clark entered the convention with twice as many delegates as Wilson, but, with the help of the two-thirds rule, Wilson's supporters swung the convention to their man on the 46th ballot. The introduction of primaries had clearly not caused the national nominating convention to wither away as Progressives had hoped. If anything, the convention's power over the nomination process seemed stronger than ever.[69]

Seeing this, Progressives pushed for an expansion of the primary system. After his election in 1912, President Woodrow Wilson called on Congress to enact legislation that would establish primary elections in every state so that voters could "choose their nominees for the presidency without the intervention of nominating conventions."[70] Congress ignored Wilson's recommendation, although 20 states opted to hold primary elections in 1916. Yet the convention remained the locus of power. In the Republican convention in 1916, no candidate on the first ballot garnered more than a quarter of the delegates needed to secure the nomination. On the third ballot, the convention chose Supreme Court Justice Charles Evans Hughes, who had not expended a single day on campaigning or appealing to the people for votes.

By 1920, enthusiasm for the direct primary had cooled considerably, especially on the Democratic side. Many states that had embraced presidential primaries during the Progressive Era proceeded to do away with them, in large part because voters showed scant interest in participating. In 1920 only 570,000 voters turned out in Democratic primaries, less than half the number of Democratic voters who had gone to the polls in 1916 when President Wilson ran essentially unopposed. More than 3 million Republicans turned out in the primary elections of 1920, but the top primary vote-getter, California's Hiram Johnson, was never a serious contender for the nomination. Instead the nomination went to Warren Harding, who had not campaigned in any primaries.

By the time Franklin Roosevelt was seeking his party's nomination in 1932, candidates knew that, while primaries could not be ignored, the road to the nomination still relied far more heavily on the inside game of negotiating with party notables than it did on an outside game of direct appeals to voters. Roosevelt certainly understood this, which is why in the summer of 1931 he dispatched his political ally James Farley on a tour of 18 states to talk with state and local party leaders and line up support. The following summer, at the Democratic national convention, a reporter wanted to know why the Iowa delegation was backing FDR. "Well," one replied, "Jim Farley came out and asked us and nobody else did."[71]

Neither Roosevelt nor any of his main rivals campaigned actively during the primaries; instead, FDR largely "tended to state business and let his lieutenants represent him." Nonetheless, even without actively campaigning, Roosevelt prevailed in virtually every state primary except in a handful of states that chose a "favorite-son" candidate—that is, a candidate who hailed from the state. Although many of these primaries were only "preferential primaries" that did not bind the states' delegates to vote for the primary winner, several party bosses were sufficiently impressed by Roosevelt's vote-getting appeal that they lined up behind him.[72]

Under the nomination system that emerged in the first half of the twentieth century, primaries could boost a candidate's prospects by enabling him to demonstrate his vote-getting ability in strategic locales. In 1948, for example, New York's Thomas E. Dewey campaigned hard in Oregon, and his victory there over Minnesota governor Harold E. Stassen helped Dewey secure the Republican nomination, albeit on the third ballot. In 1960, John F. Kennedy's nomination prospects were bolstered by his primary victory in West Virginia, an overwhelmingly Protestant state in which anti-Catholic sentiments were presumed to run strong. If Kennedy could carry a state like West Virginia, party leaders reasoned, perhaps the candidate's Catholicism was not the barrier to election many had presumed it would be. By enabling candidates to demonstrate their vote-getting abilities in selected states, primaries helped party leaders make a more informed decision about who would make the most formidable candidate in the general election.[73]

Although primaries could play a pivotal role in campaigns during this era, they were never a substitute for the central task of winning over the support of state and local party leaders. In 1952, for example, Illinois' Adlai E. Stevenson II secured the Democratic Party's nomination without entering a single primary, besting Tennessee's Estes Kefauver, who had received two-thirds of the votes cast in Democratic primaries. Unlike Kennedy, who selectively entered primaries to demonstrate his strength to party leaders, Kefauver entered every primary in an effort to maximize his delegates at the convention. Kefauver played the same outsider game that Theodore Roosevelt had tried in 1912, with the same unsuccessful result. Kennedy, in contrast, mixed the occasional timely shot from the outside with a powerful inside game of meeting and currying favor with state and local party notables.[74]

The 1968 Democratic contest revealed both the power and limits of primaries in this mixed system. Dissatisfaction with the Vietnam War fueled the insurgent campaign of Minnesota senator Eugene McCarthy, who challenged incumbent president Lyndon Johnson in the New Hampshire primary. Although McCarthy lost to Johnson in New Hampshire—receiving 42 percent of the vote to the president's 49 percent—the strength of McCarthy's showing was widely perceived as a sign of the president's weakness. Buoyed by McCarthy's showing, Robert Kennedy jumped into the race four days later. Two weeks after that, Johnson announced he would not seek reelection. The primary result had clearly mattered. Yet when the dust had settled, the winner of the Democratic nomination was a man who had not entered a single primary: Vice President Hubert Humphrey.

Had Robert Kennedy not been assassinated, perhaps the result might have been different, but probably not. For even at the moment of Kennedy's greatest triumph—his narrow victory over McCarthy in the California primary on June 4—he lagged well behind Humphrey in the delegate count. Humphrey's muscular inside game was more than a match for the flashy outside game of McCarthy and Kennedy. Although McCarthy received 39 percent of the vote in the primaries (Kennedy won 31 percent), Humphrey won easily on the convention's first ballot, securing more than two-thirds of the delegates.[75]

Humphrey's selection angered many Democrats, who questioned the fairness of having party insiders control the nomination. They advocated reforms that would make the nomination process more responsive to the preferences of rank-and-file party members. In an effort to unite his fractured party, Humphrey consented to a commission (known as the McGovern–Fraser Commission) charged with making the delegate-selection process more transparent and more democratic. Much as the 1824 election had precipitated the collapse of King Caucus and the rise of the national nominating convention, the 1968 election sounded the death knell of the national nominating convention and triggered the rise of the modern primary-centered selection process.[76]

THE CONTEMPORARY NOMINATION PROCESS

The reforms initiated after 1968 revolutionized the delegate-selection process. Power shifted from party leaders to party voters in primaries and caucuses. Selective participation in a few strategic primaries was no longer a viable option for candidates. Now they had to compete in virtually every primary if they were to secure the nomination. The Democratic Party leaders who had selected Humphrey in 1968 found themselves powerless to stop the outsider campaigns of George McGovern in 1972 and Jimmy Carter in 1976. The dramatic change in the rules of the game was captured in the bewilderment expressed by party elder statesman W. Averell Harriman at the news of Carter's sudden emergence as frontrunner after victories in the Iowa caucuses and New Hampshire primary: "How can that be? I don't even know Jimmy Carter, and as far as I know, none of my friends know him either."[77]

The Not-so-Super Superdelegates

After President Carter's loss to Ronald Reagan in 1980, Democratic Party leaders tried to write themselves back into the nomination process by guaranteeing that a certain percentage of delegates at the national convention were set aside for state party officials and members of Congress. Party leaders hoped that these "superdelegates" would make it more likely that the party's nominee would be acceptable to party insiders. Party officials also hoped that superdelegates could broker the selection of a nominee in the event that no candidate entered the convention with a majority of the delegates. Superdelegates made their first appearance in the 1984 Democratic convention, in which they made up about 14 percent of the convention's delegates. By 2008, they made up 20 percent of Democratic delegates.

Superdelegates, however, did little to revive the power of party officials or the national nominating convention. In 1984, superdelegates did break overwhelmingly for former vice president Walter Mondale, helping him to defeat the insurgent campaign of Colorado senator Gary Hart. But Mondale gained more primary votes than Hart, too, and likely would have won even without superdelegates. In any event, the 1984 election discredited the idea that party leaders were better suited to picking an electorally viable candidate. Mondale was crushed by President Reagan, carrying only the District of Columbia and his home state of Minnesota, for a total of 13 electoral votes. No Democratic nominee in American history, including McGovern, has received fewer electoral college votes than Mondale.

In 2008, the primary battle between Illinois senator Barack Obama and New York senator Hillary Clinton put superdelegates back in the spotlight. Early on, many superdelegates lined up behind the frontrunner Clinton, just as they had backed Mondale over Hart in 1984. Like Hart's supporters, Obama's backers assailed superdelegates as undemocratic. However, unlike Hart, Obama used his strength in primaries and especially caucuses, as well as his fundraising prowess, to persuade many superdelegates to back the newcomer. Most revealing of all, however, was the large number of superdelegates who insisted that they would support whichever candidate received the most pledged delegates or the most popular votes. As superdelegate and Pennsylvania congressman Jason Altmire told the *New York Times*: "If we get to the end and Senator Obama has won more states, has more delegates and more popular votes I would need some sort of rationale for why at that point any superdelegate would go the other way, seeing that the people have spoken." Viewed this way, of course, there was no rationale at all for the existence of superdelegates. Who needs superdelegates if their only job is to rubberstamp the choice made by primary and caucus voters?[78]

The 2008 election exposed the essential character of the post-1968 system, a system in which the legitimacy of the nominee depended entirely on delegates accumulated in the caucuses and primaries prior to the convention. Few superdelegates wanted a brokered convention, which would have exacerbated and highlighted fault lines within the party. Party officials understood that a nominee emerging from a brokered convention would be crippled, a compromised and illegitimate offspring of elite bargaining. Only a nominee selected by the voters would be accepted as the party's legitimate standard-bearer. And only a carefully scripted convention would enable the party to present a united front to the televised audience tuning into the convention.

The Invisible Primary

Although no amount of superdelegates will bring back the brokered conventions of yesteryear, superdelegates' candidate endorsements are not without significance. They are a visible sign of the unseen power of parties during the aptly named "invisible primary"—the critical year or more prior to the first caucuses and primaries. Also called the "money primary," this is the period in which party insiders—elected officials, activists, and fundraisers—have played a crucial role in shaping the field and settling upon a front-runner.

The Republican Party proved particularly adept in the post-1968 era at using the invisible primary to coalesce around its preferred candidate. Between 1972 and 2004, the party insiders' preferred candidate (Nixon in 1972, Ford in 1976, Reagan in 1980 and 1984, George H.W. Bush in 1992, Bob Dole in 1996, and George W. Bush in 2000 and 2004) won the Republican nomination each time, which perhaps explains why Republicans never felt the need to introduce superdelegates into their nomination process.[79]

In 2008, however, for the first time in the post-1968 era, Republican Party activists and officials failed to coalesce around a candidate during the invisible primary. Three leading candidates—Arizona senator John McCain, New York City mayor Rudy Giuliani, and former Massachusetts governor Mitt Romney—jostled for the support of party insiders during 2007, but none had emerged as the party's clear favorite by the time the voting began in the Iowa caucuses, which were won by the relatively unknown Arkansas governor Mike Huckabee. Conservative activists distrusted all three of the party's leading men, including the eventual nominee, John McCain. In winning his party's nomination, McCain became the first Republican in the post-1968 era to be nominated "despite intense opposition within his party."[80]

McCain's nomination was aided by the fact that several key early Republican primaries were open primaries, in which individuals who were not registered Republicans could vote. In New Hampshire, for instance, exit polls showed that McCain fared marginally less well than Romney among the 60 percent of primary voters who identified as Republicans. Yet McCain carried the state because he did much better than Romney among those who identified as independents. In the pivotal South Carolina primary ten days later, McCain received fewer votes from self-identified Republicans than did Huckabee, yet once again McCain's strength among those who considered themselves independents enabled McCain to win the primary. In 2008, not only did party leaders lose control of the nomination process but, arguably, rank-and-file party voters did as well.

In 2012, party insiders appeared to regain control of the nomination process. In the months leading up to the Iowa caucuses, the eventual Republican nominee, Romney, racked up the lion's share of elite endorsements and raised far more money than his chief rivals, Ron Paul, Newt Gingrich, and Rick Santorum, none of whom had significant support from party insiders. The gap in endorsements and money between the party frontrunner and party insurgents only grew wider after the voting got underway. Yet despite broad support from party insiders, Romney struggled in the early going, losing to Santorum in Iowa and to Gingrich in South Carolina. In the end, though, the party establishment's preferred candidate ran out a comfortable winner over his three insurgent rivals.[81]

Does the Party Still Decide? The Gatekeepers and the Party Crashers in 2016

Any notion that Mitt Romney's nomination in 2012 signaled a restoration of a nomination process favorable to insider-backed frontrunners was quickly dispelled during the

2016 Republican primary contest. Six months before a single primary vote had been cast, Jeb Bush's team announced that it had raised an unprecedented 114 million dollars from top party donors, part of a "shock and awe" launch to a campaign that was supposed to attract elite endorsements and scare away potential rivals, as his brother George W. Bush had done in 1999. But neither Jeb Bush's fundraising edge nor his endorsements translated into popular support or deterred other candidates from entering the race. A total of 17 Republicans threw their hat into the ring, and 12 were still in the race on the first day of February 2016 when Iowa Republicans caucused. Two of those candidates, Texas senator Ted Cruz and businessman Donald Trump, were anathema to the party establishment, yet they sat atop the polls in January 2016 and finished first and second in the Iowa caucuses.[82]

After Bush's disastrous sixth-place finish in Iowa (where he won less than 3 percent of the vote), party insiders immediately began lining up behind Florida senator Marco Rubio. Over the next three weeks, more than 30 US House members, senators, and governors from across the ideological spectrum endorsed Rubio; during that same three-week period not a single member of Congress or governor endorsed Trump and only five endorsed Cruz. But elite endorsements appeared to count for little as Trump rolled to decisive victories in New Hampshire on February 9 and South Carolina on February 20. By the middle of March, the party establishment's best hope had left the race (Bush dropped out after the South Carolina primary) and party insiders were reduced to spectators in a contest between two candidates they disliked and distrusted (Cruz and Trump) and a third (John Kasich) who had no viable path to the nomination. The party's gatekeepers could do nothing to stop Trump from crashing their party. The question is: why?[83]

Some maintain that Trump's nomination was a freak accident produced by a highly fractured field and strategic miscalculations by rival candidates who failed to take Trump seriously and so attacked each other rather than him. But this analysis mistakes cause for effect. The fractured field was itself a sign of the party insiders' inability to coalesce around a candidate who could attract support from the party rank-and-file. And the candidates' reluctance to criticize Trump was an effect of the party's fear of alienating Trump's core supporters. The reasons why the party's gatekeepers could not stop the Trump nomination, in short, run deeper than strategic missteps and idiosyncratic circumstances or events.

Part of the explanation for the declining influence of the party gatekeepers lies in changes in campaign finance. The rise of Super PACs—political action committees that spend money on behalf of a candidate—essentially allows campaigns to raise unprecedented sums of money, since there is no limit on what an individual or corporation can give to a Super PAC (individuals can only give $2,700 directly to a candidate and corporations are barred from contributing directly to candidates).[84] Republican insiders might not have liked Ted Cruz but they couldn't stop three billionaire families, including the hedge fund magnate Robert Mercer, from contributing more than 30 million dollars to Cruz Super PACs within weeks of the announcement that Cruz was running for the presidency.[85] That so many Republican candidates threw their proverbial hat in the ring —and stayed in the ring for as long as they did—was no historical accident, but rather a direct consequence of the fact that Super PACs made it much easier for candidates to tap into the money they needed to wage a campaign.

But Super PACS were hardly the major story of the 2016 nomination process. After all, Trump won the Republican nomination without relying on Super PAC money,[86] and on the Democratic side Vermont senator Bernie Sanders nearly toppled the party establishment's preferred candidate, Hillary Clinton, despite largely eschewing Super PAC money. Whereas Sanders did battle with the party's chosen one by relying largely on internet fundraising (Sanders used the social media fundraising site ActBlue to help him raise more than 200 million dollars from roughly 2.4 million donors),[87] Trump's primary campaign was largely self-financed (as was Romney's losing effort in 2008). But Trump did not spend his way to victory. Rather, Trump's candidacy was propelled by an unprecedented amount of free media. In the year leading up to Super Tuesday on March 1, Trump spent far less on television advertising than Bush, Rubio, and Cruz—and less even than Kasich and Chris Christie—but benefitted from an estimated $2 billion worth of free media, a number nearly ten times as great as that of the party insiders' preferred candidates, Bush and Rubio.[88] Both Trump and Sanders utilized the new media environment to bypass the party's traditional gatekeepers and communicate directly with their passionate supporters.[89]

Trump's nomination, however, speaks to more than a transformation in campaign finance and communication technologies. It also reveals a loss of public trust in the party's established leaders. Elite endorsements only help candidates if voters trust the elites who are doing the endorsing. When that trust breaks down, elite endorsements cease to matter and may even become counterproductive. The loss of trust is what enabled Trump to point to the party establishment's antipathy to his candidacy as "proof that he really was untouched and untainted by the unpopular GOP establishment." And that deep suspicion of the GOP establishment enabled Trump, a candidate who had never before held public office and who had switched his party affiliation multiple times over the past several decades, to execute what most party insiders experienced as a hostile takeover.[90]

After the party reforms of 1968, critics warned that the new candidate-centered primary process would undermine the power of party insiders to screen out inexperienced candidates who would be unable to govern (Carter), extremist candidates who could not get elected (McGovern), or charismatic demagogues who might undermine the country's democracy.[91] Up until 2016, the case for this critique seemed weak. Especially on the Republican side, as Marty Cohen and his coauthors showed in *The Party Decides: Presidential Nominations Before and After Reform* (2008), party insiders showed an impressive ability in the post-1968 universe to control nomination outcomes through a mix of money, media attention, and endorsements. But Trump's nomination, unimaginable in a pre-1968 universe in which candidates were vetted and largely chosen by party elites, indicates that critics of the 1968 party reforms were prescient to worry about a nomination politics that sidelined party officials and entrusted the vetting of a party's candidates to the mass public and the mass media. And, paradoxically, weak parties may be especially problematic in an era of extraordinarily high partisanship in which partisans so loathe the other party that most will reflexively vote for their party's standard-bearer no matter their own candidate's flaws.[92]

The Contemporary Debate over the Electoral College

If the contemporary nomination process raises the question of whether the nation suffers from an excess of democracy, the general election requires us to ask whether the electoral process—specifically the electoral college—is insufficiently democratic. Unlike the nomination process, which has continuously evolved over the past two centuries, the electoral college has barely changed at all. Because the Constitution makes no provision for party nominations, the process has been continually recreated to meet the needs and interests of parties and candidates. In contrast, the strategy and tactics of general election candidates remain governed, for better or worse, by the electoral college established by the Constitution and modified by the Twelfth Amendment.

Over the years there have been hundreds and hundreds of amendments introduced in Congress to reform and even abolish the electoral college. Those who advocate fixing or eradicating the electoral college typically target four problems: (1) the problem of "faithless electors"—that is, electors chosen to support one candidate who cast their vote for another candidate; (2) the undemocratic nature of the House contingency election; (3) the allocation of electors based on states, in violation of the principle of one person, one vote; and (4) the possibility that the electoral college winner might diverge from the popular vote winner.

Defenders of the electoral college counter that the alleged problems of the electoral college are largely hypothetical and that critics underestimate the college's virtues. From this perspective, faithless electors are a nonproblem since relatively few electors have been unfaithful and none of these breaches of faith have affected the outcome (though it is more difficult to be as sanguine about faithless electors in the wake of the 2016 election, in which there were seven faithless electors, including five who refused to vote for Democratic nominee Hillary Clinton). Defenders of the electoral college typically concede that it is difficult to justify the contingency election in the House, particularly the unit rule that gives each state delegation one vote. But they note that the danger is largely theoretical in a stable two-party system; after all, the last time a presidential election was decided by the House was in 1824, before a two-party system had taken shape. Moreover, defenders argue, the strength and stability of the two-party system is itself a product, at least in part, of the winner-take-all nature of the electoral college. Absent the electoral college, they maintain, the country would be riven by single-issue candidacies and a proliferation of third parties.

How the Electoral College Worked in the Twentieth Century

During the twentieth century, the electoral college's defenders emphasized the low probability of the electoral college winner being different from the popular vote winner. Yes, the electoral college vote diverged from the popular vote twice in 12 years in the late nineteenth century, but that seemed more a remote historical curiosity than a fundamental weakness. The twentieth century witnessed its share of close elections, but not once did the electoral college fail to match the popular vote winner. Moreover, the electoral college consistently rendered a more decisive judgment than the popular vote. Between 1900 and 1996, the electoral vote winner averaged 76 percent of the vote, while the average vote for the winner in the popular vote was only about 53 percent. On seven occasions (Wilson in 1912 and 1916, Truman in 1948, Kennedy in 1960, Nixon in 1968, and Clinton in 1992 and 1996) the popular vote winner failed to get a majority of the vote, yet the electoral college produced a majority winner every time.

The electoral college's effects were particularly impressive when a competitive third party was in the field. In 1980, with the independent John Anderson taking nearly 7 percent of the popular vote, the Republican nominee Ronald Reagan was able to parlay 50.7 percent of the popular vote into a whopping 91 percent of the electoral votes. In 1912, with former president and Progressive Party nominee Theodore Roosevelt taking more than 27 percent of the vote, Democrat Woodrow Wilson received 82 percent of the electoral vote despite getting only 42 percent of the popular vote. The framers had envisioned the electoral college as a system that would work without political parties, but ironically its effect has been to powerfully reinforce a two-party system.

The irony goes deeper, however. The framers were most concerned with the emergence of sectional parties and candidacies. Yet while the electoral college is a powerful deterrent to third parties that have a national appeal and constituency, it rewards regionally based third parties. In 1992, for instance, Independent candidate Ross Perot got an impressive 19 percent of the vote but failed to secure a single electoral vote; in 1996, Perot's popular vote total was 8.4 percent and he was still shut out of the electoral college. In total, Perot received 28 million votes without garnering one electoral vote. In contrast, the segregationist George Wallace won 46 electoral votes in 1968 by winning five southern states (Alabama, Arkansas, Georgia, Louisiana, and Mississippi), and in 1948 the racist Dixiecrat Strom Thurmond parlayed a little more than 1 million votes into 39 electoral votes by carrying Alabama, Louisiana, Mississippi, and South Carolina.

Both the 1948 and 1968 elections were close contests: Nixon won 43.4 percent to Humphrey's 42.7 percent in 1968, and Truman won 49.5 percent of the vote to Republican Thomas Dewey's 45.1 percent in 1948. Either election could easily have produced a result in which the regional third party candidate was positioned to play kingmaker after the election. Thurmond's 39 electoral votes would have been decisive if 3,000 Truman voters in Idaho, fewer than 1,000 in Nevada, and 9,000 in California had preferred Dewey. Wallace would have controlled the outcome in 1968 had Humphrey carried Missouri and Ohio, states he lost by 1 and 2 percent, respectively. In both elections, then, thanks to the electoral college, the nation came perilously close to enabling a reactionary arch-segregationist to pick the president. So, while the electoral college generally does work to maintain the two-party system, it does not deter regional third parties. On the contrary, it provides an incentive for them to enter the contest.

Even without robust third parties in the game, the electoral college twice in the twentieth century came extraordinarily close to producing a winner who lost the popular vote. In 1916, the electoral college nearly gifted the election to President Woodrow Wilson's opponent Charles Evans Hughes, despite Wilson's 600,000-vote margin in the popular vote. That outcome was averted only because Wilson carried California by fewer than 4,000 votes out of nearly 1 million votes cast in the Golden State—a victory that many historians attribute to Hughes' decision to snub California's governor Hiram Johnson. Had Hughes met with the California governor and carried the state, the electoral college would have produced a president who lost the national popular vote by more than 3 percent. The margin of victory in the 1976 election was narrower than in 1916, but Democrat Jimmy Carter nonetheless bested Republican Gerald Ford by nearly 1,700,000 votes. But had 5,550 Carter voters in Ohio and another 3,700 in Hawaii voted for President Ford, Carter would have lost. Still, at the end of the twentieth century these near-misses could mostly be dismissed as hypothetical speculation. In the twenty-first century, however, the nation's luck ran out, as twice in sixteen years—first in 2000 and then again in 2016—the presidential candidate with the most popular votes lost in the electoral college.

The 2000 Election: Court Picks President

In 2000, Vice President Al Gore received 500,000 more votes than the electoral college winner, Governor George W. Bush. Bush was able to win a slim majority in the electoral college—he gained 271 electors, one more than the 270 required—despite losing the popular vote because he carried 30 states to Gore's 20 plus the District of Columbia. By winning more states than his Democratic rival, Bush received a bonus of 18 electoral votes, which was sufficient to turn defeat into victory.[93]

Everyone had expected the contest between Bush and Gore to be close, but nobody anticipated that the contest would be decided by 0.009 percent of the nearly 6 million votes cast in Florida and that it would take more than a month before a winner would be declared. In the initial count, Bush had about a roughly 1,800-vote lead in Florida, a margin that was sufficiently close to trigger an automatic statewide machine recount. After the recount, Bush's margin shrank to a little more than 300 votes. However, the Florida Democratic Party, at the behest of the Gore campaign, had also petitioned to have votes recounted by hand in four populous counties in which Gore had fared well—Broward, Miami-Dade, Palm Beach, and Volusia. Under Florida law, if a candidate requests a manual recount, the county canvassing board may authorize such a recount if it finds evidence of "an error in the vote tabulation which could affect the outcome of the election." Each of the four counties determined that a full manual recount was warranted, but counting votes by hand takes time, and Florida law required counties to certify results within a week of the election. Faced with the task of recounting between roughly 200,000 (in the case of Volusia) and 600,000 (in the case of Miami-Dade) votes, county officials sought an extension of the certification deadline of November 14.[94]

Secretary of State Katherine Harris, who was co-chair of Bush's Florida campaign, refused to extend the deadline absent a showing of voter fraud, "substantial non-compliance with statutory election procedures," or "an act of God" that prevented election officials from complying with the statutory deadline. Florida law empowered the secretary of state to ignore late returns and to fine canvassing board members who missed the filing deadline, so county officials were compelled to submit their final results before completing the recount (except Volusia County, which completed their manual recount before the deadline). On November 18, after completing the count of absentee ballots,

Harris certified Bush the winner, by 930 votes. The Gore campaign, however, had taken their case to the courts in an attempt to compel the secretary of state to allow the county canvassing boards to finish their recounts. The suit was initially rejected by the trial court judge but the Florida Supreme Court (all seven of whom were Democratic appointees) overturned the lower court, ruling unanimously that Harris had been wrong not to allow the recounts to continue. The court allowed the counties five additional days, until November 26, to finish their manual recounts.

On November 26, Harris certified Bush the winner by a 537-vote margin. Gore's legal team then challenged the vote counts in three counties: Palm Beach, Miami-Dade, and Nassau. Gore's request for a hand count of 14,000 disputed ballots in Miami-Dade and Palm Beach counties was rejected by circuit court judge Sanders Saul on December 4. Four days later, on December 8, the Florida high court reversed Judge Saul's ruling. Whereas Judge Saul argued that the certification decisions of the canvassing boards could be invalidated only if there was evidence of "a clear abuse of discretion," the Florida Supreme Court insisted that the judge was required to make his own independent ("de novo") review of the evidence.[95]

Florida law stated that "No vote shall be declared invalid or void if there is a clear indication of the intent of voters," and that an incorrectly marked ballot should not be discarded unless "it is impossible to determine the elector's choice." Using this "clear intent of the voter" standard, the Florida high court found that the disputed votes should be recounted, as Gore requested. It also found that Secretary Harris had been wrong to invalidate recounted votes that had been completed after she certified the vote, which brought Gore to within 154 votes of Bush. Bush's legal team argued that if a recount was to be attempted, it should be done on a statewide basis, not just in the counties Gore had targeted. The court rejected the idea that Florida law required a statewide recount but agreed that it would be fairer in this particular case. Therefore, relying on its statutory authority "to provide any relief appropriate under the circumstances," the court (in a 4–3 vote) ordered a statewide manual recount of "undervotes."[96]

The problem of undervotes was particularly acute in counties using punch-card ballots. The primary purpose of the court-ordered manual recount was to examine those ballots in which a voter had punched out a "chad" next to the name of either Gore or Bush but the machine had not counted the vote because the "hanging chad" had not fully detached. Some states had laws that gave voting officials clear guidance about how to discern the intent of the voter on a punch-card ballot in the event of a manual recount. Texas, for instance, had a law (signed, ironically, by then governor George W. Bush) that specified that for a hanging chad to count as a vote, "at least two corners of the chad are detached" and that "light is visible through the hole," or that "indentation on the chad from the stylus or other object is present and indicates a clearly ascertainable intent of the voter to vote." Florida, however, had no such standards about discerning the voter's intent, thus leaving county officials to decide what should qualify as clear evidence of a voter's intent.[97]

After all the legal challenges and delays, however, time was running out. Federal law required all states to cast their electoral votes on December 18. Failure to meet that deadline could mean that Florida's votes would not be counted, which would leave neither candidate with a majority in the electoral college, thereby placing the decision in the hands of Congress. If that happened, Bush would almost certainly win, as Republicans controlled a majority of state delegations. Further complicating matters was that the Florida state legislature, also controlled by Republicans, was threatening to choose the state's electors itself, based on its authority in Article II, which provided that a state's electors be selected "in such Manner as the Legislature thereof may direct." Whether the legislature could legally do that after it had already opted to have the electors chosen by popular vote was unclear, like so much else in the conflict.

Immediately after the Florida Supreme Court ordered the statewide recount, Bush's lawyers asked the US Supreme Court to intervene to stop the recount and reverse the ruling. On the following day, a Saturday, the Court announced that it would hear oral arguments on Monday morning and issued a stay that brought an immediate halt to the manual recount.

On December 12, the day after oral arguments, a sharply divided Court announced its decision. The four most liberal justices argued that the Court should permit Florida officials to devise uniform statewide standards for a recount and finish that process before December 18. Perhaps Florida could even extend the recounting until January 6, 2001, which was when Congress would actually count the votes. However, the conservative majority ruled that Florida could not recount its votes because there was not sufficient time for the state to conduct a fair statewide recount.

The most criticized aspect of the Court's decision was its central holding, accepted by seven of the nine justices, that the recount process ordered by the Florida Supreme Court violated the US Constitution's equal protection clause because not all votes were being counted using the same standard. Bush's lawyers had proposed this argument to the Court but they relegated it to a secondary position in their brief, perhaps because they thought it unlikely that the Court, particularly its most conservative members, would accept an argument that invited a dramatic escalation of the federal government's role in regulating state and local elections. If the Constitution forbade counties from using different standards in discerning the intent of voters, then the entire crazy-quilt patchwork of American election laws was suspect. The Bush legal team may also have been reluctant to rely too heavily on the equal protection argument because it did not require the Court to nullify the Florida high court's recount plan. Rather, it only required that the case be sent back to the Florida Supreme Court, which could then either devise guidelines for the recount consistent with equal protection or decide that such a recount was not possible and that the election was therefore over. Indeed, this is exactly what Justices David Souter and Steven Breyer argued the Court should do.[98]

That the Court's conservative justices used the equal protection clause to stop the recount was more than a little ironic. Liberals have long worried about the inequalities that result from a decentralized electoral system that leaves the choice of voting machines to state and local authorities. They point out that nonwhite and poor Americans are more likely to live in precincts that use antiquated punch-card voting systems that are prone to produce spoiled or mismarked ballots, whereas Americans in wealthier precincts are more likely to use more reliable voting technologies such as touch-screen computers or optically scanned ballots. These inequities help to explain why half of the spoiled ballots in Florida were cast by African Americans even though only about one in ten Florida voters were African American. Ironically, the Court's unprecedented intervention in the name of the equal protection clause prevented Florida from attempting to rectify the unequal advantage that decentralized administration of election laws had given to more affluent and whiter precincts.[99]

In the eyes of many observers, the Court seemed to be animated more by partisan politics than constitutional principle. Its two most liberal justices (John Paul Stevens and Ruth Bader Ginsburg) rejected an equal protection argument to which they were normally sympathetic, while the Court's five most conservative justices embraced a radical reading of the Equal Protection Clause that was—at least in the case of William Rehnquist, Antonin Scalia, and Clarence Thomas—wholly inconsistent with their jurisprudence. Even more troubling was the conservative majority's insistence that their decision was "limited to the present circumstances." That is, although equal protection could be used as a tool to settle this election dispute, it could not serve as a precedent for future cases.

Imagine a simple thought experiment. Reverse the situations of the two candidates. If Gore had been certified the winner and Bush was challenging the vote, is it conceivable that the conservative majority would have reached for the equal protection clause to ensure a Gore victory? University of Virginia law professor Michael Klarman is surely right that there is not another Supreme Court decision "about which one can say with equal confidence that switching the parties to the litigation, and nothing else, would have changed the result."[100]

In the end, an election in which more than 100 million people participated was decided by nine unelected judges, who split along ideological and partisan lines. Each of the five judges who awarded the election to Bush was a Republican appointee, and the four who rejected this course were the Court's most liberal judges. But even had the justices not so clearly followed their own ideological and partisan proclivities, the outcome of the election would still be troubling. Although liberals condemned the US Supreme Court and conservatives excoriated the Florida Supreme Court, the real culprit was arguably the electoral college, specifically its winner-take-all nature that meant that 25 electoral votes—nearly 10 percent of the total number needed to win the presidency—depended on a tiny handful of votes.

The 2016 Election: Making Winners of Losers

No electoral system is perfect. And one electoral college misfire every hundred or so years is perhaps the kind of error rate a political system can tolerate. Moreover, in a razor-close election it may be a mistake to see the discrepancy between popular vote winner and electoral college vote winner as an error at all. After all, presidential candidates organize their campaigns in a quest to obtain a majority of electoral votes, not a majority of popular votes. Had George W. Bush and Al Gore been competing for popular votes, they would have spent less time, for instance, campaigning in swing states such as Florida, Ohio, and Pennsylvania and invested far more resources in getting out the vote in solidly red and blue states. It is certainly plausible that under these different rules, Bush would have made up the deficit of 500,000 popular votes and won the election.[101] The 2016 election, however, is more difficult to defend on these terms.

Democrat Hillary Clinton lost to Republican Donald Trump in the electoral college despite winning the popular vote by nearly 3 million votes, a margin of victory that was almost six times as great as Al Gore's in 2000. In fact, Clinton's popular vote margin was essentially the same as the popular vote margin that George W. Bush secured in winning reelection in 2004, and only 2 million lower than Barack Obama's 5-million-vote advantage over Mitt Romney in 2012. While we cannot know for certain how an election determined by popular vote would have affected the candidates' vote totals, it seems unlikely that it could have netted Trump a plurality of the popular votes. What we do know for certain is that Democrats won the popular vote in six of the seven elections between 1992 and 2016, netting 30 million more popular votes in the process, yet won the presidency on only four of those elections.[102]

So how was Trump able to win the election while losing the popular vote? Like Bush in 2000, he benefitted from winning more states than his Democratic opponent. In fact, Trump won exactly the same number of states as Bush (30—Iowa, Michigan, Pennsylvania, and Wisconsin switched from the Democratic to Republican column, while Colorado, New Hampshire, Nevada, and Virginia moved in the opposite direction). But while Bush's narrow electoral college victory in 2000 would not have happened without the electoral bonus he received by winning nine more contests than Gore, Trump's decisive electoral college victory (Trump received 306 electoral votes to Clinton's 232) did not depend on the small-state bonus built into the electoral college. Instead Trump's victory hinged on narrowly winning a handful of highly competitive rustbelt states, notably Michigan (which he won by 0.2 percent), Pennsylvania (0.7 percent), and Wisconsin (0.8 percent). A shift of 40,000 votes from Trump to Clinton in these three states (137 million votes were cast nationwide) would have been sufficient to make Clinton president.

Some observers, such as political analyst Michael Barone—noting Clinton's massive 4.2-million-vote margin in left-leaning California—argued that the 2016 election vindicated the framers' design because the state-based electoral college prevented the nation's largest state from being able to "impose something like colonial rule over the rest of the nation." It is true that about one in ten of the nation's votes were cast by Californians, but one in ten of the nation's votes also came from what journalist Nate Cohn calls "Appalachafornia" (West Virginia, Kentucky, Tennessee, Arkansas, Alabama, Oklahoma, Kansas, Nebraska, Wyoming, Montana, Idaho, North Dakota and South Dakota), and Trump won that (overwhelmingly white) region of the country by the same massive 30-point margin by which Clinton won the more racially and ethnically diverse state of California (Clinton received 55 electoral votes for the 14 million votes cast in California, whereas Trump received 73 electoral votes for the 14 million votes cast in Appalachafornia). One could complain with at least as much justification that the electoral college had fostered "colonial rule" by white, rural America.[103]

In the end, though, California and Appalachafornia cancelled each other out. Eliminate those states and Clinton still would have won the popular vote by about two percentage points and Trump still would have come out on top in the electoral college. The fundamental reason why Trump was able to lose the popular vote but still win the presidency was that he won the key battleground states. Two-thirds of campaign events in 2016 took place in six states—Florida, North Carolina, Pennsylvania, Ohio, Virginia, and Michigan—and Trump won five of those six states. The nation did not choose the president; voters in battleground states did. That is the way presidential elections work in the United States.[104]

The Future of the Electoral College

The historic discrepancy in 2016 between the popular vote and the electoral college vote spurred a spate of calls from Democrats for the abolition of the electoral college, including a bill introduced the week after the election by California senator Barbara Boxer that proposed a constitutional amendment to end the electoral college. Republicans, meanwhile, rallied to the electoral college's defense. On the same day that Boxer proposed to abolish the electoral college, president-elect Donald Trump tweeted that the electoral college was "actually genius" because "it brings all states, including the small ones, into play."

Ironically, over the preceding decade it had often been Republicans who were most vocal about the unfairness of the electoral college. Their nervousness about the electoral college dated back to the near-miss of the 2004 election, when George W. Bush won the popular vote by a comfortable 3 million votes but would have lost the presidency had 60,000 Ohio voters switched their choice from Bush to John Kerry. In the lead-up to and aftermath of the 2012 election, Republicans fretted about the Democrats' allegedly impregnable blue wall: the nineteen states totaling 242 electoral college votes that had voted Democratic in every presidential election between 1992 and 2012 (in contrast, the Republicans' only protection was a "small red picket fence" of 13 states totaling 102 electoral votes). On election night in 2012, Trump gave expression to this simmering Republican anxiety about the Democrats' unfair electoral college advantage. Convinced that Romney had won the popular vote "by a lot," Trump tweeted that the electoral college was "a disaster for democracy" that had made "a laughing stock out of our nation." The following day, Trump tweeted: "More votes equals a loss ... revolution!"[105]

It is easy to lampoon Trump's flip-flop on the electoral college, but it is hardly surprising that partisan calculations inform the way politicians see the electoral college and the desirability of reform. But, hyperbolic partisan rhetoric notwithstanding, the evidence that the electoral college systematically benefits one party over the other is relatively weak, although if Republican-dominated states continue to make it more difficult to vote by enacting, for instance, strict voter identification laws and shrinking early voting opportunities, and Democratic-controlled states continue to expand voter access through mechanisms such as automatic voter registration, then the likelihood of the Democratic Party winning the popular vote while losing the electoral college will increase. But whatever the real effects of the electoral college on party fortunes, partisan fears and ambitions are likely to continue to color the debate over the electoral college and impede the bipartisan consensus that would be necessary to replace or reform the electoral college.[106]

Only once in the past half-century—in 1969—has the nation come anywhere close to doing away with the electoral college, and, ironically, that effort was prompted by an election in which the electoral college worked to elect the popular vote-winner. But while the 1968 election ultimately gave Nixon a cushion of 31 electoral votes, the third party candidacy of segregationist George Wallace came harrowingly close to throwing the election into the House of Representatives. The prospect of an avowed segregationist being empowered to choose the president and, worse, extracting political concessions for his support, sufficiently alarmed leaders in both parties to prompt Congress to take action.

In the spring of 1969, by a vote of 28–6, the House Judiciary Committee approved a constitutional amendment to replace the electoral college with a direct popular vote. Under the proposed amendment, if no candidate received 40 percent of the vote there would be a runoff between the top two candidates. In September, the House passed the amendment by a huge (338–70) margin and President Nixon endorsed the plan. In the Senate, however, the measure ran into a filibuster spearheaded by senators from small and southern states. A vote to end the filibuster gained the support of only 60 percent of those voting, short of the two-thirds needed at that time to cut off debate.

But even had the Senate overcome the filibuster, it is unlikely the amendment would have been ratified by the requisite number of states. A *New York Times* survey of state legislative leaders after the House vote found that three-fifths of state legislatures were "either certain or likely to approve a constitutional amendment embodying the direct election plan if it passes its final Congressional test in the Senate." Passage of a constitutional amendment, though, requires the approval of 38 state legislatures, and the *Times* counted 14 states that were either leaning or solidly against the amendment. Opposition was concentrated, not surprisingly, among the least populous states, such as Idaho, Montana, Nevada, Nebraska, North Dakota, South Dakota, and Utah. A number of southern states were also resistant to the reform, which they saw as an attempt to frustrate the political ambitions of segregationist candidates with a strong regional appeal.[107]

Over the past half-century, large bipartisan majorities of the American public have continued to tell pollsters that they favor abolishing the electoral election, but the high hurdles of the constitutional amendment process virtually guarantee that the American people are unlikely to get their wish. Former president Jimmy Carter is likely right in predicting that "200 years from now we will still have the Electoral College." Some reformers, though, have pinned their hopes on establishing popular election of the president without a constitutional amendment through an "interstate compact." Under this plan, states agree to allocate their electors to the candidate who gains a plurality of the popular vote, but the compact only becomes binding on the states that have signed it when the compact includes states possessing the 270 electoral votes needed for victory. As of September 2017, ten states and the District of Columbia have signed the compact, leaving the proposal 105 electoral votes short of going into effect. So far, though, interest in the plan has been limited to states that vote Democratic in presidential elections; legislators in Republican-leaning states have shown little or no interest in replacing an institution that has helped to hand their party the presidency twice in two decades.[108]

OBSTACLES TO REFORM IN A STATE-BASED ELECTORAL SYSTEM

"If we had an opportunity to design from scratch a way to pick a president," writes political scientist Thomas Mann, "it is inconceivable that we would arrive at our present system."[109] Whatever the merits of the electoral college, there is little question that a constitution drafted today would not include an electoral college. Instead, almost certainly, it would establish direct election of the president. Similarly, it is hard to imagine anyone today devising a nomination process that resembles what we have now—a system of such incredible complexity that only a handful of experts can fully comprehend or explain it.

Simplicity is not necessarily better than complexity, of course. And rationally planned systems need not work better than rules and practices that have evolved gradually without an overarching design. There is ample reason to beware the unintended consequences of reform and the limits of human reason. Experience also counsels that reform efforts will be dictated as much by political interests and ambitions as by a desire to build better institutions. Yet even skeptics of election reform can hardly help but marvel at how dramatically the presidential selection process diverges from what most Americans say they prefer: namely, a national primary and direct election of the president.

Americans think of the president as a representative of the people, but in truth the presidential selection process remains fundamentally state-based. From its inception, the electoral college has violated the principle of one person, one vote by overrepresenting voters in smaller states. In 2000 that overrepresentation of small-state voters produced the election of a president who got 500,000 fewer votes than his opponent. And in 2016 the state-based electoral college helped to elect a president who got nearly 3 million fewer votes than his opponent.

Although an eighteenth-century relic that few Americans understand, the electoral college is never likely to be abolished because of another undemocratic, state-based feature of the Constitution: Article V, which requires that three-quarters of the state legislatures ratify any constitutional amendment. Leaving aside that the vote for ratification is placed in the hands of state legislators rather than the people—itself a strikingly undemocratic feature—the fundamental problem is that the 13 smallest states—the number needed to block a constitutional amendment—represent only about 5 percent of the population. On most issues this may not be a problem, since small states do not necessarily share interests based on their size, but small states do share an interest in perpetuating an electoral college that overrepresents their citizens.

When it comes to the electoral college, the Constitution, for better or for worse, is clearly responsible for keeping reform out of the people's hands. The Constitution, however, cannot be faulted, at least not directly, for the nation's collective inability to fix the nomination process. For the Constitution is silent about political parties—understandably so, since the framers penned their document before the nation had familiarity with organized, popularly based political parties. The framers lived, as Larry Sabato observes, in "a pre-party, pre-popular-democracy age," and they wrote a constitution suited to that age.[110]

Although the Constitution says nothing about parties, let alone how parties should regulate nominations, the presidential nomination process is even more state-based than the electoral college, and here, too, small states—particularly New Hampshire and Iowa—wield influence that is disproportionate to their numbers. States largely control when they will schedule their nominating events, and the result has been a frontloaded schedule of primaries and caucuses that almost all observers of the process believe is undesirable. The only effective way to resolve the frontloading problem is to adopt, as political scientists William Mayer and Andrew Busch conclude, "some kind of centrally directed calendar" that would be able to impose a rational order on "the autonomous, uncoordinated way that states decide when to schedule their primaries and caucuses."[111]

But from where is this central direction to come? The federal government? Mayer and Busch think that the federal government lacks the constitutional authority to regulate the nomination process.[112] The national political parties? To make their rules effective they would have to coordinate their efforts, which is unlikely given that the two parties have different rules, incentives, and cultures. Even if the two parties did coordinate their efforts, they would not be able to impose their preferences on states without the aid of Congress. And even if Congress has the authority to do this, it will be reluctant to wade into terrain that traditionally has been left to states and state parties. Once again systemic reform seems to be beyond the reach of the people and their representatives.

The end result is that the only nationally elected office in the United States remains, in ways that are rarely acknowledged in our public discourse, a creature of a state-based election system—a system that sits uneasily at best with contemporary democratic norms of one person, one vote.

NOTES

1 Observations on Jefferson's Draft of a Constitution for Virginia, October 15, 1788, in William T. Hutchinson et al., eds., *The Papers of James Madison* (Chicago: University of Chicago Press, 1962), 11:289. Max Farrand, ed., *The Records of the Federal Convention* (New Haven: Yale University Press, 1937), 2:53 (July 19, 1787).

2 Harold L. Syrett, ed., *The Papers of Alexander Hamilton* (New York: Columbia University Press, 1961–1987), 5:248.

3 Richard P. McCormick, *The Presidential Game: The Origins of American Presidential Politics* (New York: Oxford University Press, 1982), 52–58.

4 Bruce Ackerman, *The Failure of the Founding Fathers: Jefferson, Marshall, and the Rise of Presidential Democracy* (Cambridge, MA: Harvard University Press, 2005), 37.

5 Ackerman, *Failure of the Founding Fathers*, 33.

6 Ackerman, *Failure of the Founding Fathers*, 37–39.

7 Ackerman, *Failure of the Founding Fathers*, 34.

8 Ackerman, *Failure of the Founding Fathers*, 40.

9 Ackerman, *Failure of the Founding Fathers*, 87–91.

10 Ackerman, *Failure of the Founding Fathers*, 320.

11 Ackerman, *Failure of the Founding Fathers*, 89, 320. Bernard A. Weisberger, *America Afire: Jefferson, Adams, and the Revolutionary Election of 1800* (New York: William Morrow, 2000), 275.

12   Ackerman, *Failure of the Founding Fathers*, 104–06, Weisberger, *America Afire*, 275.

13   Ackerman, *Failure of the Founding Fathers*, 106.

14   McCormick, *Presidential Game*, 83–84. The Twelfth Amendment also limited the House to the top three rather than the top five vote-getters in those cases where no candidate received a majority of the electoral votes. Federalists objected that this, too, disadvantaged small states because it reduced the possibility that a candidate from a small state would be eligible in the House election.

15   McCormick, *Presidential Game*, 86.

16   McCormick, *Presidential Game*, 86–87.

17   The 1-in-100 estimate is by historian Lynn W. Turner, as quoted in Evan Cornog and Richard Whelan, *Hats in the Ring: An Illustrated History of American Presidential Campaigns* (New York: Random House, 2000), 46.

18   In *The One-Party Presidential Contest: Adams, Jackson, and 1824's Five-Horse Race* (Lawrence: University Press of Kansas, 2015), Donald Ratcliffe shows that the conventional view that Andrew Jackson was the clear choice of the people is misleading because the popular vote totals did not include six states—most importantly New York, where one in seven Americans lived—in which the electors were selected by state legislatures. Ratcliffe makes the case that if those six states had chosen electors by popular vote, then Adams would have ended up with more popular votes than Jackson.

19   McCormick, *Presidential Game*, 149.

20   Richard Hofstadter, *The Idea of a Party System: The Rise of Legitimate Opposition in the United States, 1789–1840* (Berkeley: University of California Press, 1969), 200. Also see James W. Ceaser, *Presidential Selection: Theory and Development* (Princeton, NJ: Princeton University Press, 1979), 124.

21   Van Buren to Thomas Ritchie, January 13, 1827, quoted in Ralph Ketcham, *Presidents above Party: The First American Presidency, 1789–1829* (Chapel Hill: University of North Carolina Press, 1984), 145.

22   McCormick, *Presidential Game*, 124, 135–36.

23   McCormick, *Presidential Game*, 130.

24   McCormick, *Presidential Game*, 154. Delaware switched to popular vote in 1832, while South Carolina adhered to legislative selection until it seceded from the Union in 1860.

25   The Jacksonians held a convention not because there was any doubt that Jackson would be their standard-bearer but to help the party unite around a vice-presidential candidate. By 1832, Vice President Calhoun was a staunch enemy of the president and so was out of the running. Hammering out an agreement on the vice presidency was vital for two reasons. First, Jackson's supporters worried that sectional divisions and state favorites could result in no vice-presidential candidate receiving a majority of electoral votes. That would hand the decision to the United States Senate, which the Constitution tasked with choosing from the top two vote-getters in the event that no vice-presidential candidate received a majority of electoral votes. Second, the vice-presidential choice was widely understood to be a choice for Jackson's probable successor.

26   Richard P. McCormick, "Political Development and the Second Party System," in William Nisbet Chambers and Walter Dean Burnham, eds., *The American Party Systems: Stages of Political Development* (New York: Oxford University Press, 1975), 98.

27   McCormick, "Political Development and the Second Party System," 98–101.

28   McCormick, "Political Development and the Second Party System," 97, 112.

29   In 1876 the Democratic ticket paired New York's Samuel Tilden with Indiana's Thomas Hendricks; in 1880 Pennsylvania's Winfield S. Scott ran with Indiana's William Hayden English; in 1884 Hendricks was again the party's vice-presidential nominee with another

New Yorker, Grover Cleveland, at the top of the ticket; in 1888 Cleveland's running mate was Ohio's Allen Thurman and in 1892 it was Illinois's Adlai Stevenson.

30   This effect was not part of the framers' original plan, however. The electoral college com-pelled presidential campaigns to focus on battleground states only because states chose to apportion electors on a winner-take-all basis. And while the Constitution was silent on how electors should be apportioned, Madison reported that the framers generally assumed that states would apportion electors by electoral district. In the opening decades of the nineteenth century, a number of states did apportion delegates by district; in the election of 1824, for instance, six states apportioned electors by electoral district. And during the early 1820s there was talk of a constitutional amendment to require every state to allocate electors in this manner. But the rise of party competition brought a halt to these efforts. By 1836 no state allocated electors by districts, and it stayed that way for the rest of the nineteenth century. See Richard J. Ellis, ed., *Founding the American Presidency* (Lanham, MD: Rowman & Littlefield, 1999), 123–25.

31   Michael F. Holt, *By One Vote: The Disputed Presidential Election of 1876* (Lawrence: University Press of Kansas, 2008), 175.

32   Holt, *By One Vote*, 192, 195.

33   Holt, *By One Vote*, 167, 175, 181–82. If African Americans had been free to vote, Republicans would almost certainly have won not only Louisiana and South Carolina but probably also Mississippi and maybe even Alabama (181). Whether that would have been enough to give Hayes a majority of the popular vote is more difficult to estimate.

34   Holt, *By One Vote*, 184, 194, 201–02.

35   Holt, *By One Vote*, 207. In 1800, then vice president Thomas Jefferson used his position as the Senate's presiding officer to count Georgia's four electoral votes for himself even though none of the four electors had complied with the constitutional requirement that they sign their names to the ballot. See Ackerman, *Failure of the Founding Fathers*, ch. 3 ("Jefferson Counts Himself In").

36   Holt, *By One Vote*, 213.

37   Holt, *By One Vote*, 214–15.

38   Ari Hoogenboom, *The Presidency of Rutherford B. Hayes* (Lawrence: University Press of Kansas, 1988), 40–50.

39   "Mr. Polk's Acceptance of the Nomination," *Niles's National Register*, July 6, 1844, 294. "The Republican Campaign," *New York Times*, June 18, 1876, 1.

40   Gil Troy, *See How They Ran: The Changing Role of the Presidential Candidate* (New York: Free Press, 1991), 78. Hoogenboom, *Presidency of Rutherford B. Hayes*, 17–18.

41   Michael E. McGerr, *The Decline of Popular Politics: The American North, 1865–1928* (New York: Oxford University Press, 1986), 72, 75–76. Hoogenboom, *Presidency of Rutherford B. Hayes*, 18. Troy, *See How They Ran*, 78–79.

42   Troy, *See How They Ran*, 78, 83.

43   Alexander Clarence Flick, *Samuel Jones Tilden: A Study in Political Sagacity* (New York: Dodd, Mead, 1939), 299; emphasis in original. On the evolution of the acceptance letter, see Richard J. Ellis. "Accepting the Nomination: From Martin Van Buren to Franklin Delano Roosevelt," in Richard J. Ellis, ed., *Speaking to the People: The Rhetorical Presidency in Historical Perspec-tive* (Amherst: University of Massachusetts Press, 1998), 112–33. The Tilden and Hayes acceptance letters can be found in the *New York Times*, August 5, 1876, 1, and July 10, 1876, 1, respectively.

44   Troy, *See How They Ran*, 89–90. This and subsequent paragraphs also draw from Richard J. Ellis and Mark Dedrick, "The Presidential Candidate, Then and Now," *Perspectives in Pol-itical Science* (Fall 1997), 208–16.

45 Troy, *See How They Ran*, 92–93.

46 Troy, *See How They Ran*, 95–96.

47 Troy, *See How They Ran*, 102–05.

48 Troy, *See How They Ran*, 93, 104.

49 Troy, *See How They Ran*, 109–10.

50 McGerr, *The Decline of Popular Politics*, 171–72. Troy, *See How They Ran*, 114.

51 "Leaders Urge Parker to Take the Stump," *New York Times*, September 10, 1904, 1. Troy, *See How They Ran*, 115–17.

52 Troy, *See How They Ran*, 121.

53 Troy, *See How They Ran*, 127. George E. Mowry, "Election of 1912," in Arthur M. Schlesinger, Jr., ed., *History of American Presidential Elections, 1789–1968* (New York: Chelsea House, 1985), 2156.

54 Troy, *See How They Ran*, 128–29.

55 Troy, *See How They Ran*, 135, 137–38, 140. Arthur Link et al., ed., *The Papers of Woodrow Wilson* (Princeton, NJ: Princeton University Press, 1982), 38:287.

56 Troy, *See How They Ran*, 139–40. "Wilson Will Talk on Business Today," *New York Times*, September 25, 1916, 3. "Big Crowds Cheer Wilson on His Trip," *New York Times*, October 5, 1916, 1. On the finger protector, see the photograph, dated October 28, 1916, on the website of the Wisconsin Historical Society, www.wisconsinhistory.org/whi/fullRecord.asp?id=9675. For Wilson's campaign speeches at Shadow Lawn, see Link, *The Papers of Woodrow Wilson*, 38:212–19, 301–12, 362–68, 430–38, 500–09, 549–59, 608–15.

57 Troy, *See How They Ran*, 143–45.

58 Troy, *See How They Ran*, 156, 165–66.

59 Troy, *See How They Ran*, 168–69.

60 The phrase "campaigning by governing" is from Troy, *See How They Ran*, 174.

61 Quotation is from Ceaser, *Presidential Selection*, 214.

62 Marty Cohen, David Karol, Hans Noel, and John Zaller, *The Party Decides: Presidential Nominations Before and After Reform* (Chicago: University of Chicago Press, 2008), 82.

63 Cohen, Karol, Noel, and Zaller, *The Party Decides*, 94.

64 Quotation is from Ceaser, *Presidential Selection*, 214.

65 John F. Reynolds, *The Demise of the American Convention System 1880–1911* (Cambridge: Cambridge University Press, 2006).

66 *Selecting the President: From 1789 to 1996* (Washington, DC: Congressional Quarterly, 1997), 17.

67 Sidney M. Milkis, *Theodore Roosevelt, the Progressive Party, and the Transformation of American Democracy* (Lawrence: University Press of Kansas, 2009), 98. Lewis L. Gould, *Four Hats in the Ring: The 1912 Election and the Birth of Modern American Politics* (Lawrence: University Press of Kansas, 2008), 65.

68 Milkis, *Theodore Roosevelt*, 103. Gould, *Four Hats in the Ring*, 66–67. The title of ch. 3 of Milkis's book is "The First Primary Campaign."

69 Gould, *Four Hats in the Ring*, 79.

70 *New York Times*, December 3, 1913, 2.

71 Donald A. Ritchie, *Electing FDR: The New Deal Campaign of 1932* (Lawrence: University Press of Kansas, 2007), 80. Steve Neal, *Happy Days Are Here Again: The 1932 Convention, the Emergence of FDR—and How America Was Changed Forever* (New York: William Morrow, 2004), 28–32.

72 Ritchie, *Electing FDR*, 85, 87.

73 Cohen, Karol, Noel, and Zaller, *The Party Decides*, 125–26.

74 Cohen, Karol, Noel, and Zaller, *The Party Decides*, 127.

75 Even in primary states that McCarthy won, Humphrey sometimes won the lion's share of the delegates. Thanks to the support of New Jersey's governor Richard Hughes, for instance, Humphrey gained better than three-quarters of New Jersey's delegates, even though Mc-Carthy won that state's primary.

76 In truth, the nominating convention had already begun losing its grip on American presidential politics well before 1968. In the seven nomination contests between 1932 and 1952 in which no incumbent president was running, four required multiple ballots at the convention to select a winner. And twice the first ballot leader was not the ultimate winner: in 1940 the Republican convention began with more delegates preferring Dewey before ultimately choosing Wilkie on the sixth ballot, and in 1952 the Democrats selected Stevenson on the third ballot after he had trailed behind Kefauver on the first two ballots. After 1952, in contrast, no party convention required more than one ballot to pick its nominee. With the exception of Kennedy in 1960, moreover, each nominee between 1956 and 1968 received at least two-thirds of the delegates on the first ballot. See Byron E. Shafer, *Bifurcated Politics: Evolution and Reform in the National Party Convention* (Cambridge, MA: Harvard University Press, 1988), 17–19.

77 Cohen, Karol, Noel, and Zaller, *The Party Decides*, 158.

78 Adam Nagourney and Jeff Zelent, "For Democrats, Increased Fears of a Long Fight," *New York Times*, March 16, 2008.

79 Cohen, Karol, Noel, and Zaller, *The Party Decides*, 352. At the end of the invisible primary in the 2000 campaign, for instance, Texas governor and eventual nominee George W. Bush "had the support of all but one Republican governor and 65 percent of other public endorsements." His closest rival, Arizona senator John McCain, netted fewer than one-sixth as many endorsements (225).

80 Cohen, Karol, Noel, and Zaller, *The Party Decides*, 339.

81 Barbara Norrander, *The Imperfect Primary: Oddities, Biases, and Strengths of U.S. Presidential Nomination Politics* (New York: Routledge, 2015; second edition), 45.

82 Ben White and Marc Caputo, "Inside Jeb's 'Shock and Awe' Launch," *Politico*, February 18, 2015. Ed O'Keefe and Matea Gold, "Jeb Bush and Allied Super PAC Raise an Unprecedented $114 Million War Chest," *Washington Post*, July 9, 2015. More than 90 percent of that total was raised by Bush's Super PAC, Right to Rise. Polling data can be found in William G. Mayer, "The Nominations: The Road to a Much-Disliked General Election," in Michael Nelson, ed., *The Elections of 2016* (Washington, DC: Congressional Quarterly, 2018), 37–38. The term "insider-backed front-runners" is from Cohen, Karol, Noel, and Zaller, *The Party Decides*, 336.

83 Aaron Bycoffe, "The Endorsement Primary," *FiveThirtyEight*, updated June 7, 2016, https://projects.fivethirtyeight.com/2016-endorsement-primary/. Trump won the nomination despite finishing the primary season having received the endorsement of only one US senator (Jeff Sessions, whom Trump would pick as his attorney general), three governors, and 11 members of Congress.

84 Super PACs emerged in the wake of the Supreme Court's ruling in *Citizens United v. FEC* (2010) and the subsequent decision two months later by the Court of Appeals for the DC Circuit, *SpeechNow.org v. FEC* (2010).

85 Eric Lichtblau and Alexandra Stevenson, "Hedge-Fund Magnate Robert Mercer Emerges as a Generous Backer of Cruz," *New York Times*, April 10, 2015. Nicholas Confessore, Sarah Cohen, and Karen Yourish, "Small Pool of Rich Donors Dominates Election Giving," *New York Times*, August 1, 2015.

86 Trump-allied Super PACs raised only about 2.5 million during the primary season, compared with 65 million for Cruz, 62 million for Rubio, and 127 million for Bush. Of all the Republican hopefuls, 13 raised more via Super PACs than did Trump.

87 Seema Mehta et al., "Who Gives Money to Bernie Sanders," *Los Angeles Times*, June 3, 2016. Marian Currinder, "Campaign Finance: Where Big Money Mattered and Where It Didn't," in Nelson, ed., *The Elections of 2016*, 145.

88 Nicholas Confessore and Karen Yourish, "$2 Billion Worth of Free Media for Donald Trump," *New York Times*, March 15, 2016.

89 Writing in 2008, Cohen, Karol, Noel, and Zaller acknowledged the impact of the "new communications environment" but concluded that it is "probably marginally less friendly to front-runners—and the party establishments that help create them—than what existed in the past" (*The Party Decides*, 337). In the wake of the 2016 elections, that conclusion seems to significantly understate the impact of new communication technologies on party insiders' ability to decide the nominee.

90 Ezra Klein, "Donald Trump's Success Reveals a Frightening Weakness in American Democracy," *Vox*, November 7, 2016.

91 See Nelson Polsby, *Consequences of Party Reform* (New York: Oxford University Press, 1983).

92 Klein, "Donald Trump's Success Reveals a Frightening Weakness in American Democracy." Julia Azari, "Weak Parties and Strong Partisanship are a Bad Combination," *Vox*, November 3, 2016.

93 Jack N. Rakove, "The E-College in the E-Age," in Jack N. Rakove, ed., *The Unfinished Election of 2000* (New York: Basic Books, 2001), 205.

94 Larry D. Kramer, "The Supreme Court in Politics," in Rakove, *Unfinished Election of 2000*, 108–09.

95 Kramer, "The Supreme Court in Politics," 132–33.

96 Kramer, "The Supreme Court in Politics," 133–35.

97 Abner Greene, *Understanding the 2000 Election: A Guide to the Legal Battles That Decided the Presidency* (New York: New York University Press, 2001), 34–36.

98 Kramer, "The Supreme Court in Politics," 145. The Bush team's primary legal argument had been that the state supreme court misinterpreted Florida's election law. Specifically, Bush's lawyers argued that the Florida court should have deferred to canvassing board certifications absent a showing that the board had abused its discretion, and that the court should not have counted "dimpled" ballots since these did not reveal the clear intent of the voter, as required by Florida law. Both of these arguments were plausible and perhaps compelling, but in neither case were the relevant state statutes unambiguously clear. The difficulty for the Bush team was that it was asking the US Supreme Court to take the highly unusual step of assuming the position of final arbiter of Florida state law. Only three justices (William Rehnquist, Antonin Scalia, and Clarence Thomas) were willing to accept the Bush team's invitation to have the Supreme Court second-guess a state supreme court's interpretation of its own state laws.

99 Stephen Holmes, "Afterword: Can a Coin-Toss Election Trigger a Constitutional Earthquake?" in Rakove, *The Unfinished Election of 2000*, 236.

100 Howard Gillman, *The Votes That Counted: How the Court Decided the 2000 Presidential Election* (Chicago: University of Chicago Press, 2001), 189. Kramer, "The Supreme Court in Politics," 147.

101 Gary L. Gregg II, "Con: Resolved, the Electoral College Should Be Abolished," in Richard J. Ellis and Michael Nelson, eds., *Debating Reform: Conflicting Perspectives on How to Fix the American Political System* (Washington, DC: CQ Press, 2017; third edition), 299.

102 In contrast, in the six elections prior to 1992 the Republican presidential nominees garnered 60 million more popular votes than the Democratic nominees, losing only in 1976 when Carter defeated Ford by 1.5 million votes.

103 Michael Barone, "The Electoral College Prevents California from Imposing Imperial Rule on the Country," *National Review*, December 6, 2016. Nate Cohn, "Why Trump Had an Edge in the Electoral College," *New York Times*, December 19, 2016.

104 "Two-Thirds of Presidential Campaign Is in Just 6 States," *National Popular Vote*, www.nationalpopularvote.com/campaign-events-2016. Cohn, "Why Trump Had an Edge."

105 Chris Weigant, "A Hard Look at the Big Blue Wall," *Huffpost*, June 8, 2015, www.huffingtonpost.com/chris-weigant/a-hard-look-at-the-big-bl_b_7029602.html. Glenn Kessler, "Trump's Flip-Flop on the Electoral College: From 'Disaster' to 'Genius,'" *Washington Post*, November 15, 2016.

106 On the spread of automatic voter registration, see www.brennancenter.org/analysis/automatic-voter-registration.

107 Warren Weaver, Jr., "A Survey Finds 30 Legislatures Favor Direct Vote for President," *New York Times*, October 8, 1969, p. 1.

108 Carter is quoted in Rakove, "The E-College in the E-Age," 201. The ten states that have signed the National Popular Vote bill are California, Hawaii, Illinois, Maryland, Massachusetts, New Jersey, New York, Rhode Island, Vermont, and Washington. The fate of the compact can be followed at www.nationalpopularvote.com. Ideas for achieving popular election without a constitutional amendment, including the interstate compact, are discussed in Robert W. Bennett, *Taming the Electoral College* (Stanford, CA: Stanford University Press, 2006), 161–78.

109 Thomas Mann, "Is This Any Way to Pick a President? Lessons from 2008," in Steven S. Smith and Melanie J. Springer, eds., *Reforming the Presidential Nomination Process* (Washington, DC: Brookings Institution Press, 2009), 168.

110 Larry J. Sabato, "Picking Presidential Nominees: Time for a New Regime," in Smith and Springer, eds., *Reforming the Presidential Nomination Process*, 145.

111 William G. Mayer and Andrew E. Busch, *The Front-Loading Problem in Presidential Elections* (Washington, DC: Brookings Institution Press, 2004), 158.

112 Mayer and Busch, *The Front-Loading Problem in Presidential Elections*, 153.

CHAPTER 3

THE PUBLIC PRESIDENCY

INTRODUCTORY PUZZLE: WHY DID LINCOLN PLAY SECOND FIDDLE AT GETTYSBURG?

There was a time in the not so distant past when schoolchildren all across the United States were required to memorize the 250 or so carefully chosen words that Abraham Lincoln spoke on November 19, 1863, to commemorate the Union soldiers who died in the Battle of Gettysburg. Although Americans today rarely commit the Gettysburg Address to memory, most can still recognize its iconic phrases and passages, from the familiar strains of the opening sentence—"Four score and seven years ago our fathers brought forth on this continent, a new nation, conceived in Liberty, and dedicated to the proposition that all men are created equal"—to the instantly recognizable closing line—"that this nation, under God, shall have a new birth of freedom, and that government of the people, by the people, for the people, shall not perish from the earth."

So familiar are Lincoln's famous words at Gettysburg that it is easy to forget that his speech was not the main event of the dedicatory program. The focal point was instead a two-hour oration by a 69-year-old former United States senator, Edward Everett, who was widely acknowledged to be the nation's most accomplished orator. Lincoln was asked only to deliver "a few appropriate remarks" formally dedicating the cemetery. To describe Lincoln's remarks as *the* Gettysburg Address is thus an historical anachronism. If a speech deserves the moniker of "the Gettysburg Address" it is Everett's oration, not Lincoln's brief dedicatory remarks.[1]

Today it is hard to imagine the president of the United States taking second billing to a senator, let alone a former senator. In the nineteenth century, however, this was not uncommon. Nineteenth-century Americans were accustomed to hearing far less from their president than from prominent cabinet officers and national legislators. When "carousing crowds" at Gettysburg could not induce Lincoln to speak the night before the dedicatory ceremonies, they called on Secretary of State William Henry Seward, who gratified them with an impassioned speech. Back in July, when news of Lee's defeat at Gettysburg first reached the capital, serenaders managed to extract a 500-word impromptu speech from Lincoln, who delighted the crowd by crowing that "those who opposed the declaration that all men are created equal [had] 'turned tail' and run." But only upon parading over to the nearby home of the secretary of state did they get treated to an extended speech. Seward's speech to the serenaders that July night was reprinted in full in the *New York Times*; Lincoln's was not even mentioned.[2]

Not that presidential rhetoric was unimportant in the nineteenth century. By the middle of the war, as historian Douglas Wilson notes, Lincoln had become convinced that "opinion forming [was] a primary presidential task." Lincoln well understood the power of words and spent many hours painstakingly crafting and polishing his public communications. In order to gauge public reactions and "to see how [the words] sounded," he invariably read aloud drafts to one or more trusted friends or political aides, or even the entire cabinet.[3]

Legend has it that as President Lincoln delivered his speech at Gettysburg, a photographer in front of the speaker's platform readied his equipment in order to snap a picture of the historic occasion. But so brief was Lincoln's two-and-a-half-minute address that by the time the photographer had the camera set up, the president had already finished and returned to his seat. The photograph above, discovered in 1952, is the only authenticated picture of President Lincoln at Gettysburg. It was likely taken sometime before the ceremony got under way. Lincoln appears near the center of the photograph. To Lincoln's left in the stovepipe hat is Ward Hill Lamon, marshal of the District of Columbia and Lincoln's de facto bodyguard.

Courtesy: Library of Congress, Prints and Photographs Division, LC-B8184–10454.

Contemporaries may have paid relatively little heed to Lincoln's short speech at Gettysburg, but the president's inaugural addresses and annual messages to Congress were extensively discussed in the press. The periodic public letters he wrote defending his administration's policies—such as his response to *New York Tribune* editor Horace Greeley's "The Prayer of Twenty Millions" in August 1862 and his missive to Erastus Corning and the Albany Democrats in June 1863—were also much talked about and praised by political allies for their beneficial effects on public opinion.

In penning these public letters, however, Lincoln pushed the boundaries of what was considered proper for a president. Although presidents had long employed partisan newspapers to defend their policies, it was not customary for the president to directly engage critics in the newspapers. Many approved of Lincoln's bold "violation of precedent" as appropriate to the exigencies of the Civil War. Others wagged their fingers in disapproval. The Harvard-educated Ralph Waldo Emerson, for instance, lamented that Lincoln "will not walk dignifiedly through the traditional part of the President of America" but instead "will cheapen himself" by sending "letters to Horace Greeley, and any editor or reporter or saucy party committee that writes to him."[4]

Emerson's comments reflected his elitism—he disdained "universal suffrage" for producing "coarse men" like Lincoln rather than "fine gentlemen"—but they also provide a clue to the code of rhetorical conduct that constrained nineteenth-century presidential behavior. They help us to understand why Lincoln "accepted any and all requests to speak" as an aspiring Illinois politician, yet as president waited more than two and a half years to travel outside of Washington to deliver a speech—and then spoke for only two and a half minutes. They help us to understand, too, why President Lincoln generally avoided saying anything of substance when he was serenaded, telling crowds who wished to hear from him that in his "present position" it was "not proper ... to make speeches."[5]

Lincoln's rhetorical restraint, particularly in impromptu settings, was in part a strategic calculation that such speeches, as Lincoln often explained, were too risky during a war in which his "every word" would be "so closely noted." But these political calculations were made in the context of a shared understanding of how presidents should behave. Lincoln's reluctance to be drawn out by crowds of well-wishers revealed the constraints imposed by contemporary standards of presidential dignity.[6]

Lincoln elected to go to Gettysburg because it enabled him to speak to the American people about the war's meaning in a solemn, nonpartisan setting. But he understood the importance of maintaining a "dignified" deportment, which is why on the evening before the ceremonies Lincoln refused to give the boisterous crowd the speech for which it clamored. It is also why at the dedication ceremony he kept his remarks spare, even at the risk of leaving his audience disappointed by their brevity.

THE GAUNTLET OF CONFLICTING PUBLIC EXPECTATIONS

Lincoln was an extraordinary wordsmith, but like every other mid-nineteenth-century president he struggled to pick his way through the minefield of conflicting public expectations and demands. On the one hand, presidents were supposed to accent their plebeian origins and downplay the distance between leader and led. This was an era in which presidents were commonly referred to by nicknames—Andrew Jackson was widely known as Old Hickory or the Old Hero; Zachary Taylor went by Old Rough and Ready as well as Old Zack; James Polk was called Young Hickory; William Henry Harrison was famously Tippecanoe or just Old Tip; and Lincoln was affectionately addressed as Old Abe, Honest Abe, or Uncle Abe. Emerson might not have liked it, but a democratic people did not want a president who would not deign to talk with the people.

On the other hand, the president of the United States was more than just another politician. He was also the head of state, a role that was seen to require an appropriate level of personal dignity and a certain distance from vulgar partisan appeals. That was no easy matter for a president at a time when political speech-making was public entertainment. Serenading crowds who called for speeches were generally in various stages of intoxication, as were many of the obliging speakers. Even at Gettysburg, where politicians had come to consecrate a cemetery for fallen soldiers, the atmosphere the night before was like a grand carnival. "Patriotism on dress parade," notes historian Gabor Boritt, "mingled with drunken vulgarity." Many suspected that Seward's "lively" speech that night owed more than a little to the imbibing of alcohol. Presidents, in short, had to connect with the people while avoiding rhetorical appeals that degraded the office.[7]

Some of what Lincoln faced is not unfamiliar to us today. Presidents must still negotiate the conflicting demands that stem from being both party leader and head of state. And we still want presidents who have the common touch but are at the same time uncommon leaders. But in other ways, the nineteenth century seems almost like a foreign country. Few looked to Lincoln to give an inspiring speech at Gettysburg. And while Lincoln tried to shape public opinion through proclamations, letters, and formal messages to Congress, he rarely attempted to do so through speeches, apart from his two inaugural addresses. Compare that to the torrent of presidential speech-making to which we have grown accustomed. Today it seems that whenever a president faces a problem, he is urged to deliver a speech to make things right. When members of Congress waver in their support, the president is expected to take his case directly to the American people—a phenomenon that political scientists sometimes refer to as "the rhetorical presidency" or "going public." To appreciate how far we have come, for better or for worse, it is necessary to journey back to the founding period, to what political scientist Jeffrey Tulis labels "the old way."[8]

THE OLD PATRICIAN WAYS

We are habituated to thinking of the constitutional period in terms of "founders" and "framers," terms that encourage us to imagine that the United States has remained fundamentally the same regime it always was. But this way of thinking about the past obscures the radical disjunction between the plebiscitary presidency with which we are familiar and the patrician presidency envisioned by the creators of the Constitution.[9]

The Constitutional Presidency: A President above Party

The Constitution says surprisingly little about presidential communications. Only two sections direct the president to communicate. The first is Section 7 of Article I, which commands that when the president vetoes a bill he must return it to Congress "with his Objections." The second is Section 3 of Article II, which mandates that the president "shall from time to time give to the Congress Information of the State of the Union and recommend to their Consideration such measures as he shall judge necessary and expedient." Both provisions direct the president to communicate his views to Congress.

Does this mean that the framers of the Constitution did not want presidents speaking to the people about public policy? The debates at the Constitutional Convention provide little direct help in answering this question. The delegates debated how much power the president should have and how the president should be selected, but not how much, when, or to whom the president should speak. However, the framers' writings suggest that even those delegates who backed a strong, popularly elected president did not appear to envision a president who would take an active role in leading and shaping public opinion. Instead they tended to associate popular appeals with divisive demagoguery. Nor did they envision a president who would closely reflect public opinion. Instead they sought a president who could stand above the passions and interests of the moment.[10]

In *Federalist* No. 71, for instance, Alexander Hamilton famously poured scorn on those who were "inclined to regard the servile pliancy of the executive to a prevailing current, either in the community or in the legislature," as desirable. Hamilton conceded that elected officials should be governed by "the deliberate sense of the community," but that did not require them to show "an unqualified complaisance to every sudden breeze of passion." Instead the presidency must be constituted "to withstand the temporary delusion, in order to give [the people] time and opportunity for more cool and sedate reflection."

To be sure, one of the convention delegates, Pennsylvania's James Wilson, maintained that the president ought to be "the man of the people" (rather than "the Minion of the Senate"), but the populist-sounding language is misleading. As Wilson explained to the Pennsylvania ratifying convention, the president may "be justly styled the man of the people" because "being elected by the different parts of the United States, he will consider himself as not particularly interested for any one of them, but will watch over the whole with paternal care and affection." Wilson's conception of the presidency is more paternal than populist; the president looks out for the people's interests in the same way that a father looks out for the interests of his family.[11]

The Constitutional Convention's other main proponent of a powerful, popularly elected president, Pennsylvania's Gouverneur Morris, expressed an equally paternal conception of the relationship between the presidency and the public. "The executive Magistrate," he told the convention, "should be the *guardian* of the people, even of the lower classes, against Legislative tyranny, against the Great and the wealthy who in the course of things will necessarily compose the Legislative body." The executive, Morris reiterated, ought to be "the great *protector* of the Mass of the people." The strong president that Morris envisioned was more akin to a monarch looking out for the people's enduring interests than a populist leader empowered by an election to give voice to the will of the people.

In short, the framers' conception of executive leadership, as historian Jack Rakove has pointed out, "remained, in a sense, apolitical. They saw the president not as a leader who would mobilize governing coalitions but as an executive who would rise like a patriot king above party." This was certainly the conception of the office harbored by the nation's first president, George Washington.[12]

Washington's Way

Because the Constitution said next to nothing about the forms of presidential communication, Washington assumed the burden of crafting appropriate rhetorical practices and establishing a proper relationship with the public. He was acutely conscious that his actions would create precedents for future generations to follow.

The First Inaugural Address

Washington's first act as president was to speak immediately after he was sworn in—setting the precedent for what we now call the Inaugural Address. Washington took the oath of office on the second-floor balcony of the Senate chamber, in full view of a large crowd that had gathered to witness the historic event. However, he delivered the speech inside the Senate chamber before a joint session of the two Houses of Congress and addressed not his fellow citizens but rather his "Fellow Citizens of the Senate and of the House of Representatives."[13]

Washington spoke of having been called to his position by the "voice of my country," but he did not claim that his election communicated anything about the people's political preferences or that it empowered him to pursue a particular policy agenda. The election was instead "transcendent proof of the confidence" that his fellow citizens placed in Washington's character.

There was never any danger that somebody would accuse the austere and imposing Washington of being a demagogue. The challenge that Washington faced instead was to project dignity without parroting monarchy. That was no easy task in the early republic, for British practices were often second nature to Americans. After Washington took the oath of office, for instance, the person who administered the oath—New York's highest ranking judicial officer, Robert Livingston—cried out, to tremendous cheers from the crowd, "Long live George Washington." The audience and venue for Washington's inaugural speech—a joint session of Congress delivered in the Senate chambers—mirrored the king's accession speech to Parliament, which he addressed to the membership of both houses but delivered in the House of Lords.[14]

The uncomfortable parallels between the coronation of a monarch and the inauguration of the president weighed on many people's minds. The Senate minutes referred to Washington's address as "his most gracious speech," an appellation that was commonly used to describe the king's speech to Parliament. Pennsylvania's William Maclay asked his Senate colleagues to strike the offending words from the minutes because they were "the same that are usually placed before the speech of his Britannic Majesty." Maclay predicted that they would offend the American people, who now "abhorred" all the trappings of monarchy. John Adams objected strenuously. It was senseless, in Adams's view, to throw out phrases and practices derived from a political system "under which we had lived so long and happily formerly." The Senate sided with Maclay.[15]

Fellow Citizens of the Senate
and
of the House of Representatives.

Among the vicissitudes incident to life, no event could have filled me with greater anxieties than that of which the notification was transmitted by your order, and received on the fourteenth day of the present month: — On the one hand, I was summoned by my Country, whose voice I can never hear but with veneration and love, from a retreat which I had chosen with the fondest predilection, and, in my flattering hopes, with an immutable decision, as the asylum of my declining years: a retreat which was rendered every day more necessary as well as more dear to me, by the addition of habit to inclination, and of frequent interruptions in my health to the gradual waste committed on it by time. — On the other hand, the magnitude and difficulty of the trust to which the voice of my Country called me, being sufficient to awaken in the wisest and most experienced of her citizens, a distrustful

The first page of the first speech ever delivered by an American president: Washington's Inaugural Address of 1789. It was addressed not to the American people but to the "Fellow Citizens of the Senate and of the House of Representatives."

Courtesy: Records of the US Senate, US National Archives.

Congress might balk at a specific phrase, but the British model inevitably constrained Americans' political imagination. Washington, for instance, delivered each of his annual addresses (Washington's first inaugural essentially doubled as an annual message) at the opening of the legislative session, just as the king did at the opening of Parliament. And each house of the legislature composed a reply to the president's address, just as each house of Parliament composed an address replying to the British monarch.

Addressing the President

The task of responding to the president's message embroiled the Senate in a prolonged discussion about how to address the president. Adams firmly believed that "a royal or at least princely title" was necessary "to maintain the reputation, authority, and dignity of the President." The title of "president" was far too common, Adams thought. Ambassadors were generally addressed "Most Illustrious and Most Excellent" and it would be demeaning, Adams reasoned, for the nation's chief executive to have a title that "was less than those of even our own diplomatic corps." A Senate committee endorsed Adams's view and proposed to address Washington as "His Highness, the President of the United States of America, and Protector of their Liberties." After a prolonged debate, with Maclay again spearheading the opposition to "the fooleries, fopperies, fineries, and pomp of royal etiquette," the Senate opted to follow the House of Representatives (and the Constitution) and address their message simply to the "President of the United States."[16]

President Washington was annoyed by the fuss that Adams made in the Senate over a "superb but superfluous title." Far more attuned to public perceptions than his politically tone-deaf vice president, Washington understood that a splendorous title would provide ammunition to the new government's adversaries while doing nothing to boost public confidence in the president or the government. The dignity of the office, Washington calculated, could be better enhanced in other, more democratic ways.[17]

Although certain that he did not need a fancy title, Washington was unsure about how to interact with the public. If he neither extended nor accepted public invitations, Washington worried that it would be considered "an ostentatious show of mimicry of sovereignty" and that he would cut off "the avenues to useful information from the many, and make me more dependent on that of the few." However, if he made himself too readily accessible to the public he might diminish the office and be unable to carry out the administrative work his high office required.[18]

Seeking an appropriate balance between public accessibility on the one hand and dignified reserve on the other, Washington decided to hold a weekly afternoon levee at which the public, at least those who were "respectably dressed," were offered the opportunity of being introduced to the president. Polite bows and pleasantries were exchanged, but there was no shaking of hands. Moreover, no chairs were placed in the room, so that citizens would not make the mistake of sitting in the president's presence. Vigilant as ever about not taking that "first step of the ladder in the ascent to royalty," Maclay was scathing. In his view, the president's afternoon levees were "certainly anti-republican," even if others were afraid to say so out of "fear of being charged with a want of respect to General Washington."[19]

"Seeing and Being Seen": The President on Tour

Another way that Washington made himself accessible to the people was by touring the country. Two weeks after the adjournment of the first session of the first Congress, Washington left the nation's capital for a month-long tour through New England. The aim of the tour was both "to acquire knowledge of . . . the temper and disposition of the Inhabitants towards the new government" and to make himself "more accessible to numbers of well-informed persons, who might give him useful information and advice on political subjects." Washington did not envision his travels as a speech-making tour, but rather as an opportunity for "seeing and being seen" by the American people.[20]

Again, Washington had to reckon with the specter of monarchy. Queen Elizabeth I, after all, had undertaken a "royal progress" almost annually during her 44-year reign, also for the purpose of seeing and being seen by her subjects. Washington was acutely conscious of these parallels and sought to counteract such comparisons by traveling simply. Whereas Elizabeth was typically accompanied in her travels by an immense retinue of court officials, councilors, courtiers, clergymen, and servants, Washington kept his traveling party relatively small: six servants and several personal assistants. Informed by Massachusetts governor John Hancock of the elaborate arrangements being made for his visit, Washington notified the governor that he preferred that his tour be "without any parade, or extraordinary ceremony."[21]

Washington's attempt to travel with a minimum of ceremony was largely ineffectual, however. Towns across New England welcomed the president with odes sung in his honor, the discharge of artillery, the parading of state militia, welcoming addresses by local officials, escorts in and out of town, elegant public dinners, and cheering crowds. When Washington embarked on a second tour, this time of the southern states, the carefully choreographed pageantry was even more magnificent. In Charleston, South Carolina, the president was fêted with a magnificent ball, which featured "256 elegantly dressed and handsome ladies," each of whom wore ribbons "with different inscriptions expressive of their esteem and respect for the president," such as "Rejoice, the hero's come" and "Shield, oh shield him from all harm."[22]

As Jeffrey Tulis points out, "public speaking [on these tours] was not as important as public appearances." The speeches by both the welcoming committee and the president were not designed to advance a political argument, stake out a political position, or persuade an audience. The exchange of speeches was instead an integral part of an elaborate ceremony that affirmed and enacted relationships of deference between leader and led. The town's leaders welcomed Washington by paying homage to his character, his public service, and his high office. For his part, Washington graciously accepted the tribute in a manner that affirmed the local dignitaries' authority. He studiously refrained from direct appeals to the people, either over the heads of Congress or local officials. He spoke as a dignified and unifying chief of state, a symbol of the new Constitution and government, not as the head of a party or the advocate of a particular ideology.[23]

The Farewell Address

Only once as president did Washington issue a direct appeal to the people. That was in his famous Farewell Address. Although we call it an address, it was not a speech. Rather, it was a written, untitled message, printed in a "reliably Federalist" newspaper, the *American Daily Advertiser*. In contrast to his first inaugural address or his annual messages to Congress, the Farewell Address was directly addressed "To the People of the United States, Friends and Fellow Citizens."[24]

The Farewell Address is perhaps best remembered for its warnings against "the baneful effects of the Spirit of Party." Yet Washington's message, drafted largely by the Federalist Party's chief propagandist Alexander Hamilton, was undeniably partisan. When Washington assailed "all combinations and associations, under whatever plausible character," which were designed "to direct, control, counteract, or awe the regular deliberation of the constituted authorities," he was not only voicing a traditional eighteenth-century fear of "faction" but also taking direct aim at the Democratic-Republican Societies that had sprung up across the nation during his second term. When Washington warned against "passionate attachments" to any foreign country, he was plainly criticizing Republicans for their attachment to France. And when he complained of "inveterate antipathies" to other nations he was again targeting Republicans for their hostility to Great Britain and their opposition to the Jay Treaty that had gone into effect the preceding year. Moreover, by waiting until September 19 to publish the address—in which he announced that he would not run for a third term—Washington severely hampered Republican efforts to organize a presidential campaign.[25]

One reading of Washington's Farewell Address is that he used "a stance of non-partisanship to achieve partisan ends." Washington, however, would not have seen his rhetoric in these purely instrumental terms. He sincerely believed that he had served as a president above party and faction. As he explained to Jefferson a few months before publication of the Farewell Address: "I was no party man myself, and the first wish of my heart was, if parties did exist, to reconcile them." Washington found the opposition's harsh criticisms of his administration utterly unfathomable. Why, he asked, did Republican newspapers persist in savaging him with the "grossest and most insidious mis-representations"? Why did they give "one side only of a subject, and that too in such exaggerated and indecent terms as could scarcely be applied to a Nero, a notorious defaulter, or even to a common pickpocket"? For Washington, this was simply not the way gentlemen behaved.[26]

Washington was caught between two different political worlds: a familiar one governed by patrician leaders and hierarchical norms and an emergent one structured by political parties and democratic sentiments. Intended to shore up traditional understandings of politics, the Farewell Address ironically presaged new understandings of the presidency's relationship to public opinion. One can see in Washington's address, more clearly than in anything else he penned, a glimmer of the presidency as bully pulpit. Here, for the first time in the nation's history, was the president of the United States directly addressing the people of the United States.

However, Washington's address should not be wrenched out of its historical context. Washington understood his address not as a revolutionary act but rather as an instance of a rhetorical genre familiar from European politics: the political testament in which a departing leader offers disinterested advice to guide the nation's future path. When Washington resigned at the end of the Revolutionary War, he had written just such a valedictory message, addressed to the 13 state governors, in which he laid out his conception of what was necessary for the long-term safety and welfare of the nation. The Farewell Address was not, in Washington's eyes, a model for how presidents should behave in the day-to-day process of governing. Instead it was a peculiar duty that the greatest statesmen discharged only once, as they left office. Under these peculiar circumstances, he hoped, none could accuse him of demagoguery or of having ulterior political motives.[27]

Jefferson and "the Revolution of 1800"

At the age of 76, Thomas Jefferson wrote to the eminent Virginia jurist Spencer Roane to express his conviction that "the revolution of 1800 ... was as real a revolution in the principles of our government as that of 1776 was in its form." Jefferson's formulation pointed toward a new understanding of the relationship between the public and the president. Whereas the framers of the Constitution saw the presidency as an honor bestowed on a man of sterling character and impressive achievements, Jefferson framed the presidential contest as a choice between rival principles. For the founding fathers, elections were, of course, a source of legitimacy—since in a republic, authority must ultimately derive from the people—but election results were not seen as empowering the president to pursue particular policies. In contrast, Jefferson's formulation suggested that election results could be examined to divine the political preferences of the people.[28]

Yet in likening 1800 to 1776, Jefferson showed that he remained wedded to the anti-party ethos that structured the founders' political world. Jefferson was convinced that Hamilton, Adams, and other Federalist leaders were, quite literally, trying to overturn the Revolution of 1776 by resurrecting monarchy. He believed that Federalists' monarchical principles were as un-American as the British form of government, and so his aim was not just to defeat the Federalist Party but to eradicate it from the American political landscape. Once the Federalist "monocrats" had been routed, Jefferson believed that traditional politics could be restored, a politics in which presidential choice would once again be based on individual character and merit rather than political principles.

Jefferson's First Inaugural Address

This blending of new understandings and traditional sensibilities was evident in Jefferson's First Inaugural Address, in which he described the recently concluded election as a "contest of opinion" but at the same time famously insisted, "We have called by different names brethren of the same principle. We are all republicans, we are all federalists." It is tempting to dismiss this pronouncement as merely a rhetorical ploy to assuage the bruised feelings of his defeated opponents. But while Jefferson privately acknowledged the existence of a small "phalanx of old tories and monarchists" who could not be redeemed, he did earnestly believe that "the great body" of the American people could be united once the malign influence of a reactionary few had been removed. Jefferson interpreted the election of 1800 as a revolutionary act because it ushered in a nationwide return to republican principles.[29]

Jefferson's conciliatory inaugural message was embellished by gracious praise for Washington, the "first and greatest revolutionary character, whose preeminent services had entitled him to the first place in his country's love." At the same time, however, Jefferson used the inaugural ceremony to draw a sharp contrast with his Federalist predecessors. Whereas Washington and Adams had been driven to their inauguration in a magnificent European-made coach, Jefferson walked. And while Washington and Adams had been adorned with a dress sword, Jefferson appeared as a plain citizen, sans sword.

Jefferson delivered his inaugural address within the halls of Congress, just as Washington and Adams had. Unlike his predecessors, however, Jefferson forthrightly spoke to the people of the United States. Washington's first inaugural had been respectfully addressed to members of Congress, while Jefferson addressed his "Friends and Fellow Citizens." Although Washington and Jefferson both spoke inside the Senate chamber (Washington at Federal Hall in New York City and Jefferson at the Capitol in Washington, DC), Jefferson's audience included more than one thousand citizens who had crammed into the chamber. It was "so crowded," reported Margaret Bayard Smith, that "not another creature could enter." Members of the House gallantly relinquished their seats to the many women in attendance.[30]

Jefferson was a brilliant writer and polemicist but a terrible public speaker. According to Smith, Jefferson's speech was delivered in "so low a tone that few heard it." That mattered little, however, because Jefferson's primary audience was not those inside the Senate chamber but the newspaper-reading public beyond the marbled walls. Washington uttered only 37 words in his second inaugural address, not so much a speech as a ceremonious acknowledgment of the oath of office that he was about to take. Jefferson, in contrast, used his inaugural address to articulate the principles that he believed defined America and by which he would govern. It was a message Jefferson wanted broadcast to the nation, which is why he distributed an advance copy of the speech to the *National Intelligencer*.[31]

The Emergence of Partisan Newspapers

In an age before radio and television, newspapers were the only way political leaders could communicate with a national audience. Writing under the cover of pseudonyms, the American colonial elites relied on newspapers to turn public opinion against the British and in favor of rebellion. During the debates over ratification of the Constitution, pseudonymous political elites once again utilized newspapers to mobilize public support.[32]

Newspapers at the beginning of the nineteenth century looked markedly different from the twenty-first-century newspapers with which we are familiar. Today we expect newspapers to report the news in an unbiased fashion; the editors' political opinions are supposed to remain on the editorial page. Politically biased news coverage is considered unprofessional. In the early nineteenth century, by contrast, newspapers were inseparable from partisan politics. By one count, 90 percent of American newspapers in 1810 were associated with either the Federalist or Republican parties.

Jefferson was keenly aware of the importance of newspapers in communicating with the public. Upon becoming president, he immediately made the *National Intelligencer* the administration's quasi-official organ and ensured the *Intelligencer's* financial viability by granting its editor Samuel Harrison Smith the contract for the printing of all federal laws and the printing business related to each of the government departments. Throughout his presidency, Jefferson relied on the *Intelligencer* to communicate his administration's positions to the public, even while he publicly distanced himself from the partisan press.[33]

Jefferson even wrote for and supplied information to Republican newspapers, though he was always careful to cover his tracks. In 1803, for instance, Jefferson penned a small "treatise" in defense of the administration's patronage policies and plotted with his attorney general Levi Lincoln on how to get it published in New England's leading Republican newspaper, Boston's *Independent Chronicle*, "divested of the evidence of my handwriting." So that no reader would suspect Jefferson was the author, he wrote the essay "under the character of a Massachusetts citizen." By the end of the month, the scheme had succeeded; with only minor modifications, the essay, signed "Fair Play," appeared in the *Independent Chronicle*.[34]

Why was Jefferson, a master wordsmith, so determined not to take credit for his words and to distance himself from the newspapers in which those words appeared? The answer is that Jefferson, like Washington before him, adhered to the conventions of a patrician political culture in which gentlemen were, as historian Jeffrey Pasley observes, "to act the part of self-abnegating patriotic statesmen." Republican gentlemen, like Federalist gentlemen, viewed party newspapers and their printers as indispensable but rather vulgar. The president of the United States was supposed to carry himself with a dignity and decorum that hardly seemed compatible with the vituperatively partisan newspaper politics that developed in the 1790s. Jefferson understood that his "reputation would suffer terribly if he or his cabinet ministers openly shilled for themselves in the newspapers."[35]

This was more than just adroit political strategy. Notwithstanding his boasts about the Revolution of 1800, Jefferson shared many of the traditional prejudices of his class about licentious newspapers and rabid partisanship. That was why he opted not to invite the recent Irish émigré William Duane, the radical editor of the Philadelphia *Aurora*, to come to Washington, even though the *Aurora* was widely recognized as the hub of the Republican press network. Instead Jefferson favored Smith, a respectable young gentleman with an impeccable family pedigree, whose new wife (and second cousin) Margaret Bayard Smith was the daughter of a distinguished Federalist family. Duane ridiculed Smith's "silky milky ways," but Smith's insistence on avoiding "all personal slander and vulgar language" in the pages of the *Intelligencer* suited Jefferson perfectly.[36]

When a 17-year-old Virginian, a descendant of one of the original trustees of Williamsburg, wrote to the president for advice on managing a newspaper, Jefferson's reply was scathing. A paper that stuck to "true facts and sound principles," as it should, would lamentably "find few subscribers." Almost all newspapers, Jefferson believed, had become "prostitute[d] to falsehood." The man who never reads a newspaper, declared Jefferson, "is better informed than he who reads them; inasmuch as he who knows nothing is nearer to truth than he whose mind is filled with falsehoods & errors."[37]

All presidents, of course, complain about the media and its unfair coverage. And in the early republic political leaders often had good cause to complain. Federalist and

Republican newspapers launched uncompromising and sometimes scurrilous personal and political attacks on elected officials, including the president. Even the revered Washington was boldly insulted, and "old, querulous, bald, blind, crippled, toothless" Adams was shown no mercy by the Republican press. The Federalist response to these assaults on presidential dignity had been to pass the Alien and Sedition Acts in 1798.[38]

Although Jefferson fiercely opposed the Alien and Sedition Acts, he supported prosecuting Federalist Party newspapers for their "licentiousness & ... lying." Jefferson believed that while the First Amendment prevented the *federal* government from prosecuting newspapers, there was no bar on state governments doing the same. Prosecuting "a few ... of the most prominent offenders," Jefferson told Pennsylvania's Republican governor, "would have a wholesome effect" and restore public confidence in the press.[39]

At least as surprising as President Jefferson's willingness to endorse government repression of the opposition press was his reluctance to embrace the partisan editors that carried him to the presidency and supported him in office. During Jefferson's presidency, few Republican editors were rewarded with government posts. In Jefferson's view, government was for gentlemen. The Revolution of 1800 had not changed that. Editors and printers were simply not the gentlemen "of respectable standing in society" that Jefferson sought for his government.[40]

The Rhetorical Limits of "the Revolution of 1800"

When Jefferson spoke of the Revolution of 1800, he had in mind a repudiation of those Federalist practices and principles that he associated with monarchy. He did not foresee forging a new party-centered, democratized political system. Rejecting monarchy and returning to republicanism meant, for instance, refusing to follow President Washington's precedent of delivering the State of the Union address as a speech—which Jefferson felt was too much like the "British 'Speech from the Throne' that opened each session of Parliament"—and instead transmitting it to Congress as a written message. It did not mean rejecting the patrician ideal of a president above party or embracing a populist vision in which the president openly seeks to rally popular support for himself and his programs.[41]

Consider, for instance, the manner in which Jefferson responded to the opposition he encountered to the embargo on trade that was enacted during the final year of his presidency. The embargo was deeply unpopular, particularly in New England, where it was having a devastating effect on the economy. Yet the president gave no speeches and delivered no messages to Congress explaining why he was asking Americans to sacrifice. He did pen a public letter in response to petitions of protest he received from three Massachusetts port towns, including Boston, but the letter was not written until eight months after the embargo had gone into effect. Jefferson worked furiously behind the scenes to line up legislative support, but he retained a public pose of "almost sphinxlike silence."[42]

Jefferson's reluctance to go public to explain the embargo reveals the strength of the rhetorical norms of the founding era, even after the supposed Revolution of 1800. Preserving the dignity of the office required the president to avoid getting into a partisan scrap with critics and to avoid public campaigns of self-promotion or self-defense. The gentleman statesman was supposed to take "the calm, rational view of public affairs" and to avoid demagogic appeals that played on emotions. Jefferson's Revolution of 1800 did not transform these rhetorical conventions, nor did it fundamentally alter the relationship between the presidency and the people.[43]

"Talents and Virtue Alone": James Monroe and John Quincy Adams

Jefferson's letter to Judge Roane hailing the Revolution of 1800 was penned in September 1819, near the end of James Monroe's first term as president. Monroe was determined to consolidate Jefferson's revolution by bringing "the whole [of the nation] into the republican fold." Parties, in Monroe's view, were neither inevitable nor desirable. By governing not as "the head of a party, but of the nation," Monroe believed that he could "exterminate all party divisions."[44]

The unanimity with which the nation embraced Monroe's reelection in 1820 was hailed by those Jeffersonian gentlemen who believed in what one historian mockingly describes as a "one-party system of Republican saints." Having exterminated party divisions, many Republican political leaders expected that the presidency would once again be bestowed, as the framers originally intended, as "a reward for meritorious service or as an honor [to be granted to] a respected public servant, rather than as a prize to be carried by the strongest party."[45]

There was nothing unanimous about the selection of Monroe's successor, John Quincy Adams, yet Adams tenaciously held to Monroe's vision of a president above party. In his inaugural address, Adams urged his fellow Americans to discard "every remnant" of partisan rancor. Adams went even further than Monroe, insisting that appointments should be made without regard to party. In the past, Adams explained, when politics was marked by "contention for principle," offices were "bestowed only upon those who bore the badge of party communion," but now that the "baneful weed of party strife" had been uprooted, appointments could once again be based on "talents and virtue alone."[46]

Not everybody, however, was pleased with the attempt by Monroe and Adams to eradicate "the remnant of old party distinctions." Spearheading the resistance were newspaper editors who were "emotionally and financially invested in ... party conflict." While Monroe and Adams attempted to tamp down partisan differences, editors often labored to sharpen and exaggerate those differences. At stake was not merely the legitimacy of political parties but the shape of the nation's politics. Was the nation to be governed by a disinterested elite, selected for their good character and services to the nation, or was the nation's politics to be animated by shifting popular majorities, who would select and evaluate leaders based on how well they responded to public opinion?[47]

Adams appeared almost a caricature of the genteel republican understanding of executive leadership. Although he had taught rhetoric and oratory at Harvard and was an accomplished public speaker (as he would demonstrate during a distinguished post-presidential career in the House of Representatives), Adams seemed to regard public communication as beneath the dignity of his high office. He resisted efforts to, as he put it, "exhibit himself to the people"; to do so, he believed, was not only unseemly but a distraction from the serious business of administering the government.[48]

Adams also showed little interest in mobilizing public opinion indirectly through partisan surrogates. Before becoming president, Adams vowed that he would "have no stipendiary editor of newspapers to extol my talents and services and to criticize or calumniate my rivals." In fact, Peter Force's *National Journal* did serve as the Adams administration's quasi-official newspaper—replacing the *National Intelligencer*, which had fulfilled this function for the previous three administrations—but the paper did "little more than [carry] the official notices of the executive branch." And Adams took no steps to forge a close behind-the-scenes relationship with Force or to use the *National Journal* to marshal public support for his preferred policies.[49]

When faced with a recalcitrant Congress, modern presidents frequently resort to "going public," that is, appealing directly to the public in order to put pressure on members of Congress. Adams, in contrast, lectured Congress that neither the executive nor the legislature should be "palsied by the will of our constituents." Governance was neither about heeding the people's will nor pursuing a partisan agenda. Instead it was about enlightened leaders making wise decisions that were in the long-run interests of the people. It was a patrician conception of leadership that was increasingly out of step with the "democratic ferment of the 1820s."[50]

THE NEW PARTISAN WAYS

Andrew Jackson's triumph over Adams in 1828 ushered in a new era of presidential politics, one that was both more populist and more partisan. Unlike his predecessors, Jackson invited a host of partisan newspaper editors into his government. More than 70 partisan editors were appointed to federal office in reward for their support of Jackson's candidacy, and several played key roles in the administration. Kentucky's Amos Kendall, editor of the fiercely partisan *Argus of Western America*, was given a post in the Treasury Department and became one of Jackson's most trusted advisors. Jackson also handpicked Francis Preston Blair, a colleague of Kendall's at the *Argus*, to be editor of the administration's mouthpiece, the Washington *Globe*. Blair and Kendall, both members of Jackson's so-called Kitchen Cabinet, met with Jackson almost daily to formulate political strategy and tactics. By rewarding loyal party editors with lucrative and politically prominent government posts, Jackson announced a new kind of president—one who did not seek to remain austerely above party but instead embraced the role of party leader.[51]

Speaking for the People: Andrew Jackson and the Making of the Mandate

Jackson also advanced a new understanding of the relationship between the presidency and the American people, particularly in his second term as he faced growing congressional resistance to the war he had declared on the national bank. When Congress voted to renew the bank's charter in the summer of 1832, Jackson fashioned a populist veto message that took aim at "the rich and powerful" who "too often bend the acts of government to their selfish purposes." Jackson claimed to speak for "the humble members of society—the farmers, mechanics, and laborers" who had "neither the time nor the means of securing like favors to themselves." After defeating Henry Clay in the 1832 election, Jackson pressed further, arguing that the people had given him a mandate to destroy the national bank.[52]

Brushing aside the objections of most of his cabinet members, including his secretary of the treasury, Jackson decided to remove all government deposits from the bank. Never mind that the House of Representatives had recently affirmed that the deposits were safe where they were. In Jackson's view, members of Congress were mere "Bank agents." The only way to slay the "hydra of corruption," Jackson told his vice president, was by going over the head of Congress and "placing the whole matter before the people."[53]

With the assistance of Blair and Kendall, Jackson prepared a statement explaining to the people why he was ordering the removal of government deposits from the bank. Published in the *Globe,* Jackson's message maintained that the question of whether the bank should be rechartered had been settled in the last presidential election, which was, according to Jackson, "a decision of the people against the bank." The people had "sustained the President" in the anti-bank course that he had promised to chart in his veto message and now Jackson was determined to carry their will into effect. "The decision of the country," Jackson explained, was that the bank shall "cease to exist" when its charter expires, and so the only remaining question was whether to withdraw the public deposits at that point or when the bank's charter officially expired. Having examined the question "carefully and deliberately," Jackson had come to the conclusion that immediate removal was the most effective means to the end chosen by the people. It was the people who had decided against the bank; the president, Jackson insisted, was only "carrying into effect their decision."[54]

If inviting partisan newspaper editors into his government had shocked traditional sensibilities, Jackson's insistence that the president was the "direct representative of the American people" and that Congress was a corrupt bastion of special interests presented an even more bracing challenge to republican orthodoxy. So jarring in fact was Jackson's claim to possess a popular mandate that, as political scientist Stephen Skowronek points out, it "galvanized the disparate strands of resistance to Jackson's leadership and forged the ideological foundation of the Whig party."[55]

The Whig Dissent

Senator Henry Clay spearheaded the resistance to this recasting of the relationship between the president and the people. In a three-day oration on the Senate floor, Clay sounded the alarm at the "new source of executive power which is found in the result of a presidential election." The Constitution and the laws, Clay countered, were "the sole source of executive authority." The purpose of presidential elections, Clay insisted, was "merely to place the Chief Magistrate in the post assigned to him," not to empower him to pursue particular policies.[56]

Presidential elections, in Clay's view, were judgments on a candidate's character and experience, not decisions about public policy. The people had reelected Jackson on account of "his presumed merits"; they "had no idea," according to Clay, "of expressing their approbation of all the opinions which the President held." As evidence, Clay pointed to Pennsylvania, which had voted overwhelmingly for Jackson, but which by all accounts was strongly supportive of the bank.[57]

Many of the objections that Clay and others raised against Jackson's mandate claim were valid. They were right that Jackson almost certainly would have won with or without his veto, and that he might have won by more had he not vetoed the bank. They were also right to point to the inherent fallacies in the mandate concept, since one could not know with any certainty which of the many issues, events, and personalities had motivated which voters. In short, the Whigs were right to doubt that the people spoke through the president. However, Whigs failed to offer a satisfying alternative interpretation of the meaning of presidential elections. Their insistence that presidential elections revealed nothing about the people's preferences was out of step with a more democratic and partisan age.

Speaking to the People: The Partisan President on Tour in the Age of Jackson

In claiming to speak *for* the people, Jackson transformed the relationship between the presidency and the public. Yet in speaking *to* the people, particularly when on tour, Jackson and his nineteenth-century successors continued to be constrained by traditional understandings of the presidential role as well as by available transportation and communications technologies.

Of the first six presidents, only Washington and Monroe toured the nation. Neither envisioned their tours as an occasion for speech-making. Like Washington, Monroe toured as a dignified president above party, though Monroe also came to see the tours as a way to mobilize public support for strengthening the nation's coastal and interior fortifications. Whenever a welcoming committee commended Monroe for his attention to shoring up the nation's defenses, Monroe eagerly accepted the invitation to instruct his fellow citizens on the "necessity of being better prepared [for war]."[58]

Both Washington and Monroe had the advantage of touring at a time in which national political parties were essentially moribund. Washington's tours took place before the formation of the first party system pitting Jeffersonian Republicans against Federalists, and Monroe's tours were conducted while the first party system lay in ruins. And neither Monroe nor Washington had to worry much about accusations of electioneering, since in neither case was their reelection ever in doubt. But the rise of organized, national political parties and competitive presidential elections in the late 1820s and 1830s greatly complicated the political calculus of presidential travel and speech-making. Presidents were still expected to be dignified—which usually meant nonpartisan—but they were also expected to be party leaders. The trick for the traveling president was to satisfy his partisans without offending traditional sensibilities regarding presidential dignity.[59]

Jackson's 1833 Tour

Jackson faced precisely this dilemma in 1833 when a committee of Connecticut Democrats extended him an invitation to visit New England. The invitation, accompanied by a letter praising Jackson's policies, placed the president in uncharted territory. Was it proper for the president to accept a partisan invitation from a partisan body? The president-above-party model that guided Washington and Monroe would have suggested that Jackson decline an avowedly partisan invitation. Yet after conferring with advisors Jackson accepted, and in June 1833 he embarked on a month-long tour of New England.[60]

The contrast between Jackson's trip to New England and the tours of Monroe and Washington was on display from the outset. In Philadelphia, the second stop on Jackson's tour, the reception was directed almost entirely by the president's political allies. When the citizens of Philadelphia gathered to make "the necessary arrangements for the patriotic reception," the meeting was attended exclusively by Jackson supporters, who selected a Jackson loyalist, Henry Horn, to orchestrate the president's visit. Upon arriving in Philadelphia, the president placed himself "in [the] charge" of Horn and a "committee of arrangements" composed entirely of Democrats. Not until two days after his arrival was Jackson introduced to the elected city authorities, most of whom, including the mayor, were anti-Jackson. Throughout his travels, Jackson was flanked by loyal Democrats. When the president entered Hartford, Connecticut, for instance, the procession was a veritable who's who of prominent Democrats, including the Democratic governors of New York and Connecticut as well as two of Hartford's most prominent Democrats, John Niles and Gideon Welles.

Jackson was careful, however, to avoid partisan speeches. His public remarks were so brief and inconsequential that newspapers rarely bothered to record them. Even in Concord, New Hampshire, speaking to a legislature dominated by Democrats, Jackson said little, and what little he did say avoided any hint of partisanship. Jackson's reticence was a tribute to the continuing hold of the president-above-party ideal.

Jackson's rhetorical restraint, however, did not obscure the political objective of his tour, which was to underscore the themes of national unity and federal supremacy that he had laid down in the Nullification Proclamation. Jackson had issued the proclamation in December 1832 in response to South Carolina's declaration that the tariffs enacted by the federal government in 1828 and 1832 were "null and void" in the state of South Carolina. No state, Jackson insisted, could nullify federal laws or secede from the Union.

Everywhere the president traveled, he encountered the words of his famous toast at an 1830 Jefferson Day dinner: "The Union. It must be preserved." Towns erected arches emblazoned with the president's rebuke to the nullification doctrines championed by his then vice president John Calhoun. In Norwich, Connecticut, the civic procession welcoming Jackson included several hundred women, "each of whom bore a banner inscribed with the words of the memorable toast." The triumphal arches and the women adorned with inscribed ribbons and banners had been familiar fixtures in the tours of Washington and Monroe; the novelty was that the arches and banners greeting Jackson did not celebrate his character or past services but affirmed the president's words and endorsed his policy.

Virtually every president after Jackson toured the nation in an effort to meet and communicate with the American people, though few were as successful as Jackson in navigating the conflicting roles of party leader and head of state. Each of Jackson's successors received partisan invitations to travel, and was confronted with the difficult choice of disappointing fellow partisans or inviting opposition charges that the president was degrading his office.

Van Buren's 1839 Tour

Jackson's successor, Martin Van Buren, embraced political parties more unapologetically than any previous president. Unlike many of his contemporaries, Van Buren believed that party competition was vital to democracy. But even Van Buren did not believe that the president should travel as a mere partisan. When he headed north in the summer of 1839, he strove to tear a page from Monroe's playbook by traveling virtually as a private citizen. When the "Democratic citizens" of York, Pennsylvania, invited Van Buren "to partake of a public dinner," he declined their offer, opting instead to stay in his lodgings where "citizens without distinction of party" could call upon him "to pay their respects."[61]

But 1839 was not 1817. Unlike Monroe, Van Buren received an endless stream of overtly partisan invitations. And New York's Whigs were loath to join in welcoming a Democratic president, particularly one who had been a leading architect of the state Democratic Party's ascendance. From the moment that the Whigs learned that Van Buren intended to travel through New York, they suspected that "an election tour" was in the cards. Nor were they wrong. The president's decision to return to New York for the first time since his election in 1836 was an attempt to shore up his political standing in the Empire State and unite the warring factions of the state Democratic Party behind his plan to deposit public monies in an "Independent Treasury."

The partisan dimensions of the tour became evident as soon as the president crossed over from Pennsylvania into New York toward the end of the tour's second week. Upon touching shore in New York City, Van Buren was greeted by Tammany leader John W. Edmonds, who welcomed the president on behalf of "your Democratic Fellow Citizens." Speaking "in the name of those who are ... the supporters of your principles and your policy," Edmonds offered a sustained defense of the administration's policies, most especially Van Buren's Independent Treasury plan.

Edmonds's welcome came as no surprise to Van Buren, who had been sent an advance copy of the welcoming address so he would have time to compose his response. Taking Edmonds's praise of the Independent Treasury as his cue, Van Buren delivered a strongly partisan speech on behalf of his administration's policy. The question, Van Buren insisted, was whether government was to work "for the safety of the many or the aggrandizement of the few." The opposition, he said, wanted the public's money to be controlled by "private corporations, irresponsible to the people," whereas the administration wanted it to be in the hands of the people and their elected representatives.

The president's speech confirmed the Whigs' suspicions that Van Buren had come "among us as a politician and not as President of the United States." Van Buren's partisan rhetoric emboldened several Whig-controlled town councils to refuse the president an official civic welcome. Among these was the council of Hudson, the town in which Van Buren had begun his political career nearly 30 years earlier. The Hudson council explained that they could not appropriate public monies "for the glorification of party men, or the furtherance of party measures."

Democrats defended Van Buren on the grounds that the president traveled as both head of the party and head of state, and so long as the lines separating the two roles remained distinct there was no breach of custom or decorum. It would be bad form to deliver a partisan speech to an official audience, the Democrats conceded, but there was nothing wrong with the president tailoring a partisan message to an audience made up of his political friends.

The sharply divergent reactions to Van Buren's tour reveal how the emergence of organized political parties had complicated presidential travel. Monroe's preeminent challenge while on tour had been to reassure his fellow citizens that he was not aping monarchical practices. Van Buren, too, had to fend off charges that he was "playing the Monarch," but his main difficulty was navigating the conflict between his partisan supporters, who urged him to raise high the party banner, and his political opponents, who insisted he should appear as "president of all the people." Van Buren and his supporters hoped to use the president's trip to energize and organize his political base. His opponents hoped either to tether him to a nonpolitical conception of his role that would restrict his political maneuvering or, alternatively, to use the nonpolitical norm as a stick with which to beat him for violating accepted canons of presidential behavior.

Zachary Taylor's 1849 Tour

When the Whig president Zack Taylor embarked on a tour of the northern states a decade later, the parties seamlessly swapped positions. Whigs now pointed to the president's willingness to converse with the people about important public policy issues as evidence of Old Zack's democratic manners. What Whigs saw as democracy in action, Democrats portrayed as an undignified "bid for votes." The Democratic Party flung at Taylor the same electioneering charge that Whigs had hurled at Van Buren a decade earlier, except that the transgressions of the war hero Taylor were largely attributed to the machinations of his political handlers, whereas Van Buren, widely regarded as a wily politician, was held personally responsible for his political tactics.[62]

It is tempting to see this rhetoric as little more than rank hypocrisy and partisan gamesmanship. Eager to constrain or discredit Taylor, Democrats invoked the same conceptions of presidential dignity that the Whigs had peddled when the Democrats controlled the White House. Meanwhile, Whigs, who had previously kept a vigilant watch against all violations of an austere standard of presidential propriety, now urged their president to mingle freely with the people and to communicate openly with them about public policy. Whether a speech was deemed undignified electioneering or a laudable democratic communion between president and people depended less upon rhetorical norms than raw partisan interests.

The contradictory responses to presidential tours did not mean that rhetoric was merely a cover for underlying political interests. Instead, the language with which presidents were praised and condemned reveals the power that two contradictory ideas exerted on the nineteenth-century political imagination. On the one hand, the American people now expected their president to be in close conversation with the people. This populist vision of the presidential tour coexisted, however, with an older understanding that prescribed that the president keep a dignified distance from the partisan passions that roiled a vibrant democratic community. Too much distance and a president attracted accusations that he harbored monarchical pretensions or was out of touch with the people. Solicit the people too assiduously and charges of electioneering or demagoguery were immediately hurled at the president. No nineteenth-century president who toured the nation found this an easy gauntlet to run, but none failed as spectacularly as Andrew Johnson.

Andrew Johnson's Swing around the Circle

Jeffrey Tulis has described President Johnson as "the great exception." Johnson's "popular rhetoric," writes Tulis, "violated virtually all of the nineteenth-century norms" regarding presidential speech-making. So profound was Johnson's transgression that when the House of Representatives drew up articles of impeachment against him, the tenth article condemned the president's speeches on tour for having "brought the high office of the President of the United States into contempt, ridicule and disgrace."[63]

Johnson's tour began much like many other nineteenth-century presidential tours, with an invitation. This one came from Chicago, an entreaty to participate in the dedication of a monument to Stephen Douglas. As soon as it was announced that the president would travel to Chicago, other cities extended invitations of their own and formed committees to arrange for a reception of the president "in fitting accordance with the respect due the Chief Magistrate of the Union." At stops along the way, Johnson's train was boarded by delegations charged with escorting the president to their city or town.

Johnson's tour created the same sense of high excitement and eager anticipation as previous presidential tours. Crowds seemed as eager to see and touch Andy Johnson as they had been Old Zack and Old Hickory. Johnson's supporters highlighted the importance of having the president "mingle freely with the people." For the *New York Times*, the tour provided the president a valuable opportunity for "talking with the multitude who are not politicians" while also giving the people a chance to see Johnson as he really was, rather than as he had been rendered in the opposition press. Meanwhile, the opposition predictably criticized the tour as thinly veiled electioneering.

Much that transpired on Johnson's tour, however, was anything but typical. Americans were, as the *National Intelligencer* put it, "accustomed to turn out to see and hear their Chief Magistrate," but they were not accustomed to watching their president act as Johnson did. Even many of the president's supporters were dismayed to find Johnson behaving in a manner that they deemed beneath "the dignity of his station."

The problem was never that Johnson spoke about public policy. Presidents since Monroe had done that without being pilloried, let alone impeached. Many of Johnson's supporters were in fact eager to use the tour as an opportunity to affirm the president's policies, specifically his commitment to bring southern states back into the Union with all possible speed. The problem was instead that Johnson engaged in vituperative rhetoric, much of which even today would be regarded as unbecoming of the president of the United States.[64]

Johnson's replies to the formal welcomes extended to him by civic leaders were generally short and dignified, and provoked little controversy. What got him in trouble were the long, extemporaneous speeches the president delivered from hotel balconies, often late in the evening in response to serenades from Johnson supporters, many of whom had been drinking. Speaking from a New York City hotel balcony near midnight, for instance, Johnson told a crowd that he would defend the Union and the Constitution against "the traitors in the North" with the same vigor with which he had fought "the rebels of the South." The Republican press clucked its disapproval at the president's "shamefully abusive language," but press accounts also show that Johnson's speeches were continually interrupted by loud cheering and long applause from boisterous and sympathetic crowds.

In Ohio, however, the crowds became more hostile and Johnson's rhetoric increasingly angry and vitriolic. He spent his first night in the Buckeye State in Cleveland, a bastion of anti-slavery sentiment, and at about ten o'clock at night appeared at the hotel balcony to address a large crowd that had gathered outside. Johnson began, as he almost always did, by declaiming any desire to give a speech. Mentions of Grant and Douglas brought cheers from the crowd, but the trouble began when Johnson invoked Lincoln, that "distinguished fellow-citizen who is now no more." When a voice cried out "unfortunately," Johnson shot back: "Yes, unfortunate for some that God rules on high and deals in right." The suggestion that the assassination of Lincoln and Johnson's ascension to the presidency were part of a divine plan riled the audience. And Johnson compounded the problem by insisting that had Lincoln lived, the Republican press would have "poured out" their "vials of wrath" on Lincoln just as they were now doing to him. Johnson's claims brought angry denials from the crowd. "Never," shouted some. "Three cheers for the Congress of the United States," bellowed another.

Johnson waded deeper into the fight. He challenged the crowd, just as he had done many times in New York, to name one pledge that he had ever violated, one place where he had ever departed from the platform upon which Lincoln and he were elected. Previous crowds had roared their approval at this but, offered the chance to name Johnson's transgressions, Cleveland's citizens were only too ready to oblige: "How about New Orleans?" shouted one, a reference to the bloody events of the past summer in which 34 blacks and 3 whites were killed by former Confederates who were trying to prevent the Radical Republicans from convening a constitutional convention that had as its aim the enfranchisement of blacks. That was followed immediately by other voices: "Hang Jeff Davis" and then a shout of "Hang Thad Stevens and Wendell Phillips," the former the House leader of the Radical Republicans and the latter a leading abolitionist. "Why not hang Thad Stevens and Wendell Phillips," agreed Johnson.

After briefly collecting himself, promising to "permit reason to resume her empire," Johnson descended again into the gutters of political invective. Those in the crowd responsible for the "discordant notes," he charged, were just as much traitors as Davis, Phillips, and Stevens. In fact, the "hecklers ... were cowards, too" since they "remained safely at home" while "brave Americans fought and died for their country." Johnson's tirade brought outraged cries of "Is this dignified?" The president was undeterred: "You may talk about the dignity of the president," he responded. "I care not for dignity."

This was too much even for the president's staunchest supporters. In an editorial entitled "The President's Mistake," the *New York Times*, one of the president's most steadfast backers, disavowed his remarks. "The President of the United States," the *Times* counseled, "cannot enter upon an exchange of epithets with the brawling of a mob, without seriously compromising his official character."

Rather than sidestep the demagogue label that his critics hurled at him, Johnson embraced it. If believing that "the great mass of the people ... will do right" was a demagogical idea, then he was proud to call himself a demagogue. If declaring "the great truth" that "the voice of the people is the voice of God" was demagogical then he was indeed a demagogue. If only, he thundered, there "were more demagogues in our land."

The American people had never seen anything like this from a president: a president denouncing political opponents as traitors, inciting crowds to hang a leading member of Congress, insisting that he cared nothing for the dignity of his office, and embracing the appellation of demagogue. Americans in the age of Jackson wanted their presidents to be close to the people, to mingle with the people, to talk with the people, and to speak for the people. But they still wanted their presidents to attend to the demands of presidential dignity and decorum.

"To Act and Speak with Reserve": In Johnson's Shadow

Johnson's disastrous speaking tour helped to swing the pendulum of opinion, at least for a time, in the direction of dignified reserve. That did not mean that presidents stopped touring the country. Aided by the development of the railroads, presidents after the Civil War traveled unprecedented lengths to meet the people. Johnson's successor, Ulysses S. Grant, visited 22 states and territories, getting as far west as Salt Lake City. Grant was on the road so often that questions were raised in Washington about his "absenteeism." Rutherford Hayes, the first president to make it all the way to the Pacific Ocean, traveled so frequently that wags dubbed him "Rutherford the Rover." President Benjamin Harrison was equally adventurous, embarking on a nearly 3,000-mile tour of the Midwest in 1890 and a 9,000-mile journey to the West Coast the following year.[65]

Each of these presidents was called upon to speak at stops all along the way, but Johnson's experience provided a bracing reminder of the need to avoid remarks that might be seen as undignified or unduly partisan. The lesson was especially vivid for Grant, who had accompanied Johnson for much of the 1866 tour and witnessed firsthand the adverse reaction to Johnson's theatrics. When President Grant traveled he spoke when he could not avoid it, but almost invariably he kept his comments terse and noncontroversial. Grant knew that by refusing to be drawn into a speech he would disappoint many Americans who were accustomed to listening to politicians speak. As he acknowledged to an enthusiastic crowd in Cincinnati, "you never can get half a dozen American citizens together without their wanting a speech." But Grant also believed that the bitter animosities unleashed by the Civil War made it imperative that the president act as a unifying figure who stayed above the political fray.

Unlike Grant, President Harrison was a practiced and talented public speaker, and delivered hundreds of speeches while on tour in order to satisfy the "all-pervading

American habit of demanding a speech on every occasion." Although less reticent than Grant, Harrison trod gingerly upon partisan issues. As he confessed to a gathering in Kingston, New York:

> You ask for a speech. It is not very easy to know what one can talk about on such an occasion as this. Those topics that are most familiar to me, because I am brought in daily contact with them, namely, public affairs, are in some measure prohibited to me, and I must speak therefore only of those things upon which we agree.

Harrison's philosophy, stated at the outset of his 1891 tour, was that the president "should always act and speak with a reserve," and since he was being welcomed by "men of all parties," he must not "say anything anywhere that makes a line of division."[66]

In their vigilance to avoid divisiveness and to preserve presidential dignity, late nineteenth-century presidents courted the opposite danger of appearing to be out of touch with the people's interests and wants. Harrison, for instance, was dubbed the "human iceberg" and the "refrigerator" for his aloof and frosty manner. Jackson had unleashed the power of the presidency by forging a direct connection between the presidency and the people, but presidents in the late nineteenth century, unable to escape the shadow thrown by Andrew Johnson's impeachment, typically shied away from populist appeals to the people. The result was a substantially weaker and more deferential presidency.

GOING PUBLIC IN THE PROGRESSIVE ERA

During the 1870s and 1880s, no reporters covered the White House on a daily basis. The burgeoning core of Washington correspondents largely looked to Congress for their supply of news, not only because the House and Senate dominated policymaking during this period but also because the legislature was far more open to the press than was the presidency. Washington correspondents watched legislative debates from the press gallery, mingled with members in the halls, and regularly talked on the record with legislative leaders. In contrast, reporters rarely talked with the president, and virtually never for attribution. Grover Cleveland, president from 1885 to 1889 and again between 1893 and 1897, was so uncommunicative that the press, according to one reporter, were forced to gather news from the administration "much after the fashion in which highwaymen rob a stage-coach."[67]

This complaint, however, was a sign of a change already underway in presidential–press relations. At the close of the nineteenth century, reporters increasingly looked to the presidency for news. Refused space within the Cleveland White House, journalists such as *Washington Evening Star*'s William Price waited outside "the Executive Mansion," as it was then officially called, to interview the president's visitors. Not until the presidency of William McKinley, however, did the media's growing demand for routine presidential news coincide with a president prepared to give the media regular access to the White House.[68]

William McKinley and the Origins of the Media Presidency

A former member of Congress, McKinley was comfortable with reporters in a way that Cleveland had never been. McKinley set aside a small area on the second floor of the Executive Mansion where journalists from the news services and largest newspapers could write their stories and talk with the president's visitors. McKinley's personal assistant—first John Addison Porter and later George Cortelyou—briefed reporters twice a day, once at noon and then again at four. In those cramped quarters were seen the first glimmers of a White House press room.[69]

McKinley was careful to maintain a dignified distance between the president and press. Although allowed office space in the Executive Mansion, reporters were not permitted to address the president unless he spoke to them first. Yet McKinley also strove to lower the social barriers that Cleveland had erected between president and press. Unlike Cleveland, McKinley accepted an invitation to attend dinner at the Gridiron Club, which was founded by the capitol's leading journalists in 1885 and which continues to this day as a place for politicians and journalists to mix socially. McKinley reciprocated by inviting correspondents to an inaugural reception in the East Room as well as to an end-of-the-year holiday function. When McKinley embarked on his first speaking tour in the summer of 1897, he not only invited correspondents to accompany him on the trip but wandered into the press railcar, took "a seat in the midst of the party ... threw the hat aside and chatted without reserve for over an hour." Reporters saw McKinley's openness as a sign that "friendliness between public men and newspaper reporters will be restored."[70]

But the presidency of McKinley was less a restoration of an old relationship than the establishment of a new one. For most of the nineteenth century, the relationship between the president and the press had been based on partisan affinities or antipathies. Although the dedicated administration newspaper disappeared after 1860, most newspapermen in the 1860s and 1870s continued to see themselves more as party servants than as disinterested professionals. By the 1880s, however, the ideal of unbiased, professional reporting had become increasingly influential, particularly among Washington correspondents. Turnover among the Washington press corps dropped sharply during this period: whereas in the mid-1860s about three-quarters of the correspondents turned over between one Congress and the next, by the early 1890s nearly two-thirds of the correspondents carried over between Congresses.[71]

A media increasingly independent of parties created new challenges as well as opportunities for the nation's chief executive. Unable to count on a partisan press as its public rooting section, presidents were compelled to devise media strategies that accommodated the needs of Washington correspondents. McKinley understood that reporters wanted to be supplied with daily news, so he invited them into the White House. He knew it was better to hand-feed the beast in hopes of taming it than force it to forage on its own for inconvenient scraps of information. Of course, granting correspondents regular access to the White House was no guarantee that they would take the administration's point of view, but having the president's assistant talk with reporters twice a day gave the administration a regular opportunity to place their own spin on the day's news.

McKinley and his de facto press secretary Cortelyou were equally solicitous of the needs of the Washington press corps when the president toured the country, which McKinley—unlike the generally reclusive Cleveland—did with great frequency. Up to six stenographers accompanied the president on his travels so that reporters would have an exact text of the president's speech shortly after the president finished speaking. The reports Cortelyou furnished to the press included both the president's remarks and charming anecdotes of the crowd's response—such as a young man crying out, "Here, McKinley, give us a shake, please." Harnessing the new media's desire for human interest stories enabled Cortelyou to broadcast flattering images of the president.[72]

McKinley also used the press and his speaking tours to pressure Congress, something that his Republican predecessors Hayes and Harrison, for all their travels and public speaking, had carefully avoided. In fact, McKinley's final speech before his assassination, in front of 50,000 people at the Pan-American Exposition in Buffalo, included a vigorous defense of a number of reciprocal trade treaties that were languishing in the Senate.[73]

Much of McKinley's public speaking was aimed at persuading the American people and Congress to embrace the imperialistic fruits of the Spanish–American War. In October 1898, on the eve of congressional midterm elections, McKinley launched a speaking tour through the nation's heartland in which he touted the "great glory" that the war with Spain had brought to the nation. As soon as Spanish negotiators signed the treaty in December, capitulating to Americans' demands that Spain cede not only Guam and Puerto Rico but also the Philippines, McKinley embarked on a tour of the South, hoping to nudge wavering senators to back the controversial treaty. After the Senate narrowly approved the treaty in February, McKinley frequently went public to press the case for holding on to the Philippines.[74]

The Spanish–American War contributed significantly to making a presidency-centered media and a media-centered presidency. The moment the battleship *Maine* exploded and sank in the Havana harbor in February 1898, the media rushed to the White House for immediate answers. Scores of reporters camped out "on the porch, in the front lobby, on the landings, even on the stairs" awaiting news. Twice-daily briefings were no longer sufficient to satisfy the press's appetite for information. With the war underway, McKinley expanded the White House press facilities, released official statements daily, and made sure that "little information was available except through the Executive Mansion."[75]

By the end of McKinley's presidency, as historian Lewis Gould points out, the White House had become "the nation's major center for political news." Testament to the heightened public attention fixed on the presidency were the 30 clerks McKinley needed to sort and respond to the more than 100,000 letters the White House received from the American people each year. Although an immensely popular president, McKinley instinctively drew back from the media spotlight, trusting instead in what one reporter described as those "shrewd processes of indirection" by which he "put out ... whatever news would best serve the ends of the administration." McKinley's successor Theodore Roosevelt, in contrast, adored the glare of public attention and famously celebrated the presidency as the nation's "bully pulpit."[76]

Theodore Roosevelt's Bully Pulpit

Throughout his public life, Roosevelt was drawn to "the spotlight of publicity." When he led "the Rough Riders" into battle in Cuba in June 1898, he made sure that he was followed by a bevy of reporters and photographers who could publicize his heroics. Only a few days before a triumphant Roosevelt returned home from his "bully fight" to find himself "the most famous man in America," President McKinley had barred photographers and reporters from attending the signing of a peace accord with Spain because he felt that their presence might "mar the dignity of the occasion."[77]

As president, Roosevelt saw no conflict between dignity and publicity. The power of the presidency, in Roosevelt's view, lay in the power of publicity. Public confrontations with powerful interests, such as the showdown with the Northern Securities Company in 1902, provided the staging for "moral melodramas in which citizens rooted for and against what Roosevelt was doing." Like Andrew Jackson (and Andrew Johnson), Roosevelt welcomed the public enemies he made for the opportunity they provided to cast himself as the tribune of the people. Roosevelt's keen sense of the symbolism of the public presidency was evident in one of his earliest decisions: dumping the stuffy, stately title of "Executive Mansion" and substituting in its stead the "White House."[78]

Shaping the news was as important to Roosevelt as it had been to McKinley, but Roosevelt took a far more direct approach than his predecessor. Whereas McKinley spoke with journalists only occasionally, preferring instead to funnel information to the press through his aides, Roosevelt delighted in talking with journalists. Roosevelt's favored reporters—derided by the less favored as the president's "fair haired boys" or "cuckoos"—were routinely ushered in to watch the president get shaved and listen to him talk "a blue streak." Reporters were treated to a daily "barrage of presidential advice, leaks, story ideas, gossip, [and] instructions on how to write their stories." The ground rules, however, remained the same as they had under McKinley: all conversations with the president were off the record and he could neither be quoted nor identified as the source of a reporter's information.[79]

Most Washington reporters respected and even liked McKinley—and they often shared his politics as well. Roosevelt, however, had a magnetic effect on reporters. The influential Progressive editor William Allen White testified that "Theodore Roosevelt bit me and I went mad." Correspondents admitted to Roosevelt's "shaving hour" briefings were dazzled by the president's energy and ebullience—it was "more fun than a circus," one noted. Flattered by the confidences that the president entrusted to their keeping, the press rewarded him with highly favorable press coverage.[80]

Wooing and wowing the media was only half of Roosevelt's equation for fostering favorable press coverage. Reporters who displeased the president by writing unfavorable news stories were banished to what Roosevelt called the Ananias Club—so christened after a character in the Bible who lied and was struck dead by God. Reporters understood that printing stories that were "objectionable to or censorious of the administration" would result in them being cast out of the president's circle of favorites and could even get them barred from the White House. On occasion, a displeased Roosevelt would even appeal directly to a publisher to have a reporter taken off the White House beat.[81]

The president's divide-and-rule tactics worked, as historian George Juergens explains, because of "the unequal relationship between Roosevelt and a not yet fully mature press corps" that lacked both a well-developed professional code of ethics and organizations through which they could assert their collective interests as reporters. That would soon change, as the founding of the National Press Club in 1908 and the White House Correspondents Association in 1914 enabled reporters to establish and enforce professional standards of behavior and thereby solve the collective action problem that Roosevelt so deftly exploited.[82]

Inducing journalists to report the news as Roosevelt wanted it written was a crucial element in the president's battle to mobilize public opinion in favor of progressive reform. But Roosevelt also pursued more direct approaches to rallying public opinion. Although press briefings were strictly off the record, Roosevelt made himself a fixture on the front pages through "an uninterrupted series of presidential announcements, statements, interviews, controversies, stunts, and trips." Roosevelt believed in the power of repetition. His philosophy, as one sympathetic Washington correspondent rendered it, "was that if you wished the people to understand your attitude, you must constantly, insistently, remind them of it."[83]

Roosevelt worked constructively with congressional leaders when he could, but when he ran into resistance, he did not hesitate, as he explained in his autobiography, to appeal "over the heads of the Senate and House leaders to the people, who were masters of both of us." When the Senate balked at Roosevelt's proposal to tighten government regulation of railroads, Roosevelt took his case for the Hepburn Act directly to the people who had just reelected him by an overwhelming margin. A trip to San Antonio, Texas for a Rough Riders reunion in the spring of 1905 became a cross-country campaign on behalf of the blocked legislation, with well-publicized speeches in Dallas, Denver, and Chicago. Roosevelt took to the stump again early in the fall of 1905, using a trip to his mother's family in Georgia as a pretext for a speech-making campaign throughout the Southeast that featured several major speeches touting railroad regulation.[84]

When Congress reconvened in December, recalcitrant senators were feeling the heat from constituents stirred up not only by Roosevelt's rhetorical appeals but also by his carefully orchestrated media campaign in the nation's newspapers and magazines. As one railroad executive lamented, the president had so "roused the people that it was impossible for the Senate to stand against the popular demand." A bill that only months before had been widely viewed as doomed was ultimately enacted into law with only three senators daring to vote against it. In securing passage of the Hepburn Act over the vehement objections of some of the Senate's most powerful leaders, Roosevelt dramatized more clearly than any president before him the power of the bully pulpit.[85]

"With the Nation behind Him": Woodrow Wilson and the Limits of the Rhetorical Presidency

Among those transfixed by Roosevelt's kinetic presidency was prominent political scientist Woodrow Wilson. As a graduate student at Johns Hopkins University during Chester Arthur's presidency, Wilson had written a celebrated dissertation that excoriated

WHEN THE PRESIDENT MAKES A SPEECH

Theodore Roosevelt's public speaking captured the imagination of the American people and the press in a way that no previous president's had. This two-page spread that appeared in *Harper's Weekly* in January 1907 captures the expressiveness, energy, and ebullience of Roosevelt's speech-making.

Courtesy: *Harper's Weekly*, 1907.

"Congressional Government" for its fragmentation of power and division of responsibility. The presidency barely figured in the young Wilson's thinking. The remedy that Wilson prescribed was not a more energetic presidency but instead a more cohesive, centralized Congress modeled on the British parliamentary system.[86]

Twenty years later, as the president of Princeton University, Wilson had come to a different view, one powerfully shaped by the example of Roosevelt's leadership. In 1908, during Roosevelt's final year in office, Wilson published *Constitutional Government in the United States*, a collection of lectures that distilled his new thinking about American politics. Whereas previously he had argued that only constitutional amendment could rescue an archaic constitutional structure, Wilson now saw the rhetorical presidency as the engine that could carry the nation safely through the challenges of the twentieth century.

Wilson began from the Jacksonian axiom that only the president "represents the people as whole, exercising a national choice." Congress represented parochial and special interests, whereas the president possessed the "only national voice in affairs." Having watched Republican congressional opposition to the Hepburn Act wilt under the heat of Roosevelt's relentless publicity campaign, it now seemed to Wilson that party elites could not withstand a president able to "win the admiration and confidence of the country." So long as the president "rightly interpret the national thought and boldly insist upon it," his rhetoric would make him "irresistible."[87]

As a young political scientist, Wilson had seen the Constitution as a straitjacket, but now he perceived the framing document as sufficiently "elastic" to enable the presidency to be "anything [its incumbent] has the sagacity and force to make it." The president, Wilson famously concluded, "is at liberty, both in law and conscience, to be as big a man as he can. His capacity will set the limit; and if Congress be overborne by him, it will be ... because the President has the nation behind him, and Congress has not." Four years after publishing *Constitutional Government*, Wilson got a chance to try out his theory when he was elected the nation's 28th president—ironically, with an inadvertent assist from Roosevelt, whose third party candidacy divided the Republican Party and doomed the ineffectual incumbent, William Howard Taft, to defeat.[88]

As president, Wilson underscored the importance he attached to public opinion and public speaking by dramatically breaking with tradition and delivering his annual message to Congress in person—rather than having a lowly legislative clerk read it aloud, as had been the case since Jefferson's day.[89] The trouble was that Wilson's model of public opinion leadership was premised on the president as great orator, and while Wilson was a persuasive public speaker, the only people who could hear or see him speak—in an age without television or radio—were the fortunate few in the room. However compellingly he delivered his annual message, or any other speech, members of the public would only know it by the words they read in the next day's newspapers. And even that would only occur if newspaper editors chose to print the text of the speech, rather than summarizing it or ignoring it altogether.[90]

Mobilizing public opinion thus required more than inspirational or visionary rhetoric that spoke the "common meaning of the common voice," as Wilson had put it in a Lincoln Day tribute in 1909;[91] it required a media strategy that accommodated the needs of an increasingly professionalized press corps while controlling and managing the president's message. At the suggestion of Wilson's self-styled "publicity director" Joseph Tumulty, Wilson held regularly scheduled presidential press conferences that were open to the entire press corps, something that no president had done before—Taft's press conferences had been sporadic at best and Roosevelt's regular shaving sessions had been for favored reporters only.[92]

The press corps appreciated Wilson's willingness to meet with them regularly—initially twice a week—but relations between president and press were far less chummy and convivial than they had been under Roosevelt. This was due not only to differences in personality but also to the much larger group of reporters meeting with the president. Roosevelt talked freely and easily with reporters because he invited only those he trusted. Wilson, in contrast, faced a room full of reporters, many of whom he did not even know, and his comments were naturally more guarded and less revealing. More than one hundred correspondents showed up at Wilson's first press conference. Everybody stood, the president behind his desk and the correspondents on the other side, arrayed in "a thickened crescent." The atmosphere, one participant wrote, was "chill and correct." While Roosevelt had been a geyser of information, Wilson waited for questions and then "answered crisply, politely, and in the fewest possible words." Reporters were grateful for the information the president provided but neither the president nor the press seemed to enjoy the experience.[93]

With all comers welcome—200 correspondents attended the president's second press conference—it became almost impossible for the president to enforce ground rules, which included not quoting the president without his permission. After the inevitable unauthorized quotations, Wilson threatened to discontinue the press conferences unless all journalists adhered to the president's ground rules. The result was the formation of the White House Correspondents' Association and the promulgation of rules of conduct and a process of accrediting reporters. Only those accredited by the White House Correspondents' Association would be permitted to attend the president's press conferences, and violators of the code of conduct could be stripped of their accreditation.[94]

Although professional self-regulation helped to ameliorate the problem of unauthorized information appearing on the front pages, Wilson nonetheless grew increasingly frustrated with the press conferences as well as with press coverage. "Do not believe anything you read in the newspapers," he counseled a close friend, less than six months into his presidency. He bristled at reporters' questions that he felt were trivial—as, for instance, when a reporter asked his opinion about Groundhog Day—or that intruded on his family. Reporters were equally unhappy. They could forgive the "cold and challenging eye," the occasional outbursts of pique, even the barely disguised condescension, but not the president's evasive and often misleading replies. The conferences became less frequent and less well attended until finally, a little more than two years into his presidency, Wilson abandoned them altogether, leaving the task of briefing reporters to the affable, media-savvy Tumulty.[95]

Frustrated by a press corps that seemed to report "everything ... erroneously," Wilson looked for ways to bypass Washington's correspondents, particularly as his attention turned increasingly to the war in Europe. Wilson even entertained the idea of a government-owned newspaper that would faithfully publicize and explain the government's position. After Congress declared war in April 1917, one of Wilson's first acts was to sign an executive order establishing the Committee on Public Information, through which the administration launched an unprecedented propaganda campaign to "arouse ardor and enthusiasm" for the war. The committee strove to shape public opinion not only via newspapers and magazines but through a blitz of "advertisements, books, pamphlets, billboards, placards, speeches, and films." At Wilson's urging, the committee also published the *Official Bulletin*, a collection of government statements and announcements that were distributed to newspapers and public officials and displayed in post offices across the country.[96]

After the war was over, Wilson traveled to Paris to ensure that the treaty would include a League of Nations, and so make good on his pledge to make World War I the "war to end all wars." Some 150 correspondents followed Wilson to Europe but the president refused to take reporters into his confidence during the many months he remained in France. From the other side of the Atlantic Ocean, Tumulty implored the president to court the press in order to garner more positive coverage in the nation's newspapers. Wilson brushed aside Tumulty's concerns. He had a different idea: if the Senate would not ratify the Versailles Treaty then he would take his case directly to the American people in a nationwide speaking tour.[97]

That is exactly what he did upon returning to the United States. On September 3, 1919, accompanied by two dozen reporters, Wilson embarked on a cross-country train trek that was scheduled to take him nearly 10,000 miles en route to virtually every state west of the Mississippi. He pitched the League through the Midwest, in cities and towns in Ohio, Indiana, and Iowa, into the Far West, in places such as Billings, Montana and Coeur d'Alene, Idaho, onto Seattle and Tacoma, down through Portland and San Francisco, as far south as San Diego, before heading east again through Nevada and Utah. By the time Wilson reached Pueblo, Colorado, on September 25, he had given 37 major addresses as well as innumerable short speeches, mostly from the rear of the train. "In city after city," writes historian Thomas Knock, Wilson "endured countless parades, stood in open cars for hours at a time, shook hands with hundreds of well-wishers, and spoke to crowds as large as 40,000 without the aid of an electronic public address system." The pace was punishing. Unwell when he began the tour, Wilson became seriously ill shortly after leaving Pueblo and was forced to cancel the remainder of the tour. Less than a week later, Wilson suffered a massive stroke that left him incapacitated and the treaty dead.[98]

Wilson's tour is sometimes seen, with good reason, as a lesson in the limits of the rhetorical presidency, a cautionary tale for presidents who are tempted to override legislative deliberation through impassioned public appeals.[99] Certainly the tour showed that popular rhetoric is rarely sufficient to make any president "irresistible," no matter how "boldly" the president articulates his position. But Wilson's grueling tour also revealed how difficult it was for nineteenth- and early twentieth-century presidents to make oratory the centerpiece of public opinion leadership. Like his predecessors, Wilson could only make his voice widely heard—as opposed to his words being read—by traveling immense distances by train. Even when the president attracted large crowds, only a fraction of those present could get close enough to hear the president's words. In this respect, Wilson had more in common with the rhetorical ways of his nineteenth-century predecessors than his twentieth-century successors.

BROADCASTING THE PRESIDENCY

The 1920s don't get their due. Squeezed between the Progressive Era and the New Deal, the decade is generally neatly packed away in our historical memory as one of little relevance to American political development. We may recall it as the Roaring Twenties or the Jazz Age, or with stock images of flappers, bootleggers, and mobsters, but politically it seems a placid interlude between the innovative progressive presidencies of Teddy Roosevelt and Woodrow Wilson on the one side and FDR's monumental New Deal on the other. William Harding's 1920 campaign slogan, "a return to normalcy," becomes an easy shorthand for a decade's supposedly static, even backward-looking politics. The reality is that the 1920s were a crucial period in the development of the public presidency.

For all his dedication to the arts of rhetorical persuasion and his insistence on the president as a leader of public opinion, Woodrow Wilson was stubbornly resistant to utilizing new technologies of mass communications, such as movies, newsreels, and phonograph recordings. When Hollywood producers approached him about filming cabinet meetings. Wilson rejected the idea. He thought posing for cameras contrived and undignified, and he worried that his "self-consciousness in the face of the camera" would "make the whole thing awkward and ineffective." Warren Harding and Calvin Coolidge, in contrast, had no such reservations about staged photo ops. Coolidge, who became president after Harding died during a cross-country speaking tour in 1923, proved particularly adept at using the emerging tools of mass communications to broadcast his image and message to the American people.[100]

Calvin Coolidge's "Magnificent Propaganda Machine"

Although overshadowed in our imaginations by the imposing figures of Theodore Roosevelt and Woodrow Wilson, Calvin Coolidge's voice, face, and gestures would have been more familiar to his contemporaries than were those of TR or Wilson. Coolidge was the first president to rely on radio to communicate regularly with the American people. His 1925 inaugural address, the first to be broadcast by radio, may have reached as many as 25 million Americans. More people likely heard "Silent Cal" speak on that single day than had heard Wilson or TR speak on tour in eight years in office. Certainly, the listening audience for Coolidge's address dwarfed that of the preceding 34 inaugural addresses combined.[101]

Coolidge even more eagerly embraced the public relations possibilities of moving pictures. A month after delivering his inaugural address—and two years before the appearance of the first feature-length "talkie," *The Jazz Singer*—Coolidge starred in a talking film in which "the tones of his voice came clear and synchronized perfectly with the movement of his mouth." Newsreels, their quality rapidly improving during the 1920s, prominently featured Coolidge's comings and goings, making him "as recognizable a figure in the nation's theaters as the film celebrities with whom he consorted." Coolidge went to extraordinary lengths to accommodate the camera, so much so that the posse of motion picture and still photographers who followed him around joked that Coolidge "would don any attire or assume any pose that would produce an interesting picture." His readiness to pose for the camera made him, in the judgment of one observer, "the most photographed man who ever occupied the White House."[102]

Coolidge wooed print White House newspaper reporters with the same solicitousness that he bestowed upon photographers. Unlike Wilson, who largely abandoned presidential press conferences midway through his first term, Coolidge stuck to a twice-a-week schedule throughout his five and a half years in the White House. By the time he left office in 1929, Silent Cal had held 520 press conferences, at a rate of eight a month—more than any president before or since. The presidential press conference, however, remained shielded from public view; the president could not be quoted, and anything quotable the president might utter had to be attributed to a "presidential spokesman." Nonetheless, Coolidge's biweekly exchange with reporters helped to put the president and his views on the front pages of America's newspapers.[103]

Coolidge's skillful management of the news media and assiduous cultivation of his public image helped to make the president immensely popular but also induced tremendous anxiety among critics who worried, as political scientist Lindsay Rodgers did, that Coolidge's "government by favourable publicity" was turning the president into "the most powerful elected ruler in the world" and eclipsing Congress in the public imagination. This fear of "government by publicity" was echoed by the editors of the *New Republic*, who pronounced it "an innovation unique in all history." Although Roosevelt

President Coolidge's penchant for providing the media with an "interesting picture" was on display during his vacation in the Black Hills of South Dakota in the summer of 1927, when he donned the cowboy look for the benefit of the still and newsreel photographers. Throughout his time in the Black Hills, he was accompanied, according to one account, by "some thirty-odd newspaper correspondents, a group of a dozen or more moving-picture men, several unofficial ... press agents disguised as syndicate writers, a number of expert telegraph operators, camera men representing the photo syndicates ... every last man of them devoted to the task of publicity for Mr. Coolidge" (Greenberg, *Republic of Spin*, 165).

Courtesy: Library of Congress, Prints and Photographs Division, LC-USZ62-29740.

"was once thought to be something of an expert at such business," the editors judged TR a novice compared to Coolidge. "No ruler in history," they concluded, "ever had such a magnificent propaganda machine as Mr. Coolidge."[104]

The Progressives had put great store in presidential leadership of public opinion to change America for the better. They had faith that public opinion, as Theodore Roosevelt expressed it, "if only sufficiently enlightened and aroused, is equal to the necessary regenerative task" facing the nation. But during the 1920s, Progressives increasingly worried that a politics suffused with ad men and publicists would deceive and mislead the American people. Progressives fretted that Coolidge and his advisers—particularly the media-savvy adman Bruce Barton—had constructed a popular persona that bore "no relation to the man in the White House" and were selling Coolidge's character "as though he were a new breakfast food or fountain pen." Distracted by the appealing image, Progressives worried, Americans had lost sight of the important issues at stake.[105]

Much of the Progressives' critical reaction to Coolidge's news management can be put down to ideological sour grapes. What had looked like noble education of the public during the Roosevelt or Wilson administration now seemed like deceptive spin.[106] But if we discount for hyperbole and hypocrisy, the contemporary reactions to the Coolidge administration usefully alert us to how well established the media-centered presidency and presidency-centered media were before FDR took office, and how much the conservative

Republican presidents of the 1920s contributed to institutionalizing the development of the public presidency.

Radio Days: FDR's Fireside Chats

FDR did not invent the modern media presidency but he was the first to master it. Coolidge was the radio pioneer, but failed to take full advantage of its potential. Coolidge's media guru, Bruce Barton, had stressed that radio was a game changer because it "enables the President to sit by every fireside and talk in terms of that home's interest and prosperity," to talk personally with "folks" rather than "address" them in a formal speech. Barton implored Coolidge to expand his use of radio beyond broadcasting live speeches and instead utilize the medium to converse directly with the radio audience on a monthly basis. But as fond as Coolidge was of using radio rather than a "rousing" stump speech to "get [his] message across," he resisted Barton's advice, believing that frequent radio talks would be expensive as well as unnecessary given the free positive coverage he already received from the daily press.[107]

Coolidge's successor, Herbert Hoover, received much the same advice from CBS's William Paley, who urged the new president to craft "exclusive radio talks to the whole Nation ... from your study in the White House" rather than using the medium merely to broadcast speeches the president gave to this or that audience in different locations. Speaking directly to the radio audience would allow Hoover to capitalize on "radio's intimate relationship to the home" and "bring out [the president's] personality." Radio, in short, could both nationalize the president's audience and make the connection between the president and the people seem more personal and intimate. Although Hoover broadcast by radio around 80 speeches during his term (more than twice Coolidge's total), he lacked the inclination or skill to follow Paley's advice and largely continued throughout his four years to treat radio audiences as "eavesdroppers."[108]

FDR lost no time in doing what Barton and Paley had tried in vain over the preceding eight years to get Coolidge and Hoover to do: talk directly and exclusively to a radio audience from the White House using an intimate, conversational style. On his ninth day in office, speaking from a makeshift studio in the Lincoln Study, FDR delivered his first "fireside chat." "My friends," he began, "I want to talk for a few minutes ... about banking, ... to tell you what has been done in the last few days, why it was done, and what the next steps are going to be." Americans had never experienced a president speaking to them in this way. One listener marveled that the president seemed to be "sitting by my side talking in plain simple words with me." Another listener wrote to the president after the first fireside chat: "Until last night, to me, the president of the United States was merely a legend. A picture to look at. But you are real. I know your voice [and] what you are trying to do." FDR demonstrated what Barton and Paley had understood: that radio had the capacity to transform the connection between the president and the American public.[109]

FDR's fireside chats were broadcast on each of the national networks, usually at around 10pm eastern time so to attract the largest possible listening audience. The networks would also typically rebroadcast the talk the following day for the benefit

While Calvin Coolidge was the first president to regularly use radio to address the nation, FDR was the first to master the medium. Unlike his predecessor Herbert Hoover, Roosevelt was thoroughly at ease behind the microphone. FDR understood that radio required a more relaxed, conversational style of speaking than the typically grandiloquent platform oratory. During his twelve years as president, Roosevelt delivered approximately thirty radio addresses—also known as "fireside chats"—to the nation.

Courtesy: The Granger Collection, NYC—All rights reserved.

of those who may have missed the initial airing. The talks were generally short—his first fireside chat was just under 15 minutes and rarely lasted more than a half hour—and delivered calmly and slowly, at a pace of around 100 words a minute. In contrast to Hoover's speeches broadcast over radio, which were filled with long words, bewildering facts, and complex arguments that at once "demanded and discouraged close listening attention," Roosevelt used the simplest and clearest language possible to make people feel they were almost in conversation with the president—"I found myself answering you, nodding to you, chatting to you, and agreeing with you," wrote one listener.[110]

Although now legendary, FDR's fireside chats were not all that frequent. During his first term, he delivered only eight. In fact, historian Douglas Craig calculates that FDR actually "spent less time on the airwaves during his first term than Herbert Hoover." Supporters often urged Roosevelt to take to radio more often. The president of NBC even offered him free airtime to speak to the American people once a week. Roosevelt's refusal in part reflected the immense amount of preparation that went into each talk. "Every time I talk over the air," Roosevelt explained, "it means four or five days of long, overtime work in the preparation of what I say." FDR's main reason for not speaking more often, however, was his concern that it would diminish the importance and impact of the fireside chats. "The one thing I dread," he explained, "is that my talks should be so frequent as to lose their effectiveness."[111]

FDR's embrace of radio reflected not only his mastery of the medium but also an awareness that the majority of newspapers were owned by Republicans who were skeptical of or hostile to the New Deal. Whereas Coolidge believed he could rely on largely favorable publicity from the newspapers, FDR was convinced he needed radio to bypass newspaper owners, editors, and columnists and to establish "a direct contact with the people." When, in 1939, FDR directed his cabinet members to do a series of national radio talks, he explained that "in some communities it is the unhappy fact that only through the radio is it possible to overtake loudly proclaimed untruths or greatly exaggerated half-truths." Presidents' anxiety about "fake news" did not begin with Donald Trump.[112]

Not that FDR wrote off the print media. Indeed, he was as dedicated to cultivating the Washington press corps as Coolidge and as skillful as Theodore Roosevelt. By the end of his twelve years as president he had conducted almost 1,000 press conferences, an average of nearly seven a month. Unlike Coolidge and Harding, Roosevelt did not require questions be submitted in advance, but he refused to allow follow-up questions—what he called "cross-examination"—and the president still could not be directly quoted, unless he permitted it. But for Roosevelt, who believed that most Americans now "make their decisions on what they hear rather than what they read [in] the editorials and the news columns of the daily press," the print media had become secondary to radio as a way of communicating with the American people.[113]

FDR viewed radio not only as a more reliable way to inform the American people but also as a better means of gauging what people thought. In his radio talks, he encouraged listeners to "write or telegraph to me personally at the White House," even "to tell me your troubles." And write they did, in unprecedented numbers—a rate ten times higher than during Hoover's presidency. Roosevelt delighted in the deluge of mail the White House received after his radio talks. He boasted to a group of newspaper editors that the thousands upon thousands of letters that flooded into the White House put him "more closely in touch with public opinion in the United States than any individual in this room." Those thousands upon thousands of letters, he insisted, represented "a better cross section of opinion" than could be found in any newspaper. Letters also poured into Congress in unprecedented numbers, many of them urging members to "stand by the President" and even threatening to vote against them if they didn't. [114]

Roosevelt believed that radio promoted democracy. In an age in which "so many developments ... lead away from direct government by the people," FDR wrote while still governor of New York, "radio is one which tends to restore direct contact between the masses and their chosen leaders." Radio certainly enabled FDR to help the people feel, as one appreciative listener wrote, "that we have a real share in our government." But Roosevelt's was also a vision of democracy that sidelined the legislature and elevated the executive. Indeed, for FDR, radio was vital to democracy precisely because it gave the president the means not only to bypass a biased print media but also "to appeal for public support over the heads of the Legislature."[115]

Staging the TV Presidency

At the time of FDR's death in 1945, 90 percent of American households had a radio, which had eclipsed the newspaper as Americans' principal source of national and international news. But radio's preeminence was short-lived. Following World War II, television rapidly became a fixture in American homes. In 1946 only a few thousand homes had a television set, but by 1954 more than half of all homes had a television and by 1960 there was a TV in nine out of every ten households. But while Americans couldn't wait to get their hands on a television set, presidents were slow to figure out how best to use the medium.[116]

Harry Truman permitted cameras to film his 1947 State of the Union address but there were no cue cards or teleprompters and the audience saw a president peering "down into his typescript, scarcely bothering to conceal his turning of pages." Through coaching and the use of "oversized cue cards" Truman learned to look directly at the camera, but he generally only televised his most important speeches. Television cameras were still not allowed in the presidential press conference.[117]

Dwight Eisenhower's team was determined to make Ike the first real TV President. His press secretary James Hagerty suggested that Eisenhower take advantage of the "new age" of presidential television by doing a monthly half-hour television program, but Eisenhower scorned the idea: "I can think of nothing more boring for the American public than to have sit in their living rooms for a whole half hour and look at my face on their television screens." The administration experimented with bringing television cameras into cabinet meetings, but that experiment flopped as the stilted dialogue and hokey staging made for dull television that was almost as awkward to watch as it was to participate in. When the administration invited television cameras to film a wonkish discussion about NATO between the president and Secretary of State John Foster Dulles, the split screen showed the television audience a president sitting "passively, playing with his eyeglasses, tugging on his suit and scanning the room as if uninterested in following his secretary's blather." And when the president got the chance to speak, the cameras caught Dulles "looking at his watch."[118]

The problem, as Hagerty soon realized, was that "nobody on the [White House] press staff knew much about telecasting." To help the White House produce better presidential television they brought on board the Hollywood actor, director, and producer Robert Montgomery, who not only worked with the president to improve his on-camera delivery but stage-managed the lighting, camera angles, makeup, even the color of the president's suits. The making of a more relaxed, smiling, telegenic president struck some critics—especially print journalists—as contrived and artificial. Some even saw the staging as "undignified," a charge leveled by one reader who disapproved of having Eisenhower talk to the audience while perched on the edge of his desk. But most of the American people liked the image of Ike they saw on television.[119]

While Hagerty had been quick to see the need for Montgomery's expertise, both he and Eisenhower were slow to warm to the idea of allowing television cameras into the press conferences. By mid-century, presidential press conferences were no longer the confabs they had been in the early twentieth century. The growth in the White House press corps led Truman in 1950 to move the press conference out of the Oval Office and into a cavernous room in the Executive Office Building, which required the introduction of microphones. Truman also finally allowed press conferences to be recorded and transcribed, though the press could only air or print excerpts that the White House approved. But Truman had drawn the line at television cameras, and initially Eisenhower and Hagerty, fearing that the presidential conference would be lit up "like a Hollywood premiere," drew the same line.[120]

What helped to change the administration's mind was not only its growing confidence that it could use television to its advantage, but also its increasing frustration at the White House press corp's escalating criticism of Eisenhower's unwillingness to publicly challenge the anti-Communist demagogue Senator Joseph McCarthy. Eisenhower fumed that the press conferences were becoming "a waste of time" because reporters were only interested "in some cheap political fight." "To hell with slanted reporters," Hagerty determined. "We'll go directly to the people who can hear exactly what [the president] said without reading warped and slanted stories."[121]

On January 9, 1955, at Eisenhower's 58th press conference, television cameras were finally admitted, "turning a meeting with the press into a straight-to-the-people political production." Hagerty was delighted with what seemed to be a "very potent way of getting the President's personality and viewpoints across" and thought it "almost the same thing as the start of Roosevelt's fireside chats on radio." Some observers saw "democracy at work" in the televised news conference, while others worried that the press conference would descend into showmanship without substance or candor. But while the press conference became a made-for-television affair, the White House retained control over what could be aired on television. Just as the White House provided the official transcript of the press conference from which print reporters could quote, so all film of the press conference had to be submitted to Hagerty, who had the final say on what to cut and what to keep. Neither Hagerty nor Eisenhower contemplated allowing live coverage of the president's press conference.[122]

The idea of doing press conferences live was put to John F. Kennedy shortly after his election in 1960 by his press secretary, Pierre Salinger. Many of Kennedy's confidants hated the idea. They feared it could lead to a gaffe that might embarrass the president or even possibly trigger an international incident. Other advisors worried about overexposure. The idea was also vociferously opposed by print journalists. Richard Strout of the New Republic huffed, "If Kennedy wants to revive FDR's fireside chats—fine, but he shouldn't use the press conference as a vehicle. The best conference is the one where reporters remain anonymous, where they can ask unselfconscious questions without being unpaid radio or TV actors." Kennedy, supremely confident in his abilities in front of the television camera, brushed aside these objections and embraced Salinger's proposal. The networks, in exchange, agreed to preempt their regular programming to air the live press conferences.[123]

Live press conferences made for more dramatic television. But they were also higher-stakes events, which meant the president needed to spend more time preparing. That in turn led presidents to hold fewer press conferences. Truman had already reduced the frequency of press conferences to once a week, and under Kennedy and Eisenhower it dropped to about twice a month. Over the subsequent decades, the numbers dropped still further. Richard Nixon heightened the visibility of the presidential press conference by moving them from the afternoon to prime time and simultaneously cutting back to about one press conference every two months. The same pattern was followed by Ronald Reagan, who typically blocked out two to three days to prepare for his elaborately staged prime-time press conferences. What had begun as a forum for reporters to meet with the president became, under the hot lights of television, a means for presidents to speak directly to the American people in a carefully orchestrated public event that reduced reporters to the role of "one of the props."[124]

As press conferences became another forum for presidents to appeal directly for public support, the media became ever more vocal in their criticism of White House "spin." Television at once elevated the importance the White House attached to image-making and fostered a determination among the media to uncover the truth they believed lay concealed beneath the image. While the relationship between the media and president had never been the "partnership" that Woodrow Wilson naively hoped for, it became more adversarial during the 1960s. The media's dedication to unspinning the presidential spin helped to hold presidents accountable, but also engendered in the country "a world weary view of presidential politics as merely a competition of images and messages."[125]

Attention to presidential image-making, both by the White House and by the media, reached new levels of manipulation and distrust during Nixon's presidency. Publicly, Nixon insisted he didn't worry about images, but behind the scenes he devoted unprecedented energy and resources to conjuring up favorable news coverage and crafting an image of a hard-working president, cool under pressure and above partisan politics. As one top aide later wrote, Nixon "seemed to believe there was no national issue that was not susceptible to public-relations treatment." And he was certainly convinced that no president had ever faced a more hostile Washington press corps. Nixon "hired more media and image consultants than any of his predecessors" and chose as his chief of staff (H.R. Haldeman) a man who had spent the previous 20 years as an advertising executive. Daily staff meetings focused on crafting the "line of the day" that the administration wanted to lead the evening news broadcast. The administration also established the White House Office of Communications, which was tasked not only with coordinating the administration's short-term and long-term public relations strategies but also with creating "a kind of quasi-journalistic operation" that could circumvent the White House press corps and provide presidential news directly to local media outlets and the American people.[126]

Nixon's enormous investment of energy in managing the news may have been born of a conviction that he faced unprecedented media persecution, but his institutional innovations—from the Office of Communications to the "line of the day"—established enduring precedents that subsequent presidents would build on, none more adroitly than the former actor Ronald Reagan. Reagan's media-savvy team also began their days establishing a line of the day, but focused increased attention on the visual images they hoped to see on the nightly news. The president's speeches, too, were crafted with detailed attention to the visual dimension. Speechwriter Peggy Noonan recalled that she "was thinking cinematically" as she drafted Reagan's dramatic 1984 speech commemorating D-Day, delivered atop a "windswept" Normandy cliff that American soldiers had scaled with grappling hooks 40 years before.[127]

As important as Reagan's skill in delivering lines before a camera and the White House team's careful attention to stagecraft were the changes in television news during the 1980s, specifically the emergence of cable news. The arrival of CNN, which first broadcast in June 1980, enabled the Reagan White House to "produce dramatic settings for the president to deliver carefully scripted appearances for delivery throughout the day, not just for evening news broadcasts." The proliferation of cable news channels over the subsequent decades multiplied the opportunities for presidents to speak to the people with the television cameras rolling. Reagan's successors have generally given about 500 speeches and remarks a year, more than six times the number that Eisenhower gave.[128]

FAITH IN WORDS: THE EFFECTS OF PRESIDENTIAL RHETORIC

Does all this speaking help a president? Presidents and their aides certainly think so. David Gergen, who worked in the Nixon, Ford, Reagan, and Clinton administrations, insists that in the modern presidency "there is no weapon more powerful than persuasion by speech." Presidents as different as Nixon, Reagan, Clinton, Bush, and Obama have all expressed great faith that they could boost public support for their policies or themselves through their rhetoric.[129]

However, empirical studies show that presidential speeches rarely shift public opinion significantly. In *On Deaf Ears: The Limits of the Bully Pulpit* (2003), George Edwards examined all nationally televised presidential addresses between 1981 and 2002 and found that they typically had little or no impact on presidential approval ratings. The president's approval rating was generally not much different after the speech than it had been before it. Similarly, in a study of every State of the Union message between 1953 and 2008, Kathryn Dunn Tenpas found that these high-profile speeches had no significant impact on presidential approval ratings. According to a study by Matthew Baum and Samuel Kernell, even Franklin Roosevelt's famous fireside chats did not significantly boost the president's approval ratings.[130]

Evidence that the president can use rhetoric to increase public support for his policies is also scant. Edwards shows that even Reagan, the "Great Communicator," was generally unable to use televised appeals to boost public support for his policies. Reagan's 1981 proposal to cut taxes across the board was undeniably popular, but survey research offers little reason to believe that Reagan's speeches increased public support for tax cuts. Reagan had the nation's nearly undivided attention when he appeared before Congress on April 28—his first public appearance after being shot and very nearly killed by John Hinckley—to deliver a nationally televised address in which he pitched his tax-cut plan to the American people. An NBC News/Associated Press poll conducted less than three weeks after the speech showed that 61 percent of the American people supported a tax cut—6 percent fewer than the week before the speech.[131]

Most people didn't need Reagan to persuade them that a tax cut was a good idea. They did need Reagan to persuade them that cuts in domestic spending were desirable. At the time of Reagan's election in 1980, about one in three Americans supported a reduction in government spending on services, including health and education. In 1984, after a steady barrage of speeches in which Reagan highlighted the problems with big government and the need to cut spending to balance the budget, the number of Americans who supported a reduction in spending remained unchanged. Four years later, at the end of Reagan's presidency, there was still no change in Americans' views about the need to reduce domestic spending.[132]

Why do presidents have such a difficult time persuading the public to follow their lead? Part of the problem is that people often aren't paying close attention to what the president says—and those who pay the closest attention to the president's words are the ones who are most difficult to convert, since they tend to be the best informed and most partisan segments of the American public. People also have a difficult time following the president's lead on issues because many misperceive the president's position. In 1981, Reagan's pollster Richard Wirthlin tried to gauge public support for Reagan's proposal to cut taxes by 10 percent over three years, and found that only a bare majority (51 percent) believed that this was Reagan's policy. Fully 45 percent of those whom Wirthlin surveyed thought that Reagan opposed this tax cut.[133]

In foreign policy, the Great Communicator had even more difficulty convincing the American people to follow his lead. In his memoirs, Reagan expressed his profound frustration at being unable to persuade the American public to rally behind his policy of aiding the rebels—known as the "Contras"—who were fighting to bring down Nicaragua's leftist government:

> Time and again, I would speak on television, to a joint session of Congress, or to other audiences about the problems in Central America, and I would hope that the outcome would be an outpouring of support from Americans. ... But the polls usually found that large numbers of Americans cared little or not at all about what happened in Central America—in fact, a surprisingly large proportion didn't even know where Nicaragua and El Salvador were located.[134]

If presidential rhetoric so often falls on deaf ears, why do presidents give so many speeches? Edwards suggests that part of the answer is habit. "Presidents *become* president by going public" and so they keep behaving that way once they are in the White House. That is, presidents govern in much the same way that they campaign. Going public has also become routine because presidents have "institutionalized a public relations infrastructure." Political scientist Martha Joynt Kumar calculates that in 2005, at the outset of George W. Bush's second term, full-time communications employees outnumbered staffers working full-time on domestic and economic policy. Her conservative estimate is that 350 people in the Bush White House "worked in communications and supporting operations, from senior communications officials down to the military personnel who operate the recording equipment for presidential speeches, press conferences, and briefings and who transcribe the sessions."[135]

But there is more to the story than ingrained habit and bureaucratic routine. As Edwards also points out, presidents often aren't trying to change people's minds when they go public. Instead they use their bully pulpit to preach to the converted and to mobilize the faithful. When, for instance, Reagan delivered a nationally televised plea on behalf of his tax cut plan on July 27, 1981, he did not change the public's mind, but he did spur many thousands of those who agreed with him to contact their member of Congress about the pending vote. The speech, according to the Democratic Speaker of the House Tip O'Neill, induced "a telephone blitz like this nation had never seen." Two days later, the House passed the president's tax cuts—though even here public pressure appears to have been secondary to bargains that the administration struck with wavering members of Congress before Reagan's speech.[136]

Presidents also can succeed in setting the agenda, though here too there are sharp limits to a president's power. Political scientist Jeffrey Cohen, for instance, finds that State of the Union addresses impact what people regard as the nation's most important problem, but the effect is generally short-lived. Part of the problem with State of the Union messages is that presidents generally discuss a wide range of policy areas that affect the state of the union, which makes the speech a poor vehicle for focusing public attention on any one issue.[137]

Getting the public to focus on the president's agenda is the work not of a single speech but of relentless repetition. As David Gergen points out, "almost nothing a leader says is heard if spoken only once." "For the truth to sink in," President George W. Bush agreed, "you got to keep repeating things over and over again." Today's sophisticated White House communications operations are dedicated to ensuring that the president's message is amplified and echoed across the mass media. But while setting the media's agenda and framing the terms of debate is a modern White House's constant preoccupation, the obstacles to success are formidable.[138]

Presidents are forever attempting to shape the way an issue gets defined or labeled, but more often than not their efforts are frustrated. The mass media, particularly television, frequently frames issues in terms of the political effects—which party or politicians gain and which lose—rather than policy consequences. In 1993, the Clinton White House hatched a plan to sell health care reform to the American people by focusing on a health insurance card that would bring "Security for All," thereby priming citizens to think of health care security in the same positive way that they thought of Social Security. The media, however, framed the conflict over health care in terms of the political strategies and political motives of the two sides. And the fiercer the political battle became, the more the media fixated on a strategic framing and the less it focused on the policy effects of health care reform.[139]

Presidents invariably grow frustrated by the distortions of the media "filter," just as the media grow cynical about the incessant White House "spin." The conflict is structural: the mass media define news in terms of the novel—new arguments, new policies, new directions—whereas presidents require relentless repetition to reach an inattentive public.[140]

Although presidents speak more often than ever before, viewers of the network news and readers of national newspapers are increasingly likely to hear only fragments of what the president says. When presidential candidates Richard Nixon and Hubert Humphrey squared off in 1968, the average "sound bite"—"a block of uninterrupted speech by a candidate on television news"—was 42 seconds; today it is less than 8 seconds. Newspapers show the same trend. In 1960, "the average continuous quote or paraphrase of a newsmaker's words in a front-page story was 20 lines," whereas by the end of the twentieth century "the average had fallen to 7 lines, usually in paraphrased form." Both electronic and print journalism, moreover, have become increasingly interpretive and less descriptive; journalists see their job as not merely reporting what the president (or his critics) said but revealing the political motives and maneuvers behind the president's words. Little wonder that presidents (and presidential candidates) have increasingly sought out ways to bypass the mainstream media filter by appearing on daytime and late-night talk shows and utilizing new media such as YouTube, Twitter, and Facebook.[141]

Even when presidents give nationally televised speeches, their task of reaching the public has become much more difficult than it was during the 1960s and 1970s. The explosive growth in cable channels has given viewers options that they did not have in an age of broadcasting in which the three major networks—ABC, CBS, and NBC—ruled the airwaves. When Nixon delivered his State of the Union message in 1971, two-thirds of homes with television were tuned in to hear the president speak. Three decades later, presidents could count on only half that many tuning in to hear a State of the Union message. And the State of the Union message is generally as good as it gets for presidents, since other nationally televised speeches typically have even smaller audiences. Of course, occasionally events conspire to give the president a large audience. Half the nation's households with television (totaling 88 million viewers), for instance, tuned in on September 21, 2001, to watch George W. Bush explain how the United States would respond to the terrorist attacks that had killed nearly three thousand people. But that is the exception. Far more typical is the approximately one in four households (41 million viewers) with television that tuned in on December 1, 2009, to hear Obama announce his new Afghanistan strategy or the one in five households (32 million viewers) who tuned in on September 9, 2009, to hear Obama pitch health care reform to a joint session of Congress.[142]

In delivering his Afghanistan and health care speeches, Obama at least had the advantage that they were covered, live and uninterrupted, by ten networks. Presidents, however, can no longer automatically assume, as they could in Nixon's day, that the networks will cover every national address the president wishes to make. In the 1970s and 1980s, network executives began to be more selective about which presidential addresses they would broadcast. All three of the major networks, for instance, turned down President Carter's request for airtime on July 4, 1978, to speak to the nation about his first year and a half in office, prompting the administration to cancel the speech. The three networks also twice refused to broadcast Oval Office addresses by President Reagan that made the case for aiding the Contras. When President Clinton held a prime-time news conference in April 1995 to respond to the Republicans' "Contract with America," CBS was the only major network to carry it live. Not that most Americans seemed to mind: fewer than 7 percent of households with a television opted to spend part of their Saturday evening listening to the president insist that he was not "irrelevant." In October 2002, the three major networks and

PBS chose not to televise a national address by George W. Bush—delivered in Cincinnati—in which he explained to the American people why his administration believed that military action against Iraq was probably going to be necessary.[143]

As the audience for national televised addresses has shrunk, presidents have increasingly sought out other ways of going public. As Cohen argues, presidents in "the post-broadcast age" increasingly need to "go local" to communicate with the public. During his first term George W. Bush traveled around the country about one hundred days out of each year, making 180 appearances a year outside the DC area annually. Presidents Carter and Reagan, in contrast, averaged fewer than 40 days a year on the road and about 80 local public events annually. Even in 1980, when Carter was running for reelection, he traveled the country less often than Bush and Clinton did in their least peripatetic years.[144]

At the beginning of his second term, George W. Bush made going local the centerpiece of his effort to persuade the American people to support his plan to reform Social Security by partially privatizing it. Bush unveiled his proposal for individual retirement accounts in his 2005 State of the Union message, which attracted about 38 million viewers. The speech, however, was only a prelude to the real public relations push, a frenetic "60 Stops in 60 Days" campaign in which Bush and a small army of administration officials fanned out across the country to promote the administration's plan. Even after the 60 days were up, Bush kept on traveling. Between February and July, he pitched his proposal at 37 events in 29 states plus the District of Columbia. When asked at the beginning of June why he kept "plugging away" at these local events, Bush explained: "I'm going around the country ... because most people get their news from the local news. And if you're trying to influence opinion, the best way to do it is to travel hard around the country."[145]

In the end, however, even "perhaps the most extensive public relations campaign in the history of the presidency" failed to persuade the American people. In fact, the more Bush spoke, the more skeptical Americans seemed to become. In December 2004, before the president launched his campaign on behalf of personal Social Security accounts, the public was about equally divided between support and opposition. By the early summer, after more than four months of carefully orchestrated public events, a clear majority of the American people had lined up in opposition. The percentage of the American people who disapproved of Bush's handling of Social Security also increased steadily, from 48 percent in the days immediately after his State of the Union message to 64 percent by the end of June. Going local may be, as Cohen argues, a necessary—and sometimes successful—adaptation to a fragmented media environment, but it is clearly no guarantee of success.[146]

In 2010 Barack Obama did succeed in persuading Congress to pass health care reform, but he was no more successful in changing the minds of ordinary Americans than Bush had been in 2005. When the House of Representatives passed the Patient Protection and Affordable Care Act on March 22, Rasmussen tracking polls showed that only a little over 40 percent of the American people supported the plan. During the preceding two weeks Obama had taken his case to the country, speaking to enthusiastic audiences in Missouri, Ohio, Pennsylvania, and Virginia, yet the poll numbers barely budged. Obama's public relations push may have galvanized the faithful but it did not sway the undecided. Certainly he did not convert the disbelievers; that seems beyond the reach of any president, no matter how eloquent or popular, particularly in the hyper-polarized environment fueled by partisan political media.[147]

The Twitter Presidency of Donald Trump

Is Donald Trump different? Is Twitter a game changer that returns to the presidency an effective bully pulpit that can command public attention and move public opinion?[148] People may not listen to long, flowery speeches but a 140-character limit seems made to order for a public with a limited attention span for politics. Millions of people can now hear directly from the president rather than relying on morsels of media-selected sound bites.

There is no denying the centrality of Twitter and social media to Trump's rise to the presidency. "Without the tweets," the newly elected Trump admitted, "I wouldn't be here." While immediately after the election Trump suggested that he would be "very restrained" in his use of Twitter as president, in fact Twitter has been just as central to his presidential communications as to his campaign communications. In Trump's view, Twitter is his "voice" and his way to "fight back" against the "dishonest media."[149]

This cartoon conveys Donald Trump's aspiration to use social media as a means to bypass television and print reporters and communicate directly with the American public. Although the content of Trump's late-night tweetstorms has invited plenty of criticism, the quest to use new communications technologies to achieve an unmediated relationship with the American public had become a defining feature of the contemporary presidency well before Trump assumed the office, and will undoubtedly continue to be a defining characteristic of the public presidency long after Trump leaves office.

Courtesy: Dana Summers of Tribune Media Services.

The outlandish claims that Trump sometimes makes in his tweets (e.g., "Just found out that Obama had my 'wires tapped' in Trump Tower . . . This is McCarthyism!") can distract attention away from those aspects of the Twitter presidency that represent the logical culmination of longstanding developments of the public presidency. Trump's unyielding campaign to discredit mainstream media coverage as dishonest has been far more combative than the rhetoric of other recent presidents who have complained about unfair or overly critical media coverage. But in embracing Twitter, Trump has done what all recent presidents have increasingly sought to do, namely, bypass the media gatekeepers—especially the White House press corps (eight months into his presidency, Trump had held only one solo press conference)—and speak directly to the American people. Moreover, Trump's outsized personality has not reversed the trend of declining viewership for presidential speeches. Whereas one-third of American households with a television tuned in to hear Obama's first presidential address before a joint session of Congress in February 2009, Trump's first address to a joint session of Congress in February 2017 was viewed by only 28 percent of households.[150]

The spread of social media undeniably gives American presidents new ways to communicate with the public without their words being filtered by the national media. It is less clear, though, that social media platforms such as Twitter enable presidents to overcome the most important limits on the bully pulpit. Twitter has not helped Trump boost his own popularity, which remained at historically low levels throughout the opening year of his presidency. Nor has Trump has been able to use his tweets to garner greater public support for his policy agenda.

If the essential problem facing presidents in today's polarized environment is to reach and then persuade those who are on the fence or on the opposing side, then Twitter only exacerbates the problems presidents face in an increasingly fragmented media environment characterized by ideological niche programming—often called narrowcasting (as distinct from broadcasting). The many millions who follow the president on social media are overwhelmingly those who already agree with him. To be sure, some of Trump's tweets go viral and reach a politically more diverse audience (think the "covfefe" tweet that was retweeted more than 100,000 times within a matter of hours), but these are hardly the kind of utterances likely to persuade people to support Trump or his policies. However, even if Twitter is of limited value as a way of persuading the public, it has been a vital way for Trump to communicate with and mobilize his most intense followers. And in a polarized environment, activating core supporters may be precisely what a president needs to put pressure on and persuade his fellow partisans in Congress.

President Trump views Twitter not only as "his direct pipeline to the American people" but as a way to shape what the media talks about. As Trump explained his agenda-setting strategy: "I can go bing bing bing and . . . and they put it on and as soon as I tweet it out—this morning on television, Fox—'Donald Trump, we have breaking news.'" However, many of the president's tweets seem to react to what he has seen on television news programs—and by all accounts he watches enormous quantities of television.[151] Moreover, the president's tweeting has not stopped the media from focusing on issues, such as Russia's meddling in the election, that the president has desperately wanted the media not to talk about. In fact, the president's compulsive tweeting has often made it more difficult for the White House to control the agenda, because the tweets have frustrated the task of crafting a consistent communications message. The Nixon, Reagan, and George W. Bush administrations controlled the media agenda through a carefully orchestrated focus on the "message of the day," but the Trump communications team has often scrambled to clarify or correct the latest presidential tweet. Twitter has seemed better suited to venting presidential frustrations than to focusing the nation's attention on the Trump administration's policy agenda.

Of course, there is more to Trump's rhetorical presidency than Twitter. Nor should the impact of presidential rhetoric be measured solely by its effects on presidential approval or public opinion about policies. Measuring the long-term impact of Trump's bombastic and bullying rhetoric on the nation's public culture is not easy to quantify, but that does not make it any less important. If presidential rhetoric is supposed to model character and virtue, as Glen Thurow argues, then a president who routinely demeans political opponents (Crooked Hillary, Lyin' Ted, Little Marco, Low-Energy Jeb) and media critics (Psycho Joe, low I.Q. Crazy Mika) is failing in his role as a teacher of democratic virtues.[152]

Trump has sometimes sought to identify himself with Andrew Jackson as a man of the people and a man of action unafraid to disrupt the DC establishment. But with respect to Trump's rhetoric and the responses to it, the far closer historical parallel is Andrew Johnson. Indeed, not since Andrew Johnson's ill-fated Swing around the Circle has there been such widespread concern about undignified presidential rhetoric. Much of the condemnation of Trump's "unpresidential" rhetoric has been in response to his mocking and demeaning tweets, but his speeches, too, have frequently been criticized as wildly inappropriate, from his "free-wheeling, narcissistic diatribe" in front of the memorial wall at CIA headquarters on his first day on the job to his rambling address to the 2017 Boy Scouts National Jamboree, which one critic likened to a "third world authoritarian's youth rally" and another described as "so far beyond the usual bounds of even vulgar politicians' vulgarity."[153] Like Johnson (and totally unlike Jackson), Trump seems to "care not for dignity."

Of particular concern to many are Trump's attacks on the legitimacy of American political institutions, most especially the news media, which Trump routinely denigrates as "fake news." Some see Trump's success in taking a term that "initially referred to intentionally false reports from online sources posing as genuine news sites" and making it "into a pejorative for news reports and organizations he doesn't agree with" as evidence that he is "a master of language." But while this example may illustrate the salesman's grasp of "the power of labelling" and branding, it also illuminates anew the limits of presidential rhetoric.[154]

After Trump tweeted that "the FAKE NEWS media (failing @nytimes, @CNN, @NBC News and many more) ... is the enemy of the American People. SICK!" in February 2017, Quinnipiac University polling found that not only did nine in ten respondents say it was important for the media to hold public officials accountable, but also that far more Americans (53 percent) trusted the media to "tell you the truth about important issues" than trusted Trump (38 percent)—and by May 2017 the gap between those who trusted the media and those who trusted Trump had grown even larger, and two-thirds of respondents disapproved of the way Trump talked about the media. Not surprisingly, views about the media were sharply divided by partisanship, with Republicans overwhelmingly trusting Trump more than the media and Democrats overwhelmingly trusting the media more than Trump. Whatever adverse impact President Trump's rhetoric has had on perceptions of the media, the effect appears to have been limited to Republicans. Moreover, there is little evidence that Trump's criticisms of the media have changed that many Republican minds; instead they have largely reinforced and amplified longstanding Republican distrust of the "liberal media"—or what Sarah Palin derided in 2009 as the "lamestream media."[155]

Trump's extraordinary rhetoric should not obscure the conceit he shares in common with his otherwise very different Democratic predecessors: namely, an unshakable faith in the power of words. True, Obama's language was finely literate whereas Trump's is laced with crude insults and simplistic intensifiers (as in that "very, very, very amazing man" and that "great, great developer"). And certainly Bill Clinton's elaborate discourses on policy could not be more different than Trump's short, "almost infinitely compressible" sentences and his almost total lack of interest in the complexities of public policy. But both Clinton and Obama, like Trump, were convinced that they were masters of the language (Trump loves to boast that he's been called the "Ernest Hemingway of 140 characters") and that their political success owed to that mastery—a view reinforced by pundits impressed by their successful presidential campaigns. Each assumed that the rhetoric that enabled (or appeared to enable) him to win the presidency was also the key to success in the presidency. Each learned the same hard lesson: governing is different from campaigning. The battle over language is important, but no president can govern by words alone. Twitter doesn't alter the fact that politics cannot be reduced to rhetoric.[156]

Notes

1 Garry Wills, *Lincoln at Gettysburg: The Words That Remade America* (New York: Simon & Schuster, 1992), 34–35. Ronald C. White, Jr., *The Eloquent President: A Portrait of Lincoln through His Words* (New York: Random House, 2006), 229.

2 *New York Times*, July 9, 1863, p. 5. Doris Kearns Goodwin, *Team of Rivals: The Political Genius of Abraham Lincoln* (New York: Simon & Schuster, 2005), 534. Gabor Boritt, *The Gettysburg Gospel: The Lincoln Speech That Nobody Knows* (New York: Simon & Schuster, 2006), 77.

3 Douglas L. Wilson, *Lincoln's Sword: The Presidency and the Power of Words* (New York: Vintage, 2006), 231, 180–81.

4 Wilson, *Lincoln's Sword*, 150, 197.

5 Wilson, *Lincoln's Sword*, 197. White, *The Eloquent President*, 225–26. Second Speech at Frederick, Maryland, October 4, 1862, in Roy P. Basler, ed., *The Collected Works of Abraham Lincoln* (New Brunswick, NJ: Rutgers University Press, 1953), 5:450.

6 Speech at Frederick, Maryland, October 4, 1862, *Collected Works*, 5:450.

7 Boritt, *The Gettysburg Gospel*, 60, 77, 79–80, 88.

8 Thomas E. Cronin, *The State of the Presidency* (Boston: Little, Brown, 1980; second edition), 13. Samuel Kernell, *Going Public: New Strategies of Presidential Leadership* (Washington, DC: CQ Press, 2007; fourth edition).

9 Jeffrey K. Tulis, "Reflections on the Rhetorical Presidency," in Richard J. Ellis, ed., *Speaking to the People: The Rhetorical Presidency in Historical Perspective* (Amherst: University of Massachusetts Press, 1998), 221. Also see Stephen Skowronek, *The Politics Presidents Make:*

Leadership from John Adams to George Bush (Cambridge, MA: Harvard University Press, 1993), 53.

10 Jeffrey K. Tulis, *The Rhetorical Presidency* (Princeton, NJ: Princeton University Press, 1987), 27–45.

11 Richard J. Ellis, ed., *Founding the American Presidency* (Lanham, MD: Rowman & Littlefield, 1999), 94, 149.

12 Ellis, *Founding the American Presidency*, 74; also see 165. Jack N. Rakove, *Original Meanings: Politics and Ideas in the Making of the Constitution* (New York: Knopf, 1996), 268.

13 Tulis, *The Rhetorical Presidency*, 48.

14 Tulis, *The Rhetorical Presidency*, 48. James Hart, *The American Presidency in Action, 1789: A Study in Constitutional History* (New York: Macmillan, 1948), 11.

15 Hart, *American Presidency in Action*, 29.

16 Page Smith, *John Adams* (Garden City, NY: Doubleday, 1962), 2:753–55. Gordon S. Wood, *Empire of Liberty: A History of the Early Republic, 1789–1815* (New York: Oxford University Press, 2009), 83–84. Stanley Elkins and Eric McKitrick, *The Age of Federalism: The Early American Republic, 1788–1800* (New York: Oxford University Press, 1993), 47–48. Kathleen Bartoloni-Tuazon, *For Fear of an Elective King: George Washington and the Presidential Title Controversy of 1789* (Ithaca: Cornell University Press, 2014).

17 Elkins and McKitrick, *Age of Federalism*, 48. James MacGregor Burns and Susan Dunn, *George Washington* (New York: Henry Holt, 2004), 56.

18 Elkins and McKitrick, *Age of Federalism*, 49.

19 Terri Bimes, "The Practical Origins of the Rhetorical Presidency," *Critical Review* 19 (2007), 247. Elkins and McKitrick, *Age of Federalism*, 49. Hart, *American Presidency in Action*, 29. Richard J. Ellis, *Presidential Travel: The Journey from George Washington to George W. Bush* (Lawrence: University Press of Kansas, 2008), 22. Also see Sandra Moats, *Celebrating the Republic: Presidential Ceremony and Popular Sovereignty: From Washington to Monroe* (DeKalb, IL: Northern Illinois University Press, 2009).

20 Ellis, *Presidential Travel*, 20. Tulis, *The Rhetorical Presidency*, 69. Richard Norton Smith, *Patriarch: George Washington and the New American Nation* (Boston: Houghton Mifflin, 1993), ch. 5. Also see T.H. Breen, *George Washington's Journey: The President Forges a New Nation* (New York: Simon & Schuster, 2016).

21 Ellis, *Presidential Travel*, 18–20.

22 Ellis, *Presidential Travel*, 24.

23 Tulis, *The Rhetorical Presidency*, 69. Stephen E. Lucas, "George Washington and the Rhetoric of Presidential Leadership," in Leroy Dorsey, ed., *The Presidency and Rhetorical Leadership* (College Station: Texas A&M University Press, 2002), 62.

24 Smith, *Patriarch*, 278.

25 Richard Hofstadter, *The Idea of a Party System: The Rise of a Legitimate Opposition in the United States, 1789–1840* (Berkeley: University of California Press, 1969), 96.

26 Bimes, "Origins of Rhetorical Presidency," 249. Elkis and McKitrick, *Age of Federalism*, 495–97.

27 Lucas, "George Washington and the Rhetoric of Presidential Leadership," 50. Felix Gilbert, *To the Farewell Address: Ideas of Early American Foreign Policy* (Princeton, NJ: Princeton University Press, 1961), 100. Matthew Spalding and Patrick J. Garrity, *A Sacred Union of Citizens: George Washington's Farewell Address and the American Character* (Lanham, MD: Rowman & Littlefield, 1996), 61.

28 Jefferson to Judge Roane, September 6, 1819, in Thomas Jefferson Randolph, ed., *Memoirs, Correspondence, and Private Papers of Thomas Jefferson* (London: Henry Colburn and Richard Bentley, 1829; 4 vols.), 4:324. James W. Ceaser, *Presidential Selection: Theory and Development* (Princeton, NJ: Princeton University Press, 1979), 74.

29 Jefferson's first inaugural address, along with every other inaugural address, can be accessed at http://avalon.law.yale.edu/subject_menus/inaug.asp. Jefferson to P. Mazzei, July 18, 1804, in Randolph, ed., *Memoirs, Correspondence, and Private Papers of Thomas Jefferson*, 4:20.

30 Editorial Note, First Inaugural Address, *The Papers of Thomas Jefferson*, Vol. 22: 17 February to 30 April 1801 (Princeton, NJ: Princeton University Press, 2006), https://jeffersonpapers. princeton.edu/selected-documents/first-inaugural-address.

31 Margaret Bayard Smith, *The First Forty Years of Washington Society, Portrayed by the Family Letters of Mrs. Samuel Harrison Smith*, ed. Gaillard Hunt (New York: Scribner, 1906), 26.

32 Jeffrey L. Pasley, *"The Tyranny of Printers": Newspaper Politics in the Early American Republic* (Charlottesville: University of Virginia Press, 2001), 33–35, 42–43.

33 Noble E. Cunningham, Jr., *The Jeffersonian Republicans in Power: Party Operations, 1801–1809* (Chapel Hill: University of North Carolina Press, 1963), 260–61. Pasley, *Tyranny of Printers*, 259. Mel Laracey, *Presidents and the People: The Partisan Story of Going Public* (College Station: Texas A&M University Press, 2002), 59–61.

34 Cunningham, *Jeffersonian Republicans in Power*, 255–56; for other examples of Jefferson's surreptitious use of the partisan press, see 257–58, 261–62.

35 Pasley, *Tyranny of Printers*, 206.

36 Pasley, *Tyranny of Printers*, 259–60. Jeffrey L. Pasley, "1800 as a Revolution in Political Culture: Newspapers, Celebrations, Voting, and Democratization in the Early Republic," in James Horn, Jan Ellen Lewis, and Peter S. Onuf, eds., *The Revolution of 1800: Democracy, Race, and the New Republic* (Charlottesville: University of Virginia Press, 2002), 141. Catherine Allgor, *Parlor Politics: In Which the Ladies of Washington Help Build a City and a Government* (Charlottesville: University of Virginia Press, 2000), 5. Cunningham, *Jeffersonian Republicans in Power*, 265–66.

37 Jefferson to John Norvell, June 14, 1807, cited in Pasley, *Tyranny of Printers*, 258.

38 Graham G. Dodds and Mark J. Rozell, "The Press and the Presidency: Then and Now," in Phillip G. Henderson, ed., *The Presidency Then and Now* (Lanham, MD: Rowman & Littlefield, 2000), 142.

39 Pasley, *Tyranny of Printers*, 265.

40 Pasley, *Tyranny of Printers*, 295–97. Leonard White, *The Jeffersonians: A Study in Administrative History, 1801–1829* (New York: Free Press, 1951), 548–50. For instance, only one newspaper editor was given a position of postmaster in the Jefferson administration, and he was a "young Virginia gentleman" (Pasley, *Tyranny of Printers*, 297).

41 Laracey, *Presidents and the People*, 62.

42 Leonard W. Levy, *Jefferson and Civil Liberties: The Darker Side* (New York: Quadrangle, 1963), 96. Also see Dumas Malone, *Jefferson the President, Second Term, 1805–1809* (Boston: Little, Brown, 1974), 576; and Jeremy D. Bailey, *Thomas Jefferson and Executive Power* (New York: Cambridge University Press, 2007), 272.

43 Pasley, *Tyranny of Printers*, 259.

44 Monroe to General Andrew Jackson, December 14, 1816, in *The Writings of James Monroe*, ed. Stanislaus Murray Hamilton (New York: G.P. Putnam's Sons, 1901), 5:345–46.

45 H.W. Brands, *Andrew Jackson: His Life and Times* (New York: Doubleday, 2005), 317. Harry Ammon, *James Monroe: The Quest for National Identity* (Charlottesville: University of Virginia Press, 1990), 357.

46 Inaugural Address of John Quincy Adams, March 4, 1825.

47 Hofstadter, *The Idea of a Party System*, 233. Pasley, *Tyranny of Printers*, 364–65.

48 Tulis, *The Rhetorical Presidency*, 72–73.

49 Laracey, *Presidents and the People*, 66.

50 Sean Wilentz, *The Rise of American Democracy: Jefferson to Lincoln* (New York: Norton, 2005), 260.

51 Pasley, *Tyranny of Printers*, 349, 392. Laracey, *Presidents and the People*, 73.

52 An extended discussion of Jackson's invention of the mandate and the nineteenth-century evolution of that idea can be found in Richard J. Ellis and Stephen Kirk, "Presidential Mandates in the Nineteenth Century: Conceptual Change and Institutional Development," *Studies in American Political Development* 9 (Spring 1995), 137–51. Modern presidents' use of mandates is explored in Julia R. Azari, *Delivering the People's Message: The Changing Politics of the Presidential Mandate* (Ithaca: Cornell University Press, 2014) and Patricia Heidotting Conley, *Presidential Mandates: How Elections Shape the National Agenda* (University of Chicago Press, 2001).

53 Jackson to Van Buren, September 15, 1833, in John Spencer Bassett, ed., *Correspondence of Andrew Jackson* (Washington, DC: Carnegie Institution, 1928), 5:187. Jackson to Polk, December 16, 1832, *Correspondence of Jackson*, 4:501.

54 Message Read to the Cabinet on Removal of the Public Deposits, September 18, 1833. Online by Gerhard Peters and John T. Woolley, The American Presidency Project, www.presidency. ucsb.edu. All presidential messages and addresses cited in this book, unless otherwise indicated, are drawn from the invaluable American Presidency Project website.

55 Skowronek, *Politics Presidents Make*, 150. The first quote is from Jackson's April 15, 1834 message of protest in response to the Senate's censure of the president.

56 Ellis and Kirk, "Presidential Mandates in the Nineteenth Century," 152.

57 Ellis and Kirk, "Presidential Mandates in the Nineteenth Century," 153.

58 Daniel Preston, ed., *The Papers of James Monroe: A Documentary History of the Presidential Tours of James Monroe, 1817, 1818, 1819* (Westport, CT: Greenwood Press, 2003), 649. Washington undertook three tours: a month traveling through New England in the fall of 1788, a two-month sojourn through the southern states in the spring of 1791, and a shorter trip to Rhode Island in August 1790. Monroe also undertook three tours: a three-and-a-half month tour of 13 northern states plus the territory of Michigan in the summer of 1817, several weeks traveling through the Chesapeake Bay region in June 1818, and a four-and-a-half month journey in 1819 through eight southern states.

59 Although the code of presidential dignity in the early republic required that presidents avoid electioneering, it apparently did not require presidents to avoid speaking about public policy. Indeed, decorum at times demanded that the president respond to policy concerns raised in the welcoming addresses. In Lexington, Kentucky, for instance, Monroe was invited by the welcoming committee to give his views on federally funded internal improvements, an issue of pressing importance to the citizens of western states who were plagued with dreadful roads. Monroe obliged, telling the citizens of Lexington that he did not believe the Constitution gave Congress "the power to adopt an extensive system of federally funded internal improvements." However, he pledged to work for a constitutional amendment that would give Congress that power. See *Papers of James Monroe*, 714. The ways in which nineteenth-century presidents used speaking tours to advance policy and electoral objectives are surveyed in Anne C. Pluta, "Presidential Politics on Tour: George Washington to Woodrow Wilson," *Congress & the Presidency* (September–December 2014), 335–61.

60 On Jackson's tour, see Fletcher M. Green, "On Tour with President Andrew Jackson," *New England Quarterly* (June 1963), 212–13, as well as Ellis, *Presidential Travel*, ch. 2.

61 On Van Buren's tour, see Ellis, *Presidential Travel*, ch. 2.

62 Taylor's tour is discussed in more depth in Ellis, *Presidential Travel*, ch. 3, and Richard J. Ellis and Alexis Walker, "Policy Speech in the Nineteenth Century Rhetorical Presidency: The Case of Zachary Taylor's Tour," *Presidential Studies Quarterly* 37 (June 2007), 248–69.

63 Tulis, *The Rhetorical Presidency*, 87. The analysis of Johnson's tour is derived from Ellis, *Presidential Travel*, 82–97. Also see Eric L. McKitrick, *Andrew Johnson and Reconstruction* (Chicago: University of Chicago Press, 1960), 428–38.

64 On Monroe's policy speech, see Ellis, *Presidential Travel*, 35–37. Also see Ellis and Walker, "Policy Speech in the Nineteenth Century Rhetorical Presidency."

65 Ellis, *Presidential Travel*, 6. Laracey, *Presidents and the People*, 131.

66 Tulis, *The Rhetorical Presidency*, 86. Laracey, *Presidents and the People*, 132–33.

67 Stephen Ponder, *Managing the Press: Origins of the Media Presidency, 1897–1933* (New York: Palgrave, 2000), 2, 4. Lewis L. Gould, *The Modern American Presidency* (Lawrence: University Press of Kansas, 2003), 1. Samuel Kernell and Gary C. Jacobson, "Congress and the Presidency as News in the Nineteenth Century," *Journal of Politics* (November 1987), 1027. Also see Donald A. Ritchie, *Press Gallery: Congress and the Washington Correspondents* (Cambridge, MA: Harvard University Press, 1991).

68 Ponder, *Managing the Press*, xiv, 4. Gould, *Modern American Presidency*, 1. Rodger Streotmatter, "William W. Price: First White House Correspondent and Emblem of an Era," *Journalism History* 16 (Spring/Summer 1989), 32–41. Martha Joynt Kumar, "The White House Beat at the Century Mark," *Harvard International Journal of Press/Politics* 2 (Summer 1997), 10–30.

69 Ponder, *Managing the Press*, 5. Gould, *Modern American Presidency*, 10–11.

70 Ponder, *Managing the Press*, 5–6.

71 Kernell, *Going Public*, 80–81. Also see Mark Wahlgren Summers, *The Press Gang: Newspapers and Politics, 1865–1878* (Chapel Hill: University of North Carolina Press, 1994).

72 Ponder, *Managing the Press*, 12. Gould, *Modern American Presidency*, 12. Kernell, *Going Public*, 135.

73 Gould, *Modern American Presidency*, 8. Kernell, *Going Public*, 134.

74 Gould, *Modern American Presidency*, 7–8. Kernell, *Going Public*, 134–38. Ponder, *Managing the Press*, 11–12. Also see Robert P. Saldin, "William McKinley and the Rhetorical Presidency," *Presidential Studies Quarterly* 41 (March 2011), 119–34.

75 Ponder, *Managing the Press*, 7–9.

76 Gould, *Modern American Presidency*, 11, 14. Ponder, *Managing the Press*, 14.

77 Ponder, *Managing the Press*, 17, 9; also see 18–19. Edmund Morris, *The Rise of Theodore Roosevelt* (New York: Ballantine Books, 1979), 664–65.

78 Gould, *Modern American Presidency*, 20, 16.

79 Ponder, *Managing the Press*, 18, 24. Gould, *Modern American Presidency*, 21. Lewis L. Gould, *The Presidency of Theodore Roosevelt* (Lawrence: University Press of Kansas, 1991), 153.

80 Ronald Steel, "Theodore Roosevelt, Empire Builder," *New York Times*, Sunday Book Review section, April 21, 2010. Ponder, *Managing the Press*, 18, 23–25.

81 Gould, *Modern American Presidency*, 21–22. Gould, *Presidency of Theodore Roosevelt*, 154. Ponder, *Managing the Press*, 25–26.

82 Kernell, *Going Public*, 83–87. George Juergens, *News from the White House: The Presidential–Press Relationship in the Progressive Era* (Chicago: University of Chicago Press, 1981), 17. Ponder, *Managing the Press*, 23.

83 Ponder, *Managing the Press*, 34, 25. Also see the quotation by David Barry in Kernell, *Going Public*.

84 *Theodore Roosevelt: An Autobiography* (New York: Charles Scribner's Sons, 1920), 352. Tulis, *The Rhetorical Presidency*, 98. Also see Elmer E. Cornwell, Jr., *Presidential Leadership of Public Opinion* (Bloomington: Indiana University Press, 1965), 24–26.

85 George E. Mowry, *The Era of Theodore Roosevelt, 1900–1912* (New York: Harper & Brothers, 1958), 203. Sidney M. Milkis and Michael Nelson, *The American Presidency Origins and Development, 1776–2002* (Washington, DC: CQ Press, 2003), 207. John Morton Blum, *The Republican Roosevelt* (New York: Atheneum, 1963), 92. Tulis, *The Rhetorical Presidency*, 19, 99, 101.

86 Woodrow Wilson, *Congressional Government: A Study in American Politics* (Boston: Houghton Mifflin, 1885).

87 Woodrow Wilson, *Constitutional Government in the United States* (New York: Columbia University Press, 1908), 68–69.

88 Wilson, *Constitutional Government in the United States*, 57, 69–70.

89 Wilson discontinued the practice of delivering the annual message in person after suffering a stroke in 1919. President Warren Harding resumed the practice in 1921 but Calvin Coolidge reverted to the older Jeffersonian custom in 1924 (after delivering the first State of the Union broadcast over radio the year before). President Herbert Hoover never delivered an annual message to Congress in person. Not until 1934, with Franklin Roosevelt as president, did Wilson's innovation become a permanent feature of American politics. See Michael Kolakowski and Thomas H. Neale, "The President's State of the Union Message: Frequently Asked Questions," Congressional Research Service Report for Congress, March 7, 2006, www.senate.gov/artandhistory/history/resources/pdf/stateoftheunion.pdf.

90 Ponder, *Managing the Press*, 78.

91 Woodrow Wilson, "Abraham Lincoln: A Man of the People," in Mario R. Dinunzio, ed., *Woodrow Wilson: Essential Writings and Speeches of the Scholar-President* (New York: New York University Press, 2006), 103.

92 Gould, *Modern American Presidency*, 45.

93 Ponder, *Managing the Press*, 80.

94 Ponder, *Managing the Press*, 83. Kernell, *Going Public*, 85.

95 Ponder, *Managing the Press*, 79–84. Kernell, *Going Public*, 84.

96 Ponder, *Managing the Press*, 84, 93–94, 96–97. Gould, *Modern American Presidency*, 45.

97 Ponder, *Managing the Press*, 105–06.

98 Gene Smith, *When the Cheering Stopped: The Last Years of Woodrow Wilson* (New York: William Morrow, 1964), 60–82. Kendrick A. Clements, *The Presidency of Woodrow Wilson* (Lawrence: University Press of Kansas, 1992), 196. Thomas J. Knock, *To End All Wars: Woodrow Wilson and the Quest for a New World Order* (Princeton, NJ: Princeton University Press, 1992), 262.

99 Tulis, *The Rhetorical Presidency*, 147–61.

100 David Greenberg, *Republic of Spin: An Inside History of the American Presidency* (New York: Norton, 2016), 87–88, 79. Gould, *Modern American Presidency*, 57. Ponder, *Managing the Press*, 113–14. President Taft, too, complained of "the sacrifice of dignity" in posing for photographers (Ponder, *Managing the Press*, 113).

101 Ponder, *Managing the Press*, 123. Also see Gould, *Modern American Presidency*, 69–70; Cornwell, *Presidential Leadership of Public Opinion*, 91–92; and Greenberg, *Republic of Spin*, 157, 165.

102 Greenberg, *Republic of Spin*, 165. Gould, *Modern American Presidency*, 69–70.

103 Greenberg, *Republic of Spin*, 161, 164. Gould, *Modern American Presidency*, 67–69. Ponder, *Managing the Press*, 121, 123.

104 Ponder, *Managing the Press*, 123, 147. Greenberg, *Republic of Spin*, 162, 164. Lindsay Rodgers' *The American Senate* was published in 1926 and the quoted *New Republic* article was published September 22, 1926.

105 Greenberg, *Republic of Spin*, 39, 158, 163–64.

106 Greenberg, *Republic of Spin*, 163.

107 Douglas B. Craig, *Fireside Politics: Radio and Political Culture in the United States, 1920–1940* (Baltimore, MD: Johns Hopkins University Press, 2000), 145–46, 142.

108 Craig, *Fireside Politics*, 150–51.

109 Amoz Kiewe, *FDR's First Fireside Chat: Public Confidence and the Banking Crisis* (College Station, TX: Texas A&M University Press, 2007), 1. Lawrence W. Levine and Cornelia R. Levine, *The People and the President: America's Conversation with FDR* (Boston: Beacon

Press, 2002), 3. Greenberg, *Republic of Spin*, 194. Subsequent fireside chats were, with a few exceptions, broadcast from the Diplomatic Reception Room on the ground floor of the White House.

110 Levine and Levine, *The People and the President*, 3, 13, 15–16. Craig, *Fireside Politics*, 150, 155–56.

111 Craig, *Fireside Politics*, 156. Levine and Levine, *The People and the President*, 11, 12, 18.

112 Levine and Levine, *The People and the President*, 15. Craig, *Fireside Politics*, 156. Also see Greenberg, *Republic of Spin*, 196.

113 Gould, *Modern American Presidency*, 85–86. Levine and Levine, *The People and the President*, 11–12. Also see Samuel Kernell, *Going Public: New Strategies of Presidential Leadership* (Washington, DC: CQ Press, 2007; fourth edition), 87–90.

114 Levine and Levine, *The People and the President*, 5, 9–10.

115 Arthur M. Schlesinger, Jr., *The Coming of the New Deal, 1933–1935* (Boston: Houghton Mifflin, 1958), 559 (FDR to Ralph W. Farell, March 28, 1932). Greenberg, *Republic of Spin*, 195. Levine and Levine, *The People and the President*, 2–3, 14–15.

116 Levine and Levine, *The People and the President*, 23; Kernell, *Going Public*, 132–133.

117 Greenberg, *Republic of Spin*, 257–58. Kernell, *Going Public*, 133. Gould, *Modern American Presidency*, 113.

118 Greenberg, *Republic of Spin*, 294–96. Kernell, *Going Public*, 133.

119 Greenberg, *Republic of Spin*, 298–99.

120 Greenberg, *Republic of Spin*, 256, 296. Gould, *Modern American Presidency*, 104.

121 David A. Nichols, *Ike and McCarthy: Dwight Eisenhower's Secret Campaign against Joseph McCarthy* (New York: Simon & Schuster, 2017), 133, 175. Greenberg, *Republic of Spin*, 295–97.

122 Craig Allen, *Eisenhower and the Mass Media: Peace, Prosperity, and Prime-Time TV* (Chapel Hill: University of North Carolina Press, 1993), 60–61. Greenberg, *Republic of Spin*, 297. Initially the television networks aired the entire press conference, or at least the entire White House-edited press conference, but as the novelty quickly faded the two major networks, CBS and NBC, started to exercise editorial control by typically airing only excerpts from the press conferences. Allen, *Eisenhower and the Mass Media*, 62.

123 Greenberg, *Republic of Spin*, 340–41. Kernell, *Going Public*, 94–95.

124 Kernell, *Going Public*, 93, 96–97. Gould, *Modern American Presidency*, 116. Martha Joynt Kumar, "W.H. Press Conferences Turn 100," *Politico*, March 28, 2013, www.politico.com/story/2013/03/wh-press-conferences-turn-100-089402. Reagan's successors held solo press conferences significantly more often than Nixon and Reagan had, but these rarely took place in prime-time, in part because the media wasn't interested in giving the president a prime time platform for a scripted White House media event and in part because presidents have found alternative venues to reach the public where they could better control the message. Obama, for instance, after his first year did not hold a single prime-time press conference but held a very large number (Martha Kumar counts 674) of interviews with selected journalists, including seven with Steve Kroft of CBS's *60 Minutes*.

125 Greenberg, *Republic of Spin*, 401; also see 348, 354, 363. Kernell, *Going Public*, 101, 103. Martha Joynt Kumar, "W.H. Press Conferences Turn 100."

126 Greenberg, *Republic of Spin*, 398. Gould, *Modern American Presidency*, 157, 160. John Anthony Maltese, *Spin Control: The White House Office of Communications and the Management of Presidential News* (Chapel Hill: University of North Carolina Press, 1994; second edition), 2, 5.

127 Greenberg, *Republic of Spin*, 410, 413. Martha Joynt Kumar, *Managing the President's Message: The White House Communications Operation* (Baltimore: Johns Hopkins University Press, 2007), xxx. Gould, *Modern American Presidency*, 195.

128   Kumar, *Managing the President's Message*, xxxi–xxxii. Kathryn Dunn Tenpas, "The State of the Union Address: Process, Politics and Promotion," in Michael Nelson and Russell L. Riley, eds., *The President's Words: Speeches and Speechwriting in the Modern White House* (Lawrence: University Press of Kansas, 2010), 154.

129   David Gergen, *Eyewitness to Power: The Essence of Leadership* (New York: Simon and Schuster, 2000), 210. George C. Edwards III, *The Strategic President: Persuasion and Opportunity in Presidential Leadership* (Princeton, NJ: Princeton University Press, 2009), 20. On Nixon's faith in his ability to use public speeches to "turn around public opinion," see Nelson and Riley, *The President's Words*, 185. On Clinton's "'unbelievable arrogance' regarding his ability [to use rhetoric] to change public opinion," see Lawrence R. Jacobs and Robert Y. Shapiro, *Politicians Don't Pander: Political Manipulation and the Loss of Democratic Responsiveness* (Chicago: University of Chicago Press, 2000), 106.

130   George C. Edwards III, *On Deaf Ears: The Limits of the Bully Pulpit* (New Haven: Yale University Press, 2003), 29–34. Tenpas, "The State of the Union Address," 156–59. Matthew A. Baum and Samuel Kernell, "Economic Class and Popular Support for Franklin Roosevelt in War and Peace," *Public Opinion Quarterly* 65 (Summer 2001), 198–209.

131   Edwards, *The Strategic President*, 37–39. Also see B. Dan Wood, *The Myth of Presidential Representation* (New York: Cambridge University Press, 2009), esp. ch. 5.

132   Edwards, *The Strategic President*, 49; also see Edwards, *On Deaf Ears*, 60–64.

133   Edwards, *The Strategic President*, 39, 74–75; also see Edwards, *On Deaf Ears*, 201–11.

134   Edwards, *The Strategic President*, 43.

135   Edwards, *On Deaf Ears*, 242–44. Kumar, *Managing the President's Message*, 4–5, 88.

136   Edwards, *On Deaf Ears*, 244. Edwards, *The Strategic President*, 39–41.

137   Jeffrey E. Cohen, *Presidential Responsiveness and Public Policymaking: The Public and the Policies That Presidents Choose* (Ann Arbor: University of Michigan Press, 1997), 56–58, 60–63, 65. Also see Edwards, *The Strategic President*, 79, and Edwards, *On Deaf Ears*, 246.

138   Edwards, *The Strategic President*, 105.

139   Jacobs and Shapiro, *Politicians Don't Pander*, 106–10, 177–79. Edwards, *The Strategic President*, 74.

140   Kumar, *Managing the President's Message*, xv. Edwards, *The Strategic President*, 71–72.

141   Edwards, *The Strategic President*, 72–73. Thomas E. Patterson, *The Vanishing Voter: Public Involvement in an Age of Uncertainty* (New York: Alfred E. Knopf, 2002), 68–69. Also see Thomas E. Patterson, *Out of Order* (New York: Alfred E. Knopf, 1993).

142   Samuel Kernell, *Going Public: New Strategies of Presidential Leadership* (Washington, DC: CQ Press, 2007; fourth edition), 139, 141. Edwards, *On Deaf Ears*, 190, 196–97. Matthew Eshbaugh-Soha and Jeffrey Peake, *Breaking Through the Noise: Presidential Leadership, Public Opinion, and the News Media* (Stanford University Press, 2011), 85.

143   Kernell, *Going Public*, 136–37, 139. Edwards, *On Deaf Ears*, 212–13.

144   Jeffrey E. Cohen, *Going Local: Presidential Leadership in the Post-Broadcast Age* (New York: Cambridge University Press, 2010), esp. 47–50. Brendan J. Doherty, "POTUS on the Road: International and Domestic Presidential Travel, 1977–2005," *Presidential Studies Quarterly* 39 (June 2009), 324–25, 336–38. Also see Kernell, *Going Public*, 125–29.

145   George C. Edwards III, *Governing by Campaigning: The Politics of the Bush Presidency* (New York: Pearson Longman, 2007), 38, 85, 215–80. Cohen, *Going Local*, 2.

146   Edwards, *Governing by Campaigning*, 252, 256–59. Also see Cohen, *Going Local*, 46–47.

147   The impact of partisan media on polarization is explored in Matthew Levundusky, *How Partisan Media Polarize America* (University of Chicago Press, 2013).

148   Trump's former campaign manager Corey Lewandowski called Trump's Twitter account "the greatest bully pulpit that has ever existed." Philip Rucker and Danielle Paquette, "How a

Week of Tweets by Trump Stoked Anxiety, Moved Markets and Altered Plans," *Washington Post*, January 7, 2017.

149   Lionel Barber et al., "Donald Trump: Without Twitter, I Would Not Be Here—FT Interview," *Financial Times*, April 2, 2017. Reena Flores, "In '60 Minutes' Interview, Donald Trump Weighs Twitter Use as President," CBS News, November 12, 2016, www.cbsnews.com/news/donald-trump-60-minutes-interview-weighs-twitter-use-as-president/. Mark Leibovich, "This Town Melts Down," *New York Times Magazine*, July 11, 2017. Avi Selk, "Twitter Cofounder: I'm Sorry If We Made Trump's Presidency Possible," *Washington Post*, May 21, 2017.

150   Useful historical data can be found in Callum Borchers, "The TV Audience for Trump's First Address to Congress Was Smaller than Obama's and Clinton's," *Washington Post*, March 2, 2017.

151   Sean Spicer, quoted in Andrew Blame, "Sean Spicer: Donald Trump's Twitter Usage Will Be 'Really Exciting Part' of Administration," *Washington Examiner*, December 27, 2016. Trump quoted in Mathew Ingram, "Here's Why Donald Trump Says He Loves Twitter and Plans to Keep Tweeting," *Forbes*, January 17, 2017.

152   Martin J. Medhursht, "Afterword: The Ways of Rhetoric," in Medhurst, ed., *Beyond the Rhetorical Presidency* (College Station, TX: Texas A&M University Press, 1996), 220. Also see the chapter in that volume by Glen E. Thurow titled "Dimensions of Presidential Character."

153   Andrea Mitchell and Ken Dilanian, "Ex-CIA Boss Brennan, Others Rip Trump Speech in Front of Memorial," *NBC News*, January 22, 2017, www.nbcnews.com/news/us-news/ex-cia-boss-brennan-others-rip-trump-speech-front-memorial-n710366. John McLaughlin and Bill Kristol, quoted in Caitlin Yilek, "Ex-CIA Official: Trump's Boy Scouts Speech Felt Like a 'Third World Authoritarian's Youth Rally,'" *Washington Examiner*, July 25, 2017.

154   William Cummings, "Analysis: Trump Is a Master of Language," *USA Today*, February 17, 2017.

155   Michael M. Grynaum, "Trump Calls the New Media the 'Enemy of the American People,'" *New York Times*, February 17, 2017. Brett Edkins, "Poll: More Americans Trust the Media than Donald Trump," *Forbes*, February 23, 2017. Rebecca Savransky, "Poll: Most Disagree with Trump that Media is 'Enemy of the People," *The Hill*, March 7, 2017. Quinnipiac University Poll, May 10, 2017, https://poll.qu.edu/national/release-detail?ReleaseID=2456. Also see the Gallup poll data reported in Art Swift, "Americans' Trust in Mass Media Sinks to New Low," *Gallup*, September 14, 2016, www.gallup.com/poll/195542/americans-trust-mass-media-sinks-new-low.aspx.

156   Sam Leith, "Trump's Rhetoric: A Triumph of Inarticulacy," *Guardian*, January 12, 2017. Mark Thompson, *Enough Said: What's Gone Wrong with the Language of Politics?* (New York: St. Martin's Press, 2016), 71.

PART II

THE PRESIDENT AND CONGRESS

PART III

THE PRESIDENT AND
CONGRESS

CHAPTER 4

THE LEGISLATIVE PRESIDENCY

INTRODUCTORY PUZZLE: LESSONS FROM OBAMA'S JOE WILSON MOMENT

"You lie!" The two words stunned the nation. Politicians and pundits across the political spectrum deplored them. Nearly nine in ten Americans agreed that they were inappropriate. South Carolina Representative Joe Wilson rushed to apologize for his "lack of civility," calling his outburst "inappropriate and regrettable."[1]

President Barack Obama had been accused of far worse by his political opponents during the debate over health care reform, yet Wilson's accusation instantly became a media sensation because he shouted it out in the midst of the president's speech to a joint session of Congress. On such occasions the president appears as a special guest of the House and Senate. Decorum requires that when the president enters the chamber, all members rise from their seats and applaud. Members may tweet while the president speaks but they may not question or challenge him. They are the ceremonial backdrop to the presidential pageant.

Not that the president's opponents have always behaved themselves. When President Bill Clinton appeared before a joint session of Congress in 1993 to promote his health care plan, television cameras caught a few Republican legislators "snickering, shaking their heads skeptically, and making faces at each other." And when George W. Bush used his 2005 State of the Union address to press for Social Security reform, a posse of Democrats booed. Such naughty behavior is not altogether novel. In 1950, for instance, Harry Truman's criticism of what he called Congress's "ill-considered" tax cuts brought "boos and jeers and dismissive laughter" from Republicans. However, these partisan contretemps are the exception rather than the rule. Legislators unhappy with the president generally confine themselves to looking dour.[2]

The dignified atmosphere in the House chamber on these occasions is worlds apart from the raucous confrontations in the British House of Commons during Prime Minister's Questions. Once a week, the prime minister is peppered with caustic queries, most of them from the opposition leader sitting directly across the table from the prime minister. No member of Parliament rises when the prime minister enters. The prime minister's comments are often met with jeers from the opposition. The rowdy proceedings are punctuated with cries of "order, order" by the speaker of the House of Commons, who has the thankless task of refereeing the shouting match.

The president of the United States is treated with more dignity and deference than a British prime minister not because American legislators have better manners than their British counterparts but rather because of the different roles played by the American president and the British prime minister. The prime minister is a member of the legislature, as are all the members of the prime minister's cabinet. The president, in contrast, is not a part of the legislature, and nor are any of the members of his administration. In fact, Article I, section 6 of the United States Constitution forbids any executive officer from simultaneously holding a legislative office, tearing asunder what the British system joins together.

The prime minister leads the government by virtue of her party's majority in the legislature; the only British citizens who may vote directly for the prime minister are those who hail from the prime minister's local constituency. Thus when the prime minister appears at Prime Minister's Questions, she appears unabashedly as the head of the political party that has selected her as its standard-bearer. She sits on the front bench flanked by her fellow cabinet members. Arrayed behind her are all the other members of her legislative majority, the so-called "backbenchers." When the prime minister rises to speak she faces, directly in front of her, the opposition leader, who is backed by his partisan troops. In contrast, when the president speaks to a joint session of Congress he

South Carolina Representative Joe Wilson shouts out "You lie" during President Barack Obama's address to a joint session of Congress on September 9, 2009.

Courtesy: Getty Images.

speaks from an elevated dais in the House, facing the legislators of both parties. He inevitably speaks as a partisan, of course, but he appears also as something more exalted: the head of state.

The closest British equivalent to a president's speech before a joint session of Congress is not Prime Minister's Questions but the queen's annual speech from the throne in the House of Lords, in which the monarch announces the government's legislative agenda for the coming year. In contemporary Britain, the monarch's role is purely ceremonial, and the speech read by the monarch is penned by the leadership of the governing party. No opposition leader or member would dream of booing or heckling the queen.

The president is no more a monarch than he is a prime minister. Yet the emotionally charged reaction to Joe Wilson's "moment of madness" reminds us that an American president is asked to bridge ceremonial and partisan roles that in Great Britain have been strictly separated. Americans see the president as a symbol of national unity and identity, yet they also expect the president to stake out positions on a range of divisive public policies. Although styled the nation's chief executive, a president is rarely selected on the basis of his executive or administrative skills. Presidential contests are instead centered on the candidates' advocacy of rival legislative agendas. In the eyes of most Americans, the president is the chief legislator, responsible not just for proposing a legislative program but for pushing it through Congress. Politicians and pundits judge presidents on how successful they are in getting Congress to approve their program.

Obama understood these expectations, which is why he had taken the extraordinary step of asking to address a joint session of Congress on September 9, 2009. The momentum behind health care reform, the new president's signature issue, had stalled over the summer. Senate Finance Committee chairman Max Baucus's efforts to secure bipartisan support for the legislation had proven fruitless. Republicans sensed an opportunity not only to defeat the health care bill, but to deal a body blow to the Obama presidency. Home for the August recess, members of Congress hosted town hall meetings dominated by "tea party" protesters angrily denouncing the "government takeover of health care." As the voices of opposition to "Obamacare" became louder and more strident, public support for reform eroded and Democratic members of Congress became increasingly anxious about the electoral cost of voting with the president.[3]

This was the political backdrop for Obama's speech, delivered on Congress's first day back to work after its month-long recess. To salvage comprehensive health care reform and perhaps his presidency, Obama felt he needed to confront his critics and "stiffen the spines of nervous Democrats." In his speech, Obama sharply criticized those "prominent politicians" whose "bogus claims" were made only "to kill reform at any cost." His opponents' claim that his health care plan would "set up panels of bureaucrats with the power to kill off senior citizens" was "a lie, plain and simple," a lie that "would be laughable if it weren't so cynical and irresponsible." Next the president took aim at "those who claim that our reform efforts would insure illegal immigrants." That, too, Obama underlined, was "false." It was at this point that Wilson shouted out his two-word retort.[4]

Obama came to Congress not only to lead his fellow partisans into legislative battle but also to position himself as the only adult in the room, a parent come to sort out squabbling children—and Wilson's outburst played directly into the president's narrative. Obama presented himself as a unifying and moderate voice of reason, in contrast to the "unyielding ideological camps" within Congress. And unlike members of Congress, who were interested in scoring "short-term political points," the president said he was focused on solving the "long-term challenge" of rising health care costs. Obama vowed not to sit back and watch "special interests use the same old tactics" to preserve the status quo. In sum, whereas Congress embodied special interests, partisan squabbling, and short-sightedness, the president represented an enduring national interest.

No prime minister would speak this way to Parliament. The prime minister does not denigrate or hold herself above the legislature—for she is Parliament's leader, responsible for its policies. Should Parliament fail to enact central planks of the prime minister's legislative agenda, there would be no questions about where to lay the blame: the fault would lie squarely with the prime minister and her party.

The legislative responsibility of the president, in contrast, is far more ambiguous. Presidents frequently confront a Congress in which one or both houses are controlled by the opposition party. But even when the same party controls the presidency, the House, and the Senate—as was true during the first two years of Obama's presidency—the president can still plausibly blame Congress for its failure to act. For the president has no formal power to compel obedience from members of his own party, and in the Senate the minority party has the power to filibuster and obstruct legislation in ways that are unimaginable in a parliamentary system.

Although presidents can blame Congress for failing to act, they must also expect that legislative inaction will be widely seen as a failure of their leadership. This might seem surprising to those who have carefully studied the text of the Constitution, which gives the president only two roles in the legislative process: (1) the power to veto bills, subject to an override by a two-thirds vote of both houses of Congress; and (2) the obligation "from time to time [to] give to the Congress Information of the State of the Union, and recommend to their Consideration such Measures as he shall judge necessary and expedient." How did American politics evolve from these spare constitutional clauses to the contemporary understanding that the president is responsible for shepherding legislation through Congress? This is the puzzle to which we now turn.

THE CONSTITUTIONAL BRAKES

Americans are proud that they have the oldest Constitution in the world and that their political institutions have endured through four centuries, two world wars, and one civil war. The system's longevity, as well as the freedom and prosperity it has engendered, are seen as vindication of the framers' system of separation of powers and checks and balances, a system in which ambition is made to counteract ambition, as James Madison famously put it in *Federalist* No. 51.

The durability of the framers' design—"a government of separated institutions sharing powers," in Richard Neustadt's apt description—is certainly remarkable, but so too is the dramatic change in Americans' understanding of the relationship between the executive and legislative branches. The modern understanding is captured by political scientist Robert Dahl's description of the president as "the motor in the system."

Congress, in contrast, "applies the brakes." The president, writes Dahl, "gives what forward movement there is to the system" whereas Congress is "the force of inertia." The framers of the Constitution, in contrast, conceived of the relationship in almost diametrically opposite terms. For them, Congress was the motor force and the president the necessary brake on ill-conceived legislation.[5]

The Veto Power

For the framers, the president's chief legislative function was the power to veto bills. The veto, as Alexander Hamilton explained in *Federalist* No. 73, served two purposes, both of which were defensive. First, it enabled the president "to defend himself" against laws that might encroach on his power. Second, it enabled the president to stop "bad laws" that had been enacted "through haste, inadvertence, or design."

In some ways, it seems puzzling that the framers were willing to grant the president a veto power. After all, when the colonists drew up their list of grievances in the Declaration of Independence, their first complaint was that George III had "refused his Assent to Laws, the most wholesome and necessary for the public good." When new state constitutions were drawn up in 1776 and 1777, only South Carolina vested the power to veto legislation in a governor, and that decision was quickly reversed in its revised constitution of 1778. Yet only a decade later, the debate at the Federal Convention focused less on whether to give the president a veto—though a significant minority of delegates did oppose granting the president a veto—than on whether the power should be absolute or qualified, and, if qualified, whether the override should require a vote of two-thirds or three-fourths of the legislature. There was also a persistent minority, headed by Madison, who favored giving the veto power to a "council of revision" that would consist of the president and several members of the judiciary.

Madison's preferred council of revision formed the basis for the eighth resolution of the Virginia Plan, which called for "the Executive and a convenient number of the National Judiciary" to exercise a veto over legislation. However, the idea ran into stiff opposition. Judges, argued Massachusetts' Nathaniel Gorham, are "not to be presumed to possess any peculiar knowledge of the mere policy of public measures." Involving judges in the making of legislation, moreover, would bias them when they were later asked to determine the constitutionality of a law. A majority of the delegates agreed and voted to place the veto power in the hands of the executive.[6]

Although most delegates preferred to give the veto power to the president acting alone, few wanted to give the president an absolute veto. Hamilton, Pennsylvania's James Wilson, and Gouverneur Morris were vocal exceptions, but they failed to persuade a single state to back their idea. Fears of executive power had not receded so far since the end of the Revolution that the delegates were willing, as Connecticut's Roger Sherman put it, to enable "one man to stop the will of the whole." A large majority of the delegates agreed that a two-thirds vote of both branches of the legislature should be sufficient to override a veto.[7]

However, in the middle of August, more than two months after the convention had settled on a two-thirds override, the delegates reconsidered their position. Madison, Wilson, and Morris had continued to press for some variant on a council of revision but with little success. However, their insistence that the real threat to liberty in a republic lay not in a tyrannical executive but in an unchecked legislature capable of "swallowing up all the other powers" resonated with many of the other delegates, even those who were unsympathetic to the idea of a council of revision. Four states that had earlier supported the two-thirds override now switched their position and endorsed a three-fourths threshold.[8]

On September 12, the five-person Committee of Style, charged with polishing the convention's handiwork, presented the delegates with the final draft of the Constitution. As soon as it was laid before the convention, North Carolina's Hugh Williamson urged the delegates to reconsider their decision to require three-fourths of both houses to override the president's veto. Williamson had been the one to propose the three-fourths threshold back in August, but now pronounced that this higher threshold gave the president too much power.

Morris, Hamilton, and Madison, each of whom served on the Committee of Style, labored to defend the higher threshold. Morris suggested that the difference between the two figures only amounted to a handful of votes, which invited Virginia's George Mason's scathing reply that "little arithmetic was necessary to understand that 3/4 was more than 2/3." Morris tacked back to the more compelling argument that the higher threshold was necessary to avert "the instability of laws" that was the danger "most to be guarded against" in a republic. However, Morris failed to convince the delegates, and Williamson's proposal to revert back to the two-thirds threshold was carried by a 6–4 vote.[9]

Several aspects of this debate are noteworthy. First, the United States came very close to requiring three-quarters of both houses of Congress to override a presidential veto—a decision that would have greatly strengthened the president's hand. Second, many delegates had a difficult time deciding whether two-thirds or three-fourths was a preferable threshold for overriding a veto. Every state but Georgia switched their position at least once, and two states—North Carolina and South Carolina—swung from one pole to the other with each of the three votes (on June 4, August 15, and September 12). Third, votes by state delegations on the veto threshold were often anchored less in abstract views of the relative merits of executive and legislative power than in political calculations about state interests. The decision made on September 12 to reverse the earlier vote in favor of a three-fourths threshold was triggered by the previous week's change to the mode of presidential selection. With the president now to be elected by the electoral college rather than by the legislature, the two most populous northern states—Massachusetts and Pennsylvania—switched to support the three-fourths threshold (and thereby strengthen the president), while three southern states with substantial slave populations—Maryland, North Carolina, and South Carolina—switched in the other direction.

"Measures … Necessary and Expedient"

The vigorous debates over the veto power—which received extensive discussion on five separate days—stand in marked contrast to the almost complete silence among the delegates about the only other constitutional provision that directly involved the president in the legislative process: Article II, section 3, which states that the president "shall from time to time give to the Congress Information of the State of the Union, and recommend to their Consideration such Measures as he shall judge necessary and expedient." Introduced by the Committee of Detail in early August, the provision attracted no comment from the delegates apart from Morris's suggestion that "may recommend"—the committee's original language—be altered (by dropping the word "may") so that recommending measures became a duty of the president. Otherwise, Morris counseled, the legislature would likely take "umbrage and cavil at his doing it." Morris's change was accepted without debate or objection.[10]

The reason that delegates fought bitterly over the veto power and paid almost no attention to Article II, section 3 is that few if any saw the latter as a grant of significant power, whereas all understood that the veto strengthened the executive branch at the expense of the legislature. Obligating the president to recommend laws did not weaken the legislature because it was under no obligation to heed the president's recommendations. Delegates saw this provision as an uncontroversial part of good government. Responsible for implementing the laws, the president was ideally positioned to alert Congress to a law's defects and to suggest possible modifications. And providing Congress with information could only help the legislative body better carry out its task. The absence of any objection or comment about this provision, even among the most militantly anti-executive delegates, indicates that the framers had no intention of making the president the legislator-in-chief.

"FROM MOTIVES OF RESPECT": GEORGE WASHINGTON'S RELATIONS WITH CONGRESS

Having presided over the Constitutional Convention, George Washington was acutely conscious that fears of executive power—and a jealous solicitousness of legislative prerogatives—remained a potent part of American political culture, nowhere more so than in his native Virginia. At the Virginia ratifying convention, Patrick Henry and Washington's longtime friend and neighbor George Mason had spearheaded an attack that nearly derailed the proposed new constitution. Washington understood that building support for the new government and fostering trust in the presidency would require him to exercise restraint in his interactions with the legislative branch.

Presidential restraint, first and foremost, dictated sparing use of the veto. To his old friend Edmund Pendleton, Washington explained: "From motives of respect to the legislature (and I might add from my interpretation of the constitution), I give my signature to many Bills with which my Judgment is at variance." During eight years as president, he vetoed only two bills. The first was an apportionment bill that Secretary of State Thomas Jefferson persuaded Washington to veto on the grounds that the bill was unconstitutional and that the president's "non-use" of the veto was beginning "to excite a belief that no President will ever venture to use it." Washington did not exercise his second veto—of a bill that disbanded two dragoon companies—until four days before he left office.[11]

Washington's public communications with Congress were unfailingly deferential, never scolding or confrontational. In his inaugural address he paid "tribute ... to the talents, the rectitude, and the patriotism" of the representatives and senators "selected to devise and adopt" the nation's laws. In his first annual message, he dutifully drew Congress's attention to those issues that he believed required legislative action but scrupulously avoided specifying the policy he thought should be adopted. For instance, while Washington opined that "nothing ... can better deserve your patronage than the promotion of science and literature," he did not tell Congress that it should establish a national university, even though that was a cause dear to his heart. Instead he said only that "whether this desirable object will be best promoted by affording aids to seminaries of learning already established, by the institution of a national university, or by any other expedients will be well worthy of a place in the deliberations of the legislature."[12]

Behind the scenes Washington was not entirely passive in giving shape to legislation, particularly on matters relating to national defense. For instance, although his first annual message only vaguely referenced the need to establish a "uniform and well-digested plan" for a militia, Washington had already drawn up a more specific plan that he sent to Secretary of War Henry Knox "to be worked into the form of a Bill with which to furnish ... Congress." The first Congress, however, did not share the president's sense of urgency about the need for a uniform militia and took no action on the bill. Although deeply disappointed, Washington bore the setback stoically and did not attempt to lobby legislators on behalf of his preferred plan.[13]

Washington had strategic reasons for wishing to avoid being drawn too deeply into the legislative process. For one, taking sides in fractious legislative debates would jeopardize his carefully cultivated reputation as a president above party and faction. In addition, he believed that attempting to influence Congress would be counterproductive because it would trigger charges of executive usurpation and arouse legislative resentment. Finally, Washington feared that intervening in the legislative process could damage the prestige of his presidency. Since he lacked the formal powers to compel Congress to heed his counsel, he was reluctant to place himself in a position where his views could be disregarded and he could be made to appear weak.[14]

Washington's restraint was more than just a tactical or political calculation, however. It also reflected his strict interpretation of the separation of powers. Washington believed that the Constitution required the executive not to encroach on legislative powers just as much as it commanded the legislature not to encroach on executive powers. When he thought Congress had trespassed on executive powers he was quick to protest. For instance, when the House of Representatives passed a resolution congratulating the French on their new constitution, Washington complained bitterly to Jefferson that the legislature was "endeavoring to invade the executive." But he also showed a principled regard for legislative prerogatives. When his attorney general Edmund Randolph suggested an administrative fix to a law, Washington demurred, insisting that as the Constitution "must mark the line of my official conduct, I could not justify my taking a single step in any matter, which appeared to me to require [the legislature's] agency, without its being first obtained." Congress and the president, in Washington's view, properly occupied separate spheres of action.[15]

Alexander Hamilton: Walpole to Washington's George II

Although Washington was careful not to "invade" the legislative domain, the story of legislative–executive relations during Washington's presidency is anything but one of strict separation. For while Washington maintained a respectful distance from legislative deliberations, he permitted his department heads, particularly Treasury Secretary Alexander Hamilton, to assume an active leadership role in the legislative process.

The Treasury Department's Duty to "Digest and Prepare Plans"

The Treasury Department's relationship to Congress was a point of contention from the start, particularly in the House of Representatives, which jealously guarded its constitutional monopoly on the power to initiate tax legislation. Anxious to ensure that the treasury secretary be made accountable not only to the president but also to Congress, the House bill establishing the Treasury Department required that the secretary "digest and report plans" to Congress for "the improvement and management of the revenue, and the support of the public credit." No comparable reporting provision was contained in the bills creating the other two departments, State and War.[16]

As soon as the Treasury bill was introduced on the floor of the House, Jefferson's close friend John Page jumped to his feet to object to this "dangerous" encroachment upon legislative autonomy. A treasury secretary might be safely entrusted with the "duty of making out and preparing estimates," Page allowed, but to require him to report plans would grant him "undue influence" in House deliberations. Page worried that members "might be led, by the deference commonly paid to men of abilities, who give an opinion in a case they have thoroughly studied, to support the minister's plan, even against their own judgment." This precedent, he warned, "might be extended, until we admitted all the ministers of the Government on the floor, to explain and support the plans they have digested and reported: thus laying a foundation for an aristocracy or a detestable monarchy."[17]

Others in the House, including Madison, professed that they could not understand what all the fuss was about. Surely, scoffed Massachusetts' Benjamin Goodhue, we "carry our dignity to the extreme when we refuse to receive information from any but ourselves." By providing the House with "well-formed and digested plans," the treasury secretary would not encroach on Congress's power so much as enhance its ability to make sound decisions about the nation's finances. Drawing upon the treasury secretary's experience and expertise, the bill's defenders insisted, would enable Congress to achieve its goals more efficiently and effectively. The secretary, in short, would be the agent of the House, not its master.[18]

To mollify the critics, compromise wording was proposed. Instead of "digest and report," the bill was changed to read "digest and prepare," so as to make clear that the secretary was only to report plans to the legislature when directed to do so by Congress. The change in wording was approved by a large majority, though it failed to appease Page and his allies, who believed that the alteration did nothing to diminish the danger of ministerial influence in Congress.[19]

"Mr. Hamilton is All Powerful"

After signing the bill establishing the Treasury Department, Washington nominated Hamilton to serve as the department's first head. The selection surprised nobody. Just as the delegates at the Constitutional Convention in Philadelphia debated the presidency in the near certain knowledge that Washington would be its first occupant, so the House debated the duties of the treasury secretary knowing that Hamilton was likely to be named to the post.[20]

Some scholars suspect that Hamilton actually had a hand in shaping the legislation that established the Treasury Department.[21] Certainly, the "digest and prepare" clause fit perfectly with Hamilton's vision of his role as an indispensable bridge between the executive and legislative branches. Hamilton was an ardent admirer of the British political system—"the best in the world," he called it in his June 18, 1787, speech at the convention. What made the British system effective, in Hamilton's view, was not only that the nation was symbolically united in its attachment to a monarch but that the executive and legislative powers were knitted together through the great ministers of state, particularly the prime minister who served both as a leader in Parliament and as the Chancellor of the Exchequer. Hamilton envisioned himself, as historian Forrest McDonald puts it, as "Sir Robert Walpole to Washington's George II." That is, Washington would be the symbolic, unifying force that commanded the nation's love and respect while Hamilton would be the government's prime minister, directing the new nation's economic policies.[22]

Confirmed by the Senate the same day Washington nominated him, Hamilton immediately went to work, on a Sunday no less. Putting the nation's financial house in order was recognized as an urgent priority. The Revolutionary War had been waged through massive borrowing, and creditors were clamoring to be paid. Lacking the time and understanding to formulate a solution, members of Congress turned to Hamilton for answers. Shortly before adjourning, the House of Representatives instructed Hamilton to prepare a plan that would make "adequate provision for the support of the public credit" and to report the plan to Congress when it reconvened in January. The House also dissolved the Ways and Means Committee that it had set up only a few months earlier. Rather than build up its own institutional expertise, Congress seemed ready to rely on Hamilton's expert judgment, just as Page had feared.[23]

Hamilton's report was "humbly submitted" but the plan he proposed was anything but modest. It was hugely ambitious and complex. Hamilton hoped that the House would allow him to present and explain his plan for rebuilding the nation's credit in person—just as a British minister would do in Parliament. That way he could answer members' questions and help them better "comprehend so intricate a subject." However, the prospect of a department head mimicking the behavior of a British minister troubled even Hamilton's supporters. The House insisted that Hamilton's report be received in writing.[24]

But while the House denied Hamilton the opportunity to present and defend his plan in person, he was not kept away from the floor of Congress nor prevented from lobbying on behalf of his proposals. On February 1, 1790, for instance, Pennsylvania senator William Maclay recorded in his diary that Hamilton was "here early to wait on the Speaker, and . . . spent most of his time in running from place to place among the members." Members turned to Hamilton because he understood the implications of the plan in a way that they did not; as South Carolina's Aedanus Burke groused, there was "no man in either house, who is not totally at a loss on this important subject." Hamilton's effort to forge close connections with the legislature was also helped by the fact that Congress and the department heads as well as the president were all housed in the same building, New York City's Federal Hall.[25]

Each of the legislative proposals included in Hamilton's first report was adopted by Congress with only small changes.[26] When Congress resumed work in December 1790, Hamilton was ready with two more reports: one proposing a tax on hard alcohol to pay for the interest on the state debts that the federal government had assumed, the other providing a detailed plan for a national bank. Both proposals sparked sharp ideological debates, but Congress ultimately enacted Hamilton's proposals pretty much as he had drafted them. To Maclay, writing in the closing days of the first Congress, it seemed that "Nothing is done without . . . Mr. Hamilton. [He] is all-powerful, and fails in nothing he attempts."[27]

Hamilton's extraordinary influence on the financial legislation enacted by the first Congress exposed the naiveté (or disingenuousness) of those members who had brusquely dismissed Page's fears about ministerial influence. New York's John Laurance had insisted that so long as Congress retained "the power of deciding what shall be law [the Treasury secretary] may give us all the information possible, but can never be said to participate in legislative business; he has no control whatever over this House." Hamilton showed, however, that information was power. Although possessed of no vote, he had exerted more influence on the financial legislation enacted by the first Congress than any elected legislator. Not only did he participate in the legislative business—conferring continually with members on the floor and in committees—but he essentially crafted the laws, which was precisely how, Hamilton believed, the American political system should work.[28]

Madison's "Troops" Push Back

Madison and Jefferson were becoming increasingly alarmed at Hamilton's policies and his influence in Congress. Secretary of State Jefferson took his concerns directly to the president. He told Washington that "there was a squadron devoted to the nod of the treasury, doing whatever he had directed and ready to do what he should direct." The result, Jefferson lamented, was that "the Executive had swallowed up the legislative branch." Madison, initially so sanguine about the treasury secretary's influence in Congress, dramatically reversed course in the second Congress and joined forces with Jefferson to organize an opposition party that could arrest the Hamiltonian system.[29]

One way that Madison and his allies tried to blunt Hamilton's influence was to stop the House from asking the secretary to provide financial plans. When the first Congress asked Hamilton to submit reports to Congress, those requests had sparked no organized opposition or debate. In the second Congress, in contrast, the requests met with fierce opposition. For instance, a proposal that the treasury secretary "report a plan for the purpose of reducing the debt" provoked vehement disagreement and carried only narrowly, 31–25, with "Hamilton's people"—as Maclay called them—on one side and Madison's "troops"—as Hamilton called them—on the other.[30]

Hamilton's defenders emphasized that Congress was free to reject or ignore anything that they didn't like in Hamilton's plans. But for Madison and his allies, this seemed to turn the Constitution on its head by giving Congress only "the right of a negative" rather than the power to initiate legislation. As Madison now saw it, Congress had an obligation to deliberate on the broad shape of public policy before the executive became involved. The information the executive provided should be limited "to statements of facts and details of business" and should not attempt to set the legislative agenda or provide "matured plans." Madison complained that Hamilton had used the broad language of the Treasury bill to introduce an executive-centered legislative system that was never anticipated by Congress.[31]

In combating Hamiltonian methods, Madison and his followers drew upon ideological arguments against executive power that had been honed during the American Revolution. They argued that Hamilton's influence corrupted the integrity and independence of the legislature. They insisted, as Georgia's Abraham Baldwin put it, that the people's "interests and wishes, joys and sorrows must be better known to their Representatives than it is possible for any Executive officer to be acquainted with," particularly in such a large country. And they insisted on the strictest possible understanding of the separation of powers—the barriers between the branches, Baldwin said, need not be "like the wall of China, to keep out the Tartars" but they should be made "strong and impregnable."[32]

The anti-executive bias of the opposition coalition's ideology took shape during the second Congress, but Hamilton's supporters remained firmly in control of both houses, limiting the opposition's ability to counter Hamilton's executive influence. In the third Congress, however, the anti-administration forces secured a majority in the House, enabling Madison and his allies to make institutional relations more closely correspond to Jeffersonian theory.[33]

Rather than ask Hamilton to prepare a report on the public credit, as past Congresses had done, the House instead established a select committee to investigate what revenues might be needed, leaving Hamilton "cursedly mortified." The following year, the House established for the first time a standing (that is, permanent) Ways and Means Committee that could provide a "counterweight to executive influence." Its charge was to report to the House "on the state of the Public Debt, revenues, and expenditures."[34]

In addition to fostering legislative self-reliance, Republicans put Hamilton on the defensive by launching investigations into his conduct in the Treasury Department. A select committee of 15 representatives, made up almost entirely of Madison and Jefferson's allies, spent close to three months scrutinizing the Treasury Department's transactions, forcing Hamilton to expend huge sums of energy and time documenting his actions and answering committee questions. The investigations turned up no wrongdoing on

Hamilton's part but Republicans made his life a misery. Halfway through the third Congress, Hamilton announced his resignation, putting an end to his bold experiment in ministerial government.[35]

Under the adroit leadership of Madison and Jefferson, Republicans had thwarted what they saw as Hamilton's effort "to administer the Government into what he thought it ought to be." The formation of the Republican opposition, Jefferson later explained, was grounded in a desire "to preserve the legislature pure and independent of the Executive" and to prevent the new constitution from being "warped in practice into all the principles and pollutions of [the Federalists'] favorite English model." An ideology that preached vigilance against improper executive influence suited the needs of an opposition party, but how well would it serve the Republicans when they controlled the executive branch? How effectively could a legislature function without what Hamilton called the "Executive impulse"?[36]

THE HIDDEN-HAND LEADERSHIP OF THOMAS JEFFERSON

When Jefferson assumed the presidency in 1801, he faced the daunting task of leading a party that, by his own admission, had as its raison d'être a commitment to guarding the legislature against executive influence. Not all Republicans were doctrinaire about preserving legislative autonomy—least of all Jefferson—but nor was the Republicans' anti-executive ethos merely a ruse to thwart Federalist policies that could be casually tossed aside now that the Republicans controlled the executive branch. If Jefferson was to lead Congress he would need to do so in a way that respected his party's commitment to legislative autonomy. His solution was to adopt a "hidden-hand" strategy, to lead without appearing to do so, to guide while seeming to defer.[37]

Jefferson's public pronouncements breathed deference to Congress, that "great council of our nation." Behind the scenes, however, Jefferson worked assiduously to guide legislative proceedings. Unlike his predecessors, Jefferson sought to bridge the constitutional divide between the legislative and executive branches by recruiting legislators willing to act as his agents on Capitol Hill. He looked to them, he explained, to "give cohesion to our rope of sand." As the metaphor of a rope of sand suggests, Jefferson was keenly aware that he could not trust his legislative agenda to the inherent wisdom and good sense of the legislature, despite large Republican majorities in both houses of Congress. Indeed, as the Republican majorities became increasingly lopsided—by the beginning of his second term Republicans outnumbered Federalists by about four to one in both the Senate and the House—the task of keeping the legislature from splintering into warring factions became more urgent.[38]

Jefferson understood that the constitutional duty to recommend measures to Congress was woefully inadequate to his purposes. As Jefferson explained to one of his chosen lieutenants, "If the members are to know nothing but what is important enough to be put into a public message, and indifferent enough to be made known to all the world, if the Executive is to keep all other information to himself, and the house to plunge on in the dark, it becomes a government of chance and not of design." Jefferson had no intention of leaving the Republican agenda to chance.[39]

Virtually every important piece of legislation passed during Jefferson's tenure originated with the administration. In messages to Congress, Jefferson typically indicated
only the broad outlines of his program, leaving the specific details to private communications with trusted legislators. On those occasions when Jefferson drafted legislation he impressed upon his confidants the importance of concealing his involvement.
Typical was the note that Jefferson attached to the draft of a bill he sent to Virginia
congressman John Dawson: "be so good as to copy the within and burn this original, as he
[Jefferson] is very unwilling to meddle personally with the details of the proceedings of
the legislature."[40]

Jefferson's efforts to conceal his legislative leadership did not prevent Federalists from
complaining vociferously about his influence. Massachusetts congressman Samuel
Taggart, for instance, lamented that Republican legislators "receive all the impressions
from the Executive with the same facility that the wax receives from the seal." From
"behind the curtain," concurred Massachusetts senator Thomas Pickering, Jefferson
"directs the measures he wishes to have adopted; while in each house a majority of
puppets move as he touches the wires." Federalists were not wrong to detect Jefferson's
guiding hand behind the actions of Congress, but they exaggerated the president's
control over legislative proceedings and underestimated the difficulties Jefferson faced in
exercising legislative leadership.[41]

Few of the legislators whom Jefferson relied on to shepherd bills through Congress
could be called presidential puppets. Certainly not the fiercely independent John Randolph, the closest thing Jefferson had to an administration spokesperson and floor leader
in his first term. Jefferson had felt compelled to take Randolph into his confidence not
because they had a close personal relationship but because Randolph was a force to be
reckoned with on the House floor. In addition to being a brilliant debater, Randolph
chaired the House Ways and Means Committee, a position he owed to the Speaker of the
House rather than to the president. How far Randolph was from a presidential pawn
became evident when he broke with the administration in Jefferson's second term,
launching a blistering attack on the president's "backstairs influence—of men who bring
messages to this House, which, although they do not appear on the Journals, govern its
decisions."[42]

Jefferson found it hugely frustrating that he could not communicate more openly and
frequently with members of Congress. Shortly after Randolph's outburst, an exasperated
Jefferson explained his dilemma to the *Aurora*'s William Duane. "Whatever we do is
liable to the criticisms of those who wish to represent it awry. If we recommend measures
in a public message, it may be said that members are not sent here to obey the mandates of
the President, or to register the edicts of a sovereign. If we express opinions in conversation, we have then our ... back-door counselors. If we say nothing, 'we have no
opinions, no plans.'" These are not the words of a man who found Congress to be putty in
his hands.[43]

It didn't help Jefferson's cause that in the new capital the Executive Mansion and Capitol
Hill were a mile and a half apart, much of it a swampland bridged only by a "rutted
causeway." In Philadelphia, in contrast, the president's house had been just a stroll around
the corner from Congress Hall. Even more important than the Tiber swamp, however,

were the "tacit rules ... and community custom" that compelled the president to keep his distance from Capitol Hill.[44]

Jefferson was able to break down some of these barriers by inviting small groups of legislators to dine at the Executive Mansion. Virtually every night during the months that the legislature was in session, Jefferson gathered a clutch of legislators around a circular table where they could eat and talk as equals. Jefferson's store of fine French wine flowed freely through the evening, helping to loosen even the most guarded of tongues. Legislators did not come to Jefferson's dinners to talk politics—indeed, for the president to have hosted a political dinner for members of Congress would have been deemed grossly improper and greeted with peals of calumny. Yet though the gracious host steered the conversation safely away from politics, these gatherings helped to forge bonds that were politically useful to the president.[45]

The impact these dinners had on the views or voting habits of legislators is impossible to gauge, but there is no doubt that they provided Jefferson an invaluable opportunity to take the measure of both his supporters and opponents. They enabled Jefferson to judge for himself a legislator's sagacity and temperament, foibles and talents. They gave Jefferson, in other words, exactly the sort of fine-grained information about individuals that he needed if he was to lead in a system that denied him the power to command or coerce.[46]

Although Jefferson found these dinners politically beneficial, he necessarily relied on his department heads to handle most of the informal communications with legislators. Treasury Secretary Albert Gallatin played a particularly pivotal role as the president's legislative liaison. During the Adams administration, Gallatin had been the de facto leader of the House Republicans and had forged close ties with many influential Republican legislators, including Randolph and Speaker of the House Nathaniel Macon. Moreover, unlike Jefferson's other department heads, who chose to reside near the executive buildings in which they worked, Gallatin continued to live on Capitol Hill. Throughout Jefferson's presidency, Gallatin's home served as the main meeting place for the Republican leadership. Virtually every evening, Republican legislative leaders allied with the administration would drop by Gallatin's house to discuss events of the day and to plot political strategy.[47]

Unlike Jefferson, department heads did not need to conceal their involvement in the legislative process. Congressional committee chairs routinely invited department heads, particularly Gallatin, to assist in the preparation of legislation and to recommend amendment to bills under consideration. Whereas Jefferson had to soft-pedal his legislative proposals as merely "private suggestions," Gallatin openly drafted legislation without apologies.[48]

Congressional Republicans were every bit as reliant on Gallatin's financial expertise as Federalists had been on Hamilton's. Indeed, many of the same legislators who had railed against Hamilton's legislative influence in the 1790s now eagerly solicited Gallatin's participation in crafting legislation. Abraham Baldwin, for instance, one of Hamilton's severest critics in the early 1790s, sent Gallatin a bill in the spring of 1802 with a request that the treasury secretary "note on the bill any amendments which you think proper to recommend to [the committee's] consideration." Not for the last time in American history, partisan attitudes toward executive power were recast to suit altered political circumstances and interests.[49]

But while Gallatin's relationship with members of Congress was at least as close and influential as Hamilton's had been, there was a crucial difference in how the two men conceived of their roles. Gallatin never saw himself as akin to a prime minister.[50] He never would have referred to "my administration," as Hamilton did. It was always Jefferson's administration. In Gallatin's mind, Jefferson was the party's head while he was the president's "eyes and ears" on the Hill and his chief legislative lobbyist. Hamilton, in contrast, envisioned himself as the leader of the Federalist Party—a view shared by most Federalists in Congress, even during the Adams administration when Hamilton was in private practice. Hamilton viewed Washington as "an aegis very essential to me," a protective shield that helped lend legitimacy to his financial policies—policies with which the president was certainly in sympathy, but which Hamilton crafted with little or no input from the president. In short, whereas Hamilton saw the president's role in instrumental terms, Gallatin saw himself as an instrument of the president.[51]

One of the great ironies of American presidential history is that a party dedicated to the proposition that the legislature should be free of executive control yielded a presidency that exercised a degree of influence over the legislative branch that exceeded anything the nation would see for another century. It is tempting to see this paradox as evidence that the Republicans didn't really mean what they said about executive power and legislative autonomy. That would be a mistake, however, both because it fails to do justice to Jefferson's skillful exercise of political leadership and because it leaves us unprepared for the collapse of presidential influence in Congress after Jefferson left office.

CONGRESS RESURGENT

None of Jefferson's successors—not James Madison, not James Monroe, and certainly not John Quincy Adams—exercised anything like the influence over Congress that Jefferson had done. Each was possessed of great talents and intelligence and each had extensive experience in both the national legislature and executive: Madison served eight years as Jefferson's secretary of state and another eight as the leader of the House Republicans; Monroe was a United States senator before becoming secretary of state and of war, and in between he had two stints as Virginia's governor as well as serving as the American ambassador to France and Britain; Adams had been a United States senator, secretary of state, and ambassador to the Netherlands, Prussia, Russia, and Britain. Yet each struggled to lead Congress. Why?

Was Jefferson to Blame?

Some scholars blame Jefferson for his successors' difficulties with Congress. According to this view, Jefferson's personal power over Congress was purchased at the cost of weakening the institution of the presidency. Rather than publicly justify his leadership of Congress, Jefferson hid behind an "affected modesty and deference" toward the legislature. Rather than teach the virtues of executive leadership, he misled the country into thinking that Congress did not need presidential direction. Moreover, by relying on legislators to serve as his "trusty lieutenants" he severely compromised the presidency's independence and diminished its responsibility for governance.[52]

The trouble with this argument is that it mistakes the consequences of Jefferson's leadership for its causes. Jefferson's reliance on personal influence did not create a weak presidency vis-à-vis Congress; rather, a weak presidency compelled Jefferson to lead Congress in the indirect manner that he did.[53]

Certainly he could not rely on his constitutional powers to compel legislative compliance with his wishes. Granted, Jefferson never vetoed a bill, but nor did his Federalist predecessor John Adams. And in any event, while useful in thwarting unwanted legislation, the veto was ill-suited to advancing Jefferson's legislative agenda. Perhaps it might be thought that Jefferson should have used the appointment power to secure votes, but had he done so he would have been roundly denounced for corrupting the legislature. Bartering executive patronage for legislative support was, in Republican eyes, among the most odious features of the British political system.[54]

To suggest that Jefferson should have raised high the banner of presidential leadership of Congress is to slight the powerful norms that governed presidential behavior during the early republic. Presidents could propose measures, but they were not supposed to pressure Congress or interfere with legislative judgments. Both Washington and Adams observed that convention as much as Jefferson. Rather than fault Jefferson for failing to behave like a modern president in the mold of Franklin Roosevelt or Lyndon Johnson, we would do better to marvel at the ingenuity with which he adapted to his political environment.

If Jefferson is to be faulted for the difficulties his successors encountered, the culprit is not his hidden-hand leadership style but rather the disastrous embargo policy he pursued in his final year as president. Desperate to avoid getting drawn into the Napoleonic wars engulfing Europe, Jefferson induced Congress to enact legislation that prohibited American ships from sailing to foreign ports. Jefferson hoped that his experiment in "peaceable coercion" would put pressure on the British government to end their policy of seizing American trading ships, but the coercion was felt most acutely by American citizens, particularly those whose livelihood depended on the shipping trade. Jefferson's policy was a complete failure. Immensely unpopular with the American people, it had no effect on British policy, compromised core Republican principles of individual liberty and limited government, revived the Federalist Party in the Northeast, and ruptured the Republican Party.

The embargo's failure was a blow not only to Jefferson and his party, but to executive leadership more broadly. Although Jefferson's public communications gave the impression that the policy was the legislature's responsibility and that he was merely executing the legislative will, in reality Jefferson designed the policy and, together with Madison and Gallatin, drafted the legislation that gave the administration unprecedented coercive powers. Trusting in Jefferson's judgment, congressional Republicans had acquiesced to each of the president's requests for enhanced enforcement authority. The collapse of the embargo in the waning days of the Jefferson presidency led many in Congress to reconsider the wisdom of allowing the president to chart the nation's course.[55]

"Ah, Poor Jemmy" Madison

Even without the embargo fiasco, James Madison would have been hard-pressed to emulate Jefferson's success. Although possessed of a razor-sharp intellect, the reserved Madison lacked Jefferson's silky interpersonal skills and political adroitness. Still more important, Madison could not don Jefferson's mantle as the undisputed party leader. Jefferson was the party's symbolic head; virtually all Republican legislators would have defined themselves as Jeffersonian Republicans, but few if any would have called themselves Madisonian Republicans. At best, Madison could lay claim to being a factional leader beset with a "number of strong enemies and rivals" within the Republican ranks.[56]

Jefferson sought out strong congressional leaders because he could be confident in their loyalty to him and the party. Madison did not have this luxury. For two years Congress drifted without strong leadership, and when a strong leader finally did emerge it was not a Madison loyalist who took command but a rival for party leadership, Speaker of the House Henry Clay. Hitherto, the Speaker of the House had been more of a presiding officer than a floor leader, much like the speaker in the British Parliament, but Clay transformed the speakership into a position of genuine power. And unlike the informal floor leaders of Jefferson's presidency, Clay did not take his cues from the White House. Madison tried to induce Clay to join his administration, but Clay spurned the offer, preferring to direct the nation's affairs from his post as Speaker of the House—a decision that was itself a sign of a resurgent Congress, confident in its own powers and jealous of its prerogatives.[57]

The legislative eclipse of the executive after Jefferson left office was fueled, too, by the emergence of the congressional nominating caucus. As we saw in Chapter 2, the collapse of the Federalist Party at the presidential level meant that the key electoral decision was the selection of the Republican Party nominee, and that decision was in the hands of the congressional Republican caucus. This had two direct effects on presidential power. First, it denied the president an independent popular basis of authority of the kind that Jefferson could claim after his victory over John Adams in 1800. Second, it gave congressional Republicans leverage over a president who wished to be reelected. Indeed, some historians think that Clay pushed Madison into war in 1812—an election year—in part by cautioning the president that if he continued to delay he could not count on legislators supporting his renomination at the upcoming party caucus. The congressional nominating caucus also undermined the president's ability to command the loyalty of department heads, whose presidential prospects also depended on ingratiating themselves with members of Congress. This had a debilitating effect on the president's ability to lead Congress because presidents in the early republic had to rely on department heads to bridge the separation of powers, as the Washington community still frowned upon presidents meddling directly in legislative deliberations.[58]

Consider the case of Robert Smith, Secretary of the Navy under Jefferson and Secretary of State under Madison. Like all of Jefferson's cabinet members, Smith functioned as a legislative liaison, faithfully transmitting Jefferson's program to Congress through the relevant committees. But when Madison asked Smith to contact key members of

Congress, he refused, insisting that such interference with the legislative process would be improper. An exasperated Madison protested that "the conveniency of facilitating business in that way was so obvious that it had been practiced under every past administration." Unable to enlist Smith's cooperation, Madison fired him. That relieved Madison of a particularly nettlesome cabinet member but did not solve the fundamental structural problem, which helps to explain why Madison went through two secretaries of state, three secretaries of the navy, four secretaries of the treasury, and four secretaries of war during his eight years. In contrast, Jefferson had no turnover in these same four departments.[59]

The Audacity of James Monroe

Monroe was a more capable and forceful administrator than Madison, but he had at least as much difficulty inducing his department heads to do his bidding rather than collude with Congress. For much of Monroe's presidency, particularly in his second term, his treasury secretary (William Crawford), secretary of state (Adams), and secretary of war (John Calhoun) jockeyed relentlessly to line up the congressional support they would need to secure the Republican presidential nomination. The result, Adams lamented, was "a thousand corrupt cabals between the members of Congress and the heads of the Departments." The problem during this period, in short, was not a lack of communication between the legislative and executive branches, but rather that the close bonds forged between department heads and legislative factions more often frustrated than furthered the president's legislative program.[60]

Unlike Jefferson, Monroe could not lean on party loyalty or the specter of monarchical Federalism to rally Republicans in Congress. With the old party lines now blurred, legislative politics became structured largely by personal allegiances and factions, and no factional leader, including Clay, commanded anything approaching a legislative majority. Monroe's strategy was to lead Congress by drawing into his cabinet factional leaders who could bring with them the support of their legislative allies, a strategy that depended on Monroe being able to forge a policy consensus within his cabinet. Sometimes this worked, as when he crafted a cabinet consensus that enabled him to defeat Clay's effort to censure General Andrew Jackson for exceeding his orders during the Seminole War. But the presidential ambitions of his department heads more often frustrated Monroe's best efforts to find a consensus—"Crawford's opinion," Adams groused in 1819, "is becoming whatever is not mine"—and absent that consensus, Monroe's program stood little chance in Congress.[61]

The development of standing committees compounded the difficulty of forging cabinet unity and influencing Congress. By the end of Monroe's presidency the House of Representatives possessed almost three times the number of standing committees it had at the end of Jefferson's presidency, including new standing committees on expenditures, one for each of the five executive departments. More committees in a larger House (213 members in 1824 as compared to 142 in 1808) allowed for greater specialization, which in turn endowed Congress with greater policy expertise while also increasing the number of possible veto points within the legislative process. More specialized committees also enabled Congress to keep a closer watch on the executive departments' daily activities—much closer than one man devoid of any staff could possibly do. Not surprisingly, department heads decided that "keeping in the good graces of their superintending congressional committees [took] priority over keeping in the good graces of the President."[62]

Monroe was not a passive president. Nor was he, as he is sometimes portrayed, a true believer in "legislative supremacy."[63] He threatened to veto legislation he did not like, something Jefferson never did.[64] He worked behind the scenes—in vintage hidden-hand style—to secure support for the Missouri Compromise.[65] He urged Congress to repeal all internal taxes, which Congress did with the same enthusiasm as when Jefferson proposed the idea in 1801. He wrote annual messages that were longer than any of his predecessors' because he felt it his duty to provide legislators the reasons behind his recommendations. In Britain, he explained to Adams, the executive's speech at the opening of Parliament could afford to consist only of "short allusions to the principal topics of public affairs, and in general terms . . . because if the Government was attacked the Ministers were in Parliament to defend themselves." Under the American system, in contrast, Monroe said, presidents needed to explain themselves fully in their messages because they had "no one in the legislature to support them, except members who occasionally appear as volunteers."[66]

The fundamental problem for Monroe, as it had been for Jefferson and Madison, was that members of Congress still regarded presidential influence as suspect. If Monroe had been in any doubt about this, Speaker Clay gave the president a refresher course after Monroe dared to venture the opinion in his first annual message that Congress lacked the constitutional power to build roads and canals. Madison's veto of an internal improvements bill at the end of the previous congressional session had come as an unwelcome shock to many legislators—"not even an earthquake that should have swallowed up one half of this city could have excited more surprise," said Clay—and Monroe felt that it would be better for the president and Congress if legislators were informed from the outset that his "settled conviction" on the subject would prevent him from signing similar legislation. Freely acknowledging the tremendous value to the nation of having good roads and canals, Monroe recommended that Congress should pass a constitutional amendment granting the federal government the authority to finance such improvements.[67]

Clay waxed indignant at Monroe's audacity. How dare the president "tell . . . us what we may or may not do," he thundered. For the president to express an opinion to Congress prior to passage of the legislation, Clay argued, was "irregular and unconstitutional." It "inverted the order of legislation, by beginning where it should end." A president was at liberty to give his opinion upon vetoing a bill, but to offer it before that point prevented each house of Congress from giving its "free and unbiased consideration" to a measure. The president, in short, had no business intervening in the legislative process until after Congress had finished its work.[68]

Things only got worse for Monroe in his second term. His virtually unanimous reelection had no effect on his legislative influence. Just days after Monroe's second inaugural address, Clay announced that the president "had not the slightest influence in

Congress." A similar judgment was rendered by New York senator Rufus King, who noted that despite Monroe's resounding reelection "the plans or measures of Government are without friends in Congress; by which I mean no one offers himself to explain or to support those measures which are supposed to have the recommendations and favor of the Executive." Whereas Clay reveled in the president's lack of influence, King—who had served as a senator during Washington's presidency and had been among the leading advocates of a strong presidency at the Constitutional Convention—was deeply concerned by this development.[69]

"Deserted by All": The Presidency of John Quincy Adams

John Quincy Adams fully shared King's concerns. From the outset of Monroe's presidency, Adams had sounded the alarm about "Clay's project" of attempting "to control or overthrow the Executive by swaying the House of Representatives." But the problem went beyond Clay. "Every day," Adams complained, he was "witnessing ... a perpetual struggle in both Houses of Congress to control the Executive—to make it dependent upon and subservient to them." When Adams became president he was determined to stamp presidential authority onto the political system—and with Clay safely ensconced as his secretary of state he at least would not have to contend with Clay railing against executive influence.[70]

In his first annual message, Adams recommended that Congress embark on an ambitious program of internal improvements as well as establish an interior department, a naval academy, a national university, a federal astronomical observatory, a bankruptcy law, a uniform national militia law, and a uniform system of weights and measures. Adams's legislative agenda was bold, but though he hoped to make a daring show of presidential leadership he ended up only exposing presidential weakness. Legislators received Adams's message with a mixture of scorn and disdain. Virtually nothing that Adams proposed was passed, or even voted upon, by Congress. Things went from bad to worse after the midterm elections, when both houses fell into the hands of the president's avowed enemies. From that point on, as political scientist Wilfred Binkley put it, "Congress spent its energy in grand inquest into the conduct of the Executive" and Adams spent his by "reigning not ruling and deserted by all." The presidency seemed to have reached the nadir of its influence.[71]

Just how low was dramatized by the so-called "Tariff of Abominations," a transparent political effort by Adams's congressional opponents to pick up votes for Andrew Jackson in crucial swing states. With Adams a nonfactor, Jackson's legislative allies passed a "ghastly, lopsided, unequal tariff bill" that slighted the interests of southern and New England states—which could be counted on to vote for Jackson and Adams respectively—while imposing heavy duties that benefitted key constituencies in competitive states such as New York (wool farmers), Pennsylvania (iron makers), and Kentucky (hemp growers). If ever there was a case for a presidential veto, this legislative monstrosity was it. Not only was the bill calculated to hurt the president politically, but it was universally regarded as bad public policy. Yet at no point did Adams even threaten to veto the legislation. In fact, Adams never vetoed any legislation during his four years as president, even though Congress was firmly in control of his political enemies during his final two years.[72]

The Veto: Whig Theory and Democratic Practice

That John Quincy Adams vetoed no bills is less surprising than it might at first appear. His father John Adams, though a proponent of an absolute veto at the time of the Constitution's framing, never vetoed a bill either. Neither did Jefferson. Even Monroe used the veto only once, for an internal improvements measure that he deemed unconstitutional. Of the early presidents, only Madison used the veto with any frequency, striking down legislation on seven occasions. Although there were no hard-and-fast rules in the early republic about when it was proper to veto legislation, presidents clearly regarded the veto as a power to be exercised "with great reserve."[73]

The other notable feature of the veto in the early republic is how rarely it became the focus of controversy. Several of Madison's vetoes were strongly criticized, particularly his veto of the national bank and his striking down of an internal improvements measure, but Madison's critics rarely if ever focused their objections on the veto power itself. Their objections instead were with the merits of Madison's policy positions. Only Monroe's first annual message—in which, recall, the president forewarned Congress that he could not in good conscience sign internal improvements legislation that he regarded as unconstitutional—provoked any significant, albeit short-lived, effort to restrict the veto power. Not until Andrew Jackson's presidency did the veto power become a source of sustained conflict between the president and Congress and between the political parties.[74]

Andrew Jackson v. Henry Clay

In the course of three days during his second year as president, Jackson vetoed four bills, more than the combined total during the 32 years served by Washington, Adams, Jefferson, Monroe, and Adams. The most controversial of the four was his veto of the Maysville bill, which would have extended a federal road 60 miles through Clay's home state of Kentucky. Unlike Monroe and Madison, whose vetoes of internal improvement legislation had rested solely on constitutional objections, Jackson objected on policy grounds as well. The Maysville bill, Jackson argued, was unacceptable because it would lead to either higher taxes or a larger national debt, neither of which Jackson was willing to accept for federal projects of a "purely local character."[75]

Jackson's veto enraged Clay. As Clay saw it, the central issue transcended the constitutional and policy arguments that had swirled around internal improvements legislation during the previous two decades. The larger problem was Jackson's use of executive power. Clay proposed a constitutional amendment to enable a simple majority in Congress to override an executive veto. Clay was certain that political hay could be made out of Jackson's veto in states in which internal improvements were popular, but he told Daniel Webster that was "a collateral consideration." The main focus of the anti-Jackson forces should be in "contending against a principle which wears a monarchical aspect."[76]

Jackson's veto of the national bank in July 1832 led Clay to escalate his assault upon the veto power. On the floor of the Senate, Clay charged that this "extraordinary power" could only be safely employed if it was used sparingly, reserved for those rare cases "of precipitate legislation, in unguarded moments." To employ the veto in "ordinary cases" of political disagreement, as Jackson was doing, was "totally irreconcilable" with republican government. Not only did the veto enable "one man to overrule" a "deliberatively expressed" legislative judgment, it also distorted that legislative judgment because legislators were compelled to anticipate what a president would or would not veto. The veto, Clay reminded his fellow senators, had been "borrowed from a prerogative of the British King," but whereas in England the veto had "grown obsolete," in the United States Jackson was making it an instrument of executive usurpation.[77]

Clay spoke not only as a United States senator defending legislative prerogatives, but also as the National Republican presidential nominee kicking off his 1832 campaign against "King Andrew." The private phase of that campaign had begun earlier in the year when Clay pressured the bank's president Nicholas Biddle to apply for recharter immediately, even though the bank's charter was not due to expire until 1836. Clay told Biddle that Jackson would not dare to veto the bank before the election, but in truth Clay was counting on Jackson's veto. Without it, Clay felt he had no chance of defeating the popular president. Clay hoped that a bank veto would fracture the Jacksonian coalition—one-third of Jackson's supporters in Congress had voted for recharter—and enable Clay to recast the narrative of the presidential election as a contest between the people and their representatives on the one side and the tyrannical King Andrew on the other.[78]

Clay's gambit failed in its immediate objective of unseating Jackson, in part because Jackson's veto message provided a compelling counter-narrative that cast the president as the people's champion in a battle against the "money power." But Clay did succeed in giving the disparate anti-Jackson forces a unifying credo as well as a new name: the Whigs. Those who stood firm against executive encroachment, Clay announced in 1834, were the "the whigs of the present day." As far back as England's Glorious Revolution of 1688, the Whigs had been the defenders of representative government, and the sworn enemies of "royal executive power." In Clay's eyes, Jackson was no man of the people; rather he and his supporters were latter-day Tories, presenting "boundless" claims for executive power while making the president's "sole will the governing power."[79]

Jackson's followers dismissed Clay's historical analogy. In their view, Whigs were merely latter-day Federalists. But the division between Clay's Whigs and Jackson's Democrats was not simply a replay of the old division between Hamilton's Federalists and Jefferson's Republicans. No longer was there a party like the Federalists that advocated a strong government coupled with a strong executive. Nor was there a party like the Republicans that joined fear of government power with distrust of executive power. Instead there were partisans who described themselves as Whigs and supported a weak executive at the head of a relatively active federal government, and partisans who labeled themselves Democrats and defended a strong president and a limited central government.

The Democratic vision was less paradoxical than it might at first appear, for the instrument of presidential power that Jacksonians were most intent on defending was the negative power of the veto. Jackson's supporters insisted that the veto was necessary to

BORN TO COMMAND.

KING ANDREW THE FIRST.

A famous drawing from the 1832 campaign that condemns President Andrew Jackson for his use of the veto power to thwart the will of Congress. Underneath the picture was posed the question: "Shall he reign over us, or shall the People Rule?"

Courtesy: Library of Congress, Prints and Photographs Division, LC-DIG-ppmsca-15771 DLC.

curb government power and to check the wasteful expenditures produced by the corrupting mix of public and private power in the halls of Congress. Too often, as Jackson told Congress in his second annual message, "combinations of small minorities" in the legislature entered into corrupt arrangements—known then and now as "logrolling"—that enabled passage of measures "which, resting solely on their own merits, could never be carried." Originally designed by the Federalists as a check upon impulsive majorities, the executive veto was refashioned by Jackson into the people's most potent weapon in the battle against special interests.[80]

William Henry Harrison Preaches the Whig Philosophy

So long as Democrats controlled the presidency, there was no contradiction between the Whigs' commitment to a weak president and a strong government. But what would happen to their anti-executive commitments if the Whigs were to capture the presidency, as they finally did in 1840 when William Henry Harrison defeated incumbent Martin Van Buren? Harrison's inaugural address provided an answer: executive power would be rolled back and the nation's slide toward "a virtual monarchy" arrested. Part of the problem Harrison attributed to a defect in the Constitution, specifically the provision allowing the president to be reelected. Harrison pledged to do his bit to remedy this constitutional shortcoming by serving only one term. But the larger problem, Harrison explained, stemmed from the Democrats' departure from the original understandings of the Constitution.[81]

Harrison took particular exception to the Jacksonian notion that the president was a more authentic representative of the people than was Congress. It was "preposterous," Harrison declared, to suppose that the framers could have entertained the notion "that the President, placed at the capital, in the center of the country, could better understand the wants and wishes of the people than their own immediate representatives, who spend a part of every year among them, living with them, often laboring with them, and bound to them by the triple tie of interest, duty, and affection." The veto power, Harrison reasoned, must therefore never be used to "assist or control Congress . . . in its ordinary legislation." Equally pernicious, in Harrison's view, was the idea that the president should be "a part of the legislative power." Although the Constitution made it the president's duty to communicate information and recommend measures to Congress, that clause "was not intended to make him the source in legislation." It was particularly important that the executive "should never be looked to for schemes of finance." Lawmaking, Harrison preached, should be left to the lawmakers.

Unfortunately, the nation was denied the opportunity to find out if President Harrison would practice what he professed. Less than one month after delivering the longest inaugural address in American history—nearly two hours, in a snowstorm no less—Harrison died of pneumonia, making John Tyler president.

John Tyler's "Abusive Exercise" of the Veto

Tyler was a Whig in name only. He had supported Jackson in 1828 and 1832, and only left the Democratic fold after becoming disenchanted with Jackson's forceful response to

South Carolina's flirtation with nullification. Although Tyler switched parties, he never recanted his longstanding view that Clay's "American System" of a national bank, protective tariffs, and federal internal improvements was unconstitutional. Nor, it turned out, did he share the Whig view of legislative supremacy articulated by Harrison.[82]

Tyler immediately inserted himself into the legislative process by informing Congress of which parts of the Whig legislative agenda he would accept and which parts he would be compelled to veto. Tariffs he was willing to support, but only if they did not exceed 20 percent. And he would not accede to the establishment of a national bank if he deemed it unconstitutional. Under the leadership of Clay, congressional Whigs were in no mood to take dictation from a president who owed his position to mere accident, and they pushed through a bank bill that made only minor concessions to Tyler. When "His Accidency" followed through on his veto threat, Clay tried again with a compromise measure that seemed to meet Tyler's constitutional objections by forbidding the bank from establishing local branches without a state's consent. As a further concession to Tyler, the Whigs renamed the national bank a "fiscal corporation." However, the changes made no difference to Tyler, who vetoed the Fiscal Corporation bill just as he had the Fiscal Bank bill.[83]

Tyler's second veto left him, quite literally, a man without a party. Within 48 hours of the second veto, every member of Tyler's cabinet but one had resigned. A few days later a caucus of congressional Whigs voted to expel the president from the party. After Tyler vetoed tariff legislation in the next session of Congress, some Whigs began to entertain ideas of expelling Tyler from the presidency. "The more Vetoes the better," Clay counseled. "The inevitable tendency of events is to impeachment." In January 1843, Virginia's representative John Minor Botts formally moved to impeach Tyler for "an arbitrary, despotic and corrupt abuse of the veto power." Almost two-thirds of House Whigs voted in favor of referring Botts's impeachment resolution to committee, though that was not nearly enough to overcome the united opposition of Democrats.[84]

The Whigs did not have the votes to drive Tyler out of office but they continued to hammer away at the president for his "abusive exercise" of the veto power. After Tyler vetoed a second tariff bill in August 1842, the House took the unusual step of referring Tyler's veto message to a select committee. Chaired by ex-president John Quincy Adams and composed almost entirely of Whigs hostile to Tyler, the committee issued a report that excoriated Tyler for having perverted the proper relationship between legislature and president. Under the Constitution, the committee declared, the executive was supposed to be "dependent upon and responsible to" the legislature. Indeed, prior to Jackson's presidency, "all reference, in either House of Congress, to the opinions or wishes of the President, relating to any subject in deliberation before them, was regarded as an outrage upon the rights of the deliberative body." Restoring the original constitutional relationship between president and Congress, the committee argued, required changing the Constitution so that a majority of Congress could override the president's veto.[85]

This idea was not new. Clay had first floated the idea after Jackson's Maysville veto and the same amendment was introduced on three occasions in Jackson's second term and once during Van Buren's presidency. The amendment recommended by Adams's House committee carried 98–90, far shy of the two-thirds required for a constitutional amendment to move forward, but nonetheless a dramatic statement of the depth of Whig opposition to the veto power.[86]

Here to Stay: The Veto Vindicated

The Whigs' relentless criticism only seemed to heighten Democratic appreciation of the veto. Every Democratic Party platform between 1844 and 1856 included a vigorous defense of the veto power. The genius of the veto, as Democratic senator and future president James Buchanan expressed it, was that it was merely the power "to arrest hasty and inconsiderate changes, until the voice of the people, who are alike the masters of Senators, Representatives and President, shall be heard." There was thus nothing tyrannical or monarchical about its use. Its exercise only suspended government action until, in the words of the 1844 platform, "the judgment of the people can be obtained." Even when being wielded by a president who had not been elected, the veto was thus an essential part of popular rule.[87]

With Democrats united in their support of the veto, the Whigs could never come close to securing a constitutional amendment to rein in the veto. But Congress was hardly as defenseless as the Whigs claimed. For starters, Congress was learning to avoid vetoes by tacking objectionable and sometimes unrelated provisions onto essential appropriations measures. In 1848, for instance, Congress faced a veto threat from President James Polk over a bill to appropriate $50,000 to dredge the Savannah River, precisely the sort of internal improvement measure that Polk had vetoed twice before. In Polk's view, such improvements were a state, not a federal, responsibility. Yet Polk felt compelled to swallow his objections and sign the bill after Congress added it onto an appropriations bill that provided essential funding for civil and diplomatic officers.[88]

Moreover, the Constitution's two-thirds override threshold proved less insurmountable than Whigs initially feared. The Whigs' belief that the two-thirds override was essentially equivalent to an absolute veto was grounded in experience. Congress had failed to override any of the 18 presidential vetoes between 1787 and 1844—and that doesn't count the 14 pocket vetoes that Congress had no chance to override. (The president exercises a pocket veto by taking no action on a bill passed within ten days of Congress's adjournment.) Tyler's final veto, in February 1845, was Congress's first successful veto override. After that, however, veto overrides became more common. Congress overrode five of the nine bills that Democrat Franklin Pierce (1853–1857) vetoed, and 15 of the 21 bills vetoed by Andrew Johnson (1865–1869). Clearly the veto power fell well short of the dictatorial power that Whigs imagined it to be.

Yet the Whigs were not wrong to sound the alarm. American presidents have vetoed more than 2,500 bills and Congress has mustered the votes needed to override only 110 times. Even if one excludes from that total the more than 1,000 pocket vetoes, the president's will has been upheld 93 percent of the time. If one also excludes vetoes of private bills[89]—which constitute close to two-thirds of the total number of vetoes—the president's winning percentage remains an impressive 80 percent. But perhaps that is the way the founders would have wanted it.[90]

Certainly, Whigs who argued that the framers intended the veto to be limited to those circumstances in which the president judged a bill to be unconstitutional or an encroachment on presidential power were wrong. Virtually all the framers agreed that the veto's purpose was to check not just unconstitutional but also hastily considered or "unjust and pernicious laws." Washington and Madison, both of whom were at the Constitutional Convention, vetoed bills without lodging constitutional objections or expressing concerns about encroachment on executive power. Nonetheless, the restraint of each of the first six American presidents—with the possible exception of Madison—seems closer in spirit to the Whig philosophy than the Democratic practice.[91]

Whatever its merits, the Whig reading of the proper scope of the veto power expired with the party's demise in the 1850s. The last Whig presidents—Zachary Taylor and Millard Fillmore—were also the last United States presidents to refrain from vetoing legislation. After the Civil War, presidential vetoes became commonplace, and fundamental debate over the veto power faded away as Americans of all political stripes came to accept the veto as a legitimate weapon in the presidential arsenal. Presidential vetoes were still capable of igniting legislative wrath, but legislators no longer questioned the president's authority to issue a veto, even when, as during Grover Cleveland's first term, the president struck down an average of more than one hundred bills a year.[92]

ABRAHAM LINCOLN: WHIG IN THE WHITE HOUSE?

Although the Whigs lost the argument over the veto power, their suspicion of executive influence in the legislative process continued to color American politics long after the party's demise. The Whig Party expired in the 1850s, rent asunder by the conflict over slavery, and in its place emerged the Republican Party, which was dedicated to halting the spread of slavery. Anti-slavery Democrats—men such as Ohio's Salmon Chase, Connecticut's Gideon Welles, and Massachusetts' Ben Butler—joined the fledgling Republican Party, but most Republicans were former Whigs, including the first Republican president, Abraham Lincoln. In the mid-1850s, Lincoln and other ex-Whigs began to call themselves Republicans, but they did not cease to think like Whigs.

As a congressman during Polk's presidency, Lincoln had adhered to the orthodox Whig understanding of the executive's place in the legislative process. Lincoln vigorously defended Zachary Taylor's pledge to defer to Congress should he be elected in 1848. To "transfer" legislative power to the president, Lincoln argued, would be "to take it from those who understand, with minuteness, the interests of the people, and give it to one who does not, and cannot so well understand it." En route to Washington, DC, thirteen years later, president-elect Lincoln told a gathering in Pittsburgh that his "political education" strongly inclined him to the view that "as a rule" it was "better that congress should originate, as well as perfect its measures" without interference from the president.[93]

Lincoln's Whiggish deference to Congress tends to get overlooked in the rush to celebrate our sixteenth president's greatness. Yet, as David Donald pointed out in his seminal essay "A Whig in the White House," Lincoln involved himself little in the making of the nation's domestic policies. He largely left economic policy to Congress and his secretary of the treasury, Salmon Chase. He watched passively as Congress voted for "tariff increase after increase," pushing rates to unprecedented levels. He did little but affix his signature to the landmark pieces of legislation that created land-grant colleges and authorized the construction of a railroad from the Missouri River to the Pacific Ocean.[94]

On extraordinary occasions, Lincoln did exert influence on economic legislation that he deemed vital to the war effort. For instance, when Congress balked at enacting Chase's plan to create a centralized national banking system, Lincoln sent both houses of Congress a sharply worded message that urged the legislation's prompt passage. Lincoln's breach of his customary Whiggish decorum was sufficiently irksome to the Republican-controlled Senate that the legislature refused to have the message printed. Undeterred, Lincoln discreetly dispatched his private secretary William O. Stoddard to meet with two undecided senators and communicate to them the president's "deeply" held views on the bill. Aware that he was treading on perilous ground, Stoddard assured the senators that the president "is always cautious, and rightly so, about saying or doing anything which can be construed as Executive interference with the independence of the legislature." The pressure paid off, however, and Lincoln secured the couple votes he needed to ensure the measure squeaked through the Senate.[95]

A fundamental precept of Lincoln's Whiggish "political education" had been that the president should exercise the veto power sparingly, if at all. As president, Lincoln generally kept faith with this precept; he typically refrained from vetoing legislation or from threatening a veto to get a bill he preferred. The exception that proves the rule was Lincoln's pocket veto of the Wade–Davis bill, an effort by Republicans in Congress to dictate the terms on which Confederate states should be reintegrated into the Union.[96]

Eager to encourage southern states to lay down their arms, Lincoln had announced a plan in December 1863 by which southern states could establish new state governments and be entitled to representation in Washington if 10 percent of the number of white male citizens who had voted in 1860 pledged their loyalty to the Union and renounced slavery. The Wade–Davis bill, passed in the summer of 1864 with virtually unanimous Republican backing, would have increased the requirement to 50 percent and also barred any individual who had supported the rebellion from participating in the formation of the government. By placing the threshold so high, Congress's plan ensured that Reconstruction of Confederate states would not commence until after the Confederacy was defeated. Lincoln's more lenient Ten Percent Plan, in contrast, was designed to induce states—or factions within a state—to renounce the Confederacy and thus bring the war to a speedier end.[97]

Lincoln viewed his pocket veto of the Wade–Davis bill as in keeping with long-established Whig doctrine, which acknowledged that the president could veto legislation, as Zachary Taylor put it in his first annual message, to "defend the executive against encroachments of the legislative power." In Lincoln's view, so long as the nation was at war, Reconstruction was the responsibility of the commander in chief. Since the Wade–Davis plan undermined a central piece of his strategy for winning the war, Lincoln believed that he was not interfering with legislative powers but defending the executive against legislative encroachment.[98]

Lincoln's pocket veto nonetheless invited the fury of the bill's primary sponsors, Senator Benjamin Wade and Representative Henry Winter Davis, both former Whigs.

They published a manifesto—known as the Wade–Davis Manifesto—assailing Lincoln for "grave Executive usurpation." In hyperbole typical of the entire manifesto, Wade and Davis insisted that "a more studied outrage on the legislative authority of the people has never been perpetrated." Lincoln, they lectured, "must confine himself to his executive duties—to obey and execute, not make the laws." The president's job was to suppress the rebellion; the "political reorganization" of the South was the job of Congress.

If being a Whig in the White House required leaving Reconstruction to Congress then Lincoln was unwilling to play the part, certainly not while the Civil War continued. When Congress reconvened in December 1864, Lincoln vowed to veto any legislation that did not recognize the legitimacy of the new government in Louisiana, which had followed Lincoln's Ten Percent Plan. The Republican-controlled Congress adjourned without passing new legislation, leaving Reconstruction firmly in Lincoln's hands.[99]

After his emphatic reelection in November 1864, Lincoln became bolder about departing from Whig orthodoxy, particularly on the matter of a constitutional amendment to abolish slavery. When Lincoln had first broached the idea in his 1862 annual message, he had seemed almost apologetic for his intrusion, pleading with members not to see "any undue earnestness" on his part as a sign of "want of respect" for members of Congress, many of whom, he allowed, had far "more experience than [he did] in the conduct of public affairs." When Congress took up the amendment in the summer of 1864, Lincoln reiterated his support, but he did little to influence legislative deliberations and watched helplessly as House Democrats defeated the amendment.[100]

After the November elections, however, Lincoln acted more in the mold of the Whigs' old nemesis Andrew Jackson than Lincoln's lifelong political idol Henry Clay. Just as Jackson made the 1832 election a referendum on his bank veto, so Lincoln made the 1864 election a referendum on the abolition of slavery. As a young congressman in 1848, Lincoln had parroted the Whig notion that "Presidential elections, and the legislation of the country [should be] distinct matters; so that the people can elect [as president] whom they please, and afterwards, legislate just as they please, without any hindrance." But now, in his fourth annual message in December 1864, Lincoln insisted that Congress should heed the people's verdict in the election: "It is the voice of the people now, for the first time, heard upon the question."[101]

Lincoln supplemented public pressure with private meetings with individual House members he thought could be persuaded to change their vote. For example, Lincoln made a personal appeal to Congressman James Rollins, who represented the most pro-slavery district in Missouri and was himself a large slave owner. Like Lincoln, Rollins was Kentucky-born and a former Whig, and Lincoln traded on their shared background as "old Whigs" and "followers of that great statesman, Henry Clay" to make his pitch. Assuring Rollins that passage of the amendment was the surest way "to bring the war to a speedy close," Lincoln secured not only his vote but also a commitment from Rollins to talk up the amendment with others in the Missouri delegation.[102]

In the end, through a deft combination of public exhortation, personal persuasion, and backroom deals, Lincoln managed to secure the votes necessary for the amendment's passage. Before the year was out, the Thirteenth Amendment had been ratified by the requisite three-fourths of the states, making it the nation's first constitutional amendment in more than 60 years.[103]

In securing the Thirteenth Amendment, Lincoln's behavior had been anything but Whiggish. However, a constitutional amendment was no ordinary piece of legislation. Moreover, Lincoln was fresh from a resounding triumph over General George McClellan after having waged a campaign centered on the amendment. And Lincoln was still a war president, and able to lean upon his role as commander in chief in making the argument that the amendment was necessary to bring about a quick end to the war. What would happen, however, when the war came to an end, when there was no mandate to invoke, and when attention reverted to ordinary legislation? After Robert E. Lee's surrender, followed a week later by Lincoln's assassination, the nation would find out the answer.

CLAY'S REVENGE: AN ERA OF LEGISLATIVE SUPREMACY

Andrew Johnson had been Lincoln's running mate in 1864, but he was also a lifelong Democrat and fervent admirer of his fellow Tennessean Andrew Jackson. Johnson's "political education" was as Jacksonian as Lincoln's was Whiggish. Johnson instinctively employed Jacksonian rhetoric, styling himself "the Tribune of the people," even though nobody had voted for him for president. Unlike Lincoln, who was always publicly respectful of Congress, Johnson openly denigrated the legislature. Oppression, Johnson insisted, "can be exercised by many more rigorously, more vigorously, and more tyrannically, than by one." And Johnson did not hesitate to use the veto, rejecting more bills in one term than the previous six presidents combined.[104]

No president who wished to shape the post-war Reconstruction of the South could have avoided clashing with Congress, not even one as popular and as attuned to legislative sensibilities as Lincoln. But Johnson's castigation of Congress and his frequent direct appeals to the people induced a ferocious reaffirmation of Whig dogma by congressional Republicans. Leading the way was Thaddeus Stevens, an ex-Whig for whom it was an article of faith that under the Constitution not "one particle of legislative power" rested with the president. The people were indeed the sovereign masters, but according to Stevens they "speak through Congress" alone. Johnson was the people's "servant," and "as Congress shall order he must obey." When Johnson refused to change his ways, Stevens and his fellow House Republicans impeached him, and they came within one Senate vote of removing him.[105]

Less than a week after Johnson's acquittal, the Republican Party nominated as their presidential candidate Ulysses S. Grant, a 46-year-old general who had never before held elected office. In accepting the nomination, Grant described the president as a "purely administrative officer," thereby signaling to Republicans that they could expect him to be far more deferential toward Congress than Johnson was.[106] But, contrary to what historians have frequently implied, Grant was not a latter-day Whig—his first presidential vote was actually cast for Democrat James Buchanan in 1856.[107] In his inaugural address, Grant let it be known that he would veto any measure he opposed if he thought it advisable. Grant was as good as his word, vetoing 93 bills during his two terms, more than his 17 predecessors combined.[108]

Grant also pledged that "on all leading questions agitating the public mind" he would "always express [his] views to Congress." The problem for Grant was that Congress routinely disregarded his recommendations. This was partly because legislators viewed him as a political neophyte, an impression the fumbling Grant did little to dispel. But it was also because congressional Republicans, particularly in the Senate, continued to see the presidency through the prism of Whig ideology. Typical was the view expressed by Ohio's John Sherman, a Whig turned Republican who served as chairman of the Senate Finance Committee throughout Grant's tenure. "The executive department of a republic like ours," Sherman declared, "should be subordinate to the legislative department. The President should obey and enforce the laws, leaving to the people the duty of correcting any errors committed to their representatives in Congress."[109]

Even had Grant been a more skilled politician and possessed more legislative experience, he would still have found influencing, let alone leading, Congress a tall order. Veteran Massachusetts legislator George Frisbie Hoar, who served in Congress from 1869 to 1904, put his finger on the problem that confronted not only Grant but his immediate successors as well:

> The most eminent Senators ... would have received as a personal affront a private message from the White House expressing a desire that they should adopt any course in the discharge of their legislative duties that they did not approve. If they visited the White House, it was to give, not to receive advice.

Even patronage, that dread tool of executive influence, had become an instrument more of legislative than executive power, as Grant himself acknowledged shortly after leaving office. "The President," he conceded, "very rarely appoints, he merely registers the appointments of members of Congress."[110]

By the end of Grant's administration it seemed obvious to many observers, including a precocious Princeton undergraduate by the name of Woodrow Wilson, that Congress was "the ruling body of the nation" and the president "merely the executor of the sovereign legislative will." The Whigs had lost the argument over the veto power and their party had long since expired, but their vision of legislative supremacy and executive subordination had proven far more enduring. Somewhere, surely, Henry Clay was smiling.[111]

THE NEW SCHOOL OF EXECUTIVE LEADERSHIP

The heavily whiskered presidents of the late nineteenth century are little remembered and much maligned, but few, if any, were actually as docile as Wilson's judgment suggested or Whig doctrine demanded. Indeed, during the very months that Wilson was penning his senior thesis, President Rutherford Hayes was engaged in a dramatic showdown with the Democratic Congress over civil rights legislation that authorized the government to use federal troops and marshals at polling places to protect the voting rights of blacks. Democrats attached the law's repeal as a rider to vital appropriations legislation in an effort to force Hayes to acquiesce to their wishes. Bridling at Congress's attempt at "coercive dictation," Hayes vetoed the appropriations, daring Congress to shut the government down. Democrats tried the same basic ploy three more times, but each time Hayes refused to sign the legislation and each time congressional Republicans rallied around the president to sustain his veto. Eventually, Congress backed down and Hayes got his way.[112]

Grover Cleveland: Cultivating the "Habit of Independent Initiative"

Even less pliable was Grover Cleveland, the only Democrat to be elected president in the 50 years between the onset of the Civil War and the election of Woodrow Wilson in 1912. Cleveland was a Whig's worst nightmare. No president before or since has wielded the veto more freely. On average, Cleveland vetoed 73 bills a year. Admittedly, more than 80 percent of Cleveland's vetoes struck down private bills, typically bills granting pensions to disabled veterans of the Union army, but even excluding these Cleveland still vetoed more than one hundred bills.[113]

During his second term, Cleveland was even less inclined to follow the legislative will. Cleveland returned to office in 1893, after a four-year hiatus, just as the nation was becoming enveloped in financial panic. Stocks plunged, banks closed, businesses failed, and unemployment climbed. Cleveland believed that the chief culprit was the Sherman Silver Purchase Act of 1890, which, by requiring the government to purchase silver, had drained the Treasury's gold reserves. Cleveland called a special session of Congress and demanded the act's immediate repeal. Although the Democrats had a majority in both the House and the Senate, the silver issue divided the party down the middle. Cleveland played hardball, letting it be known that he would ignore patronage requests from any Democratic legislator who failed to back repeal. Cleveland's close ally William L. Wilson shepherded the measure through the House, but repeal was derailed in the Senate by a filibuster. When Democratic senators tried to craft a compromise measure that would break the deadlock, the president repudiated their handiwork and vowed to make no patronage appointments until the Senate passed his original repeal bill. The Senate caved, passing the repeal in exactly the form that Cleveland had requested. The president's will had prevailed.[114]

Although repeal failed to reverse the economic downturn and ruptured the Democratic Party, Cleveland's resolute leadership captured the imagination of Woodrow Wilson, now a professor of political science at Princeton University. In an essay penned for the *Atlantic Monthly* in 1897, Wilson hailed Cleveland for having "refreshed our notion of an American chief magistrate." Wilson acknowledged that at first Cleveland had labored under a traditional view of his office as "essentially executive," with the exception of his liberal use of the veto power. But Cleveland was unwilling to "stand by and see the policy of the country hopelessly adrift," and so, almost "in spite of himself," abandoned "his role of simple executive" and his posture as "a power standing aloof from Congress," and became instead a legislative "leader and master." What Wilson admired about Cleveland was not the president's hundreds of vetoes, but rather that he had developed "the habit of independent initiative in ... legislative policy." Under Cleveland's leadership, Wilson marveled, "power had somehow gone the length of the avenue, and seemed lodged in one man."[115]

Why would Wilson, a devout Democrat, celebrate a president who, in having "forced the fight" on the silver issue, fractured his party and directly contributed to the Republican rout in 1896? Wilson acknowledged that Cleveland was something of a blunt instrument—a "direct, fearless, somewhat unsophisticated man of action"—but believed that was precisely the sort of leadership needed to smash the entrenched power of party bosses. The problem with American politics, in Wilson's view, was that parties were not held together by shared political principles but were instead loosely bound congeries of local and state interests that only pulled together every four years for the purpose of winning presidential elections and dividing the spoils. Cleveland's leadership thrilled Wilson because Cleveland had decided that "if the party would not act with him, he must act for it," even if it meant forcing party leaders, "for their own good," to forsake short-term political advantage. Wilson saw Cleveland as a heroic figure because, as political scientist Daniel Stid explains, he had "cleared the way for the rise of a new, more principled party."[116]

Once principled parties were in place, Wilson intimated, Cleveland's style of leadership would no longer be necessary or even desirable. Cleveland led his party and Congress "through mastery [rather] than through persuasion" because party politicians who cared only about the spoils of office were not amenable to rational persuasion. Once political parties had been remade, then presidents could lead through persuasion, acting with their fellow partisans rather than on their behalf. The new politics Wilson envisioned would require a different type of president, one more schooled in the arts of politics and persuasion.[117]

The Strategic Sense of William McKinley

Wilson's ode to Cleveland appeared in the same month that William McKinley took the oath of office, becoming the nation's 25th president. McKinley was Cleveland's antithesis, as tactful and conciliatory as Cleveland was blunt and confrontational. Prior to becoming president, Cleveland had never served in a legislature and had no national political experience: he had been sheriff of Erie County for two years; mayor of Buffalo for less than a year, where he was known as "His Obstinacy"; and governor of New York for two years, where he earned the tag of "the veto governor." McKinley, in contrast, had a wealth of experience in national politics, having served in the House of Representatives during four different presidencies, including a stint as chairman of the powerful House Ways and Means Committee. He also had experience as a chief executive, having served four years as governor of Ohio prior to running for president.[118]

Wilson never took much interest in McKinley's presidency, perhaps because he thought McKinley represented the old-style politics of a president beholden to party barons in Congress. But in fact McKinley displayed precisely the sort of legislative initiative and party leadership that Wilson sought in a president. McKinley wasted no time in his inaugural address in charting a legislative direction and invoking a popular mandate for the policies he had pledged to pursue in the campaign. Rather than have the new Congress wait until December to begin its work, as was customary, McKinley announced his intention to call Congress into session immediately to write legislation that raised tariffs. Congress had no choice but to act, McKinley insisted, because "the voice of the people" had declared that "such legislation should be had."[119]

McKinley worked closely with Republican legislators during the special session, though he refrained from trying to dictate specific tariff rates. The precise rates were far less important to McKinley than securing a bill that unified the party and that included a reciprocity provision giving the president discretion to negotiate rate adjustments. The bill that Congress finally delivered to McKinley's desk set rates significantly higher than the president desired, but he signed the Dingley Act because it delivered on his core strategic objectives.[120]

Not since Jefferson had the nation had a more skilled legislative and party leader in the White House. McKinley understood, in a way that Cleveland never had, the strategic tradeoffs that leadership in a system of separated powers required. "I could ride a white horse in this situation and pass the original bill," McKinley confided to a reporter, but "the vital thing is to keep as many votes as possible in Congress back of the whole pro-gramme of the Administration." Or, as McKinley put it to a friend, "a personal triumph . . . would weigh little against the demoralization and disorganization of his own party in the legislative branch of Government upon which he must depend." In other words, McKinley had no intention of behaving like Cleveland and allowing a misguided sense of courage to cripple his party and his future effectiveness as a leader. Whereas Cleveland's righteous rectitude had contributed to Democrats losing an unprecedented 113 seats in the House in the 1894 congressional elections, McKinley's finely honed strategic sense enabled Republicans to sustain their majorities in both houses of Congress throughout his presidency and laid the groundwork for a period of sustained Republican dominance in national politics.[121]

By the end of McKinley's presidency, the Whig doctrine that the president's job was merely to execute "the sovereign legislature's will" had been well and truly laid to rest. When Admiral George Dewey, the most celebrated war hero of his day, announced his candidacy for the presidency in 1900, he found himself the butt of widespread ridicule for suggesting that the presidency was "not such a very difficult" job since it required little more than faithfully executing the law of Congress.[122] Careful observers of the presidency during the McKinley years noted the executive's growing influence in the lawmaking process, some with alarm, others with approval.[123] And it was not the presidency alone where this transformation in thought and deed was taking place. At the state level, too, governors were increasingly looked to as a source of legislative leadership, particularly from self-styled "progressives" who saw party bosses and party machines as the chief obstacles to reform.[124]

Theodore Roosevelt: "That Fellow ... Wants Everything"

No governor during McKinley's presidency attracted more attention than New York's Theodore Roosevelt. In his autobiography, Roosevelt recalled that while "in theory the Executive has nothing to do with legislation," in practice "more than half" of his work as governor involved securing support for legislation. Much of that work took the form of "repeated private conversations" with legislators to convince them to follow his lead. When that tactic failed—as it often did when his agenda conflicted with the interests of the Republican machine headed by party boss Thomas Platt—Roosevelt shifted to "arousing the people, and riveting their attention" on the legislation he desired. Tired of Roosevelt beating up on his machine, Platt helped to engineer a scheme by which Governor Roosevelt would be kicked upstairs to the vice presidency, where he would be out of Platt's way. The devious plan backfired, however, when McKinley was killed and Vice President Roosevelt became President Roosevelt.[125]

We are accustomed to thinking of Roosevelt as a pioneer in the presidency. And in some ways he was, as we saw in the previous chapter. But fascination with Roosevelt's flamboyant personality obscures the rest of the story, namely that Roosevelt often found himself fending off charges from Progressives that he was not leading Congress aggressively enough. For instance, when the rector of St. George's Episcopal Church in New York City chided the president for a lack of specifics regarding antitrust legislation in his 1902 annual message to Congress, Roosevelt strove to teach the clergyman the facts of political life in the nation's capital: "Are you aware," Roosevelt asked, "of the extreme unwisdom of my irritating Congress by fixing the details of a bill, concerning which they are very sensitive, instead of laying down a general policy?"[126]

Roosevelt is so closely associated with the "bully pulpit" that we tend to overlook the tremendous political skill he showed in working with members of Congress, particularly the leadership of his own party. Roosevelt assiduously cultivated the so-called Republican "old guard" in the Senate, powerful legislators with a strong sense of senatorial prerogative and who were deeply suspicious of Progressive reform. Roosevelt worked particularly hard at courting Joseph Cannon, probably the most powerful Speaker in the history of the House of Representatives. Realizing that no bill could get a hearing, let alone pass the House, without Cannon's approval, Roosevelt was careful to consult with Cannon before recommending measures and to give him an advance copy of each of his messages to Congress.[127]

During the final two years of his presidency, Roosevelt's relations with legislators frayed as he pushed Congress harder to enact his proposals. Members expressed exasperation after receiving five special messages from Roosevelt in a single week in December 1906. "That fellow at the other end of the Avenue," Cannon groused, "wants everything, from the birth of Christ to the death of the devil." The more publicly and insistently he pushed, the more resistant Congress became. As time ticked down on his tenure, Roosevelt's agenda became increasingly ambitious and his approach less patient and cautious, while members of Congress felt more emboldened to oppose a president they knew would soon be leaving office. Roosevelt's war of words with Congress in his final year didn't hurt the president's popularity—"When Roosevelt attacks Congress," reported one paper, "the people feel that he is making their fight"— but the standoff meant that the president got little of what he wanted during his final years in office. Roosevelt hoped, however, that his protégé William Howard Taft would succeed where he had failed.[128]

William Howard Taft: A Failure of Politics, Not of Ambition

Few presidents have been more misunderstood or unfairly caricatured than Taft, who had the misfortune of being sandwiched between two of the twentieth century's most colorful presidents. Most Americans would be hard-pressed to remember anything about Taft apart perhaps from his massive girth—he weighed over 330 pounds when he left office— and his alleged difficulty extracting himself from the White House bathtub. Many scholars, misled by Taft's post-presidential writings in which he spelled out a narrow reading of presidential power, have mistakenly seen Taft as a passive president who had more in common with the Whigs than with Roosevelt or Wilson. But although Taft was not a success in the White House, his failure, as political scientist Peri Arnold rightly argues, "was not a failure of ambition. It was a failure of politics."[129]

In his inaugural address, Taft laid out an ambitious, detailed legislative agenda. Identifying downward tariff revision as the nation's most urgent priority, he immediately called Congress into session to enact the necessary changes. To the modern ear, tariff reform hardly sounds like a boldly progressive call to arms, but Taft's announcement was a daring break with Republican orthodoxy, which for decades had equated high tariffs with prosperity. Progressives, in contrast, believed that the tariff was an insidious source of monopolistic power—"the mother of trusts," they called it.[130]

In championing tariff revision Taft was venturing onto terrain that Roosevelt had deemed too perilous to traverse. Roosevelt had shied away from a showdown over the tariff for fear that it would rupture his relationship with Republican leaders, particularly Speaker Cannon—instead, the canny Roosevelt used periodic threats of tariff revision as a way to leverage concessions from the Republican leadership on other parts of his agenda, most notably railroad regulation. Taft also rushed in where Roosevelt had feared to tread by trying to oust Cannon as Speaker of the House and replace him with someone more sympathetic to his reform agenda. Roosevelt was the voice of caution, warning Taft that insurgents lacked the votes to dislodge Cannon and that if he alienated the powerful Speaker his broader reform agenda would be stymied.[131]

Taft belatedly realized that Roosevelt was right: if he wanted tariff reform he would have to withdraw his support from the anti-Cannon insurgency. When Taft capitulated to "the hard fact of Cannon's position," Progressives felt betrayed and the new president looked weak. Taft's problem was not that he was in the thrall of an outdated Whig orthodoxy but that he was an inexperienced politician—the presidency was his first elected office—who misjudged what was possible and raised expectations that he could not meet.[132]

Taft allowed the House and Senate to hash out most of the details of the tariff legislation, but this was not on account of a Whiggish sensibility but rather because Cannon and Senate Majority Leader Nelson Aldrich persuaded the naive Taft that it would be best if he weighed in at the conference committee stage, where, they promised, his views would exert "great influence." Taft thought this would be sufficient to get the tariff reform he wanted—and in fact his intensive negotiations with the conference committee resulted in some substantial rate reductions. But Taft misjudged how much could be achieved in conference committee, which was limited to reconciling the differences between the House and Senate bills, both of which set tariff rates at relatively high levels.[133]

The bill that emerged from conference committee was a far cry from the sweeping tariff reduction Taft had promised the country. Progressives urged Taft to veto the bill, as he had earlier promised to do if the bill failed to measure up to his campaign pledge. But Taft had boxed himself in. If he vetoed the bill, he would permanently alienate the Republican congressional leadership, which had spent five months crafting legislation that had overwhelming support among Republicans. Taft did not see how he could enact the rest of his reform agenda if he had to rely on the "broken reed" of the Democratic Party plus a handful of noisy Republican insurgents. Progressives urged Taft to take his case to the people, but the president had little faith in his rhetorical abilities—for good reason—and in any event it was doubtful that public pressure would have influenced Republican legislators, most of whom represented districts in which high tariffs were popular. Having already invested countless hours negotiating the bill's details, Taft judged he had no alternative but to sign the bill.[134]

Taft compounded his political problems by offering an extravagant defense of the Payne–Aldrich Act as "the best tariff bill" ever enacted. Those ill-chosen words helped to fix Taft in the public mind as the patsy of the "standpat" conservatives and an apologist for Cannonism and eastern corporate interests. Taft's bungling of the tariff issue drove Progressives from the Republican Party in droves and helped Democrats in 1910 win control of a congressional chamber for the first time in 15 years. Two years later, with the Republican Party hopelessly split between Taft and the Progressive Party candidate Theodore Roosevelt, Democrats secured the White House for the first time since Grover Cleveland.[135]

WOODROW WILSON: THE PRESIDENT AS PRIME MINISTER

By the time Woodrow Wilson assumed the presidency in 1913, the idea that the president was responsible for leading the legislature had become firmly fixed in the public mind, particularly among Progressives. For an executive to remain "scrupulously loyal to the old theory of the separation of powers," wrote progressive Herbert Croly, was to be seen as "weak and poor-spirited." Although Roosevelt's legislative achievements had been modest, his mesmeric leadership made people look to the executive as the initiator of reform. And Taft, despite his fumbling, conscientiously advanced a legislative agenda, sometimes even providing Congress with drafts of proposed legislation, including what became the Mann–Elkins Act, which strengthened government regulation of railroads. Moreover, activist governors across the nation—Robert La Follette in Wisconsin, Charles Evans Hughes in New York, Hiram Johnson in California, and Wilson himself in New Jersey—were transforming the way that Americans thought about the relationship between the executive and legislature.[136]

Although Wilson was the beneficiary of this shift in public expectations, his open leadership of Congress transcended anything the nation had seen before. Like Taft, he immediately called Congress into special session to fulfill his campaign promise to lower tariffs. But from then on Wilson's performance was in a league of its own. Where Taft had followed a century of precedent by sending his tariff message to be read to Congress by a congressional clerk, Wilson went to the Capitol and read it himself. He did this, he explained, to show that the president is "not a mere department of the government hailing Congress from some isolated island of jealous power" but rather is "a human being trying to cooperate with other human beings in a common service."[137]

Scholars have sometimes interpreted Wilson's speech to Congress as a milestone in the development of the rhetorical presidency but, in Wilson's own mind, coming to Congress was an attempt not to reach over the heads of members of Congress but rather to bridge the separation between the legislature and the executive that he had long believed was the root cause of the nation's inability to address its problems. As a young political scientist, he had admired the British parliamentary system and dreamed of breaking down the separation through constitutional amendment; as president he saw the opportunity to remake the relationship between the president and Congress so that they worked for a common purpose rather than at cross purposes.[138]

Wilson understood that the American people were increasingly looking to the president for legislative leadership. As he expressed it in a letter written to a House committee chair only a month before his inaugural address, the nation expected the president to be "the prime minister, as much concerned with the guidance of legislation as with the just and orderly execution of the law." If the president was going to be judged on what the legislature did—as all prime ministers were—then the president could ill afford, as Taft had done in the case of the tariff, to sit idly by while the legislature did its work. Roosevelt had shown Wilson that appealing to public opinion was one way that a president could push Congress, but Wilson understood that public pressure of this sort was generally insufficient and often counterproductive, particularly in dealing with the Senate. Insulated by staggered six-year terms, Wilson explained, the Senate "is not so immediately sensitive to opinion and is apt to grow, if anything, more stiff if pressure of that kind is brought to bear upon it." To prevail in Congress, Wilson believed, required the president to establish "intimate relations of confidence" with legislators. And that is exactly what Wilson set out to do from the moment he was elected.[139]

Even before taking the oath of office, Wilson conferred privately with Democratic leaders of Congress about the special session that he intended to call. And the day after his dramatic special message on the tariff, he journeyed back to the Capitol to discuss tariff legislation with members—another symbolic departure from precedent, which dictated that while legislators could visit the White House, the president should generally stay away from Capitol Hill.[140] Wilson also had a direct phone line installed between the White House and the Capitol to facilitate communication between the president and legislators.[141]

Whereas Taft was persuaded to wait until the conference stage to place his stamp on tariff legislation, Wilson engaged Congress at every stage of the legislative process. When the House Ways and Means Committee produced an initial bill that retained protective tariffs on products that were important to the Democratic base in the South and West—such as farm products, leather, wool, and sugar—Wilson pushed back, persuading the committee chair that such protections were not only economically harmful but compromised the party's core commitment to abolish "privileges and exemptions from competition." Behind the persuasion was the implicit threat of a veto.[142]

Presidential success in Congress is rarely if ever down to a president's skill or persuasive power alone. Wilson's ability to lead where Taft had failed was due also to the preferences and organization of his followers in Congress. Taft tried to take his party in a direction—lower tariffs—that only a minority of Republicans were inclined to follow, whereas Wilson strove to lead Democrats in a direction that was consonant with their party's ideology dating to the days of Jackson. Moreover, House Democrats could call upon the discipline of the Democratic caucus. Formed in 1911 after Democrats took control of the House, the caucus committed Democratic legislators to back any legislation that had the support of two-thirds of House Democrats. These caucus rules greatly facilitated Wilson's ambition to function as a prime minister leading his party.[143]

The Underwood Tariff Act—which not only lowered tariffs to rates that the nation had not seen since before the Civil War but also included the nation's first progressive income tax—was an historic achievement, but Wilson did not stop there. Three months after pitching tariff reform in a special message, he returned to Congress, "as the head of the Government and the responsible leader of the party in power," to call for banking and currency reform. In the case of tariff reform, Wilson's task was relatively straightforward: ensure that Democrats in Congress adhered to their longstanding anti-tariff principles. With banking and currency reform, however, the challenge was more formidable, since there was no agreement within the Democratic Party, let alone the nation, on what such reform should look like. Some Democrats feared government control of banking while others followed William Jennings Bryan in demanding public control. The final product— the creation of a Federal Reserve that was a government entity but insulated from political control through fixed terms and long tenure—was largely a product of Wilson's intensive negotiations with Democratic legislators to find a compromise that different factions within the party could accept.[144]

After deftly shepherding into law the Underwood Act and the Federal Reserve Act, Wilson spent the following year assembling a coalition to pass the Clayton Anti-Trust Act and the Federal Trade Commission Act. Wilson's remarkable success in working with the 63rd Congress was widely praised, but—ironically, in view of Wilson's reputation as the progenitor of the rhetorical presidency—he was criticized by some Progressives for working too closely and cooperatively with Congress. The editors of the *New Republic*, for instance, admired Wilson's "adroit leadership" but also expressed concern that "a closer relationship between President and Congress [could] mean a remoter relationship between the President and popular opinion." The presidency, they concluded, "cannot afford to become too intimately associated with Congress [because] the Presidency depends for its primary strength and great usefulness upon its ability to lead the dominant element in public opinion." Wilson's model of "a responsible Prime Minister," they believed, was less desirable than an "independent executive whose power rests on his direct influence on popular opinion."[145]

Wilson found the prime minister model of diminished relevance in his second term, when the Democratic Party no longer commanded majorities in both houses of Congress. In addition, America's involvement in World War I meant that Wilson was increasingly drawn away from domestic policy, where he believed the president should work collaboratively with his fellow partisans in Congress, and toward foreign policy, where he believed partisanship had no place and the president's power was close to absolute. Behaving as a surrogate prime minister, Wilson compiled a legislative record in his first two years that ranks among the most impressive in American history. In his last two years, acting as the independent executive who would brook no compromise with the Republican-controlled Senate over the Versailles Treaty, Wilson experienced among the most devastating legislative defeats of any president.[146]

MORE WILSONIAN THAN WHIG: FROM HARDING TO HOOVER

Executive action has often produced legislative reaction, and Wilson's presidency was no different. In 1920, Republican presidential nominee Warren Harding promised to leave the legislating to the legislators. Indeed, the party's enthusiasm for Harding reflected a feeling among legislators that the amiable Harding would "sign whatever bill the Senate sent him and not send bills for the Senate to pass."[147]

But there was no rolling back the clock and resurrecting Whiggery. Only a few months into his presidency, Harding concluded that he could not stick to his "preelection ideals of an Executive keeping himself aloof from Congress." Unannounced, he marched over to the Senate and dressed down the august body for failing to enact tax reform and for promoting a profligate "bonus" bill for veterans that "no thoughtful person, possessed with all the facts" could endorse. Unable to persuade the legislature to relent on the bonus bill, Harding vetoed it.[148]

Calvin Coolidge generally thought the less legislation the better, but his understanding of the president's relationship with Congress was more Wilsonian than Whiggish. In his autobiography, Coolidge explained that it was "the business of the President as party leader to do the best he can to see that the declared party platform purposes are translated into legislative and administrative action." Coolidge said that he preferred to work cooperatively with legislators through "personal discussion," but in Congress's "hours of timidity," when it became "subservient to the importunities of organized minorities," the president necessarily had to act as "the champion of the rights of the whole country."[149]

Herbert Hoover failed to arrest the country's slide into an economic depression, but that failure cannot be traced to any lingering traces of Whiggery. Whereas Whigs and neo-Whigs trusted in Congress to legislate in the public interest, Hoover had a barely disguised contempt for the political horse-trading, partisanship, and special interests that he believed dominated the legislature. As one biographer put it, Hoover "felt that he represented the welfare of the people and that Congress represented the politicians." In 1931 Hoover refused to call Congress into special session to deal with the worsening depression because he feared that legislators would only make the economic situation worse by passing laws that pandered to constituents and interest groups.[150]

When Congress finally convened in December 1931, Hoover was anything but deferential, demanding that Congress take action on 16 proposals. That Congress passed only a small fraction of what Hoover wanted was testament not to any outdated respect for legislative autonomy but to Hoover's weaknesses as a politician and to Democrats' control of the House. An engineer by training and a man of "extreme reserve" by nature, Hoover invested little energy in building personal relationships with members of Congress. It was enough, in Hoover's mind, that the policy he proposed was the correct one. Logic and facts, Hoover believed, not promises of patronage or personal charm, should determine public policy.[151]

FDR: LEGISLATOR IN CHIEF

Hoover's failure looks all the greater because it preceded the most startling burst of legislative productivity in the nation's history. In his first hundred days Franklin Delano Roosevelt steered 15 major pieces of legislation through Congress, including: the Economy Act, which delegated to the president the power to cut veterans' benefits and the salaries of government workers; the Civilian Conservation Corps Reforestation Act, which put the jobless to work planting trees and arresting soil erosion; the Agricultural Adjustment Act, which sought to arrest falling farm prices by paying farmers not to grow crops; and the National Industrial Recovery Act, which established the National Recovery Administration, rolled back anti-trust regulations, guaranteed collective bargaining for workers, and allocated more than 3 billion dollars in spending for public works projects. With a few exceptions, the early New Deal legislation—unlike Wilson's New Freedom legislation—was drawn up by the executive branch, not Congress.[152]

So productive was FDR's first hundred days that they have become the standard by which presidents are now judged. Some presidents have been only too eager to be measured against the hundred-day test. In 1965, Lyndon Johnson urged his aides to "jerk out every damn little bill" so that his administration could boast of having bested Roosevelt's record. In 1992, candidate Bill Clinton vowed that the day after he took office his legislative program would be sent to Congress and he would produce "the most productive hundred-day period in modern history." Presidential candidate Donald Trump made the same vow, even releasing a "Contract with the American Voter" that detailed a "100-day action plan to Make America Great Again" that included repealing Obama's signature legislative accomplishment, the Affordable Care Act. Only when it became clear that he would not achieve repeal in the first hundred days—or much of any other legislative accomplishments—did Trump reverse course and slam the test as a "ridiculous standard" of presidential performance. Other presidents have tried from the outset to play down the importance of the first hundred days, as John F. Kennedy did in his 1961 inaugural address when he allowed that his vision of reform would not be finished in the first hundred days nor even in the first thousand days, "nor in the life of this Administration, nor even perhaps in our lifetime on this planet." Knowing that he could not match Roosevelt's legislative record, Richard Nixon created a "Hundred Days Group," which he charged with publicizing the administration's legislative actions while getting it "off the hook on quantity of legislation." But no amount of rhetoric or public relations spin has been able to persuade the media to abandon their focus on the first hundred days as a test of presidential mettle.[153]

Measuring presidents by how they stack up against Roosevelt's first hundred days ignores the unique economic crisis that made possible his unprecedented legislative success. The country was so desperate for leadership, said humorist Will Rogers, that if Roosevelt "burned down the capitol we would cheer and say 'well, we at least got a fire started anyhow.'" No personal or public appeals from the president were necessary, for instance, to secure—on the opening day of the special session—passage of the first emergency banking bill, which passed unanimously in the House after a mere 40 minutes of debate. The Senate rushed the bill through the same day, with only seven dissenting votes, so that the president could sign the bill into law later that evening.[154]

Designed to staunch financial panic and restore public confidence in the banks, the emergency banking bill was admittedly exceptional in its urgency, but other major bills too were rushed through with relatively little debate. The House allocated an average of only about four hours of debate to the administration's major measures. Debate in the Senate was typically much longer, but five major bills—including the act that established the Civilian Conservation Corps (CCC), the Home Owners' Loan Act, and the Federal Emergency Relief Act—were passed in the Senate by voice vote.[155]

Roosevelt also had the advantage of overwhelming Democratic majorities in both chambers. In the House, there were nearly 200 more Democrats than Republicans. Not that all Democrats blindly followed Roosevelt. In fact, the Economy Act, which was introduced the morning after Roosevelt signed the emergency banking bill, met stiff resistance from many Democrats opposed to the cost-cutting measure. In the Senate, too, the support of conservative Republicans was pivotal in beating back liberal Democratic amendments designed to weaken the economy bill. On most issues, however, particularly in the House, Roosevelt's legislative success in his first hundred days was constructed upon the loyalty of the party's huge majorities.[156]

To emphasize the conditions that made possible Roosevelt's unparalleled success with Congress is not to take away from Roosevelt's consummate skill in exploiting those circumstances. It is instead to remind ourselves that political skill alone is insufficient for presidential leadership. The disposition of the followers is at least as important as the talents of a leader.

Moreover, what we remember today as "Roosevelt's Hundred Days" or "Roosevelt's New Deal" was not the work of a heroic chief legislator. The emergency banking bill was not drafted by Roosevelt or even his aides, but by Walter Wyatt, general counsel for the Federal Reserve Board, where he had served since the Harding administration. Several Roosevelt officials—specifically Raymond Moley and Treasury Secretary William Woodin—were involved in negotiating the bill's contents, but the bill was largely the handiwork of holdovers from the Hoover Treasury Department. The president's direct involvement in the formulation and passage of the bill was minimal. His main role instead was to use what Moley called the "magic [of] that calm voice" to reassure Americans, in the first of his storied fireside chats, that the banks were solvent and their savings secure. That famous fireside chat took place several days *after* Roosevelt had signed the bill into law.[157]

One of Roosevelt's only direct contributions to the emergency banking legislation was to scotch the idea of government insurance of bank deposits. He disliked the idea that the government should "guarantee bad banks as well as good banks" because he thought "the weak banks will pull down the strong"—the same position taken by the big New York banks and the American Bankers Association. Roosevelt stuck to this view when Congress began work on a permanent banking bill, one that included federal deposit insurance. Roosevelt vowed to veto the entire bill—which had been drafted by Congress—if federal deposit insurance was not removed. Congress refused to back down and appeared to have the votes to override a presidential veto, prompting Roosevelt to yield. The Federal Deposit Insurance Corporation (FDIC) has been justly hailed as "one of the most brilliant and successful of the accomplishments of the Hundred Days," but it was enacted in spite of, not because of, Franklin Roosevelt.[158]

Another signature piece of New Deal legislation that Roosevelt resisted was the National Labor Relations Act, penned by New York senator Robert Wagner. Roosevelt did not want government siding with labor or business; rather, he saw the role of government as helping to mediate disputes between employers and employees, so as to avoid the disruption of strikes and work stoppages. Wagner, however, attached greater value to a strong labor movement, and his bill empowered government to protect labor's right to unionize and bargain collectively. Only after the bill had passed the Senate 63–12 and been reported out of a House committee did Roosevelt reverse course and, bowing to the inevitable, decide to back the Wagner Act.[159]

Even when the initiative came from the president, the final product often reflected legislators' preferences at least as much as the president's. For example, in June 1935, the president sprung a surprise by proposing to dramatically increase taxes on the wealthy. He called upon Congress to enact inheritance and gift taxes (the latter for those trying to evade the former), a graduated tax on large corporations (the larger the corporation the higher the tax), and a surtax for the very wealthy. When Congress was finished with the Wealth Tax Act, however, the inheritance tax had been axed and the corporate income tax reduced to "no more than symbolic importance." Congress did raise the surtax rate on the wealthy, as Roosevelt asked, but it also added elements that Roosevelt had not asked for, including a surtax on "excess" profits—companies making more than 10 percent were levied a 6 percent surtax and companies making more than 15 percent had to pay a 12 percent surtax.[160]

Congress, in sum, "played a vital and consistently underestimated role in shaping the New Deal." Even during the first hundred days, when deference to the president's wishes was at its peak, Congress was no doormat. After the first hundred days, as the sense of national emergency started to fade, Congress became increasingly assertive about putting its mark on Roosevelt's legislative agenda. By his second term, FDR found that often, no amount of personal charm or soaring rhetoric was sufficient to persuade Congress to follow his lead.[161]

Roosevelt's second inaugural address famously called attention to "one-third of a nation ill-housed, ill-clad, ill-nourished," yet as historian William Leuchtenburg notes, Roosevelt "got almost nothing" he asked for from Congress to address these problems. One of the few exceptions was the Housing Act of 1937, which provided public housing for low-income families. But public housing legislation is hardly a tale of heroic presidential leadership. Senator Wagner, not Roosevelt, was the driving force behind the legislation. Wagner had introduced public housing legislation several times in Roosevelt's first term but the president had been uninterested. Roosevelt worried that low-cost housing would undermine real estate values and preferred plans that sent the urban poor into the countryside—such as the CCC—to plans for urban renewal. Roosevelt's decision to support Wagner's bill in the summer of 1937—after it had passed the Senate—was crucial to its passage in the House, but the measure that ultimately came to the president's desk was a shadow of Wagner's original bill, which had been "emasculated" by legislators representing rural America.[162]

Roosevelt's second-term difficulties with Congress are particularly notable in view of the shattering defeat Republicans experienced in 1936. Roosevelt's Republican opponent, Alf Landon, received only eight electoral votes and Democrats picked up seats in both houses. When Roosevelt took the oath of office for a second time, Democrats had a better than four-to-one advantage in the Senate and not far off that in the House. But conservative Democrats, particularly in the South, had soured on the New Deal. Worried that the federal government "had gone far enough—or too far," congressional conservatives stymied Roosevelt at almost every turn, so that by the end of the first year of his second term, Leuchtenburg writes, Roosevelt seemed "a thoroughly repudiated president."[163]

The difficulties Roosevelt encountered in getting his way with Congress, despite partisan majorities that no president since has come close to matching, make the nation's wait for the next FDR all the more puzzling. Analyzed rather than mythologized, the Roosevelt presidency has at least as much to teach us about the limits of presidential influence in Congress as it does about the power of presidential persuasion.

In the Shadow of FDR

Every president since Harry Truman has operated in FDR's shadow, perhaps none more so than Barack Obama, who inherited an economic crisis that invited comparisons to the depression of the 1930s. Although inaugurated more than a half-century after Roosevelt's death, Obama continually found himself measured against FDR. Initially, many of these comparisons were intended as compliments. But when Obama failed to deliver the hoped-for reforms, comparisons with FDR took on a more critical edge. If only Obama had acted more boldly, like FDR, we were told, things would have turned out so much differently.[164]

Disappointed liberals complained not only about Obama's unwillingness to champion a single-payer—that is, government-run—universal health care plan but also about his unwillingness to fight for the so-called "public option"—a government-run insurance plan that would compete with private insurance companies. They complained, too, about his willingness to cater to conservative Democratic committee chairmen, and were especially appalled at his insistence on trying to forge a bipartisan plan that would attract Republican support. They also faulted him for cutting deals with drug company CEOs that protected the companies' profits in return for their political support. FDR, they insisted, would never have behaved this way. Whereas Obama tried to placate his political enemies, Roosevelt invited their hatred, flogging them publicly as "economic royalists." Roosevelt, in short, had made the New Deal by being "a divider, not a uniter," drawing a clear line between the forces of reform and the forces of reaction.[165]

However, this narrative mistakes the way Roosevelt campaigned for reelection in 1936 with the way he governed in his first term. Roosevelt's famous applause line welcoming the hatred of his enemies—"They are unanimous in their hate for me, and I welcome their hatred"—came in a Madison Square Garden campaign speech only three days before the 1936 election, and his powerful jab at economic royalists was delivered in his 1936 acceptance speech at the Democratic national convention. This divisive rhetoric was calculated to rally the party faithful and turn out Democratic voters, but it was not how the New Deal was won.

During his first two years FDR was as focused as Obama on not allowing his reform agenda to be cast in purely partisan terms. Invited in 1934 to participate in the Democratic Party's annual Jefferson Day celebrations, Roosevelt declined, explaining that "our strongest plea to the country . . . is that the recovery and reconstruction program is being accomplished by men and women of all parties." Roosevelt did not see himself as charting a partisan, let alone leftist, course, but rather as setting a middle course between partisan and ideological extremes. Those on the left complained constantly about what they perceived as Roosevelt's moderation and conservatism.[166]

The mythical version of FDR's presidency also obscures the many compromises that went into the making of New Deal legislation, including its most storied element: the Social Security Act of 1935. Just as Obama's health care plan compelled Americans to buy health insurance, so the Social Security Act required employees to contribute to a national system of old-age insurance. But this landmark legislation was laced with compromises and concessions to powerful interests and congressional conservatives. The first was the exclusion of health insurance reform, which Roosevelt calculated would attract fierce opposition from the medical profession and Congress. Moreover, against the advice of his top aides, Roosevelt insisted on regressive payroll taxes to finance old-age insurance because he believed an apparently self-supporting system would be easier to sell to Congress and because politicians would find it more difficult to scrap a program if citizens believed they had "earned" their pensions through payroll contributions they had made throughout their working life. The president's Social Security plan also left out the most vulnerable employees and those least likely to be white, such as farm workers and domestics, in order to make the legislation more palatable to southern Democrats. Judged by the other welfare systems of the world, in the words of a sympathetic Roosevelt biographer, the Social Security Act was "astonishingly inept and conservative."[167]

To remember the concessions that Roosevelt made is not to deny that the New Deal greatly expanded the role of the federal government in protecting citizens from what FDR famously termed the "hazards and vicissitudes of life." The New Deal transformed, moreover, how Americans thought about the government's responsibilities for the economy—a change in expectations that was recognized in the Employment Act of 1946, which directed the federal government to "promote maximum employment, production, and purchasing power." Of course, the extent to which the federal government should intervene in the economy has continued to be a fault line dividing the two parties. Democrats have strived to extend the New Deal, never with more success than in 1965 when Lyndon Johnson leveraged huge Democratic majorities in both houses of Congress to secure legislation that, among other things, provided medical insurance for the elderly (Medicare) and the poor (Medicaid). Republicans, in contrast, have generally resisted the expansion of the welfare state. But while the two parties continue to disagree about the

This Richard Thompson cartoon from the *New Yorker* (November 17, 2008) captures the widespread view in the media that Obama had an opportunity to be a transformative leader in the mold of FDR. The following week, *Time* magazine traded on the same trope with a Photoshopped cover image of a grinning Obama, riding in an open car, with the trademark Roosevelt cigarette holder protruding from his lips. The cover story's title was: "The *New* New Deal: What Barack Obama Can Learn from FDR—and What the Democrats Need to Do."

Courtesy: Richard Thompson for the *New Yorker*.

scope of the federal government's domestic responsibilities, there is no longer any partisan disagreement about the president's responsibility to initiate legislative policy.

After FDR, American government textbooks routinely described the president as the "chief legislator," a term that was first used in the 1920s during the Coolidge administration.[168] Of course, as we have emphasized at length, FDR was not the first president to initiate legislation. Theodore Roosevelt, Taft, and Wilson all had executive branch officials draft bills that were then introduced in Congress, as did Harding, Coolidge, and Hoover. Changes in congressional and public expectations, as well as presidential behavior, occurred gradually, not in one dramatic historical moment. Nonetheless, under FDR, starting with the flurry of legislation during his first hundred days, the practice of initiating bills in the executive branch became far more common and widely accepted.

When Taft or Wilson submitted the draft of a bill to a congressional committee, opponents accused them of usurping congressional authority, whereas presidents after FDR were more likely to be charged with the reverse sin of failing to provide sufficiently specific legislative language. In 1947, for instance, President Harry Truman was publicly rebuked by a Republican senator for failing to provide Congress with the draft of a bill that laid out "exactly" what he wanted in the way of anti-inflation legislation. And in 1953, the Republican chair of the House Foreign Affairs Committee privately upbraided the Eisenhower administration for not providing the committee with a specific bill on foreign aid legislation: "Don't expect us to start from scratch on what you people want," the chair fumed. "That's not the way we do things here—you draft the bills and we work them over."[169]

This shift in expectations has been accompanied by institutional innovations designed to facilitate a president's ability to lead Congress. In FDR's day, there was no White House office devoted to legislative relations. Roosevelt did not do it all himself, of course—he dispatched aides to the Hill when he thought it would help, and cabinet members and agency heads were in close communication with congressional committees, as they had been since the beginning of the republic. Nonetheless, Roosevelt devoted a tremendous amount of his time during his first term to congressional relations—three or four hours a day was Roosevelt's estimate. Today, in contrast, presidents rely heavily on the White House Office of Legislative Affairs to handle relations with Congress—an innovation that dates to the Eisenhower presidency.[170]

Congress has also taken steps that have enhanced the president's capacity to meet the increased expectations. In the Employment Act of 1946, for instance, Congress required the president to submit an annual economic report that included a review of economic conditions in the country, an economic forecast of "foreseeable trends," and "a program for carrying out the policy ... of maintaining maximum employment, production, and purchasing power." To help the president meet these statutory obligations, the act created a three-person Council of Economic Advisors to be housed in the Executive Office of the President, and placed under the sole control of the president. Passage of the 1946 act did not mean, however, that members of Congress were now prepared to be dictated to by the president, or that they were abdicating their policymaking role. Instead, as political scientist James Sundquist points out, Congress passed the law because it sought "a solid base of information and concrete recommendations from which to work."[171]

The 1946 act signaled a new era of legislative–executive relations in which Congress wanted to know the president's views "across-the-board and in detail" before they began to legislate.[172] However, the desire to have the president initiate a comprehensive legislative program did not necessarily herald a greater disposition to follow the president's lead. The president was expected to supply a roadmap and set the departure point, but members of Congress did not feel obligated to take the president's preferred route. Indeed, members of Congress continued to take great pride in striking out on their own, even when the president was of their own party. For instance, when Democratic House Ways and Means chairman Charlie Rangel was asked whether he supported President Obama's proposal to raise taxes on families earning more than $250,000, he replied that he would "have to study it" but that he didn't "take presidents' recommendations that seriously." And that was only six weeks into Obama's administration, when the president's public approval rating was over 60 percent.[173]

Rangel's remark is a reminder of how radically different presidential leadership of Congress is from a prime minister's leadership of Parliament, even when a president's party has majorities in both houses of Congress. Indeed, the burdens of being legislator-in-chief are often felt most acutely by a president whose party controls Congress. Backed by partisan majorities in both houses, a president is more likely to get what he wants, but he also runs a far greater risk of being judged weak if Congress resists, as Jimmy Carter discovered. A president boldly brandishing the veto or lambasting a "do-nothing" or irresponsible Congress may, ironically, find it easier to be perceived as a strong or resolute leader.

But living in FDR's shadow means that the "classic test" of presidential greatness is not the capacity to block Congress from acting foolishly but the ability to lead it to act wisely. Every president since FDR, Republican and Democrat alike, has confronted the challenge of trying to meet the greatly increased expectations for legislative leadership while functioning within an unchanged constitutional structure that grants the president no power to command legislative obedience. The mismatch between public expectations and presidential power is only made worse by FDR's other unintended legacy: a greatly exaggerated belief in the power of presidential persuasion to produce policy change.[174]

Those who expect presidents to transform the nation's politics or policies are likely to be disappointed. No matter how skilled a politician or charismatic an orator, a president is a facilitator more than a director of legislative change. That is, presidents typically lead, as political scientist George Edwards has shown, by exploiting opportunities "to help others go where they want to go anyway," not by heroically "leading others where they otherwise would not go." Nor is that such a bad thing in a democracy, unless we assume that the president knows best—a premise, we can be sure, that none of the framers would have been willing to grant.[175]

Notes

1   Carl Hulse, "In Lawmaker's Outburst, a Rare Breach of Protocol," *New York Times*, September 9, 2009.
2   Hulse, "In Lawmaker's Outburst." "Where's the Line between Dissent and Disrespect?" *Talk of the Nation*, September 14, 2009, www.npr.org/templates/story/story.php?storyId=112819190.

3   Ben Smith, "Health Reform Foes Plan Obama's Waterloo," *Politico*, July 17, 2009.

4   Jonathan Cohen, "How They Did It: The Inside Account of Health Care Reform's Triumph," *New Republic*, June 10, 2010, 22.

5   Richard E. Neustadt, *Presidential Power: The Politics of Leadership from FDR to Carter* (New York: Wiley, 1980), 26. Robert A. Dahl, *Pluralist Democracy in the United States: Conflict and Consent* (Chicago: Rand McNally, 1967), 136.

6   Max Farrand, *The Records of the Federal Convention*, volume 4 (New Haven, CT: Yale University Press, 1937), 2:73, 79 (July 21). Farrand's *Records* are also available at http://memory.loc.gov/ammem/amlaw/lwfr.html. The five days (June 4, 6, July 21, August 15, September 12) of debate over the veto power are also available in Richard J. Ellis, ed., *Founding the American Presidency* (Lanham, MD: Rowman & Littlefield, 1999), 134–44.

7   Farrand, *Records of the Federal Convention*, 1:99 (June 4).

8   Farrand, *Records of the Federal Convention*, 2:300 (August 15).

9   Farrand, *Records of the Federal Convention*, 2:585–87 (September 12).

10 Farrand, *Records of the Federal Convention*, 2:405 (August 24).

11 Forrest McDonald, *The American Presidency: An Intellectual History* (Lawrence: University Press of Kansas, 1994), 223. To Edmund Pendleton, September 23, 1793, in *The Writings of George Washington*, ed. Worthington Chauncey Ford (New York: G.P. Putnam's Sons, 1891), 12:327. Robert J. Spitzer, *The Presidential Veto: Touchstone of the American Presidency* (Albany: State University of New York Press, 1988), 28.

12 Not until his Farewell Address and final annual message did Washington recommend that Congress establish a national university.

13 First Annual Message, January 8, 1790. Donald Jackson and Dorothy Twohig, eds., *The Diaries of George Washington* (Charlottesville: University Press of Virginia, 1979), 5:507–08 (December 18–19, 1789).

14 See Communication of Sentiments to Benjamin Hawkins, *Writings of George Washington*, 12:72–73; and Leonard D. White, *The Federalists: A Study in Administrative History* (New York: Macmillan, 1948), 55.

15 White, *The Federalists*, 55, 53. Also see James Thomas Flexner, *George Washington and the New Nation, 1783–1793* (Boston: Little, Brown, 1970), 221.

16 Freeman W. Meyer, "A Note on the Origins of the 'Hamiltonian System,'" *William and Mary Quarterly* 21 (October 1964), 582.

17 *Annals of Congress*, June 25, 1789, 615–16.

18 *Annals of Congress*, June 25, 1789, 617, 628.

19 *Annals of Congress*, June 25, 1789, 628–29, 632.

20 Madison to Jefferson, May 27, 1789, in James Morton Smith, ed., *The Republic of Letters: The Correspondence between Thomas Jefferson and James Madison, 1776–1826* (New York: Norton, 1995), 1:613. Forrest McDonald, *Alexander Hamilton: A Biography* (New York: Norton, 1982), 128.

21 The original bill detailing the treasury secretary's duties was introduced by Hamilton's close friend and ally Elias Boudinot. We know, too, that Hamilton was in New York City—the seat of the federal government until December 1790—during the legislative debates and that his legal work during the spring and summer of 1789 was "much interrupted by daily conferences" with members of Congress. It is difficult to believe that Hamilton—a master at wielding political influence throughout his career—would not have attempted to use his connections and influence to shape a position that was his for the asking, particularly since his decision to accept the job hinged in part on how Congress drew up the position. See McDonald, *Alexander Hamilton*, 11, 128–29. White, *The Federalists*, 118. Meyer, "A Note on the Origins of the 'Hamiltonian System,'" 585.

22 McDonald, *American Presidency*, 228. Also see McDonald, *Alexander Hamilton*, 125–26; and Wilfred E. Binkley, *President and Congress* (New York: Vintage Books, 1962; third revised edition), 46.

23 McDonald, *Alexander Hamilton*, 133, 142. Alvin M. Josephy, Jr., *On the Hill: A History of the American Congress* (New York: Touchstone, 1979), 65. Jacob E. Cooke, ed., *The Reports of Alexander Hamilton* (New York: Harper Torchbooks, 1964), x.

24 Cooke, ed., *Reports of Alexander Hamilton*, 45. *Annals of Congress*, January 9, 1790, 1080–81.

25 *Journal of William Maclay*, entry of February 1, 1790, http://memory.loc.gov/ammem/amlaw/lwmj.html. Robert J. Spitzer, *President and Congress: Executive Hegemony at the Crossroads of American Government* (New York: McGraw-Hill, 1993), 22–23.

26 McDonald, *American Presidency*, 229. Hamilton's plan to have the national government assume the state's debts passed only after he struck a famous deal with Madison and Jefferson. The two Virginians pledged to secure southern votes for assumption and in return Hamilton agreed to round up northern votes in support of making a spot along the Potomac River the permanent capital of the United States.

27 *Journal of William Maclay*, entries of February 4 and February 9, 1791.

28 *Annals of Congress*, June 25, 1789, 626.

29 Notes of a Conversation with George Washington, October 1, 1792, *The Papers of Thomas Jefferson*, ed. John Catanzariti et al. (Princeton, NJ: Princeton University Press, 1990), 24:435. *Annals of Congress*, June 25, 1789, 629.

30 Joseph Cooper, "Jeffersonian Attitudes toward Executive Leadership and Committee Development in the House of Representatives, 1789–1829," *Western Political Quarterly* 18 (March 1965), 47. *Annals of Congress*, November 19–20, 1792, 696–708. *Journal of William Maclay*, entry of February 25, 1791; also see July 6–7, 1790. Noble E. Cunningham, Jr., *The Jeffersonian Republicans: The Formation of a Party Organization, 1789–1801* (Chapel Hill: University of North Carolina Press, 1957), 21.

31 *Annals of Congress*, November 19–20, 1790, 698–700 (Madison), 703–04 (Abraham Baldwin).

32 *Annals of Congress*, November 20, 1792, 705. Like Madison, Baldwin was a signer of the Constitution, a supporter of the original Treasury bill, and now an ardent opponent of Hamilton's fiscal agenda.

33 Cooper, "Jeffersonian Attitudes toward Executive Leadership," 52.

34 *Annals of Congress*, March 26, 1794, 531. White, *The Federalists*, 73. Cooper, "Jeffersonian Attitudes toward Executive Leadership," 54–55. *Annals of Congress*, December 21, 1797, 159.

35 McDonald, *Alexander Hamilton*, 286–87; also see 258–61.

36 Madison, quoted in Gordon S. Wood, *History of the Early Republic, 1789–1815* (New York: Oxford University Press, 2009), 149. Jefferson and Hamilton, quoted in White, *The Federalists*, 95, 54.

37 Richard Ellis and Aaron Wildavsky, *Dilemmas of Presidential Leadership: From Washington through Lincoln* (New Brunswick, NJ: Transaction Publishers, 1989), 68. Fred I. Greenstein first used the "hidden hand" label to describe the presidency of Dwight Eisenhower in *The Hidden-Hand Presidency: Eisenhower as Leader* (New York: Basic Books, 1982). See also Noble E. Cunningham, Jr., *The Process of Government under Jefferson* (Princeton, NJ: Princeton University Press, 1978), 193.

38 Robert M. Johnstone, Jr., *Jefferson and the Presidency: Leadership in the Young Republic* (Ithaca, NY: Cornell University Press, 1978), 128–31. Ellis and Wildavsky, *Dilemmas of Presidential Leadership*, 69. Noble E. Cunningham, Jr., *Jeffersonian Republicans in Power: Party Operations, 1801–1809* (Chapel Hill: University of North Carolina Press, 1963), 76. Also see James Sterling Young, *The Washington Community, 1800–1828* (New York: Harcourt Brace Jovanovich, 1966), 130.

39 Johnstone, *Jefferson and the Presidency*, 130–31. Young, *The Washington Community* (New York: Harcourt Brace Jovanovich, 1966), 130.

40 Cunningham, *Process of Government*, 188, 192.

41 Johnstone, *Jefferson and the Presidency*, 148–49. Cunningham, *Process of Government*, 193.

42 Cunningham, *Process of Government*, 188. Also see Johnstone, *Jefferson and the Presidency*, 132–36.

43 Jefferson to William Duane, March 22, 1806, in Cunningham, *Process of Government*, 193.

44 Young, *Washington Community*, 158–59. Also see Jefferson to John Randolph, December 1, 1803, quoted in Cunningham, *Jeffersonian Republicans in Power*, 95.

45 Young, *Washington Community*, 168–69. Also see Johnstone, *Jefferson and the Presidency*, 144–48.

46 See Jefferson to David R. Williams, January 31, 1806, in Cunningham, *Jeffersonian Republicans in Power*, 95–96.

47 Cunningham, *Process of Government*, 211–12. Johnstone, *Jefferson and the Presidency*, 141. Young, *Washington Community*, 166. Leonard D. White, *The Jeffersonians: A Study in Administrative History, 1801–1829* (New York: Free Press, 1951), 50–51.

48 Cunningham, *Process of Government*, 192–93, 203; also see 200–01, 205–06.

49 Cunningham, *Process of Government*, 200.

50 During Jefferson's presidency, the figures likened to a prime minister or premier were not department heads but legislative leaders known to have Jefferson's confidence. In early 1802, a Federalist identified Virginia's representative William Branch Giles as the "premier or prime minister of the day" (Johnstone, *Jefferson and the Presidency*, 133). After Giles moved over to the Senate, he was judged to have assumed the role of "the Ministerial leader in the Senate" (Cunningham, *Jeffersonian Republicans in Power*, 93). With Giles gone from the House, Randolph was seen to have assumed the role of "our great premier" (76). After Randolph's fall from grace, speculation grew that Representative Barnabus Bidwell was angling to become "primus inter pares" (89).

51 McDonald, *Alexander Hamilton*, 292 n18. Johnstone, *Jefferson and the Presidency*, 141. Ellis and Wildavsky, *Dilemmas of Presidential Leadership*, 43.

52 This is the position advanced, for instance, by Clinton Rossiter in *The American Presidency* (New York: Harcourt, Brace & World, 1960), 94–95.

53 Johnstone, *Jefferson and the Presidency*, 302–03.

54 White, *Jeffersonians*, 43. Young, *Washington Community*, 174–75.

55 White, *Jeffersonians*, 34. Ellis and Wildavsky, *Dilemmas of Presidential Leadership*, 75. Johnstone, *Jefferson and the Presidency*, esp. 305–06.

56 Johnstone, *Jefferson and the Presidency*, 304–05.

57 Robert V. Remini, *Henry Clay: Statesman for the Union* (New York: Norton, 1991), 72–93, esp. 81–82. White, *Jeffersonians*, 53.

58 Remini, *Henry Clay*, 91. White, *Jeffersonians*, 54.

59 Cunningham, *Process of Government*, 197. Ralph Ketcham, *James Madison: A Biography* (Charlottesville: University of Virginia Press, 1990), 488–89. Young, *Washington Community*, 234–35.

60 *Memoirs of John Quincy Adams*, ed. Charles Francis Adams (Philadelphia: J.B. Lippincott, 1875), 4:242 (February 2, 1819). Young, *Washington Community*, 223–24.

61 *Memoirs of John Quincy Adams*, 4:451 (November 27, 1819). Harry Ammon, *James Monroe: The Quest for National Identity* (Charlottesville: University of Virginia Press, 1990), 380, 384–85, 423. Ellis and Wildavsky, *Dilemmas of Presidential Leadership*, 95–96. Young, *Washington Community*, 235–36. Noble E. Cunningham, Jr., *The Presidency of James Monroe* (Lawrence: University Press of Kansas, 1996), 126–27.

62 White, *Jeffersonians*, 101. Cooper, "Jeffersonian Attitudes toward Executive Leadership," 61. Young, *Washington Community*, 244.

63 Sidney M. Milkis and Michael Nelson, *The American Presidency: Origins and Development, 1776–2002* (Washington, DC: CQ Press, 2003; fourth edition), 111; also see White, *Jeffersonians*, 38.

64 See, for example, *Memoirs of John Quincy Adams*, 4:67 (March 23, 1818); and Cunningham, *Presidency of James Monroe*, 101–02.

65 Ammon, *James Monroe*, 450–57. Cunningham, *Presidency of James Monroe*, 93–103. Fred I. Greenstein, *Inventing the Job of President: Leadership Style from George Washington to Andrew Jackson* (Princeton, NJ: Princeton University Press, 2009), 70. Compare White, *Jeffersonians*, 38–39; and Milkis and Nelson, *American Presidency*, 111.

66 *Memoirs of John Quincy Adams*, 4:457 (November 29, 1819). Ammon, *James Monroe*, 382–83. Cunningham, *Presidency of James Monroe*, 45.

67 *Annals of Congress*, March 13, 1818, 1371. James Monroe, First Annual Message, December 12, 1817.

68 *Annals of Congress*, March 13, 1818, 1373–74.

69 Cunningham, *Presidency of James Monroe*, 127.

70 *Memoirs of John Quincy Adams*, 4:28 (December 6, 1817); 4:497 (January 8, 1820).

71 Stephen Skowronek, *The Politics Presidents Make: Leadership from John Adams to George Bush* (Cambridge, MA: Harvard University Press, 1993), 118. John Quincy Adams, First Annual Message, December 6, 1825. Binkley, *President and Congress*, 82. Young, *Washington Community*, 248; also see 188–89.

72 Remini, *Henry Clay*, 329. Also see Daniel Walker Howe, *What Hath God Wrought: The Transformation of America, 1815–1848* (New York: Oxford University Press, 2007), 274; and Sean Wilentz, *The Rise of American Democracy: Jefferson to Lincoln* (New York: Norton, 2005), 299–300.

73 Spitzer, *Presidential Veto*, 30. *Memoirs of John Quincy Adams*, 8:230 (June 6, 1830). In 1789, John Adams had considered the absence of an absolute veto to be one of the greatest defects of the new Constitution. See his letter to Roger Sherman, July 18, 1789, quoted in White, *The Federalists*, 93 n18.

74 Spitzer, *Presidential Veto*, 30–32.

75 Andrew Jackson, Veto Message, May 27, 1830.

76 Remini, *Henry Clay*, 362.

77 *Register of Debates*, July 12, 1832, 1265–66.

78 Remini, *Henry Clay*, 379–80; Michael J. Holt, *The Rise and Fall of the American Whig Party: Jacksonian Politics and the Onset of the Civil War* (New York: Oxford University Press, 1999), 15–16. Richard J. Ellis and Stephen Kirk, "Presidential Mandates in the Nineteenth Century: Conceptual Change and Institutional Development," *Studies in American Political Development* (Spring 1995), 138.

79 *Register of Debates*, April 14, 1834, 1314. Also see Remini, *Henry Clay*, 457–63; and Holt, *Rise and Fall of the American Whig Party*, 16–17, 26–30.

80 Andrew Jackson, Second Annual Message, December 6, 1830. Ellis and Wildavsky, *Dilemmas of Presidential Leadership*, 114–15.

81 William Henry Harrison, Inaugural Address, March 4, 1841.

82 Holt, *Rise and Fall of the American Whig Party*, 128.

83 Remini, *Henry Clay*, 581–96. Holt, *Rise and Fall of the American Whig Party*, 128–35. Howe, *What Hath God Wrought*, 591–92.

84 Remini, *Henry Clay*, 597, 605. Howe, *What Hath God Wrought*, 594. Spitzer, *Presidential Veto*, 51.

85 *Congressional Globe*, August 16, 1842, 894–96.

86   Spitzer, *Presidential Veto*, 38. David P. Currie, *The Constitution in Congress: Democrats and Whigs, 1829–1861* (Chicago: University of Chicago Press, 2005), 165. *Congressional Globe*, August 16, 1842, 907.

87   Spitzer, *Presidential Veto*, 44, 53. James Polk's final State of the Union message (December 5, 1848) also included a lengthy defense of the president's veto power. The people, Polk reminded the Whigs, "have commanded the President, as much as they have commanded the legislative branch of the Government, to execute their will." Like Jackson, Polk suggested that the president was the more authentic representative of the people's will because only he was "responsible ... to the people of the whole Union," whereas legislators often fell prey to "combinations of individuals and sections" and so sacrificed the people's interest on the altar of special or parochial interests.

88   Spitzer, *Presidential Veto*, 54–55.

89   A private bill is defined in the United States Code as "bills for the relief of private parties, bills granting pensions, bills removing political disabilities, and bills for the survey of rivers and harbors" (Spitzer, *Presidential Veto*, 81).

90   Spitzer, *Presidential Veto*, 73–74.

91   Ellis, *Founding the American Presidency*, 132. Washington's veto of legislation that would have reduced the size of the army by two dragoons contained no constitutional arguments. President Madison vetoed a bill to recharter the national bank, even though he conceded in the message that the bank was constitutional.

92   Spitzer, *Presidential Veto*, 59. Leonard D. White, *The Republican Era: 1869–1901: A Study in Administrative History* (New York: Macmillan, 1958), 39–40. President James Garfield also never vetoed a bill but he served only a few months before being assassinated.

93   Fragment: What General Taylor Ought to Say, [March ?] 1848; Speech in the US House of Representatives on the Presidential Question, July 27, 1848; and Speech at Pittsburgh, Pennsylvania, February 15, 1861 in Roy P. Basler, ed., *The Collected Works of Abraham Lincoln* (New Brunswick, NJ: Rutgers University Press, 1953), 1:454, 504, 4:214.

94   David Donald, *Lincoln Reconsidered: Essays on the Civil War Era* (New York: Vintage; second edition, enlarged), 191–92. G.S. Boritt, *Lincoln and the Economics of the American Dream* (Memphis: Memphis State University Press, 1978), 209.

95   Boritt, *Lincoln and the Economics of the American Dream*, 201–02.

96   Speech at Wilmington, Delaware, June 10, 1848, *Collected Works of Abraham Lincoln*, 1:476. Donald, *Lincoln Reconsidered*, 192–93.

97   Wade–Davis Bill, entry in Mark E. Neely, Jr., *The Abraham Lincoln Encyclopedia* (New York: McGraw-Hill, 1982), 322.

98   Zachary Taylor, Annual Message, December 4, 1849.

99   David Herbert Donald, *Lincoln* (New York: Simon and Schuster, 1995), 561–62.

100 Abraham Lincoln, Second Annual Message, December 1, 1862.

101 Speech in US House of Representatives on the Presidential Question, July 27, 1848, *Collected Works of Abraham Lincoln*, 1:506. Abraham Lincoln, Fourth Annual Message, December 6, 1844, American Presidency Project, www.presidency.ucsb.edu/ws/index.php?pid=29505.

102 J.G. Randall and Richard N. Current, *Lincoln the President: Last Full Measure* (New York: Dodd, Mead, 1955), 309–10.

103 Lincoln also appears to have dangled patronage to induce Democrats to switch their votes, particularly those who had not been reelected. For instance, Brooklyn Democrat Moses Odell switched his vote and immediately after the legislative session was installed in a lucrative federal post as a New York City naval agent. Randall and Current, *Lincoln the President*, 310. Also see Philip Shaw Paludan, *The Presidency of Abraham Lincoln* (Lawrence: University Press of Kansas, 1994), 301.

104   Paul Bergeron, ed., *The Papers of Andrew Johnson*, volume 10: February–July 1866 (Nashville: University of Tennessee Press, 1992), 10:426.

105   Speech on Congressional Sovereignty, September 27, 1866, Lancaster, Pennsylvania, in Beverly Wilson Palmer and Holly Byers Ochoa, eds., *The Selected Papers of Thaddeus Stevens*, volume 2: April 1865–August 1868 (Pittsburgh: University of Pittsburgh Press, 1998), 2:198.

106   To Joseph R. Hawley, President National Union Republican Convention, May 29, 1868, in John Y. Simon, ed., *The Papers of Ulysses S. Grant*, volume 18: October 1, 1867–June 30, 1868 (Carbondale, IL: Southern Illinois University Press, 1991), 18:264.

107   This misconception can be traced to a much quoted essay—written in the second year of Grant's presidency—by one of the president's severest critics, Henry Adams. Adams wrote that Grant believed "as it was the duty of every military commander to obey the civil authority without question, so it was the duty of the President to follow without hesitation the wishes of the people as expressed by Congress" ("The Session," *North American Review*, July 1870, 34). This quote was recycled and endorsed in White's influential book *The Republican Era*, 23–24. Wilfred Binkley also relied heavily on Adams's essay in rendering his own conclusion that "except on rare occasions [Grant] was ... disposed to accept without question the work of Congress as the authoritative expression of the will of the American people" (*President and Congress*, 181). For a corrective, see Brooks D. Simpson, *The Reconstruction Presidents* (Lawrence: University Press of Kansas, 1998), esp. 135.

108   Ulysses S. Grant, Inaugural Address, March 4, 1869. Spitzer, *Presidential Veto*, 72. Grant was also the first president to ask for an item veto—that is, the power to approve some parts of a bill while negating others. In his 1873 annual message he explained to Congress that an item veto would enable the president to "protect the public against the many abuses and waste of public moneys which creep into appropriation bills and other important measures during the expiring hours of Congress." Fifth Annual Message, December 1, 1873.

109   Grant, Inaugural Address. John Sherman, *Recollections of Forty Years in the House, Senate, and Cabinet*, volume 2 (Chicago: Werner, 1895), 1:447.

110   George Frisbie Hoar, *Autobiography of Seventy Years*, volume 2 (Charles Scribner's Sons, 1905), 2:46. White, *The Republican Era*, 24.

111   Woodrow Wilson, "Cabinet Government in the United States" (1879), in Ronald J. Pestritto, ed., *Woodrow Wilson: The Essential Political Writings* (Lanham, MD: Lexington, 2005), 137.

112   Simpson, *Reconstruction Presidents*, 220–24. The quotations are from Hayes's diary entry of March 18, 1879, in volume 3 of *Diary and Letters of Rutherford B. Hayes*, www.ohiohistory.org/onlinedoc/hayes/Volume03/Chapter37/March181879.txt.

113   Spitzer, *Presidential Veto*, 74–75. Roosevelt vetoed marginally more bills than Cleveland but was in office significantly longer. Roosevelt's per year average, Spitzer calculates, was a little over 50 vetoes a year. Nearly 80 percent of FDR's vetoes also involved private bills.

114   Richard E. Welch, Jr., *The Presidencies of Grover Cleveland* (Lawrence: University Press of Kansas, 1988), 115–19, 122–23. Also see Karen S. Hoffman, "'Going Public' in the Nineteenth Century: Grover Cleveland's Repeal of the Sherman Silver Purchase Act," *Rhetoric and Public Affairs* (Spring 2002), 57–77.

115   Woodrow Wilson, "Mr. Cleveland as President," *Atlantic Monthly* (March 1897), 289, 292, 294–96. Also see Daniel D. Stid, *The President as Statesman: Woodrow Wilson and the Constitution* (Lawrence: University Press of Kansas, 1998), 36–40.

116   Wilson, "Mr. Cleveland as President," 289, 291, 296, 300. Stid, *The President as Statesman*, 39.

117   Wilson, "Mr. Cleveland as President," 296.

118   Alyn Brodsky, *Grover Cleveland: A Study in Character* (New York: St. Martin's Press, 2000), 44, 57.

119   Stid, *The President as Statesman*, 191 n59. William McKinley, Inaugural Address, March 4, 1897.

120   Lewis L. Gould, *The Presidency of William McKinley* (Lawrence: University Press of Kansas, 1980), 42–44.

121   Gould, *Presidency of William McKinley*, 209; also see 2–5. On the comparison with Jefferson, see Binkley, *President and Congress*, 231. Further testimony to McKinley's legislative influence is offered in Hoar, *Autobiography of Seventy Years*, 46–47. A more recent appreciation of McKinley's legislative and party leadership is Kevin Phillips, *William McKinley* (New York: Times Books, 2003).

122   Gould, *Presidency of William McKinley*, 214. "How Admiral Dewey's Announcement is Received," *The Literary Digest*, April 14, 1900, 443.

123   Gould, *Presidency of William McKinley*, 240, 243. In "The Growing Powers of the President," for example, Washington journalist Henry Litchfield West noted with alarm that "the executive ... influences, if it does not control, the action of Congress." *The Forum* (March 1901–August 1901), 25.

124   See Saladin M. Ambar, *How Governors Built the American Presidency* (Philadelphia: University of Pennsylvania Press, 2012).

125   Theodore Roosevelt, *An Autobiography* (New York: Charles Scribner's Sons, 1920), 282; also see 280.

126   Joseph Bucklin Bishop, *Theodore Roosevelt and His Time Shown in His Own Letters*, volume 2 (New York: Charles Scribner's Sons, 1920), 1:233–34.

127   Binkley, *President and Congress*, 240–42. McDonald, *American Presidency*, 357.

128   Lewis L. Gould, *The Presidency of Theodore Roosevelt* (Lawrence: University Press of Kansas, 1991), 244, 277, 294.

129   Peri Arnold, *Remaking the Presidency: Roosevelt, Taft, and Wilson, 1901–1916* (Lawrence: University Press of Kansas, 2009), 116. On Taft's post-presidential views of presidential power, see William Howard Taft, *Our Chief Magistrate and His Powers* (New York: Columbia University Press, 1916), esp. 139–40.

130   Arnold, *Remaking the Presidency*, 106–07, 109–11. William Howard Taft, Inaugural Address, March 4, 1909.

131   Arnold, *Remaking the Presidency*, 107, 109. John Morton Blum, *The Republican Roosevelt* (New York: Atheneum, 1963), esp. 75–85. George E. Mowry, *The Era of Theodore Roosevelt, 1900–1912* (New York: Harper & Brothers, 1958), 238–41.

132   Lewis L. Gould, *The Presidency of William Howard Taft* (Lawrence: University Press of Kansas, 2009), 54. Mowry, *Era of Theodore Roosevelt*, 240. Arnold, *Remaking the Presidency*, 111.

133   Mowry, *Era of Theodore Roosevelt*, 246. Arnold, *Remaking the Presidency*, 113.

134   Arnold, *Remaking the Presidency*, 114–15. Gould, *Presidency of William Howard Taft*, 52.

135   Gould, *Presidency of William Howard Taft*, 60, 62. Arnold, *Remaking the Presidency*, 116.

136   Herbert Croly, *Progressive Democracy* (New York: Macmillan, 1914), 296. Joseph E. Kallenbach, *The American Chief Executive: The Presidency and the Governorship* (New York: Harper & Row, 1966), 336. On the Taft administration's drafting of the Mann–Elkins Act, see Lawrence H. Chamberlain, *The President, Congress and Legislation* (New York: Columbia University Press, 1946), 420–22.

137   Stid, *The President as Statesman*, 91.

138   Stid, *The President as Statesman*, 91–92.

139   Stid, *The President as Statesman*, 89. Daniel Stid, "Rhetorical Leadership and 'Common Counsel' in the Presidency of Woodrow Wilson," in Richard J. Ellis, ed., *Speaking to the People: The Rhetorical Presidency in Historical Perspective* (Amherst: University of Massachusetts Press, 1998), 167.

140   An exception to this general rule was at the end of the legislative session when the president would come to the Capitol—using the "President's Room" in the Senate—to sign legislation.

141 Stid, "Rhetorical Leadership and 'Common Counsel,'" 169.

142 Arnold, *Remaking the Presidency*, 171–72. Arthur S. Link, *Wilson: The New Freedom* (Princeton, NJ: Princeton University Press, 1956), 179–80.

143 Arnold, *Remaking the Presidency*, 173.

144 Arnold, *Remaking the Presidency*, 175–80. Stid, *The President as Statesman*, 92.

145 Stid, "Rhetorical Leadership and 'Common Counsel,'" 172–73. On Wilson's leadership in securing the Clayton Act and the Federal Trade Commission Act, see Arnold, *Remaking the Presidency*, 181–90.

146 Stid, "Rhetorical Leadership and 'Common Counsel,'" 175.

147 Binkley, *President and Congress*, 266.

148 Robert K. Murray, *The Politics of Normalcy: Governmental Theory and Practice in the Harding–Coolidge Era* (New York: Norton, 1973), 56.

149 Calvin Coolidge, *The Autobiography of Calvin Coolidge* (New York: Cosmopolitan Book Corporation, 1929), 223, 229, 231.

150 Martin L. Fausold, *The Presidency of Herbert C. Hoover* (Lawrence: University Press of Kansas, 1985), 51, 147–48. Jordan A. Schwarz, "Hoover and Congress: Politics, Personality, and Perspective in the Presidency," in Martin L. Fausold and George T. Mazuzan, eds., *The Hoover Presidency: A Reappraisal* (Albany: State University of New York Press, 1974), esp. 88–90, 93, 99.

151 McDonald, *American Presidency*, 364. Schwarz "Hoover and Congress," 91. Also see E. Pendleton Herring, "First Session of the Seventy-Second Congress, December 7, 1931, to July 16, 1932," *American Political Science Review* (February 1934), esp. 855–58.

152 Arthur M. Schlesinger, Jr., *The Coming of the New Deal* (Boston: Houghton Mifflin, 1959), 21. Anthony J. Badger, *FDR: The First Hundred Days* (New York: Hill & Wang, 2008), 52–53, 55.

153 Badger, *FDR*, xiv. David Greenberg, "The Folly of the 'Hundred Days,'" *Wall Street Journal*, March 21, 2009, W3. Louis Nelson, "Trump Scoffs at 100-Day Mark as 'Ridiculous Standard,'" *Politico*, April 21, 2017. Also see Jeff Greenfield, "Why the First 100 Days Concept is Bogus," *Politico*, April 12, 2017.

154 Badger, *FDR*, xv. George C. Edwards III, *The Strategic President: Persuasion and Opportunity in Presidential Leadership* (Princeton, NJ: Princeton University Press, 2009), 112–13, 115. Badger, *FDR*, 26, 40–41. Pendleton Herring, "First Session of the Seventy-Third Congress, March 9, 1933 to June 16, 1933," *American Political Science Review* (February 1934), 75. Also see John Frendreis, Raymond Tatalovich, and Jon Schaff, "Predicting Legislative Output in the First One-Hundred Days, 1897–1995," *Political Research Quarterly* (December 2001), 853–70.

155 Herring, "First Session of the Seventy-Third Congress," 75. Sylvia Snowiss, "Presidential Leadership of Congress: An Analysis of Roosevelt's First Hundred Days," *Publius* (1971), 62.

156 Herring, "First Session of the Seventy-Third Congress," 70–72. Edwards, *The Strategic President*, 113. Badger, *FDR*, 52–53. Snowiss, "Presidential Leadership of Congress," 81–83. Schlesinger, *Coming of the New Deal*, 552–53.

157 On the drafting of the emergency banking bill, see Badger, *FDR*, 25–26, 38; and Amos Kiewe, *FDR's First Fireside Chat: Public Confidence and the Banking Crisis* (College Station: Texas A&M University Press, 2007), esp. 62–63. The Moley quote can be found in the latter on p. 60.

158 Badger, *FDR*, 43. Adam Cohen, *Nothing to Fear: FDR's Inner Circle and the Hundred Days That Created Modern America* (New York: Penguin Press, 2009), 278. Schlesinger, *Coming of the New Deal*, 443.

159 Schlesinger, *Coming of the New Deal*, 400–06. William E. Leuchtenburg, *Franklin D. Roosevelt and the New Deal, 1932–1940* (New York: Harper & Row, 1963), 150–51. James MacGregor Burns, *Roosevelt: The Lion and the Fox* (New York: Harcourt, Brace & World, 1956), 219.

160 Leuchtenburg, *Franklin D. Roosevelt and the New Deal*, 152–54. James T. Patterson, *Congressional Conservatism and the New Deal: The Growth of the Conservative Coalition in Congress, 1933–1939* (Lexington: University of Kentucky Press, 1967), 59–69.

161 Schlesinger, *Coming of the New Deal*, 554. Badger, *FDR*, 74.

162 Leuchtenburg, *Franklin D. Roosevelt and the New Deal*, 134–36, 231, 250. Patterson, *Congressional Conservatism and the New Deal*, 155, 183.

163 Patterson, *Congressional Conservatism and the New Deal*, 75. Leuchtenburg, *Franklin D. Roosevelt and the New Deal*, 251.

164 William E. Leuchtenburg, *In the Shadow of FDR: From Harry Truman to Barack Obama* (Ithaca, NY: Cornell University Press, 2009; fourth edition), 302.

165 Jean Edward Smith, "Roosevelt: The Great Divider," *New York Times*, September 2, 2009, A31.

166 Burns, *Roosevelt: The Lion and the Fox*, 184.

167 Leuchtenburg, *Franklin Roosevelt and the New Deal*, 132. Schlesinger, *Coming of the New Deal*, 308–09, 313–14. Edwards, *The Strategic President*, 116. Lawrence R. Jacobs, "The Promotional Presidency and the New Institutional Toryism: Public Mobilization, Legislative Dominance, and Squandered Opportunities," in George C. Edwards III and Desmond S. King, eds., *The Polarized Presidency of George W. Bush* (New York: Oxford University Press, 2007), 303–07.

168 In *The Living Constitution*, published in 1927, Howard Lee McBain described the president as "a Chief Legislator rather than a Chief Executive." According to McBain, the notion that the president was the chief executive was little better than a "gentle fraud" because "the prime function of the President is not executive at all. It is legislative. ... We elect the President as a leader of legislation. We hold him accountable for what he succeeds in getting Congress to do and in preventing Congress from doing" (115–17).

169 Kallenbach, *American Chief Executive*, 340. Richard E. Neustadt, "Presidency and Legislation: Planning the President's Program," *American Political Science Review* (December 1955), 1015.

170 Schlesinger, *Coming of the New Deal*, 554. On the Office of Legislative Affairs—initially called the Office of Congressional Relations—see Russell Riley, ed., *Bridging the Constitutional Divide: Inside the White House Office of Legislative Affairs* (College Station: Texas A&M University Press, 2010); Kenneth F. Collier, *Between The Branches: The White House Office of Legislative Affairs* (Pittsburgh: University of Pittsburgh Press, 1997); and Eric L. Davis, "Congressional Liaison: The People and Institutions," in Anthony King, ed., *Both Ends of the Avenue: The Presidency, the Executive Branch, and Congress in the 1980s* (Washington, DC: American Enterprise Institute, 1983), 59–95.

171 James L. Sundquist, *The Decline and Resurgence of Congress* (Washington, DC: Brookings Institution Press, 1981), 65.

172 Neustadt, "Presidency and Legislation," 1015. Also see Andrew Rudalevige, *Managing the President's Program: Presidential Leadership and Legislative Policy Formulation* (Princeton, NJ: Princeton University Press, 2002).

173 Jonathan Chait, "Why the Democrats Can't Govern," *New Republic*, April 15, 2009.

174 The gap between public expectations and the president's formal powers is the starting point of Neustadt's *Presidential Power*. Neustadt's emphasis on the president's power of persuasion is critiqued in Edwards, *The Strategic President*, and George C. Edwards III, *At the Margins: Presidential Leadership of Congress* (New Haven, CT: Yale University Press, 1989). In *Roosevelt: Lion and the Fox*, James MacGregor Burns describes "the chief executive's capacity to lead Congress" as "the classic test of greatness in the White House" (186).

175 Edwards, *At the Margins*, 4–5. Andrew Rudalevige, "The Executive Branch and the Legislative Process," in Joel D. Aberbach and Mark A. Peterson, eds., *The Executive Branch* (New York: Oxford University Press, 2005), 445.

CHAPTER 5

THE WAR-MAKING PRESIDENCY

INTRODUCTORY PUZZLE: WHY DIDN'T TRUMAN CALL A WAR A WAR?

"Mothers and fathers all over our beloved land are spending sleepless nights worrying again over their boys being sent to fight wars on foreign soil—wars that are no concern of ours." To this American citizen, writing to her president, it seemed plain that young Americans were being sent to fight in a war. Yet President Harry Truman denied that was the case.[1]

"We are not at war," Truman declared at a press conference on June 29, 1950, just days after he had authorized United States air and naval forces to assist the South Korean government in repelling the surprise invasion by North Korea. South Korea, Truman explained, had been attacked by "a bunch of bandits," and the United States, together with other members of the United Nations, was simply suppressing "a bandit raid." He was not taking the country into war but rather participating in a United Nations "police action."[2]

Even after large numbers of American ground forces began to fight and die in Korea, Truman continued to avoid the "W" word. In an address to the nation on July 19, 1950, Truman spoke to the country for the first time about what he called "the situation in Korea." Earlier that same day he sent a special message to Congress in which he referred to "the Korean operation" and "the Korean crisis." Neither in his address to the American people nor in his message to Congress did Truman speak of war, even though just three days earlier more than 400 American soldiers had been killed, most of them in a battle at Kum River. Indeed, by the time Truman addressed the nation, some 1,200 Americans had already been killed in Korea. Before the Korean "situation" was finally brought to a close in 1953, 33,000 Americans had died in combat and more than three times that many had been wounded. Only the Civil War, World War I, World War II, and the Vietnam War have produced more American casualties.[3]

Why, then, did President Truman rely on euphemisms to cover up what was plain to every American: that the nation was engaged in a war with North Korea? It was not that Truman was trying to disguise from the American people or from Congress the severity of the situation or the sacrifices that would be required. In his July 19 address, he forthrightly told the American people that to halt the "Communist invasion" would "take a hard, tough fight." He also made no effort to hide that a large military buildup would be required and that "substantial" tax increases would therefore be necessary. He even warned that rationing and price controls might be required in "the stern days ahead."[4]

The main reason for Truman's verbal evasion lies in the text of Article I, section 8 of the United States Constitution, which gives Congress the power to declare war. Not having asked Congress to declare war on North Korea, Truman felt it necessary to deny that the nation was at war. But that only pushes the puzzle back a step: why did Truman not ask Congress to declare war?

If Truman thought that Congress would refuse to declare war, then it is easy to understand why he would avoid going to Congress, particularly since he believed that

Speaking from the White House on July 19, 1950, President Harry Truman addresses the nation on "the situation in Korea."

Courtesy: Time & Life Pictures/Getty Images.

Korea was a vital test of American resolve. However, there is no evidence that Congress would have refused the president had he asked for a formal declaration of war or a resolution approving or authorizing the use of force. In fact, Truman's determination to draw the line against Communist expansion in Korea was strongly supported by both congressional Republicans and Democrats.[5]

Perhaps Truman felt that the situation in Korea was so urgent that even a small delay would have calamitous consequences. But even if saving South Korea required the president to act quickly, it does not explain why Truman did not subsequently seek legislative authorization or approval. Why then did Truman not seek retroactive legislative authorization when even his severest Republican critics had pledged to back it?

Congress must shoulder some of the blame. For while some Republicans—most notably Ohio's influential senator Robert Taft, a.k.a. "Mr. Republican," and Senate minority leader Kenneth Wherry—insisted that the president was required by the Constitution to get legislative authorization for his actions, other Republicans accepted that Truman's police action did not require a declaration of war. Moreover, no Democratic legislator—and Democrats controlled both the House and the Senate—pressed Truman to seek congressional approval or authorization for his actions. Indeed, the day after the North Korean invasion, Truman asked the Democratic chairman of the Senate Foreign Relations Committee, Tom Connally, whether he would need a declaration of war from Congress if he decided to commit American forces to Korea, and Connally reassured the president that would not be necessary since the president had "the right to do it as commander in chief and under the UN charter." We all know, Connally said, that "if a burglar breaks into your house, you can shoot him without going down to the police station and getting permission."[6]

Truman did experience pressure from within his administration to seek a war resolution from Congress, most especially from Averell Harriman. A savvy politician and experienced diplomat, Harriman urged the president to go to Congress while legislative support was there for the taking, arguing that if the war dragged on it would be better to have Congress implicated in the decision. Uncertain about the best course, Truman directed Secretary of State Dean Acheson to draft a congressional resolution approving the use of military force in Korea.[7]

Acheson, however, strongly opposed asking for congressional approval of the president's actions. A distinguished lawyer, Acheson argued that the president should stand upon his constitutional powers as commander in chief. To bolster his case, Acheson produced 87 past instances in which the president had ordered American troops into combat without getting congressional approval. He pointed out, for instance, that President William McKinley had ordered 5,000 soldiers to China in the Boxer Rebellion and that Franklin Roosevelt had sent troops to Iceland in 1941 without getting authorization from Congress.[8]

On July 3, Truman summoned his advisors—and the Senate majority leader—to discuss how best to handle Congress. Although Truman is often celebrated for his decisiveness, in this case he hesitated, preferring to defer a decision until after Congress returned from a week-long recess. But by the time Congress returned, casualties were mounting and the prospect of a unified congressional front no longer seemed as certain.

The situation in Korea was rapidly looking less like a "police action" or any of the 87 precedents identified by Acheson, and more like a protracted war. To invite Congress to debate a war resolution at this juncture, Acheson later explained, would have sown division in the country and undermined the "shaken morale of the troops."[9]

Ultimately, however, Truman's reluctance to ask for congressional approval owed less to tactical calculations about whether such a resolution would help or hinder the war effort and more to a concern with protecting presidential prerogative. Truman opted not to follow Harriman's political counsel because—as Harriman put it—Truman "always kept in mind how his actions would affect future presidential authority." Acheson agreed that the determinative factor was Truman's desire not to establish a precedent that would restrict future presidents' capacity to respond to military emergencies. "His great office," Acheson explained, "was to him a sacred and temporary trust, which he was determined to pass on unimpaired by the slightest loss of power or prestige."[10]

Herein lies a critical difference between the president and Congress. Whereas presidents frequently attend to the precedent their decisions may establish for future presidents, individual members of Congress are rarely concerned with how their actions will affect congressional power over the long run. Even if a president is not inclined to focus on the longer-term institutional implications of a decision, the many lawyers at his disposal are there to press him not to establish precedents that might handicap future incumbents. And presidents know that history—or at least historians—will judge their "greatness" on whether they strengthened or weakened their office. No individual member of Congress carries the same burden.[11]

THE WAR POWERS DEBATE

Acheson went to great lengths to persuade Truman that sending troops abroad without congressional authorization was consistent with precedents dating back to the earliest days of the republic. In turn, Truman's intervention in Korea has been seized upon by subsequent presidents to justify their own decisions not to seek declarations of war from Congress. In fact, no president since Truman has deemed a declaration of war from Congress to be constitutionally necessary, no matter the number of troops or the circumstances, although several—notably Lyndon Johnson in the Vietnam War, George Herbert Walker Bush in the Gulf War, and George Walker Bush in the Iraq War—have sought and received legislative authorization for their actions.

During the Vietnam War, liberals who had vigorously defended Truman's constitutional authority to intervene militarily in Korea began to have second thoughts about the scope of presidential war powers. Having in 1951 derided Robert Taft's reading of the Constitution as having "no support in law or in history," historian Henry Steele Commanger told Congress in 1971 that the "warmaking power is lodged and was intended to be lodged in the Congress" and that it was "very dangerous to allow the president to, in effect, commit us to a war from which we cannot withdraw." Similarly, historian Arthur Schlesinger Jr., who in 1951 had criticized Taft's position as "demonstrably irresponsible," belatedly found a prescient wisdom in Taft's warnings against allowing an "imperial presidency" to take the nation into war anywhere in the world. And whereas in 1951

Democrats in Congress had strenuously resisted Republican efforts to pass a joint res-olution that would have required congressional assent before the president sent troops into harm's way, congressional Democrats in 1973 pushed through the War Powers Resolution, which limited the president's ability to send troops into combat without legislative approval.[12]

Ironically, just as liberal Democrats were rediscovering the sagacity of "Mr. Repub-lican," conservative Republicans began to unearth the virtues of a resolute President Truman. In taking decisive action in Korea, on this view, Truman was not usurping constitutional power but instead vigorously exercising the powers that the framers had wisely granted the commander in chief. Had Truman—and his successors in the White House—not unilaterally wielded the presidential war power, the United States would have been ill-equipped to meet the threat of the Soviet Union and likely could not have prevailed in the Cold War. Moreover, Congress acted its constitutional part by appro-priating funds for the Korean War. Had Congress wished to do so, it could have termi-nated the war by refusing to pay for it. On this reading, both the president and Congress acted as the framers intended. If Congress chose not to end the Korean War, the failing was "a lack of political will rather than a defect in the constitutional design."[13]

Who should we believe? When Truman intervened in Korea did he usurp congressional powers, as Taft claimed? Or did the framers intend to give the commander in chief the power to defend the nation's interests abroad? Were Truman's actions a dramatic departure from well-established historical precedent or were they consonant with two centuries of American history? Our inquiry must begin with the making of the Constitution.

ORIGINAL UNDERSTANDINGS

In eighteenth-century Britain, the power to make war and negotiate peace was lodged in the monarch. In the nation's "intercourse with foreign nations," explained the eighteenth-century English jurist William Blackstone, the monarch was "the delegate or representative of his people." From this stemmed the king's "sole prerogative of making war and peace," sending and receiving ambassadors, and making treaties. Parliament had no power to reject a treaty, declare war, or make peace, although it could use the "check of parliamentary impeachment" to "call the king's advisers to a just and severe account . . . for improper or inglorious conduct in beginning, conducting, or concluding a national war." The king was also "the generalissimo, or the first in military command," with the power to direct "the united strength of the community" against foes internal and external. In his capacity as "general of the kingdom," the monarch possessed "the sole power of raising and regulating fleets and armies."[14]

Fighting a revolutionary war against what they perceived to be a tyrannical king compelled Americans to rethink the wisdom of entrusting one man with the power to wage war. Indeed, in forming a government of their own, the American revolutionaries did away with a chief executive altogether, leaving all executive powers in the hands of the Continental Congress. While the delegates who gathered in Philadelphia in the summer of 1787 knew that they did not want an executive with the prerogative powers of George III, they also did not want to repeat the mistakes of the Articles of Confederation.

The Virginia Plan: The Convention's Starting Point

Prior to laying the Virginia Plan before the convention delegates on May 29, 1787, Edmund Randolph enumerated the leading "defects of the confederation." The first defect was that the confederation "produced no security against foreign invasion." The problem was twofold. First, the federal government was dependent on the states to raise and maintain an army and navy, and thus could not muster the military forces necessary to protect the nation. As a result, the government was too weak to repel Indian attacks, compel the British to relinquish northern outposts, or open up the Mississippi to American trade. Second, national security was jeopardized because the central government lacked the authority to prevent states from provoking a war or violating national treaties. For instance, Congress's inability to compel states to pay prewar debts to British merchants, as required by the peace terms of 1783, gave the British an excuse to renege on their pledge to relinquish control of strategically important northern forts.[15]

The Virginia Plan proposed to solve these problems by freeing the central government from its dependence on the goodwill of states to raise armies and execute treaties. Under the Virginia Plan, Congress was empowered to "negative" any law that it deemed in contravention of the Constitution and "to call forth the force of the Union" against any state that failed to fulfill its constitutional duty, as defined by Congress. The Virginia Plan also departed from the Articles in creating a separate executive branch, but it did not spell out whether the powers of war and peace should be lodged in the legislature or the executive. Instead the Virginia Plan noted only that "the National Legislature ought to be impowered [sic] to enjoy the Legislative Rights vested in Congress by the Confederation" and that "a National Executive ... ought to enjoy the Executive rights vested in Congress by the Confederation."[16]

Legal scholar John Yoo, who served in the Office of Legal Counsel in George W. Bush's administration, reads the spare language of the Virginia Plan as maintaining "the traditional vesting of formal war and treaty powers to the executive." More likely, however, the authors of the Virginia Plan were putting off the decision about where to vest these powers, either because of disagreement within the Virginia delegation or because the Virginia delegates were unsure about where these powers should be lodged. Randolph, after all, was no friend of a strong executive. And James Madison, the primary author of the Virginia Plan, had admitted to George Washington just two weeks before arriving in Philadelphia that he had "scarcely ventured as yet" to form an opinion on the powers that should be given to the national executive.[17]

Although most eighteenth-century political philosophers, such as Blackstone and Montesquieu, regarded the powers of war and peace as executive in nature, few framers shared this view. When the convention took up the Virginia Plan's proposal for a national executive on June 1, South Carolina's Charles Pinckney leapt to his feet to object that the executive rights referred to in the Virginia Plan might be construed to "extend to peace & war," which would make the executive "a Monarchy, of the worst kind, to wit an elective one." Pinckney's sentiments were echoed by his widely respected South Carolina colleague John Rutledge and underscored even more emphatically by James Wilson, perhaps the convention's most vocal champion of a vigorous chief executive. The prerogatives of the British monarch, Wilson emphasized, were not "a proper guide in defining the Executive powers" for "some of these prerogatives were of a Legislative nature," most notably the powers of war and peace. "The only powers" that Wilson "conceived [as] strictly Executive were those of executing the laws, and appointing officers." Madison agreed with Wilson, and proposed substitute language that reflected Wilson's definition of executive powers. Madison's motion carried with the support of every state but Connecticut, whose delegates were divided on the motion.[18]

The Committee of Detail's First Draft

The delegates did not return to the subject of war and peace until August, when the five-member Committee of Detail—which was chaired by Rutledge and included Wilson and Randolph as members—reported a first draft of the Constitution based on the decisions reached in the convention over the previous two months. The Committee of Detail granted the legislature the power "to make war," as well as the power to raise armies, build and equip fleets, and "call forth the aid of the militia, in order to execute the laws of the Union, enforce treaties, suppress insurrections, and repel invasions." An early draft of the committee's report, in Randolph's hand, also vested the treaty-making power in the legislature, but the committee decided it would be wiser to give this power to the Senate alone. The committee also entrusted the Senate with appointing ambassadors and the president with receiving ambassadors. In addition, the committee made the president "the commander in chief of the Army and Navy of the United States, and of the Militia of the Several States."[19]

When the convention took up the committee's handiwork in the middle of August, delegates immediately zeroed in on the war-making provision. Pinckney objected to allowing the House to participate in war-making because it would be too large and its decision-making too slow. Pinckney proposed that the Senate should be given the power to make war, especially since it already had been granted the power to make treaties. Nobody seconded Pinckney's proposal, however. Pierce Butler, another South Carolinian, pointed out that even the Senate was too unwieldy and suggested that the power to make war should instead be entrusted to the president, who would "not make war but when the Nation will support it." Butler's proposal garnered no support, only the scorn of Massachusetts' Elbridge Gerry, who said he "never expected to hear in a republic a motion to empower the Executive alone to declare war." The delegates did, however, back a motion by Gerry and Madison to change "make war" to "declare war."[20]

From "Make War" to "Declare War"

What did the convention delegates intend by giving Congress the power to "declare war" rather than to "make war"? According to Yoo, this change radically shrank congressional war powers, since to declare war at that time did not mean to "authorize" or "commence" a war but rather to "announce," "publish," or "proclaim" hostilities that had already begun. The convention debates, however, provide no support for Yoo's interpretation. In offering their substitute wording, Gerry and Madison explained that the change was intended only to make it clear that the executive retained "the power to repel sudden attacks." And in admonishing Butler, Gerry plainly used "declare war" as a synonym for initiating, not announcing war. Moreover, Connecticut's delegation was persuaded to vote in favor of the Gerry–Madison motion only after Rufus King pointed out that "make war" could be misconstrued to include "conduct war," which everybody agreed was the commander in chief's job. In addition, George Mason saw no conflict between his support for the wording change and his unwavering opposition to "giving the power of war to the Executive." Indeed, after the Gerry–Madison motion carried by an 8–1 vote, Butler proposed that since the convention had decided to give the legislature the power of war it should also give the legislature the "power of peace"—that is, the power to make treaties.[21]

In short, the delegates believed that they had empowered Congress to take the nation into war while leaving the president with the authority to repel invasions and to conduct a war once it had been authorized by the legislature. But the Constitution's spare language and the delegates' hurried debate left many vital questions unanswered. For instance, did the president have to wait for the nation to be attacked or could he mount a preemptive attack if an invasion was imminent? And did the power to defend the nation against sudden attack extend to protecting American citizens or interests abroad?[22]

In view of the controversies that have swirled around presidential war powers for more than two centuries, one might wish that the framers had probed the implications of the "declare war" clause more deeply and carefully. But at least the delegates did briefly debate the change in wording, leaving us vital clues as to what they had in mind. In contrast, the commander-in-chief clause was not debated at all during the convention.

The Commander-in-Chief Clause

A narrow reading of the commander-in-chief clause highlights the common eighteenth-century Anglo-American practice of designating a military commander as a commander in chief (each fleet in the British navy had a commander in chief) and placing the commander in chief under the control of a political superior. During the Revolutionary War, for instance, George Washington was styled "General and Commander in Chief," and was instructed "punctually to observe and follow such orders and directions" as Congress might choose to transmit. The trouble with this interpretation is that the president is not a naval or military commander but an independent branch of government.[23]

Contemporary presidents have preferred an expansive interpretation of the commander-in-chief clause that essentially grants the president an unrestricted authority to do with the armed forces whatever he deems in the national interest. On this reading, the delegates made the president the commander in chief because they intended to give the president the power of the sword while reserving to Congress the power of the purse. But if the commander-in-chief clause was intended to be an expansive grant of war-making power, why did those delegates who were most suspicious of executive power raise no objections to making the president commander in chief? Even more puzzling, why were the delegates convinced that they had vested the war power in the legislature?

And why did they bother to give Congress the power to declare war if the commander-in-chief clause essentially nullified that power?

No delegates took exception to the commander-in-chief designation, because the term was familiar to them from their own state constitutions. Each state constitution placed the governor at the head of the state's military forces and all but two called him the commander in chief. The commander in chief's job, everybody understood, was to direct the military in order to protect the nation in case of war, invasion, or rebellion. But no delegate would have equated this role with the traditional "prerogative of making war and peace," which was understood as the power to commence and end war. In fact, the president's power as commander in chief was in some ways even more restricted than that of state governors, because while state governors could call out the state militia on their own authority, the president could only command the state militias—which at that time were largely what passed for a military in the United States—when Congress called them into national service to "execute the Laws of the Union, suppress Insurrections and repel Invasions."

In making the president commander in chief, in sum, the framers clearly did not intend to vest the president with the traditional prerogative of taking the nation into war. Rather, they were endeavoring to ensure civilian control over the military and an effective marshalling of the nation's fighting forces. After all, how could a national legislature that would consist of hundreds of people and be in session no more than three or four months in a year effectively direct and supervise military forces in the event of an invasion or rebellion, let alone a lengthy war? The advantage of making the president commander in chief seemed too obvious to the delegates to warrant discussion or debate.

The "Power of Peace"

Although the convention delegates had little difficulty agreeing that the power to initiate or authorize war should be vested in Congress and that the power to conduct or direct war belonged to the commander in chief, the delegates were deeply divided over how to allocate the power of peace, particularly the power to make treaties. Some delegates argued that the president alone should be responsible for making treaties, while others, including Madison, thought the power was best shared between the president and the Senate. In early September, the Committee on Postponed Matters reported a compromise proposal that granted the president the power to make treaties "by and with the advice and consent" of the Senate. Moreover, two-thirds of senators present needed to consent for a treaty to be consummated. After considerable wrangling and many failed motions, the delegates ultimately decided to accept the committee's compromise.[24]

Less contentious was the committee's proposal to change the way ambassadors were chosen. Rather than have the Senate appoint ambassadors, as the Committee of Detail had proposed, the president would do so "by and with the advice and consent of the Senate." In granting the president a central role in the appointment of ambassadors as well as the making of treaties, the Committee on Postponed Matters decisively shifted the balance of power between the Senate and the president. At the end of August the power to conduct foreign relations still lay almost entirely in the hands of the Senate, with the president possessing little more than the power to receive ambassadors. In contrast, by the time the Constitution was finished in the middle of September, the making of treaties and appointing of ambassadors were listed under Article II, which specified executive powers, rather than Article I, which delineated legislative powers.[25]

These late changes greatly enhanced presidential power in foreign affairs. Yet, as historian Jack Rakove has pointed out, these important last-minute changes were attributable "more to doubts about the Senate"—particularly the fact that it represented the interests of small states better than large states—than enthusiasm for a strong executive. Moreover, the framers' final formulation was a far cry from the traditional royal prerogative over the power of peace. What Blackstone granted to the king alone was now to be shared between the president and the Senate. The result, as political scientist Edward Corwin famously wrote, was "an invitation to struggle for the privilege of directing foreign policy."[26]

DEBATING WASHINGTON'S NEUTRALITY PROCLAMATION: HELVIDIUS V. PACIFICUS

A common contemporary conceit is that we live in a world far more dangerous than anything our forefathers could have imagined. Certainly nuclear, biological, and chemical weapons are capable of causing destruction on a scale that would have been unimaginable to people living two hundred years ago. But in other ways, Americans of the founding generation faced threats to the nation's existence that were more profound than those we face today. The United States had two established European powers ensconced along its borders—Britain to the north and Spain to the south and west—not to mention a host of Indian tribes. When Washington took office in 1789, the nation had a regular army numbering in the hundreds to defend vast borders that stretched for thousands of miles. Moreover, the nation's economic fortunes hinged on trade yet it had no navy to protect its shipping against foreign powers and pirates.

For a new nation with no navy and a tiny regular army, the world became a whole lot more perilous when republican France—having guillotined their king the week before—declared war on Britain in February 1793. Taking sides in a war between the world's two superpowers that was engulfing the European continent was clearly not in America's interests, especially if it backed the losing side. Making matters particularly vexing for the United States was that the French—with whom the Americans had signed a treaty of "perpetual alliance" in 1778—wanted the United States to aid them in their quest to extend the republican "empire of liberty" across monarchical Europe and its far-flung colonies. And many Americans, fresh off a revolutionary war with the British, instinctively sympathized with the French cause. To solicit American help, the French government sent to the United States a special envoy, Edmond Genet, who was tasked with authorizing American citizens—using letters of marque—to seize British trading ships off the Atlantic coast and recruiting American citizens to fight against the Spanish (with whom France was also at war) in the territories of Florida and Louisiana.[27]

Genet's actions—and the rapturous reception that he received upon his arrival—alarmed the Washington administration, which worried that private citizens heeding

Genet's call might provoke the British to declare war on America. Washington asked his cabinet two key questions: Should he call Congress into session? And should he issue a proclamation to prevent "interferences of the Citizens of the United States in the War between France and Great Britain"? The cabinet—which included Treasury Secretary Alexander Hamilton and Secretary of State Thomas Jefferson—agreed that Congress did not need to be called back into session, and that Washington should issue a proclamation that made it clear that the United States would not take sides in the war between France and Britain and threatened criminal prosecution of American citizens who violated the proclamation.[28]

Issued on April 22, 1793, Washington's Proclamation of Neutrality was generally well received. Nobody wanted another war, least of all with Britain. And yet for many Jeffersonian Republicans, who loathed Britain and sympathized with the French republic, strict neutrality was, as Jefferson told Madison, "a disagreeable pill." Jefferson had reluctantly swallowed his misgivings because he felt the proclamation "necessary to keep out of the calamities of a war," but many of Jefferson's supporters were appalled. How, Madison asked Jefferson, could the American republic be neutral in a contest that pitted republican liberty against monarchy? Moreover, how could the United States ignore the duties it owed to France under the Treaty of Alliance it signed in 1778? And what gave the president the right to declare peace without consulting Congress? A policy of neutrality seemed in reality a pro-British policy.[29]

Madison's skepticism about the wisdom of the proclamation was mild compared with the zeal with which some in the Republican press attacked it. These partisan attacks on the administration provided Hamilton an excuse to enter the fray, writing a series of seven tightly argued essays under the pseudonym "Pacificus" that aimed to vindicate both the president's policy of neutrality and the president's constitutional authority to declare neutrality.

Hamilton argued that the Constitution made the president "the organ of intercourse between the United States and foreign nations." It was the president's job to declare "the existing condition of the nation with regard to foreign powers," and to interpret and enforce the obligations and duties that citizens had under existing international law and treaties. Hamilton found this authority not only in specific grants of power—the power to receive ambassadors, the power to make treaties with the advice and consent of the Senate, the commander-in-chief clause, and the power to execute the laws—but also in what is often referred to as the "vesting clause," which declares that "the executive power shall be vested in a president of the United States." According to Hamilton's reading, whereas the Constitution enumerated the legislative powers that were granted to Congress (Article I begins, "All legislative powers herein granted shall be vested in a Congress of the United States"), the Constitution did not enumerate "all the cases of executive authority." On Hamilton's construction, anything that was in its nature an executive power therefore belonged to the president, except where the Constitution explicitly specified a role for Congress, as it did in granting the legislature the power to declare war and giving the Senate a role in the appointment of officers and the making of treaties.[30]

Hamilton's arguments appalled Jefferson. Like most of his contemporaries, Jefferson believed that the first sentence of Article II ("The executive power shall be vested in a

President of the United States") was not an expansive warrant for presidential power, but rather a statement that executive power would be wielded by a single person called a president. Jefferson had been willing to mute his philosophical differences with Hamilton in pursuit of a foreign policy goal that they both believed was necessary to national security, but he believed Hamilton had gone too far in using the policy dispute to aggressively push his vision of enhanced executive power. Knowing Madison's strong disapproval of the neutrality proclamation, Jefferson now wrote to his friend: "For god's sake, my dear Sir, take up your pen, select the most striking heresies, and cut him to pieces in the face of the public."[31]

Using the pen name of "Helvidius," Madison took up Jefferson's challenge. The normally mild-mannered Virginian came out swinging: only "the foreigners and degenerate citizens among us who hate our republican government and the French revolution," Madison wrote, could applaud the principles advanced by Pacificus. Madison rejected Hamilton's argument that the power to declare war and the power to make treaties were inherently executive powers—only those with their "eyes too much on monarchical governments" could believe such an absurdity. The "natural province" of the executive was to execute laws, Madison reasoned, and there was nothing about making a treaty or declaring war that involved the execution of laws. If these powers were to be assigned to "their most natural department" then the legislature, which is tasked with the making of laws, had the far stronger claim to being the natural home of such powers. As authority, Madison called upon Hamilton himself, who in *Federalist* No. 75 had proclaimed that the treaty-making power, although neither strictly legislative nor executive, partook "more of the legislative than of the executive character."[32]

Madison objected not only to Hamilton's expansive reading of the vesting clause but also to his claim that specific grants of executive power in Article II, particularly the power to receive ambassadors, made the president "the organ of intercourse" with other nations. Madison was willing to grant that the executive was "a convenient organ of preliminary communications with foreign governments," but that did not give the president the power to conduct foreign policy on his own. For support Madison again appealed to Hamilton's own words, this time in *Federalist* No. 69, where Hamilton had argued that the power to receive ambassadors and other public ministers was "more a matter of dignity than of authority." Receiving ambassadors, Hamilton had assured critics during the debate over ratification, "will be without consequence in the administration of government," since it was not a grant of broad power in foreign policy but merely a recognition that it would be inconvenient to convene the legislature every time a foreign minister arrived in the country.[33]

Madison relished exposing the inconsistencies and opportunism in Hamilton's position, but he was less effective in explaining why Washington's proclamation unconstitutionally encroached upon Congress's power to declare war. Underneath Hamilton's more provocative constitutional argumentation was a more modest claim that the president had an obligation to keep the peace until Congress decided to take the country into war. Nothing in Washington's proclamation prevented Congress from declaring war with Britain or France. Moreover, Madison went too far in suggesting that the president's role in the conduct of foreign relations did not extend beyond the merely ceremonial or convenient. After all, the framers lodged the treaty-making power in Article II and clearly envisioned that the president would play an indispensable part in what Hamilton called "the management of foreign negotiations." In arguing that the Constitution lodged the powers of making war and peace almost entirely in the legislative branch, Madison did as much violence to the framers' intent as Hamilton did in claiming that the vesting clause was an untapped reservoir of powers to decide questions of war and peace.[34]

Ultimately Hamilton's reading would prove far more influential than Madison's, but neither had any discernible effect on Washington's decision-making. Although Washington may have sympathized with Hamilton's expansive reading of Article II, he steered a prudent course that avoided an institutional showdown with Congress. He sided with Jefferson and against Hamilton in deciding not to abrogate the 1778 treaty with France, and when Congress convened in December 1793 he offered to leave it to "the wisdom of Congress to correct, improve, or enforce" the policy he had announced in the proclamation. Washington knew that he needed Congress's cooperation for not only political but also legal reasons, because the administration could not get juries to convict violators of the proclamation in the absence of a federal statute. For its part, Congress gave Washington's proclamation its "hearty approbation," since the "maintenance of the peace" was among "the most important duties of the Magistrate charged with the faithful execution of the laws." At Washington's suggestion and using its constitutional authority in Article I, section 8, "to define and punish ... offenses against the Law of Nations," Congress passed the Neutrality Act of 1794, which enabled the administration to successfully prosecute violators.[35]

FIGHTING INDIANS AND PIRATES IN THE EARLY REPUBLIC

The war of words between Madison and Hamilton obscured the cooperation and mutual deference that characterized the relationship between the president and Congress on questions of war and peace during the Washington administration. Just as the president and Congress worked together to keep the country out of the war between France and its European neighbors, so they worked together to wage war against Indian tribes on the western frontier. Although Congress never formally declared war on the Indians, Washington sought and received authorization from Congress at virtually every step of the rapidly escalating conflict.

Protecting the Frontiers in the Washington Administration

From the outset of the new government, the administration came under intense pressure to protect the lives and property of Americans living on the frontier. Without a significant military presence on the border, moreover, the government could not stop frontiersmen from attacking Indians and provoking a wider war. In response, Congress temporarily authorized the president to call into service "such part of the militia of the states ... as he may judge necessary ... for the purpose of protecting the inhabitants of the frontiers of the United States from the hostile excursions of the Indians." The following year, and again the year after, Congress reauthorized the president to call out the militia to protect those living on the frontiers.[36]

State militias, however, proved ineffective in fighting the Indians, and Congress refused to accede to the president's repeated recommendations to enact legislation that would knit diverse state militias into a more uniform and reliable fighting force. The combination of poorly trained militia units and a tiny standing army contributed to embarrassing losses to Indian forces in the Northwest Territory, most spectacularly on the morning of November 4, 1791 when a surprise attack by 1,000 Indians devastated the 1,400-man army commanded by General Arthur St. Clair. A total of 600 Americans died and another 300 were wounded in a defeat that stunned the country and provoked furious criticism of the administration's military strategy and diplomatic efforts.[37]

As soon as the president learned of St. Clair's defeat he promised to send the Senate and the House "all such matter as shall be necessary to enable the Legislature to judge of the measures which it may be proper to pursue." Within a month the president had sent Congress "a flood of documents" that demonstrated the steps the administration had taken to secure peace and the obstacles it faced in defending frontier inhabitants with an inadequate military force. The only way to subdue "the Indian enemy," the administration argued, was to create a large professional army that could take the offensive and compel the Indians to "listen to the dictates of peace." To that end, Washington asked Congress to triple the military budget and give him a standing army of over 5,000 soldiers.[38]

The president's plan faced strong opposition in Congress, not only within the emerging Republican Party, which expressed fear of a standing army under executive control, but also from northeastern Federalists who were not enthusiastic about waging war against the Indians to aid western settlers. Congress ultimately gave the president the 5,000-man army he asked for, but with one crucial restriction: the new troops were to be disbanded "as soon as the United States shall be at peace with the Indian tribes."[39]

Congress recognized that the nation was at war with Indian tribes that lay east of the Ohio River but never seriously considered issuing a formal declaration of war. Nor did the president seek such a declaration. Few Americans believed that a limited war against small bands of Indian tribes should be dignified with a declaration of war; such declarations were reserved for a "full-dress war" against a foreign state. But, in Washington's view, that did not relieve the president of his constitutional obligation to seek authorization from Congress for military actions, particularly offensive ones. The deference that Washington showed to Congress's constitutional prerogatives was reciprocated by the legislature, which rejected any attempt to prescribe how the commander in chief should conduct military operations against the Indians.[40]

Admittedly, Washington had little choice but to seek Congress's prior approval for any significant military campaign, since without cooperation from Congress he would have had no army to command. But Washington's actions also reflected his understanding of where the Constitution had lodged the power to initiate "an offensive war," declared or not. Governors from the Southwest pleaded constantly with the Washington administration to help them to dispossess the Indians, particularly the Creeks, but always received the same answer from Washington and his secretary of war. "The Constitution," Washington explained to South Carolina's governor William Moultrie in 1793, "vests the power of declaring war with Congress; therefore no offensive expedition of importance can be authorized until after they have deliberated upon the subject, and authorized such a measure."[41]

Buying Off the Barbary Pirates

Washington adopted the same position in dealing with the Barbary pirates off the North African coast. The Barbary powers of Algiers, Tripoli, Tunis, and Morocco had a long history of capturing merchant ships in the Mediterranean, seizing their cargos, and ransoming their crews. Many European nations, including the British, negotiated treaties with the Barbary states that committed them to pay the pirate nations an annual tribute, in exchange for which the pirates would leave the Europeans' trading vessels alone. When Washington took office the United States had no treaties with Algiers, Tunis, or Tripoli, and this prevented American vessels from safely trading in the Mediterranean. In addition, 21 Americans who had been taken captive by pirates in 1785 were still being held for ransom. Previous efforts to secure their release from Algiers had foundered on the $60,000 asking price, which was well over ten times what the all-star negotiating team of Thomas Jefferson, John Adams, and Benjamin Franklin had been commissioned to pay by the Continental Congress.[42]

In his second annual message in 1790, Washington drew Congress's attention to the "distressful" condition of the nation's trade in the Mediterranean, and Secretary of State Jefferson prepared a comprehensive, secret report for Congress that demonstrated the serious threat to American interests posed by the Barbary pirates. If Algiers secured peace with Portugal, Jefferson warned, the "Algerines" would immediately begin to prey on American trading ships in the Atlantic Ocean. Jefferson told Congress that the United States could try to "obtain peace by purchasing it"—he estimated that peace with Algiers alone would cost about $1 million. Alternatively, Jefferson suggested, the nation could "repel force by force," which would require building a navy. Perhaps, too, Jefferson suggested, the United States could forge a military alliance with other nations whose interests were also harmed by the pirates. Jefferson laid out the facts and the options, but made clear that the decision rested with Congress. "Upon the whole," his report concluded, "it rests with Congress to decide between war, tribute, and ransom, as the means of re-establishing our Mediterranean commerce."[43]

Jefferson's clear preference was to use force—giving in to extortion, Jefferson believed, would just encourage the pirates to plunder. However, Congress was unwilling to authorize war or to allocate sufficient funds to negotiate a peace treaty that would secure the release of American captives. Only after Algiers—having secured the truce with Portugal of which Jefferson had warned—seized 11 American ships and more than one hundred American seamen in the Atlantic in the fall of 1793 did Congress finally take action. First, it appropriated $1 million—one-sixth of the federal budget—to "defray any expenses which may be incurred in relation to the intercourse between the United States and foreign nations," and then it authorized the construction of six naval vessels at a cost of nearly $700,000. In Washington's final year in office, the administration at last secured the release of the captives and a peace agreement, in exchange for a $650,000 payoff to the Algiers leader as well as a hefty annual tribute. Similar though less expensive deals were struck with Tunis and Tripoli.[44]

The problem with the policy of tributes and appeasement, as Jefferson had foreseen, was that the Barbary nations were forever raising their demands. By the end of the 1790s, the Washington and Adams administrations had paid out close to $10 million to the leaders of the Barbary nations. To make matters worse, these tributes hadn't stopped the Barbary nations from humiliating the United States, perhaps in part because the American government had fallen behind on its promised payments. In September 1800, for instance, the US frigate *George Washington,* in Algiers to deliver the nation's belated tribute, was forced by the Dey of Algiers to sail under an Algiers flag and transport to Constantinople the Algiers ambassador and nearly a million dollars in coins and jewels, as well as 100 African slaves, 60 "harem women," and a menagerie of sheep, horses, cattle, lions, tigers, antelope, ostriches, and parrots.[45]

"To Chastise Their Insolence": Jefferson and the First Barbary War

Upon becoming president, Jefferson was determined to put an end to the escalating demands and "insolencies," and the only way to do that, he believed, was by dispatching a naval force to the Mediterranean. Jefferson convened his cabinet on May 15, 1801, to discuss whether a squadron capable of deterring the pirates should be sent "to cruise in the Mediterranean." The cabinet agreed that a mission to protect American commerce was desirable but disagreed about how far the president could go in authorizing the use of force. All concurred with Treasury Secretary Albert Gallatin that the president could "not put us in a state of war," and everybody also agreed that American ships must be permitted to repel attacks. But the cabinet disagreed about what would happen in the event that a Barbary nation declared war on the United States. Attorney General Levi Lincoln, Jefferson's chief legal advisor, insisted that only Congress could take the United States into a state of war and that while American ships could repel an attack, they could "not proceed to destroy the enemy's vessels generally" without congressional authorization. Gallatin, in contrast, maintained that the United States would enter a state of war if one of the Barbary nations declared or made war on the United States ("to declare war & to make war," Gallatin insisted, "is synonymous"), at which point the "command & direction of the public force then belongs to the Executive."[46]

Five days later, naval commander Richard Dale received his orders to embark for the Mediterranean. The secretary of navy's directive to Dale mirrored Gallatin's position rather than Lincoln's. If Dale found that the Barbary nations were at peace with the United States, he was to avoid any warlike acts. If, however, Dale found that the Barbary nations had declared war against the United States, he was authorized "to chastise their insolence by sinking, burning or destroying their ships and vessels, wherever [he] shall find them." If only one of the Barbary nations had declared war, he was also instructed to establish a blockade that would prevent vessels from entering or leaving enemy ports.

Any prisoners taken were to be treated with "humanity and attention" and landed on any part of the Barbary Coast, except for Christians, who were to be treated "kindly" and deposited on "some Christian shore."[47]

Upon reaching the Mediterranean in early July, Dale discovered that the Bashaw of Tripoli had already declared war on the United States, and so immediately set up a blockade of Tripoli. On a resupply mission, one of the American ships, the *Enterprise*, pursued and opened fire on a Tripolitan warship, killing or wounding nearly two-thirds of the enemy crew. After throwing overboard the enemies' guns and dismantling its masts—all except "an old sail and spar"—the *Enterprise* allowed the ship and its surviving crew to hobble home.[48]

When the new Congress convened in December 1801, Jefferson recounted the actions his administration had taken during the past nine months while the legislature had been out of session. He informed Congress that he had sent "a small squadron ... to protect our commerce" against the threat of attack. The mission's purpose, he emphasized, was purely defensive. The *Enterprise*, for instance, had "liberated" the Tripolitan ship and crew once the enemy ship had been "disabled from committing further hostilities" because the American ship was "unauthorized by the Constitution, without the sanction of Congress, to go beyond the line of defense." It was now up to Congress, Jefferson said, to decide whether to "authorize measures of offense also," a power that was "confided by the Constitution to the Legislature exclusively."[49]

Jefferson's account was misleading in several respects. Jefferson reported that the *Enterprise* had "fallen in with" the Tripolitan ship when in fact the *Enterprise* had pursued the enemy vessel and initiated the resulting three-hour gun battle. Furthermore, the *Enterprise* let the enemy's ship and crew go free not because the president had forbidden the squadron to go beyond defensive actions but rather because the *Enterprise* was on the outward leg of its resupply mission. Had the *Enterprise* been on the homeward leg of its mission, the ship's captain was under orders to capture enemy warships so long as they could be safely transported back. More important, nothing in the secretary of the navy's original instructions would have prevented Dale from ordering the *Enterprise* to sink any Tripolitan warship it encountered. Commodore Dale, in short, exercised considerably more restraint than he needed to under the rules of engagement that the administration issued to him.[50]

Jefferson's stance has perplexed many scholars, just as it exasperated some of his contemporaries. Writing under the pseudonym "Lucius Crassus," Alexander Hamilton assailed the president for his exaggerated deference to Congress and his narrow reading of executive power. When the nation was at peace, Hamilton acknowledged, the Constitution gave Congress the exclusive power of taking the nation into a state of war. But it was absurd, Hamilton insisted, to suggest that the executive needed congressional authorization "to capture and detain [enemy] cruisers with their crews" when the enemy had already declared war on the United States. The United States was at war with Tripoli whether or not Congress acknowledged it, and thus legislative authorization of war was pointless or at least unnecessary.[51]

That Jefferson and Hamilton would disagree about executive power is not surprising. But what makes Jefferson's position puzzling is that Hamilton's argument was essentially the same one that Gallatin had made nine months before and which underlay the administration's orders to Dale. So why did Jefferson now insist that he needed congressional approval for offensive actions that, as he stressed in his annual message, were essential to put the American "force on an equal footing with that of its adversaries"? Jefferson's position particularly bewildered Gallatin, who continued without success over the next year to try to persuade Jefferson that he did not need legislative authorization for offensive action against Tripoli. The executive conduct, he told Jefferson in August 1802, must be the same whether war is declared by Congress or by the enemy: "to fight, take, and destroy the armed vessels of the enemy."[52]

What makes Jefferson's behavior startling to us is that we have become accustomed to presidents and their lawyers insisting on expansive interpretations of presidential power. At a minimum, we expect presidents to avoid actions that might erode the power of their office. Truman's determination not to go to Congress for authorization in the war with Korea is a case in point. Hamilton was appalled at Jefferson's message for precisely this reason: by asking Congress for authorization rather than acting alone, Hamilton believed that Jefferson weakened the presidency and hampered future presidents' ability to protect national security.

But building a stronger presidency was not part of Jefferson's political agenda. What Jefferson wanted was to end the pirates' extortion, and he believed he had a better chance of achieving that goal if he acted with Congress than if he acted unilaterally. Moreover, Jefferson was confident that the new Republican Congress would give him the support he needed, as indeed it quickly did. In February 1802, Congress authorized the president to "subdue, seize, and make prize of all vessels, goods, and effects, belonging to the Bey of Tripoli ... and also to cause to be done all such other acts of precaution or hostility as the state of war will justify and may in his opinion require." The deference that Jefferson showed Congress regarding the decision about whether to make war was more than reciprocated in the broad discretion that Congress granted Jefferson in prosecuting the war.[53]

THE CONGRESSIONAL "PROPENSITY TO WAR"

Jefferson's reluctance to wage war without legislative authorization reflected deeply seated republican fears that war was "the true nurse of executive aggrandizement." As Madison explained in 1793,

> In war, a physical force is to be created; and it is the executive will, which is to direct it. In war, the public treasures are to be unlocked; and it is the executive hand which is to dispense them. In war, the honours and emoluments of office are to be multiplied; and it is the executive patronage under which they are to be enjoyed. It is in war, finally, that laurels are to be gathered, and it is the executive brow they are to encircle.

Because war invariably increased executive power, executives had an institutional incentive to start wars. That was why Madison believed it to be an "axiom" of political science that the executive was the department "most distinguished by its propensity to war" and why it was "the practice of all states, in proportion as they are free, to disarm" the executive's capacity to wage war without the authorization of the people's representatives in the legislature.[54]

In the early republic, however, Madison's axiom proved a poor predictor of presidential behavior. Early American presidents were more often a brake on Congress's desire to engage in war. This was particularly true of the war between France and Britain that lasted from 1793 to 1815. We have already seen that Washington's Proclamation of Neutrality in 1793 frustrated many congressional Republicans who would have preferred to side with France even at the risk of war with Britain. And Washington's Farewell Address in 1796 famously warned his fellow citizens against being drawn into the wars of Europe and reminded them of the dangers that "overgrown military establishments" posed to republican liberty. President John Adams, too, kept the nation from rushing into a full-fledged war with France, despite strong support for war in Congress. Indeed, Adams chose peace over war even though he knew that it would divide and demoralize his party and likely wreck his chance for reelection. Nor did the axiom fare better during Jefferson's presidency. As we saw in the previous chapter, Jefferson went to extraordinary lengths in his second term to avoid war with Britain, persisting in a quixotic and disastrous embargo policy that crippled the economy, divided his party, and destroyed his presidency. However, it was Madison's own presidency that most dramatically revealed the limitations of republican orthodoxy.

James Madison and the "War Hawks"

Just days before Madison took the oath of office, Congress finally repealed the hated embargo that forbade American trading ships from leaving port. However, lifting the embargo did not stop the British and French from seizing American merchant ships and restricting American trade. Madison still hoped to pursue a modified policy of commercial coercion that could induce the belligerents to change their policy toward neutral trading vessels. Congress, however, was increasingly adamant that the United States must insist on free trade, backed by armed force. Some members advocated arming merchant vessels, but while this could deter privateers it would do little to hinder the British navy. Others had come to the view that only war would compel the British to respect what Tennessee congressman Felix Grundy called the American "right of exporting the productions of our own soil and industry to foreign markets."[55]

The trumpet of war was clearly sounded in February 1810 by the 34-year-old senator from Kentucky, Henry Clay. Three weeks after taking his seat, Clay rose to call for "resistance by the sword." In place of Madison's tedious policies of commercial pressure and diplomatic negotiation, Clay offered his countrymen the prospect of "deeds of glory and renown" that would rival those of "the illustrious founders of our freedom." He urged the United States to strike at Britain through the conquest of Canada—which would be a simple matter for a virile "race of heroes." The Kentucky militia on its own, Clay boasted, could "place Montreal and Upper Canada at your feet."[56]

Clay's speech encapsulated the country's mounting frustration at the government's inability to halt the "injuries and indignities" visited on the United States by its former colonial master. Americans resented not only Britain's restrictions on their trade but also the impressment of their sailors. Those from the western United States also blamed the British for instigating Indian attacks on frontier settlements. This popular discontent made itself felt in the 1810 midterm elections. When the 12th Congress convened in November 1811, close to half of the House was composed of newly elected members, many of whom were younger and more militantly nationalistic than the representatives they replaced.[57]

Known as the "War Hawks," they pushed relentlessly for war with Britain. Although newcomers to Congress, they were immediately thrust into positions of influence. Clay had quit the Senate for the House and was promptly elected Speaker, a position he used to ensure that War Hawks were amply represented on key committees. Among those Clay took under his wing was a 29-year-old Anglophobe from South Carolina, John Calhoun, who was placed on the Foreign Relations Committee. When the House came to declare war in June 1812 it would be Calhoun—as acting chair of the Foreign Relations Committee—who would deliver the committee's thunderous call for an "immediate appeal to arms" to halt "the mad ambition, the lust of power, and commercial avarice of Great Britain."[58]

President Madison was not the bumbling weakling that historians have sometimes made him out to be, but he was a reluctant warrior. He shared the War Hawks' concerns that the British—as he expressed it in his message to the new Congress in November 1811—were "trampling on rights which no independent nation can relinquish." But unlike the War Hawks, who went to war with their heads crammed with extravagant visions of glory and conquest, Madison's vision of the war was more modest and his rhetoric always more restrained. When Madison finally asked Congress to declare war on Britain on June 1, 1812, he did so believing that the British and his own party had left him with no other choice.[59]

Most historians agree that going to war with Britain in 1812 was a misguided, nearly suicidal act. In 1812, the United States possessed a tiny navy made up of mostly small gunboats that were no match for the world's most powerful navy. By one count, the British had three naval warships, each of which typically had 74 cannons for every one cannon the American possessed. On land, too, the Americans faced long odds. Even with the troop buildup authorized by Congress in the spring of 1812, the American regular army was still only about one-tenth the size of the British army, which numbered 250,000 men. In declaring war on Britain, as Yoo points out, the United States had managed to select the one foe in the world that "could directly threaten the nation's security"—indeed, the nation's very existence.[60]

Whatever indignities the Americans had suffered at the hands of the British in the years leading up to the war, they hardly compared to the humiliation of having the British torch the White House and the Capitol while the president and his cabinet fled for the hills of Virginia. And the economic hardships that American commerce had suffered as a neutral nation were dwarfed by the suffocating blockade that the British imposed on the eastern seaboard during the war. The discontent that was felt so acutely before the war in the southern and western states was mild compared to the secessionist movement that the war precipitated in several northeastern states. And, notwithstanding the visions of territorial conquest that so captivated the congressional War Hawks, most of the war was spent trying to win back territory the nation had lost during the war. The War of 1812, in short, was precisely the sort of ill-conceived and avoidable war that the framers presumably hoped to avoid in designing a new constitution.

The flaw in the framers' system was that it was designed primarily to check presidential war-making, while the War of 1812 was at least as much or more a war of Congress's making. Certainly the war with Britain was jointly embarked upon by the legislature and the executive, but it was the House of Representatives, not the executive, that had proved to be "most distinguished by its propensity to war." And lest it be thought ironic that the government entity closest to the people proved to be the most warlike, it seems rather that House members were more strongly committed to war precisely *because* they more closely reflected the sentiments of their constituents, particularly Republican voters in southern and western states. Once again, Madison's republican axiom proved an unreliable guide to understanding war-making in the early republic.

The First Presidential War: Polk's War with Mexico

That Madison's axiom fared so poorly in the early republic is a tribute to the restraint of the nation's first presidents—a restraint rooted in the widely shared understanding that the decision to make war was vested in Congress.[61] Unilateral executive war-making was also inhibited by the popular fear of a standing army and a professional navy, a distrust that severely limited the armed forces at the president's disposal. And in the eyes of Jefferson and Madison, the axiom's failure was due to the Republican Party's triumph over Hamilton and his Federalist followers, a triumph that ensured the new nation would not follow down the old-world path of executive aggrandizement, an overgrown military establishment, and ruinous taxes.

The words of the Constitution mattered, but time would prove that their effectiveness as a check on presidential war-making depended on the informal norms and unwritten rules of the political culture. The conflict with Mexico in the 1840s demonstrated that a president determined to start a war would not find the text of the Constitution a barrier, particularly if his party controlled Congress.

The Mexican republic had something that the new president, James Knox Polk, wanted very much: California. He hoped to buy it for $20 million but Mexico wasn't interested in selling. So Polk's mind turned to thoughts of war. The problem was that Mexico and the United States were at peace and he lacked grounds for going to war—apart from desiring territory that belonged to Mexico.[62]

Polk saw his opportunity in the annexation of Texas, which had been approved by Congress in the final days of John Tyler's administration. The annexation of Texas had been plenty controversial in the United States, particularly among northerners who feared that acquiring Texas would increase the power of slave states. Indeed, annexing Texas had required an audacious end run around the Constitution after the Senate rejected a treaty of annexation negotiated by the administration. Bypassing the treaty-making provision, which required approval by two-thirds of the Senate, Tyler secured annexation by getting a majority in both houses to pass a joint resolution. It was the first but hardly the last time that a president would sidestep the Senate's treaty-making power to secure an international agreement.[63]

The annexation of Texas presented Polk with the opportunity to pick a fight with Mexico since Texas and Mexico had very different ideas about the boundary separating them. When Texas was part of Mexico, the boundary was the Nueces River. After winning their independence, however, Texans insisted that the boundary lay further south, along the Rio Grande. Polk's plan was simple: send American troops, under the command of General Zachary Taylor, as near to the Rio Grande as was feasible and provoke the Mexicans into an attack. The administration instructed Taylor that if the Mexican army crossed the Rio Grande he was to regard it as an invasion of the United States and an act of war.[64]

Both the Mexicans and Taylor exercised tremendous restraint at first, much to Polk's frustration. Taylor hung back, reluctant to cross into what the rest of the world recognized as Mexican territory. When he finally marched into the disputed territory in early 1846, a Mexican force confronted Taylor and ordered him to halt. When Taylor refused, the Mexicans retreated without firing, allowing the Americans to march unimpeded to the Rio Grande, as Polk had ordered. Once Taylor had reached the Rio Grande, the Mexicans again demanded that Taylor's army withdraw to the Nueces River. Polk's orders made that impossible, however, and Taylor responded with a further provocation by setting up a blockade at the mouth of the Rio Grande, an act of war under international law. An officer in Taylor's army confided the obvious to his diary: "We have not one particle of right to be here. It looks as if the government sent a small force on purpose to bring on a war, so as to have a pretext for taking California and as much of this country as it chooses."[65]

Finally, two weeks after Taylor established his blockade, the Mexican president caved in to intense public pressure to respond to the American invasion. He authorized the army to undertake "defensive" operations to drive out the Americans. Two days later, on April 25, 1,600 Mexican cavalry crossed the river and ambushed two small American regiments, killing 16 men and capturing almost 50 others. Polk at last had the provocation he needed to justify war with Mexico and seize California.[66]

Polk rushed to Congress with a war message. He told Congress that Mexico had "invaded our territory and shed American blood upon the American soil." Mexico, Polk lied, had commenced war "notwithstanding all our efforts to avoid it." He did not ask Congress to declare war but rather only "to recognize the existence of the war" and then to place at his disposal "the means of prosecuting the war with vigor, and thus hastening the restoration of peace."[67]

The administration's disinformation whipped the nation up into a frenzy of indignation. Large pro-war rallies were held across the country. Anxious to avoid any awkward questions about the president's action, House Democrats allotted only two hours for debate, all but 30 minutes of which was taken up with reading documents furnished by the administration. Twenty-four hours after receiving Polk's war message, both houses of Congress endorsed the president's claim that Mexico had initiated war with the United States and provided Polk with $10 million and authorization to enlist an additional 50,000 troops.[68]

Congressional Whigs tried in vain to slow the stampede to war. But even Whigs who blamed Polk for starting the war were unwilling to vote against the troops now that the president had placed them in harm's way. The Whigs attempted to separate the resolution that essentially declared war on Mexico, which they almost all opposed, from the funding bill, which only a few dared oppose. But on an almost strictly party-line vote, Democrats succeeded in attaching the authorization for war as a preamble to the appropriations bill. Outmaneuvered, the Whigs felt compelled to swallow the Democratic package for fear of being branded weak or unpatriotic. Only 16 legislators in both houses, all fiercely anti-slavery Whigs, voted against the final measure. The Constitution's checks on executive war-making proved to be no barrier to a president determined to take the nation to war.[69]

But there is more to the story of the Mexican War. Back in the 1790s, Madison had fretted that it was in war that "laurels are to be gathered, and it is the executive brow they are to encircle." Yet it did not work out that way for Polk and the Democrats, even though the war against Mexico was a spectacular military success. Victory after victory ensued, often against much larger forces. By September 1847 the American flag was flying atop Mexico City and the only question that remained was how much territory Mexico would have to yield to the United States. Yet Polk grew steadily more unpopular, and Whigs as well as many northern Democrats became increasingly vocal in their opposition to the commander in chief—"Polk the Mendacious," they christened him.[70]

In the 1846 midterm elections, the Whigs capitalized on the disaffection with Polk and picked up 40 seats to take control of the House of Representatives. When the new Congress convened in December 1847—three months after the fall of Mexico City—the House censured Polk for starting the war "unnecessarily and unconstitutionally." On the floor of the House, Illinois freshman Abraham Lincoln lashed Polk for his lies and deceptions: "the blood of this war, like the blood of Abel," Lincoln declared, "is crying to heaven against him." So ferocious was the attack that some of Lincoln's friends worried for the young congressman's political future.[71]

Among the concerned was Lincoln's law partner William Herndon, who cautioned Lincoln that blaming the United States for the war against Mexico could hurt him with voters. Herndon also tried to persuade Lincoln that the president must be "the sole judge" of whether it was necessary to cross into another country to defend against invasion. After all, even if one accepted Lincoln's premise that the land between the Rio Grande and Nueces River belonged to Mexico—which, Lincoln wrote, was as easy to prove as it was to "prove that your house is not mine"—the Mexicans had not given up hope of taking back all of Texas.[72]

Lincoln was aghast at his friend's reasoning. "Allow the President to invade a neighboring nation, whenever *he* shall deem it necessary to repel invasion," Lincoln responded, "and you allow him to make war at pleasure." Imagine if tomorrow the president "should choose to say he thinks it necessary to invade Canada, to prevent the British from invading us, how could you stop him?" The Constitution, Lincoln lectured his partner, gave the "war-making power to Congress" because its framers believed that monarchs were always "involving and impoverishing their people in wars." Because they understood this "to be the most oppressive of all Kingly oppressions," continued Lincoln, "they resolved to so frame the Constitution that *no one man* should hold the power of bringing this oppression upon us." Herndon's view, Lincoln scolded him, "places our President where kings have always stood."[73]

Polk was no George III, but he had unlocked latent powers of the presidency that were, as Alexis de Tocqueville had spied a decade earlier, "almost royal in magnitude." Whatever the intent of the framers, as a practical matter the president stood roughly where kings had always stood when it came to waging war. Requiring Congress to declare war was not going to deter presidents from making war.[74]

In conducting the war and negotiating the peace, Polk was barely hindered by Congress, which was only in session for six of the sixteen months between the start of the war in May 1846 and the fall of Mexico City in September 1847. Even the war's most bitter critics consistently voted to fund the troops. Polk alone decided on military strategy and troop deployment. After the fall of Mexico City, he unilaterally determined the occupation policy. Polk ordered the military to collect and confiscate Mexico's tariff's revenues, which enabled the government to raise more than $500,000 to pay for the cost of occupation. The president also kept tight control over the peace negotiations. The envoy that Polk secretly sent to negotiate peace terms with Mexico was paid out of executive funds and his name was never submitted to the Senate for confirmation. And Polk alone provided the envoy written instructions about what territories were to be demanded and the price that was to be paid for them.[75]

Nonetheless, Congress did play some part in ending Polk's war before the president was quite ready to bring down the curtain, thanks to the disobedience of Polk's envoy, Nicholas Trist. Polk had sent Trist to Mexico in April 1847 to offer Mexico $20 million if it would cede what is today California, Nevada, Utah, Arizona, New Mexico, and part of Colorado. However, the military's successes led Polk to think his initial territorial aims were overly modest and he now set his sights on acquiring Baja California as well as much of northern Mexico. Polk recalled his envoy but Trist, who sympathized with the Mexicans' plight, defied the president's order. Using his recall as leverage, he warned the Mexicans that if they did not accept his original deal, Polk would likely force them to accept even more disadvantageous terms in the future. With great reluctance but with little choice, the Mexicans accepted Trist's terms for peace, and on February 2, 1848, they signed the peace agreement.[76]

The treaty's arrival in Washington on February 19 came as an unpleasant shock to Polk. He wanted more of Mexico and had been prepared to prolong the occupation and send troops to Baja in order to force Mexico's submission to his new demands. Two days earlier, the House had finally authorized the borrowing of $16 million dollars to support the war—less than he had asked for but a clear victory nonetheless. The Whigs' bite, Polk was finding, was a lot less ferocious than their bark. But Trist's treaty transformed the political dynamic, and Polk knew it.[77]

A couple of members of his cabinet—most vociferously his secretary of the treasury, Robert Walker, who wanted to seize all of Mexico (an aim not shared by Polk)—urged the president to tear up the treaty without submitting it to the Senate, but Polk understood that doing so would jeopardize everything he had gained since the beginning of the war. Congress—especially now that the House of Representatives was controlled by the Whigs—was not going to support a war when the government had already secured a peace treaty giving Polk everything he had originally asked for—and for $15 million rather than the $20 million he had authorized Trist to pay. And without the funding he needed, he told his cabinet, his army of occupation would be "constantly wasting and diminishing in numbers," forcing him ultimately to withdraw the army and thereby weaken the government's bargaining position. Polk fretted, too, that if the Whigs won the next presidential election he might lose all the territory that Mexico had ceded in the treaty. It was time, Polk calculated, to cash in his chips and submit the treaty to the Senate, which ratified it by a vote of 38–14, despite intense opposition from southern Democrats who wanted more territory and northern Whigs who wanted less.[78]

In the end, then, Congress and the Constitution did matter. Had Polk been king, Baja California might very well be part of the United States today, as conceivably might large chunks of present-day Mexico. Polk was ultimately constrained by Congress's power of the purse, though only because the Whigs had taken control of the House and because his envoy had disobeyed his instructions. Although Congress never voted to cut off funding for the war, its power of the purse affected Polk's calculations about what he could achieve militarily and induced him to accept a peace treaty that he otherwise might not have agreed to. In contrast, ironically, Congress *had* voted to declare (strictly speaking, recognize) a war, yet it played no meaningful role in the decision to initiate the war with Mexico. It was a war solely of the president's choosing, and exposed the framers' naiveté in thinking that the "declare war" clause could check presidential war-making.

FIGHTING THE CIVIL WAR

The Mexican War was a calamity for Mexico, which lost 40 percent of its territory. But in the short term at least it also had a disastrous effect on the United States. The new territory acquired by Polk ignited a ferocious fight over the spread of slavery that propelled the country toward a Civil War that would claim over 600,000 lives, nearly as many Americans as have been killed in all the other nation's wars combined. One out of every 50 Americans was killed in the Civil War—a rate more than six times as great as in World War II and 20 times greater than in World War I.

A war unlike any the nation had previously known, the Civil War made the commander in chief more important and more powerful than ever before. Ironically, that power was wielded by one of Polk's severest congressional critics, Abraham Lincoln. Equally ironically, the president who watched passively as seven states, including Texas, seceded from the Union and established a new Confederate government was James Buchanan, who as Polk's secretary of state had advocated rejecting the Treaty of Guadalupe Hidalgo and continuing the Mexican War so that the United States might acquire vast swaths of what is today northern Mexico.[79]

Responding to Secession

Secession paralyzed Buchanan. He believed that states did not have a right to secede but he also believed that the Constitution did not give the federal government the power to compel them to remain in the Union. After South Carolina seceded and it became clear that other states from the Deep South would soon follow, Buchanan sent a special message to Congress explaining that the crisis had reached "such vast and alarming proportions as to place the subject entirely above and beyond Executive control." Only Congress, he declared, possessed the constitutional authority to deal with secession and "to authorize the employment of military force."[80]

Lincoln acted on a very different understanding of the powers of the federal government and the president to respond to secession. He had none of Buchanan's strict constructionist misgivings about the federal government's powers over the states. If states had no right to secede, then the government must have the power to prevent states from leaving the Union. Nor did he believe that only Congress could deal with a crisis that threatened the existence of the nation. Indeed, since Congress was no longer in session, Lincoln knew that only the president could save the Union.

By the time Lincoln called Congress into special session on July 4, 1861, he had already taken the nation to war. It was Lincoln who decided, over the heated objections of his secretary of state, William Seward, and his top general, Winfield Scott, to resupply Fort Sumter, even though he knew that it would likely provoke a Confederate attack on the fort. Immediately after the Confederates attacked Fort Sumter on April 12, Lincoln declared a state of rebellion in seven southern states. Invoking the authority vested in him by the Militia Act of 1795—which empowered the president to call out state militias "whenever the laws of the United States shall be opposed or the execution thereof obstructed, in any state, by combinations too powerful to be suppressed by the ordinary course of judicial proceedings"—Lincoln ordered the Union states to provide 75,000 troops, an act that provoked four additional southern states to secede.[81]

In calling out the militia, Lincoln acted with specific legislative authorization, but other actions that he took during the first months of the war not only lacked statutory authorization but seemed at odds with the Constitution. Article I gives Congress the exclusive power to raise and pay for an army and navy, yet Lincoln unilaterally expanded the army and navy by 40,000, called for another 40,000 volunteers, and paid $2 million out of the treasury to facilitate military recruiting. Lincoln also imposed a naval blockade on all southern ports, which under international law placed the Union in a state of war with the Confederacy.

When the 37th Congress finally gathered in Washington for a one-month special session in July 1861, Lincoln knew he had some explaining to do. Resupplying Fort Sumter, he stressed, was a purely defensive action. The southern rebels had initiated the hostilities and left him "no choice ... but to call out the war power of the Government; and so to resist force, employed for its destruction, by force, for its preservation." Lincoln acknowledged that in calling up volunteers to serve for three-year terms and expanding the regular army and navy, his actions went beyond what was perhaps "strictly legal." But "whether strictly legal or not," Lincoln said, these measures "were ventured upon, under what appeared to be a popular demand, and a public necessity; trusting, then as now, that Congress would readily ratify them."[82]

By a nearly unanimous vote, Congress retroactively approved the president's military "acts, proclamations, and orders ... as if they had been issued and done under the previous express authority and direction of the Congress of the United States." In addition, Congress gave Lincoln everything he asked for to suppress the rebellion, and sometimes more. Where the president requested $400,000 to fund an army of 400,000 three-year enlisted troops, Congress supplied him with $500,000 to support 500,000 soldiers. Legislators did not want a debate over constitutional war powers but rather a quick end to the rebellion.[83]

However, Congress did more than just authorize Lincoln's actions and fund the army. It also moved to define the war's aims. Anxious to reassure the strategically vital border states of Kentucky, Missouri, and Maryland, Congress passed a joint resolution (the Crittenden–Johnson Resolution) stating that the war was to preserve the Union, not to eradicate slavery. And on the last day of the emergency session—over the bitter opposition of Democrats and border state Republicans—Congress passed the Confiscation Act, which stated that a master would forfeit ownership of any slave "employed in hostile service against the government of the United States." Lincoln signed the act, albeit reluctantly.[84]

The Wartime Role of Congress

When Congress convened again in early December, the mood in the country had dramatically darkened. The nation's initial confidence in a quick war had been shattered by the military setbacks suffered by Union armies in the summer and fall of 1861. The surge of patriotic enthusiasm that greeted Lincoln's July 4 message had dissipated and been replaced by rising anxiety that this inexperienced frontier lawyer was not up to the task. During the fall, with Congress out of session, Republican legislative leaders had met with both Lincoln and General George McClellan—commander of the 200,000-strong Army of the Potomac—to press for more urgent prosecution of the war. Now with Congress in session again, disgruntled legislators looked for more formal means "to invigorate a timid administration." And so was born the Joint Committee on the Conduct of the War.[85]

Historians disagree sharply in their evaluations of the committee. Some argue that its wide-ranging investigations were useful in ferreting out inefficiency and corruption in the military. Others suggest that the committee's effect was detrimental because it politicized military appointments and promotions and spawned factionalism and distrust among the Union's military commanders. Some fault the committee for pressuring the administration and military officers to mount "foolish, premature maneuvers," whereas others credit it for inducing a cautious administration and its reluctant generals to wage a more aggressive war against the South. In one reading, the committee was a constant thorn in Lincoln's side, forcing continual and unwelcome changes in the president's military policy; in another, the committee more closely resembled a tool at the president's disposal, which he unleashed "on generals unwilling to fight." Whatever the committee's impact on Lincoln's war policies, one thing is clear: many in Congress did not believe that being commander in chief made the president solely responsible for conducting the war.[86]

Congressional Republicans were even less willing to leave to the president the most important war policy question of all: what to do about slavery. This was a question both of military strategy and of the war's ultimate objectives. The strategic question involved a tradeoff: striking at slavery would weaken a pillar of the southern economy and could boost the morale of the North, but risked driving the border states into the arms of the

Confederacy. The larger question was whether the war was to be limited to restoring "the Union as it was" or whether it was to destroy slavery and remake the South.[87]

History justly remembers Lincoln's Emancipation Proclamation, issued on September 22, 1862, declaring that on January 1, 1863, any slave residing in an area still in rebellion would be "thenceforward, and forever free." Less often recounted are the many steps that the 37th Congress took before adjourning in July 1862 to make emancipation both the means and ends of the Civil War. In March, Congress prohibited the military from returning fugitive slaves. In April, it freed all slaves in the District of Columbia. In June, it outlawed slavery in the territories. In July, it amended the Militia Act to allow "persons of African descent" to serve in the armed forces and to provide for emancipation of any slave (and their family members) who enlisted in the Union army, provided the slave's master was a rebel. And most dramatically, that same month Congress passed the Second Confiscation Act, which declared that slaves encountered by the Union army "shall be deemed captives of war, and shall be forever free of their servitude"—so long as the slave belonged to a person "engaged in rebellion" or who "in any way gave aid or comfort" to the rebellion. This act of emancipation was passed not only at Congress's initiative but in the face of a veto threat from the Great Emancipator, who insisted that the federal government lacked the power to abolish slavery in the states.[88]

"By Virtue of the Power in Me Vested as Commander in Chief"

So if Congress could not abolish slavery in the states, on what grounds did Lincoln propose to do so? In his original Emancipation Proclamation the answer was not entirely clear. The closest Lincoln came to a justification was his opening declaration that "I, Abraham Lincoln, President of the United States of America, and Commander-in-chief of the Army and Navy thereof, do hereby proclaim ... " Making matters more confusing, he sought to buttress the proclamation's authority by invoking several acts of Congress, most notably the Second Confiscation Act. Only in the final Emancipation Proclamation, issued on January 1, 1863, did Lincoln fully articulate the basis for his action. He issued the proclamation, he now explained, "by virtue of the power in me vested as Commander-in-Chief ... in time of actual rebellion against the authority and government of the United States, and as a fit and necessary war measure for suppressing said rebellion." Emancipation was justified, in short, because as commander in chief he had decided that it was necessary to defeat the Confederacy.[89]

The Emancipation Proclamation was a watershed moment in the development of the American presidency. Never before had a president invoked the commander-in-chief clause as a source of such sweeping power. Previous presidents, including Polk, rarely relied on the commander-in-chief clause.[90] Initially, even Lincoln hardly mentioned the commander-in-chief clause in his public communications. In fact, the only proclamation issued in the war's first year in which Lincoln mentioned the commander-in-chief clause was a proclamation of May 3 ordering an increase in the size of the military—and in that case Lincoln clearly did not believe that the commander-in-chief clause was a sufficient warrant for his action, since he also pledged to submit this directive for Congress's approval "as soon as [Congress] assembled."[91]

Early on, Lincoln relied less on the commander-in-chief clause than on the constitutional injunction that the president "take care that the Laws be faithfully executed." He presented the blockade of southern ports, for instance, not as an act of war but as an effort to quell "unlawful" and "disorderly proceedings" and to protect "the public peace and the lives and property of quiet and orderly citizens pursuing their lawful occupations." In Lincoln's mind, the government was not engaged in war with another government, but rather was confronted with "a combination of persons" engaged in an "insurrection" against the government. Lincoln never really abandoned this understanding of the conflict, always preferring to call it a rebellion rather than a civil war.[92]

But as the war wore on, Lincoln turned to the commander-in-chief clause with increasing regularity to justify his actions. For instance, when critics objected to the arrest and banishment of Ohio Democrat Clement Vallandigham for "declaring disloyal statements," Lincoln defended his actions on the grounds that, "The people have, under the constitution, made the commander-in-chief, of their Army and Navy . . . the man who holds the power, and bears the responsibility of making" the determination of what the public safety requires in times of rebellion or invasion. If the president abused that power, Lincoln said, the people could impeach or defeat him.[93]

Lincoln's critics were right to worry about a construction of the commander-in-chief clause that entitled the president to unilaterally decide what the public safety requires. But Lincoln's words and deeds need to be placed in context. What Lincoln faced was not a border scuffle or small-scale revolt but, as he said, a "clear, flagrant, and gigantic case of rebellion." If the rebellion succeeded, the nation would cease to exist in its former form, a result that Lincoln and almost everybody else in the North regarded as unacceptable.[94]

The problem with Lincoln's reading comes when the extraordinary becomes a precedent for the ordinary and routine. The danger to American constitutional democracy would arise when future presidents and their aides exhumed Lincoln's words and actions to bolster their authority in situations that bore little or no relationship to the crisis that Lincoln faced. In the short term, however, there was little danger of that. As Lincoln accurately predicted in his final annual message, executive power was "greatly diminished by the cessation of actual war." In the immediate wake of the Civil War, there was no gradual accretion to presidential power. Instead Lincoln's broad construction of executive war powers stimulated a powerful backlash, both from Congress as well as from the Supreme Court. By 1875, as political scientist Theodore Lowi has written, an observer looking only at the presidency "would not have known there had been a war or a Lincoln." And that is probably the way that an old Whig like Lincoln would have wanted it.[95]

Becoming a World Power

Writing in 1835, Alexis de Tocqueville was struck by the weakness of executive power in the United States relative to his native France. The underlying cause of that weakness,

Tocqueville believed, lay not in the Constitution but in geopolitics. The executive in France was powerful because the country was surrounded by enemies. The United States, in contrast, was "separated from the rest of the world by the Atlantic Ocean and still too weak to seek to rule the sea." It had "no enemies, and only rarely [did] its interests intersect with those of other nations of the globe." These reflections prompted Tocqueville to offer a prediction: "If the existence of the Union were under constant threat, if its great interests were daily intertwined with those of other powerful nations, the executive power would take on increased importance in the public eye, because people would expect more of it, and it would do more." In this instance, as in so many others, Tocqueville was prophetic.[96]

Of course, Tocqueville exaggerated. The Atlantic Ocean separated the United States not from the rest of the world but from Europe and Africa. Although too weak to rule the sea, the United States was not too weak to invade Mexico. But from a European perspective, Tocqueville was surely right, particularly after the Napoleonic Wars came to an end in 1815. After 1815, none of Europe's many nineteenth-century wars threatened the national security of the United States. And America's rapid territorial expansion meant that the United States no longer had European powers on its doorstep. The American army remained tiny by European standards. A decade after the end of the Civil War, the United States' army was 20 times smaller than the French army and half the size of the Belgian army. The American navy had fewer ships than at least a dozen other countries, including Turkey and Sweden.[97]

Following the Civil War, Americans were especially preoccupied with their internal affairs. Reconstructing the South was a massive undertaking but not an emergency requiring swift executive action. During the 1870s and 1880s—the so-called "Gilded Age"—the nation's restless energies were absorbed in building railroads that knit together the nation's vast territories and building factories that employed millions in the teeming cities of the Northeast. The major parties argued largely about domestic issues, such as tariffs, monetary policy, and civil service reform. Foreign affairs seemed a distant concern to most Americans.

One should not overstate the point. American business remained as reliant as ever on securing foreign markets for its products. The Civil War and Reconstruction did not extinguish the dreams of territorial expansion that captivated so many Americans in the antebellum period. Indeed, when Ulysses S. Grant became president in 1869, he promptly tried to annex Santo Domingo (known today as the Dominican Republic), which he saw as a desirable destination for freed slaves as well as a site for a valuable naval base in the Caribbean. While negotiating the treaty of annexation, Grant—without seeking congressional authorization—dispatched several naval ships to defend the Santo Domingo government against a possible invasion by Haiti. The Senate responded by rejecting the treaty and condemning Grant's "usurpation of power" in using the navy "without the authority of Congress in acts of hostility against a friendly foreign nation." Grant backed down, reversing his naval order and giving up on the acquisition of Santo Domingo.[98]

Throughout the latter part of the nineteenth century, the Senate aggressively used its power over treaties to frustrate presidential initiatives in foreign policy. In fact, between 1871 and 1897 the Senate ratified no treaties of consequence. In *Congressional*

Government, published in 1885, political scientist Woodrow Wilson complained that the treaty ratification process compelled the president to "approach [the Senate] as a servant conferring with his master." The Senate, moreover, did not merely vote treaties up or down, but felt at liberty to rewrite and amend them, much to the frustration of the diplomats charged with negotiating treaties. Writing in 1899, President McKinley's secretary of state John Hay lamented the Constitution's "irreparable mistake" of giving a minority in the Senate the power to block any treaty, no matter how advantageous or prudent or popular that treaty. The Senate's recalcitrance, Hay complained, made "all serious negotiation impossible."[99]

Hay's frustration at the power of the Senate was understandable. By enabling one-third of the Senate to veto treaties, the Constitution placed a tremendous roadblock in the way of the government's ability to make treaties. But Hay's lament obscures that presidents by the end of the nineteenth century were finding creative ways around that roadblock. In 1898, when Senate Democrats thwarted the McKinley administration's treaty annexing Hawaii, the president did what Tyler had done more than a half-century earlier with Texas: annex by a joint resolution of Congress, which required only a majority vote in both houses. McKinley and Theodore Roosevelt also relied heavily on executive agreements, which enabled them to bypass Congress entirely. In 1905, for instance, when the Senate balked at a treaty with Santo Domingo that gave the United States control over its customhouses, Roosevelt simply "put the agreement into effect" on his own. Between 1889 and 1939, according to one study, nearly two-thirds of international compacts were executive agreements rather than treaties.[100]

The resurgence of presidential power in foreign affairs at the turn of the twentieth century was not just a matter of more savvy or assertive presidents. It was also, as Tocqueville predicted, a product of new circumstances, specifically America's emergence as a great power with interests that stretched across the globe. Ironically, Congress was the catalyst for this development by pushing the country into a war against Spain that both President Cleveland and President McKinley had resisted.

The Spanish–American War

The Spanish–American War of 1898 stemmed from a popular revolt in Cuba. Cubans wanted independence from Spanish rule, and the Spanish government wished not to lose control of a lucrative territory that had been part of its empire for centuries. Americans were outraged at reports of Spanish atrocities and sided overwhelmingly with the Cuban insurgents. Throughout the last two years of his presidency, Cleveland strenuously resisted congressional efforts to involve the country in the Cuban revolt, reportedly telling a delegation of legislators that if Congress declared war on Spain he would refuse to mobilize the army.[101]

McKinley too, though more sympathetic to Cuba and imperialistic expansionism than Cleveland, worked diligently during his first year in office to avoid war with Spain. McKinley had no interest in annexing Cuba, but he did have a strong interest in bringing an end to the violence in Cuba, which was damaging American economic interests and endangering American lives. Cuba was a Spanish colony, but 90 percent of its exports went to, and about half of its imports came from, the United States. Moreover, American business had some $50 million invested in Cuba, much of it in sugar and tobacco plantations. McKinley pressured Spain to grant Cuba limited autonomy, but his diplomatic efforts met increasing resistance, both from members of Congress, who wanted McKinley to align the government with the Cuban rebels, and from the Spanish government, which resented the United States intervening in what it regarded as its internal affairs.[102]

Under pressure from Congress to take action and anxious to protect the thousands of Americans who lived in Cuba, McKinley ordered an American battleship, the *Maine*, into the harbor of Havana in January 1898. Three weeks later, with pressure for war mounting both in Spain and the United States, the *Maine* exploded, killing 266 Americans. Although almost certainly an accident caused by an internal explosion, an American inquiry board concluded that a Spanish submarine mine was the likely culprit. Even after receiving the board's report, McKinley held out hope that "something may yet happen to avert hostilities," but there was little he could do to prevent war since Spain was unwilling to accept Cuban independence and the Cuban rebels were unwilling to accept half-measures.[103]

The Spanish–American War lasted only a few months but it announced America's arrival as an imperial power. Defeated Spain not only agreed to Cuban independence but also ceded the Philippines, Puerto Rico, and Guam to the United States. In a preface to the fifteenth printing of *Congressional Government*, written in 1900, Woodrow Wilson identified the war with Spain as the source of "the most important change" in American government since the book's publication 15 years earlier because it led the nation to "plunge into international politics and into the administration of distant dependencies." Echoing Tocqueville, Wilson observed that "when foreign affairs play a prominent party in the politics and policy of a nation, its Executive must of necessity be its guide: must utter every initial judgment, take every first step of action, supply the information upon which it is to act, suggest and in large measure control its conduct." In Wilson's view, the president was now "at the front of affairs, as no president, except Lincoln, has been since the first quarter of the nineteenth century."[104]

Although McKinley had worked to avert war with Spain, he pounced on the opportunity to expand the war to Spanish possessions in the Far East. He ordered a naval fleet to the Philippines to "capture . . . or destroy" Spanish warships based in Manila Bay. After the American fleet, under the command of Admiral George Dewey, destroyed the Spanish fleet, McKinley dispatched American troops to Manila to "complete the reduction of Spanish power in the archipelago." Manila fell the day after the Spanish and American governments signed an armistice, and Spain demanded that Manila be returned. McKinley refused, instructing his five-man negotiating team in Paris to insist that Spain must cede not only Manila but all of the Philippines. He would brook no compromise. Lacking "the material means to defend [her] rights," Spain capitulated to "the law of the victor," taking the $20 million on offer rather than continue a war it was bound to lose.[105]

Little Wars of Empire

The Treaty of Paris marked the end of one war but the start of another, much longer war in the Philippines. Almost twice as many Americans died in the Philippine–American

War as the Spanish–American War, yet McKinley never considered seeking congressional authorization for the war in the Philippines. Because the Philippines belonged to the United States, McKinley reasoned that the executive was quelling a rebellion, not waging war against a foreign state.

Nor did McKinley seek congressional approval in the summer of 1900 when he ordered American troops stationed in the Philippines to China as part of an international force to quell the Boxer Uprising, a quixotic effort by poorly armed peasants to drive out Westerners and Christian missionaries. The Chinese empress sided with the Boxers and declared war on the foreign powers, including the United States, yet McKinley insisted to Congress that the actions he had taken "involved no war against the Chinese nation." American forces had been sent to China, he explained, not to make war but to restore order, protect American life and property, and ensure that the United States was compensated for its losses in the violent uprising. It was, in short, an international police action, not a war.[106]

Over the next several decades, American presidents repeatedly sent United States military forces to intervene in the affairs of other nations, especially in Central America and the Caribbean. None of the many "Banana Wars," in countries such as Nicaragua, the Dominican Republic, and Haiti, were declared or authorized by Congress. Indeed, presidents never referred to these interventions as wars at all, but instead described them as "police actions" aimed at protecting American citizens and property as well as ensuring that these nations honored their foreign debts and protected foreign property so that European nations would not have an excuse to intervene in the region.[107]

Members of Congress periodically objected to the executive's increasing willingness to deploy American forces overseas without consulting Congress. In 1912, the Senate debated an amendment that would require presidents to seek congressional approval before committing American military forces abroad, except in cases of genuine emergency when Congress was not in session. The amendment was easily defeated, as most senators were unwilling to restrict the commander in chief's ability to protect American lives and property. But even those senators who objected to the amendment conceded two points: (1) Congress possessed the power to pass a law forbidding troops from being sent out of the country, and (2) although the president could send troops "into any country" to protect Americans, he could not send them "for the purpose of making war." Making war, declared New York senator (and former secretary of war and state in the McKinley and Roosevelt administrations) Elihu Root, was "of course" an act that required congressional authorization. Congress, then, as much as the president, conspired in the fiction that the United States was not engaged in war when it intervened in the affairs of sovereign nations.[108]

On rare occasions, a president did go to Congress before sending in troops. In 1914, for instance, President Woodrow Wilson called a joint session of Congress to ask members to approve using the armed forces against Mexico. Wilson said military action was necessary because the Mexican president had refused to permit a requested 21-gun salute to show contrition for the wrongful arrest of nine American seamen in Tampico. Although the American seamen had been quickly released, the Mexican commander had immediately apologized, and the Mexican president had expressed his regrets, this was apparently not enough to preserve the dignity of the United States. Wilson made plain that he did not have to ask Congress for its blessing, but said he did "not wish to act in a manner possibly of grave consequence except in close conference and co-operation with both the Senate and the House." The House immediately authorized the use of the armed forces, but the Senate took two days to consider whether such a trivial incident justified a military response. That was one day too long for Wilson, who ordered the Marines to land at Veracruz without waiting for authorization from the Senate. The American occupation of Veracruz lasted for seven months, and ended only after Wilson's real purpose had been achieved: the overthrow of the Mexican president General Victoriano Huerta (Wilson never did get his 21-gun salute).[109]

World War I

In 1917, Wilson again appeared before a joint session of Congress to request authorization for military action, this time to arm American merchant vessels that were being attacked by German submarines. As in 1914, Wilson insisted that he came to Congress not because he was required to by the Constitution but because he thought it would be politically advantageous. "No doubt," Wilson lectured Congress, "I already possess that authority without special warrant of law, by the plain implication of my constitutional duties and powers." But he preferred to know that Congress was behind him "in whatever it may become necessary for me to do." When the authorization that Wilson sought was blocked by a Senate filibuster, the president armed the vessels anyway.[110]

Few Americans, members of Congress included, were desperate to prevent the president from intervening militarily in the affairs of far weaker nations, particularly in the American hemisphere. Some thought the bullying morally wrong and others found the president's actions constitutionally suspect. But these protests were generally muted because the interventions involved relatively small numbers of troops and posed little direct risk to American life or national security. Americans took a much more skeptical view, however, of involvement in the wars of Europe. While American Marines landed in Veracruz within two weeks of the arrest of the seamen in Tampico, World War I went on for nearly three years before Wilson finally asked Congress to declare war on Germany.[111]

Although Congress formally declared war against Germany on April 6, 1917, Wilson made the key decisions that took the United States into World War I. It was Wilson who proclaimed neutrality in 1914 while tilting the nation's foreign policy ever more steeply in favor of the British and against Germany. It was Wilson who broke off diplomatic relations with Germany and armed American merchant ships, authorizing them to attack any German submarine that was submerged or engaged in any "unlawful act" that might jeopardize the ship or its passengers. And it was Wilson who called Congress into session to "formally accept the status of belligerent which [had] been thrust upon it" as a result of German submarine attacks on American merchant ships in the war zone around the British Isles.[112]

Unlike the nation's three previous declared wars—the War of 1812, the Mexican–American War, and the Spanish–American War—each of which had been motivated by and/or resulted in the acquisition of territory, the United States did not stand to gain any territory from going to war with Germany. Perhaps that explains why Wilson insisted that this was to be a war unlike any other war, "a war to end all wars" and "to make the world safe for democracy." If those were the war's aims, the war failed spectacularly, despite the defeat of Germany and its autocratic allies. Wilson's blueprint for a new world order, the League of Nations, was rejected by the United States Senate, and the less than magnanimous peace terms offered to Germany laid the groundwork for the rise of Nazism and the coming of World War II.

After the war, many Americans could not understand why more than 100,000 Americans had to die—another 200,000 were wounded—to sort out Europe's squabbles. The war had brought higher taxes, military conscription, increased government control of the economy, and domestic repression, with little or nothing on the benefit side of the ledger. To many Americans, the war seemed a colossal waste of lives and resources, a blunder they vowed never to repeat. Almost everybody, it seemed, blamed Wilson. The result was a powerful backlash in Congress and the country against both presidential control of foreign policy and military intervention in Europe. By aggressively wielding executive power, Wilson ironically made it more difficult for the next Democratic president, Franklin Roosevelt, to respond to a genuinely profound threat to democratic freedom and American national security.

ENTERING WORLD WAR II

During the 1930s, Congress reacted to the alarming rise of Nazism in Germany by clinging ever more tightly to isolationism. Legislators were determined not to let Roosevelt do what Wilson had done: drag the country into a fruitless European war. When FDR asked Congress in 1934 for the authority to impose an arms embargo on nations the president judged to be the aggressors in a military conflict, the Senate balked. To give the president that sort of broad, discretionary authority, complained the chair of the Senate Foreign Relations Committee, would "have a strong tendency" to draw the United States into war.[113]

Between 1935 and 1939, Congress passed four neutrality acts that were designed to keep the president from involving the nation in the fight against Nazism. So powerful were the currents of isolationism that Gallup polls found that about three-quarters of the public backed a "Peace Amendment" that would require a nationwide popular referendum before a congressional declaration of war could take effect, except in cases of invasion. The amendment—known as the Ludlow Amendment—came close to getting a majority of the House to support it, despite vigorous opposition from the Roosevelt White House.[114]

Even after Germany invaded Poland in September 1939, the American public and Congress continued to resist being drawn into war. Only after Japan's attack on Pearl Harbor in December 1941, more than two years into World War II, did Roosevelt ask Congress to declare war. During the preceding two years, however, Roosevelt did what he could to aid the Allied forces, often in clear violation of neutrality laws he had signed as well as international laws that forbade a neutral nation from supplying a belligerent nation with arms.

In May 1940, for instance, British Prime Minister Winston Churchill pleaded with Roosevelt to send his country 40 or 50 "older destroyers" to replace those the Germans had destroyed. FDR initially resisted, telling Churchill that he needed congressional authorization for such a transaction and that he doubted Congress would approve it, particularly with an election approaching. But with Britain's survival appearing to hang in the balance, Roosevelt was desperate to find a way to get Churchill the destroyers he needed. The solution that the administration came up with was an executive agreement giving Britain 50 "over-age" destroyers, in exchange for which the United States would receive permission to use British bases in the Atlantic and Caribbean. In announcing the agreement in September 1940, Roosevelt explained that he had made the deal because using Britain's bases was essential to the nation's ability to defend itself against "overseas attack." Fifty aging destroyers, Roosevelt reasoned, was a small price to pay for the defense of the United States. Legal experts assailed the president's subterfuge as illegal and unconstitutional, but the public backed the deal.[115]

After his reelection in November 1940, Roosevelt—much like Wilson after his reelection in 1916—felt emboldened to align the United States more openly with the Allied cause. In a speech in December 1940, he vowed to make the United States the great "arsenal of democracy" in the fight against the Nazis. Some of this he did with Congress's explicit approval, such as the president's famous Lend-Lease program, by which the nation "lent" weapons and ammunitions to a bankrupt British government. Many other actions he took without asking Congress's approval or authorization, including sending 4,000 US Marines to Iceland, freezing German and Japanese assets in the United States, ordering the navy to "shoot on sight" any German vessels in the North Atlantic, and directing the navy to protect convoys taking supplies and war matériel to Iceland.[116]

However, Congress was far from powerless and significantly constrained Roosevelt's ability to deploy American forces, particularly through its control over conscription. Britain had wanted Roosevelt to send 20,000 troops to Iceland, thereby enabling Britain to redeploy the 20,000 men it had stationed there. But Roosevelt could only scrape together 4,000 Marines, in large part because the Selective Service Act, passed by Congress in September 1940, made it illegal to deploy draftees outside the Western Hemisphere, which was commonly understood at the time to exclude Iceland. The act also limited the term of duty for draftees to one year, which forced Roosevelt to return to Congress in the summer of 1941 to plead for an extension of the draftees' term of duty. Roosevelt urged Congress to extend draftees' tour of duty for the duration of the emergency (Roosevelt had declared an "unlimited national emergency" at the end of May) and to remove the limitation on where they were deployed. Congress refused to budge on the restriction on sending draftees outside the Western Hemisphere, but consented to extend service to 18 months, a compromise that carried in the House by a single vote, despite the Democrats' 100-vote majority. The recalcitrance of Congress reflected the mood of the American public, 70 percent of whom still opposed American entry into the war.[117]

Roosevelt was determined to take the nation to war, but he knew that he could not wage war effectively against Nazi Germany without the support of Congress and the American people. And that support, Roosevelt understood, required the enemy to attack American forces. That attack came on the "day that would live in infamy," December 7, 1941.

But the Japanese attack on Pearl Harbor did not just happen; it was provoked by policies Roosevelt pursued, particularly an oil embargo against Japan. There was no conspiracy. Roosevelt did not know the Japanese were going to attack Pearl Harbor, but he made demands on Japan that he knew would make an attack on American forces more likely. Roosevelt also pursued policies in Europe that he knew would provoke German attacks. By providing naval convoys for British ships crossing the Atlantic, Roosevelt sparked an "undeclared shooting war" with Germany in September 1941 that resulted in the deaths of more than a hundred American sailors and which enabled Roosevelt to prevail upon Congress to amend the neutrality acts to allow for the arming of American merchant ships.[118]

Congress declared war against Japan and Germany immediately after the attack on Pearl Harbor, but the president made the decisions that marched the United States into war. Congress and the public opinion it reflected undoubtedly provided a powerful brake on the president's desire to go to war. Had Roosevelt not had to worry about Congress or his own reelection, the American military would surely have intervened much earlier. The same had been true in World War I, but the lessons the nation drew from these two world wars would be very different.

After World War I, the nation blamed a high-handed and arrogant president for needlessly involving the nation in the affairs of Europe and looked to Congress to prevent it from happening again. After World War II, the lesson most people drew was that isolationism was no longer viable in an increasingly dangerous world and Congress was too parochial to be trusted to make farsighted decisions about national security. The triumph over Nazism and the preservation of the world's liberal democratic nations seemed to demonstrate that the president knew best—or at least better than Congress— what was in the national security interests of the United States.

THE COLD WAR AND THE ORIGINS OF THE NATIONAL SECURITY STATE

World War II was unlike any previous war in American history, less because of what happened during the war than what happened afterward. During World War II there was the same enhancement of government power as in World War I. During both wars, government created agencies, directed industry, mobilized national resources, cranked out propaganda, drafted citizens, and suppressed civil liberties. However, in World War I, as in the Civil War, the wartime measures ended when the fighting stopped: conscription ceased, defense expenditures were slashed, government restrictions were lifted, agencies were abolished, and executive power was rolled back. After the emergency was over, there was a "return to normalcy." But after World War II, the nation slid seamlessly from world war into Cold War, a state of nearly perpetual emergency that justified a permanent national security state, with the commander in chief at its helm.

Consider military spending. After World War I, the defense budget quickly shrank to levels that were not dramatically different than before the war. In constant dollars (that is, controlling for inflation), the amount that the United States spent on national defense in 1924 or 1934 was only marginally more than it had been spending in 1914, the year that war broke out in Europe. In contrast, the United States spent more than 20 times more in constant dollars in 1954 or 1964 than it spent in 1939, the year that World War II began.[119]

The same picture is displayed if one looks at the number of military personnel. When FDR took office in 1933, the military had about 244,000 soldiers on active duty, a number that was not dramatically different than the 154,000 personnel on duty when Woodrow Wilson became president in 1913. In contrast, when Dwight Eisenhower became president in 1953 the United States armed forces numbered over 3.5 million, more than ten times the number in uniform the year that World War II broke out. A decade later, in 1963, when Lyndon Johnson took the oath of office, the United States still had about 2.7 million military personnel on active duty. For the first time in American history, the country was maintaining a massive standing army in peacetime, precisely the thing that had so worried the framers of the Constitution.[120]

As the framers anticipated, a large standing army dramatically increased the power of the executive. With millions of troops at his disposal, the commander in chief could send the American military to anywhere in the world. Indeed, that was precisely the point. The Cold War was a global struggle between Communism and "the Free World." If Communist aggression was not arrested, then countries would fall like dominos. The widely accepted lesson of World War II, after all, was that appeasement and avoidance only strengthened the enemy and put off the day of reckoning. Containment of the Soviet bloc therefore required that the United States respond immediately to Communist incursions anywhere in the world, even in far-off places like Korea and Vietnam.

"Technology Has Modified the Constitution"

But it was more than just an increase in the size of the military that swelled presidential power. It was also the nature of the weapons now at the president's disposal, most especially the atom bomb, which was developed without the involvement or knowledge of Congress. The Constitution gave Congress the authority to declare war, but the atom bomb gave the president the power to destroy another nation without asking Congress's permission. The framers' intentions were no longer relevant to war-making because, as political scientist Richard Neustadt told a Senate committee in 1963, "technology has modified the Constitution." The president, Neustadt explained, "perforce, becomes, the only ... man in the system capable of exercising judgment under the extraordinary limits now imposed by secrecy, complexity, and time."[121]

The Cold War and the atom bomb transformed the nation's understanding of the role of the commander in chief. After World War II, it became commonplace for Americans to refer to the president as the commander in chief, whether or not the United States was actually at war. Moreover, the president became not the commander in chief of the armed forces, but *our* commander in chief. When Lyndon Johnson was running for reelection in 1964, for instance, he repeatedly referred to himself, in campaign stops all across the country, as "your commander in chief," even though he was addressing civilians. Before the Cold War, no president would have dreamed of telling American civilians that he was their commander in chief.[122]

Originally conceived as a part-time position, commander in chief had become a full-time role. Ever since Truman ordered atom bombs dropped on Nagasaki and Hiroshima, the president has been shadowed around the clock by a military aide who carries the "football" containing the nuclear codes. In every presidential election of the past 60 years, voters have been asked to consider whether a candidate is the sort of person they would trust as the commander in chief whose finger would be on "the button" at all times. The symbolic link in the public mind between the president and the commander in chief was forged even more tightly once presidents, beginning with Ronald Reagan in 1981, began routinely returning military salutes as they alighted from Marine One, the White House helicopter operated by the Marine Corps. War or no war, the president in the nuclear age was always the commander in chief.[123]

The Spread of Executive Secrecy

The Cold War did far more than elevate the commander in chief's symbolic role. It also increased executive secrecy. Some level of secrecy has, of course, always been essential to military operations and foreign negotiations. After World War II, however, the scope of secrecy expanded beyond anything the nation had known before. This was not simply an executive power grab. Congress and the public shared a belief that clandestine tactics, classified information, and secret agents were necessary to counter the Soviet threat. In 1947, Congress passed the National Security Act, which established the National Security Council as well as the nation's first peacetime intelligence agency, the Central Intelligence Agency. Although the CIA's statutory mandate was initially vague, Congress soon passed the Central Intelligence Agency Act, which exempted the new agency from normal budgeting reporting requirements. How the CIA spent its money and how much it spent could therefore be hidden from the American people and from Congress.[124]

Under Truman, the CIA expanded dramatically. By the last year of Truman's presidency, the CIA's covert office had nearly 6,000 agents scattered across 47 nations, and a budget over $80 million. Initially the CIA's focus was spying and propaganda. In 1948, for instance, the CIA secretly funneled millions of dollars into Italian elections in order to support the Christian Democratic Party and defeat the Italian Communist Party, which was covertly funded by the Soviet Union. Under Eisenhower, the CIA began to engage in covert operations using paramilitary forces, which went well beyond what Congress envisioned in establishing the agency. At Eisenhower's direction, the CIA orchestrated the overthrow of leftist leaders in Iran and Guatemala and replaced them with governments more friendly to American interests. Eisenhower also authorized the CIA's failed attempts to engineer coups in Indonesia and Cuba. Each of these covert military operations was executed without congressional knowledge, let alone congressional approval. Indeed, neither Congress nor the public became aware of the CIA's involvement in these coups until congressional investigations in the 1970s.[125]

During the 1950s and the first half of the 1960s, those on both sides of the political aisle seemed to agree that national security required trusting the president. After all, only the president had access to the vast flow of classified information gathered by the nation's burgeoning intelligence community, which included not only the Central Intelligence

Upon exiting Marine One in January 1988, President Ronald Reagan returns the attending Marine's salute. Today the presidential military salute has become commonplace, but no president before Reagan—not even Dwight Eisenhower, who spent a lifetime in the military—offered a military salute. Prior to Reagan, the military salute was deemed suitable only for those in uniform.

Courtesy: AFP/Getty Images.

Agency but also the various intelligence agencies in the Department of Defense, including the National Security Agency (created in 1952) as well as the Defense Intelligence Agency and National Reconnaissance Office (both formed in 1961). Speaking in 1961, Arkansas senator William Fulbright admitted that it was "distasteful" and even a little bit dangerous to trust the president with powers "unchecked and unbalanced," but like so many others he believed the nation had no choice. As Fulbright put it, "The price of democratic survival in a world of aggressive totalitarianism is to give up some of the democratic luxuries of the past." An eighteenth-century constitution, Fulbright believed, was simply ill-suited to cope with twentieth-century dangers.[126]

THE VIETNAM WAR: ORIGINS AND AFTERMATH

When President Lyndon Johnson appeared before the American people on August 4, 1964, nobody doubted his version of events. The North Vietnamese, Johnson reported, had launched unprovoked torpedo attacks on two American naval vessels in the Gulf of Tonkin, the first on August 2 and the second on August 4. Congress complied immediately with Johnson's request for a joint resolution in support of the president taking "all necessary measures to repel any armed attack against the forces of the United States and to prevent further aggression." Drafted by the White House months earlier, the resolution was approved unanimously by the House and passed 88–2 in the Senate.[127]

The Gulf of Tonkin Resolution

Before voting on the Gulf of Tonkin Resolution, members of Congress were assured by the administration that the *Maddox* was fired upon while on a "routine patrol in international waters." In reality, as the administration knew full well, the ship was off the North Vietnamese coast to provide electronic reconnaissance for secret CIA-backed commando raids on North Vietnam, a policy (called 34-A) that the president had secretly authorized more than six months earlier. Nobody in Congress or the public knew about this covert CIA operation, which included using small boats manned by South Vietnamese and foreign mercenaries to attack North Vietnam. In fact, the August 2 attack was, as Defense Secretary Robert McNamara informed the president the following day, a direct response to a 34-A strike on two North Vietnamese islands in the Gulf of Tonkin two nights before. Moreover, after the August 2 attack the administration ordered the *Maddox* and a second destroyer, the *C. Turner Joy*, to move to within 11 miles of the North Vietnamese coast in a deliberate effort to provoke a second attack. The administration, as Walter Cronkite concluded 40 years after the incident, was clearly "laying bait for the fox, American bait to justify American retaliation."[128]

The North Vietnamese attack of August 4, which Johnson offered as the primary rationale for the joint resolution, almost certainly never happened. The two American destroyers did initially think they were under attack, and when the president spoke to the country on August 4 he likely did believe that there had been a second attack. Hindsight, of course, is 20–20, but there were lots of reasons to be skeptical at the time. Johnson had received a cable to Washington from the commander of the two-destroyer task group,

A gaggle of congressmen look on as President Johnson affixes his signature to the Gulf of Tonkin Resolution, which stated that "Congress approves and supports the determination of the President, as Commander in Chief, to take all necessary measures to repeal any armed attack against the forces of the United States and to prevent any further aggression."

Courtesy: Getty Images.

notifying his superiors that reports of fired torpedoes and enemy sightings may have been due to "freak weather effects" and an "over-eager sonarman." The cable advised a "complete evaluation before any further action" was taken. But neither McNamara nor Johnson was interested in doing a complete evaluation. They already had what they wanted: a second attack to justify a retaliatory strike and secure the support of Congress.[129]

It was not that Johnson ever believed he was required to get congressional authorization to attack North Vietnam. When Johnson addressed the American people on August 4 it was to inform them that he had already ordered retaliatory air strikes on North Vietnam. The Gulf of Tonkin Resolution was not passed until three days later. A couple years later, Johnson was asked at a press conference whether the Gulf of Tonkin Resolution provided a sufficient justification for the massive escalation of the war that Johnson had carried out. Few congressmen, after all, believed that in voting for the resolution they were approving a long, protracted land war in Asia. Johnson's answer was that congressional support, while politically "desirable," was not constitutionally "necessary to do what we did and what we are doing." As commander in chief, Johnson insisted, he was already vested with the authority to deter "Communist aggression."[130]

At first, few members of Congress seemed disposed to dispute the president's broad claims of executive power. In fact, Congress deserves at least as much blame as the president for the Gulf of Tonkin Resolution. Congress made no attempt to investigate Johnson's version of events, just as it had made no effort to oversee the covert operations that had provoked the crisis in the first place. Nor did Congress attempt to define or delimit the military response that it was approving. On the flimsiest of pretexts—even by the administration's own misleading account, the North Vietnamese attacks had not wounded or killed a single American soldier nor damaged or hit an American ship or installation—Congress gave the president advance blessing for any attacks he might deem necessary to prevent further aggression. The Gulf of Tonkin Resolution revealed at least as much about congressional abdication during the Cold War as it did about executive aggrandizement.[131]

To the War Powers Resolution

As American involvement in the Vietnam War escalated and the body count climbed, Congress became increasingly skeptical of both the war in Vietnam and the presidential war-making power. By 1968, when Johnson announced that he would not run for reelection, 500,000 American troops were in Vietnam and 35,000 American soldiers had died. Even before Senate hearings in 1968 revealed that Johnson had not told the whole truth about the Gulf of Tonkin, his efforts to conceal the war's escalation and then finesse its failures had engendered talk of the president's "credibility gap." That pillar of the post-World War II national security state—the notion that the commander in chief could and must be trusted to do what is best for the nation's security—appeared to be crumbling.

Johnson's lies and half-truths engendered a growing appreciation in Congress for what Senator Fulbright now hailed as the "great merit in the checks and balances of our 18th century Constitution." In 1969, Fulbright sponsored a "sense of the Senate" resolution declaring that the armed forces should not be dispatched abroad without the approval of the legislature and executive. The nonbinding resolution passed overwhelmingly in the Senate, but the new president Richard Nixon paid it no heed.[132]

Nixon had campaigned in 1968 on a pledge to bring a swift end to the Vietnam War, but instead the war widened. In the spring of 1970, Nixon ordered an invasion of Cambodia—a neutral country through which the North Vietnamese were transporting troops and supplies—without asking for congressional authorization or support, not even after the fact. Congress signaled its disapproval by revoking the Gulf of Tonkin Resolution and attaching an amendment—called the Mansfield Amendment—to an essential military procurement bill that declared it was the policy of the United States to "terminate at the earliest practicable date all military operations ... in Indochina." The Mansfield Amendment also called upon the president to set "a date certain" for the "prompt and orderly withdrawal of all United States military forces."[133]

Nixon brushed aside Congress's objections. In a signing statement, Nixon declared that the amendment was "without binding force or effect," and vowed that it would not change his administration's policies. Revoking the Gulf of Tonkin Resolution made no difference either, since the administration rejected the notion that it needed congressional approval or permission for military actions in Southeast Asia. As commander in chief, Nixon insisted, he had the right and responsibility under the Constitution to do whatever he deemed necessary to protect American forces in South Vietnam. Even after the last American forces had been withdrawn from Vietnam in March 1973, Nixon initiated another massive bombing campaign in Cambodia without seeking legislative approval.[134]

The bombing of Cambodia was brought to a halt in the summer of 1973 only after a veto-proof majority in Congress passed the Case–Church Amendment that cut off all funding for any further United States combat operations in Southeast Asia. The amendment showed that Congress's power of the purse was still a formidable weapon in restricting presidential war-making, but the circumstances of the amendment and the length of the Vietnam War also revealed the limits of the power of the purse. The amendment passed only after all American troops had been withdrawn from Vietnam, thus inoculating Congress against charges that it was endangering the lives of American troops. While troops remained in harm's way, however, it had been difficult if not impossible for Congress to cut off funding, even for an unpopular war.

Determined to rein in unilateral presidential war-making, Congress in November 1973 passed the War Powers Resolution (WPR). The law required that the president report to Congress within 48 hours of committing troops to combat, and mandated that American troops be brought home after 60 days if Congress has not "declared a war or ... enacted a specific authorization." The resolution was enacted over the vehement objections and veto of President Nixon, who insisted that the act was not only unconstitutional but would also cripple the nation's ability to respond to international crises.[135]

The WPR was Congress's attempt to breathe life into the all but moribund "declare war" clause and to ensure that future presidents could not engage in war without the consent of Congress. The effort failed. The WPR has had little effect on presidential or congressional behavior. In the decades after passage of the WPR, presidents deployed troops abroad with the same regularity they had before its enactment. President Reagan, for instance, ordered American military forces into Grenada, Lebanon, and Libya, without complying with the WPR. In response to Iraq's invasion of Kuwait in 1990, President George Herbert Walker Bush dispatched more than 430,000 troops to the Middle East, and only five months after the beginning of the troop buildup did he seek authorization from Congress. Even then, Bush maintained that he did not need congressional authorization to make war on Iraq since as commander in chief he already possessed the "constitutional authority to defend vital U.S. interests." Clinton launched military operations in Haiti and Kosovo without getting authorization from Congress, and Barack Obama did not get congressional approval for US military operations in Libya. The decision about when and where to dispatch troops remained as firmly in the president's hands as it had been before the WPR.[136]

CONGRESSIONAL CHECKS ON PRESIDENTIAL WAR POWERS

Congressional checks on presidential war powers have not been totally lacking, however. Studies of American military actions in the half-century after World War II have shown a positive correlation between the strength of the president's party in Congress and the frequency with which the president deployed the US military to respond to an international crisis. That is, the more members of the president's party were in Congress, the more likely a president was to commit American forces abroad. Studies have also shown that the duration and scale of a military action were also affected by the partisan composition in Congress. That is, the more fellow partisans the president could count on in Congress, the greater the likelihood that the president would engage in longer and larger military actions.[137]

These studies suggest that although post-World War II presidents consistently claimed not to need congressional authorization or approval for military actions, they generally did take into account the level of congressional support in deciding on the use of force, particularly when it carried the risk of prolonged military involvement. Even if the "declare war" clause had become a dead letter during the Cold War and the War Powers Resolution had proven to be merely "a toy handcuff," Congress still factored into presidents' calculations about responding militarily to crises. Ironically, then, congressional checks on presidential war-making remained relevant during the Cold War chiefly on account of an institution that the framers of the Constitution failed to anticipate and tried to discourage: political parties.[138]

The prospects for more robust congressional checks on presidential war powers were enhanced by the collapse of the Soviet Union in 1991. The end of the Cold War raised questions about whether the national security state that had existed for the previous 40 years was still necessary. Having triumphed over Soviet Communism, did the United States still need an army of several millions and an extensive network of secret intelligence agencies? If the nation's security was no longer implicated in the conflicts of far-off countries, then the familiar rationale for military intervention no longer seemed to apply. And if national security was not at stake, why should Congress defer to the president on questions of when and where to send American troops?

The congressional response to events in Somalia in 1993 suggested that the institutional dynamics of the post-Cold War era might indeed be different from that of the preceding four decades. In the closing days of his presidency, George Herbert Walker Bush, acting at the request of the United Nations, sent 25,000 troops to Somalia to protect relief workers delivering humanitarian aid to the people of the war-torn nation. When Clinton became president, he scaled back the American troop commitment while still retaining American forces in Somalia. However, after 18 American soldiers were killed and their bodies dragged through the streets in October 1993, Congress turned up the pressure on the president. Clinton promised to have all troops out by the end of March 1994, and Congress made sure he kept his promise by cutting off all funding for military actions in Somalia after March 31, 1994. Six months later, the Democratic-controlled Congress passed another defense appropriations act that cut off funding for any US military role for humanitarian relief efforts in Rwanda. Since what was at stake was not national security but humanitarian missions, Congress—even one controlled by the president's own party—seemed more willing to challenge the president over troop deployments than had generally been the case during the Cold War. But then came the terrorist attacks of September 11, 2001.

THE WAR ON TERROR: THE PRESIDENCY IN PERPETUAL WAR

Almost 3,000 people died on that tragic Tuesday when al-Qaeda hijacked four airliners, flying two of them into the World Trade Center and another into the Pentagon. Terrorism was not new, of course: about a thousand people had been injured in the bombing of the World Trade Center in 1993, and 168 people were killed in 1995 in the Oklahoma City bombings. But the scale of 9/11 was unlike any terrorist attack the nation had experienced before.

After 9/11, far-off conflicts once again seemed critical to national security. During the 2000 presidential campaign, candidate George W. Bush had derided "nation-building" as a kind of liberal social engineering applied to the international arena. But after 9/11, failed states seemed to be no longer of merely humanitarian concern but rather a threat to the security interests of the United States. The "war on terror," as the Bush administration dubbed it, would be a global war, just as the war against communism had been. Terrorist attacks by stateless actors possessing biological, chemical, or nuclear weapons seemed every bit as terrifying as the prospect of a nuclear war with the Soviet Union had been during the Cold War. Combating shadowy terrorist groups meant that covert operations and secret intelligence seemed as imperative as they had been at the height of the Cold War. And like the Cold War, a global war against terror promised to endure for generations.

The Wars in Afghanistan and Iraq

Three days after 9/11, Congress passed a joint resolution authorizing the president to use

> all necessary and appropriate force against those nations, organizations, or persons
> he determines planned, authorized, committed, or aided the terrorist attacks that

occurred on September 11, 2001, or harbored such organizations or persons, in order to prevent any such future acts of international terrorism against the United States by such nations, organizations, or persons.

The Authorization for Use of Military Force (AUMF) plainly permitted the president to use force against al-Qaeda, which planned and carried out the attacks, and against the Taliban government in Afghanistan, which provided a safe haven for al-Qaeda terrorists. In launching Operation Enduring Freedom in Afghanistan, with the aim of defeating the Taliban regime and finding Osama bin Laden and other al-Qaeda leaders, the Bush administration acted in close accord with the congressional resolution.[139]

Operation Enduring Freedom drove the Taliban from power by the end of 2001, but most al-Qaeda leaders, including bin Laden, eluded capture. More clearly needed to be done to bring the perpetrators of 9/11 to justice. But the Bush administration adopted a more expansive conception of the task ahead. "Our war on terror," Bush promised the country, "begins with Al Qaeda, but it does not end there." Preventing terrorism, Bush announced in his January 2002 State of the Union message, required not only hunting down the perpetrators of 9/11 but preventing any "regimes that sponsor terror from threatening America or our friends and allies with weapons of mass destruction." Bush singled out three regimes in particular: Iran, Iraq, and North Korea. "States like these and their terrorist allies," Bush explained, "constitute an axis of evil, arming to threaten the peace of the world." The enemy in the war on terror thus included not only terrorists but all regimes that potentially could provide weapons of mass destruction to terrorists. In the name of preserving peace, Bush seemed to be committing the United States to perpetual war.[140]

It is tempting to dismiss Bush's "axis of evil" speech as a rhetorical ruse, aimed less at justifying war against evil regimes than at laying the groundwork for the invasion of one particular regime, the Iraqi government of Saddam Hussein. We know that immediately after 9/11, Bush ordered subordinates to prepare invasion options. And we know too that well before 9/11, top officials in the Bush administration were already discussing ways to effect "regime change" in Iraq. An expansive war on terror that encompassed evil regimes capable of funneling weapons of mass destruction to terrorists thus gave the Bush administration the opportunity to achieve what many administration officials had long sought: justification to forcibly remove Saddam Hussein from power.[141]

Although Bush's 2002 State of the Union message was undoubtedly composed with an eye to justifying war with Iraq, it also reflected the administration's conviction that the attacks of September 11 demonstrated that conventional ways of thinking and acting were no longer sufficient to safeguard the United States. During the Cold War, defensive doctrines of deterrence and containment had protected the nation, but the war on terror, Bush explained, could "not be won on the defensive." The AUMF acknowledged that the president had the constitutional authority "to take action to deter and prevent acts of international terrorism against the United States," but Bush believed that to win the war on terror the government could no longer be merely "reactive." Bush maintained that the president must have the authority—and did not need Congress to give it to him—to protect the nation by acting "against such emerging threats before they are fully formed."

Even if Saddam Hussein did not pose an imminent threat to the United States, the president claimed the constitutional power and responsibility to remove him before his regime posed such a threat.[142]

It was often said that 9/11 changed everything. However, the politics of war-making after 9/11 mirrored institutional patterns etched during the Cold War. The Bush administration invaded Iraq in March 2003 when Republicans commanded majorities in both the House and Senate. The administration loudly touted the executive's wartime prerogatives but also knew that Republican legislative leaders and committee chairs would back the president, providing the administration political cover. So long as Republicans controlled Congress, there would be minimal congressional oversight of a Republican president's conduct of the war. And when Democrats took control of Congress in 2007, they immediately launched committee hearings into nearly every aspect of the wars in Iraq and Afghanistan, including the government's reliance on Blackwater private security contractors, the White House's role in the disclosure of Valerie Plame's identity as a CIA agent, the use of "enhanced interrogation" techniques, the administration of the detention center at Guantánamo Bay, and even whether Bush's abuses of executive power rose to the level of an impeachable offense.[143]

But if the Iraq War showed that party control of Congress still mattered in checking executive war-making, it also underscored the formidable powers of the modern president at war. Democrats interpreted their victory in the 2006 midterm elections as a mandate to end the war in Iraq, and public opinion polls showed that sizable majorities of the public wanted the United States out of Iraq. Yet only a week after the new Democratic Congress convened, Bush announced that he was ordering 20,000 more troops to Iraq and extending the tour of duty of the troops already in Iraq, a strategy described as a "surge." Although outraged by what they saw as an escalation of the war, congressional Democrats could do little more than pass a nonbinding resolution in the House expressing disapproval of the decision while promising "to continue to support and protect the members of the United States Armed Forces who are serving or who have served bravely and honorably in Iraq." The Senate couldn't even manage that much because Democrats fell four votes short of the 60 votes needed for cloture. Resolutions to cut off funding for the troop surge went nowhere in both chambers.

Iraq, in fact, looked a lot like Vietnam, not in the number of US casualties (the 4,500 American soldiers who died in Iraq pale in comparison to the 58,000 American soldiers who died in Vietnam) but in the institutional dynamics. In both wars, the president secured congressional authorization while denying he needed it to commence hostilities. In both wars, the president tailored the facts to suit his objectives: Johnson misled the nation about events in the Gulf of Tonkin; Bush misled the country about Iraq's supposed possession of weapons of mass destruction. In both wars, once troops were committed, members of Congress had to contend with the charge that their criticisms undermined troop morale and would prolong the war by giving aid and comfort to the enemy. And, finally, in both wars, so long as troops were on the ground, Congress's power of the purse was hardly a credible threat, let alone a realistic option.[144] The events of September 11, 2001, did not so much usher in a new era of unconstrained presidential war-making as revive the Cold War pattern.

"The Tools Necessary ... to Defeat the Enemy"

The war on terror not only provided the Bush administration with the opportunity to topple Saddam Hussein, but also presented the chance to reverse what some in the administration, particularly Vice President Dick Cheney, saw as the "constant, steady erosion of the prerogatives and powers of the president" dating back to the end of the Vietnam War. Cheney had in mind not only the War Powers Act but also a host of other laws enacted during the Nixon, Ford, and Carter administrations that sought to establish congressional oversight over covert operations and foreign intelligence gathering. After revelations in the 1970s about CIA abuses, Congress set up intelligence committees to oversee CIA activities, and the Intelligence Oversight Act of 1980 required the president to keep the intelligence committees "fully and currently informed of all covert actions" carried out by the government. In 1978, in response to disclosures that the Nixon administration had used warrantless wiretaps on war protesters, Congress enacted the Foreign Intelligence Surveillance Act (FISA) of 1978, which required that the government obtain permission from a special court (the Foreign Intelligence Surveillance Court) before conducting domestic surveillance aimed at uncovering clandestine operations conducted by a foreign government or preventing acts of terrorism or sabotage by a foreign power or its agent.[145]

Immediately after 9/11, the administration pushed through the USA Patriot Act (a.k.a. the Uniting and Strengthening America by Providing Appropriate Tools Required to Intercept and Obstruct Terrorism Act of 2001), which gave the executive branch sweeping new powers of surveillance, detention, and prosecution. The need for such legislation was urgent, Bush explained, because "we're at war. ... And in order to win the war, we must make sure that the law enforcement men and women have got the tools necessary, within the Constitution, to defeat the enemy." After signing the bill, Bush vowed to "enforce this law with all the urgency of a nation at war."[146]

A nation at war, the president and his lawyers insisted, could not afford—and constitutionally did not need—to play by the same rules as a nation at peace. According to the administration's lawyers, a wartime president could designate individuals as "unlawful enemy combatants" and hold them indefinitely without bringing them to trial, charging them, or allowing them legal representation. The determination of who was an enemy combatant was "a quintessentially military judgment" that could be made only by the commander in chief. The Office of Legal Counsel also claimed that Congress could not interfere with interrogations ordered by the president during wartime. As commander in chief, the president's lawyers argued, the president possessed the constitutional authority "to order interrogations of enemy combatants to gain intelligence information concerning the military plans of the enemy." Any legislation that compromised the commander in chief's power to conduct interrogations of enemy combatants, including bans on torture, was therefore unconstitutional. The president had to be free to do what was necessary to win the war.[147]

Lawyers in the Office of Legal Counsel scoured past precedents, particularly from the Civil War and World War II, to support the notion that the president in war had broad powers unavailable to peacetime presidents. They pointed to Lincoln's Emancipation

Proclamation and to FDR's establishment of a military commission to try and execute Nazi saboteurs apprehended on United States soil in 1942. But the analogies to the Civil War and World War II were in tension with the Bush administration's oft-repeated assertion that the war on terror was "a different kind of war," against an enemy unlike any the nation had faced before. If the war on terror was like no other the nation had previously experienced, did it make sense to look to the past for guidance?[148]

Arguments about the president's war powers take on a different meaning in the context of a military conflict likely to last a generation or more than in the context of a Civil War that lasted four years (and killed over 600,000 Americans) or a world war in which the United States was at war for less than four years (and resulted in the death of over 400,000 Americans). When Roosevelt and Lincoln claimed extraordinary war powers, they were claiming temporary powers to meet a national emergency, powers that were to be relinquished with the surrender of readily identifiable enemies. In contrast, Bush and his legal advisors argued that the president and the federal government should be vested with extensive war powers for an indefinite period of time that would come to a close not with the surrender of a specific enemy but with a determination by the executive branch that "every terrorist group of global reach" had been vanquished.[149]

Barack Obama: The Promise and the Legacy

As a presidential candidate in 2008, Barack Obama strongly criticized the Bush administration's expansive arguments about executive power in wartime. The former law professor stressed that the president did not have the constitutional power to authorize a military attack unless it was to stop "an actual or imminent threat to the nation" and rejected the idea that the Constitution permitted the president to disregard congressionally defined limits on troop deployments or interrogation techniques. Candidate Obama also repudiated the idea that the Constitution gave the president inherent wartime authority to detain US citizens without charge as unlawful enemy combatants. As president, Obama also cautioned against facile use of the term "war on terror," arguing that rather than "define our effort . . . as a boundless 'Global War on Terror,'" the nation should instead think of the challenge it faced "as a series of persistent, targeted efforts to dismantle specific networks of violent extremists that threaten America."[150]

While Obama's rhetoric departed significantly from Bush's, scholars debate about how different their actions were.[151] Critics who accent the continuity between Bush and Obama as commanders in chief note that, just as Bush sent 20,000 additional troops to Iraq without seeking congressional support, so Obama sent 30,000 additional troops to Afghanistan in a unilateral "surge" of his own. Even if Obama avoided using the term "war on terror," he continued to vigorously prosecute the war against not only al-Qaeda but also its many "affiliates" and "offshoots," most notably the Islamic State (a.k.a ISIS or ISIL), but also other Islamist militant groups such as al-Shabaab in Somalia. Whatever doubts Obama may have had about capturing and indefinitely detaining individuals in an ill-defined war on terror, he appeared to have few compunctions about targeted killings of suspected terrorists, including, in one case, an American citizen (see Chapter 10).

Despite Obama's criticism of the secrecy of the national security state, he massively expanded the CIA's reliance on drone strikes to kill suspected terrorists, particularly in Pakistan but increasingly in countries far from the Afghanistan battlefield, including Somalia, Yemen, and Libya. It was with much fanfare, on the second day of his presidency, that Obama reversed the Bush-administration directives authorizing torture and ordered the shuttering of the CIA's overseas "black site" prisons. But the very next day Obama authorized two secret drone attacks in Pakistan that killed at least a dozen civilians. Unlike Bush, Obama publicly (albeit belatedly) acknowledged the existence of the drone program and pressed for tighter rules governing drone attacks to minimize civilian deaths, but by the end of his presidency Obama had authorized over 500 drone strikes—ten times the number Bush had authorized—and killed an estimated 3,800 people, including hundreds of civilians.[152]

Obama's justification for all this killing was the AUMF. Nobody could doubt that when the Obama administration tracked down and killed the 9/11 mastermind bin Laden it was acting pursuant to Congress's intent in crafting the AUMF. However, the more the battle turned from fighting the perpetrators of 9/11 to fighting groups that didn't even exist at the time Congress enacted the AUMF, the more the administration had to stretch its interpretation of the AUMF. Although Obama, in a much publicized speech at the National Defense University in May 2013, spoke of his "desire to refine, and ultimately repeal, the AUMF's mandate" in order to get the nation off a "perpetual wartime footing," he found that far easier said than done. For starters, many Republicans in Congress would have gladly repealed the AUMF and replaced it with a more explicitly open-ended authorization to fight "a multigenerational, existential war with radical Islam." But adopting a more open-ended AUMF would only legitimate the "Forever War" that Obama hoped to wind down in his second term.[153]

Obama could be eloquent in warning against the dangers to democracy of a perpetual war on terror that would draw the nation "into more wars we don't need to fight, or continue to grant presidents unbound powers more suited for traditional armed conflicts between nation states." And his efforts to wind down the 9/11 war were not only rhetorical. After eight years of Obama's presidency, the number of US troops in war zones was reduced from 150,000 troops to 14,000. But if Obama's aim was to move the country away from a permanent wartime footing and rein in unilateral presidential war-making, he largely failed.[154]

Obama well understood that bringing the 9/11 war to a close required clearly distinguishing between al-Qaeda and other Islamist groups that sprang up. But in practice, driven by military and political exigencies, Obama played a crucial role in collapsing that distinction and thereby extending the 9/11 war. The stunning military successes (and horrific massacres) of the Islamic State in Iraq and Syria in 2014 presented Obama with a stark choice between two theories that could justify taking military action against the Islamic State: (1) treat it as a new phase in the same war that Congress had authorized in the AUMF, or (2) treat it as a new conflict against a new enemy that required new authorization from Congress. The second theory would recognize that the Islamic State had been excommunicated from al-Qaeda and that the two groups were now sworn enemies. It was also consistent with Obama's urgent call the year before regarding the need to bring to an end the country's seemingly endless 9/11 war. However, by this point in his presidency Obama had (for good reason) come to the conclusion that Congress was so mired in partisanship that it could not or would not act. And so, to the surprise and disappointment of many who had applauded his 2013 National Defense University speech, Obama stuck with the first theory—thereby embracing, in the words of one critic, "presidential unilateralism masquerading as implausible statutory interpretation."[155]

Ironically, the Obama administration's reliance on creative statutory interpretations was in some ways related to Obama's reluctance to embrace sweeping arguments about inherent presidential war powers. In Libya, for instance, when the air war that Obama carried out against Colonel Muammar Gadhafi's regime in 2011 exceeded the 60 days allowed by the War Powers Act, the administration did not dismiss the act as an unconstitutional intrusion on presidential war powers. Instead it concocted the theory that the air strikes did not count as "hostilities" under the War Powers Act because the American mission was a limited one and there were no American troops on the ground, no real risk of American casualties, and no exchanges of fire. In other words, because pro-Gadhafi fighters could not shoot back at American missiles, the administration did not need congressional approval. Members of Congress denounced this "preposterous" theory but failed to take any action to check the administration as they were unable to agree on whether to end the strikes or authorize them.[156]

Obama did not disguise his frustration at what he saw as a dysfunctional dynamic in which Congress sniped from the safety of sidelines, leaving the president to "stretch the boundaries of his authority as far as he can" in order to take necessary military action. But even as Obama lamented the legal stretching of presidential war-making authority, his administration's legal theories and actions created precedents that future presidents will undoubtedly use to justify unilateral military actions. Although the Obama administration was fond of drawing an invidious contrast between its own desire to act pursuant to statutory law and the Bush administration's assertion of an inherent executive power and defiance of Congress, Obama's stretching of the 2001 AUMF to wage war against the Islamic State did as much as any action taken by the Bush administration to perpetuate the 9/11 war and to enable unilateral presidential war-making. At the end of Obama's eight years, the nation was no closer to "turning the page" on the Forever War than it had been at the beginning of his term.[157]

Some now question whether it is even possible to draw a "clear distinction between war and not-war." Rather than expend energy on "the Sisyphean effort to 'end' war"—or debate what counts as a war—one former Obama official argues that the nation's policymakers would be better off "developing norms and institutions that support rights and the rule of law, but are not premised on a sharp line between war and peace." Arguably, this is what the Obama administration tried to do, for instance, in drawing up more exacting rules and procedures governing the use of drones in ways that better protected civilians. But the pressing challenge confronting Congress, the courts, and the country remains, as it has since the beginning of the Cold War, how to define and delimit presidential war powers in the context of perpetual war.[158]

Notes

1   David McCullough, *Truman* (New York: Simon & Schuster, 1992), 790–91. The letter, from a Mrs. Mary K. Albert, is dated July 11, 1950, and is in the Harry S. Truman Papers: Official File: OF 471–B.

2   The President's News Conference, June 29, 1950.

3   Special Message to the Congress Reporting on the Situation in Korea, July 19, 1950; Radio and Television Address to the American People on the Situation in Korea, July 19, 1950. For American casualties in the major US wars, see table Ed1–5—Military personnel and casualties, by war and branch of service: 1775–1991 in *Historical Statistics of the United States*, Millennial Edition Online.

4   Radio and Television Address to the American People on the Situation in Korea, July 19, 1950. McCullough, *Truman*, 792.

5   John W. Spanier, *The Truman–MacArthur Controversy and the Korean War* (New York: W.W. Norton, 1965), 29–30, 62–63. McCullough, *Truman*, 781–82.

6   Spanier, *The Truman–MacArthur Controversy and the Korean War*, 62. Robert J. Donovan, *Tumultuous Years: The Presidency of Harry S. Truman, 1949–1953* (New York: Norton, 1982), 222.

7   McCullough, *Truman*, 789. Donovan, *Tumultuous Years*, 223.

8   Dean Acheson, *Present at the Creation: My Years in the State Department* (New York: Norton, 1969), 414–15. Arthur M. Schlesinger, Jr., *The Imperial Presidency* (Boston: Houghton Mifflin, 1973), 132. Donovan, *Tumultuous Years*, 224.

9   Donovan, *Tumultuous Years*, 223–24. Acheson, *Present at the Creation*, 414–15.

10   Acheson, *Present at the Creation*, 415. McCullough, *Truman*, 789.

11   Ironically, while Truman's refusal to seek legislative authorization for the Korean War was motivated by a desire to protect presidential prerogatives, the administration simultaneously argued that in "the present crisis ... *any* debate over prerogatives and power [was] essentially sterile, if not dangerous to the success of our foreign policy" (Schlesinger, *Imperial Presidency*, 135). That is, while it was fine for the president to base his actions on a desire to preserve or enhance the constitutional and legal foundations of presidential power, it was unproductive if not unpatriotic for members of Congress to question the constitutionality or legality of committing American troops without legislative approval.

12   Louis Fisher, *Presidential War Power* (Lawrence: University Press of Kansas, 2004; second edition), 102, 113. Louis Fisher, "The Law: Scholarly Support for Presidential Wars," *Presidential Studies Quarterly* 35 (September 2005), 593–96. Schlesinger, *Imperial Presidency*, 139.

13   John Yoo, *The Powers of War and Peace: The Constitution and Foreign Affairs after 9/11* (Chicago: University of Chicago Press, 2005), 143. John Yoo, *Crisis and Command: The History of Executive Power from George Washington to George W. Bush* (New York: Kaplan, 2009), esp. 334–40.

14   William Blackstone, *Commentaries on the Laws of England* (New York: Garland Publishing, 1978; reprint of ninth edition, 1783), 252–63. First published in 1765, Blackstone's commentaries were enormously influential in colonial America. On Blackstone's influence on Hamilton see Gerald Stourzh, *Alexander Hamilton and the Idea of Republican Government* (Palo Alto, CA: Stanford University Press, 1970).

15   Max Farrand, ed., *The Records of the Federal Convention* (New Haven, CT: Yale University Press, 1937; 4 vols.), 1:18–19, 24–25 (May 29). Frederick W. Marks, *Independence on Trial: Foreign Affairs and the Making of the Constitution* (Baton Rouge: Louisiana State University Press, 1973), 5–15.

16   Farrand, *Records of the Federal Convention*, 1:21 (May 29).

17   Yoo, *Powers of War and Peace*, 91. William T. Hutchinson et al., eds., *The Papers of James Madison* (Chicago: University of Chicago Press, 1962), 9:385.

18   Farrand, *Records of the Federal Convention*, I: 65–66, 70 (June 1). Yoo's conclusion that "at this point in the debate, the Framers seemed to agree that vesting the president with all the 'executive powers' of the Articles of Confederation would include the power over war and peace" (*Powers of War and Peace*, 92) is wrong. Yoo is also mistaken in suggesting that it was not until July 26, when the convention sent specific resolutions to the Committee of Detail, that the Virginia Plan's language granting the National Executive "the Executive rights vested in Congress by the Confederation" was replaced by a definition of executive power as limited to the "Power to carry into Execution the national laws" and "appoint to Offices in Cases not otherwise provided for" (Farrand, *Records of the Federal Convention*, 1:21; 2:132). In fact, this change, as we have seen, was approved by the convention on June 1 upon Madison's motion. Also misleading is Yoo's claim that the resolutions sent to the Committee of Detail on July 26 "failed to transfer the old Congress's executive powers, including those of making war and peace, to any institution within the new government" (*Powers of War and Peace*, 93). In fact, the debate and vote on June 1 made it clear to the Committee of Detail that the convention desired the powers of war and peace to be vested in the legislature.

19   Farrand, *Records of the Federal Convention*, 2:143–44, 155, 182–83, 185.

20   Farrand, *Records of the Federal Convention*, 318.

21   Yoo, *Powers of War and Peace*, 145. Farrand, *Records of the Federal Convention*, 2:318–19 (August 17). In support of his interpretation, Yoo contends that in the ratifying conventions the supporters of the Constitution "did not argue that Congress's power to declare war … would check the President" (*Crisis and Command*, 50; also see Yoo, *Powers of War and Peace*, 142). Instead, Yoo maintains, the Constitution's defenders relied exclusively on the argument that the legislature's power of purse would check the executive's power of the sword. While supporters of the Constitution did point to the power of the purse as a check on the president's power to conduct war, it is not true that they ignored the "declare war" clause. James Wilson, for instance, made this argument at the Pennsylvania ratifying convention ("It will not be in the power of a single man, or a single body of men, to involve us in [war]; for the important power of declaring war is vested in the legislature at large") as did James Iredell in the North Carolina ratifying convention and Charles Pinckney in the South Carolina ratifying convention (Fisher, *Presidential War Power*, 9–10).

22   Forrest McDonald, *The American Presidency: An Intellectual History* (Lawrence: University Press of Kansas, 1994), 173–74.

23   Fisher, *Presidential War Power*, 13. Richard J. Ellis, *Founding the American Presidency* (Lanham, MD: Rowman & Littlefield, 1999), 158–59. Also see Francis D. Wormuth and Edwin B. Firmage, *To Chain the Dog of War: The War Power of Congress in History and Law* (Dallas: Southern Methodist University Press, 1986), 106–07.

24   Farrand, *Records of the Convention*, 2:297 (August 15), 2:319 (August 17), 2:392–93 (August 23), 2:498–99 (September 4), 2:538 (September 7).

25   Farrand, *Records of the Convention*, 2:498 (September 4), 2:538–39 (September 7).

26   Jack N. Rakove, *Original Meanings: Politics and Ideas in the Making of the Constitution* (New York: Alfred A. Knopf, 1996), 267. Edward S. Corwin, *The President: Office and Powers, 1787–1957* (New York University Press, 1957), 171. Also see Jack N. Rakove, "Solving a Constitutional Puzzle: The Treatymaking Clause as a Case Study," *Perspectives in American History* (1984), 233–81.

27   McDonald, *American Presidency*, 236. Also see Stanley Elkins and Eric McKitrick, *The Age of Federalism: The Early American Republic, 1788–1800* (New York: Oxford University Press, 1993), 333–35.

28 Martin S. Flaherty, "The Story of the Neutrality Controversy: Struggling over Presidential Power outside the Courts," in Christopher H. Schroeder and Curtis A. Bradley, eds., *Presidential Power Stories* (New York: Foundation Press, 2009), 25.

29 Elkins and McKitrick, *The Age of Federalism*, 333, 358.

30 Pacificus No. 1, available at the Online Library of Liberty, http://oll.libertyfund.org.

31 Jefferson to Madison, July 7, 1793, in John Catanzariti, et al., eds., *The Papers of Thomas Jefferson*, Volume 26, May 1793 to August 1793 (Princeton, NJ: Princeton University Press, 1995), 444.

32 Helvidius No. 1, available at the Online Library of Liberty, http://oll.libertyfund.org.

33 Helvidius No. 1, 3.

34 *Federalist* No. 75.

35 Fisher, *Presidential War Power*, 28. Flaherty, "The Story of the Neutrality Controversy," 43, 48.

36 Richard H. Kohn, *Eagle and Sword: The Federalists and the Creation of the Military Establishment in America, 1783–1802* (New York: Free Press, 1975), 96–97. Fisher, *Presidential War Power*, 17.

37 Allan R. Millett and Peter Maslowski, *For the Common Defense: A Military History of the United States* (New York: Free Press, 1994), 95–97. Kohn, *Eagle and Sword*, 106, 115–16. Yoo, *Crisis and Command*, 78.

38 Fisher, *Presidential War Power*, 18. Kohn, *Eagle and Sword*, 120.

39 Kohn, *Eagle and Sword*, 120–23. Yoo, *Crisis and Command*, 79.

40 Schlesinger, *Imperial Presidency*, 21.

41 Yoo, *Crisis and Command*, 75–76. Fisher, *Presidential War Power*, 19. David P. Currie, *The Constitution in Congress: The Federalist Period, 1789–1801* (Chicago: University of Chicago Press, 1997), 84.

42 Gerhard Casper, "The Washington Administration, Congress, and Algiers," in David Gray Adler and Larry N. George, eds., *The Constitution and the Conduct of American Foreign Policy* (Lawrence: University Press of Kansas, 1996), 260.

43 Casper, "The Washington Administration, Congress, and Algiers," 260–61.

44 Casper, "The Washington Administration, Congress, and Algiers," 261–68. Max Boot, *The Savage Wars of Peace: Small Wars and the Rise of American Power* (New York: Basic Books, 2002), 10–11.

45 Boot, *The Savage Wars of Peace*, 11–12. Fisher, *Presidential War Power*, 33. Montgomery N. Kosma, "Our First Real War," *Green Bag* (Winter 1999), 170.

46 Notes on a Cabinet Meeting, May 15, 1801, in Barbara B. Oberg, et al., eds., *The Papers of Thomas Jefferson*, Volume 34: May 1 to July 31, 1801 (Princeton, NJ: Princeton University Press, 2008), 34:114–15. Compare Yoo, *Crisis and Command*, 113.

47 Extract of a Letter from the Secretary of the Navy to Commodore Dale, May 20, 1801, in *American State Papers, Foreign Relations* (Washington, DC: Gales and Seaton, 1832), 7th Congress, 1st Session, 2:359–60. The complete text of the letter can be found in *Naval Documents Related to the United States Wars with the Barbary Powers* (Washington, DC: United States Government Printing Office, 1939), 1:465–69.

48 Lieutenant Andrew Sterrett to Commodore Dale, August 6, 1801, *American State Papers*, 2:360. Boot, *The Savage Wars of Peace*, 14.

49 Thomas Jefferson, First Annual Message, December 8, 1801.

50 Kosma, "Our First Real War," 174. Yoo, *Crisis and Command*, 113.

51 Fisher, *Presidential War Power*, 34–35. Kosma, "Our First Real War," 176–77. Yoo, *Crisis and Command*, 114.

52 Thomas Jefferson, First Annual Message, December 8, 1801. Gallatin to Jefferson, August 16, 1802, quoted in Robert M. Johnstone, Jr., *Jefferson and the Presidency: Leadership in the Young Republic* (Ithaca: Cornell University Press, 1978), 65.

53 Kosma, "Our First Real War," 177.

54 Fisher, *Presidential War Power*, 28. Helvidius No. 4 (September 14, 1793). Also see Madison's "Political Observations," April 20, 1795, in William T. Hutchinson, et al., eds., *The Papers of James Madison*, Congressional Series (University Press of Virginia, 1985), 15:51.

55 Drew McCoy, *The Elusive Republic: Political Economy in Jeffersonian America* (New York: Norton, 1980), 233. Also see J.C.A. Stagg, *Mr. Madison's War: Politics, Diplomacy, and Warfare in the Early American Republic, 1783–1830* (Princeton, NJ: Princeton University Press, 1983), 27–28, 51.

56 Robert V. Remini, *Henry Clay: Statesman for the Union* (New York: Norton, 1991), 59–60. Alvin M. Josephy, Jr., *On the Hill: A History of the American Congress* (New York: Touchstone, 1979), 141–42. Also see Steven Watts, *The Republic Reborn: War and the Making of Liberal America, 1790–1820* (Baltimore: Johns Hopkins University Press, 1987), 91–92.

57 Fisher, *Presidential War Power*, 37–38. Sean Wilentz, *The Rise of American Democracy: Jefferson to Lincoln* (New York: Norton, 2005), 147. Wood, *Empire of Liberty*, 660–61.

58 Donald R. Hickey, *The War of 1812: A Forgotten Conflict* (Urbana: University of Illinois Press, 1989), 44. Wilentz, *Rise of Democracy*, 147. Wood, *Empire of Liberty*, 660–61.

59 Wilentz, *Rise of Democracy*, 154. Robert Allen Rutland, *The Presidency of James Madison* (Lawrence: University Press of Kansas, 1990), 86.

60 Yoo, *Crisis and Command*, 140–41. Hickey, *The War of 1812*, 34. Wood, *Empire of Liberty*, 659, 672.

61 This understanding was affirmed by the federal courts on numerous occasions in the early republic. See Fisher, *Presidential War Power*, 25, 30, and Peter Irons, *War Powers: How the Imperial Presidency Hijacked the Constitution* (New York: Metropolitan Books, 2005), 35–42.

62 Yoo claims that Polk won the election on a platform that included acquiring California (*Crisis and Command*, 191) but the acquisition of California was not discussed during the 1844 presidential campaign. See Daniel Walker Howe, *What Hath God Wrought: The Transformation of America* (New York: Oxford University Press, 2007), 708.

63 Howe, *What Hath God Wrought*, 699. Schlesinger, *Imperial Presidency*, 40–41. Yoo, *Crisis and Command*, 192.

64 Howe, *What Hath God Wrought*, 733–34, 738–39.

65 Howe, *What Hath God Wrought*, 739.

66 Howe, *What Hath God Wrought*, 740.

67 James K. Polk, Special Message to Congress on Mexican Relations, May 11, 1846.

68 Wilentz, *Rise of Democracy*, 582, Howe, *What Hath God Wrought*, 741.

69 Howe, *What Hath God Wrought*, 741–42. Fisher, *Presidential War Power*, 42. Wilentz, *Rise of Democracy*, 582.

70 Wilentz, *Rise of Democracy*, 602–03. Charles Sellers, *James K. Polk: Continentalist, 1843–1846* (Princeton, NJ: Princeton University Press, 1966), 478, 484.

71 Donald, *Lincoln*, 123–25. Howe, *What Hath God Wrought*, 796–97.

72 Donald, *Lincoln*, 125–26. Lincoln to William H. Herndon, February 15, 1848, in Roy P. Basler, ed., *The Collected Works of Abraham Lincoln* (New Brunswick, NJ: Rutgers University Press, 1953), 1:451.

73 Lincoln to Herndon, February 15, 1848, in Basler, ed., *Collected Works*, 1:451–52.

74 Alexis de Tocqueville, *Democracy in America* (New York: Library of America, 2004), 142.

75 Howe, *What Hath God Wrought*, 797, 800, 811–12. Robert W. Merry, *A Country of Vast Designs: James K. Polk, the Mexican War, and the Conquest of the American Continent* (New York: Simon & Schuster, 2009), 340–42. Donald, *Lincoln*, 126. Yoo, *Crisis and Command*, 196

76 Howe, *What Hath God Wrought*, 800–05.

77 Merry, *A Country of Vast Designs*, 426. Howe, *What Hath God Wrought*, 797.

78 Merry, *A Country of Vast Designs*, 427–28. Howe, *What Hath God Wrought*, 803, 806. James K. Polk, *The Diary of James K. Polk During His Presidency, 1845–1849* (Chicago: A.C. McClurg, 1910), 347–48.

79   Jean H. Baker, *James Buchanan* (New York: Times Books, 2004), 42.

80   James Buchanan, Special Message, January 8, 1861. Yoo, *Crisis and Command*, 206.

81   The original 1792 Militia Act had made the president's power to call out the militia in such cases contingent on authorization "by an associate justice [of the Supreme Court] or district judge," but that restriction was dropped when the act was amended in 1795.

82   Message to Congress in Special Session, July 4, 1861, in Basler, *Collected Works*, 4:426, 429.

83   Philip Shaw Paludan, *The Presidency of Abraham Lincoln* (Lawrence: University Press of Kansas, 1994), 81–82. Donald, *Lincoln*, 305.

84   Paludan, *The Presidency of Abraham Lincoln*, 83–84. Donald, *Lincoln*, 314.

85   Bruce Tap, *Over Lincoln's Shoulder: The Committee on the Conduct of the War* (Lawrence: University Press of Kansas, 1998), especially 14–24.

86   Tap, *Over Lincoln's Shoulder*, 4, 8, 256. Also see T. Harry Williams, *Lincoln and the Radicals* (Madison: University of Wisconsin Press, 1941); and Hans Trefousse, *The Radical Republicans: Lincoln's Vanguard for Racial Justice* (New York: Knopf, 1969).

87   James M. McPherson, *Battle Cry of Freedom: The Civil War Era* (New York: Oxford University Press, 1988), 500.

88   Paludan, *The Presidency of Abraham Lincoln*, 133–35, 145–47. James G. Randall, *Constitutional Problems under Lincoln* (Urbana: University of Illinois Press, 1964; revised ed.), 356–65, esp. 358. McPherson, *Battle Cry of Freedom*, 500. Donald, *Lincoln*, 365–66.

89   Preliminary Emancipation Proclamation, September 22, 1862; and Emancipation Proclamation, January 1, 1863, in Basler, *Collected Works*, 5:433–36; 6:28–30. Also see Lincoln's public letter to James C. Conkling, August 26, 1863 and his letter to Treasury Secretary Salmon Chase, September 2, 1863. Basler, *Collected Works*, 6:408, 428.

90   In the early republic, nobody called the president the commander in chief except in wartime, and sometimes not even then. The term was instead most commonly used to refer to the army's top general. In his annual message of 1806, for instance, Jefferson referred to "our commander in chief" and did not mean himself but rather General James Wilkinson, commander in chief of the US army. Similarly, on the eve of the Mexican War, President Polk in his diary used the phrase "commander in chief of the army" to refer to his top general, Winfield Scott, and continued to do so even after Congress had declared war on Mexico. Polk, *Diary*, 1:395–96 (May 13, 1846), 1:414–15 (May 21), 1:420 (May 23), 2:268 (December 9), 2:293 (December 25).

91   Basler, *Collected Works*, 4:354. Also see Schlesinger, *Imperial Presidency*, 61–63.

92   Proclamation of a Blockade, April 19, 1861, in Basler, *Collected Works*, 4:338–39.

93   To Matthew Birchard and Others, June 29, 1863, in Basler, *Collected Works*, 6:303.

94   To Erastus Corning and Others, June 12, 1863, in Basler, *Collected Works*, 6:264.

95   Schlesinger, *Imperial Presidency*, 66, 68. Sidney M. Milkis and Michael Nelson, *The American Presidency: Origins and Development, 1776–2002* (Washington, DC: CQ Press, 2003; fourth edition), 163.

96   Tocqueville, *Democracy in America*, 141–42.

97   David J. Silbey, *A War of Frontier and Empire: The Philippine-American War, 1899–1902* (New York: Hill & Wang, 2007), 17. Boot, *Savage Wars of Peace*, 62.

98   Schlesinger, *Imperial Presidency*, 78. Also see William S. McFeely, *Grant: A Biography* (New York: Norton, 1982), 336–44.

99   Schlesinger, *Imperial Presidency*, 80–81. Woodrow Wilson, *Congressional Government: A Study in American Politics* (Boston: Houghton Mifflin, 1885), 233. W. Stull Holt, *Treaties Defeated by the Senate* (Baltimore: Johns Hopkins University Press, 1933), 178–79.

100   Schlesinger, *Imperial Presidency*, 85–88.

101   Fisher, *Presidential War Power*, 52.

102   Lewis L. Gould, *The Spanish-American War and President McKinley* (Lawrence: University Press of Kansas, 1982), 24, 29. Fisher, *Presidential War Power*, 52.

103   Gould, *Spanish-American War and President McKinley*, 32–33, 35, 41. G.J.A. O'Toole, *The Spanish War: An American Epic 1898* (New York: Norton, 1984), 21, 225–26. Evan Thomas, *The War Lovers: Roosevelt, Lodge, Hearst, and the Rush to Empire, 1898* (New York: Little, Brown, 2010), 225–26.

104   Woodrow Wilson, Preface to Fifteenth Printing (August 15, 1900), in *Congressional Government: A Study in American Politics* (Baltimore: Johns Hopkins University Press, 1981), 22.

105   Fisher, *Presidential War Power*, 54. Boot, *Savage Wars of Peace*, 104. Leon Wolff, *Little Brown Brother: How the United States Purchased and Pacified the Philippine Islands at the Century's Turn* (New York: Doubleday, 1961), 172.

106   Fisher, *Presidential War Power*, 58. Boot, *Savage Wars of Peace*, 78–79. William McKinley, Fourth Annual Message, December 3, 1900.

107   Boot, *Savage Wars of Peace*, 129. Fisher, *Presidential War Power*, 58–59, 65–66.

108   Schlesinger, *Imperial Presidency*, 90–91.

109   Fisher, *Presidential War Power*, 62–63. Boot, *Savage Wars of Peace*, 150–51, 155. Woodrow Wilson, Address to a Joint Session of Congress on the Tampico Incident, April 20, 1914.

110   Fisher, *Presidential War Power*, 68. Woodrow Wilson, Address to a Joint Session of Congress: "Request for Authority," February 26, 1917. The filibuster led directly to a rule change that same year that allowed the Senate to bring a filibuster to a close ("cloture") if two-thirds of voting senators agreed to end the filibuster.

111   Boot, *Savage Wars of Peace*, 155.

112   Fisher, *Presidential War Power*, 66–69. Woodrow Wilson, Address to a Joint Session of Congress Requesting a Declaration of War on Germany, April 2, 1917.

113   Schlesinger, *Imperial Presidency*, 96.

114   Schlesinger, *Imperial Presidency*, 97–98. Ole R. Holsti, *Public Opinion and American Foreign Policy* (Ann Arbor: University of Michigan Press, 2004; revised edition), 17–18.

115   Schlesinger, *Imperial Presidency*, 105–08. Yoo, *Crisis and Command*, 298–302. Fisher, *Presidential War Power*, 76–77.

116   Yoo, *Crisis and Command*, 303–05. Fisher, *Presidential War Power*, 78–79. Schlesinger, *Imperial Presidency*, 111–12.

117   Robert Dallek, *Franklin D. Roosevelt and American Foreign Policy, 1932–1945* (New York: Oxford University Press, 1979), 276–77. Yoo, *Crisis and Command*, 305, 308. "National Affairs: Lesson in Geography," *Time*, July 21, 1941. Also see Steven Casey, *Cautious Crusade: Franklin D. Roosevelt, American Public Opinion, and the War against Nazi Germany* (New York: Oxford University Press, 2001).

118   Yoo, *Crisis and Command*, 304–10.

119   Table Ed146–54—National defense outlays and veterans' benefits: 1915–1995, in *Historical Statistics of the United States*, Millennial Edition Online.

120   Table Ed26–47—Military personnel on active duty, by branch of service and sex: 1789–1995, in *Historical Statistics of the United States*, Millennial Edition Online. Yoo, *Crisis and Command*, 332.

121   Schlesinger, *Imperial Presidency*, 166. Richard E. Neustadt, *Presidential Power: The Politics of Leadership from FDR to Carter* (New York: Wiley, 1980), 159. Also see Garry Wills, *Bomb Power: The Modern Presidency and the National Security State* (New York: Penguin Press, 2010), 1–4.

122   The *Public Papers of the Presidents* include 14 campaign speeches by Johnson in October 1964 in which he described himself as "your commander in chief." Also see Wills, *Bomb Power*, 47–49.

123   Garry Wills, "At Ease, Mr. President," *New York Times*, January 27, 2007, A17.

124 Douglas T. Stuart, *Creating the National Security State: A History of the Law That Transformed America* (Princeton, NJ: Princeton University Press, 2008), 268–69. Fisher, *Presidential War Power*, 241–42. Also see David F. Rudgers, *Creating the Secret State: The Origins of the Central Intelligence Agency, 1943–1947* (Lawrence: University Press of Kansas Press, 2000).

125 Amy B. Zegart, *Flawed by Design: The Evolution of the CIA, JCS, and NSC* (Stanford, CA: Stanford University Press, 1999), 188–89. Fisher, *Presidential War Power*, 242–43. Yoo, *Crisis and Command*, 344. Schlesinger, *Imperial Presidency*, 167.

126 Schlesinger, *Imperial Presidency*, 170. Fisher, *Presidential War Power*, 242.

127 Fisher, *Presidential War Power*, 129–31. Lyndon Johnson, Radio and Television Report to the American People following Renewed Aggression in the Gulf of Tonkin, August 4, 1964.

128 Fisher, *Presidential War Power*, 132. Robert McNamara, "The Tonkin Gulf Resolution," in Andrew J. Rotter, ed., *Light at the End of the Tunnel: A Vietnam War Anthology* (Wilmington, DE: Scholarly Resources, 1999; revised edition), 78. Walter Cronkite, "Gulf of Tonkin's Phantom Attack," *All Things Considered*, NPR, August 2, 2004, www.npr.org/templates/story/story.php?storyId=3810724.

129 Fisher, *Presidential War Power*, 132.

130 Schlesinger, *Imperial Presidency*, 180–81. Lyndon Johnson, The President's News Conference, August 18, 1967.

131 Fisher, *Presidential War Power*, 131. Schlesinger, *Imperial Presidency*, 181.

132 Fisher, *Presidential War Power*, 138–39.

133 Richard M. Pious, *The Presidency* (Boston: Allyn & Bacon, 1996), 455. Yoo, *Crisis and Command*, 352.

134 Richard Nixon, Statement on Signing the Military Appropriations Authorization Bill, November 17, 1971. Schlesinger, *Imperial Presidency*, 187–88, 194–98.

135 Richard L. Madden, "House and Senate Override Veto by Nixon on Curb of War Powers," *New York Times*, November 8, 1973, 1.

136 William G. Howell and Jon C. Pevehouse, *While Dangers Gather: Congressional Checks on Presidential War Powers* (Princeton, NJ: Princeton University Press, 2007), 5–6, 68. Yoo, *Crisis and Command*, 482–83, n37. For an indictment of the WPR as an abdication of Congress's constitutional power, see Fisher, *Presidential War Power*, 145–48. For an indictment of the WPR as an unconstitutional invasion of presidential power, see Terry Eastland, *Energy in the Executive: The Case for the Strong Presidency* (New York: Free Press, 1992), 123–24.

137 Douglas L. Kriner, "Presidents, Domestic Politics, and the International Arena," in George C. Edwards III and William Howell, eds., *The Oxford Handbook of the American Presidency* (New York: Oxford University Press, 2009), 671. Also see Howell and Pevehouse, *While Dangers Gather*; and Douglas L. Kriner, *After the Rubicon: Congress, Presidents, and the Politics of Waging War* (Chicago: University of Chicago Press, 2010).

138 The phrase "toy handcuff" is Arthur Schlesinger's, from the 1989 epilogue he wrote for his 1973 classic *The Imperial Presidency*. See Arthur M. Schlesinger, Jr., *The Imperial Presidency* (New York: Mariner Books, 2004), 433.

139 Andrew Rudalevige, *The New Imperial Presidency: Renewing Presidential Power after Watergate* (Ann Arbor: University of Michigan Press, 2005), 215.

140 George W. Bush, Address before a Joint Session of the Congress on the United States Response to the Terrorist Attacks of September 11, September 20, 2001; and Address before a Joint Session of the Congress on the State of the Union, January 29, 2002.

141 Rudalevige, *The New Imperial Presidency*, 218–19.

142 Rudalevige, *The New Imperial Presidency*, 216, 218. Fisher, *Presidential War Power*, 202–04.

143 Howell and Pevehouse, *When Dangers Gather*, 23. Norman Ornstein and Thomas Mann, "When Congress Checks Out," *Foreign Affairs* (2006), 68.

144   Rudalevige, *The New Imperial Presidency*, 219, 221–22. On the president's strategic advantages in war-related matters, see Howell and Pevehouse, *When Dangers Gather*, 6–9.

145   George W. Bush, Remarks at a Reception for Senatorial Candidate John Cornyn in Houston, Texas, September 26, 2002. Rudalevige, *The New Imperial Presidency*, 112–13, 120–24, 211. Fisher, *Presidential War Power*, 246–48. In addition, in 1974, Congress enacted the Hughes–Ryan Amendment, which required that no covert action could be carried out in a foreign country without the president expressly affirming, in writing, that such an action was necessary to national security. The act also required the executive branch to report the president's "finding" to the appropriate congressional committees "in a timely fashion."

146   Rudalevige, *The New Imperial Presidency*, 244–46.

147   Rudalevige, *The New Imperial Presidency*, 228–29, 248. Office of Legal Counsel, Memorandum for Alberto R. Gonzales, Re: Standards of Conduct for Interrogation under 18 U.S.C. Sections 2340–2340A, August 1, 2002, p. 31. The memo is reprinted in Karen J. Greenberg, ed., *The Torture Debate in America* (New York: Cambridge University Press, 2006), 344.

148   George W. Bush, Address before a Joint Session of the Congress on the United States Response to the Terrorist Attacks of September 11, September 20, 2001. John Yoo, *War by Other Means: An Insider's Account of the War on Terror* (New York: Atlantic Monthly Press, 2006), 17. Rudalevige, *The New Imperial Presidency*, 227.

149   Bush, Address before a Joint Session of the Congress on the United States Response to the Terrorist Attacks of September 11, September 20, 2001.

150   Charlie Savage, "Barack Obama's Q&A," *Boston.com*, December 20, 2007, http://archive. boston.com/news/politics/2008/specials/CandidateQA/ObamaQA/. Barack Obama, Remarks at National Defense University, May 23, 2013. Also see Jay Solomon, "US Drops 'War on Terrorism' Phrase, Clinton Says," *Wall Street Journal*, March 31, 2009.

151   See, for instance, the debate between Daniel Wirls and Daniel J. Tichenor in Richard J. Ellis and Michael Nelson, eds., *Debating the Presidency: Conflicting Perspectives on the American Executive* (Washington, DC: CQ Press, 2015; third edition), 185–205 ("Resolved, President Barack Obama Has Followed President George W. Bush's Approach to the War on Terror"). Also see Trevor McCrisken, "Ten Years On: Obama's War on Terrorism in Rhetoric and Practice," *International Affairs* (July 2011), 781–801.

152   Micah Zenko, "Obama's Embrace of Drone Strikes Will Be a Lasting Legacy," *New York Times*, January 12, 2016. Micah Zenko, "Obama's Final Drone Strike Data," January 20, 2017, www.cfr.org/blog-post/obamas-final-drone-strike-data.

153   Charlie Savage, *Power Wars: Inside Obama's Post-9/11 Presidency* (New York: Little, Brown, 2015), 684. Obama, Remarks at National Defense University, May 23, 2013.

154   Obama, Remarks at National Defense University. Christi Parsons and W. J. Hennigan, "President Obama, Who Hoped to Sow Peace, Instead Led the Nation at War," *Los Angeles Times*, January 13, 2017.

155   Savage, *Power Wars*, 685–88, 638. In early 2015, seven months after the bombing campaign had begun, Obama reversed course and did ask Congress to authorize an air war against the Islamic State. In announcing his proposal, Obama explained, "I do not believe America's interests are served by endless war, or by remaining on a perpetual war footing" (689). Congress took no action.

156   Savage, *Power Wars*, 645, 647. Also see Louis Fisher, "Military Operations in Libya: No War? No Hostilities?" *Presidential Studies Quarterly* (March 2012), 176–89. This "not hostilities" theory was also rejected by Obama's own Office of Legal Counsel, but Obama overruled the OLC's legal conclusions, siding instead with the State Department's legal advisor Harold Koh.

157   Savage, *Power Wars*, 653, 696, 690, 698.

158   Savage, *Power Wars*, 690–91.

CHAPTER 6

THE UNILATERAL PRESIDENCY: LEGISLATING FROM THE OVAL OFFICE

INTRODUCTORY PUZZLE: WHY THE GLOBAL GAG RULE IS ENACTED OR REPEALED EVERY EIGHT YEARS

In 1973, Congress passed, and President Richard Nixon signed, the Foreign Assistance Act, an overhaul of an act of the same name passed by Congress in 1961. The 1973 act reflected a bipartisan consensus that America's political and economic interests, as well as the welfare of the world's poor and even the planet's survival, depended on government-sponsored family planning in developing countries. Section 104 of the act, titled "Population Planning and Health," stipulated that "in order to increase the opportunities and motivation for family planning, to reduce the rate of population growth, to prevent and combat disease, and to help provide health services for the great majority," the president was "authorized to furnish assistance on such terms and conditions as he may determine, for population planning and health." Congress set the goals—and appropriated the funds—and tasked the president with devising the means best calculated to carry out those ends. This is the way the textbooks say it should be: Congress legislates and the president executes.[1]

While the act gave the president broad administrative discretion to spend the appropriated money as he saw fit, it tied the president's hands on one matter. The president could not use any of the money "to pay for the performance of abortions as a method of family planning or to motivate or coerce any person to practice abortion." Known as the Helms Amendment after its sponsor, freshman senator Jesse Helms (R-NC), the restriction was a response to the Supreme Court's ruling in *Roe v. Wade*, the landmark 1973 case that made abortion a constitutional right. Again, textbook stuff: Congress legislates and the president executes the law.[2]

For social conservatives, however, the Helms Amendment did not go nearly far enough. They objected that the US government could still fund organizations that performed or advocated abortions so long as US funds were not used for those activities. Conservative Christian groups pressed Congress to change the policy so that no international organization that performed or advocated abortions could receive federal funding. But with the House of Representatives firmly in the hands of the Democratic Party, their lobbying efforts were unsuccessful. Stymied in the legislature, conservative groups switched their focus to the executive branch. They pressed Republican president Ronald Reagan, elected in 1981, to take unilateral action to achieve their policy goal of defunding all organizations that supported or were complicit in providing abortions to women of the world. Their lobbying efforts reached fruition in 1984 when Reagan issued a directive that did exactly that. Known as the Global Gag Rule to critics and the Mexico City policy to supporters (because it was publicly unveiled at the 1984 World Population Conference in Mexico City), it cut off government funding to nongovernmental organizations (NGOs) that advocated abortion or provided abortion services, information, counseling, or referrals.[3]

The policy remained in place until January 22, 1993, when newly elected Democratic president Bill Clinton—on his second day in office and the twentieth anniversary of the *Roe v. Wade* decision—issued a presidential memorandum repealing the Global Gag Rule. Clinton's policy stood for eight years, until the election of President George W. Bush, who made reinstating the Mexico City policy one of his first acts as president. A further eight years later, new president Barack Obama waited only a few days before ordering a repeal of the Global Gag Rule. And as soon as Donald Trump took office in 2017 he reinstated the ban.

This is decidedly not the way the textbooks say American government should work. Separation of powers and checks and balances are supposed to make policy changes slow and arduous. Some deplore this because they feel it prevents the government from taking necessary action and enables powerful groups to preserve the status quo. Others celebrate

On Monday, January 23, 2017, three days after taking the oath of office, President Donald Trump reinstates the Global Gag Rule with a stroke of the pen.

Courtesy: AP Photo/Evan Vucci.

it because building consensus and constructing coalitions creates policies that will be more broadly accepted, durable, and effective. Yet neither judgment seems to apply here. There is neither consensus nor stalemate. Instead we find public policy swinging wildly between one extreme and the other depending on the will of one individual: the president.

Nor is it the case that Congress has made the important policy-setting decisions and the executive is simply working out the administrative details. On the contrary, the Helms Amendment enacted by Congress had little effect on NGOs that provided family planning assistance to women across the globe. In contrast, the Mexico City policy, enacted by executive fiat, transformed NGOs' ability to fulfill their missions of promoting family planning and protecting women's health.

So how did we get to this point, where presidents can unilaterally make public policy? Did the framers of the Constitution intend for American public policy to be made by executive order or is this a power grab by modern presidents? In Chapter 4, we saw that during the twentieth century, Congress and the public increasingly looked to the president to initiate and lobby for legislation. Does the unilateral presidency parallel the development of the legislative presidency or does it follow a different path? Before answering these questions, it is necessary to clarify what we mean by "the unilateral presidency."

DEFINING THE UNILATERAL PRESIDENCY

Tracing the development of the unilateral presidency is complicated because unilateral directives come in many guises. A 2007 Congressional Research Service study counted more than two dozen kinds of presidential directives, including proclamations, national security directives, military orders, and presidential memoranda.[4] The most widely known is the executive order—indeed, for many people the terms "executive order" and "unilateral executive action" are likely synonymous. However, many unilateral actions described in the press as executive orders are in fact presidential memoranda. Each of the Global Gag Rule directives, for instance, was a presidential memorandum, not an executive order.

The difference between these various terms is often opaque, even to those who pay close attention to government. Indeed, presidents themselves have been known to mistakenly describe their own memoranda as executive orders. The only definitive difference between a presidential memorandum and an executive order is that the latter (like proclamations) must be published in the *Federal Register*. But even that difference is hardly absolute. Prior to 1935, there was no requirement that executive orders be published. And today memoranda are sometimes published in the *Register* and routinely (though not invariably) published in the *Weekly Compilation of Presidential Documents* and listed on the White House website. Certainly, the presidential memoranda repealing and reinstating the Global Gag Rule did not lack for publicity. Little wonder that one scholar of unilateral directives describes presidential memoranda as "executive orders by another name."[5]

Distinguishing between presidential proclamations and executive orders is also difficult. The most frequently cited rule is that a proclamation is addressed to the general public whereas an executive order is directed to government officials and agencies. However, this neat distinction often breaks down in practice. At the outset of his presidency, Franklin Roosevelt used a proclamation to close every bank in the country and then five days later used an executive order to permit those same banks to open. President Eisenhower issued an executive order to enforce the integration of southern schools whereas his successor President Kennedy achieved the same end through a proclamation. Equally confounding is President Andrew Johnson's "Executive Order 6," which takes the form of a proclamation announcing ratification of the Fourteenth Amendment.[6]

Even less accurate is the notion that proclamations are largely ceremonial or symbolic whereas executive orders involve public policy. In fact, of the more than 8,000 presidential proclamations issued since 1789, roughly 40 percent are policy-based, among them some of the most famous presidential directives, including Washington's Proclamation of Neutrality, Jackson's Nullification Proclamation, and Lincoln's Emancipation Proclamation. Moreover, some executive orders have little to do with public policy, such as President George Herbert Walker Bush's order establishing "the Military Outstanding Volunteer Service Medal" or President James K. Polk's order announcing the death of former president Andrew Jackson. Not surprisingly, all three branches of government have concluded that the two terms are nearly interchangeable, the difference being, in the words of a 1957 House report, "more one of form than substance."[7]

How a directive gets named, moreover, is ultimately up to the president. As political scientist Kenneth Mayer explains, "The lack of any agreed-upon definition means that, in essence, an executive order is whatever the president chooses to call by that name." What matters most is not the name we give to these different directives but the uses to which presidents put them. By whatever name, unilateral directives enable the president to legislate—that is, to create public policy that carries the force of law.[8]

Of course, courts may conclude that a president lacks the statutory or constitutional authority to issue a particular order. Donald Trump's executive order banning refugees and immigrants from seven Muslim-majority nations from entering the US was blocked by the courts, leading the president to issue what he later complained was a "watered-down" version of his travel ban—and that version too was held up and redefined in the courts. The courts also blocked Barack Obama's directive that would have allowed undocumented immigrants whose children were citizens or legal residents to be shielded from deportation.[9]

Congress can also nullify a presidential directive by passing legislation that contravenes the order. For instance, when President Clinton rescinded (by presidential memorandum) President Reagan's 1988 directive banning privately funded abortions for US servicewomen at overseas US military hospitals, Congress nullified Clinton's directive by enacting legislation that codified Reagan's ban. Congress also can use its power of the purse to block an executive order of which it disapproves, as it did in stymieing President Obama's directive ordering the closing of the detention facility at Guantánamo Bay. By refusing to fund the closing of the prison and by barring the use of any federal funds to transfer any Guantánamo detainees to the United States, Congress ensured that the prison was still open when Obama left office.

Unilateral presidential directives, then, do not give the president absolute or unchecked power. But they do, as political scientist William Howell emphasizes, give the president a strategic advantage, because he initiates the action to which the other branches must respond. Judicial power is limited because only a relatively small number of presidential directives are challenged in court, and more often than not the courts defer to the president. By one count, only about 2 percent of executive orders in the latter half of the twentieth century were challenged in court. When the orders were challenged, the president prevailed almost nine times out of ten. Another study that examined executive orders over the nation's first 150 years found only 16 executive orders overturned in court.[10]

Congressional power is limited, too, because while the president can legislate at the stroke of a pen, Congress must mobilize majorities in both houses—and if Congress is to overcome a presidential veto it must garner a two-thirds supermajority in both houses. Not surprisingly, the legislative record is replete with failed congressional efforts to revoke unpopular directives. Bills to permanently repeal or establish the Global Gag Rule, for instance, have been introduced in Congress countless times without ever coming close to mustering the necessary votes to create new law. So have unilateral presidential directives upset the balance of the framers' carefully constructed constitutional order? Or are they instead an integral part of that constitutional order?[11]

"FOLLOW OUR #CONSTITUTION"

On February 12, 2014, President Barack Obama issued Executive Order 13658, which raised the minimum wage of employees of government contractors by almost 40 percent, to $10.10 an hour, and indexed the minimum wage to inflation. The president did everything he could to publicize the order, including announcing it in his State of the Union address several weeks prior to formally promulgating the order. Republicans howled in protest. "Mr. President we are a nation of laws & we are supposed to follow our #Constitution," tweeted Kentucky senator Rand Paul. "You do not get to 'act alone.'"

Obama's defenders countered that the president was not behaving any differently than President Bush, who, for instance, used one of his earliest executive orders (EO 13202) to prohibit federal dollars from going to construction projects in which a contractor had signed a "project labor agreement" with a labor union (an order that Obama repealed shortly after assuming office).[12] Moreover, Obama's critics fell silent in the face of Donald Trump's slew of consequential executive orders (Trump issued 42 executive orders in his first six months in office, nearly twice the 22 executive orders that Obama issued in his first six months). Exposing partisan motives, however, does not settle the question of whether Paul's reading of the Constitution is correct.

Another favorite defense was to point out that Obama had issued fewer executive orders than most of his predecessors. Indeed, Obama issued fewer executive orders annually than any president since Grover Cleveland.[13] However, that defense is hardly adequate either, since executive orders are only one of the many labels that presidents attach to their unilateral directives. That Obama issued fewer executive orders does not mean his presidency was necessarily less reliant on unilateral directives. A simple count of executive orders is inadequate, too, because it takes no account of what is being ordered. Two days before issuing EO 13658, Obama issued EO 13657, which changed the name of

Obama's executive orders often angered Republicans, who accused the president of abdicating his responsibility to enforce the laws and follow the Constitution. That outrage is captured by this Michael Ramirez cartoon lampooning Obama's use of executive orders to get what he wanted but otherwise couldn't achieve.

Courtesy: *Investor's Business Daily.*

the National Security Staff to the National Security Council Staff. Yet nobody suggested that "acting alone" in that instance violated the Constitution.

So where is the line between those areas in which the president can lawfully act alone and those in which he cannot—and on what side of that line should we place an executive order such as Obama's increase of the minimum wage for federal contractors? Is Paul right that Obama's directive violated the separation of powers inscribed in the Constitution?

The argument for separation of powers is expressed in Montesquieu's famous precept that "there can be no liberty where the legislative and executive powers are united in the same person." This principle underlies the claim that by unilaterally raising the minimum wage, President Obama acted as a tyrant or dictator. There is no denying that legislating via executive directive "violates a strict separation of powers," but the Constitution did not in fact establish a strict system of separation of powers. Instead, in Richard Neustadt's famous formulation, it established a system of "separated institutions sharing powers."[14]

In insisting on an absolute separation of powers, Obama's critics sounded more like the Anti-Federalists who opposed the Constitution than the Federalists who wrote it. One of the Anti-Federalists' chief complaints against the proposed constitution was that it invited tyranny because it failed to adhere to the maxim that the legislative and executive powers must be "separate and distinct." James Madison's task, in *Federalist* No. 47, was to refute this criticism. While acknowledging that the "accumulation of all powers, legislative, executive, and judiciary, in the same hands . . . may justly be pronounced the very definition of tyranny," Madison argued that the Anti-Federalists had "totally misconceived and misapplied" Montesquieu's celebrated maxim. According to Madison, in insisting that liberty depended on a separation of powers, Montesquieu "did not mean that [the different branches] ought to have no partial agency in, or no control over, the acts of each other." Instead, "the fundamental principles of a free constitution are subverted" only "where the whole power of one department is exercised by the same hands which possess the whole power of another department."

Judged by the Madisonian standard, then, Obama's unilateral hike in the minimum wage did not subvert the fundamental principles of the Constitution. Nothing in Obama's directive prevented Congress from enacting a law that overrode Obama's order. If Obama's directive had been concealed from Congress—as is the case with almost all national security directives—so that the legislative body had no opportunity to override the presidential order, then one could make a strong case for constitutional subversion. Instead, Obama not only published the order, as required by law, but actually announced to Congress and the nation his intention to issue the order in the most public way possible: in a State of the Union message.

Moreover, even though Obama had pledged to "act on [his] own . . . when Congress isn't acting," a careful look at Executive Order 13658 shows that Obama did not actually claim to "act alone." Obama's order began by invoking "the authority vested in me as President by the Constitution" *and* the authority he derived from a specific statute: the Federal Property and Administrative Services Act. George W. Bush cited the same statute in justifying Executive Order 13202—as did Obama's repeal of Bush's order. Indeed, few executive orders involving contested domestic policy fail to invoke the authority of a legislative statute.

Of course, one might object that invoking statutory authority is more a strategic effort to cloak unilateralism than evidence refuting unilateralism. Certainly, the fact that presidents can appeal to the same statute and draw opposite conclusions—as is true of the Global Gag Rule and project labor agreements—suggests that statutes often do little to constrain presidents intent on taking unilateral actions that fit their ideological predilections.

The fundamental difficulty, though, for critics who contend that a unilateral directive—by Obama or Trump or any other president—does not "follow our Constitution" is that the Constitution does not mention such directives, let alone prescribe whether or when a president can issue such a directive. That the Constitution does not mention executive directives is hardly a reason to believe that they are illegitimate—after all, the Constitution also makes no mention of judicial review, but few contend that judges are failing to follow the Constitution when they pass judgment on a law's constitutionality. Nor will it profit us to examine the debates at the Constitutional Convention, because the framers of the Constitution never discussed the legitimacy of executive orders, presidential proclamations, and the like.

The constitutional silence, though, invites the question of how it is that a practice that was never addressed in the Constitution or at the Constitutional Convention became such an integral part of the presidential arsenal. Do contemporary complaints about presidents' willingness to "act alone" indicate a new development in the American presidency, either in the form of a heightened sensitivity to unilateral presidential action or a more robust assertion of unilateral presidential powers—or both? Or is partisan sparring over presidential directives merely part of the same constitutional tug-of-war that has been going on since the nation's founding? Since the text of the Constitution and the framers' debate do little to illuminate these questions, we turn directly to the historical development of unilateral presidential directives.

Measuring the Rise of Unilateral Directives

There is no difficulty identifying the first presidential veto: it occurred on April 5, 1792. Nor is it difficult to tally up the total number of vetoes in American history (2,572 as of October 2017) or count the precise number issued by each president. Anyone can find those numbers on Wikipedia. But getting an accurate count of unilateral presidential directives is far more difficult, particularly in the eighteenth and nineteenth centuries. Even if we limit our inquiry to executive orders, the obstacles to obtaining an accurate count are formidable, at least prior to passage of the Federal Register Act of 1935, which mandated that executive orders—unless they were classified or pertained only to particular individuals—be published.[15]

In the nineteenth century there was no central repository for collecting executive orders and there were no uniform procedures for identifying them. Indeed, what counts as an executive order in the nineteenth century is often far from clear. Some early orders consist of little more than a president scrawling "Approved" or "Let it be done" atop a recommendation emanating from a cabinet secretary. In fact, the words "executive order" don't appear on any order until the presidency of Ulysses Grant, and only in 1907 did the federal government—specifically the State Department—begin to assign numbers to executive orders. Theodore Roosevelt's Executive Order 709 was the first to be issued with a number; the preceding 708 orders were retroactively assigned a number. But the State Department's retroactive numbering was radically incomplete: it only went back to 1862 and excluded thousands of orders that were not submitted to the State Department. Estimates of how many nineteenth-century executive orders are excluded from the official count of executive orders vary wildly (one estimate puts the number at somewhere between 15,000 and 50,000), but everybody agrees that "the precise numbers of these directives are simply not known."[16]

We do know, however, that at least some directives not included in the standard counts of nineteenth-century executive orders—both the numbered and unnumbered series of presidential executive orders—were highly important. Take, for example, Grover Cleveland's "famous order" on April 28, 1887, instructing the secretary of the interior to change the way the government handled public lands that railroad companies received as compensation (known as indemnity) for having been denied the use of some part of another land grant. Noting that under the existing policy "hundreds of thousands if not millions of acres" of public lands had been placed "beyond the reach of our citizens," Cleveland ordered the executive branch to adopt the position that the railroads should surrender indemnity lands that rightfully belonged to the government and that those lands should instead be opened to homesteaders. Yet because the order took the form of a letter it was never counted as an executive order, even though, as historian Allan Nevins observed long ago, it plainly had "the effect of an executive order."[17]

Any conclusions about the development of the unilateral presidency premised on a simple count of executive orders must therefore be regarded with great skepticism. Nonetheless, most tallies of recorded executive orders (counting both the numbered and unnumbered series) suggest that such directives were uncommon in the early republic, were more common in the decades after the Civil War, and exploded in the early twentieth century (see Figure 6.1). Every president between Theodore Roosevelt and Franklin Roosevelt averaged between 150 and 300 executive orders a year, whereas presidents between Lincoln and McKinley never exceeded an average of 40 a year, and presidents in the first half of the nineteenth century rarely averaged more than a few each year.

Jeremy Bailey and Brandon Rottinghaus's count of proclamations (see Figure 6.2) suggests a similar developmental pattern: relatively few proclamations in the early republic, a growing number in the latter half of the nineteenth century, and a surge in the opening decades of the twentieth century.[18] To be sure, counting proclamations in the nineteenth century is susceptible to many of the same methodological problems that afflict the counting of executive orders. One scholar estimates "that 4,500 or more may have been lost." Flawed as these measures are, the data in Figures 6.1 and 6.2 would seem to support two conclusions.[19]

First, the rise of the unilateral presidency is not a recent phenomenon. Instead, its roots extend deep into the presidential past. That much is crystal clear, no matter how

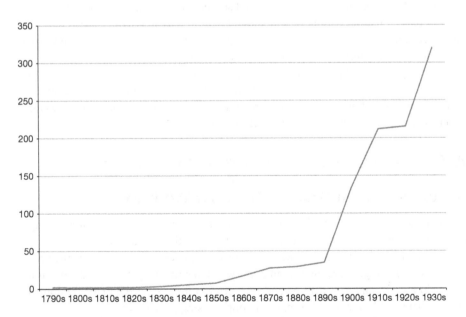

FIGURE 6.1 Average Annual Number of Executive Orders by Decade, 1790s–1930s

Source: Calculated from data in Lyn Ragsdale, *Vital Statistics on the Presidency: Washington to Clinton* (Congressional Quarterly, 1996), 337–41.

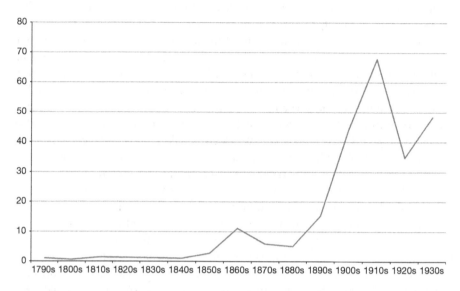

FIGURE 6.2 Average Annual Number of Proclamations by Decade, 1790s–1930s
Source: Data provided to the author by Jeremy Bailey and Brandon Rottinghaus.

many nineteenth-century executive directives have been lost. Second, presidents in the early republic appear to have been far less disposed to act unilaterally than twentieth-century presidents. If true, that might support a more thoroughgoing version of Rand Paul's critique: one that indicted not just Obama but all twentieth-century (and maybe even a few late nineteenth-century) presidents for failing to follow the original understanding of presidential power. Before reaching any conclusions, however, it is necessary to take a closer look at the ways in which nineteenth-century presidents actually used executive orders and presidential proclamations. We begin with a little-known executive order by the nation's eighth president, Martin Van Buren.

A Tale of Two Nineteenth-Century Executive Orders

Martin Van Buren Orders a Ten-Hour Work Day

President Martin Van Buren had the misfortune of running for reelection during a disastrous economic downturn. With the election less than a year away, the economic outlook appeared bleak. Unemployment and bankruptcies were climbing, while prices, production, and wages were falling. Van Buren was under intense pressure to do something to ameliorate working-class distress, and panicked Democrats urged him to take dramatic actions that would shore up his support among working people.

But what could Van Buren do? The Keynesian understanding that government spending and tax cuts could stimulate an ailing economy was still a century away. And government spending on relief was anathema to Democrats. Van Buren had made his laissez-faire position clear in his message to the special session of Congress, called in the wake of the 1837 Panic: "all communities," he lectured,

> are apt to look to government for too much ... especially at periods of sudden embarrassment and distress. ... The framers of our excellent Constitution and the people who approved it [acted] on a sounder principle. They wisely judged that the less government interferes with private pursuits the better for the general prosperity.

Van Buren's strategy had been to affix blame for the downturn on the banking industry—and the special privileges it received from government—but that narrative was wearing thin as the economy continued its tailspin.[20]

Hoping to stem the erosion of working-class support, Van Buren turned his attention to an issue that was dear to labor groups in the industrial Northeast: the ten-hour work day. Some workers had already secured the right to a ten-hour day—including federal workers in the Philadelphia and Brooklyn naval yards—but no state had a law mandating a ten-hour work day (the first state to pass such a law would be New Hampshire in 1847). Certainly, there was no prospect of Congress enacting a law establishing a ten-hour work day. But the fact that federal workers in the naval yards in Philadelphia and New York were protected by a ten-hour day provided Van Buren the political cover to take action.[21]

On March 31, 1840, a few days after receiving a report from his secretary of the navy that showed that workers' hours were sunrise to sunset at naval yards in Boston, Norfolk, Pensacola, Portsmouth, and Washington, DC, while they were limited to ten hours a day in Brooklyn and Philadelphia, Van Buren issued the following executive order:

> The President of the United States, finding that different rules prevail at different places as well in respect to the hours of labor by persons employed on the public works under the immediate authority of himself and the Departments as also in relation to the different classes of workmen, and believing that much inconvenience and dissatisfaction would be removed by adopting a uniform course, hereby directs that all such persons, whether laborers or mechanics, be required to work only the number of hours prescribed by the ten-hour system.

With the stroke of a pen, Van Buren had mandated the ten-hour work day for all those laboring on federal public works. Historian Arthur Schlesinger Jr. perhaps goes overboard in rhapsodizing that the order "was an unmistakable declaration that the people's government would act on behalf of people as freely as in the past the capitalists' government had acted on behalf of the capitalists," but there is no question that the president had unilaterally enacted into law one of labor's most cherished objectives.[22]

The directive attracted plenty of criticism from the opposition. Horace Greeley, for instance, responded that the length of the work day should be a matter of "mutual agreement" between laborers and employers. "What have Governments and Presidents to do with it?" he asked. The *Essex Gazette* charged Van Buren with trying to "bribe" the laboring class at a "ruinous cost" to the public treasury. But notably absent was the charge that Van Buren had acted unconstitutionally. The opposition disagreed with Van Buren's policy but did not question his power to "act alone."[23]

The parallels between Van Buren's and Obama's directives are striking. Both Van Buren's ten-hour work-day directive and Obama's directive boosting the minimum wage were aimed at improving the lot of workers employed using federal dollars. And both were motivated by electoral politics: Obama's order was clearly part of an effort to help Democratic congressional candidates by focusing the 2014 midterm elections on the minimum wage and Van Buren's was a transparent attempt to boost his electoral support in the 1840 election. One would be hard-pressed to find greater unilateralism in Obama's order than in Van Buren's. Indeed, if anything, Van Buren's order appears more unilateral. Unlike Obama's order, which grounded the president's authority to act in a specific statute, Van Buren made no reference to any legislative enactment. Instead he premised his order purely on his own judgment about what would be fairest and most appropriate for workers.

Was Van Buren's unilateralism exceptional? The evidence suggests not. In a study of policy-related presidential proclamations, political scientists Jeremy Bailey and Brandon Rottinghaus found that nineteenth-century presidents were "much more likely" than modern presidents to act unilaterally—that is, to act without invoking explicit statutory authority. Indeed, according to Bailey and Rottinghaus's count, about seven in ten of the 166 unilateral policy proclamations in American history occurred between 1789 and 1900, even though seven-eighths of policy proclamations occurred after 1900. A narrower study of "settle down" proclamations (those proclamations issued as "warnings to the public") found a similar pattern: only one of every six such proclamations issued between the presidencies of Washington and McKinley cited a statute or Congressional resolution, whereas modern presidents more often than not invoked the authority vested in them by a particular statute.[24]

That Van Buren's order did not invoke a statute whereas Obama's did may admittedly reveal less about a decline in executive unilateralism than it does about the growing formalization and systematization of proclamations and executive orders. In the nineteenth century, few guidelines governed the form that executive orders and proclamations should take. In contrast, ever since Harry Truman's Executive Order 10006, issued in 1948, presidents have been instructed to cite "the authority under which the order or proclamation is issued." Moreover, twenty-first-century presidents have the institutional capacity, particularly with the development of the Office of Legal Counsel (see Chapter 10), to locate the relevant statutes that can buttress the president's authority to act. Although these modern developments in institutional capacity are undeniable, they also suggest that, paradoxically, increasing administrative and legal professionalization may constrain the unilateral presidency.[25]

Andrew Johnson Amends the Freedmen's Bureau Bill

The conventional contrast between modern presidential unilateralism and nineteenth-century presidential passivity also fails to take into account a fundamental feature of the nineteenth-century political system: namely, Congress was frequently not in session.

Typically, Congress met for a "long" session that lasted about six months and a "short" session that lasted about three months. As a result, a nineteenth-century president could govern without Congress for as much as two-thirds of his term. During Obama's presidency, in contrast, there were only a handful of days when Congress was not in session. To see why "being there" matters, consider the case of the Freedmen's Bureau Act of 1865.

On March 3, 1865, President Abraham Lincoln signed into law "an Act to Establish a Bureau for the Relief of Freedmen and Refugees." The statute established a federal agency that was entrusted with "the supervision and management of all abandoned lands" in the South and "the control of all subjects relating to refugees and freedmen ... under such rules and regulations as may be prescribed by the bureau and approved by the president." The Bureau of Refugees, Freedmen, and Abandoned Lands—popularly known as the Freedmen's Bureau—was to be headed by a presidentially appointed (and Senate-confirmed) commissioner, and to remain in existence for the duration of the war and for one year thereafter.[26]

Section 4 of the new law granted the commissioner, "under the direction of the President, ... the authority to set apart, for the use of loyal refugees and freedmen, such tracts of land within the insurrectionary states as shall have been abandoned, or to which the United States shall have acquired title by confiscation or sale." The law also directed that "to every male citizen, whether refugee or freedman ... there shall be assigned not more than forty acres of such land." Moreover, any freedman or refugee assigned land was to be "protected in the use and enjoyment of the land for the term of three years at an annual rent not exceeding six per centum upon the value of such land." If no appraisal of the land's value was available, the method of ascertaining its value was left up to the commissioner. At any point during those three years, the occupant of the land would be allowed to purchase it. The law effectively placed more than 850,000 acres under the control of the Bureau and the president.[27]

The day that Lincoln signed the bill was the last for the 38th Congress. The new 39th Congress, as was customary in the nineteenth century, would not convene until December. For the next nine months, the president would necessarily "act alone"—or at least without Congress. However, that president would not be Abraham Lincoln, who was assassinated less than six weeks after signing the bill, but Andrew Johnson, who took the oath of office just hours after Lincoln was pronounced dead on April 15, 1865.

We will never know what Lincoln would have done with the sweeping power vested in him by this statute, but we know what Johnson did. Relying on his constitutional power to grant pardons (Article II, Section 2, clause 1), Johnson issued a proclamation at the end of May that granted amnesty to a wide swath of southern whites who had fought in the Civil War so long as they took an oath of loyalty to the Constitution. Crucially, the pardon called for a "restoration of all rights of property, except as to slaves." The bureau's commissioner, O.O. Howard, thus confronted two conflicting imperatives: a legislative directive to redistribute abandoned and confiscated lands to freed slaves and an executive directive to return those lands to white masters. Without consulting the president, Howard issued a directive in late July (Circular 13) that instructed his subordinates to proceed with "as little delay as possible" in implementing the law by setting aside land for the "immediate use" of refugees and freedmen. The president's pardon, Howard ordered, "will not be understood to extend to the surrender of abandoned or confiscated property which by law has been 'set apart for Refugees and Freedmen.'" On Howard's reading, the Constitution gave the president the power to pardon former Confederates but it did not give him the power to override the law regarding the disposal of property that had been taken from former Confederates.[28]

Johnson disagreed. He ordered that the directive be rescinded and a new one promulgated. Drafted in the White House, the new order (Circular 15) instructed bureau officers that any persons pardoned by the president should have their lands restored to them. With the president liberally granting special pardons to wealthy Southerners throughout the summer and fall of 1865 (those planters worth more than $20,000 had been excluded from the general amnesty proclamation issued in May), the supply of land available for redistribution shrank dramatically. Under Johnson's policy, even blacks who had already been settled on confiscated land—most notably the roughly 40,000 freedmen who occupied land along the coast of South Carolina and Georgia that had been divided into 40-acre tracts and redistributed by military order (Special Field Order No. 15) of General William Tecumsah Sherman in January 1865—were compelled to relinquish what they now thought of as their land. Howard, who thought his job was to distribute land to former slaves, instead found himself implementing a policy of evicting them.[29]

By the time the new Congress convened in December 1865, section 4 of the law that Congress had passed only nine months earlier was a dead letter. The Freedmen's Bureau Bill had given the president broad statutory authority to radically reconstruct southern society by redistributing land from the pre-war slaveholder elite to impoverished freedmen. But through executive action, as historian Eric Foner points out, Johnson had in effect "unilaterally amended" the law so that the Freedmen's Bureau could not transform the landholding patterns of southern society. "Whatever might be the views of Congress," observed a journalist, "confiscation is not possible with an Executive determinedly hostile to it."[30]

This episode shows that the textbook tale of a Congress that writes the laws and a president that executes them obscures more than it reveals about the law-making process. The power to administer laws is also the power to write them. It also shows that the notion that delegation of broad discretionary authority to the executive is a twentieth-century development is wrong. Moreover, it shows that even where a law is relatively precise, there is almost always scope for the executive to remake the law in ways that accord with the president's own political preferences.

It might be objected that the Civil War and Reconstruction were an aberration to the normal nineteenth-century patterns. Certainly, the Freedmen's Bureau was an ambitious "experiment in social policy" that seemed at odds with many nineteenth-century Americans'—very much including the president's—expectations about the role of the federal government in society.[31] But that is in many ways the point: when the federal government is called upon to act, the executive must profoundly shape the actions taken. Nothing better demonstrates the connection between government action and executive power than public land policies in the nineteenth century.

RESERVING PUBLIC LANDS FOR PUBLIC PURPOSES

The Power to "Make All Needful Rules and Regulations"

We are accustomed to thinking of the nineteenth-century federal government as small and inactive, at least as compared to the welfare (and national security) state that developed in the twentieth century. But the federal government was far from passive in one area at least: the acquisition, disposal, and reservation of public lands. More than three-quarters of the nation's 2.3 billion acres were at one point under the control of the federal government and about two-thirds of those federal lands were disposed of by the government during the nineteenth century. Unlike in other policy areas—such as internal improvements—where there were deep partisan differences about whether the federal government had the constitutional authority to act, in the area of public lands the Constitution was unambiguous: Congress had the power to "make all needful Rules and regulations respecting the Territory or other Property belonging to the United States."[32]

But of course Congress could not possibly make all "needful Rules and regulations" relating to federal lands. There was far too much land for that—by 1826, the government already owned 261 million acres of land. Congress did specify the terms for the sale of public lands, but it largely left to the executive branch to decide what lands to sell and when. For instance, in 1820, Congress enacted a law requiring that private buyers of public lands must pay in cash—previously, land could be secured just by putting 5 percent of the price down, leading to astronomically high levels of debt—while also lowering the minimum per-acre price to $1.25 (down from $2) and halving the minimum tract to 80 acres. Section 4 of the act, however, conferred upon the president the power to offer the public lands to the highest bidder "at such time, or times, as the President shall by his proclamation designate for the purpose."[33]

A decade later, Congress passed the Preemption Act of 1830, which gave "squatters" the right to purchase land (up to 160 acres) that they had cultivated. The act explicitly stipulated, though, that the law's guarantee of the "right of preemption" did not "extend to any land which is reserved from sale by act of Congress, or by order of the President." The act thereby recognized what had already become common practice: the reserving of public lands for public purposes—such as military installations, public schools, lighthouses, and mineral reservations—by order of the president. Similarly, the Preemption Act of 1841 excluded from the right of preemption all "lands included in any reservation, by any treaty, law, or proclamation of the President of the United States."[34]

Congress in the early republic could be exactingly precise about which lands were to be reserved and for what purposes. For instance, the early Congresses routinely specified that one square mile (section 16 on the surveyor's map) be reserved for public schools in each township within a given territory. Congress also usually instructed the executive branch precisely where to build lighthouses—or at least specified the land on which the lighthouse was to be built.[35]

However, Congress frequently left it up to the president to determine which public lands should be reserved, especially lands for military purposes. In 1798, for instance, Congress authorized the president to erect forts "in any ... place or places as the public safety shall require, in the opinion of the President of the United States."[36] Congress's willingness to delegate to the president was not limited to military reservations. In 1796, for instance, Congress authorized the president to establish government-owned trading posts along the frontiers in those places "as he shall judge most convenient" to carry on "a liberal trade" with Indian tribes. Legislation providing for the disposal of public lands in the territories also typically gave the president discretion over the withdrawal of lands adjacent to mineral resources. In 1804 and 1807, for example, Congress required the government to reserve land in the Indiana territory that contained salt springs and lead mines, but left it to the president to determine how much land contiguous to the mines and springs should be reserved. Other early statutes envisioned an even broader presidential authority of withdrawal for unspecified public purposes. An 1807 act regarding land grants in the Michigan Territory, for instance, exempted land "in the town of Detroit and its vicinity ... which may by the President of the United States be set aside for public use."[37]

One public use to which nineteenth-century presidents routinely put federal lands was the creation of Indian reservations. Legislation that authorized presidential action in this domain provided few if any rules and regulations to govern the president's actions. The Removal Act of 1830, for instance, empowered the president to exchange federal lands west of the Mississippi for land held by Indian tribes in the southern states, but left it to the president to decide what lands to trade, when to trade them, or whether to trade them. During the latter half of the nineteenth century, presidents liberally used executive orders to carve hundreds of Indian reservations out of federal lands—with little or no legislative authorization.[38]

Getting the Judicial Seal of Approval

Executive directives setting aside public lands encountered a number of legal challenges in the nineteenth century. The first significant case to reach the US Supreme Court (*Wilcox v. Jackson* [1839]) involved land along the Chicago River that was claimed by a settler under the Preemption Act of 1830. The government countered that the land had been reserved for military purposes (Fort Dearborn) and so the settler had no claim to the land under the 1830 act. The plaintiff insisted, however, that the land had not been reserved "by order of the President," as required by the law but instead had been reserved by the secretary of war. The Court disagreed. "The President speaks and acts through the heads of the several departments," and so the Court considered the act of the War Department in setting aside the land "as being in legal contemplation the act of the President."[39]

The Court also rejected the notion that the executive order was unauthorized simply because no statute identified Fort Dearborn by name. The Court pointed to several statutes dating back to 1798 in which Congress had given the president a free hand in deciding the location of forts. "Instead of designating the place themselves," the Court explained, Congress had "left it to the discretion of the president, which is precisely the same thing in effect" as if Congress had named the place itself. Moreover, the Court noted, the military post at Fort Dearborn was in existence at the time that Congress passed the Preemption Act in 1830. In choosing to exempt from preemption all lands that had been reserved by order of the president, Congress had implicitly authorized the president's action in reserving the lands at Fort Dearborn.[40]

Among the most influential nineteenth-century Supreme Court cases relating to executive orders was *Grisar v. McDowell* (1869), which involved land in San Francisco (the Presidio) that President Millard Fillmore had set aside for military purposes in 1850. The city of San Francisco claimed that (a) the land belonged to the city, not the federal government, and (b) even if it belonged to the government, the president exceeded his power because no statute authorized the president's land grab. The Court ruled that the Presidio was in fact federal land and so the city lacked standing to challenge the president's order. The Court nonetheless went out of its way to uphold the president's authority to reserve public lands for public purposes. "From an early period in the history of the government," the Court opined, "it has been the practice of the President to order from time to time, as the exigencies of the public service required, parcels of land belonging to the United States to be reserved from sale and set apart for public uses." Moreover, the Court continued, "the authority of the President in this respect was recognized in numerous acts of Congress," including the preemption acts of 1830 and 1841. And even if Congress hadn't explicitly authorized this particular withdrawal, Fillmore's action had been "indirectly approved by the legislation of Congress in appropriating moneys for the construction of fortifications and other public works" upon these lands.[41]

The language and reasoning in *Grisar* strongly influenced lower courts. In *U.S. v. Leathers* (1879), for instance, a Nevada district court dismissed a challenge to President Ulysses Grant's 1874 executive order, which set aside federal land to create the Pyramid Lake Indian Reservation. The defendant, who was charged with trading in "Indian country" without a license, argued that the reservation was not Indian country because Congress had neither established the reservation nor given the president permission to do so. Drawing on *Grisar* as well as a related Supreme Court case, *Wolcott v. Des Moines Navigation* (1867), the district judge rejected the idea that the president could only withhold lands if Congress had explicitly authorized the action. The judge pointed out that "no direct authority to the president to reserve lands and set them apart for public purposes is found in either *Grisar* or *Wolcott*, but in each the president's authority is recognized by acts of Congress which proceed upon the ground that he has it." Perhaps concerned that Indian reservations created by executive order invited legal challenges like the one in *Leathers*, Congress passed a law in 1887 that explicitly gave the congressional stamp of approval to all Indian reservations, past and future, created by executive order.[42]

By the end of the nineteenth century, litigation relating to the president's power to withdraw public lands had led the Supreme Court to formulate several important propositions regarding unilateral directives. Among them were: (1) directives by the executive "have all the force and effect of a law of the United States" (*Clay Peters v. United States* [1894]); (2) an order "sent out from the appropriate executive department . . . is the legal equivalent of the President's own order" (*Wolsey v. Chapman* [1880]); (3) a presidential proclamation was not legally distinguishable from an executive order (the holding in *Wolsey*); and (4) "no set form of words or phrases is necessary" for an executive directive to be valid. "It is enough if there are sufficient words to indicate the purpose of the power" (*U.S. v. Payne* [1881]). Most important, the Court had settled that Article 4, section 3, granting Congress the power to "make all needful Rules and regulations respecting the Territory or other Property belonging to the United States," should not be interpreted too literally. Congress need not in fact make all rules and regulations regarding federal lands but could instead lawfully authorize the president to make the rules, either explicitly by statute or implicitly by not repudiating the president's action.[43]

Unresolved by these nineteenth-century cases, though, was whether Congress had "*recognized*" the "authority *of* the President"—in the language of *Grisar*—or whether Congress had merely *delegated* that authority *to* the president. That is, *Grisar* could be read as stating the obvious fact that Congress, in passing the preemption acts, had wished to recognize that the withholding of public lands via executive orders that had been legally authorized by Congress was as legally valid as withdrawals ordered directly by Congress. But there was another reading of *Grisar*: that the president had an *inherent* power to withdraw land in the public interest—a power that Congress could recognize but could not take away. This more expansive reading of unilateral executive authority was integrally connected to the fight over the nation's forest lands that began in the latter part of the nineteenth century.[44]

The Fight over the Nation's Forests

Although Congress and presidents had been reserving public land for public purposes since the beginning of the republic, before the Civil War few if any Americans gave any serious thought to reserving public lands in order to conserve the nation's forests. Forests were for clearing. Felling trees was the way Americans had made farmland since the time of the pilgrims. After the Civil War, experts began to sound the alarm that the nation's forests—and its supply of cheap wood—would vanish if the government did not take steps to protect forest lands, but federal politicians were slow to heed the call. Settlers voted; trees did not.[45]

The catalyst for change was the Land Revision Act of 1891, a multi-faceted effort to modernize the complex "conglomeration of land laws that had accumulated" over the past half-century. Tacked on to the bill at the eleventh hour—at the urging of President Benjamin Harrison, who privately threatened to veto the bill if it was not included—was a final section that gave the president broad authority to protect the nation's forests. Neither debated by Congress nor printed before the final vote on the bill, section 24 consisted of only a single sentence:

> That the President of the United States may, from time to time, set apart and reserve, in any State or Territory having public land bearing forests, in any part of the public lands wholly or in part covered with timber or undergrowth, whether of commercial value or not, as public reservations, and the President shall, by public proclamation, declare the establishment of such reservations and the limits thereof.[46]

Little about this section fits the textbook ideal of the legislative process, in which Congress legislates and the president executes. To start with, the section appears to have been drafted by an executive branch official: Edward Bowers, an assistant commissioner in the General Land Office. More important, the section "contained neither a purpose for the reserves nor a means of administering them," let alone the constitutionally prescribed "needful Rules and regulations" that are supposed to guide the executive's enforcement of the law. Instead the hastily written and passed law left decisions about which if any forests were to be preserved entirely in the president's hands.[47]

President Harrison immediately took advantage of the law. Within a month he had created a forest reserve on public lands next to Yellowstone National Park—the nation's first national park, established by Congress in 1872. In the remaining two years of his term, Harrison unilaterally set aside 13.4 million acres of forest land in seven western states and territories, more than doubling the size of the nation's forest reserves.[48]

Harrison's Democratic successor, Grover Cleveland, carried on where Harrison left off. In four years, Cleveland reserved over 25 million acres of forest land—again more than doubling the nation's forest reserves. More than 21 million of those acres were reserved via 13 proclamations issued on a single day (George Washington's birthday—February 22, 1897) at the close of his term. Whereas Harrison's conservation directives occasioned little controversy, Cleveland's parting orders angered many in the affected western states. The Seattle Chamber of Commerce protested that even "King George had never attempted so high-handed an invasion upon the rights" of Americans. The Republican-controlled Congress retaliated against the "Washington's Birthday Reserves" by passing an amendment—written by a South Dakota senator who objected to Cleveland's reservation of 1 million acres in the Black Hills—that would undo the president's unilateral actions. Because Congress affixed the amendment to an essential government funding bill (called the Sundry Civil Appropriations Act), Cleveland was forced to choose "between funding the federal government or preserving his forest reserves." The president opted for a government shutdown, pocket-vetoing the bill on his last day in office.[49]

After William McKinley assumed office, however, Congress neither revoked Cleveland's end-of-term forest reserves nor reined in the president's power to create new reserves. In fact, Congress expanded executive control over the nation's forest lands, albeit while finally providing some statutory guidelines to inform the president's decision-making. The new law, signed by McKinley in early June 1897, reaffirmed the president's authority to create forest reserves but stipulated that such reserves could only be established if they would protect forests or watersheds and "furnish a continuous supply of timber for the use and necessities of citizens of the United States." The law also granted the secretary of the interior broad authority "to regulate ... occupancy and use" of the reserves. Congress did suspend Cleveland's "Washington's Birthday Reserves" for nine months, but it left it to the president to decide whether to abolish the reserves.[50]

In four and a half years as president, McKinley did not do away with any of Cleveland's forest reserves—or Harrison's. He did order a reduction in the size of the Olympic Forest Reserve, removing about one-third of the 2.2 million acres that Cleveland had set aside, and he shaved off some land from the 4.5 million acres that Cleveland had carved out to create the Washington Forest Reserve. Elsewhere in the west, though, he used his unilateral power to adjust boundary lines to *increase* the size of existing forest reserves, including adding 244,000 acres to the Black Hills Forest Reserve established by Cleveland.

McKinley also created 12 new forest reserves, including the 2.3-million-acre Gila River Forest Reserve in New Mexico and 1.6-million-acre forest reserves in Arizona (Black Mesa Forest Reserve) and California (Pine Mountain and Zaca Lake Forest Reserve— what is today part of the Los Padres National Forest). In total, McKinley set aside 7 million acres of forest land.[51]

In the space of just ten years, Presidents McKinley, Cleveland, and Harrison had unilaterally reserved almost 50 million acres in forest reserves—equal to about 78,000 square miles, an area the size of the state of Nebraska. Yet nothing in these presidencies could have prepared the nation for what would come next. In seven and a half years in office, Theodore Roosevelt would unilaterally reserve almost 150 million acres of forest land, an area larger than the state of California and not far off the size of Texas.

Roosevelt's aggressive expansion of the nation's forest reserves was hailed by con-servationists but many in the west were not happy about the president's actions. In a rerun of the showdown with Cleveland a decade earlier, Congress passed an appro-priations act in late February 1907 that included an amendment (sponsored by Oregon senator Charles Fulton) declaring that "Hereafter no forest reserve shall be created, nor shall any addition be made to one heretofore created, within the limits of the States of Oregon, Washington, Idaho, Montana, Colorado, or Wyoming except by act of Con-gress." Members of Congress calculated that Roosevelt would not be willing to veto the entire appropriations bill at the end of the legislative session, and they were right. What they did not count on was that while the bill lay on the president's desk awaiting his signature, Roosevelt tasked administration officials with identifying all public lands in those six states that could be placed in forest reserves. Roosevelt then issued 33 procla-mations on the first two days of March that set aside 17 million acres in the states named in the amendment. Having preserved virtually all the land that the amendment had intended to put beyond the president's reach, TR signed the bill.[52]

The 33 "midnight proclamations" show what Roosevelt meant when he later claimed to have "used every ounce of power there was in the office." Of course, what Roosevelt saw as forceful executive action in the public interest, critics denounced as lawless "usurpation" or even "dictatorship."[53] But both the president's rhetoric and that of his critics obscure several important points about Roosevelt's proclamations. First, the "midnight proclamations" were not unprecedented. Cleveland had done essentially the same thing ten years earlier—and had provoked much the same congressional reaction. Second, Roosevelt's "unilateral" directives establishing national forests were explicitly authorized by acts of Congress. Indeed, in each proclamation that established a new forest reserve, Roosevelt claimed to act "by virtue of the power in me vested by section twenty-four of the [1891] Act of Congress"—exactly the same language employed by his three predecessors. Moreover, each time Roosevelt ordered an expansion of an existing forest reserve, he, like McKinley, invoked the final clause of the 1897 act that authorized the president to adjust the boundaries of any forest reserve.

It is true, as political scientist Graham Dodds writes, that Roosevelt "justified his action in terms of stewardship," but here too Roosevelt was less innovative or unilateral than is usually thought. In a memorandum justifying his 33 proclamations, Roosevelt explained that he had reserved the forests to prevent "immense tracts of valuable timber" from falling into the hands of "the lumber syndicates" and "to keep the land for the benefit of the actual settler and home-maker" while also preserving the natural resources "in such manner as to keep them unimpaired for the benefit of children now growing up to inherit the land." But this vision of stewardship of the forests echoed the purposes articulated by Congress in the 1897 act. Moreover, beginning with Harrison in 1892, each proclamation with which the president established or expanded a forest reserve was prefaced with a "whereas" clause stipulating that "it appears that the public good would be promoted by setting apart and reserving said lands as a public reservation." We should not, in short, allow Roosevelt's larger-than-life persona to obscure the longer-term evolutionary development of the presidency.[54]

Taft and Roosevelt's Quarrel

One of the most common tropes of American presidential history is the contest between Theodore Roosevelt's expansive view of presidential power and his successor William Howard Taft's "strict construction" of presidential power. The principal texts in this narrative are two books written by Roosevelt and Taft after they left office.

In his autobiography, published in 1913, Roosevelt contrasted weak presidents of "the Buchanan-Taft schools" with strong presidents (like himself) in the mold of Jackson and Lincoln. Strong Lincoln-like presidents took the view that the president—indeed, "every executive officer in a high position"—was "a steward of the people bound actively and affirmatively to do all he could for the people." Roosevelt boasted that he had "acted for the public welfare [and] the common well-being of all our people, whenever and in whatever manner was necessary, unless prevented by direct constitutional or legislative prohibition."[55]

Taft responded with a book of his own, *The President and His Powers*, published in 1916. The president, Taft wrote, can only exercise power granted to him by the Constitution or an act of Congress. "There is," he insisted, "no undefined residuum of power which he can exercise because it seems to him to be in the public interest." The notion that the executive "is charged with responsibility for the welfare of all the people in a general way, that he is to play the part of a universal Providence and set all things right, and that anything that in his judgment will help the people he ought to do, unless he is expressly forbidden not to do it" was "an unsafe doctrine" that gave the executive unlimited power that could lead "to results of an arbitrary character."[56]

These were sincerely held views that informed their presidential actions,[57] but the philosophical debate distracts us from similarities in their behavior, at least when it came to the use of unilateral directives. Taft actually issued more executive orders per year than Roosevelt. The same is true for presidential proclamations; in fact, Taft issued more nonceremonial proclamations per year than any president in American history. And more than half of Taft's proclamations related to public lands.[58]

To be sure, Taft harbored grave doubts about the legality of some of the unilateral actions that Roosevelt had taken or allowed his subordinates to take. One such directive was Roosevelt's late-term withdrawal of huge swaths of public land along rivers and streams in seven western states. Roosevelt's purpose in withdrawing the land from

Although remembered most for his sharp criticisms of Theodore Roosevelt's unilateral exercise of presidential power, William Howard Taft was no slouch when it came to unilateral directives. In fact, Taft issued more executive orders than any of his predecessors, including Roosevelt. Here he signs Executive Order 1498, directing the Surgeon General to inspect "the sanitary or hygienic condition" of all government buildings in the District of Columbia—one of the earliest efforts to regulate health and safety in the federal workplace.

Courtesy: carlanthonyonline.com.

settlement was to prevent private interests from monopolizing control of potential water-power sites. Taft regarded this as a noble purpose but did not believe it was authorized by any statute and so, in keeping with his strict construction beliefs, one of his first executive actions was to restore the lands to private settlement.[59]

Although this incident is often offered as emblematic of Taft and Roosevelt's radically different understandings of presidential power, the story is more complex than this simple narrative would suggest. To begin with, it exaggerates Roosevelt's unilateralism. His withdrawal of water-power sites followed the recommendations of both the Reclamation Service (created by Congress in 1902) and the Inland Waterways Commission, a commission created by Congress in 1907 at Roosevelt's request. The commission's membership included four congressmen (two from each party), including the commission chair (Theodore Burton, chairman of the House Committee of Rivers and Harbors) and vice chair (Senator Francis Newlands, architect of the 1902 Reclamation Act). Upon receiving the commission's report, moreover, Roosevelt transmitted it to Congress together with a message urging the enactment of legislation that would ensure that "our waterways [are used] in the interest of all the people."[60] Roosevelt's orders were justified as temporary means of protecting lands while Congress came up with a permanent solution. As Gifford Pinchot, Roosevelt's close ally and chief of the US Forest Service, explained the administration's philosophy, Roosevelt would "withdraw sites from entry to keep them safe until Congress could act to protect them."[61]

The simple version of events also obscures Taft's own reliance on unilateral directives—not just in undoing Roosevelt's policy but in setting his own. In explaining his decision to repeal Roosevelt's order, Taft told his nephew that it was "more in accordance with the law" and that he felt it was "safer for me to find out through the [US] Geological Survey the places where there are valuable power sites and then ... set them aside out of harm's way." By Taft's own admission, then, he was prepared to set aside land for power sites on the recommendation of a bureaucratic agency, even without congressional authorization. And in fact, within days of writing this letter, he started issuing executive orders establishing power sites on many of the same lands that Roosevelt had withdrawn. By the time Congress, in the summer of 1910, got around to explicitly authorizing the president's power to withdraw public lands for power sites, Taft had already withdrawn lands for that purpose in California, Colorado, Idaho, Montana, Oregon, and Wyoming. Moreover, the 1910 law gave the president virtually unlimited discretion over the establishment of water-power sites. During the remaining two and a half years of his presidency, Taft used executive orders to establish scores of power-site reserves across the west, including many of the sites that Roosevelt had targeted for protection.[62]

In a sense, Roosevelt and Taft conspired to create the same myth: a brash Roosevelt single-handedly saving the wilderness and a plodding Taft methodically restoring a nation of laws. But contrary to Taft's storyline and Roosevelt's occasional boasts, Roosevelt typically did seek congressional authorization for his conservation directives. In 1906, for instance, he helped persuade Congress to pass the Antiquities Act, which gave the president broad authority to create national monuments on federal lands that included "historic landmarks, historic or prehistoric structures, and other objects of historic or scientific interest." In some instances, Roosevelt used this legislative authorization more aggressively than did Taft, the most storied example being Roosevelt's designation of the Grand Canyon as a national monument after Congress refused Roosevelt's entreaties to declare it a national park to protect it from private interests who wished to exploit the canyon for private gain. But for the most part Taft and Roosevelt used the authority to proclaim national monuments in similar ways: Taft proclaimed 11 national monuments in four years, fewer than Roosevelt's 18 but at the same or a greater rate than Wilson (12 in eight years), Harding and Coolidge (21 in eight years), Hoover (nine in four years), and FDR (12 in 13 years).[63]

One of the most commonly repeated stories about Roosevelt's conservation unilateralism relates to his creation, in March 1903, of the nation's first wildlife reserve at Pelican Island off the coast of Florida—it amounted to nothing less than an "executive coup," according to one admiring biographer.[64] Legend has it that Roosevelt asked a Justice Department lawyer about his authority to establish the reserve.

A few days later, a government lawyer, sallow, squinty-eyed, purse lipped . . . came to the White House. He solemnly intoned, "I cannot find a law that will allow you to do this, Mr. President." "But," replied T.R., now rising to his full height, "is there a law that will prevent it?" The lawyer, now frowning, replied that no, there was not. T.R. responded, "Very well, I so declare it."[65]

The quoted exchange is likely apocryphal, though it does accurately illustrate Roosevelt's determination to use executive authority to preserve wilderness and wildlife. But the image of a conservationist president ordering wildlife reserves all across the country without congressional sanction or approval is mostly wrong. Yes, Roosevelt used executive orders to create 51 bird reserves during his tenure as president, but only a handful of these were created before Congress had clearly recognized the president's authority to do so in a 1906 statute (the Game and Bird Preserves Protection Act) that prohibited hunting or disturbing birds on any federal lands that "have been set apart or reserved as breeding grounds for birds by any law, proclamation, or Executive order." This was no executive coup.[66]

Even more wrong is the idea that Roosevelt unilaterally decreed the creation of the nation's first game preserves. It is true that Roosevelt issued a proclamation creating the first game preserve (the Wichita Mountain Forest and Game Preserve in Oklahoma) on June 2, 1905, but that was six months *after* Congress passed an act that explicitly authorized the president "to designate such areas in the Wichita Forest Reserve as should, in his opinion, be set aside for the protection of game animals and birds and be recognized as a breeding place therefor." Similarly, establishment of the Grand Canyon Game Preserve, proclaimed by Roosevelt on June 23, 1908, was explicitly provided for by legislation enacted by Congress two years earlier (on June 29, 1906). The third game preserve—the National Bison Range in Montana—that Roosevelt allegedly "created" at the end of his term was also specifically called for by an act of Congress, which Roosevelt signed into law on May 23, 1908. The only game preserve that can be reasonably attributed to Roosevelt's executive discretion was his executive order, on February 27, 1909, which set aside Fire Island in Alaska as a preserve and breeding ground for moose—an order consistent with the congressional intent of the Game and Bird Preserves Protection Act of 1906.[67]

If Roosevelt's executive actions were nothing like as unilateral or lawless as critics such as Taft suggested, Taft's actions were not as timid or strict constructionist as his philosophical statements might suggest. No wildlife refuge created by Roosevelt compared in size, for instance, to the 2.7 million acres that Taft set aside in the Aleutian Islands. The wildlife reserve on the Aleutian Islands was one of ten bird reserves Taft created by executive order, 41 fewer than Roosevelt but using essentially the same legal authority. And if Roosevelt liberally construed the Antiquities Act in making the Grand Canyon a national monument, so too did Taft when he expanded the Natural Bridges national monument in Utah from the original 120 acres set aside by Roosevelt to a "monument" of 2,740 acres. Moreover, despite Taft's insistence that the executive could only set aside public lands when "expressly authorized by law," there were a number of times when Taft directed that lands be withdrawn by unilateral directive in the absence of any statutory authorization. One of these unauthorized directives was Temporary Petroleum

Withdrawal Order No. 5—an order that ended up being litigated in the US Supreme Court, in a case that subverts the customary storyline of the Taft–Roosevelt quarrel.[68]

The Curious Case of *United States v. Midwest Oil*

In February 1897, during the final month of Cleveland's second term, Congress passed (and the president signed) legislation specifying that public lands containing petroleum were "free and open to occupation, exploration, and purchase by citizens of the United States … under regulations prescribed by law." The law helped propel the California oil rush. Oil was being pumped out of public lands at such a rate that, according to a government report delivered to Secretary of Interior Richard Ballinger in September 1909, it would "be impossible for the people of the United States to continue ownership of oil lands for more than a few months. After that the government will be obliged to repurchase the very oil that it has practically given away." The report believed that there was an "immediate necessity for assuring the conservation of a proper supply of petroleum for the government's own use."[69]

Taft's response was indeed immediate. Upon receiving the report from Ballinger, the president issued "Temporary Petroleum Withdrawal Order No. 5," which commanded that a huge swath of public lands in California and a smaller amount in Wyoming be closed to private interests. Congress had declared these lands "free and open" and now the president unilaterally declared these same lands off limits to drilling. Taft excused the directive on the grounds that it was "in aid of proposed legislation affecting the use and disposition of the petroleum deposits on the public domain." That is, he hoped that when the 61st Congress returned in December, it would pass legislation that would explicitly authorize the president to do what he had already done—an action, he explained to Congress, that he had taken "in the interest of the public." In June 1910, the Republican-controlled Congress granted the president's wish, passing legislation (the Pickett Act) which stated "That the President may, at any time, in his discretion, temporarily withdraw from settlement, location, sale, or entry any of the public lands of the United States … and reserve the same for water-power sites, irrigation, classification of lands, or other public purposes to be specified in the orders of withdrawals, and such withdrawals or reservations shall remain in force until revoked by him or by an act of Congress."[70]

But the question remained: was Taft's Lincoln-like first order legal? Or was it, as a strict constructionist might hold, an act of usurpation? The question was put to the test when the Taft administration sued the Midwest Oil Company seeking to recover land and oil that the government alleged had been illegally taken subsequent to the president's order. The company countered that Taft's action was lawless and unconstitutional. In 1914, with Woodrow Wilson ensconced in the White House, the US Supreme Court agreed to hear the case.

The case sharply divided the Court. Of the eight justices who participated in the case, three agreed with the lower court that Taft's act of stewardship was without statutory or constitutional authorization and was therefore illegal. The other five justices—four of whom were put on the Court by Taft—upheld the legality of the president's order. Writing for the Court was Taft appointee Joseph Lamar, while the dissenting opinion was penned by Roosevelt appointee William Day.

The Roosevelt-appointed Day sounded every inch a Taft-style strict constructionist. The framers' intricate construction, Day wrote, was premised on a strict separation of powers. Each branch had to be "limited to the exercise of the powers appropriate to its own department." Moreover, it was one of the "great functions" of the Court to ensure that "each branch [be kept] within the sphere of its legitimate action, and to prevent encroachments of one branch upon the authority of another." Day underscored that it was imperative that the Constitution's "grant of authority to the Executive . . . not . . . be amplified by judicial decisions."

The Taft-appointed Lamar, in contrast, offered a reading of executive power in the spirit of Roosevelt's more elastic vision. Justice Lamar started not with clear constitutional lines of separation but rather the premise that "government is a practical affair, intended for practical men." He looked not to an original sacred text but to "long-continued practice." Over the past 80 years, Lamar wrote, there had been "scores and hundreds" of executive directives withdrawing public land from private acquisition in the absence of statutory authority. He counted about one hundred executive directives "establishing or enlarging Indian reservations" and another hundred "establishing or enlarging military reservations," as well as 44 "establishing bird reserves." Although "there was no statute empowering the President to withdraw any of these lands from settlement . . . when it appeared that the public interest would be served by withdrawing or reserving parts of the public domain, nothing was more natural than to retain what the government already owned. . . . The President was in a position to know when the public interest required particular portions of the people's lands to be withdrawn from entry or location."

The Court's contention, though, was not that the president had an inherent constitutional authority to advance the public interest but rather that congressional authorization of the president's power to withdraw public lands could be inferred from Congress's longstanding acquiescence in the practice of such executive directives. As the Court put it, Congress was the "principal" and the executive its "agent" and "in not a single instance was the act of the agent disapproved" by the principal. Since Congress had never "repudiate[d] the power claimed or the withdrawal orders made," the president could be presumed to have acted with "an implied grant of power to preserve the public interest." By not disavowing executive directives, Congress had made them legal.[71]

Questions can be asked of both opinions. The dissenters arguably clung to a rigid originalism that seemed incompatible with the demands of modern governance. Yet the majority opinion is also suspect, resting as it does on dubious history. Although nineteenth-century executive directives generally did not cite specific statutory authority, that does not mean that there were no laws authorizing the president to act. In the case of military withdrawals, for instance, Congress passed a number of laws authorizing presidential withdrawals. There is also the puzzle of why, if Taft possessed a widely recognized "implied grant of power to preserve the public interest," he (a) made his order temporary and (b) asked Congress to "affirm" his action after the fact. Taft at least seemed unaware of this allegedly well-known grant of power.[72]

However deficient may have been the history upon which the Court's opinion rested, the case came to stand for the principle that congressional silence in the face of unilateral executive actions is tantamount to congressional authorization or at least acceptance of those actions. Given the strategic advantages of the president—especially that he acts alone whereas Congress must assemble veto-proof majorities—the Court's opinion helped to lay the basis for a more liberal use of unilateral presidential directives. The outcome of the case is particularly ironic because it was President Taft who had confidently opined, in a June 1909 letter chastising the Roosevelt administration's unilateral conservation directives: "Congress has the power to dispose of lands; not the executive ... The power of the President to withdraw land appropriated to popular settlement by act of Congress is exceedingly limited under the decision of the courts." Thanks to Taft's own unilateralism, that was no longer true, if it ever had been.[73]

Executive directives setting aside public lands have continued down to the present day. Many have been of great importance and some have excited huge controversy, such as FDR's 1943 proclamation creating a 221,000 acre national monument in Jackson Hole, Wyoming; Jimmy Carter's 17 proclamations on a single day (December 1, 1978) setting aside 56 million acres through the addition of 15 national monuments and enlargement of two others; Bill Clinton's 1996 proclamation that ended coal mining in nearly 2 million acres of southern Utah by establishing the Grand Staircase-Escalante National Monument; and Barack Obama'a proclamation creating the 1.35 million acre Bears Ears National Monument. Decrying the Bears Ears monument as a "massive federal land grab," Donald Trump ordered a dramatic downsizing of the monument, an act that is sure to be challenged in court by Native American tribal groups and conservation groups who maintain that Trump lacks the legal authority to shrink the boundaries of national monuments. But while public lands directives still stir strong political emotions, they no longer define the unilateral presidency in the way that they did in the first decades of the twentieth century. Beginning in the 1930s, the locus of institutional conflict shifted from the disposal of public lands to a debate about the modern social welfare and regulatory state. One measure of the change is that during Theodore Roosevelt's second term, more than 90 percent of presidential proclamations related to public lands, whereas during Franklin Roosevelt's first term, that number plummeted to 14 percent.[74]

DELEGATING AUTHORITY IN THE NEW DEAL

Rationalizing the Executive Order: How the NRA begat the Federal Register Act

In 1933, the first year of Franklin Delano Roosevelt's presidency, Congress enacted about one hundred public laws. During that same year, FDR issued more than five hundred executive orders, well over twice the average annual number of executive orders of his immediate predecessors. Half of those executive orders promulgated or amended industry-wide "codes of fair competition" that were drafted by companies under the auspices of the National Recovery Administration (NRA), established by executive order following passage of the National Industrial Recovery Act in June 1933. Intended to promote "cooperation rather than destructive competition," the industry-wide codes established production quotas, minimum prices, maximum hours, and minimum wages.[75]

Keeping track of these many orders was no easy task. Just how difficult became clear when the Justice Department charged J.W. Smith with violating the production quotas of the petroleum industry code promulgated by executive order in August 1933. The US Supreme Court agreed to hear the case, but in preparing for oral argument the government unearthed an embarrassing fact: in September 1933 the president had issued an executive order amending the code that had "inadvertently dropped the enforcement language." The government was thus prosecuting somebody for breaking a law that didn't exist. The oversight was remedied by another executive order, but the government was compelled to drop the case.[76]

The Court was not so willing to let the matter drop. In a separate case involving another oil producer (the Panama Refining Company) accused of violating production quotas, the justices grilled the government's attorney, Harold Stephens, about how executive orders were made and recorded. They wondered how private citizens could be expected to follow the law if even the government's lawyers were having difficulty knowing what was in these directives. Justice Louis Brandeis wanted to know whether there was any "official or general publication of these executive orders." Stephens admitted there was not. Brandeis pressed, "Well, is there any way by which one can find out what is in these executive orders when they are issued?" Again Stephens was compelled to make the embarrassing admission that "it would be rather difficult," though he did suggest that it would be "possible to get certified copies of the executive orders and codes from the NRA." Justice James Clark McReynolds, no fan of the New Deal, asked Stephens how many orders and codes had been issued over the last 15 months. Stephens said he didn't know, though he guessed "several hundred."[77]

The problem of haphazard issuing and recording of executive orders did not begin with FDR. In 1927, during the presidency of Calvin Coolidge, Harvard law professor Felix Frankfurter had noted that "the formation and publication of executive orders and regulations [was] still at a primitive stage." In fact, as far back as 1873, the Supreme Court had complained about the lack of systematic record-keeping relating to executive directives. Presidents Grant, Harding, and Hoover all issued executive orders that attempted to "regularize and systematize" the process of making and recording presidential directives. But while the problem of "so many poorly catalogued and unpublicized orders" was not new, the dramatic expansion in the size and scope of the federal government's responsibilities during the 1930s made it clear that the system of unilateral directives needed to be modernized so that citizens could know the federal laws they were expected to comply with and the government the laws they were supposed to enforce.[78]

The spectacle of the government admitting that it would be "difficult" to locate directives that had the force of law—and were being used to criminally prosecute people—prompted Congress to take action and put an end to the "rather amazing informality" that had hitherto governed the process of issuing unilateral executive directives. Under the Federal Register Act of 1935, all executive orders and proclamations of general applicability were henceforth to be published in a Federal Register so that citizens would be able to know the laws they were expected to follow. At the same time, Congress clearly acknowledged what the courts had long recognized: the executive branch made law and did not simply execute it.[79]

"Dictatorial Tastes" or "Congressional Surrender"?

Congress's creation of the *Federal Register* helped to institutionalize the use of unilateral executive directives, but it did not put an end to the criticism of what J.W. Smith's lawyer called "the viciousness of governing folks by executive order." Throughout FDR's presidency, critics of the New Deal continued to insist that the president was subverting the Constitution by legislating from the White House.[80]

Among the most vocal critics was former president Herbert Hoover, who pointed to Roosevelt's "daily issuance of Executive orders," particularly in his first term, as evidence of the president's "dictatorial tastes." It is tempting to charge Hoover with hypocrisy: after all, Hoover himself issued nearly 250 executive orders a year, a rate that is outstripped only by FDR's annual average of 270. But these gross numbers tell us little. For starters, more recent presidents have often packaged their unilateral directives under other names, such as presidential memoranda. In addition, these counts include many executive orders that are not even remotely sinister or aggrandizing. For instance, many of FDR's orders were required by a 1930 statute that "established a mandatory retirement age for federal employees, but authorized the president to exempt individuals from this provision by executive order." In 1941, for instance, one in five of FDR's executive orders were retirement exemption orders. The significant decline in the number of executive orders during FDR's last years was due not to any decline in executive unilateralism but rather to a January 1942 executive order that granted a blanket exemption for all presidential appointments and thereby eliminated the need for so many orders. An indictment of Roosevelt's "dictatorial tastes" must rest not on the number of executive orders but on the substance of those orders.[81]

From the outset of his presidency, FDR certainly signaled a willingness to go it alone if need be. Everybody remembers Roosevelt's inaugural address for its intrepid insistence that "the only thing we have to fear is fear itself," but less often recalled is the president's warning that "the normal balance of executive and legislative authority" might not be "wholly adequate to the unprecedented demand and need for undelayed action." The new president said that he was prepared to work through the normal legislative process but cautioned that "in the event that the Congress shall fail" to adopt the necessary legislation, he would "not evade the clear course of duty that will then confront me. I shall ask the Congress for the one remaining instrument to meet the crisis—broad executive power to wage a war against the emergency as great as the power that would be given me if we were in fact invaded by a foreign foe." It was this line, not the remark about "fear itself," that drew the loudest and longest applause from the crowd.[82]

With Congress not yet in session, 36 hours after uttering those words, Roosevelt issued a proclamation that closed every bank in the country for the next four days. There were good reasons to take this action since if banks remained open there could be a calamitous run on the banks from panicked depositors. But did the president have the authority to order a bank holiday? When the idea was pitched to President Hoover two days before Roosevelt's inaugural, it was suggested that the president could act under the authority of a statute passed during World War I: the Trading with the Enemy Act of 1917. Hoover declined to do so after Attorney General William Mitchell questioned the legality of relying on an act that was clearly intended for other purposes, namely to restrict trade with countries at war with the United States. Roosevelt exhibited no such qualms in proclaiming to act "in view of [the] national emergency" and "by virtue of the authority vested in" him by the 1917 statute.[83]

Roosevelt's reliance on the Trading with the Enemy Act to justify the bank holiday is a textbook example of a president stretching a statute well beyond the original congressional intent. It is also a reminder of why the invocation of statutory authority in a presidential directive is not necessarily a sign that the president acted with the authorization of Congress. In declaring a bank holiday, Roosevelt was neither exercising authority that Congress had granted nor executing an action that Congress told him to take. Instead he was using an ill-fitting congressional statute as a fig leaf to try to cover the naked act of legislating from the White House.

So does the bank holiday proclamation support Hoover's charge that Roosevelt harbored "dictatorial tastes"? One reason to be skeptical of the indictment is that the idea of declaring a bank holiday and of relying on the Trading with the Enemy Act to sanction it did not come from FDR or his lawyers but rather from officials in the Hoover administration and the Federal Reserve Board. Another, more important reason for skepticism is that Roosevelt's very first unilateral directive, issued the day after his inauguration, was a proclamation calling Congress into extraordinary session, a power explicitly granted the president by Article II, section 3 of the Constitution. Roosevelt's March proclamation required Congress to begin its legislative work on Thursday, March 9, just five days after FDR's inauguration. Had the president not issued the proclamation, Congress would not have convened until December. Even more telling is the contrast with Lincoln's April 15, 1861, proclamation calling Congress into extraordinary session after the attack on Fort Sumter. Whereas Roosevelt mandated that Congress begin its work immediately, Lincoln ordered Congress to convene on July 4, giving himself more than 12 weeks to face the secession crisis without congressional interference. Moreover, all the many New Deal programs and "alphabet agencies" (e.g., NRA, WPA, CWA, AAA, FWA)—including those agencies created by executive order—originated with congressional legislation.[84]

Finally, it is difficult to see the bank holiday as dictatorial when Congress's first legislative act on its first day was to pass the Emergency Banking Relief Act, which amended the Trading with the Enemy Act by extending the president's extraordinary powers to regulate the country's international and domestic finances in wartime to include any declared national emergency. Roosevelt put the act's broad grant of authority over banking and currency to immediate use by unilaterally extending and then ending the banking holiday. Among the executive orders FDR issued under authority of the act was one that made it a crime—subject to a $10,000 fine or ten years' imprisonment, or both—for individuals to possess gold. The order essentially nationalized gold by directing all persons to deliver their gold to the Federal Reserve.[85]

The broad grant of authority to the executive branch, typical of so many important New Deal-era statutes, suggests that the Roosevelt administration's unilateral directives owed more to what Hoover derided as "Congressional surrender of responsibility" than they did to the president's allegedly "dictatorial tastes." Opponents of New Deal policies seized on the idea of congressional abdication to argue that the "doctrine of non-delegation" prevented Congress from delegating so much of its legislative power to the executive branch. The Supreme Court initially appeared receptive to this line of attack, and in 1935 it famously struck down the heart of the National Industrial Recovery Act (see Chapter 9 for a discussion of the case, *Schechter Poultry Co. v. United States*) on the grounds that Congress had unconstitutionally delegated its lawmaking responsibilities to the president. The Court's decision in *Schechter* nullified about four hundred executive orders, but the case proved to be an aberration and had little enduring impact on Congress's lawmaking or the Court's jurisprudence.[86]

Rather than follow the logic of *Schechter*, the Court rapidly reverted to its previously expressed view that it was up to Congress to decide what authority it delegated to the president, at least so long as Congress lay down a minimally "intelligible principle" that the executive could follow. The delegation to the president that Hoover saw as "Congressional surrender of responsibility" has generally been seen by the court as a necessary part of lawmaking in a modern democracy. As the Court explained in a much later case (*Mistretta v. United States*), "our jurisprudence has been driven by a practical understanding that in our increasingly complex society, replete with ever changing and more technical problems, Congress simply cannot do its job absent an ability to delegate power under broad general directives." In delegating to the president, Congress was not surrendering its lawmaking responsibility but acting in accordance with what Chief Justice William Howard Taft—in upholding a 1922 statute that gave the president broad authority to adjust tariff rates—called "the inherent necessities of ... governmental co-ordination."

COMBATING DISCRIMINATION: THE PROMISE OF UNILATERAL ACTION

FDR's Executive Order 8802: Creating the Fair Employment Practices Commission

The New Deal was made possible by huge Democratic majorities in both houses of Congress. By creating a safety net for the aged and boosting the power of labor unions, the New Deal helped to remake American capitalism. But this transformation in social welfare policy was dependent on assurances that one aspect of American society remained unchanged: race relations in the South. Southern Democrats were sufficiently numerous and strategically placed to block any policy of which they disapproved. At no point in FDR's presidency did Southerners make up less than 44 percent of Democrats in the Senate and 41 percent in the House. And because of their substantially greater seniority (a product of representing states and districts where there was virtually no partisan opposition), southern Democrats chaired most of the key committees through which New Deal legislation had to pass.[87]

Knowing that a Congress dominated by southern whites would not support civil rights legislation, African American leaders (and the president's wife) pressed Roosevelt to act on his own to prohibit racial discrimination in the military and federal agencies and to bar government contracts from being awarded to companies that discriminated on the basis of race. Roosevelt was reluctant to take any action that would alienate southern

Democrats in Congress, but his calculus began to change as his attention shifted from implementing the New Deal to preparing for a world war. Pivotal in changing the president's political calculation in the summer of 1941 was the threat of a march on Washington to publicize African Americans' demands for racial justice. Desperate to avoid an internationally embarrassing incident at a time when the appearance "of unity was most essential to national prestige," FDR agreed to issue Executive Order 8802 in exchange for the organizers calling off the march.[88]

Issued only a week before the March on Washington was scheduled to take place, EO 8802 fell well short of what civil rights groups had wanted. Indeed, Roosevelt seemed to go out of his way to downplay the order's significance, claiming that he was only "reaffirming" an existing "policy of full participation in the defense program by all persons, regardless of race, creed, color, or national origin." What was certainly new, though, was the requirement that defense contracts "hereafter negotiated" include a nondiscrimination clause and the creation of the Fair Employment Practices Commission (FEPC) to investigate complaints of discrimination in the defense industry and to take "appropriate steps to redress grievances which it finds to be valid." Modest though these steps were, the order still represented a watershed moment in civil rights. "From that moment on," writes political scientist Kenneth Mayer, "civil rights groups *expected* presidential leadership in civil rights policy." It demonstrated, too, that African Americans could successfully exert pressure on the presidency.[89]

The key role that civil rights groups played in pressuring FDR to issue EO 8802 reveals an aspect of unilateral presidential directives that is too often forgotten: namely, the directives are often anything but unilateral. The order stemmed not from the president's own wishes or desires but from intense political pressure from outside groups. Its provisions were a political compromise negotiated by a president who was trying to do just enough to mollify African Americans but not so much that it would antagonize southern Democrats. EO 8802 was not the command of an imperial president but the cautious work of a politician practicing the art of persuasion and bargaining.

The fate of FEPC is also a reminder of the difficulties of trying to enact social change without Congress. The commission was largely ineffective in ending discrimination in the defense industry because it lacked the authority to enforce the nondiscrimination clause, since only the agency contracting with the company could cancel a contract. Even investigating complaints was difficult because the FEPC's five unpaid commissioners operated on a shoestring budget with "no staff to speak of"—a consequence of being dependent on the president's discretionary "emergency" funds since Congress refused to appropriate money for the commission's work. Moreover, while the FEPC could hold hearings, it could not compel people to testify. After the first FEPC collapsed amid bureaucratic infighting and "tepid" presidential support, civil rights groups succeeded in pressuring Roosevelt to issue a second executive order resurrecting a new and more robust FEPC, which included a commissioner to be paid $10,000 a year (equivalent to nearly $140,000 in 2014 dollars). But the reconstituted and reinvigorated FEPC was promptly brought to heel by Congress, which passed an amendment (sponsored by Georgia's Democrat senator Richard Russell) that prohibited any federal money from going to "any agency that had been in existence for more than one year (including those established by executive order) without specific congressional appropriation." The law didn't mention FEPC but that was its intended target. In 1946, Congress formally abolished FEPC.[90]

Truman's Executive Order 9981: Desegregating the Military

After World War II, civil rights groups stepped up their campaign to end racial discrimination. The war shone a harsh light on the grotesque disjunction between the ideals of equality and freedom that Americans professed and the reality of racial subordination and segregation in the South. Having fought for freedom abroad, blacks now demanded freedom at home. As one black soldier wrote, "I spent four years in the Army to free a bunch of Dutchmen and Frenchmen, and I'm hanged if I'm going to let the Alabama version of the Germans kick me around when I get home." Membership in the National Association for the Advancement of Colored People (NAACP) jumped from 50,000 to 450,000 during the war years. The politics of race was changing, too, as huge numbers of blacks left the South to find work in industrialized cities in the North and West.[91]

Much had changed, but not the Senate. Southern Democrats still controlled the important levers of power in that body. When Truman took the oath of office on April 12, 1945, the Senate majority leader was a Democrat from Kentucky, the Democratic whip was from Alabama, the chair of the Senate Rules Committee and the chair of the Senate Appropriations Committee were from Virginia, and the chair of the Senate Finance Committee was from Georgia. Efforts to enact civil rights laws were repeatedly stymied by southern senators. Even after Republicans took control of the Senate in 1947, southern Democrats still managed to block all anti-segregation legislation. Numerous anti-segregation amendments to the 1948 Selective Service Bill were defeated in floor votes. Even a relatively limited proposal to exempt servicemen from paying a poll tax in federal election was dropped by Senate leaders because of the uncompromising opposition of southern senators.[92]

With no chance of achieving racial justice through the legislative process, civil rights groups focused their lobbying efforts on the president. As they had in 1941, they promised a march on Washington if no action was taken. A. Philip Randolph turned up the public pressure on the president by calling on all black males to refuse to register for the peacetime draft until the president desegregated the military. Randolph and the NAACP also informed the president that he "could not count on" the support of African Americans in the 1948 election if he did not act. So long as blacks lived overwhelmingly in the South, Democratic presidents had little reason to court black voters since the region was already overwhelmingly Democratic, but now that increasing numbers of blacks had moved to electorally competitive states (where they were not systematically disenfranchised), Truman had a far greater electoral incentive to meet their demands than Roosevelt had done. Assured by his aide Clark Clifford that black votes in key swing states "will more than cancel out any votes the President may lose in the South," Truman issued Executive Order 9981 desegregating the armed forces.[93]

The intensity of southern legislators' opposition to integration and the many veto points within Congress had helped defeat every legislative effort to end segregation in the military. Now, however, those same veto points worked to the advantage of the civil rights community. In 1948, Georgia Democrat Richard Russell had been able to block the amendment abolishing the poll tax on servicemen, but in 1950, when the Selective Service Act was up for renewal, he could not get a majority of his colleagues to vote for a "voluntary segregation" amendment that would have undercut Truman's order. Congressional gridlock for the first time now worked to further rather than retard racial justice.[94]

EO 9981 was Truman's most famous unilateral directive and the one he was most proud of. Desegregating the military, he boasted shortly after leaving the presidency, was "the greatest thing that ever happened to America." But Truman issued a number of other important, if less famous, directives that helped make the presidency "the focal point of racial progress." Among these were EO 9980, which established a Fair Employment Board charged with ending racially discriminatory hiring among all 2 million federal government employees, and EO 10308, which established a Committee on Government Contract Compliance that was charged with "investigating and reporting on the enforcement of nondiscrimination clauses in federal government contracts," which potentially affected as many as 20 million employees.[95]

By the close of Truman's presidency, civil rights groups had come to expect presidential action when their way was blocked in Congress. However, Truman's successor Dwight Eisenhower, racked by doubts about the wisdom and legitimacy of using federal and presidential power to eliminate racial discrimination, fell badly short of meeting those raised expectations. To be sure, Eisenhower did famously—though with the greatest reluctance—issue EO 10730, federalizing the Arkansas National Guard and authorizing the use of US armed forces to enforce court-ordered school desegregation in Little Rock—a court order that was being actively defied by Arkansas governor Orville Faubus. In taking this action, though, there could be no question of treading on congressional authority, nor of exceeding presidential authority, since the order was, as Attorney General Herbert Brownell assured Eisenhower, firmly rooted in the president's constitutional and statutory authority "to use militia and military forces when normal law enforcement authorities are unable to enforce the federal law."[96]

JFK's Executive Order 11063: Ending Discrimination in Public Housing

Eisenhower's reluctance to use presidential power to advance civil rights was heavily criticized in the 1960 presidential campaign by the Democratic nominee, John F. Kennedy. "Many things," Kennedy declared in an October 1960 speech, "can be done by a stroke of the presidential pen." Kennedy particularly faulted Eisenhower for not using the power of the pen to abolish discrimination in federally assisted housing programs, a step that had, he pointed out, been unanimously recommended the year before by a congressionally created civil rights commission.[97]

Promising executive action on civil rights was seen not only as an effective way to secure the support of black voters but also as a way to govern without splitting the Democratic Party. In a memo to the president-elect, Harris Wofford warned Kennedy that Congress could "go up in flames" if the president tried to push through civil rights legislation. Governing by executive order, Wofford advised, would enable the president to avoid "a party-splitting legislation battle." A strategy premised on "a minimum of legislative action and a maximum of executive action" would also be more effective since the administration lacked the votes to end the filibuster that would inevitably block any civil rights legislation. However, Wofford also counseled the president not to publicly renounce his support for "far-reaching legislation," as the threat of such legislation could be used to persuade southern Democrats to accept his executive actions. "You can explain your executive actions to them," Wofford wrote, "as the only alternative to bringing forward such legislation." Executive orders, in Wofford's view, were integral to "the recurring negotiation with southern political leaders."[98]

As a presidential candidate, Kennedy conveyed the impression that ordering non-discrimination in publicly assisted housing was as simple as wielding a pen. As president-elect, he was urged to issue the order by his principal advisor on civil rights. Yet as president, he took no action on housing for almost two years. Why?

Kennedy's campaign rhetoric suggested that President Eisenhower only had to sit down at a desk with a pen to make the housing order a reality. The truth was far more complicated. The president does not in fact govern unilaterally even when issuing executive orders. Beginning in the 1930s, all draft executive orders were required to be submitted first to the Bureau of the Budget (BOB) and the Justice Department for review—disapproval by either the director of BOB or the attorney general meant that an order could not be sent to the president unless it was "accompanied by the statement of the reasons for such disapproval." In reviewing an executive order or proclamation, BOB (and later its successor, the Office of Management and Budget) solicited comment from any executive agency that might be affected by the order. This process of review for executive orders was essentially the same as the review process for the president's legislative program.[99]

This review process invited different opinions and perspectives, and on the housing order there were sharply divergent views, particularly regarding how widely the order should apply. One especially divisive issue was whether the order should be limited to federal agencies directly involved in building or administering public housing or whether it should also direct the Federal Deposit Insurance Corporation (FDIC) to forbid federally insured banks to lend to builders who discriminated on the basis of race. Advocates of strong civil rights action, including the Civil Rights Commission, urged the broadest possible coverage, but the head of the Justice Department's Civil Rights Division questioned whether the president had the constitutional authority to issue a command of this sort to an independent agency like the FDIC. Justice Department lawyers reported there was "a substantial chance" that the courts would nullify an order that denied federal deposit insurance to banks that discriminated. There was also a substantial chance that either the FDIC would refuse to comply with the order or that Congress would refuse to appropriate funds to support this new FDIC responsibility.[100]

Almost a year passed before a compromise order finally "had been cleared through all the agencies" and landed on Kennedy's desk. But even then Kennedy was unable to wield his mighty pen. Undoubtedly the president would have liked to end racial discrimination in housing, if only to keep his campaign promise, as well as to bring an end to the thousands of mocking pens that were being sent to the White House to protest the president's failure to act. But the president also wanted other things that required congressional cooperation, including the creation of a new cabinet-level department of housing and urban development. Timing was everything, his aides counseled. And a housing executive order at this time would lose him the support of southern Democrats and doom his other legislative goals. Better, they said, not to "muddy the water right now." Better to wait until after the 1962 elections. And wait is exactly what Kennedy did.[101]

When Kennedy finally did sign EO 11063, on November 20, 1962, it was with none of the bravado and swagger of his campaign speech two years earlier. Instead the president strove to make the announcement as low-key and "as little divisive as possible." As aide Ted Sorenson later wrote, Kennedy "found the lowest-key time possible ... the night before he and country closed shop for the long Thanksgiving weekend"—and the same day that the president dramatically announced the end of the Cuban Missile Crisis. For supporters of the order, the low-profile announcement was less disappointing than its substance. Particularly bitter pills to swallow were the decisions not to cover FDIC-insured banks and not to cover existing housing stock. Essentially, the order covered only new homes built with loans guaranteed by the Federal Housing Authority or the Veterans Administration—roughly 2 percent of the nation's housing. Nobody felt much like celebrating the president's order.[102]

An action that had seemed so effortless—as easy as "a stroke of the presidential pen"—had turned into an excruciating political headache for the president. Kennedy quickly regretted ever uttering that phrase: "Who put those words in my mouth?" he was heard to grouse (Kennedy knew full well the culprit and directed that every pen sent to the White House in protest be forwarded to Harris Wofford's office).[103] In promising to resolve difficult social problems with a "stroke of the pen," Kennedy raised expectations about civil rights that he was unable to meet.[104] Having a pen did not mean that the president could rule unilaterally. Kennedy's own preferences were tightly constrained by bureaucratic processes, legal judgments, and the political preferences, power, and calculations of other elites, including those in Congress. Kennedy's experience with EO 11063 suggests that the real concern with presidents promising to rule by executive directive in the face of legislative gridlock is not that the nation will descend down a slippery slope of usurpation and dictatorship, but that the president's supporters will feel disillusioned and disappointed when the president struggles to deliver the promised outcome.

Reagan's Order That Never Was: The Failure to End Quotas

Affirmative action in employment can be traced to Executive Order 11246, issued by President Lyndon Johnson in an effort to implement the 1964 Civil Rights Act's prohibition on racial and gender discrimination in employment. The presidential order commanded government contractors to "take affirmative action to ensure that applicants are employed ... without regard to their race, color, religion, or national origin." In 1967, Johnson amended the order to include sex. What counted as affirmative action, however, was initially unclear. Admitting that there was no "fixed and firm definition of affirmative action," the director of the Office of Federal Contract Compliance told Congress that the best he could do was to "say in a general way [that] affirmative action is anything that you have to do to get results." Under President Richard Nixon, however, affirmative action was given a precise definition: it meant "specific goals and timetables" for hiring members of a minority group. Failure to have a workforce that approximated the racial composition of the company's geographic area was evidence of racial discrimination.[105]

The Nixon administration's orders were controversial from the moment they were unveiled. Members of Congress on both sides of the partisan aisle objected that Nixon's affirmative action program "was obliterating the boundaries of his constitutional powers, legislating on his own rather than enforcing congressional intent." Congressional opposition was bolstered by the comptroller general's determination that mandating goals and timetables violated the plain language and intent of Title VII of the Civil Rights Act, which prohibited discrimination on the basis of race. Yet despite widespread opposition, including vehement objections from southern Democrats and labor unions, Congress failed to overturn the administration's directives. Legislative inaction was interpreted by the courts as implicit authorization of executive action. In the name of deferring to Congress, the courts sanctioned presidential unilateralism.[106]

Affirmative action seems, at first look, to be a perfect example of the way in which presidents capitalize on their ability "to move first and act alone" to unilaterally shape public policy. But affirmative action also poses a puzzle for the unilateral presidency model. For if the model leads us to expect that the legislature and judiciary would struggle to overturn the Nixon administration directives, it also leads us to expect that a president opposed to federally mandated goals and timetables would have little difficulty ending affirmative action with the stroke of a pen. Yet when Ronald Reagan was elected president in 1980, no such order was forthcoming, even though candidate Reagan made no secret of his belief that "federal guidelines or quotas" distorted "the noble concept of equal opportunity" by requiring employers to use race and sex, "rather than ability and qualifications," as the main criteria in hiring decisions. Why, then, didn't Reagan use the power of the pen to abolish federally mandated racial preferences, as so many supporters urged him to—and so many opponents feared he would?[107]

Reagan's failure to act cannot be attributed to a change of heart. He remained as staunchly opposed to federally mandated goals and timetables on the day he left office as on the day he took office. Nor could Reagan have been deterred by public opinion, which by and large shared the president's skepticism about the use of racial preferences. After Reagan's landslide reelection in 1984, the time seemed especially ripe for the president to unilaterally enact his vision of "colorblind law" by ordering an end to federally mandated goals and timetables—or so argued Reagan's assistant attorney general for civil rights, William Bradford Reynolds.[108]

"With a stroke of a pen," Reynolds urged, the president should "replace [EO 11246] with one that makes clear that the federal government does not require, authorize or permit the use of 'goals', or any form of race or gender conscious preferential treatment by federal contractors." Reynolds had made the same pitch during Reagan's first term, but Attorney General William French Smith had resisted taking action. After the 1984 election, however, Reagan reshuffled his cabinet, replacing Smith with Edwin Meese, the president's most trusted advisor and a staunch critic of affirmative action, whose views closely mirrored the president's. Like Reagan, Meese believed that "the idea that you can use discrimination in the form of racially preferential quotas, goals, and set-asides to remedy the lingering social effects of past discrimination" was a "legal, moral, and constitutional tragedy." Meese made revision of EO 11246 a departmental priority. He authorized the drafting of a new executive order that eliminated the requirement that federal contractors must establish numerical goals for hiring racial minorities and women. The draft order also forbade the federal government from using statistical evidence to measure compliance with nondiscrimination laws.[109]

The new order seemed to comport closely with Reagan's own views. In a radio address in June 1985, the president warned against those "who, in the name of equality, would have us practice discrimination." These people, he said, had "turned our civil rights laws on their head, claiming they mean exactly the opposite of what they say." Following the Reynolds–Meese script, Reagan reminded the American people that "in 1980 and 1984 I ran for president and told you I was opposed to quotas. In response to your mandate, our administration has worked to return civil rights laws to their original meaning—to prevent discrimination against any and all Americans"—that is, not just African Americans or Latinos or women but white males as well.[110]

Not long after Reagan's speech, Meese presented the Justice Department's revision of EO 11246 to Chief of Staff Don Regan. The president would have liked nothing better than to sign the executive order that Meese and Reynolds had drawn up, yet that is not what happened. Instead the draft order sparked a bitter struggle within the administration, belying the notion that the president is a unitary actor who gets to "act alone."[111]

Leading the opposition to the draft order was Secretary of Labor William Brock, who was charged under EO 11246 with enforcing affirmative action for federal contractors. Brock rejected the Meese–Reynolds premise that hiring goals and timetables amounted to quotas and insisted that federally mandated goals and timetables were indispensable to combating racial discrimination. Brock's position was shared by a majority of Reagan's cabinet, including the influential Secretary of the Treasury James Baker and Secretary of State George Shultz, who, as Nixon's secretary of labor, had played a pivotal role in promulgating the order requiring federal contractors to provide "specific goals and timetables" in hiring.[112]

The administration tried to bridge the gap between Meese and Brock by forming a working group charged with coming up with a mutually acceptable compromise. The effort failed, leaving the White House Domestic Policy Council—chaired by Meese and consisting of seven other cabinet members with domestic policy portfolios—with the options of backing its chairman and recommending that the president issue an executive order rescinding the requirement that federal contractors employ goals and timetables, or backing Brock by recommending either that the president take no action or that he simply issue an executive order prohibiting federal contractors from using "quotas." Stymied by the conflicting views and opposing factions, the council was unable to decide on a course of action to recommend to the president.[113]

Brock's hand was strengthened by outside opposition to the Meese–Reynolds order that came not just from the civil rights community but from a core Republican constituency: big business. Over the previous decade, racial and gender goals and time-tables had become an integral part of corporate culture and procedures, which often included an "in-house affirmative action bureaucracy." Although the Meese–Reynolds order would have allowed companies to continue to use goals and timetables on a voluntary basis, the removal of the federal mandate risked exposing companies to lawsuits from white males who claimed reverse discrimination. To abandon goals and timetables would have exposed companies to other risks, including boycotts and protests from the civil rights community. It would also have jeopardized companies' ability to recruit and retain the kind of diverse workforce that executives increasingly viewed as a competitive strength. Fearing the disruption that the Meese–Reynolds order would cause to established ways of doing business, the National Association of Manufacturers (NAM) initiated a lobbying campaign to dissuade the president from signing the order.[114]

The stalemate within the Domestic Policy Council and the opposition of NAM and the civil rights community did not deter those within the administration who believed that Reagan should sign the Justice Department order. On February 12, 1986, the day after a frustrated Reagan admitted at a press conference that he was still awaiting a White House recommendation on how to amend affirmative action in employment, the Commission on Civil Rights' chairman, Clarence M. Pendleton, wrote directly to the president, urging him to sign the Justice Department order and "put the lingering debate about goals and timetables behind us, and permit all Americans to live, work, and be educated in a colorblind society free of discrimination." In Pendleton's view, the distinction that Brock and others tried to draw between quotas on the one hand and goals and timetables on the other was specious. "Goals and timetables," he declared, "mean quotas or they mean nothing." Pendleton concluded: "You can end [goals and timetables] and any other kind of government-sanctioned discrimination with a stroke of your pen. I urge you to do so immediately."[115]

Despite hitting a roadblock in the Domestic Policy Council, the Justice Department sent White House director of communications Pat Buchanan a public relations campaign to accompany the order that Meese still hoped Reagan would sign. Included among the materials sent to Buchanan was not only a presidential statement announcing the executive order revising EO 11246 but also the draft of a letter Reagan was to send to members of Congress, talking points for the media, and a White House letter to be sent to important newspaper editors. Each document made the case that Reagan's executive order was necessary to end the "government-mandated race and gender goals" that "invariably result in the very discrimination" that the Civil Rights Act of 1964 and EO 11246 intended to eliminate. "The executive order program," Reagan was to explain, "had been transformed into a bureaucratic maze where the search for numerical equivalency (or proportionality) has overtaken the only real, legitimate objective—that of ensuring equal opportunity for all individuals without regard to race or gender." The White House also prepared a national address for Reagan to deliver on the day before he issued the order that would set out the philosophical case against pursuing "color-conscious policies" to combat racism or "past injustice."[116]

The statement prepared by the Justice Department as well as the speech drafted by the White House reflected Reagan's deepest beliefs about civil rights. Yet the president never delivered the speech nor issued the statement. And he never signed the executive order revising EO 11246. Reagan's failure to issue the order frustrated many conservatives, who believed that overturning the Nixon-era orders should have been a straightforward matter of unilateral action, requiring no persuasion or bargaining or accommodation.[117] The reality, however, was that the president (and ultimately Meese too) decided that an executive order would come at too high a political price. The administration's worry was not so much that Congress might strike back by codifying the goals and timetables language—Reagan could veto any such legislation and Congress almost certainly could not have mustered the votes to override the veto. Instead the principal concern was that the order would divide and weaken the Republican Party and hurt the president's own political standing. Unable to fashion a compromise that would unite different factions within the administration and the party, the president and his advisors decided against direct executive action.[118]

The Reagan administration's failure to revise Executive Order 11246 provides a cautionary lesson regarding the "unilateral politics model"—particularly its assumption that executive directives enable the president to set policy "on their own" without bargaining and persuasion with rival views and interests.[119] The president's own policy preferences regarding affirmative action ultimately counted for little. He could not act alone because politically he could not afford to ignore the views of the business community and the civil rights community, as well as skeptical Republican leaders in Congress, such as Senate Majority Leader Bob Dole. Most important, he and his top aides could not ignore the divisions within his own administration. In short, Reagan did not revise EO 11246 because, contrary to the assumption of the unilateral politics model, the presidency is not a unitary actor.[120]

THE PARADOX OF THE MODERN PRESIDENCY: THE MULTILATERALISM OF UNILATERAL DIRECTIVES

"Stroke of the pen, law of the land. Kind of cool" is how, in 1998, Clinton aide Paul Begala memorably described the appeal of executive orders. What seems kind of cool to a lame-duck administration faced with a recalcitrant Congress understandably fills the president's opponents with alarm as they contemplate an unaccountable second-term president circumventing the normal political process to unilaterally enact his policy preferences. Both sides, though, are prone to exaggerate: executive directives are neither the panacea that the president's allies imagine nor the autocratic danger that the president's enemies fear.[121]

Both sides exaggerate because they assume that a presidential directive is a purely unilateral action, emanating from the president and commanding compliance with the president's will. But as Matthew Dickinson points out—and Reagan's failure to revise EO 11246 attests—the difference between administrative and legislative policymaking is generally not the difference between unilateral and multilateral policymaking; rather "it is a change in where, and with whom, bargaining takes place." A close examination of the formulation of executive orders shows "more consultation and less fiat" than is assumed by both critics and boosters of the unilateral presidency.[122]

Consider, for example, President Clinton's second-term executive order intended to protect children from "environmental health risks and safety risks"—that is, those risks to health and safety that are "attributable to products or substances that the child is likely to come in contact with or ingest (such as the air we breathe, the food we eat, the water we drink or use for recreation, the soil we live on, and the products we use or are exposed to)." Beginning from the premise that "a growing body of scientific knowledge" demonstrated that children "may suffer disproportionately" from such risks, Clinton directed each government agency to "make it a high priority to identify and assess" environmental health and safety risks to children and to "ensure that its policies, programs, activities, and standards address" the disproportionate risks faced by children.[123]

Issued on April 21, 1997, Executive Order 13045 seems a straightforward unilateral directive in which the president tells executive agencies what to do. But closer examination of the order shows that it reflected not so much the president's preferences as those of a particular federal agency: the Environmental Protection Agency (EPA). The order had its origins in an EPA effort to publicize environmental health risks to children. As part of that effort, EPA administrator Carol Browner proposed—in a memo addressed to 13 White House and cabinet officials—a "potential executive order" that would establish stricter regulatory standards commensurate with the "potentially heightened risks faced by children." The EPA subsequently drafted the order and (following standard procedures) sent it to the Office of Management and Budget, which then solicited feedback on the order from a broad array of affected agencies. While the draft order was circulating throughout the bureaucracy, Browner and other EPA officials lobbied the White House for support.[124]

Many agencies and offices raised concerns about the order. They worried about the practical difficulties of assessing the effects of a policy or program on children. They worried, too, that the order invited lawsuits, virtually putting a "kick-me sign" on the back of every agency that failed to adequately protect children. The Department of Health and Human Services, for instance, asked how the government could justify allowing tobacco to remain legal since smoking was so clearly detrimental to children's health. What ensued was an intensive round of negotiations over several months involving, among others, the Domestic Policy Council, the National Economic Council, the Council on Environmental Quality, and the Office of Science and Technology Policy. The order that resulted from the negotiations was significantly altered—"weakened," in the EPA's judgment—to accommodate the concerns of the various parties. In the revised order, agency compliance was demanded only "to the extent permitted by law and appropriate, and consistent with the agency's mission." Moreover, independent regulatory agencies were only "encouraged" to comply.

By the time the proposed order reached the president in mid-April, it had—as the accompanying decision memo noted—"been the subject of extensive discussion with affected agencies." Still, not everybody was happy. A few department heads now took their objections directly to the president. Clinton tried to act the peacemaker, asking for a few more changes "to ease [the] burden a bit" on the agencies. With those final changes, the executive order was at last issued.

The story of EO 13045 shows the flaws in the theoretical assumption that unilateral powers such as executive orders are distinguished by the president's ability "to move first and act alone." In reality, the "first mover" was not the president or the White House but EPA administrator Carol Browner—or, more probably, a few of her subordinates. And the president certainly did not act alone—in fact, he was barely involved in the process of formulating the order, a process that was intensely multilateral, involving at least 17 executive agencies and staff offices in the Executive Office of the President. On its face a unilateral command emanating from the president, EO 13045 was in reality the product of intensive bargaining and negotiation between rival bureaucratic interests and agendas.[125]

So how typical is EO 13045? Political scientist Andrew Rudalevige asked precisely that question in examining a random sample of 293 executive orders between the Truman and Reagan presidencies. His finding: more than six in ten executive orders resemble EO 13045 in originating outside the White House, in executive departments and agencies. Rudalevige also found that these orders are commonly "in response to congressional action, either because legislators requested an action or because they demanded it in statute." If one looks only at "significant" executive orders (an admittedly subjective measure), the percentage of executive orders originating in departments drops, but still constitutes a majority of executive orders. In many of these cases, Rudalevige suggests, what appears to be a presidential command may be better thought of as "White House ratification of what agencies wanted to do in the first place." And, of course, even when directives do emanate from the White House, they may be subject to extensive negotiation and bargaining with affected agencies and departments.[126]

If the provenance of executive orders highlights the multilateralism of formally unilateral directives, the implementation of those orders, which are by definition dependent on bureaucratic action, is even more likely to be characterized by multilateralism. The trouble with most studies of unilateral power is that they stop at the issuance of the order, apparently on the assumption that when agencies are told to "do this" or "do that," they will. More than a half-century ago, Richard Neustadt famously suggested that such an assumption was naïve: that in fact "nothing will happen" when the president issues an order to the bureaucracy. Neustadt exaggerated, but if EO 13045 is at all typical there is good reason to question how much an order will affect agencies' behavior. In the case of EO 13405, accommodating agency objections meant creating the loopholes that could be used to avoid compliance. Multilateralism in the directive's formulation begat multilateralism in the directive's implementation.[127]

The paradox of the modern presidency, then, is that, on the one hand, unilateral directives have become a defining, ubiquitous feature of presidential power. Particularly in an era of divided government and perpetual partisan gridlock, supporters of a president are increasingly prone to demand unilateral actions, just as a president's opponents are ever more vocal in deploring them. And yet, on the other hand, the same growth in the size and scope of the federal government that makes presidential directives more unavoidable and far-reaching increases the challenge of directing an anything-but-unitary executive branch that counts "nearly three million persons within its purview."[128]

The pluralism of views and interests within the executive branch does not mean that we should be unconcerned about excessive reliance on unilateral directives. The real problem with executive orders, however, may be less that they open the door to presidential dictatorship than that they produce polices that are unstable and short-term and sow administrative uncertainty and confusion. As we saw at the beginning of this chapter in the case of the Global Gag Rule, reliance on unilateral directives rather than legislation can produce dramatic swings in the law with each partisan change in the presidency. Lurching between opposing policies in this way undermines the ability of affected agencies, organizations, and individuals to plan intelligently for the future. Curtailing the exercise of unilateral powers might therefore promote more effective governance.

Signing Statements: Unilateral Power or Interbranch Dialogue?

Prior to the presidency of George W. Bush, few people paid much attention to signing statements—that is, statements presidents issue upon signing a law. Presidential scholars rarely researched their use and journalists largely ignored them. When thought of at all, signing statements tended to be regarded as largely symbolic or rhetorical—a chance for the president to praise those who made the law and to claim credit for its passage. During Bush's tenure, however, signing statements suddenly became a cause célèbre—exhibit A of the unilateral presidency run amok. Political science journals, law reviews, and op-ed columns filled up with analyses of signing statements—many positing that such statements subverted the constitutional order by enabling presidents to nullify statutory provisions and thereby rewriting laws to conform to the president's policy preferences.[129]

The most notorious Bush signing statement occurred upon the president's signing of a 2006 Department of Defense appropriations bill, which included a provision (the Detainee Treatment Act—a.k.a. the McCain Amendment) intended to forbid the torture of detainees captured in the "Global War on Terrorism." The administration lobbied vigorously against the amendment on the grounds that the interrogation of "enemy combatants" was a matter properly left to the commander in chief. Congress overwhelmingly rejected this argument; in the Senate, the amendment passed 90–9. Unable to stop the amendment from passing—or to prevent a veto override—Bush signed the law and issued a statement that in order to protect the American people from further terrorist attacks, he would interpret the torture ban "in a manner consistent with the constitutional authority of the President to supervise the unitary executive branch and as Commander in Chief." Bush's statement was widely condemned as lawless since he appeared to be reserving the right to disregard the law's restrictions on interrogation methods.[130]

Bush's aggressive use of signing statements prompted a scathing 2006 American Bar Association report that concluded that signing statements posed a "serious threat to the rule of law" and the separation of powers. During the 2008 campaign, both parties' presidential nominees pledged to eschew Bush's path. Republican nominee John McCain declared that he would "never, never, never, never" use a signing statement. If he disagreed with a law, he promised he would veto it, as the Constitution required. The Democratic nominee Barack Obama granted that signing statements had their place to "protect a president's constitutional prerogatives," but called it a "clear abuse of power" for presidents to use signing statements "to evade laws that the president does not like or as an end-run around provisions designed to foster accountability." Candidate Obama pledged that president Obama would not use signing statements "to nullify or undermine congressional instructions as enacted into law."[131]

Although intense public scrutiny of signing statements is relatively recent, their use can be traced all the way back to the nineteenth century. In 1830, for instance, Andrew Jackson signed an $8,000 appropriations bill to fund the surveying of a road to be built between Detroit and Chicago. Jackson had no objection to federal monies being used to construct roads in federal territories, and the greater part of the road would be within the federal territory of Michigan. However, to reach Chicago a small part of the road would have to pass through the states of Indiana and Illinois, and Jackson doubted that the Constitution gave the federal government the power to build federal roads in states. So along with the signed bill, Jackson sent Congress a statement declaring that he desired "to be understood as having approved this bill with the understanding that the road authorized by this section is not to be extended beyond the limits of the [Michigan] Territory."[132]

Jackson's daring statement was the exception, not the rule. The nineteenth-century custom was to have the president's private secretary orally notify Congress of a bill's signing. Presidents who departed from the custom courted congressional rebuke, as John Tyler discovered in 1842 when he issued a signing statement that communicated his "deep and strong doubts" about the constitutionality of a bill relating to the appor- tionment of congressional districts. Tyler was careful to stress that it was proper that his doubts must yield to the "solemnly pronounced opinion of the representatives of the people and of the States," and he pledged that his reservations about the constitutionality of the law would not affect his willingness to enforce it. Tyler's deferential language did little to mollify Congress. A House Select Committee report—authored by ex-president John Quincy Adams—condemned Tyler's statement as "a defacement of the public records and archives" and an "evil example for the future."[133]

If this overwrought congressional response to a relatively innocuous presidential state- ment was designed to deter future presidents from following Tyler's example, it seemed to have its desired effect. Up through the early twentieth century, signing statements remained relatively rare. Theodore Roosevelt, enamored as he was of a robust presidency, issued only one signing statement. Not until the 1930s and 1940s did signing statements begin to become commonplace. But while signing statements were common by the mid-twentieth century (Truman averaged 16 a year and Eisenhower 18) and were often used to castigate Congress (at least a third of Eisenhower's and Truman's signing statements criticized Congress for passing a flawed measure), they were generally not used to challenge the constitutionality of a law. Only about one in twenty of the more than 600 presidential signing statements issued between 1945 and 1974 raised constitutional objections to a bill.[134]

The mid-century pattern started to shift in the 1970s as Gerald Ford and Jimmy Carter confronted a "resurgent Congress" intent on clawing back power that legislators felt had been lost to the "imperial presidency" style of Lyndon Johnson and Richard Nixon. One of the ways Congress tried to reassert control over the executive branch was through greater use of the so-called "legislative veto," a procedure allowing a majority of one or both houses of Congress to "veto" an executive action if legislators disapprove of it. Ford and especially Carter often used signing statements to object to the legislative veto as an unconstitutional infringement on executive power—an argument that would ultimately be vindicated by the Supreme Court in 1983 in *I.N.S. v. Chadha*. But although Ford and Carter issued signing statements at an unprecedented rate, averaging nearly 60 a year, the great majority of their statements were still conventional rhetorical statements that praised or criticized Congress for passing a law, claimed credit for the legislation, or explained the legislation to the public. Only about one in eight of their signing statements raised constitutional challenges to the law they signed.[135]

Although Ford and Carter made greater use of signing statements than their predecessors, not until the Reagan presidency was there "a concerted effort to institutionalize and legitimize the use of presidential signing statements." Not that Reagan issued more signing statements than Carter and Ford; in fact, he issued considerably fewer. But Reagan's signing statements were far more likely—around three times as likely—to lodge constitutional objections to a law. In fact, in eight years Reagan issued roughly as many signing statements that raised constitutional objections as had been issued during the previous 200 years. The transformation was particularly marked during Reagan's second term when Attorney General Ed Meese spearheaded a Justice Department effort to make signing statements a more powerful tool of presidential power.[136]

The problem, as assistant deputy attorney general Samuel Alito expressed it in a February 1986 memo, was that courts and litigants, including executive branch lawyers, "invariably speak of 'legislative' or 'congressional' intent" rather than "the President's intent." In Alito's mind, this was unjust. "Since the President's approval is just as important as that of the House or Senate," he reasoned, "the President's understanding of the bill should be just as important as that of Congress." Alito suggested that courts focused on legislative intent rather than the president's intent in large part because Congress "churns out great masses of legislative history bearing on its intent—committee reports, floor debates, hearings," whereas presidents "created nothing comparable." Although presidents were strategically placed in the legislative process to "get the last word on questions of interpretation," Alito lamented that signing statements had failed to capitalize on this strategic advantage because they had generally been "little more than a press release." More developed and robust "interpretive signing statements," Alito argued, would help to redress the imbalance in the legislative record and thereby "increase the power of the executive to shape the law." As part of this effort to enhance the accessibility of signing statements to both lawyers and judges, Meese prevailed upon the publisher of the *United States Code Congressional and Administrative News* to include signing statements as part of its influential Legislative History section.[137]

The idea of using signing statements to "increase the power of the executive to shape the law" was heartily embraced by Reagan's successor, George Herbert Walker Bush. Faced with a Democratic-controlled Congress throughout his term, Bush relied heavily on signing statements to attempt to put his imprint on legislation. Bush issued as many signing statements in four years as Reagan did in eight. More striking, over half of Bush's statements (compared to about one-third of Reagan's) challenged the constitutionality of the law he had signed, typically on the grounds that some aspect of the law encroached on executive prerogatives.[138]

The Clinton administration, initially at least, was more restrained in its use of signing statements. Walter Dellinger, head of the Office of Legal Counsel (OLC), penned a memo at the outset of Clinton's term that refused to endorse (or reject) the Reagan–Bush agenda of using signing statements to create legislative history. However, Dellinger did accept that on "appropriate occasions" signing statements were a legitimate way for the president to inform Congress and the country that a provision in a law was unconstitutional and that it would therefore "not be given effect by the Executive Branch." Despite getting a green light on constitutional signing statements, Clinton initially used such statements far more sparingly than his predecessor, issuing in his first term less than one-quarter the number that Bush had. Indeed, in his first term Clinton issued fewer constitutional signing statements than Jimmy Carter. However, in his second term, facing a Republican-controlled Senate and House (just as Bush had faced a Democratic-controlled Senate and House), Clinton's behavior looked much more like Bush's than Carter's. In fact, in Clinton's last two years more than 50 percent of his signing statements (as opposed to 17 percent in his first term) voiced constitutional challenges to the legislation he signed.[139]

Viewed against the backdrop of the development of the preceding quarter-century, then, George W. Bush's use of signing statements was far from unprecedented. Indeed, Bush actually issued fewer signing statements annually (about 20) than any president since John F. Kennedy. Bush's father issued constitutional signing statements at nearly twice the rate of his son. What set George W. Bush apart, however, was that nearly four out of every five of his signing statements expressed constitutional objections to a law. Moreover, Bush's 125 constitutional signing statements challenged 1,200 specific clauses —twice the number of all previous presidents combined. In addition, Bush's constitutional signing statements tended to be sweeping and vague. For instance, a 2007 signing statement on an end-of-year government funding measure complained that this legislation "contains certain provisions similar to those found in prior appropriations bills passed by the Congress that might be construed to be inconsistent with my Constitutional responsibilities" and announced that "to avoid such potential infirmities the executive branch will interpret and construe such provisions in the same manner as I have previously stated in regard to similar provisions."[140]

Although Alito's 1986 memo is typically seen as having laid the groundwork for Bush's expansive use of signing statements, Bush's signing statement strategy bore little or no relation to the course that Alito recommended. The "principal objective" of the Meese Justice Department had been "to ensure that Presidential signing statements assume their rightful place in the interpretation of legislation," and Alito argued that the "first step" toward achieving that goal was "to convince the courts that presidential signing statements are valuable interpretive tools." To achieve that aim, Alito suggested, required statements that were "longer, more substantive, and more detailed." Bush's signing statements, in contrast, were typically brief but broad constitutional pronouncements of presidential authority backed with little or no detailed analysis of the statute—hardly the sort of statement calculated to persuade judges to regard them as "valuable interpretive tools."[141]

By sparking a political backlash against signing statements, moreover, the Bush administration set back the Reagan administration's goal of expanding the role of signing statements. We have already noted John McCain's pledge in 2008 never to issue a signing statement as president, but even Bush himself largely avoided using signing statements in his last year in office, issuing only five. Bush's successor Barack Obama averaged five signing statements a year, the lowest of any president since World War II.

It is less clear, though, that Obama's relatively restrained use of signing statements limited presidential power or advanced the rule of law. In 2009, for instance, Obama signed a State Department appropriations bill that included a provision forbidding department officials from participating in UN meetings presided over by nations designated by the government as sponsors of terrorism. Bush acquiesced in the same provision but, unlike Obama, issued a signing statement declaring that the provision infringed on the president's constitutional authority to conduct foreign relations and instructing the department to treat the law as advisory only. Although Obama did not object to this measure in a signing statement, he subsequently obtained an OLC opinion that came to the same conclusion as the Bush signing statement about the provision's unconstitutionality. The OLC memo also explicitly declared that department officials could "disregard" the law's restriction on attendance of UN meetings. And in both the Bush and Obama administrations, State Department officials did in fact defy the law by attending UN meetings chaired by a nation—Iran—that the government deemed a sponsor of terrorism.[142]

A case can be made that it is better for presidents to do as Bush did and use signing statements to publicly declare their constitutional objections to legislative provisions—at least so long as those statements are characterized (in the words of Obama's March 9 memo) by "sufficient specificity to make clear the nature and basis of the constitutional objection."[143] Unlike signing statements, OLC opinions are typically circulated within the executive branch and are not released to Congress or the public. Fewer signing statements may make for less rather than more accountability—particularly since signing statements have been found to increase congressional oversight in affected committees.[144] Certainly, the transparency and publicity that attaches to signing statements would seem preferable to presidents "resisting laws in silence."[145]

The main reason that fear of signing statements is at least "somewhat overblown" is, as Louis Fisher writes, that what matters most is not "what the President says at the time of a signing statement but what he does afterward." Although signing statements are often portrayed by critics as a de facto line-item veto that enables presidents to nullify those aspects of a law he disagrees with, signing statements do not in fact modify a law. Moreover, there is a world of difference between presidents claiming that a law is unconstitutional and refusing to comply with the law. One study found 93 signing statements between 1789 and 1981 that challenged the constitutionality of a law, but in only 12 of those cases (five in the Carter administration) was there evidence that the executive had disregarded the statute.[146]

Even in those cases where the words of the signing statement are followed up with actual executive noncompliance—and those cases have undeniably become more frequent over the past four decades—it is difficult to fault signing statements. As Ian Ostrander and Joel Sievert point out, "no study to date" has demonstrated a causal link. It seems more likely that noncompliance is caused not by the signing statement but by the conception of executive authority harbored by the president and his lawyers. "Blaming the signing statement for non-compliance," Ostrander and Sievert point out, is "akin to blaming the messenger for the content of a message."[147]

When presidents decline to enforce a law (or threaten not to enforce a law) it is not because of signing statements but because of OLC opinions that tell the president—as the OLC instructed Clinton in 1994—that he "has the authority to defend his office and decline to abide by [a law], unless he is convinced that the Court would disagree with his assessment." There seems no reason to believe that a world without signing statements would see less defiance of laws. If such defiance is a problem, it is due to the White House's dubious constitutional claims, not to the White House's reliance on signing statements to communicate those claims.[148]

Legal scholar Bruce Ackerman worries, though, that, precisely because signing statements are so public, they may have a deleterious effect on the way that the American people think about presidential power. Signing statements, Ackerman cautions, get "the general public in the habit of hearing presidents proclaim that they can take the briefest look at the Constitution and insist that Congress (and the rest of us) should treat their casual constitutional pronouncement with high seriousness." It is not clear, however, whether such pronouncements make the public more accepting (as Ackerman seems to fear) or more skeptical (as the backlash against Bush's statements might suggest) of executive aggrandizement.[149]

As we saw in the previous chapter and shall see again in subsequent chapters (specifically Chapters 8 and 10), presidents (and their lawyers) are certainly prone to make claims about the office's constitutional authority that are historically and legally suspect. However, it is difficult to see how abolishing signing statements would remedy this problem. Instead, there seems to be reason to credit the view that "if the President has decided to decline to enforce a statute because it's unconstitutional then it is much better that he tell the Congress and the public of his intentions, rather than keep it secret." In this way, "the checks and balances of the constitutional system can be set to work."[150] Viewed in this light, signing statements are better understood not as an instance of unilateral executive action but rather as part of a continuing dialogue—complete with a fair share of bluff and bluster—between the executive branch and Congress over their respective powers.[151]

NOTES

1 Public Law 93–189-December 17, 1973, www.govtrack.us/congress/bills/93/s1443/text. John Sharpless, "World Population Growth, Family Planning, and American Foreign Policy," in Donald T. Critchlow, ed., *The Politics of Abortion and Birth Control in Historical Perspective* (University Park, PA: Pennsylvania State Press, 1996), esp. 87–89.

2 This provision was Section 114, titled "Limiting Use of Funds for Abortions."

3 Sharpless, "World Population Growth, Family Planning, and American Foreign Policy," 95. Sneha Barot, "Abortion Restrictions in U.S. Foreign Aid: The History and Harms of the Helms Amendment," *Guttmacher Policy Review* (Summer 2013), 10, www.guttmacher.org/pubs/gpr/16/3/gpr160309.html.

4 Graham G. Dodds, *Take Up Your Pen: Unilateral Presidential Directives in American Politics* (Philadelphia: University of Pennsylvania Press, 2013), 5–6. Harold C. Relyea, "Presidential Directives: Background and Overview," Congressional Research Service Report for Congress, April 23, 2007.

5   Philip J. Cooper, *By Order of the President: The Use and Abuse of Executive Direct Action* (Lawrence: University Press of Kansas, 2002), 83–85, 81. Dodds, *Take Up Your Pen*, 7–8.

6   Dodds, *Take Up Your Pen*, 7. Cooper, *By Order of the President*, 118–19, 265 n3. Also see Kenneth R. Mayer, *With the Stroke of a Pen: Executive Orders and Presidential Power* (Princeton University Press, 2001), 34–35.

7   Dodds, *Take Up Your Pen*, 7–8. The count of proclamations is from Jeremy D. Bailey and Brandon Rottinghaus, "Reexamining the Unilateral Politics Model: Sources of Authority and the Power to Act Alone," paper delivered at the American Political Science Annual Meeting, September 2010, p. 15, at SSRN: http://ssrn.com/abstract=1643783; also see Jeremy D. Bailey and Brandon Rottinghaus, "The Development of Unilateral Power and the Problem of the Power to Warn: Washington through McKinley," *Presidential Studies Quarterly* (March 2013), 190. Bailey and Rottinghaus define "policy-based proclamations" as those relating directly to "government process, structure, or actions, including both international and domestic affairs."

8   Mayer, *With the Stroke of a Pen*, 34–36 (quotation at 34).

9   Courts' judgments about the legality of executive orders are often shaped by partisanship as much as legal principle. Each of the judges who voted to block Obama's immigration order (the district court judge, the two-judge majority at the appellate level, and four Supreme Court justices) were Republican appointees and each of the judges who voted to uphold the order (the dissenting appellate judge and four Supreme Court justices) were Democratic appointees.

10 William G. Howell, *Power without Persuasion: The Politics of Direct Presidential Action* (Princeton, NJ: Princeton University Press, 2003). Dodds, *Take Up Your Pen*, 12. The two studies referenced are Kenneth Mayer, "Executive Orders and Presidential Power," *Journal of Politics* (May 1999), 445–66 (at 448); and Terry M. Moe and William G. Howell, "The Presidential Power of Unilateral Action," *Journal of Law, Economics, and Organization* (1999), 132–79 (at 175).

11 Data on how often Congress is successful in overturning an executive order can be found in Dodds, *Take Up Your Pen*, 12.

12 Bush's executive order reinstated an order that was originally issued by his father George Herbert Walker Bush in 1992 (EO 12818) and repealed the following year by President Clinton (EO 12836). Obama repealed George W. Bush's order with Executive Order 13502.

13 See "Executive Orders: Washington–Trump," American Presidency Project, www.presidency.ucsb.edu/data/orders.php. Over his two terms, Obama issued 276 executive orders, marginally fewer than George W. Bush's 291, but substantially fewer than Clinton's 364 or Reagan's 381 orders. Carter issued 320 in just four years.

14 Dodds, *Take Up Your Pen*, 13. Richard E. Neustadt, *Presidential Power: The Politics of Leadership* (New York: John Wiley & Sons, 1960), 33.

15 Mayer, *With the Stroke of a Pen*, 70.

16 Mayer, *With the Stroke of a Pen*, 66–67. Dodds, *Take Up Your Pen*, 14–16.

17 Allan Nevins, *Grover Cleveland: A Study in Courage* (New York: Dodd, Mead, 1944), 359–60. Dodds, *Take Up Your Pen*, 99.

18 Although the total number of presidential proclamations continued to increase in the twentieth century, Bailey and Rottinghaus show that this increase is due entirely to the increase in what they code as symbolic proclamations. After the 1930s, the number of policy proclamations actually declined steadily and by the last decade of the twentieth century, there were only about 12 policy proclamations a year, which is lower than at any time since the 1880s. Whereas in the 1890s, 90 percent of proclamations were policy proclamations, by the 1990s 90 percent of proclamations were symbolic.

19 Dodds, *Take Up Your Pen*, 16.

20 Martin Van Buren, Special Session Message, September 4, 1837.

21 Donald B. Cole, *Martin Van Buren and the American Political System* (Princeton, NJ: Princeton University Press, 1984), 367. Arthur M. Schlesinger, Jr., *The Age of Jackson* (Boston: Little, Brown, 1945), 265n.

22 Schlesinger, *Age of Jackson*, 265.

23 Schlesinger, *Age of Jackson*, 266. "Ten Hour System," *Essex Gazette*, April 25, 1840.

24 Bailey and Rottinghaus, "Reexamining the Unilateral Politics Model," 19, 31 (table 1). Bailey and Rottinghaus, "The Development of Unilateral Power and the Problem of the Power to Warn," 201.

25 Dodds, *Take Up Your Pen*, 15. Bailey and Rottinghaus, "The Development of Unilateral Power and the Problem of the Power to Warn," 201.

26 U.S. Statutes at Large, 38th Cong., Sess. II, Ch. 90, pp. 507–09.

27 Eric Foner, *Reconstruction: America's Unfinished Revolution, 1863–1877* (New York: Harper & Row, 1988), 158.

28 Proclamation 134—Granting Amnesty to Participants in the Rebellion, with Certain Exceptions, May 29, 1865. Circular No. 13, July 28, 1865, National Archives and Records Administration, Record Group 105, Entry 24, No. 139, Asst Adjutant General Circulars 1865–1869, Bureau of Refugees, Freedmen, and Abandoned Lands, www.umbc.edu/che/resources/. Foner, *Reconstruction*, 159. Also see William S. McFeely, *Yankee Stepfather: General O.O. Howard and the Freedmen* (New Haven: Yale University Press, 1968), 103–06.

29 Foner, *Reconstruction*, 70–71, 159–160, 191. McFeely, *Yankee Stepfather*, 134. As much as a month prior to issuing Circular 15, which is dated September 12, 1865, Johnson had already directed Howard to restore property to individuals he had pardoned. See Endorsement re Berryman B. Leake, August 16, 1865, in Paul H. Bergeron, ed., *The Papers of Andrew Johnson* (Nashville: University of Tennessee Press, 1989), 8:603; also see McFeely, *Yankee Stepfather*, 128. Both directives are listed in Clifford Lord, ed., *List and Index of Presidential Executive Orders, Unnumbered Series, 1789–1941* (New Jersey Historical Records Survey, Work Projects Administration, 1943), 35–36.

30 Foner, *Reconstruction*, 161. Interview with Alexander K. McClure (ca. October 31, 1865), in *Papers of Andrew Johnson*, 9:310.

31 Foner, *Reconstruction*, 142. Also see Martin Abbott, *The Freedmen's Bureau in South Carolina, 1865–1872* (Chapel Hill: University of North Carolina Press, 1967), 133. On Johnson's hostility toward the Freedmen's Bureau, see his Freedmen's Bureau Veto Message, February 19, 1866, in *Papers of Andrew Johnson*, 10:120–27.

32 Karen Orren and Stephen Skowronek, *The Search for American Political Development* (New York: Cambridge University Press, 2003), 159. Brian Balogh, *A Government Out of Sight: The Mystery of National Authority in Nineteenth Century America* (New York: Cambridge University Press, 2009), 179. Also see Kristina Alexander and Ross W. Gorte, "Federal Land Ownership: Constitutional Authority and the History of Acquisition, Disposal, and Retention," Congressional Research Service Report for Congress, December 3, 2007.

33 Leonard D. White, *The Jeffersonians: A Study in Administrative History, 1801–1829* (New York: Macmillan, 1951), 513–14. Daniel Feller, *The Public Lands in Jacksonian Politics* (Madison: University of Wisconsin Press, 1984), 27. Act of April 24, 1820, ch. 51, 3 *Stat.* 567.

34 Act of May 29, 1830, ch. 208, 4 *Stat.* 421. Act of September 4, 1841, ch. 16, 5 *Stat.* 456. The 1841 act made the law permanent, until it was repealed in 1891. On the politics surrounding the passage of the 1830 preemption law, see Feller, *Public Lands in Jacksonian Politics*, 126–31.

35 Alexandra Usher, "Public Schools and the Original Federal Land Grant Program" (Center on Education Policy, 2011), esp. 22–23. Charles F. Wheatley, Jr., *Study of Withdrawals and Reservations of Public Lands*, Prepared for the Public Land Law Review Commission, 1969, 60.

36 Wheatley, *Study of Withdrawals and Reservations*, 57.

37 Wheatley, *Study of Withdrawals and Reservations*, 56, 59–60.

38 Balogh, *A Government Out of Sight*, 209. Glendon A. Schubert, Jr., *The Presidency in the Courts* (Minneapolis: University of Minnesota Press, 1957), 85.

39 *Wilcox v. Jackson* 38 U.S. 498 (1839). Also see Schubert, *Presidency in the Courts*, 67, and Dodds, *Take Up Your Pen*, 73.

40 *Wilcox v. Jackson*. Also see Wheatley, *Study of Withdrawals and Reservations*, 78–79.

41 *Grisar v. McDowell*, 73 U.S. 363 (1869). Also see Schubert, *Presidency in the Courts*, 68, and Dodds, *Take Up Your Pen*, 74. The Court provided no examples of land "set apart for public uses," but among the early executive orders withdrawing public lands for military installations are Fort Gratiot and Fort Howard (by John Quincy Adams) and Fort Brooke, Appalachicola Arsenal, Fort Jessup, Fort Winnebago, and Fort Wilkins (by Andrew Jackson). See Lord, ed., *List and Index of Presidential Executive Orders, Unnumbered Series*, 4–5.

42 *U.S. v. Leathers* 26 F. Cas. 897 (D. Nev. 1879) (No. 15,581), https://law.resource.org/pub/us/case/reporter/F.Cas/0026.f.cas/0026.f.cas.0897.html. Dodds, *Take Up Your Pen*, 76. Schubert, *Presidency in the Courts*, 85–86. A measure of the informality of nineteenth-century executive orders was that Grant's order was "inscribed upon a diagram purporting to be a map of the Pyramid Lake Indian reservation."

43 Dodds, *Take Up Your Pen*, 75–76.

44 The ambiguity in the language of *Grisar* is stressed in Wheatley, *Study of Withdrawals and Reservations*, 74–77.

45 Benjamin Horace Hibbard, *A History of the Public Land Policies* (Madison: University of Wisconsin Press, 1965; orig. pub. 1924), 529, 531.

46 Homer E. Socolofsky and Allan B. Spetter, *The Presidency of Benjamin Harrison* (Lawrence: University Press of Kansas, 1987), 70–72. The 1891 act included a repeal of the Preemption Act of 1841.

47 Socolofsky and Spetter, *Presidency of Benjamin Harrison*, 71–72.

48 Socolofsky and Spetter, *Presidency of Benjamin Harrison*, 72. Hibbard, *A History of the Public Land Policies*, 530. Anne R. Ashmore, *Presidential Proclamations concerning Public Lands: January 24, 1791–March 19, 1936: Numerical List and Index* (Washington, DC: Library of Congress Law Library, 1981), 15–16.

49 Charles F. Wilkinson, *Crossing the Next Meridian: Land, Water, and the Future of the West* (Washington, DC: Island Press, 1992), 123–24. Dodds, *Take Up Your Pen*, 100. Socolofsky and Spetter, *Presidency of Benjamin Harrison*, 73. Hibbard, *A History of the Public Land Policies*, 530. Ashmore, *Presidential Proclamations Concerning Public Lands*, 16. The forest reserves established by Cleveland's "Washington's Birthday Reserves" were "San Jacinto and Stanislaus in California; Uintah in Utah; Mt. Rainier (renamed from Pacific and enlarged) and Olympic in Washington; Bitter Root, Lewis and Clark, and Flathead in Montana; Black Hills in South Dakota; Priest River in Idaho; and the Teton and Big Horn in Wyoming." Gerald W. Williams, *The USDA Forest Service: The First Century* (Washington, DC: USDA Forest Service, 2005).

50 Wilkinson, *Crossing the Next Meridian*, 124. Williams, *The USDA Forest Service*. Act of June 4, 1897, ch. 2 *Stat.* 36.

51 The forest reserves that McKinley enlarged were Pine Mountain and Prescott (both established by McKinley), Pecos River and Trabuco Canyon (established by Harrison), and Big Horn, Black Hills, and Cascade Forest (established by Cleveland).

52 Dodds, *Take Up Your Pen*, 146. Also see Theodore Morris, *Theodore Rex* (New York: Random House, 2001), 485–87; and Lewis Gould, *The Presidency of Theodore Roosevelt* (Lawrence: University Press of Kansas, 1991), 203–04. Following Morris (487), Dodds counts 21 new forest reserves and 11 enlarged ones, but this is wrong. Of the reserves listed by Morris, nine

already existed at the time of Roosevelt's March proclamations. My own count, derived from the proclamations listed in Appendix I in Richard C. Davis, *Encyclopedia of American Forest and Conservation History* (New York: Macmillan, 1983) and Ashmore, *Presidential Proclamations concerning Public Lands*, 21–22, indicates that Roosevelt's proclamations created more like a dozen new national forests and expanded 20.

53 Roosevelt to George Otto Trevelyan, June 19, 1908, in H.W. Brands, ed., *The Selected Letters of Theodore Roosevelt* (New York, NY: Cooper Square Press, 2001), 491. Dodds, *Take Up Your Pen*, 147, 151.

54 Dodds, *Take Up Your Pen*, 147. Memorandum, March 2, 1907, in Elting E. Morison, ed., *The Letters of Theodore Roosevelt* (Cambridge, MA: Harvard University Press, 1952), 5:604.

55 Theodore Roosevelt, *An Autobiography* (New York: Scribner's, 1913), 357, 363.

56 William Howard Taft, *The President and His Powers* (New York: Columbia University Press, 1916), 140, 144.

57 Both men expressed these views while in office. See Taft's letter to William Kent, June 29, 1909, quoted in Henry F. Pringle, *The Life and Times of William Howard Taft* (New York: Farrar & Rinehart, 1939), 480, 481; also see Lewis L. Gould, *The Presidency of William Howard Taft* (Lawrence: University Press of Kansas, 2009), 45–46. On Roosevelt, see his letter to Trevelyan, June 19, 1908, in Brands, *Selected Letters of Theodore Roosevelt*, 491.

58 This count of proclamations is derived from Ashmore, *Presidential Proclamations concerning Public Lands*, 12–13, and data provided by Jeremy Bailey and Brandon Rottinghaus.

59 Hibbard, *History of Public Land Policies*, 508. Elmo R. Richardson, *The Politics of Conservation: Crusades and Controversies, 1897–1913* (Berkeley: University of California Press, 1962), 61. Pringle, *Life and Times of William Howard Taft*, 481.

60 Hibbard, *History of Public Land Policies*, 508. Gifford Pinchot, *Breaking New Ground* (New York: Harcourt, Brace, 1947), 328–29, 332–33. *Preliminary Report of the Inland Waterways Commission, 60th Congress*, 1st session, Document No. 325 (Washington: Government Printing Office, 1908), iii–vii (Message of the President, February 26, 1908).

61 Pinchot, *Breaking New Ground*, 388. Also see Roosevelt's Memorandum, March 2, 1907, *Letters of Theodore Roosevelt*, 5:604.

62 Taft to Hulbert Taft, May 12, 1909, in Pringle, *Life and Times of William Howard Taft*, 481. Taft also issued many executive orders withdrawing land for coal, potash, and phosphate reserves as well as reservoirs.

63 Dodds, *Take Up Your Pen*, 148. The count of monuments created by executive action is from National Parks Conservation Association, Factsheet: List of Proclaimed National Monuments.

64 The "executive coup" quotation is from Morris, *Theodore Rex*, 519. Although Roosevelt's order is commonly credited with creating the first federal wildlife refuge, Michael J. Bean suggests that President Benjamin Harrison "may in fact deserve that distinction" for his 1892 proclamation reserving Alaska's Afognak Island (*The Evolution of National Wildlife Law* [New York: Praeger, 1983], 22 n59).

65 Robert L. Fischman, *The National Wildlife Refuges: Coordinating a Conservation System through Law* (Washington, DC: Island Press, 2003), 35. This exchange is repeated in different forms in many Roosevelt biographies. See, for example, Morris, *Theodore Rex*, 519; William Henry Harbaugh, *Power and Responsibility: The Life and Times of Theodore Roosevelt* (New York: Octagon Books, 1975), 315; and Lewis Gould, *Presidency of Theodore Roosevelt*, 111. The likely apocryphal character of the exchange is acknowledged in "Where the Wild Things Are," *Smithsonian Magazine* (March 2003).

66 Pelican Island was created on March 14, 1903. The only other bird reserve that Roosevelt created in his first term was on Breton Island off the coast of Louisiana (October 4, 1904). The

following year he created a reserve at Stump Lake in North Dakota (March 9, 1905) and then established three reserves (Huron Islands and Siskiwit Islands in Michigan and Passage Key in Florida) on October 10, 1905. A bird reserve at Indian Key in Florida was created on February 10, 1906. See the *Report of the Acting Chief of the Bureau of Biological Survey for 1906* (Washington: Government Printing Office, 1906), 15; this and the other Bureau of Biological Survey reports cited below are available at the Biodiversity Heritage Library, www. biodiversitylibrary.org. The Game and Bird Preserve Act was passed on June 28, 1906.

67   *Report of the Chief of the Bureau of Biological Survey for 1905* (Washington: Government Printing Office, 1905), 310. Roosevelt, *Autobiography*, 421; compare Morris, *Theodore Rex*, 519; and James M. Strock, *Theodore Roosevelt on Leadership: Executive Lessons from the Bully Pulpit* (New York: Three Rivers Press, 2001), 243. Roosevelt's executive order (No. 1038) establishing the Fire Island Reservation is printed in the Bureau of Biological Survey—Circular No. 71, issued April 11, 1910.

68   Report of Chief of the Bureau of Biological Survey, September 15, 1913, in *Annual Reports of the Department of Agriculture for 1913* (Washington: Government Printing Office, 1913), 8. Pringle, *Life and Times of William Howard Taft*, 478.

69   *United States v. Midwest Oil Co.* 236 U.S. 459 (1915). Unless otherwise noted, all information and quotations in this section are from the opinions in this case.

70   William Howard Taft, Special Message, January 14, 1910. Wheatley, *Study of Withdrawals and Reservations*, 88.

71   The Wilson administration did advance the argument that "It is entirely logical to infer the power [of withdrawal] out of the Constitution, from the very necessity for its existence and from the functions of the President in our Government" (Brief for Appellant, quoted in Wheatley, *Study of Withdrawals and Reservations*, 146), but the Court declined to follow the government's invitation to rule on whether the president had an inherent, constitutionally based withdrawal power. The Court took the view that it "need not consider whether, as an original question, the President could have withdrawn from private acquisition what Congress had made free and open to occupation and purchase" because the case could be decided on narrower grounds and from "the legal consequences flowing from a long continued practice to make orders like the one here involved." The question of whether the president had an inherent, nonstatutory power to withdraw public lands was the focus of intense argument within Franklin Delano Roosevelt's administration in 1940–1941. Initially, Attorney General Robert Jackson answered the question in the negative, but strong criticisms of the attorney general's opinion by others in the administration led Jackson to reverse course and provide an affirmative answer. See Wheatley, *Study of Withdrawals and Reservations*, esp. 108–20.

72   Wheatley, *Study of Withdrawals and Reservations*, 82, 88–89. Taft, Special Message, January 14, 1910.

73   Taft to William Kent, June 29, 1909, Pringle, *Life and Times of William Howard Taft*, 481. So long as Congress could mobilize majorities, however, it retained the power to check unilateral directives. In June 1919, for instance, the Republican-controlled Congress flexed its political muscle by tacking on to an appropriations act a rider that provided no public lands could be withdrawn "by Executive Order, proclamation, or otherwise for or as an Indian reservation." And in 1927, Congress went still further by forbidding the president from making any changes to the boundaries of an Indian reservation. Schubert, *Presidency in the Courts*, 96 n32, 98 n64.

74   On the controversy surrounding the national monument proclamations of FDR, Carter, and Clinton, see Dodds, *Take Up Your Pen*, 167–68, 211, 213. My count of the percentage of public land proclamations is derived from data in Ashmore, *Presidential Proclamations concerning Public Lands*, 12–13. Also see Mayer, *With the Stroke of a Pen*, 75–76.

75   Adam L. Warber, *Executive Orders and the Modern Presidency: Legislating from the Oval Office* (Boulder, CO: Lynne Rienner, 2006), 108. Lyn Ragsdale, *Vital Statistics on the Presidency:*

Washington to Clinton (Washington, DC: CQ Press, 1996), 340–41. Cooper, *By Order of the President*, 18. Butler Shaffer, *In Restraint of Trade: The Business Campaign against Competition, 1918–1938* (Cranbury, NJ: Associated University Presses, 1997), 115.

76 Mayer, *With the Stroke of a Pen*, 68–69.

77 Dodds, *Take Up Your Pen*, 183–84. Mayer, *With the Stroke of a Pen*, 69.

78 Dodds, *Take Up Your Pen*, 182–83. Mayer, *With the Stroke of a Pen*, 66–68.

79 Dodds, *Take Up Your Pen*, 185. Mayer, *With the Stroke of a Pen*, 69–70 (quoting a March 1934 Treasury Department legal memorandum).

80 Mayer, *With the Stroke of a Pen*, 69. Also see Warber, *Executive Orders and the Modern Presidency*, 107.

81 Dodds, *Take Up Your Pen*, 220–21. Mayer, *With the Stroke of a Pen*, 74. The decline in executive orders in Roosevelt's last years was also due to an executive order on April 24, 1943, in which FDR "delegated his authority to withdraw and manage public lands to the secretary of the interior." As a result, the average annual number of executive orders relating to public lands dropped from about one hundred to closer to a half dozen (Mayer, *With the Stroke of a Pen*, 75).

82 Cooper, *By Order of the President*, 40. "Dictatorship: The Road Not Taken," www.fdrlibrary. marist.edu/archives/pdfs/dictatorship.pdf.

83 Martin L. Fausold, *The Presidency of Herbert C. Hoover* (Lawrence: University Press of Kansas, 1985), 233. Amos Kiewe, *FDR's First Fireside Chat: Public Confidence and the Banking Crisis* (College Station: Texas A&M University Press, 2007), 43–44.

84 George McJimsey, *The Presidency of Franklin Delano Roosevelt* (Lawrence: University Press of Kansas, 2000), 293.

85 Executive Order No. 6102, April 5, 1933. Also see Dodds, *Take Up Your Pen*, 163.

86 Dodds, *Take Up Your Pen*, 163–64. Edward S. Corwin, *The President: Office and Powers, 1787–1957* (New York University Press, 1957), 127.

87 Ira Katznelson, *Fear Itself: The New Deal and the Origins of Our Times* (New York: Liveright, 2013), 20, 151.

88 Mayer, *With the Stroke of a Pen*, 186–88. Dodds, *Take Up Your Pen*, 166.

89 Mayer, *With the Stroke of a Pen*, 187–88. Franklin D. Roosevelt, "Executive Order 8802—Reaffirming Policy of Full Participation in the Defense Program by All Persons, Regardless of Race, Creed, Color, or National Origin, and Directing Certain Action in Furtherance of Said Policy," June 25, 1941.

90 Mayer, *With the Stroke of a Pen*, 189–90. Franklin D. Roosevelt: "Executive Order 9346 Establishing a Committee on Fair Employment Practice," May 27, 1943.

91 James T. Patterson, *Grand Expectations: The United States, 1945–1974* (New York: Oxford University Press, 1996), 20, 23.

92 Howell, *Power without Persuasion*, 56–57.

93 Mayer, *With the Stroke of a Pen*, 191.

94 Howell, *Power without Persuasion*, 57.

95 Mayer, *With the Stroke of a Pen*, 190, 192, 193. Dodds, *Take Up Your Pen*, 198–99. The Truman quote is from an interview in the summer of 1953, according to a story ("How Fort Jackson Was Integrated in 1952") in the *Philadelphia Tribune*, July 10, 1990.

96 Mayer, *With the Stroke of a Pen*, 194. Also see Robert Frederick Burt, *The Eisenhower Administration and Black Civil Rights* (Knoxville: University of Tennessee Press, 1984).

97 Dodds, *Take Up Your Pen*, 200. Mayer, *With the Stroke of a Pen*, 195. Speech of Senator John F. Kennedy, National Conference on Constitutional Rights and American Freedom, Park-Sheraton Hotel, New York, NY, October 12, 1960.

98 Mayer, *With the Stroke of a Pen*, 197. Irving Bernstein, *Promises Kept: John Kennedy's New Frontier* (New York: Oxford University Press, 1991), 47–49.

99   Andrew Rudalevige, "Executive Orders and Presidential Unilateralism," *Presidential Studies Quarterly* (March 2012), 148–49.

100 Bernstein, *Promises Kept*, 52. Mayer, *With the Stroke of a Pen*, 198–99.

101 Mayer, *With the Stroke of a Pen*, 198–99. Bernstein, *Promises Kept*, 51–52.

102 Bernstein, *Promises Kept*, 52. Mayer, *With the Stroke of a Pen*, 200–01.

103 Bernstein, *Promises Kept*, 51. Mayer, *With the Stroke of a Pen*, 198.

104 In an article in the *Nation* published immediately after Kennedy's election, Martin Luther King, Jr., wrote: "It is no exaggeration to say that the president could give segregation a death blow through a stroke of the pen" (Mayer, *With the Stroke of a Pen*, 8).

105 Mayer, *With the Stroke of a Pen*, 203–04. Robert R. Detlefsen, "Affirmative Action and Business Deregulation: On the Reagan Administration's Failure to Revise Executive Order No. 11246," in James W. Riddlesperger, Jr., and Donald W. Jackson, eds., *Presidential Leadership and Civil Rights Policy* (Westport, CT: Greenwood Press, 1995) 63–64. The "affirmative action" language in EO 11246 was taken verbatim from President Kennedy's 1961 Executive Order 10925.

106 Ricardo Jose Pereira Rodrigues, *The Preeminence of Politics: Executive Orders from Eisenhower to Clinton* (New York: LFB Scholarly Publishing, 2007), 61–62. J. Larry Hood, "The Nixon Administration and the Revised Philadelphia Plan for Affirmative Action: A Study in Expanding Presidential Power and Divided Government," *Presidential Studies Quarterly* (Winter 1993), 152. Mayer, *With the Stroke of a Pen*, 205–06. The Nixon administration orders took the form of directives from the secretary of labor, who was charged under EO 11246 with enforcing compliance with the order.

107 Howell, *Power without Persuasion*, 15. Rodrigues, *The Preeminence of Politics*, 75, 85. Also see Nicholas Laham, *The Reagan Presidency and the Politics of Race: In Pursuit of Colorblind Justice and Limited Government* (Westport, CT: Praeger, 1998), 19; and Herman Belz, *Equality Transformed: A Quarter Century of Affirmative Action* (New Brunswick, NJ: Transaction Publishers, 1991), 181.

108 On Reagan's commitment to "colorblind law," see Laham, *The Reagan Presidency and the Politics of Race*, esp. chapter 4.

109 Terry Eastland, *Energy in the Executive: The Case for the Strong Presidency* (New York: Free Press, 1992), 355–56 n12. Laham, *The Reagan Presidency and the Politics of Race*, 23; also see 22–24, 26; and Detlefsen, "Affirmative Action and Business Deregulation," 66.

110 Laham, *The Reagan Presidency and the Politics of Race*, 73–74.

111 Laham, *The Reagan Presidency and the Politics of Race*, 23.

112 Laham, *The Reagan Presidency and the Politics of Race*, 26–27, 69, 222 n47.

113 Laham, *The Reagan Presidency and the Politics of Race*, 30, 77.

114 Detlefsen, "Affirmative Action and Business Deregulation," 67–68.

115 Laham, *The Reagan Presidency and the Politics of Race*, 77, 36.

116 Laham, *The Reagan Presidency and the Politics of Race*, 77, 85, 82, 79.

117 In *Dead Right* (New York: Basic Books, 1994), for instance, David Frum fumes that "at any moment in his presidency [Reagan] could have abolished the noxious thing [affirmative action] with a few signatures" (72).

118 Laham, *The Reagan Presidency and the Politics of Race*, 68–71, 124–25. Compare Eastland, *Energy in the Executive*, 356 n12.

119 Compare Howell, *Power without Persuasion*, 15.

120 The point is not that Reagan was powerless to affect affirmative action policy. But Reagan's greatest impact on the use of racial preferences came not through direct action—the stroke of a pen—but via the indirect route of judicial appointments. Judicial selection in the Reagan administration is discussed in Chapter 9.

121 Dodds, *Take Up Your Pen*, 5.

122   Matthew J. Dickinson, "We All Want a Revolution: Neustadt, New Institutionalism and the Future of Presidency Research," *Presidential Studies Quarterly* (December 2009), 757. Rudalevige, "Executive Orders and Presidential Unilateralism,"142.

123   Rudalevige, "Executive Orders and Presidential Unilateralism," 142. William J. Clinton, "Executive Order 13045—Protection of Children from Environmental Health Risks and Safety Risks," April 21, 1997.

124   The account of the formulation of EO 13045 in this and the subsequent paragraphs is taken from Rudalevige, "Executive Orders and Presidential Unilateralism," 142–44.

125   The quotations are from Howell, *Power without Persuasion*, 15.

126   Rudalevige, "Executive Orders and Presidential Unilateralism," 152–55.

127   Rudalevige, "Executive Orders and Presidential Unilateralism," 156–57. Richard E. Neustadt, *Presidential Power: The Politics of Leadership* (New York: John Wiley & Sons, 1960), 9.

128   Rudalevige, "Executive Orders and Presidential Unilateralism," 141, 145, 157.

129   Ian Ostrander and Joel Sievert, "What's So Sinister about Presidential Signing Statements," *Presidential Studies Quarterly* (March 2013), 59. Compare Philip J. Cooper, "George W. Bush, Edgar Allan Poe, and the Use and Abuse of Presidential Signing Statements," *Presidential Studies Quarterly* (September 2005), 516.

130   Ostrander and Sievert, "What's So Sinister about Presidential Signing Statements?" 63. Charles Savage, "Bush Could Bypass New Torture Ban," *Boston Post*, January 4, 2006.

131   Michael Abramowitz, "On Signing Statements, McCain Says 'Never,' Obama and Clinton 'Sometimes,'" *Washington Post*, February 25, 2008. American Bar Association, Task Force on Presidential Signing Statements and the Separation of Powers Doctrine, 2006, p. 20.

132   Andrew Jackson, "Special Message," May 30, 1830.

133   Christopher N. May, "Presidential Defiance of 'Unconstitutional' Laws: Reviving the Royal Prerogative," *Hastings Constitutional Law Quarterly* (1993–1994), 929–30. Christopher S. Kelley, "The Significance of the Presidential Signing Statement," in Christopher S. Kelley, ed., *Executing the Constitution: Putting the President Back into the Constitution* (Albany: State University of New York Press, 2006), 75. John Tyler, "Special Message," June 25, 1842.

134   May, "Presidential Defiance of 'Unconstitutional' Laws," 930–31. Richard S. Conley, "The Harbinger of the Unitary Executive? An Analysis of Presidential Signing Statements from Truman to Carter," *Presidential Studies Quarterly* (September 2011), 549, 554.

135   Conley, "The Harbinger of the Unitary Executive," 554. Kelley, "The Significance of the Presidential Signing Statement," 77. May, "Presidential Defiance of 'Unconstitutional' Laws," 931. Johnson and Nixon also used signing statements to object to the legislative veto: see Kevin E. Evans, "Looking before Watergate: Foundations in the Development of the Constitutional Challenges with Signing Statements, FDR–Nixon," *Presidential Studies Quarterly* (June 2012), 390–405.

136   Ostrander and Sievert, "What's So Sinister about Presidential Signing Statements?" 62. May, "Presidential Defiance of 'Unconstitutional' Laws," 931.

137   Samuel Alito to the Litigation Strategy Working Group, February 5, 1986, www.archives.gov/files/news/samuel-alito/accession-060-89-269/Acc060-89-269-box6-SG-LSWG-AlitotoLSWG-Feb1986.pdf. Cooper, *By Order of the President*, 203. Kelley, "The Significance of the Presidential Signing Statement," 79.

138   May, "Presidential Defiance of 'Unconstitutional' Laws," 931. Christopher Kelley and Bryan W. Marshall, "The Last Word: Presidential Power and the Role of Signing Statements," *Presidential Studies Quarterly* (June 2008), 260.

139   Walter Dellinger to Bernard N. Nussbaum, Re: Presidential Signing Statements, November 3, 1993, http://scholarship.law.duke.edu/cgi/viewcontent.cgi?article=2177&context=faculty_scholarship. Kelley and Marshall, "The Last Word," 260.

140 Kelley and Marshall, "The Last Word," 260. Conley, "The Harbinger of the Unitary Executive," 547. George W. Bush, "Statement on Signing the Consolidated Appropriations Act, 2008," December 26, 2007.

141 Alito to the Litigation Strategy Working Group, 1–2, 4.

142 Charles Savage, "Ignoring a Law on Foreign Relations," *New York Times*, September 15, 2009. Charles Savage, "Obama Takes New Route to Opposing Parts of Laws," *New York Times*, January 8, 2010.

143 Barack Obama, Memorandum for the Heads of Executive Departments and Agencies (Subject: Presidential Signing Statements), March 9, 2009. Presidents can also communicate their views on the constitutionality of legislation through Statements of Administration Policy (SAP), which are produced by the Office of Management and Budget and outline the administration's position on pending legislation. See Laura L. Rice, "Statements of Power: Presidential Use of Statements of Administration Policy and Signing Statements in the Legislative Process," *Presidential Studies Quarterly* (December 2010), 692. As Ostrander and Sievert point out, "many statements of administration policy read like presidential signing statements with similar language and objections raised" ("What's So Sinister about Presidential Signing Statements?" 76), but such statements do not receive anything like the publicity that signing statements do, which is part of their attraction to the White House. See Todd Garvey, "The Obama Administration's Evolving Approach to the Signing Statement," *Presidential Studies Quarterly* (June 2011), 393–407.

144 For evidence that signing statements spur congressional oversight, see Scott H. Ainsworth, Brian M. Harward, and Kenneth W. Moffett, "Congressional Response to Presidential Signing Statements," *American Politics Research* (November 2012), 1067–91. This research suggests that signing statements, contra Kelley and Marshall, do not necessarily give the president a "last-move advantage" ("The Last Word," 255).

145 Ostrander and Sievert, "What's So Sinister about Presidential Signing Statements?" 76.

146 Louis Fisher, *Constitutional Conflicts between Congress and the President* (Lawrence: University Press of Kansas, 2007; fifth edition), 124. May, "Presidential Defiance of 'Unconstitutional' Laws," 937. Ostrander and Sievert, "What's So Sinister about Presidential Signing Statements?" 66–67.

147 Ostrander and Sievert, "What's So Sinister about Presidential Signing Statements?" 65, 68–69.

148 Andrew Rudalevige, *The New Imperial Presidency: Renewing Presidential Power after Watergate* (Ann Arbor: University of Michigan Press, 2005), 177.

149 Bruce Ackerman, *The Decline and Fall of the American Republic* (Cambridge: Harvard University Press, 2010), 91.

150 David Barron et al., "Untangling the Debate on Signing Statements," Georgetown Law Faculty Blog, July 31, 2006, http://gulcfac.typepad.com/georgetown_university_law/2006/07/thanks_to_the_p.html. This statement was crafted as a response to the 2006 ABA report and was co-signed by six legal scholars, each of whom served in the Office of Legal Counsel during the Clinton administration.

151 Ostrander and Sievert, "What's So Sinister about Presidential Signing Statements?" Compare Jeffrey Crouch, Mark J. Rozell, Mitchel A. Sollenberger, "President Obama's Signing Statements and the Expansion of Executive Power," *Presidential Studies Quarterly* (December 2013), 883–99.

THE PRESIDENT AND THE EXECUTIVE BRANCH

PART III

THE PRESIDENT AND THE
EXECUTIVE BRANCH

CHAPTER 7

ORGANIZING THE PRESIDENCY

INTRODUCTORY PUZZLE: WHY DOES A "KID" GET TO TELL BILL CLINTON'S CABINET WHAT TO DO?

"Screw him. I won't go." Robert Reich had only been in the job a little over three months, but already he was fed up with those "twerps in the White House," mostly "kids about 30 or 32 years old," telling him what to do and where to go. Before accepting the job as secretary of labor, Reich was a tenured professor at Harvard University and the author of an impressive stack of books, including *The Work of Nations*, which candidate Bill Clinton pored over during the 1992 presidential campaign. Reich and Clinton had been friends since their days together as Rhodes Scholars in the late 1960s, and Clinton thought so highly of Reich that he made him head of his economic transition team before nominating him to head the Labor Department. The Senate approved Reich's appointment by unanimous consent. Yet here was Reich, head of a department of 18,000 people and responsible for a budget of $100 billion, taking orders over the phone from junior White House staffers he'd neither heard of nor met.[1]

On this occasion the directive came from "Steve somebody" in the White House Office of Cabinet Affairs. Reich's chief of staff, Kitty Higgins, relayed the message to her boss: "The White House wants you to go to Cleveland ... They called this morning." Reich was to tour a factory, get on local TV, and tout the administration's achievements during Clinton's first hundred days in office. And Reich wasn't happy about it. He felt he had more important things to do. His job was to advise the president, implement public policy, and "help people get better jobs," not parade around the country like a trained seal. He grilled Higgins: Who precisely wanted him to go to Cleveland? Did the president want him to go? Or was this a directive from the White House chief of staff or perhaps some other senior presidential advisor? Or was "the White House wants" merely code for what some midlevel White House staffer thought would be a fruitful use of the secretary's time? Or, worst of all, was the Cleveland trip simply the bright idea of some lowly White House aide, some "snotty kid" only one step removed from a campaign internship?[2]

Reich was hardly in an ideal position to find out the answer. Yes, he was a longstanding friend of the president, but he could hardly call up the president and ask, "Bill, do you

A posed photograph from January 1994 of President Bill Clinton's cabinet. Vice President Al Gore sits with President Clinton at the head of the table; Labor Secretary Robert Reich is seated, fourth to the left of Gore. Cabinet meetings in the Clinton White House were rare, but the real mystery, in Reich's view, was why Clinton *ever* bothered to meet with his cabinet. According to Reich, there was "absolutely no reason for him—for any president—to meet with the entire cabinet" because cabinet officers had "nothing in common except the first word in [their] titles."

Courtesy: Time & Life Pictures/Getty Images.

really want me to go to Cleveland?" And he wasn't likely to bump into the president or any of his top aides while at work, either. Reich's office wasn't in the West Wing or anywhere close to 1600 Pennsylvania Avenue. Instead it was about two miles down Pennsylvania Avenue, on the second floor of the Labor Department building, a massive six-story structure of more than a million square feet located only a few hundred yards from the Capitol. The president's top aides, by contrast, were just down the hall from the Oval Office, and many of those snotty young staffers that Reich so resented were housed somewhere in the West Wing or, at least, across the street, in the Eisenhower Executive Office Building.

Handicapped by the physical distance that separated his office—which he likened to "one of those hermetically sealed, germ-free bubbles they place around children born with immune deficiencies"—from the day-to-day workings of the White House, Reich struggled to stay in the information loop. Other cabinet members were finding it even more difficult. A year and a half into Clinton's first term, Reich got a desperate call from the secretary of transportation, Federico Peña. After 18 months on the job, Peña, a former two-term mayor of Denver, was still trying to figure out how to find out what was going on in the White House. Reich didn't have much of an answer. He had learned that one good spot for picking up information was the parking lot between the West Wing and the Eisenhower Building, where "dozens of White House staffers tromp every few minutes."

He'd also found that useful gossip could be had by "linger[ing] in the corridors of the West Wing after a meeting." But that required getting invited to a White House meeting, hardly a daily occurrence for most cabinet members.[3]

In Clinton's first year, the president assembled the entire cabinet only seven times. Cabinet meetings, Reich quickly learned, were "meaningless" and awkward affairs. The 14 cabinet members (today it is 15, following the creation of the Department of Homeland Security in 2002) as well as nearly a dozen other cabinet-level officers (such as the director of the Office of Management and Budget and the director of the Environmental Protection Agency) would "sit stiffly" around a large oval table, listening to the president "drone on" about current events "as if he were speaking to a group of visiting diplomats." Alternatively, meetings devolved into "show and tell" sessions, like when the administration's "AIDS czar" was invited to instruct cabinet secretaries on steps they could take to raise AIDS awareness. Cabinet meetings were obviously not the place where policy decisions were made or political influence exerted. Indeed, Reich thought it a wonder that the cabinet ever met.[4]

Far more relevant to decision-making were the Domestic Policy Council (DPC) and National Economic Council (NEC). Charged with coordinating and managing the administration's domestic policy agenda, the DPC's membership included every cabinet member except the secretaries of state and defense, with the president in the chair. At least that's the way it looked on paper, in the executive order that Clinton issued in 1993. In reality, Clinton almost never attended DPC meetings, which were instead convened and directed by White House staff. Actual control over the DPC was vested in a White House aide (Carol Rasco in Clinton's first term) with the title "assistant to the president for domestic policy," who was supported by a staff of around 30 people. Most DPC staffers were part of the 32-and-under crowd that so irritated Reich. And none of them, including the DPC head, had to be confirmed by the Senate or appear before congressional committees to testify about their actions, as Reich did.[5]

The DPC was structured, as political scientist Shirley Anne Warshaw notes, "to ensure that the White House staff controlled the [domestic policymaking] process." Bruce Reed—who took over from Rasco in Clinton's second term after serving as Rasco's deputy in the first—explained that the DPC's "primary purpose" was "to allow the Cabinet Secretaries who implement and oversee policy the opportunity to communicate with and comment to the White House staff inside the gates that design the policy." In other words, White House staff were supposed to design and develop the president's policies while the DPC generously afforded those charged with carrying out the policy—the cabinet members—the chance to come to the White House and comment on those policies. Reed made no apologies for this organizational structure. It was imperative, in Reed's view, "to center decisions in the White House" because presidents "pick their cabinets for lots of different reasons but policy development tends not to be one of them." Only staffers—even if they were young—could be trusted to know and reflect presidential preferences.[6]

To Reed—who was 32 at the outset of Clinton's presidency—this division of labor between staff and cabinet seemed the only sensible way to ensure that the administration's policies reflected the wishes of an elected president rather than the parochial concerns of a particular department or the pet projects of a cabinet head. To Reich, on the other hand, Reed's outlook exemplified the conceit of the White House staff, who viewed cabinet officials as akin to "provincial governors presiding over alien, primitive territories." In the eyes of the "arrogant center," lamented Reich, these provincial governors were important "only in a ceremonial sense. They wear the colors and show the flag. Occasionally they are called in to get their next round of orders before being returned to their outposts."[7]

The clash between cabinet and staff is endemic to the contemporary presidency. Reich's complaints about the arrogant center are as common as Reed's grumbling about the divided loyalties of cabinet chiefs. In recent decades, many presidents, Clinton included, have entered office promising to cut the White House staff or restore the integrity of "cabinet government." Yet they end up doing nothing of the sort, despite the considerable time and energy they typically devote to cabinet selection. Instead they generally grow the White House staff by creating new offices and responsibilities. Moreover, policy development and coordination has been concentrated ever more tightly in the hands of White House staff, leaving cabinet members to implement and sell policies that have been designed in the West Wing.[8]

The centralization of decision-making authority in an expanded White House staff is one of the most important institutional developments of the modern presidency. Today the White House staff includes about 135 offices, including nearly one hundred that are policy-related. By contrast, when Woodrow Wilson became president a century ago, the White House staff consisted of only one important staffer, the president's private secretary, Joseph P. Tumulty. The other dozen or so people who worked in the Wilson White House had almost exclusively clerical responsibilities. A century before Wilson, presidents who wanted secretarial help with correspondence or appointments had to pay for a secretary out of their own pockets. No statute acknowledged the existence or need for presidential staff, and the Constitution made no mention of White House staff either.[9]

How did we get from a Constitution that had no place for even the most rudimentary White House staff to a "presidential branch" that today has some two thousand employees and a budget of about $400 million? In charting this institutional evolution we begin with the framers' debates over how the presidency should be organized.

THE FRAMERS ORGANIZE THE PRESIDENCY

The question of how to organize the presidency presented itself first as a question of whether there should be one president or several. And the answer was by no means as obvious to the framers as it seems to us today.

Debating Unity in the Executive

A remarkable number of delegates at the Constitutional Convention favored a plural executive. Benjamin Franklin, for one, thought a plural executive was desirable because government policy would be more stable and predictable, traits particularly valuable in foreign policy. A plural executive, Franklin added, would also solve the problems of succession, illness, or death. John Dickinson, whose enmity for Franklin was so great that he reportedly refused to put a lightning rod on his house, agreed with his old nemesis on the dangers of lodging the executive power in a single person. Surveying all of world history, Dickinson could find "no instance of its being ever done with safety." He proposed instead a three-headed executive, consisting of one person from the eastern states, another from the middle states, and a third from the southern states. Their terms would be staggered, with the person in office the longest being styled the president, but each of the three executives would have equal power.[10]

Franklin and Dickinson were not alone in their support for a plural executive. James Wilson's motion that the executive "consist of a single person" was opposed by three (Delaware, New York, and Maryland) of the ten state delegations that voted, and a fourth (New Jersey) would have opposed the motion had they had a quorum. At least a quarter of the convention delegates supported a plural executive. Support for a plural executive was particularly strong among older delegates—those like Franklin (81 years old), Connecticut's Roger Sherman (66), and Virginia's George Mason (61), whose anti-executive views were shaped by their battles against royal governors during the colonial period.[11]

The champions of a single president were concentrated among the convention's younger generation, those like Wilson (44), James Madison (36), Gouverneur Morris (35), Alexander Hamilton (32), and South Carolina's Charles Pinckney (29). Their outlooks were forged in reaction to the weakness of executive power in the Articles of Confederation and in the revolutionary-era state constitutions. These delegates were concerned that a plural executive would invite intrigue and violence as well as diffuse responsibility. "In order to control the Legislative authority," Wilson instructed the convention, "you must divide it. In order to control the Executive you must unite it." A plural executive, Wilson argued, would be a house divided against itself, and could not stand.[12]

Mason's Lament: A President sans Council

After deciding on June 4 that the executive power should be vested in a single person, the convention sought to create an executive council to advise the president.

The idea of a council of state to advise and check the chief executive had deep roots in colonial history. Each colony had possessed an executive council, whose consent the governor needed on important matters such as making appointments. After the revolution, almost every state constitution retained a council of state that the governor was required to consult. The Virginia constitution, for instance, provided that the governor could exercise no executive functions without seeking the advice of an eight-member privy council, which was selected by the legislature.[13]

Virtually all the convention delegates seemed to assume that an executive council of some sort was desirable, but there was scant agreement about how it should be composed or the power it should wield. In the latter part of August, the Committee of Detail finally suggested a concrete plan. The president would have "a privy council," composed of the president of the Senate, the Speaker of the House of Representatives, the chief justice of the Supreme Court, and the heads of the various executive departments. The council's "duty" would be to advise the president "in matters respecting the execution of his office, which he shall think proper to lay before them." However, the council's powers were advisory only. The president would have the ultimate "responsibility for the measures which he shall adopt." The committee's proposal, however, never came to a vote, and so the issue was handed over to the Committee on Postponed Matters, chaired by New Jersey's David Brearly.[14]

The Brearly Committee's report of September 4 dropped the council, and instead provided that the president "may require the opinion in writing of the principal Officer in each of the Executive Departments, upon any subject relating to the duties of their respective offices"—the wording that is today part of Article II, section 2. The delegates who had supported a plural executive were particularly unhappy about the absence of an executive council. Virginia's George Mason fretted that the convention was "about to try an experiment on which the most despotic Governments had never ventured." Mason urged the convention to instruct the Committee on Postponed Matters to prepare a new clause that would establish an executive council. Franklin seconded Mason's motion, arguing that a council would "be a check on a bad President" and "a relief to a good one." Even Madison, no friend of a plural executive, backed his Virginia colleague's motion.[15]

Two weeks earlier, Gouverneur Morris had proposed a council of state composed of the chief justice of the Supreme Court and the heads of five executive departments, but now he defended the committee's decision not to establish a council. The committee, he assured his colleagues, had carefully considered the idea of a council of state but rejected it because they did not want to enable the president to deflect blame for his mistakes onto the council. Morris's explanation did little to assuage the delegates' misgivings about the omission of a council of state, but at this late date in the convention few delegates were prepared to tackle the formidable problems presented by the creation of a council. Who, for instance, would get a seat on the council, and who would select the council members? And would the council be a purely advisory body or would its consent be required? Unable to marshal anything approaching a consensus on these questions and desperate to wrap up the convention's business, the convention rejected Mason's motion and approved the committee's language authorizing the president to require the opinion of department heads.[16]

Ultimately, then, the Constitution provided scant guidance as to how the president should be advised and the presidency organized. There was to be one president rather than three. That much had been settled. But the document prescribed little else regarding the structure of the executive branch. The framers clearly anticipated the creation of executive departments, each headed by a "principal officer," but they left it to Congress to enumerate those departments and their duties. And, as Hamilton noted in *Federalist* No. 74, the Brearly clause seemed "a mere redundancy" since the nation's chief executive necessarily possessed the authority to get advice, written or otherwise, from the heads of executive departments.

Making the First Departments, Convening the First Cabinet

During the summer of 1789, Congress created the departments of foreign affairs, war, and treasury. Each department was to be directed by a department head, but what role department heads were to play in advising the president was unclear. The Constitution stipulated that the president could require department heads to provide a written opinion "on any subject relating to the duties of their respective offices," but that did not meet Washington's desire "always to compare the opinions of those in whom I confide with one another." If Washington only consulted the secretary whose department was most immediately affected by a policy matter, he risked becoming a prisoner to the superior expertise of that department head. By the same token, if department heads limited their advice to matters that directly affected their department, then Washington would have to reach beyond the executive branch for advice that reflected broader and diverse perspectives.[17]

Washington made it clear to his department heads that he wanted them to be more than effective administrators. In attempting to recruit Charles Cotesworth Pinckney as secretary of war, Washington explained that he was not looking for someone merely to carry out the "detail duties of the Office." Instead he wanted a department head who could advise him on all "interesting questions of National importance." Thus, while a secretary of war of course had to be "of competent skill in the Science of War," it was still more important that he possess "a general knowledge of political subjects."[18]

Washington often asked Treasury Secretary Hamilton for his views on matters of foreign policy, just as he solicited Secretary of State Jefferson's opinions on domestic policies. In 1791, when Madison raised constitutional objections to Hamilton's proposal for a national bank, Washington requested a written opinion on the bank's constitutionality from Jefferson. When Jefferson and Attorney General Edmund Randolph backed Madison's position, Washington informed Hamilton that he would veto the national bank bill unless Hamilton could demonstrate that the Virginians' reading of the Constitution was wrong. In the end, Washington signed the bill, but only after having solicited the strongest possible arguments on both sides of the question. Hamilton's position prevailed not because the bank fell within the administrative purview of the treasury secretary but because ultimately Washington agreed with Hamilton about the need for a national bank and shared his more expansive interpretation of the Constitution.[19]

The debate over whether to veto the national bank bill was typical of Washington's first-term advisory structure in that he consulted with cabinet members individually rather than collectively. In the final year of his first term, however, Washington began to experiment with a new advisory structure that promoted collective discussion and debate. Instead of relying solely on written opinions and private conversations, the president convened meetings with the three department heads and the attorney general. The gang of four—which Washington dubbed his "cabinet"—met frequently during the spring of 1793 as the president struggled to forge a policy that would keep the United States out of the war between France and Britain. During these meetings, Jefferson and Hamilton were, according to Jefferson, "daily pitted in the cabinet like two cocks." Although Washington took no pleasure in watching his two chief advisors gouge each other, he found the frank exchange of views invaluable and continued to hold cabinet meetings regularly for the remainder of his time in the presidency. And as bruising as Jefferson found the fighting, he recognized the value of meeting collectively and continued the practice during his presidency.[20]

George Mason's lament had been true enough: the framers had created a president without a "constitutional Council." He was right, too, that the president would need

WASHINGTON AND HIS CABINET.

President George Washington seated with his cabinet members: Secretary of War Henry Knox, Secretary of Treasury Alexander Hamilton (standing), Secretary of State Thomas Jefferson, and Attorney General Edmund Randolph.

Courtesy: The Granger Collection, NYC—All rights reserved.

something akin to a council of state. But Mason erred in thinking that the only way of providing for such a council was through the Constitution. Within four years, President Washington had created a de facto council of state that closely resembled the one that Gouverneur Morris had proposed at the convention. Although Washington's cabinet did not include the chief justice of the Supreme Court, it did bring together the heads of the principal executive departments. And the president was free "in all cases," as Morris had stipulated, to "exercise his own judgment, and either conform to such opinions or not as he may think proper." The president, in short, had his council, despite its being neither mentioned in nor authorized by the Constitution.[21]

"AN ALMOST INSUPPORTABLE BURDEN": THE ORIGINS OF PRESIDENTIAL STAFF

"The president needs help" are among the most famous four words ever penned about the American presidency. That plea was the opening gambit in a 1937 report issued by the Brownlow Committee, which had been appointed by President Franklin Delano Roosevelt to publicize the administrative challenges confronting the nation's chief executive. This oft-quoted cry for help, sounded on the Constitution's sesquicentennial, grabbed the nation's attention, but there was nothing novel about the lament. Since the opening days of the new republic, presidents have complained about the lack of administrative support. Indeed, a month before he had even taken the inaugural oath of office, Washington was already complaining that his correspondence had become "an almost insupportable burden."[22]

George Washington's Staff

Living in the twenty-first century, surrounded by cell phones, electronic mail, word processors, and copying devices, it is difficult for us to appreciate the burden of correspondence in the life of an eighteenth-century statesman, particularly one as famous as Washington. People from all walks of life wrote to Washington, and most expected a response. Hours were consumed deciphering illegible handwriting. Every letter Washington signed had to be written at least twice—the first one for delivery and the other entered into a letterbook that contained copies of all Washington's outgoing correspondence. If a letter was particularly important, it might be sent by different routes, which would require yet another copy to be penned. To forward a letter or report, or an extract thereof, also required copying out by hand the enclosed material.

As commander in chief of the revolutionary army, Washington had been accustomed to help of the highest quality. He relied on staff support from an array of young and talented military aides, including a future Speaker of the House (Jonathan Trumbull), US senator (William Grayson), secretary of the treasury (Hamilton), secretary of war (James McHenry), and attorney general (Edmund Randolph). The aides composed most of the general's correspondence, typically drawing from notes or instructions Washington provided. After Washington had corrected and approved the letter, his military staff took care of the final copying.[23]

As president, however, Washington had nothing like the level of staff support he enjoyed in the military. His department heads were talented and in some ways they were, as political scientist Fred Greenstein writes, the "equivalent of a modern presidential staff," particularly when it came to advising the president and writing important messages. But a department head was far too busy attending to his departmental duties to provide the president with the more routine staff support that he required.[24]

Washington brought with him to the capital his trusted personal secretary Tobias Lear, a Harvard graduate who had been with the president since 1786 and would remain at the president's side throughout his first term, acting as confidant, sounding board, courier, and letter writer. But there was far too much work even for the industrious Lear. Copying the president's letters and other documents was a full-time job, and Washington hired his young nephews—first Robert Lewis and subsequently Howell Lewis—to copy papers "from breakfast until dinner, Sundays excepted." Yet Washington found he needed still more help to keep up with his official duties.[25]

Washington's experience as commander in chief of the army had given him a clear sense of what he desired in an aide: "secrecy and prudence, attention and industry, good temper, and a capacity and disposition to write correctly and well." But recruiting and retaining such people proved difficult, even for the nation's most revered figure. In his first year in office, Washington took on young Thomas Nelson Jr., scion of a distinguished Virginia family, who showed little aptitude for the job and soon departed. The following year, Washington recruited Major William Jackson, who possessed extensive staff experience, including as secretary at the Constitutional Convention. During the president's 1791 tour of the southern states, the 30-year-old Jackson not only served as "unofficial bodyguard" but also drafted the many replies that Washington gave to welcoming remarks. Unfortunately for Washington, Jackson resigned after the tour to resume a career in law and business. Two years later, the irreplaceable Lear also left Washington's employ to pursue a career in business.[26]

The Problem of Paying for Help

Washington paid each of his secretaries out of his own pocket. They were paid anywhere from a few hundred dollars annually—his nephew Howell Lewis took the job of copyist for $300 a year—to $800 a year, in the case of Lear. That Washington footed the bill for their salaries does not mean that Congress gave no thought to providing the president with staff support or that Congress wished to discourage the president from hiring staff. On the contrary, in the legislative debate over presidential compensation, members acknowledged that the president required the assistance of at least two secretaries possessed of "abilities and information." Initially, Congress planned to provide the president a salary of $20,000 and a separate expense allowance for secretaries and clerks as well as household items such as furniture and carriages. But Congress ultimately decided against itemizing presidential expenses, preferring instead to raise the president's salary to $25,000 and leave him to decide how best to allocate his expenses. In striking out a provision for the funding of presidential secretaries and clerks, then, the first Congress sought not to hamstring or weaken the president but rather to avoid micromanaging the president's conduct of his executive duties.[27]

The trouble with this arrangement was threefold. First, by building the expense of presidential secretaries and clerks into the presidential salary it was easy to forget that Congress intended to fund staff support. What began as an effort to respect presidential discretion could easily become a way for Congress to limit presidential capacity. Second, the president's pay remained fixed even as his expenses rose. By the end of Madison's presidency, the president's salary was worth only half of what it had been at the outset of Washington's tenure, and not until 1873, during the presidency of Ulysses S. Grant, would Congress finally increase it. Third, few presidents were as wealthy as the nation's first president. Even before he became president, Washington had a personal secretary that he paid handsomely as well as an extensive household that he supported, not to mention an elegant carriage, pulled by four magnificent white horses. Even the land-rich early presidents were usually cash-poor. Jefferson had to borrow more than $4,000 in his first year in office to cover his expenses, which included a wine bill that approached

$3,000. And Monroe had to finance his first presidential tour by selling his furniture to the government.[28]

Monroe fired off a plea for help in the closing months of his presidency. The president, he told Congress, spent far too much time on "inferior details" at the expense of his "higher duties." Monroe complained, for instance, of the many hours he wasted signing land patents, military commissions, and passports. Yet it took nearly a decade, and a backlog of some 20,000 land patents, before Congress finally provided funding for a secretary of land patents authorized to sign for the president. And even then Congress refused to make the patent secretary part of the president's personal staff; instead, Congress required that his appointment be subject to the advice and consent of the Senate.[29]

Staffing from Jefferson through Buchanan

If the president was at times reduced to little more than a glorified clerk, the fault lay not only with Congress for failing to provide adequate staff support, but with some presidents for failing to delegate. Whereas Washington took immediate steps to secure secretarial help with the routine copying work of the office and relied liberally on others—both personal secretaries and cabinet members—for help in drafting messages, Jefferson insisted on doing virtually all his own writing. Little wonder that he found he spent "from 10 to 12 and 13 hours a day at [his] writing table."[30]

Jefferson did employ a private secretary, but he conceived the office as more akin to a political aide than a mere clerk. He looked to his secretary less to relieve himself of the "unceasing drudgery" of his office than to serve as liaison with the Washington community, particularly Congress. As Jefferson explained the job to William Burwell, it required not only carrying official communications between the president and Congress but also holding "occasional conferences and explanations with particular members, with the offices, & inhabitants of the place where it cannot so well be done in writing." To meet this need, Jefferson sought secretaries possessed of political skill and ambition. Burwell, for instance, served simultaneously as Jefferson's secretary and as a delegate in Virginia's General Assembly, before leaving both posts to take a seat in the United States House of Representatives.[31]

Jefferson assumed greater responsibility for his correspondence than did other nineteenth-century presidents, but he was not alone in using his personal secretary as both official and unofficial conduit to the legislature. Madison, for instance, also relied on his private secretary to transmit information to and from members of Congress. Not all secretaries were equally suited to the job of communicating with Congress. Isaac Coles, Madison's first secretary—and Jefferson's last—was forced to resign after he horse-whipped a congressman on the grounds of the Capitol. His place was taken by his more diplomatic brother, Edward Coles, who served ably as Madison's personal secretary for more than five years (and later became governor of Illinois). Much of Coles's job was taken up with routine matters—filing the president's papers, making copies of correspondence, writing routine letters, acting as messenger, and helping the president's wife (and Coles's cousin) arrange social events—but Madison also entrusted Coles with politically sensitive tasks. In the fall of 1814, for instance, in the midst of a cabinet reshuffle, Madison dispatched Coles to discreetly sound out New York's congressional delegation about the possibility of appointing the state's governor Daniel Tompkins as either secretary of state or secretary of treasury. Coles was also regularly sought out by politicians seeking jobs or favors for themselves, their friends, or their constituents.[32]

In the nineteenth century, job-seekers and favor-mongers posed as great a hindrance to the president's discharge of his "higher duties" as did the burden of official correspondence. President Washington had foreseen this problem and responded by severely limiting access to the president. He held a weekly afternoon levee at which gentlemen could pay their respects and attended a "mixed company" gathering hosted by his wife Martha on Friday evenings, but there was to be no casual "dropping in" on the president. Critics thought this policy of "seclusion from the people" smacked of monarchy, but the revered Washington could just about get away with it. The spread of democratic mores, however, compelled his nineteenth-century successors to strike a different balance, one that privileged accessibility over seclusion. But could an accessible president still find the time to carry out his executive duties?[33]

The predicament facing nineteenth-century presidents is amply documented in the diary kept by President James Polk. Entry upon entry details an unending stream of visitors, some calling "to pay their respects, but most of them seeking office." When Congress was in session, Polk typically opened his doors to visitors until noon on weekdays, with the exception of Tuesday, which was reserved for cabinet meetings. However, even when the White House was closed to the public, the president still found himself constantly "interrupted and annoyed" by callers.[34]

The task of keeping unwanted visitors out of the White House was entrusted to the porter, who was frequently circumvented. The president typically instructed the porter to admit none but cabinet members and those who had "important" official business, but a mere doorman was hardly in a position to judge what the president counted as important. In one typical diary entry, Polk vented his frustration that several members of Congress together with their friends had been admitted even though their "important business" turned out to be nothing more than "importunate applications for office." Such incidents, Polk complained, resulted in the continual "useless consumption of [his] time."[35]

In sum, the mid-nineteenth-century presidency was beset by a woeful mismatch between the extraordinary demands heaped upon the president and the meager institutional resources placed at his disposal. Little wonder that Polk frequently retired at night feeling "greatly fatigued and worn down by [his] labors" or that Andrew Jackson described the presidency as "a situation of dignified slavery." All that stood between the president and hordes of office-seekers was a lowly doorman, and for staff support the president was reliant largely on a single private secretary, almost always a young family member or relation willing to work for little more than room and board. Between 1817 and 1860, every president but one (Franklin Pierce) chose as his private secretary either a nephew, son, or son-in-law. Some of these young men were competent, but most were retained for reasons that had little to do with their aptitude for the job.[36]

No president wanted to fire a family member, no matter how ineffective they were as a secretary. Polk's life was made much more difficult, for instance, by his nephew's frequent sojourns away from the capital, on at least two occasions for as long as six weeks. One might think that the president of the United States would be able to dictate his secretary's schedule, yet Polk was powerless to stop his nephew leaving for Baltimore to attend the Democratic national convention despite the president's strong objections. On another occasion, Polk was "vexed" upon finding that his nephew had abandoned his secretarial post for "a party of pleasure" in Maryland. Yet Polk made no attempt to replace his nephew—whose wife and children also lived under the president's roof—even though his absences required Polk either "to perform the duties of secretary as well as President" or to rely on a succession of temporary replacements, typically clerks borrowed from various government departments.[37]

In 1857, Congress took an important first step in placing presidential staffing on a more stable, professional basis by authorizing an annual salary of $2,500 for the president's private secretary. Initially, however, this $2,500 appropriation had little noticeable effect on the quality of staffing; instead it merely enabled President James Buchanan to provide for his 23-year-old nephew and ward James Buchanan Henry out of the public purse. Buchanan seems to have chosen Henry, a man of limited talents and various vices, less for his secretarial abilities than out of a desire to keep a watchful eye on his ward.[38]

In ordinary times, the nation could perhaps afford a president bogged down by routine correspondence, surrounded by swarms of office-seekers, and assisted largely by inexperienced young kinsmen. But as the nation slid inexorably toward civil war, it was an open question whether the rudimentary organization of the White House would prevent the nation's new president, Abraham Lincoln, from focusing on the crucial decisions that would be necessary if the nation was to be preserved.

ORGANIZING THE LINCOLN WHITE HOUSE

On President Lincoln's first day at work, the extent of the organizational problem was glaringly obvious. Waiting on the president's desk was a letter from the commander at Fort Sumter informing Lincoln that there appeared no alternative but to surrender the fort—a rude shock for a president who had pledged only the day before to use every power at his disposal to "hold, occupy, and possess" Fort Sumter and any other property belonging to the federal government. Lincoln needed to make a decision and he needed to make it quickly, but instead of spending the day huddled with advisors he had to attend to the "crush of office seekers," hundreds of people in a line "so long that it extended down the stairs to the front entrance" of the White House. Each of them came to the president with "a story to tell, a reason why a clerkship in Washington or a job in their local post office or customs house would allow their family to survive."[39]

The situation during Lincoln's first month seemed intolerable. Supporters scolded the president for frittering away his precious time "listening to the appeals of competing office-hunters." Secretary of State William Seward thought the chaotic scenes at the White House, its "grounds, halls, stairways, [and] closets" crammed with supplicants for office, betrayed a president in over his head. Lincoln, complained Seward, had "no system" and "no conception of his situation." Unlike Lincoln, Seward had executive experience, having served two terms as governor of New York, and he fretted that the president did not understand the need to delegate. Preoccupied with "the details of office dispensation" and determined "to do all his work," the president would have no time for strategic thinking, let alone "great ideas."[40]

Historians have been quick to dismiss Seward's grousing as little more than the personal pique of a man who felt that he and not Lincoln should have been the 16th president of the United States. But Seward was right that Lincoln had never administered anything in his life. In fact, Lincoln was only the second president without prior executive experience—the only other was the forgettable Franklin Pierce. But Lincoln was a quick learner and not nearly as administratively naive as Seward and other veteran Washingtonians assumed. Lincoln was acutely aware that his open-door policy was detracting from his ability to focus on the crisis of secession. Within the month, Lincoln had curtailed his daily "promiscuous receptions" to several days a week for five hours, and before long he had cut them to three hours, from 10am to 1pm.[41]

Lincoln's Private Secretaries

Even before taking the oath of office, Lincoln had taken two crucial steps that would help him to manage the extraordinary demands on his time. First, instead of hiring an inexperienced family relation as his private secretary, as almost all past presidents had done, he tapped 29-year-old John Nicolay, whose sound judgment and work ethic had lifted him from printer's apprentice to newspaper publisher and editor at a Whig journal and landed him the post of principal clerk in the office of the Illinois secretary of state, the de facto campaign headquarters for the state's Republican Party. Second, instead of relying on one secretary, Lincoln secured the services of an assistant secretary, 23-year-old John Hay, whose impressive talents would one day lead to a distinguished diplomatic career capped by seven years as secretary of state during the McKinley and Roosevelt administrations. Because Congress only provided for one secretary, Lincoln arranged to have Hay appointed as a clerk in the Pension Office (housed within the Department of the Interior) and then detailed to the White House.[42]

Nicolay occupied the same office—adjacent to the president's—as previous private secretaries, but he filled it as nobody had before. Not everybody liked the change. The snobs who dominated the capital's social life sneered at Nicolay's appointment. In their view, the private secretary was supposed to arrange the president's dinner parties and attend social functions that the president could not attend, and thus needed to be "a man of refinement and culture and thoroughly at home in fine society," somebody like Buchanan's Princeton-educated socialite nephew. Nicolay was responsible for ensuring that seating arrangements at White House dinners accorded with rank and protocol, but he understood his preeminent duty to be "defending the President from needless intrusion."[43]

They called him "sour and crusty," "disagreeable and uncivil," "the bulldog in the ante-room," "the impassable Mr. Nicolay." With no interest in being popular and seemingly immune to charm and cajoling, the Bavarian-born Nicolay never shrank from saying "no." In fact, marveled one of Nicolay's assistants, he "could say 'no' about as disagreeably as any man" alive. Lincoln heard the grumbling about Nicolay's stern manner, but made no attempt to soften his secretary's demeanor. He understood that his fiercely loyal secretary, who "measured all things and all men by their relations to the President," was an indispensable buffer against what one White House visitor described as the "loiterers, contract-hunters, garrulous parents on paltry errands, toadies without measure, and talkers without conscience."[44]

Lincoln's secretaries also played a vital role in sifting through the huge volume of mail that poured into the White House. Unlike Polk, who "insisted on personally reading every one of the hundreds of letters he received every week," Lincoln instructed his secretaries to bring him only the letters that required his attention. The bulk of the opening, reading, sorting, filing, and disposing of the president's mail was carried out across the hall from Nicolay, in the office of assistant secretary John Hay. The deluge of mail would have overwhelmed Hay had Lincoln not recruited additional help in the form of a second assistant secretary, 25-year-old William O. Stoddard. As editor and part-owner of the *Central Illinois Gazette*, Stoddard had been an early backer of Lincoln's candidacy and Lincoln had rewarded him with the job of secretary of land patents. The $1,500-a-year post was housed in the Interior Department, but the war slowed the land office business sufficiently that Stoddard was transferred to the White House to assist Hay, who was thereby able to focus his attention on the president's most important correspondence and to assist Nicolay on pressing political matters.[45]

For the next two and a half years, until he became incapacitated by illness, Stoddard's primary responsibility was opening and processing the couple hundred pieces of mail that were dumped on his desk every day but Sunday. Among the missives in the president's bulging mail bag, Stoddard recalled, were

applications for office, for contracts, for pardons, for pecuniary aid, for advice, for information, for autographs, voluminous letters of advice, political disquisitions, religious exhortations, the rant and drivel of insanity, bitter abuse, foul obscenity, slanderous charges against public men, police and war information, military reports.

Many letters Stoddard redirected to the appropriate federal bureaus and departments, and many others were consigned to the wastebasket. Stoddard estimated that only "three or four in a hundred, properly briefed and remarked upon, were laid on the President's desk."[46]

The filtering of the president's correspondence by "mere boys" excited complaints from plain people as well as prominent politicians. Yet even when complaints reached the president, as Stoddard said they frequently did, Lincoln "never interfered" or rebuked his secretaries. In keeping unnecessary correspondence away from his desk, the president's secretaries were doing the president's bidding, just as they were in keeping unwanted visitors out of his office. The secretaries' shared understanding of their role is clear in the instructions that Hay left before embarking on a quick trip to New York: "Refer as little to the President as possible. Keep visitors out of the house when you can. [Be] inhospitable, but prudent."[47]

Lincoln's three secretaries not only protected the president's time but also defended his reputation in the press. Taking advantage of their journalistic experience and contacts,

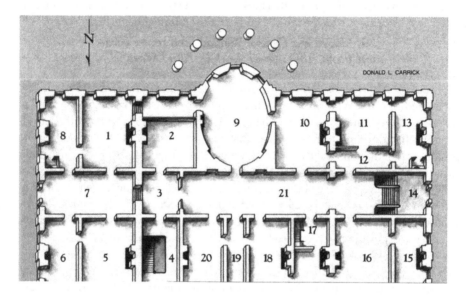

The layout of the second floor of Lincoln's White House. Room 1 is President Lincoln's office and cabinet room. Adjacent to that is John Nicolay's office (room 8). Across the hall from Nicolay's office is the office (room 6) shared by John Hay and William Stoddard. Adjacent to that, and across from Lincoln's office, was the bedroom shared by Hay and Nicolay. Room 9, today's Oval Office, was the family library, and rooms 10 and 11 were the bedrooms of Mary Todd Lincoln and Abraham Lincoln, respectively. Rooms 15 and 16 were for Lincoln's sons, and rooms 18 and 20 were guest bedrooms. Lincoln built the partition in room 2, the office reception room, so that he could slip unnoticed from his office to the family quarters.

Courtesy: Donald L. Carrick, The White House Historical Association.

Hay and Stoddard penned hundreds of anonymous or pseudonymous pro-Lincoln op-eds in newspapers across the country. Lincoln's secretaries also cultivated sympathetic journalists, scolding them when they thought their coverage of the president unfair. In the run-up to the 1864 election, for instance, Nicolay met with the *New York Tribune*'s editor Horace Greeley to protest an editorial critical of Lincoln and exacted an offer from Greeley to provide the administration space to present its point of view—an invitation that Nicolay gladly accepted.[48]

Nicolay, in particular, exercised an unprecedented degree of power for a private secretary. Lincoln often dispatched Nicolay to troubleshoot "delicate" political problems. During 1864 Nicolay even operated as "the unofficial manager" of Lincoln's reelection campaign. Nicolay's power rested on Lincoln's unshakable faith in his secretary's judgment and loyalty as well as on Nicolay's unflappable demeanor, his "gift of hearing other people talk," and his knack for taking "prompt as lightning ... a hint or an idea." But Nicolay's power was also due to the size of Lincoln's staff. Whereas presidents like Polk and Buchanan had relied essentially on a single secretary, Lincoln's staff was sufficiently large that roles became more specialized. Nicolay and even Hay could carry out important political tasks for the president, including some that took them outside of the capital, because other White House secretaries were available to execute the most routine duties.[49]

The Contrasting Administrative Styles of Lincoln and Polk

The sizable staff that Nicolay recruited to assist the president was indispensable to Lincoln's ability to focus his energies on the decisions that mattered most, but equally important was Lincoln's willingness to delegate responsibility to his department heads. Seward's early concern that the inexperienced Lincoln would try to do it all himself turned out to be misplaced. Unlike Polk, who closely supervised the work and budgets of each department, Lincoln gave a "completely free hand" to most of his department chiefs.[50]

Polk took great pride in his ability to manage the entire executive branch on his own. He boasted that he had "become so familiar with the duties and workings of the government, not only upon general principles, but in most of its minute details" that he had little need of his cabinet. In Polk's view, micromanaging administrative details was necessary to avoid mistakes. Because a president who "entrusts the details and smaller matters to subordinates" would be plagued by "constant errors," Polk preferred "to supervise the whole operations of the government [himself] rather than entrust the public business to subordinates." A heroic apostle of one-man administration, he left office a physical wreck and was dead three months later.[51]

Like Polk, Lincoln worked long hours. Neither man could be called "an idler or a lounger." And certainly the burdens of office took their toll on Lincoln just as they did on Polk. But whereas Polk aspired to supervise the entire executive branch, Lincoln largely left his subordinates alone except where it directly affected his core priorities: winning the war and ending slavery. Lincoln's attorney general, postmaster general, secretary of interior, and secretary of navy, writes historian David Donald, "conducted their department's affairs virtually without oversight or interference from the President." Even in foreign relations Lincoln was content to play a "minor role," largely ceding the conduct of diplomacy to his more experienced secretary of state.[52]

In the eyes of many of his contemporaries, Lincoln's failure to stamp his authority on each executive department was a mark of his weakness as an administrator. If presidential strength is equated with control over the executive branch, then Lincoln was undeniably weak. Judged by this standard, Polk appears far closer to the ideal administrator. But there were hidden strengths in Lincoln's administrative style. Not only did it allow Lincoln to focus the limited managerial resources at his disposal on core priorities, it also helped him to deflect blame for unpopular policies. Blame for higher taxes and the creation of the Internal Revenue Service, for instance, was laid at the door of Treasury Secretary Samuel Chase. When the administration failed to enforce congressional acts confiscating the property of slave owners, radicals blamed the conservative attorney general Edward Bates. When the war went badly, conservatives screamed for the ouster of Secretary of

War Edwin Stanton. And Secretary of State Seward, "Lincoln's evil genius," was held by many anti-slavery Republicans to be "the real cause" of what they perceived to be the president's overly cautious policies.[53]

Not all of Lincoln's department heads welcomed the autonomy Lincoln granted them. To Chase it often felt more like neglect. When Chase tried to draw Lincoln into a discussion of economics, Lincoln feigned ignorance: "You understand these things. I do not," he told Chase. So long as his treasury secretary continued to raise the revenues needed to fight the war, Lincoln was largely content to leave economic policy in Chase's capable hands. Chase resented this arrangement, however, both because his job on Capitol Hill would have been easier with the president's forthright support and because he saw himself as more than merely the administrator of the nation's economic policies. As the head of one of the two major executive departments, Chase believed he and the rest of the cabinet should be advising the president on a broad range of policies relating to the war, slavery, and the South.[54]

Lincoln's "Team of Rivals"

Lincoln, however, had a very different understanding of the cabinet's role. In sharp contrast to Polk, who met twice a week with his cabinet to solicit policy advice and listen to reports on the business of each department, Lincoln attached little value to cabinet meetings and held them as infrequently as he could. Whereas Polk insisted that each department head be present at cabinet meetings, Lincoln seemed not to care if cabinet members absented themselves. One regular absentee was Seward, who preferred to confer with the president in private where they could talk more frankly and fully. When Stanton showed up at meetings, one cabinet officer griped, it was only "to whisper to the President, or take the dispatches or papers from his pocket and go into a corner with the President." Stanton revealed next to nothing in front of his colleagues because he did not trust them to keep military plans secret, a concern that the president shared. Chase, too, stopped attending regularly once he realized that little of importance would be discussed at this "so-called cabinet." Attorney General Bates, who opposed Chase on virtually every political question, agreed with his rival: "There is, in fact, no Cabinet and the show of Cabinet-councils is getting more and more, a mere show—Little matters or isolated propositions are sometimes talked over, but the great business of the country—questions of leading policy—are not mentioned."[55]

This is not the way we usually remember Lincoln's cabinet, his so-called "team of rivals." They were certainly rivals but hardly a team. One of the most famous depictions of the Lincoln presidency is Francis Carpenter's painting that hangs today in the United States Capitol. Lincoln is seated at the cabinet table in his office, flanked by his seven department heads, four of them sitting, three of them standing. Each of them looks an impressively sage counselor to the president, who has in his hand the first draft of the Emancipation Proclamation. The painting records an actual meeting, but it obscures what actually took place, namely that the president summoned his cabinet to read a draft of a proclamation that they knew nothing about and had no hand in crafting. Before reading the document, Lincoln told them that he had "resolved upon this step, and had

not called them together to ask their advice, but to lay the subject-matter of a proclamation before them." Lincoln did accept Seward's suggestion that he wait until after a
military victory to announce the proclamation, but that was the extent of the cabinet's
influence.[56]

Lincoln's reluctance to bring "the great business of the country" before his cabinet can
be explained in part by the extraordinary circumstances of his presidency, including the
profound differences of opinion among his department heads, a polarization of opinion
that was a product of Lincoln's decision to forge a cabinet out of leaders from the party's
diverse ideological factions. Lincoln's cabinet was composed of four of his chief rivals for
the Republican nomination: Seward, Chase, Bates, and Simon Cameron. In addition,
four of his cabinet members were former Democrats and three were ex-Whigs. A
peacetime president willing or able to create a more ideologically homogeneous cabinet
would likely find it easier to use his cabinet as an advisory council and to forge a policy
consensus. But while Lincoln's situation was in many ways unique, the problems he
confronted with his cabinet would prove to be a harbinger of things to come. Chase
would not be the last to lament that while "we ... are called members of the Cabinet in
reality [we are] only separate heads of departments."[57]

Francis Carpenter's painting of President Lincoln's reading of the Emancipation
Proclamation to his cabinet. Seated, from left to right, are Secretary of War Edwin Stanton,
Lincoln, Secretary of the Navy Gideon Welles, Secretary of State William Henry Seward,
and Attorney General Edward Bates. Standing, from left to right, are Secretary of Treasury
Salmon Chase, Secretary of the Interior Caleb Smith, and Postmaster General Montgomery
Blair.

Courtesy: Getty Images.

In view of how little use cabinet meetings were to Lincoln and the department heads, perhaps the most remarkable thing is that Lincoln continued to convene the cabinet at all. Cabinet meetings were still officially held twice a week. That Lincoln felt a need to keep up appearances with "the show of Cabinet-councils" attests to how entrenched had become the notion that presidential decision-making should be shaped by cabinet deliberations. Indeed, the very term "cabinet," by now a staple of Americans' political vocabulary, implied a collective role for department heads.[58]

Twice-weekly cabinet meetings, typically on Tuesday and Friday, remained a fixture of the nineteenth-century presidential schedule, even as presidents and cabinet members complained constantly about them being a waste of valuable time.[59] Part of the problem was that the cabinet was getting steadily larger. The addition of the Department of the Navy in 1798, the elevation of the postmaster general to cabinet rank in 1829, and the creation of the Interior Department in 1849 meant that Lincoln's cabinet was nearly twice the size of Washington's four-person cabinet. And over the next half-century, the cabinet would grow by another three members: a secretary of agriculture was added in 1889, a secretary of commerce in 1904, and a secretary of labor in 1913.[60]

The underlying problem, however, was not the cabinet's size but the gravitational pull exerted on its constituent parts, the "centrifugal force" that dragged a cabinet officer away from the president's goals and toward the outlook, interests, and constituencies of the department he managed. Meeting twice a week for an hour or two was not enough to instill a collective consciousness, a feeling that each member had a shared, mutual responsibility for administration policy. From the president's vantage point, many cabinet members were simply too parochial to counsel him on what was best for the country.[61]

SALVATION BY STAFF: THE CAUTIONARY TALE OF ULYSSES GRANT

Every nineteenth-century president would have sympathized with President Ulysses S. Grant's lament about his secretary of the interior Jacob Cox, whom the president eased out after a little more than 18 months on the job. Cox, Grant fumed, "thought the Interior Department was the whole government." So where was the president to turn for counsel when his chief advisory body was a patchwork of jealous fiefdoms that had few incentives to pull together as a team or to see a problem from the president's point of view? Grant's answer was to turn to his White House staff.[62]

Although rarely remembered as an innovator, the former general was the first president to rely heavily on White House staff for policy and personnel advice. Grant's experience is often left out of the conventional narrative of the emergence of a White House staff, which is unfortunate because his troubled presidency provides a valuable cautionary tale about the perils of seeking "salvation by staff."[63]

Protecting the President from the People

As the commanding general of the Union army, Grant had been supported by a substantial staff of military aides, three of whom he brought to Washington to serve as

White House staffers. Orville Babcock, Horace Porter, and Frederick T. Dent were each West Point graduates, career military officers, and brevet brigadier generals. Porter was nearly 32 when Grant took the oath of office; Babcock was 33; and Dent, Grant's roommate at West Point, was 48—two years older than the president, who at 46 was younger than any of his predecessors. For the first time in American history, the president's aides were close enough to the president in age to be his peers rather than his sons.[64]

Congress still only provided for one private secretary, but Grant got around that by having Dent and Porter placed on the personal staff of General William Tecumseh Sherman, who then assigned them to work at the White House. Unlike Lincoln, Grant did not have to borrow clerks from other government offices because in 1867, for the first time, Congress provided funding for an assistant private secretary, a stenographer, and several executive clerks to handle the bulk of the routine work of the office.[65]

Dent was essentially the president's appointments secretary. His desk was stationed in the reception room, where all White House visitors had to report. Dent ushered a few into the president's office, others he turned away, but most were directed to see Porter or Babcock, who would decide whether a meeting with the president was warranted. Many found, as General Sherman testified, that by seeing Babcock first they could "accomplish the object of the visit without seeing the President at all."[66]

In regulating access to the president, Babcock, Porter, and Dent played a role not unlike that of Nicolay and Hay in the Lincoln administration. But Grant's staff played the part much more efficiently, largely because they had a more compliant master. Hay and Nicolay had a "four-years struggle" to keep visitors out of the president's office because Lincoln, as Hay later recalled, "would break through every Regulation" designed to keep "the people … away from him." Grant, in contrast, was never comfortable with strangers and was only too happy to have them turned away. Unlike Lincoln, who was an expansive, entertaining, and sympathetic interlocutor, Grant "was no more than quietly polite to strangers, extending his hand indifferently for a listless shake." If he "ventured a few monosyllables in reply," writes historian Mark Wahlgren Summers, "it was done with an air of resignation that made both relieved to close their conference."[67]

Orville Babcock's "Passion for Helpfulness"

Babcock's role in the Grant White House was far more than "intermediator between the people and the President." Unlike his predecessors, Babcock also played a key role as presidential advisor and surrogate. In contrast to his boss, the gregarious Babcock was a natural politician, the sort of person whom others seemed to like instantly. Possessing what Grant's son Jesse shrewdly described as "a passion for helpfulness," Babcock befriended many of Washington's most powerful congressmen, with whom he dined regularly. Beneath the genial exterior, moreover, was a quick and agile mind. Babcock graduated third in his class at West Point; Grant, in contrast, finished near the middle of his.[68]

Most important of all, Grant trusted "Bab." When Hamilton Fish refused Grant's offer to become secretary of state, the president dispatched Babcock to convince Fish to change his mind. Knowing that Fish had offered his wife Julia's poor health as the reason for his refusal, Babcock used his considerable charm to win over Julia and then enlisted her aid in persuading her reluctant husband to accept the post—thereby averting an early embarrassment for Grant, who had carelessly sent Fish's name to the Senate before receiving his acceptance.[69]

Without Babcock's intervention, Fish probably would not have accepted the president's job offer. With Babcock at Grant's side, Fish frequently had cause to regret his decision. Throughout his seven-year tenure, Fish complained bitterly about what he perceived to be Babcock's "ever-present and ever-interfering influence" in his department's affairs.

General Ulysses Grant, cigar in hand, with his trusted military aide, General Orville E. Babcock. When Grant became president in 1869, Babcock became Grant's right-hand man in the White House.

Courtesy: Missouri History Museum, St. Louis.

The problem, as Fish saw it, was that Babcock "fancies himself President of the United States." Babcock and Fish clashed repeatedly over diplomatic appointments. Babcock viewed diplomatic postings as patronage to be doled out to bolster the president's political standing, whereas Fish sought to fill the positions with "cultivated" men of distinction with diplomatic experience. Fish believed Babcock was rewarding his political cronies and degrading the foreign service. Babcock thought Fish was paying insufficient attention to the president's political interests.[70]

In prior administrations, no department head, let alone the secretary of state, had reason to complain about interference from a mere private secretary. Past secretaries had sometimes played the role of liaison with Congress, but none had dared to engage in bureaucratic turf battles with department heads. Lincoln's secretaries used the press to defend the president and his policies, but that was nothing like Babcock's use of the press in intra-administration disputes. Babcock leaked information to the press to force the ouster of one cabinet member, and he used the close relationship he had forged with the disreputable owner of Washington's *National Republican*—a quasi-official administration mouthpiece—to sanction stories that were critical of the State Department's policy toward Cuba, including one that attacked Fish personally.[71]

Babcock believed that he was looking out for the president's political interests in a way that department secretaries were not. Presumably, Grant believed that too, or he would not have allowed Babcock to exert such a strong role behind the scenes. But did Babcock's advice and machinations help the president? In securing Fish's services, he clearly advanced the president's interests. But in much else that Babcock did, he contributed materially to Grant's failed presidency.

The Whiskey Ring Scandal

No event brought into sharper relief the trouble that Grant invited by trusting in Babcock than the Whiskey Ring. At the center of the corrupt ring was John McDonald, whom Grant, at Babcock's suggestion, had installed as head of a major regional office of the Internal Revenue Service in St. Louis. McDonald's charge was not only to collect federal revenue but also to help the administration fend off the political challenge of Missouri's Carl Schurz, leader of the so-called "Liberal Republicans," a faction that was strongly opposed to Grant's renomination. McDonald's scheme, an elaborate mix of bribery and blackmail, helped distillers evade high federal whiskey taxes while funneling huge sums of whiskey money into Republican coffers. After Grant's reelection was secured in 1872, the ring morphed into an almost exclusively criminal operation that made McDonald and his cronies rich.[72]

When the newly installed treasury secretary Benjamin Bristow began to investigate the ring, he found that the trail led all the way to the White House, to the office of Orville Babcock. How much Babcock knew about the scope of McDonald's thieving is open to debate, but Babcock undoubtedly conspired to frustrate Bristow's investigation by passing information to McDonald. And if McDonald is to be believed, Babcock was rewarded for his help with as much as $25,000 in cash, a $2,400 diamond shirt stud, and the occasional hook-up with an "irresistible" St. Louis courtesan known as "the Sylph."[73]

Yet Grant's faith in Babcock remained unshakable. When Bristow initially told the president that he had arrested 350 people in connection with the ring, Grant replied that McDonald must be honest because "he [was] an intimate acquaintance and confidential friend of Babcock's." When Bristow produced the evidence that led to Babcock's indictment by a grand jury, Grant persuaded himself that the prosecution was politically motivated and that Bristow's real aim was to embarrass Grant. Babcock was in the dock, he told his cabinet, but the prosecution was really "putting [the president] on trial." Convinced of Babcock's innocence and determined to thwart his political enemies, Grant forbade prosecutors from offering immunity or plea bargains in exchange for testimony against Babcock. He told his cabinet that he was determined to go to St. Louis to testify on Babcock's behalf. A unanimous cabinet talked the president out of the "impossible and unseemly" idea but they could not deter the president from giving a deposition, which had its desired effect: Babcock was acquitted on the strength of the president's character reference.[74]

Although Babcock got off, the damage to Grant's reputation was irreparable. Most impartial observers, then as now, believed Babcock was guilty. In rushing to Babcock's defense, Grant looked at worst dishonest, at best a fool—particularly when, two months after the acquittal, Babcock was indicted again in another scandal involving burgled documents. Grant's failed presidency provides a valuable corrective to the notion that staff are a president's salvation and that cabinet members are necessarily—as Calvin Coolidge's budget director Charles Dawes famously put it—"a president's natural enemies." It was not a cabinet member but the president's top staffer and closest friend who "served more than any other man to blacken the record of Grant's administration." What hurt Grant most was not departmental parochialism but an insistence that political and personal loyalty be privileged over administrative competence and policy expertise.[75]

Settling for Second Best: Private Secretaries in the Gilded Age

Babcock is barely remembered today, but he was very much on the mind of James Garfield as he prepared to become the 20th president of the United States. As chairman of the powerful House Appropriations Committee during the Grant presidency, Garfield had closely observed the power Babcock wielded as well as the damage he did. "The man who holds that place," Garfield confided to a political ally, "can do very much to make or mar the success of an administration." So important was the position, he added, that it "ought to be held in higher estimation than Secretary of State." The man he wanted for the post was Lincoln's former aide John Hay, who was then assistant secretary of state in the Hayes administration. Garfield thought that Hay would make the position "one of power and brilliancy" and thereby "double [the president's] strength," but he also recognized that its low prestige and meager salary made Hay's acceptance improbable. Garfield was right. Hay rejected the offer, telling the president-elect that he had no desire to subject himself once again to the unremitting and "unspeakably repulsive ... contact with the greed and selfishness of office-seekers and bull-dozing Congressmen." Garfield ended up settling instead for an efficient but inexperienced 22-year-old stenographer.[76]

While late nineteenth-century presidents continued to complain about the difficulty of getting good help, few in Congress seemed overly concerned. Legislators may have agreed with Garfield's assessment that a strong private secretary could double the president's power, but they had no desire to help the president bulk up. Many in Congress believed that the president should merely execute the legislative will and therefore had no need for a politically experienced staffer who could counsel the president on policy. And few in Congress doubted that they had already provided the president with secretarial and clerical support that was more than adequate to discharge the routine duties of the office.

Presidents did not dispute the latter point. Set to begin his second stint as president in 1893, Grover Cleveland told an associate that "as the executive office is now organized it can deal, with a fair amount of efficiency, with the routine affairs of Government." During his first term, Cleveland was assisted by not only a private secretary (paid $3,250 a year) but also an assistant secretary ($2,250), two executive clerks ($2,000), a stenographer ($1,800), and three other clerks of various pay grades, not to mention a steward, three ushers, five messengers, two doorkeepers, and a watchman. Of critical importance was the dramatically increased professionalism at the level of the assistant secretary and clerks. When Rutherford Hayes became president, he promoted one of Grant's two executive clerks to the post of assistant secretary, and the assistant remained in that position for the next 25 years, until his death in 1902. The other of Grant's two executive clerks remained in the White House until his death in 1915. In short, by the latter decades of the nineteenth century the president was supported by a professional clerical staff characterized by an impressive institutional continuity, much like today's executive clerk's office.[77]

The problem facing late nineteenth-century presidents, then, was not managing the routine office work. Instead the problem, as Cleveland emphasized, was that "if the President has any great policy in mind or on hand he has no one to help him work it out." At the end of Cleveland's first term, Congress had boosted the private secretary's salary to $5,000 (the same as a member of Congress earned), but that was Congress's sole concession to the president's need for help that went beyond routine office work. What Cleveland wanted, however, was not a mere private secretary but an "assistant to the president." He suggested a salary of $10,000—which was $2,000 more than the vice president and department heads were paid—so that he could recruit from among the country's best and most experienced political operatives. His first choice had been William L. Wilson, the powerful West Virginia congressman who was about to assume the reins as chair of the House Ways and Means Committee, but Cleveland had to make do with Henry Thurber, a "well-connected and well-intentioned socialite with no political ability." The time when someone of Wilson's stature would join the president's staff was still decades away.[78]

MANAGING GOVERNMENT AND BUDGETS IN THE NINETEENTH CENTURY

No matter how efficient an administrator, a private secretary could do little to help the president direct the steadily expanding executive branch. When James Monroe took office in 1817 there were only about 4,500 federal workers in the executive branch, and three-fourths of those worked in the post office. Even at the time of Lincoln's inauguration there were fewer than 6,000 executive branch employees, not counting the post office, which employed 84 percent of executive branch workers. But by the end of the nineteenth century, as McKinley prepared to take the oath of office for the second time, the executive branch had grown substantially in size and complexity. The federal bureaucracy now counted 100,000 non-post office employees; counting the post office, the number was closer to 250,000. To put the transformation another way, in the three and a half decades before the Civil War (1826–1860) federal spending averaged $36 million and never exceeded $75 million, whereas in the three and a half decades after the war (1866–1900) federal spending averaged $325 million and never dropped below $240 million.[79]

During most of the nineteenth century, presidents made only sporadic attempts to control departmental budgets. Estimates of how much money was needed were prepared by the various bureaus, offices, and field agents that made up the executive branch. Department heads might review the estimates but rarely revised them. Instead bureau estimates were sent to the Treasury Department, which compiled them, usually with few or no changes, into a "book of estimates" that was then forwarded to Congress. The president, administrative historian Leonard White found, "had little, if anything, to do with the level or content of the estimates ... or with the actual use of the funds annually made available" by Congress.[80]

For most of the nineteenth century—the Civil War being a notable exception—Congress kept executive officials on a tight leash by avoiding lump-sum appropriations and itemizing how almost every dollar should be spent. This was especially true with respect to personnel, where "office after office had specified for it the exact number of clerks and other employees to which it was entitled, and precise pay for each one." Protecting their budgets required executive officers to plead not with the president but with members of the congressional appropriations committees that saw it as their job to "shave and reduce" the inflated estimates of the departments.[81]

Even apart from budgetary matters, presidential supervision of departmental affairs was sharply limited by institutional capacity as well as political custom. Absent more generous staff support, vigilant oversight of the executive branch could not be achieved without submerging the president in a mass of technical details, making him a slave to the "tyranny of the trivial," as arguably happened to Cleveland, who expended many hundreds of hours personally investigating the merits of pension claims by Civil War veterans. Moreover, presidents generally felt obliged to respect the convention that a president should not interfere unduly in the management of departmental affairs. Not every president went as far as Grant, of whose administration it was said that "seven Cabinet members made seven policies," but most cabinet members during this period expected to be chiefly responsible for the policies of their departments. And presidents in the late nineteenth century largely shared that expectation.[82]

"No Responsibility Exists": The Progressive Quest for Administrative Reform

Not everybody was happy with the status quo, however. The diffusion of responsibility was an increasing concern to reform-minded Americans in the late nineteenth century.

As early as 1870, Grant's second year in office, Henry Adams condemned a government that "does not govern." Congress was "inefficient" and "incompetent," while the executive, "deprived of its necessary strength by the jealousy of the Legislature," lacked "the responsibility, direct, incessant, and continuous" that a government of "over forty millions of people and an entire continent" required. In 1870, Adams was an alienated voice in the political wilderness, but by 1900 his complaint that "no responsibility exists at Washington" was being echoed across the political spectrum. Increasingly, those who styled themselves "Progressives" demanded that the president be granted the capacity to direct the executive branch and take full responsibility for its actions. The bureaucratic buck should stop at the president's desk.[83]

Calls for administrative reform were boosted by the return of budget deficits in the mid-1890s. Between 1866 and 1893 the federal government never ran a deficit, but between 1894 and 1910, the federal government operated at a deficit most of the time. Tax revenues were increasing, but government expenditures were growing even more rapidly. When McKinley took office in 1897 the government spent a little over $350 million annually, but by the time William Howard Taft entered the White House in 1909, government expenditures were nearly twice that. Many observers, Democrat as well as Republican, agreed with Henry Jones Ford that the government's inability to control expenditures showed that it had become "seriously deranged." The consensus was that government needed to be made more efficient.[84]

Administrative Reform in the Taft Administration

In 1910, Taft asked Congress for $100,000 to study how to make the government more efficient. Anxious to get government spending under control and bring an end to the deficits, Congress gave Taft the money he requested as well as complete control over the conduct of the study. Taft directed his secretary Charles Norton, a former assistant in the Treasury Department, to devise a plan for how to proceed. After spending several months talking with "efficiency experts," Norton counseled the president to avoid relying on executive branch officials for the study. To keep the study "within [the president's] own hands" and to avoid it being "blocked ... by the Cabinet," it should be entrusted to a presidential aide operating out of the White House. The best man for the job, Norton and Taft agreed, was Frederick Cleveland, a professor of finance and one of the founders of the New York Bureau of Municipal Research, a nongovernmental organization in the vanguard of the nationwide movement to make city government more efficient and accountable.[85]

Cleveland was given a White House office and a staff of ten accountants, clerks, and stenographers to help him gather data about how agencies transacted business, kept records, and prepared budgetary estimates. Cleveland spoke the language of efficiency, but his understanding of that term differed significantly from that of most members of Congress. For congressmen, efficiency meant economizing. They wanted the government's study to identify wasteful spending so it could be eliminated. For Cleveland, however, efficiency meant ending the fragmented authority that prevented coordination among the different parts of the bureaucracy. The underlying structural problem, as

Cleveland saw it, was not waste but an "atomized administrative universe dominated by congressional authority." Cleveland argued that efficiency demanded severing the close ties that bound the agencies to legislative committees and instead centralizing administrative authority—particularly over spending estimates—in the White House. Centralized executive control of the budgeting process was thus the linchpin to efficient administration of government.[86]

As the broader aims of Cleveland's investigation became clear, it ran into strong resistance from Congress as well as from the Treasury Department and individual bureaus and agencies, all of which felt threatened by the effort to centralize budgetary authority in the White House. In hopes of improving the reception on Capitol Hill, Taft transformed Cleveland's one-man show into a distinguished six-person Commission on Economy and Efficiency, with Cleveland as chair. Congress, though, remained unimpressed, particularly since the commission failed to identify any substantial cost savings. Nor did it help the commission's cause that the large deficits that had so alarmed lawmakers at the outset of Taft's term had vanished. Absent a fiscal emergency, Congress was unwilling to cede its traditional control over executive budgets.[87]

Although Congress showed no interest in the commission's recommendations, Taft had become a convert to Cleveland's vision of a centralized, executive-centered budget process. In January 1912, Taft threw down the gauntlet to Congress. "The United States," he told Congress, "is the only great Nation whose government is operated without a budget." And without such a budget, he continued, it was impossible to achieve a government that was both "responsive to public opinion and responsible for its acts." Taft could not compel Congress to adopt the commission's recommendations, but he could order his department heads to comply with the commission's budgetary recommendations. And so Taft demanded two budgets: one following the traditional method of compiling disparate agency estimates into a book of estimates and the other following the commission's recommendations for a presidential budget. Congress could not stop the president from submitting his own budget, but they could (and did) ignore it. To underscore their rejection of Taft's vision of executive reorganization, Congress also cut off further funding for the commission.[88]

Although Taft's successor Woodrow Wilson was sympathetic to the commission's vision of administrative reform, he refused to revive the commission or to follow Taft's experiment in executive budgeting. Either plan, he calculated, would upset congressional leaders and jeopardize his legislative agenda. However, by leading the nation into World War I, Wilson inadvertently revived congressional support for reform by driving government spending and budget deficits to record levels. The total national debt, which had been about $1 billion in 1916, the year before the nation entered the war, ballooned to nearly $25 billion by 1919.[89]

The President's New Management Tool: The Bureau of the Budget

The unprecedented budget deficits spurred the Republican-controlled House into action in 1919. A House select committee condemned the system of departmental and agency estimates as a "patchwork" system that compelled congressional committees to waste valuable time "exploding the visionary schemes of bureau chiefs for which no administration would be willing to stand responsible." The committee proposed that the president should be made solely responsible for all estimates emanating from the executive branch. To enable him to carry out this responsibility, the committee recommended the creation of a budget bureau that would be housed in the White House and report directly to the president. The Senate came up with a similar proposal, though their version placed the new budgetary bureau in the Treasury Department. In the end, the two houses compromised on a bill that placed the bureau in the Treasury Department but made its director a personal assistant to the president. The budget director was to report directly to the president, who was free to select anybody he wanted, without the advice or consent of the Senate.[90]

Signed into law by Warren Harding on June 10, 1921, the Budget and Accounting Act authorized the new Bureau of the Budget (BOB) "to assemble, correlate, revise, reduce, or increase the estimates" of executive departments and agencies. Harding and his first budget director, Charles Dawes, immediately put the new authority to use. The president directed Dawes to reduce all agency estimates for 1922 by 10 percent. Dawes aggressively sought to check agency autonomy and assert presidential control over the executive branch. BOB officers were assigned to oversee specific government agencies; their responsibility, Dawes explained, was "to bring to the heads of the departments and the chiefs of bureaus . . . a better realization of how the plan of their particular department can be made to better accord with the plan which the President has established." Moreover, Dawes ordered that all legislative proposals emanating from departments must first be cleared by BOB if the legislation would "create a charge upon the public Treasury or commit the Government to obligations which would later require appropriations to meet them."[91]

The new centralized budgetary process seemed to pay immediate dividends. In 1921, government expenditures still exceeded $5 billion; however, using the new budgetary tools, the Harding administration and Congress slashed government spending in 1922 by almost 40 percent, to $3.3 billion. Throughout the remainder of the Harding and Coolidge presidencies, expenditures remained stable, hovering around $3 billion. And from 1922 through 1930 the government ran unprecedented surpluses, ranging from $700 million to over $1 billion; prior to 1920 the largest annual surplus in American history was less than $145 million.

But while BOB provided the president with powerful new tools for managing the executive branch, many observers were disappointed at what they considered its narrow focus on spending reductions. Too often its leaders defined their role as policing trivial cost savings. Dawes's successor, Herbert Lord, made it his job to check employees' desks "for excessive use of official stationery, paper clips, and other government supplies." Dawes was so eager to show his commitment to economy that he spent less than half the money that Congress appropriated for his agency. Whereas Dawes and Lord believed their frugality showed they were leading by example, critics countered that they were limiting the capacity of the fledgling bureau to carry out its work and undermining the president's ability to manage the executive branch.[92]

When Franklin Roosevelt became president in 1933, he quickly became frustrated by the niggardly focus of BOB. Its director, Lewis Douglas, with whom Roosevelt initially met almost every morning, seemed interested only in cutting government spending and reducing the deficit, to the virtual exclusion of any other presidential priorities, such as helping the one-quarter of American workers who were out of work. Rather than helping the president pursue his priorities, Douglas was lobbying for his own agenda. By the summer of 1934 Douglas was out, and Roosevelt marginalized his replacement, preferring to rely on other White House assistants to shape his agenda.[93]

Moreover, Roosevelt was unhappy to find that the lightly staffed BOB was doing little to stem the tide of uncoordinated agency requests for legislation. Roosevelt demanded that BOB make legislative clearance a top priority so that the administration spoke with a single voice in Congress: the president's. Efficiency in the Roosevelt presidency was to mean more than mere economy; it was to mean, as Frederick Cleveland had envisioned, a unified, cohesive executive branch under the control of the president.[94]

FDR and the Making of the Managerial Presidency

Shortly after his reelection in 1936, Roosevelt suggested to a group of reporters that his landslide victory had been helped by Republicans' failure to focus the election on the Achilles' heel of the New Deal: administration. The president would have received no argument from students of public administration, who were often aghast at the chaotic array of overlapping agencies created during Roosevelt's first term and the absence of clear lines of authority and accountability.[95]

Administering the New Deal

The way Roosevelt administered the Federal Emergency Relief Appropriation Act of 1935, confessed Louis Brownlow, "shocked every student of public administration to the marrow of his bones." Congress had given the president almost total discretion over how to spend the nearly $5 billion lump-sum appropriation on the theory that the president and his administrators were in the best position to spend the emergency relief money where it could do the most good. What Roosevelt came up with was the so-called "five ring circus." Applications for spending projects went first to Frank Walker, a presidential assistant who headed up the Division of Applications and Information. If Walker approved the plan it was forwarded to the Advisory Committee on Allotments, a 23-person committee chaired by Interior Secretary Harold Ickes that made recommendations to the president. If the plan was approved by the president, the head of the Works Project Administration (WPA), Harry Hopkins, was responsible for implementing it. The task of keeping the financial accounts and disbursing funds was handed to Treasury Secretary Henry Morgenthau, and the acting director of the Bureau of the Budget, Daniel Bell, was responsible for "doling out a nickel here and a dime there for administrative expenses." As Brownlow noted, this labyrinthine process "confused nearly everybody."[96]

The seeds of this disorderly administrative structure were sown in the president's conviction that swift action required the creation of new agencies. Roosevelt believed that existing departments and agencies would be slowed by bureaucratic inertia and distracted by competing objectives, whereas a new agency could attack its task with single-minded zeal. And emergency agencies did sometimes act with incredible speed, none faster than the Civil Works Administration (CWA). Established in November 1933 with the goal of putting 4 million people to work during the upcoming winter, the CWA put 2 million people to work in its first ten days. "But for God's sake," CWA head Harry Hopkins told the president, "don't ask me what they're doing." By January, the CWA had shot well past the 4 million mark. But cutting through the bureaucratic red tape also invited corruption, the revelations of which helped bring about the CWA's early demise, though not before Hopkins had spent close to a billion dollars in a little over four months.[97]

The CWA was unusually short-lived. Most new agencies, even temporary ones, endured for far longer. Established in 1933, the Public Works Administration (PWA), for instance, lasted until 1939, and the WPA continued to operate from 1935 until 1943. Often the functions of new agencies overlapped, creating duplication as well as competition. Both the WPA, headed by Hopkins, and the PWA, headed by Ickes, administered public works programs, and the two leaders feuded constantly over control of the programs. Some of this overlap was administratively productive, since conflicting grants of authority pushed important decisions onto the president's desk for resolution. But the overlap and competition also confused and exasperated his subordinates and impeded the coordination of government programs. Compounding the problem, new agencies often competed and overlapped with existing agencies. Public works, for instance, was also the province of well-established agencies like the Corps of Engineers, housed in the War Department, and the Bureau of Reclamation, located in the Interior Department.[98]

During his first term, Roosevelt tried several different schemes for coordinating the federal government's response to the Great Depression. By executive order, on July 11, 1933, he created an Executive Council (EC), which consisted of the entire cabinet, the budget director, and the heads of a host of freshly minted agencies, including the Agricultural Adjustment Administration, the National Recovery Administration, the Federal Emergency Relief Administration, the Farm Credit Administration, the Home Owners' Loan Corporation, and the Tennessee Valley Authority. Composed of two dozen people, the council proved too large to coordinate policy effectively, and so five months later the president, again by executive order, formed a new group of half the size called the National Emergency Council (NEC). The NEC included only four members of the cabinet (Interior, Agriculture, Commerce, and Labor) and dispensed with the budget director and assistant secretary of the treasury as well as several agency heads. Seven months later, Roosevelt spawned yet another cabinet-level coordinating committee, the Industrial Emergency Committee (IEC). Half the size of the NEC, the IEC consisted of only two cabinet members (Interior and Labor), several agency heads, and a presidential aide.[99]

The multiplication of cabinet-level councils created overlapping membership—members of the IEC were also on the NEC and most of those on the NEC were also on the EC—and spawned confusion as to which council had jurisdiction over which activities. Roosevelt's response was to abolish the Executive Council, transferring all its duties to the NEC and giving every member of the Executive Council a place on a reconstituted NEC, which now became a 34-person "super" cabinet committee, of which the IEC was made a subcommittee. Directing both the committee and the subcommittee was Donald Richberg, who was given broad powers to carry out the council's charge to coordinate the government's policies. But this experiment faltered also; one presidential aide simply could not herd the entire government, especially when the president did not consistently back him. Within six months Richberg had announced his resignation, "a victim of sniping from cabinet members"; his successor lasted six months as well. NEC meetings became increasingly infrequent, attended more often by lower-level staff than principals. On April 28, 1936, the NEC met for the last time.[100]

Roosevelt needed help, and he knew it. Government was getting too big and its tasks too varied and complex to be administered through ad hoc cabinet councils. In 1932, the last year of Hoover's presidency, the executive branch, not counting the post office and national defense, had fewer than 200,000 employees. By 1936, at the end of Roosevelt's first term, that number had more than doubled, to 420,000 employees. The vast majority of the increase was in newly created agencies that existed outside of established departments. Interdepartmental coordinating committees, boards, and commissions proliferated— in 1934 Richberg counted a staggering 350 interdepartmental committees and sub-committees. With the NEC collapsing under its own weight, Roosevelt became increasingly receptive to arguments that administering the New Deal required rethinking the way the presidency was organized and staffed.[101]

The Brownlow Committee's Plea for Help

One month before the NEC's last meeting in April 1936, Roosevelt unveiled a committee made up of three nationally recognized students of public administration: Brownlow, Charles Merriam, and Luther Gulick. Supported by a large staff of 27, the Brownlow Committee, formally known as the Committee on Administrative Management, was tasked with discovering ways "to give the President effective managerial direction and control over all departments and agencies of the Executive Branch of the Federal Government com-mensurate with his responsibility." In private conversations with Brownlow and Merriam, Roosevelt emphasized that he was not looking for cost savings but better management tools. "We have got to get over the notion that the purpose of reorganization is economy," Roosevelt insisted. "The reason for reorganization is good management."[102]

The Brownlow Committee released its report in January 1937. Taking its cue from Roosevelt, the committee emphasized the broader purposes of executive reorganization. Managerial efficiency, the report maintained, was necessary to make good "the popular will in a people's government." The presidency, as currently organized, was an archaic institution, out of step with recent advances in administrative science and unable to meet the demands of a complex, modern society. Where else, the report asked, "can there be found an executive in any way comparable upon whom so much petty work is thrown? Or who is forced to see so many persons on unrelated matters and to make so many decisions on the basis of what may be, because of the very press of work, incomplete information?" When government was small, the nation was able to tolerate these inefficiencies. But the dramatic growth of government and multiplication of government agencies required remaking the executive branch so that its myriad activities could be directed and coordinated by the president. "Those who waver at the sight of needed power," the report closed, "are false friends of modern democracy. Strong executive leadership is essential to democratic government today."[103]

The committee's first recommendation—which immediately followed its famous plea that "The President needs help"—was the addition of up to six presidential assistants. They were to help the president make decisions by "obtaining quickly and without delay all pertinent information possessed by any of the executive departments." Then they were to help the president carry out those decisions by "seeing to it that every administrative department and agency affected is promptly informed." Unlike presidential secretaries, who served as liaisons to Congress, the press, and the public, these assistants were to "remain in the background" and "emit no public statements"—they would be possessed, the report famously declared, with "a passion for anonymity." Although these assistants would remain out of the public eye, they would not be powers behind the throne. They "would not be interposed between the President and the heads of his departments" and would "have no power to make decisions or issue instructions in their own right." They would assist the president but "they would not be assistant presidents in any sense."[104]

Roosevelt thought the report "grand," not surprisingly, since he had played a significant role in shaping the committee's agenda and refining its proposals. Congress, however, greeted the report with "sullen silence" and even overt hostility. The idea of increasing the president's staff was not particularly controversial, though many in Congress and the press scoffed at the notion that any senior presidential aides would possess a "passion for anonymity." Other parts of the report, however, were profoundly unpopular on Capitol Hill. Members of Congress particularly resented the committee's proposal to strip the comptroller general—who headed the General Accounting Office (GAO), a legislative agency established by the 1921 Budget and Accounting Act to enhance legislative control over expenditures—of the power to disallow agency expenditures that he deemed to be inconsistent with the purposes of a legislative appropriation.[105]

Congress was also strongly opposed to the proposal to give the president the power to transfer all independent boards and commissions either into existing departments or into one of three proposed new departments: Public Works, Social Welfare, and Conservation. To the Brownlow Committee, bringing the "headless 'fourth branch'" under presidential control would end the "confusion, conflict, and incoherence" produced by agencies that were independent of presidential control. Roosevelt insisted that the reforms would merely make him a better, more efficient manager of the executive branch, but members of Congress regarded the reforms as a thinly disguised presidential power grab. Despite overwhelming Democratic majorities in both houses of Congress and the president's trouncing of Republican Alf Landon, the 75th Congress refused to enact what critics dubbed the "dictator bill."[106]

The Reorganization Act of 1939

In 1939, two years after the Brownlow report's introduction, Congress finally did take action on executive reorganization. The bill, however, was only a "pale imitation" of the committee's original draft. The Reorganization Act of 1939 included no change to the duties of the GAO or the comptroller general, no new executive departments, and no sweeping overhaul of independent agencies. It did, however, authorize six new presidential administrative assistants—at a salary of up to $10,000 each—to help the president cope with his increased administrative responsibilities.[107]

On paper, the change seemed dramatic, as it tripled the number of top presidential aides. It was the first increase in senior presidential staff since 1929, when Herbert Hoover had persuaded a reluctant Congress to add two additional presidential secretaries to bring the total to three. But Roosevelt had never operated with only the three senior aides allowed by law. Like Lincoln and Grant before him, Roosevelt "borrowed" staffers from other departments. Raymond Moley was formally appointed assistant secretary of state, but his real role was as a key White House aide in the early New Deal. Rexford Tugwell, another influential Roosevelt aide in the early New Deal, was officially the assistant secretary of agriculture. In drafting New Deal legislation, Roosevelt also relied heavily on the assistance of Thomas Corcoran, whose paid position was as legal counsel to the Reconstruction Finance Corporation, and Benjamin Cohen, who worked for the Public Works Administration and later the Interior Department.[108]

Roosevelt's borrowing of staff went well beyond a few high-profile aides. Between 1933 and 1939, the size of Roosevelt's budgeted White House staff remained at around 37, the same number it had been during Hoover's last two years and only slightly higher than the budgeted staff of 31 during the Harding presidency. But the real number of individuals detailed to the White House during Roosevelt's presidency was much, much larger. In his first term, for instance, an average of around 125 people a year worked at the White House—mostly as clerical and secretarial support—while on the payroll of other departments or agencies. Some of these only worked at the White House for a few months in the year, but about half of them worked in the White House year-round.[109]

The Brownlow Committee exaggerated, then, in claiming that FDR's staff assistance was "entirely inadequate." Nor was the president desperate for the additional six staff assistants recommended by the committee. Indeed, Roosevelt acknowledged as much while lobbying for the entire package of Brownlow reforms. "I would hardly know what to do with six Executive Assistants," FDR confessed in 1937, "if I do not have any authority to put the government as a whole on a businesslike basis." After passage of the 1939 act, Roosevelt was slow to fill the new administrative assistant positions. Not until 1941 was the last of the six positions filled. Moreover, even after 1939, FDR continued to rely heavily on aides borrowed from other parts of the federal government. And after America's entry into World War II, Roosevelt took advantage of lump-sum defense appropriations to further expand the number of White House employees. By 1945, about 200 people worked in the White House, which was four times the number budgeted by Congress. The Brownlow Committee's six new assistants were not exactly a drop in the administrative bucket, but neither did they transform the workings of the Roosevelt White House.[110]

More important than the six new staff assistants was the provision of the 1939 act that granted the president the authority to reorganize the executive branch, subject to congressional veto. The Brownlow Committee had proposed that the president's reorganization authority be made permanent, but Congress consented only to a temporary, two-year grant of authority subject to specific limitations, such as not altering the number of departments and exempting 21 agencies—including the GAO—from any reorganization. Congress had actually given Roosevelt temporary reorganization authority once before, in the Economy Act of 1933, but he had used it sparingly then, in part because he was anxious to avoid controversial reorganization plans that might undermine congressional support for his economic recovery program and in part because he initially saw reorganization more as a means to secure budgetary savings than as a tool to increase his control over the executive branch. This time, however, Roosevelt was ready to take full advantage of Congress's delegation of reorganization authority.[111]

The Creation of the Executive Office of the President

Three weeks after signing the Reorganization Act into law, Roosevelt sent Congress his reorganization plan. Shortly thereafter he issued Executive Order 8248, which laid out the plan in detail. The reorganization plan had a number of provisions, but by far the most important were the creation of an Executive Office of the President (EOP) and—following the Brownlow Committee's recommendation—removing the Bureau of the Budget from the Treasury Department and making it a presidential agency, housed within the EOP.[112]

Under Executive Order 8248, the first unit within the EOP was the White House Office, which was to house the president's personal staff. The executive order subdivided the White House Office into three units: (1) the executive clerk, who was charged with providing for "the orderly handling of documents and correspondence within the White House Office" and supervising the requisite clerical support; (2) the presidential secretaries, whose job was to "facilitate and maintain quick and easy communication" with Congress, department and agency heads, the press, and the public; and (3) the new administrative assistants, whose job descriptions were left exquisitely vague: they were to "assist the President in such matters as he may direct."[113]

The executive clerk's office as a separate administrative unit within the White House Office endures to this day, but the distinction between the existing president secretaries and the new administrative assistants had "little relevance to the subsequent history of the White House Office." The administrative assistants soon became indistinguishable from presidential secretaries—and even the term "secretary" faded away as a designation among senior aides, except for the press secretary, whose work as liaison with the press remained distinctive. Had the Brownlow Committee had its way, the administrative assistants would have been markedly different from the president's political secretaries. Brownlow and his colleagues originally conceived the assistants as "career men" who would "serve through administration after administration," on the model of the British cabinet secretariat. But after Roosevelt scotched that idea, little was left that could differentiate the vaguely defined role of presidential assistant from the only slightly less vaguely defined position of presidential secretary.[114]

In designating the White House Office and its three subdivisions, Executive Order 8248 largely codified—albeit vaguely—existing roles within the president's personal staff. But in moving BOB into the newly created EOP, FDR's reorganization plan realized the Brownlow Committee's objective of arming the president with institutional staff support: career civil servants, possessed of technical expertise, administrative competence, and institutional memory, who could help the president to manage and coordinate the executive branch.

As important as moving BOB out of the treasury and into the EOP was the dramatic increase in funding for it. A year before Congress passed the 1939 Reorganization Act, FDR prevailed upon legislators to pass a supplemental appropriation that doubled the number of BOB employees, from 45 to 100. By the end of Roosevelt's presidency, the number of BOB staffers had climbed to well over 500, with an annual budget of nearly $3 million, more than 15 times higher than it had been prior to the release of the Brownlow report. The BOB that Roosevelt built endowed his successors with managerial capabilities that had been unavailable to his predecessors.[115]

RICHARD NIXON AND THE ORIGINS OF THE ADMINISTRATIVE PRESIDENCY

When Richard Nixon became president in 1969, he inherited a presidential branch unrecognizable from the one that Herbert Hoover had bequeathed to FDR. Even the EOP created by Roosevelt had been transformed beyond all recognition. Apart from the White House Office and the Bureau of the Budget, none of the other EOP units established by Roosevelt were still in existence. Moreover, the EOP had several new units that had become pillars of the modern presidency, most notably the Council of Economic Advisors, created by Congress in 1946, and the National Security Council, established by Congress in 1947. The White House Office staff was also much larger: by 1968, the White House Office had about 250 full-time employees, with another 200 or so staffers detailed to the White House while remaining on the payroll of departments or agencies.[116]

Watergate and the Alarm over the "Swelling of the Presidency"

During the 1960s, the increasing size of the president's staff attracted little attention or concern, which was a testament to the widespread belief among political elites that growing the White House staff was a safe and proven way to provide presidents with the necessary help.[117] By the time Nixon resigned in August 1974, however, there was widespread alarm at the "swelling of the presidency," thanks in large part to Watergate, the seismic scandal that forced Nixon's resignation and landed many of his top aides in jail, including Chief of Staff John Haldeman and Nixon's top domestic policy aide, John Ehrlichman.[118]

Watergate took its name from the break-in by Nixon campaign operatives at the Democratic National Committee (DNC) headquarters, which was housed in the Watergate office complex in Washington. Authorized by the chairman of the Committee to Re-elect the President, John Mitchell (who had just stepped down from the role of attorney general, the nation's top law enforcement officer), the plan was to tap the phones of DNC chairman Larry O'Brien in a bid to secure information that could be useful to the

Nixon reelection campaign or damaging to the campaign of Democratic challenger George McGovern. Unfortunately for the administration, the burglars were caught. What followed was a frantic administration cover-up involving hush money, shredded files, lies to investigators, and perjured testimony before Congress.

Despite the cover-up, investigators unearthed a lot more than one botched break-in, which may explain why Nixon risked his presidency to conceal a campaign operation of which he had no prior knowledge. What investigators found was a foul-mouthed president obsessed with enemies, conspiracies, and retribution, and a staff of eager-to-please zealots who not only compiled an "enemies list" but sought ways, as White House Counsel John Dean put it in a 1971 memo, to "use the available federal machinery"—including tax audits, federal contracts, litigation, and prosecution—"to screw our political enemies." The duo who orchestrated the DNC break-in, G. Gordon Liddy and Howard Hunt, were only reprising their role from the previous year, when as White House staffers they burgled—with Ehrlichman's blessing—the office of Daniel Ellsberg's psychiatrist. Their goal: to find information that could discredit Ellsberg, who had leaked a secret Defense Department report on Vietnam—the Pentagon Papers—to the *New York Times*.[119]

The misplaced loyalty and "blind ambition" of Nixon's many White House aides is certainly a vital part of the Watergate story. Virtually all of those who went to jail in Watergate were White House staffers or in the pay of staff. However, White House aides checked Nixon's vindictiveness at least as often as they abetted it. Several months before the Ellsberg break-in, for instance, Nixon ordered a raid on the Brookings Institution, a prominent Washington think tank that he believed possessed "tons" of classified documents in a safe. "You're to break into the place ... Blow the safe ... rifle the files, and bring them in," he instructed his aides. And make sure, he added, to have the safe "cleaned out in a way that it makes somebody else" look responsible. No aide argued against the illegal scheme but nobody carried it out either, despite Nixon repeating the directive during at least five different meetings over a two-week span, including one meeting in which he gave instructions as to the time the break-in should be carried out—"around 8:00 or 9:00 o'clock" was best, Nixon thought. The "dirty tricks" and systematic abuse of power uncovered in Watergate, in short, owed more to Nixon's personal failings than to a bloated White House staff.[120]

The drama of Watergate distracts attention from the more enduring organizational changes during the Nixon presidency, specifically the centralization of policymaking in the White House and the emphasis on placing Nixon loyalists in agencies and departments. Nixon was not the first president to care about making the executive branch responsive to presidential policy preferences, but his distrust of the bureaucracy went well beyond anything his predecessors had expressed. Nixon believed, not without reason, that the bureaucracy was colonized by liberal Democrats who were unsympathetic to his conservative policy objectives.[121]

The Promise of Cabinet Government

Candidate Nixon had been critical of President Lyndon Johnson's penchant for "taking all power" for himself and not giving cabinet members the freedom to do their jobs.

Nixon vowed that, if elected president, he would "disperse power" to his cabinet. "Creative people," Nixon explained, "can't develop in a monolithic, centralized power set-up." Having promised a return to "cabinet government," president-elect Nixon took the unusual step of unveiling his entire cabinet on national television. Every one of them, he promised the country, was "an independent thinker" who would be "urged to speak out in the Cabinet and within the Administration on all the great issues" facing the nation. He did not want "a Cabinet of 'Yes' men," he assured the country. Nor was Nixon's message about dispersing policymaking power to the departments a disingenuous public relations ploy. When Haldeman gathered White House staffers for their first post-election meeting, he underscored the president's message that their job was "not to do the work of government, but to get the work out to where it belongs—out to the Departments."[122]

Almost immediately, however, Nixon's plan to decentralize domestic policymaking ran into trouble. Although Nixon said he wanted independent thinkers in the cabinet, he also expected his administration to chart a more conservative course than LBJ, whose expansion of federal programs Nixon frequently criticized during the campaign as too expensive and too reliant on Washington for solutions. In introducing his pick to head the Department of Health, Education, and Welfare (HEW), for instance, Nixon boasted that Robert Finch would "not simply add billions to programs that have failed, but would find new ways to solve social problems." The problem, Nixon and his aides found, was that cabinet members like Finch underwent "an almost ritualistic courting and mating process with the bureaucracy" they had been chosen to lead. After going off to "marry the natives"—as Ehrlichman memorably expressed it—cabinet members returned to the White House not as independent thinkers brimming with fresh ideas for solving problems but rather as blinkered advocates for established departmental programs and interests. Making matters worse, the natives the cabinet members married, at least in departments like HEW and Housing and Urban Development (HUD), were mainly liberals who distrusted Nixon almost as much as Nixon distrusted them.[123]

Nixon and his aides complained increasingly of being "surrounded" by bureaucratic interests opposed to White House policies. Department secretaries saw the problem differently, of course. In their view, the president was becoming isolated by staffers who were shutting their boss off from expertise and diverse perspectives. As Nixon's distrust of the permanent bureaucracy grew, he demanded that his staff devise ways to make the bureaucracy more responsive to his policy preferences.[124]

The First-Term Strategy: Building a "Counter-Bureaucracy"

In Nixon's first term, the administration's primary strategy for ensuring policy responsiveness was to create a "counter-bureaucracy"—an enlarged and enhanced White House staff capable of controlling domestic policymaking. As Nixon would later explain the strategy: "bringing power to the White House [was necessary] in order to dish it out." Unable to rely on department heads to dismantle or streamline federal programs, Nixon felt he had no choice but to centralize power in the White House in order to meet his objective of dispersing power to the states and localities.[125]

A key component of the counter-bureaucracy strategy was the formation of the Domestic Council. At first glance, the Domestic Council did not seem that different from the Urban Affairs Council that the administration had initially used to coordinate domestic policy. Both councils were directed by a top White House aide (Daniel Patrick Moynihan headed the Urban Affairs Council and John Ehrlichman headed the Domestic Council) and both were made up of domestic cabinet heads, but there was a world of difference in how they functioned. Moynihan's staff was small and he mostly facilitated rather than directed the council's work. Moreover, the bulk of the Urban Affairs Council's policy initiatives were developed in subcommittees that were staffed by the departments and chaired by cabinet members. The Domestic Council, in contrast, was a cabinet council in name only. It rarely met, and when it did, Ehrlichman called the meetings, controlled the agenda, and reported to the president. The subcommittees were replaced by six project groups, each chaired by a member of Ehrlichman's Domestic Council staff, which had grown to more than 60 people by the end of Nixon's first term. Rather than a mechanism for bringing cabinet members together to coordinate policy, the Domestic Council became an instrument for the White House to bypass department heads and work directly with departmental staff to develop policy.[126]

Ehrlichman's Domestic Council did for domestic policy what Henry Kissinger's National Security Council (NSC) had already done for foreign policy: it centralized power in the White House. In both councils, real power rested not with the statutory members of the two councils—the domestic department heads in the case of the Domestic Council and the secretaries of state and defense in the case of the NSC—but with a White House aide and the staff he directed.

Formally, the Domestic Council, like the NSC, was lodged in the Executive Office of the President, not in the White House Office. In placing the Domestic Council outside of the White House Office, Nixon followed the recommendation of his Advisory Council on Executive Reorganization (better known as the Ash Council, after its chairman Roy Ash), which he had charged with devising ways to improve the functioning of the executive branch. As originally envisioned by the Ash Council, the Domestic Council was to work "in close coordination with the President's personal staff" but was to possess "its own institutional identity." The new council was to "develop and deploy the 'institutional memory' so essential if continuity is to be maintained, and if experience is to play its proper role in the policy-making process." The Ash Council hoped that the Domestic Council would allow for a leaner White House staff while providing presidents with the institutional expertise and resources to devise and coordinate effective public policy. That was the theory, at least.[127]

In practice, the Nixon White House insisted on making the Domestic Council into an extension of White House staff. The council's staff were "not subject to competitive civil service law and, therefore, could be hired or fired as [the president] saw fit." Institutional memory, one administration official reluctantly admitted, should not be "interpreted as necessarily going from administration to administration." Under Ehrlichman, the Domestic Council was staffed with Nixon loyalists rather than professional policy experts. For instance, heading the project group responsible for crime and transportation policy was Egil Krogh, an Ehrlichman protégé fresh out of law school with zero experience in transportation policy. (Ehrlichman expanded Krogh's portfolio in 1972 to include directing the White House Special Investigations Unit—popularly known as "the Plumbers"—that carried out the Ellsberg break-in.) Ehrlichman obliterated the Ash Council's distinction between the president's personal staff and the Domestic Council's institutional staff, and in the process undermined the administration's capacity to initiate and analyze domestic public policy.[128]

The Second-Term Strategy: Politicizing the Bureaucracy

Within the administration there was a growing sense that the first-term strategy of centralizing policymaking power in an expanded White House staff was not producing the desired results. A White House counter-bureaucracy seemed no match for an executive branch bureaucracy that was possessed of far superior numbers, organizational experience, and policy expertise. Moreover, a White House staff that had grown "like Topsy"—as Nixon lamented shortly after his reelection—introduced new management problems. "Staffers could not keep up with what their subordinates were doing," wrote one close observer of the administration, and "it was often impossible to find out who was handling a particular matter." In addition, as White House aides became consumed by administrative details they had less time to focus on the most important policy questions.[129]

The strategy of centralizing domestic policymaking in the White House staff seemed particularly inadequate because Democrats controlled both houses of Congress, ensuring that almost any policies—especially conservative ones—that the administration devised would be defeated. Unable to secure its domestic agenda through legislation, the Nixon administration increasingly sought ways to shape policy through administrative actions, such as writing regulations and issuing administrative rules. Political scientist Richard Nathan, who worked on domestic policy in the Nixon administration for four years, has dubbed this new strategy "the administrative presidency," because it aimed to take advantage of the broad discretion that modern legislation typically grants to executive agencies in implementing laws.[130]

If the Domestic Council had difficulty establishing itself as a mechanism of policy formulation, it was even less well equipped to monitor the thousands of rules and regulations promulgated by government agencies. Gaining control of the bureaucracy, it was decided, required colonizing the bureaucracy with Nixon loyalists rather than growing the White House staff. If the bureaucracy could be trusted to do the right thing, then the White House staff could be shrunk and power dispersed to the departments.[131]

Initially Nixon had granted department heads broad discretion to make political appointments within their departments, even encouraging them to make their choices "on the basis of ability first, and loyalty second." White House involvement in the selection of subcabinet officials remained relatively modest until the fall of 1970, when Haldeman put Fred Malek in charge of identifying, selecting, and approving the selection of important administrative posts. It was not until after Nixon's reelection, however, that the administration unleashed its new strategy of politicizing the bureaucracy as an alternative to building a White House counter-bureaucracy.[132]

The day after his reelection, Nixon directed all political appointees to submit their resignations. Those considered insufficiently loyal to Nixon were removed. Among the casualties was the highly respected secretary of commerce, Peter Peterson, who quipped that he flunked his administration physical because "his calves were too thick and he could not click his heels." Peterson, a former CEO at Bell and Howell Corporation, was replaced by Harry Dent, the White House's chief campaign strategist and a loyal Nixonian. The Domestic Council staff was pared dramatically and loyalists slotted into subcabinet positions. Krogh, for instance, was named undersecretary of transportation. Malek assured Haldeman that all appointments to the Office of Economic Opportunity (OEO)—an office created during the Johnson administration that was home to a host of Great Society programs, including Head Start, Job Corps, and the Legal Services Program—would be "known quantities" who were "100 percent responsive to the White House" and "committed to decimating OEO." In future, Ehrlichman vowed, "When we say jump, [political appointees] will only ask how high?"[133]

OMB and the Decline of Neutral Competence

The effort to make the bureaucracy more responsive to the president included a make-over of the Bureau of the Budget (BOB), which, following a recommendation by the Ash Council, was renamed the Office of Management and Budget (OMB) in 1970. BOB took great pride in its reputation for nonpartisan professionalism, but "neutral competence" did not sit well with an administration that tended to view government officials as either for or against it. To highlight OMB's ties to the president, Nixon took the unprecedented step of moving the OMB director into a coveted West Wing office. Nixon also charged the first OMB director, George Schultz, with chairing the daily morning White House staff meeting. Consistent with the first-term strategy of creating a counter-bureaucracy, OMB's staff was increased dramatically, particularly in terms of management-oriented staff, which by the end of 1971 had tripled in size from about 50 to 150 personnel.[134]

Despite Schultz's prominence in the White House and the increased resources devoted to bureaucratic management within OMB, Nixon's top aides were disappointed that the OMB wasn't doing more to monitor the bureaucracy's compliance with the president's policies. When Caspar Weinberger took over for Schultz in June 1972, Ehrlichman fired off a memo to Weinberger expressing his disappointment that OMB had "never successfully managed" the bureaucracy during Schultz's tenure. "By management," he explained, he meant "in the get-the-Secretary-to-do-what-the-President-needs-and-wants-him-to-do-whether-he-likes-it-or-not sense." Only if the OMB is "properly staffed … with loyal, highly political people," Ehrlichman insisted, could it fulfill its potential as "one of the most important tools available to the President in wheeling the bureaucracy." Only by politicizing the OMB, in other words, could the president count on it doing his bidding.[135]

In the second term, the administration acted aggressively to ensure that Nixon loyalists were "placed in the OMB and put in charge." Roy Ash was selected as OMB director and Fred Malek, chief architect of the administration's second-term politicization strategy, was made deputy director. Senior OMB positions, which had been occupied by career civil servants in the old BOB, were filled with political appointees plucked from outside OMB, who could be counted on to speak "with the voice of the White House." Under Ash and Malek, OMB assumed a leading role in carrying out Nixon's attempt to impound (that is, to refuse to spend) as much as 20 percent of discretionary spending that had been appropriated by Congress in 1973. Not surprisingly, by the time Nixon left office, the OMB was widely seen, by Congress as well as by agencies and departments, as a "partisan agent"—indistinguishable in outlook and orientation from the president's personal staff.[136]

The excesses of the Nixon administration created a backlash. The perception that OMB had become too partisan to be trusted induced Congress, in 1974, to create the Congressional Budget Office (CBO), giving legislators their own repository of budgetary expertise and analysis. The same act that created the CBO—the Congressional Budget and Impoundment Control Act of 1974—also forbade the president from impounding appropriations without specific legislative authorization. Congress also changed the law to require Senate confirmation of the OMB director and deputy director.[137]

Watergate derailed the administration's ambitious second-term plans for disciplining the bureaucracy. When Nixon was compelled to accept the resignation of his top two aides, Ehrlichman and Haldeman, he lost the driving forces behind the effort to bend the bureaucracy to the administration's will. And as Nixon's focus shifted from controlling the bureaucracy to avoiding impeachment, agency and department officials felt increasingly free to act independently of the White House. In the waning months of the Nixon presidency, many in the bureaucracy felt almost as if "there is no White House anymore."[138]

THE ADMINISTRATIVE PRESIDENCY AFTER NIXON

Although Watergate cut short Nixon's efforts to create a more responsive bureaucracy, the White House that Nixon built proved remarkably enduring. Under Nixon the White House staff assumed responsibilities that it has never relinquished: devising policy, cultivating interest group support, overseeing communications strategies, administering cabinet meetings, and providing legal advice. In the first half of the twentieth century, the primary duties of White House staff were correspondence, press relations, scheduling, and speechwriting. An "expanded and empowered" White House staff did not start with Nixon, of course—and indeed Nixon tried, as we have seen, to belatedly reverse the development—but his presidency was, as political scientist Andrew Rudalevige writes, a "tipping point" in the organization of the White House.[139]

Prior to Nixon, only one president—Dwight Eisenhower—had resorted to a chief of staff; since Nixon, every president, no matter their decision-making style, has opted for a chief of staff to manage the large White House staff and regulate access to the president. Nixon's Domestic Council is known today as the Office of Policy Development (OPD), which since 1993 has been composed of two councils, the National Economic Council and the Domestic Policy Council. While the name has changed, Nixon's model of centralizing policy development in the White House has not. The councils and working groups within OPD, as in Nixon's Domestic Council, have almost invariably been staffed and directed by White House aides rather than by department officials. Moreover, the Office of Management and Budget serves today as precisely the sort of politically responsive staff unit that Nixon imagined it should be.[140]

Presidents have also continued to strive—in the words of one George W. Bush aide— to "implant their DNA throughout the government." Nixon's speechwriter William Safire appears to have been prescient when, in 1975, he predicted that "one day the infiltration and reorganization [of the bureaucracy] which now seems so villainous will be carried out by more principled people under the banner of reform." The kinds of attempts to layer the bureaucracy with loyalists that seemed scandalous in Nixon's day are commonplace today. Indeed, Nixon's efforts to "take on the bureaucracy" seem haphazard compared to those of his Republican successors, especially Ronald Reagan and George W. Bush, who pursued the strategy of appointing loyalists earlier, more systematically, and with more far-reaching effect than Nixon.[141]

Appointing "Committed Reaganites"

At the outset of the 1980 general election campaign, Reagan made his Nixonian intentions clear. "Crucial to my strategy of spending control," he explained, "will be the appointment to top government positions of men and women who share my economic philosophy." He promised his audience that "we will have an administration in which the word from the top isn't lost or hidden in the bureaucracy." It was no empty promise. A year before the election, Reagan's most trusted aide, Edwin Meese, had already hired Pendleton James—who had been Malek's top deputy in the Nixon administration—to begin identifying "committed Reaganites" for service in a Reagan government. Once the Republican nomination had been wrapped up, the operation was stepped up, with James allotted a budget of $80,000 to open an office and hire a small staff.[142]

The day after Reagan's inauguration, James was given a West Wing office, the title of assistant to the president, and a large staff to help him identify and vet candidates for the more than 400 subcabinet positions that required Senate confirmation. Cabinet members were "consulted" in the selection process, but unlike Nixon and Carter, who began their presidencies by assuring cabinet members they would be able to pick their own subordinates, Reagan made it clear to each cabinet member at the outset that James and the White House would "control the appointment process … all the way down." Cabinet members could object to a White House choice, but rarely did. This was not surprising since the main criterion used in their own selection had been loyalty to Reagan and his conservative political philosophy, rather than their political stature or independence. In identifying candidates to fill government posts, Meese and James gravitated toward individuals who they believed would "rock the boat"—that is, upend the bureaucratic status quo rather than perpetuate it. In many cases, this meant picking individuals who were skeptical or openly hostile to the mission of the agency to which they were appointed.[143]

The Reagan administration was able to penetrate the bureaucracy more deeply than Nixon not only because it started earlier and devoted more staff resources to the task, but because the 1978 Civil Service Reform Act, passed at Democrat Jimmy Carter's behest, made many more positions in the bureaucracy amenable to presidential control. The 1978 law created a Senior Executive Service (SES), composed of about 7,000 senior management positions in the federal government, and allowed 10 percent of these posts to be designated as "noncareer"—and up to 25 percent within any given agency. Carter thought that facilitating the replacement or reassignment of ineffective administrators would make government more efficient and flexible, but the Reagan administration seized on the act to ensure the bureaucracy reflected the president's policy preferences. Almost none of the roughly 700 SES officials with noncareer status were retained when Reagan took office. In filling these positions, managerial competence sometimes seemed a secondary or tertiary concern to the White House. "'Goddamn near' every potential appointee" had to be run by Reagan's political affairs director Lyn Nofziger, who insisted on privileging Republicans who had "labored loyally in the Reagan vineyard." "As far as I'm concerned," explained Nofziger, "anyone who supported Reagan is competent."[144]

The Reagan White House also took a strong interest in the roughly 1,300 Schedule C positions in the federal bureaucracy—positions exempt from civil service regulations "because of their confidential or policy-determining character." Most of those who occupy Schedule C positions provide staff support for political appointees in EOP and the departments. By law, Schedule C positions—which were created in the Eisenhower administration—are controlled by the agencies and departments, but the Reagan administration insisted that all Schedule C positions be cleared with the White House Presidential Personnel Office (PPO), headed by James. "We wanted the receptionist who answered the secretary's telephone to have a Reagan tone to her voice," explained one White House staffer.[145]

The Reagan White House understood that appointing loyalists was important but not sufficient for controlling the bureaucracy. Loyalty also needed to be inculcated and reinforced. Nixon's aides had understood this as well, albeit belatedly. When Haldeman raised concerns about whether a potential appointee was really a "tried and true [Nixon] loyalist," Malek shot back a detailed plan for "developing intense political loyalty to the President." Whereas Malek's belated plan for instilling loyalty in political appointees was wrecked by Watergate, Reagan's staff were ready with theirs on day one, if not before. During the transition period, Reagan's cabinet picks were put through what amounted—in the words of Martin Anderson, Reagan's first director of the Office of Policy Development—to "an indoctrination course." Through pep talks, briefings, seminars, meetings, receptions, and dinners, the Reagan White House worked to instill in their recruits an allegiance to the Reagan agenda of reducing the size and scope of the federal government.[146]

To ensure that the message of smaller government was heard in the lower reaches of the bureaucracy, Reagan relied not only on the heavy hand of OPP but also on the long arm of OMB. Reagan capitalized on the more politicized Office of Management and Budget that Nixon had created to put Reagan loyalists in all the agency's top policy-making positions, which now included not only a director and deputy director and the four program associate directors (PADs) added by Nixon, but also two new executive associate directors that had been added by Carter, as well as half a dozen noncareer deputy associate directors. Reagan tapped Congressman David Stockman, a brash, young, anti-government ideologue, to direct OMB. At 34, Stockman was the youngest person ever to serve as head of OMB or BOB, as well as the first elected politician to serve in the post. Stockman quickly emerged as the administration's leading spokesman for Reagan's program of tax and spending cuts.[147]

Institutionalizing Regulatory Review: From Reagan to Trump

Stockman grabbed the headlines, but more enduring changes in OMB's role were taking place largely out of public view, most notably with the establishment in 1981 of the Office of Information and Regulatory Affairs (OIRA) and the institutionalization of regulatory review within OMB. OIRA (pronounced oh-eye-ruh) was not a Reagan invention; it was part of the Paperwork Reduction Act that Carter signed into law in the final weeks of his presidency. The statutory charge of the new office was relatively modest: to ensure that agencies complied with the new law's goal of reducing the paperwork that resulted from federal reporting requirements. However, Reagan greatly expanded OIRA's responsibilities. In an executive order issued shortly after taking office, Reagan tasked OIRA with reviewing all new government regulations and requiring agencies to submit cost–benefit analyses of all regulations to OIRA.[148]

Reagan's executive order made the oversight of administrative regulations a leading function of OMB. Staffing for OIRA ballooned to 90 people by the end of its first year. Under Reagan, OIRA reviewed an average of nearly 2,400 regulations a year. Most were ultimately issued without change, but by the second term nearly 30 percent of regulations reviewed by OIRA were either withdrawn or changed by agencies as a result of the review. The threat of OIRA review also affected agencies' behavior by inhibiting agency officials from issuing regulations that they thought might be adversely reviewed. In addition, regulations were shaped by informal interactions at the front end as agency officials sought input from OIRA in the development of regulations in order to avoid conflicts in the formal review process. "You don't spend two years thinking about a regulation without thinking about whether OMB is going to shoot it down," explained one EPA staff member.[149]

The beauty of OIRA, from the Reagan administration's perspective, was that it institutionalized Republicans' skepticism of government regulation in the EOP. Measured by the number of political appointees, OIRA has never been particularly politicized. Apart from the presidentially appointed OIRA administrator and his two Schedule C assistants, it has remained composed entirely of career civil servants. Its organizational structure and personnel have remained remarkably stable across Democratic and Republican administrations. Midway through George W. Bush's presidency, four of its top six career officials had been at OIRA since 1981. And at the heart of its organizational culture, as political scientist William West observes, remains "the belief that government action has the potential to do more harm than good and that the probable effects of regulations should therefore be considered as thoroughly and as objectively as possible."[150]

Although stacked with civil servants committed to sound cost–benefit analysis, OIRA personnel also understand their role as ensuring that agencies do not promulgate regulations that conflict with the president's stated policy preferences. And indeed the evidence suggests that OIRA was highly responsive to presidential preferences. In George W. Bush's first year, OIRA review resulted in the withdrawal of more than 150 regulations, twice as many as were withdrawn during Clinton's entire second term. This more aggressive posture by OIRA reflected the influence of new director John Graham, a sceptic of regulation who saw his role as White House "traffic cop for the entire bureaucracy." But the higher number of withdrawn regulations also reflected awareness on the part of both agency heads and OIRA officials that if a dispute was appealed, the Bush White House was likely to side with OIRA.[151]

Although OIRA was responsive to the administration's policy agenda, Bush became dissatisfied with OIRA's capacity to stem the regulatory tide. Immediately after Democrats took control of the House and the Senate in 2006, Bush moved to supplement centralized clearance of agency rules with greater politicization of the agencies' regulatory decision-making. Specifically, Bush ordered that "no rulemaking shall commence" without the prior approval of the agency's designated regulatory policy officer, who was required to be a political appointee. The requirement that every agency have a regulatory policy officer dated from the Clinton era, but Clinton's directive had left it up to the agency head to designate the regulatory policy officer, who could be a career official or a political appointee. Under Clinton, moreover, the regulatory policy officer was to be "involved at each stage of the regulatory process," but did not have a veto power over regulations.[152]

One of Barack Obama's first acts as president was to rescind Bush's controversial executive order, but Obama, like Clinton, relied heavily on White House control over administrative rules—both through directives from the White House and by installing political supporters in the agencies—to achieve policy changes that he could not hope to pass in a Republican-controlled Congress. During the Clinton presidency, Republicans in Congress sought to limit the administrative presidency by enacting the Congressional Review Act of 1996, which required agencies to submit any "major" regulatory change—defined as one that cost at least $100 million—to Congress for review. The act gave Congress 60 legislative days to override any major regulation by passing a resolution of disapproval, which was subject to veto by the president. Up until 2017, Congress had only once succeeded in using the act to overturn an administration regulation—a ruling by the Occupational Safety and Health Administration in the final days of the Clinton administration that would have set new workplace ergonomics rules to reduce repetitive stress injuries. In 2017, though, after Donald Trump's election, the Republicans in Congress used the act to repeal 14 administrative rules that were issued at the close of the Obama administration, including a Federal Communications Commission rule that protected consumers' online data from Internet providers and an Interior Department rule restricting what mining companies could dump into waterways.[153]

As a presidential candidate, Trump vowed to cut the number of administrative rules by 75 percent, and one of his first acts as president was to order agencies to revoke two regulations for every new rule they issue. This order was seen as an opening salvo in what the then White House chief strategist Stephen Bannon promised would be a "deconstruction of the administrative state." Like Nixon, Reagan, and Bush, Trump has aimed to use the tools of the administrative presidency—politicization and centralization—to rein in the administrative state.[154]

The Rationality of Politicization and Centralization

Political scientist Terry Moe has argued that it is no surprise that modern presidents, both Democratic and Republican, have sought to centralize control over policy in the White House and to politicize the bureaucracy by installing appointees who share their political goals. In Moe's view, these strategies of centralization and politicization are rational responses to the mismatch between the president's limited formal authority and the escalating public expectations of presidential performance. Since the public holds the president accountable for government outcomes, presidents naturally try to do whatever they can to control those outcomes.[155]

The normative argument for centralizing power in the White House or politicizing the bureaucracy is simple: bureaucrats aren't elected, presidents are. When candidate Reagan promised an administration in which "the word from the top isn't lost or hidden in the bureaucracy," he explained that it was vital not to lose that voice "because it is the voice of the people." George W. Bush's first OMB director, Mitch Daniels, made the same point to his staff whenever somebody took issue with the White House's position. "We all got the same number of votes for president," he would tell them: zero. In Daniels's view, OMB had an ethical obligation to be, above all else, responsive to the president's preferences.[156]

Although modern presidents have generally embraced the view that the executive branch should be broadly responsive to the president's agenda, they have not all gone about achieving responsiveness in the same way or to the same degree. The number of political appointees—which is one measure of politicization—increased markedly under George W. Bush and declined substantially under Clinton. Bush also placed far greater emphasis on installing like-minded "Bushies" to policymaking positions in the departments—another way to measure politicization—than did his father, George Herbert Walker Bush. Moe's thesis cannot explain these variations among presidents, for while presidents may be rational actors, they respond not only to broad shifts in public expectations but to historically contingent circumstances, such as party control of Congress and perceptions of whether the bureaucracy reflects their values.[157]

Politicization and centralization may be rational for individual presidents, but is it desirable for the presidency? Some evidence suggests that presidents and the political system pay a high cost for allowing responsiveness to trump competence. In a study of the Federal Emergency Management Agency (FEMA), for instance, political scientist David Lewis showed that the agency's politicization was directly responsible for its dismal performance in responding to Hurricane Katrina. A great deal of attention in the press focused on FEMA director Michael Brown, whom Bush named to the post even though he had no emergency management experience. (Brown had, however, been head of the International Arabian Horse Association and a contributor to Bush's campaign.) But the problem with FEMA went well beyond Brown's inexperience. Created as an independent agency by President Carter in 1979, FEMA had an extraordinarily high number of political appointees from the outset, almost three times as many as other agencies its size.

When Bush came to power, FEMA had 27 political appointees, slightly fewer than under Carter but still a large number for a relatively small agency. Bush, however, further degraded the agency's competence by increasing the number of political appointees by 50 percent, and packing the agency with Bush supporters with little or no experience in emergency relief.[158]

The cataclysmic impact that FEMA's response to Hurricane Katrina had on George W. Bush's second term suggests that privileging responsiveness over competence may be bad not only for American citizens but for American presidents as well. Lewis's work raises an even more profound question, however, about Moe's assumption that politicization is undertaken to enhance presidential control of the bureaucracy. Lewis finds that the increase in political appointees under Bush, almost all of which were Schedule C appointees, was driven less by a desire to gain control of the bureaucracy than by a wish to reward supporters and campaign workers with old-fashioned patronage. Such appointments do little to enhance presidential control over the executive branch and do a lot to degrade the competence of the executive branch.[159]

Indeed, some experts argue that this increased layer of political appointees—largely made up of inexperienced campaign aides and interns—actually makes the executive branch less responsive to the president's wishes. "The more people you get in these jobs," opines political scientist Paul Light, "the less presidential control you have," because it increases the layers between the president's top aides and the bureaucrats that the administration wants to control. Over the past several decades, several national commissions have recommended slashing the number of political appointees as a way to improve both administrative competence *and* political responsiveness, but neither Republican nor Democratic presidents have shown much interest in a depoliticized presidency. Rational or not, the politicized presidency is here to stay.[160]

Notes

1   Robert B. Reich, *Locked in the Cabinet* (New York: Alfred A. Knopf, 1997), 108–10. Bob Woodward, *The Agenda: Inside the Clinton White House* (New York: Simon & Schuster, 1994), 20, 59.

2   Reich, *Locked in the Cabinet*, 108–10. Frontline: The Clinton Years, www.pbs.org/wgbh/pages/frontline/shows/clinton/anecdotes/2.html.

3   Reich, *Locked in the Cabinet*, 73, 179. Shirley Anne Warshaw, *Powersharing: White House–Cabinet Relations in the Modern Presidency* (Albany: State University of New York Press, 1996), 221, 212–14.

4   Reich, *Locked in the Cabinet*, 150–51; also 77. Warshaw, *Powersharing*, 221. Stephen Hess with James P. Pfiffner, *Organizing the Presidency* (Washington, DC: Brookings Institution Press, 2002; third edition), 152, 263 n13.

5   Warshaw, *Powersharing*, 213, 215. Bradley H. Patterson, Jr., *The White House Staff: Inside the West Wing and Beyond* (Washington, DC: Brookings Institution Press, 2000), 79–80. Bradley H. Patterson, Jr., *To Serve the President: Continuity and Innovation in the White House Staff* (Washington, DC: Brookings Institution Press, 2008), 110.

6   Warshaw, *Powersharing*, 215. Patterson, *The White House Staff*, 87.

7   Reich, *Locked in the Cabinet*, 109.

8   Patterson, *To Serve the President*, 1–2. Hess, *Organizing the Presidency*, 152. Jeffrey E. Cohen, *The Politics of the U.S. Cabinet: Representation in the Executive Branch, 1979–1984* (Pittsburgh: University of Pittsburgh Press, 1988), 39.

9   Patterson, *To Serve the President*, 1–2. Lewis L. Gould, *The Modern American Presidency* (Lawrence: University Press of Kansas, 2003), 43. John Hart, *The Presidential Branch* (New York: Pergamon Press, 1987), 16. Also see Charles E. Walcott and Karen M. Hult, "The Bush Staff and Cabinet System," in Mark J. Rozell and Gleaves Whitney, eds., *Testing the Limits: George W. Bush and the Imperial Presidency* (Lanham, MD: Rowman & Littlefield, 2009), 24–26.

10 Richard J. Ellis, ed., *Founding the American Presidency* (Lanham, MD: Rowman & Littlefield, 1999), 31–32.

11 Ellis, *Founding the American Presidency*, 32–34. Of the delegates known to have voted against Wilson's motion, the average age was 55; the average age of all the delegates at the convention was about 44.

12 Ellis, *Founding the American Presidency*, 33–34.

13 Ellis, *Founding the American Presidency*, 44–45.

14 Max Farrand, ed. *The Records of the Federal Convention* (New Haven, CT: Yale University Press, 1937; 4 vols.), 2:367 (August 22). Ellis, *Founding the American Presidency*, 49.

15 Farrand, *Records of the Federal Convention*, 2:499 (September 4); 2:541–42 (September 7).

16 Farrand, *Records of the Federal Convention*, 2:541–43 (September 7). Ellis, *Founding the American Presidency*, 45, 48–50.

17 James Thomas Flexner, *George Washington and the New Nation, 1783–1793* (Boston: Little, Brown, 1970), 401. The Department of Foreign Affairs was established in July 1789 and renamed the Department of State a few months later.

18 Washington to Charles Cotesworth Pinckney, January 22, 1794, in Dorothy Twohig et al., eds., *The Papers of George Washington, Presidential Series* (Charlottesville: University Press of Virginia, 1987), 15:104.

19 Forrest McDonald, *The Presidency of George Washington* (Lawrence: University Press of Kansas, 1974), 76–77. Stanley Elkins and Eric McKitrick, *The Age of Federalism: The Early American Republic, 1788–1800* (New York: Oxford University Press, 1993), 232–33.

20 Jefferson to Doctor Walter Jones, March 5, 1810, in *The Works of Thomas Jefferson* (G.P. Putnam's Sons, 1904–1905; 12 vols.), available at *The Online Library of Liberty* (http://oll.libertyfund.org). Flexner, *George Washington and the New Nation*, 400. Richard F. Fenno, Jr., *The President's Cabinet* (Cambridge, MA: Harvard University Press, 1959), 17–18. Also see Lindsay M. Chervinsky, "George Washington and the First Presidential Cabinet," *Presidential Studies Quarterly* (March 2018).

21 Ellis, *Founding the American Presidency*, 48, 51.

22 Washington to Samuel Vaughan, March 21, 1789, quoted in Leonard D. White, *The Federalists: A Study in Administrative History* (New York: Macmillan, 1948), 496. Hart, *Presidential Branch*, 10.

23 White, *The Federalists*, 495.

24 Fred I. Greenstein, *Inventing the Job of President: Leadership Style from George Washington to Andrew Jackson* (Princeton, NJ: Princeton University Press, 2009), 2.

25 White, *The Federalists*, 496.

26 Richard Norton Smith, *Patriarch: George Washington and the New American Nation* (Boston: Houghton Mifflin, 1993), xvii, 21–22, 93, 168. White, *The Federalists*, 496 n24.

27 Flexner, *George Washington and the New Nation*, 203–24. Hart, *Presidential Branch*, 10–12. *Annals of Congress*, July 13 and 16, 1789, 657–62, 668–71 (quotation at 670). A member of Congress, by way of contrast, received $6 a day, a per diem that applied only to the days the legislature was in session. In 1789, Congress was in session for 210 days, so a member with

perfect attendance would have received a salary of $1,260, roughly one-twentieth of the president's salary. See Ida A. Burdick, "Salaries of Members of Congress: A List of Payable Rates and Effective Dates, 1789–2008," CRS Report for Congress (updated February 21, 2008).

28 Hart, *Presidential Branch*, 12. Richard J. Ellis, *Presidential Travel: The Journey from George Washington to George W. Bush* (Lawrence: University Press of Kansas, 2008), 23, 137. Noble E. Cunningham, Jr., *The Process of Government under Jefferson* (Princeton, NJ: Princeton University Press, 1978), 44–45.

29 Hart, *Presidential Branch*, 14. Leonard D. White, *The Jacksonians: A Study in Administrative History, 1829–1861* (New York: Macmillan, 1954), 83. The position of secretary of land patents was established on a temporary basis, and by the following decade the signing of land patents appears to have again become the responsibility of the president or his private secretary. See the diary entry dated September 25, 1846, in which President James Polk welcomed the return of his private secretary J. Knox Walker because it meant that he would "be relieved from the labour of signing land Patents which [he] had to perform during [Walker's] absence." Milo Milton Quaife, ed., *The Diary of James K. Polk during His Presidency, 1845 to 1849* (Chicago: A.C. McClurg, 1910), 2:155.

30 Cunningham, *The Process of Government under Jefferson*, 35–36. Rather than rely on a clerk to copy letters, Jefferson preferred to use the latest labor-saving inventions—first a letter press and later a device "by which two or more pens could be operated simultaneously to make identical copies," an invention that he celebrated as "a most invaluable Secretary, doing its work with correctness, facility and secrecy."

31 Hart, *Presidential Branch*, 13. Cunningham, *The Process of Government under Jefferson*, 36–37. Stephen E. Ambrose, *Undaunted Courage: Meriwether Lewis, Thomas Jefferson, and the Opening of the American West* (New York: Simon & Schuster, 1996), 59.

32 Robert Allen Rutland, *The Presidency of James Madison* (Lawrence: University Press of Kansas, 1990), 52. J.C.A. Stagg, *Mr. Madison's War: Politics, Diplomacy, and Warfare in the Early American Republic, 1783–1830* (Princeton, NJ: Princeton University Press, 1983), 433. Polk's diary provides countless examples of his private secretary J. Knox Walker not only transmitting presidential messages to Congress but relaying to the president information about happenings on Capitol Hill. See, for example, *Diary of James K. Polk*, 1:337, 1:343, 1:394, 1:451, 2:26, 2:51, 2:66, 2:304, 2:318, 2:320.

33 Stuart Leibiger, *Founding Friendship: George Washington, James Madison, and the Creation of the American Republic* (Charlottesville: University Press of Virginia, 1999), 112. Ellis, *Presidential Travel*, 22.

34 *Diary of James K. Polk*, 3:208 (November 11, 1847); 1:458 (June 8, 1846). Charles Sellers, *James K. Polk: Continentalist, 1843–1846* (Princeton, NJ: Princeton University Press, 1966), 303. When Congress was not in session, Polk generally opened his office to visitors in the early afternoon, usually at one or two o'clock. Saturdays were also cabinet days.

35 *Diary of James K. Polk*, 1:472 (June 16, 1846). Also see 1:457–58 (June 8, 1846), 2:212 (October 29, 1846), 2:362 (January 30, 1847), 2:436 (March 23, 1847).

36 *Diary of James K. Polk*, 4:65 (August 10, 1848). White, *The Jacksonians*, 84.

37 *Diary of James K. Polk*, 3:457 (May 21, 1848); 2:345–46 (January 21, 1847). James Polk to James Walker, August 11, 1845, in Wayne Cutler, ed., *Correspondence of James J. Polk*, Volume X, July–December 1845 (Knoxville: University of Tennessee Press, 2004), 146. Also see *Diary of James K. Polk*, 2:155 (September 25, 1846). When Polk's private secretary J. Knox Walker went to Tennessee for six weeks after the close of the legislative session in August 1846, Polk brought in as a temporary replacement William Voorhies (2:88), a clerk in the Post Office Department who had helped the president in the past with copying messages to Congress (1:103). When Walker went to Virginia to visit his relations for six weeks at the end of the

summer in 1848, Polk had "the occasional assistance" of H.C. Williams (4:145), a trusted clerk in the War Department, whom Polk had also relied upon in the past to copy confidential messages (1:102–03) and deal with backlogs of correspondence (2:395). In the case of Walker's shorter absences, Polk turned to an array of other government clerks, including in the Navy Department (3:70), the General Land Office (3:459), and the Post Office (3:483).

38 Michael Medved, *The Shadow Presidents: The Secret History of the Chief Executives and Their Top Aides* (New York: Times Books, 1979), 13.

39 Doris Kearns Goodwin, *Team of Rivals: The Political Genius of Abraham Lincoln* (New York: Simon & Schuster, 2005), 334. David Herbert Donald, *Lincoln* (New York: Simon & Schuster, 1995), 311.

40 Goodwin, *Team of Rivals*, 335, 341. Michael Burlingame, *Abraham Lincoln: A Life* (Baltimore: Johns Hopkins University Press, 2008), 2:70–72.

41 Burlingame, *Abraham Lincoln*, 2:69, 75. Harold Holzer, *Dear Mr. Lincoln: Letters to the President* (Reading, MA: Addison-Wesley, 1995), 2, 4. F.B. Carpenter, *The Inner Life of Abraham Lincoln: Six Months at the White House* (Lincoln: University of Nebraska Press, 1995), 281.

42 Michael Burlingame, ed., *An Oral History of Abraham Lincoln: John G. Nicolay's Interviews and Essays* (Carbondale: Southern Illinois University Press, 1996), xi–xii. Michael Burlingame and John R. Turner Ettlinger, eds., *Inside Lincoln's White House: The Complete Civil War Diary of John Hay* (Carbondale: Southern Illinois University Press, 1997), xii.

43 Burlingame, *An Oral History of Abraham Lincoln*, xii–xiii. Hart, *Presidential Branch*, 15, 17. David Herbert Donald, *"We Are Lincoln Men": Abraham Lincoln and His Friends* (New York: Simon & Schuster, 2003), 196. William O. Stoddard, *Abraham Lincoln: The True Story of a Great Life* (New York: Fords, Howard, & Hulbert, 1884), 243.

44 William O. Stoddard, *Inside the White House in War Times: Memoirs and Reports of Lincoln's Secretary*, ed. Michael Burlingame (Lincoln: University of Nebraska Press, 2000), 57, 109, 151. Burlingame, *An Oral History of Abraham Lincoln*, xiii. Michael Burlingame, ed., *Lincoln Observed: Civil War Dispatches of Noah Brooks* (Baltimore: Johns Hopkins University Press, 1998), 83. Holzer, *Dear Mr. Lincoln*, 12.

45 Sellers, *Polk*, 302. Holzer, *Dear Mr. Lincoln*, 24. Stoddard, *Inside the White House*, ix–xi. Harold Holzer, ed., *Lincoln's White House Secretary: The Adventurous Life of William O. Stoddard* (Carbondale: Southern Illinois University, 2007), 7.

46 Holzer, *Dear Mr. Lincoln*, 18–19. Stoddard, *Inside the White House*, 157–58. Also see John Hay to William Herndon, September 5, 1866, in Douglas L. Wilson and Rodney O. Davis, eds., *Herndon's Informants: Letters, Interviews, and Statements about Abraham Lincoln* (Urbana: University of Illinois Press, 1998), 331. Surveying the 15,000 letters in the Lincoln papers at the Library of Congress—letters that were either endorsed by the president or endorsed by one of his secretaries and then forwarded to the President—Holzer estimates that an average of 11 or 12 letters crossed Lincoln's desk each work day (*Dear Mr. Lincoln*, 25).

47 Helen Nicolay, *Lincoln's Secretary: A Biography of John G. Nicolay* (New York: Longmans, 1949), 84. Stoddard, *Inside the White House*, 159. John Hay to Edward D. Neill, July 14, 1864, in Michael Burlingame, ed., *At Lincoln's Side: John Hay's Civil War Correspondence and Selected Letters* (Carbondale: Southern Illinois University Press, 2000), 87.

48 Michael Burlingame, "Lincoln Spins the Press," in Charles M. Hubbard, ed., *Lincoln Shapes the Presidency* (Macon, GA: Mercer University Press, 2003), 65–67. Medved, *Shadow Presidents*, 21. Also see Stoddard, *Inside the White House*, xviii–xix; Donald, *We Are Lincoln Men*, 203–04; and Michael Burlingame, ed., *With Lincoln in the White House: Letters, Memoranda, and Other Writings of John G. Nicolay, 1860–1865* (Carbondale: Southern Illinois University Press, 2006), 142–43. In addition, see Michael Burlingame, ed., *Dispatches from Lincoln's White House: The Anonymous Civil War Journalism of Presidential Secretary William O.*

Stoddard (Lincoln: University of Nebraska Press, 2002); and Michael Burlingame, ed., *Lincoln's Journalist: John Hay's Anonymous Writings for the Press, 1860–1864* (Carbondale: Southern Illinois University Press, 2006).

49   Wilson and Davis, *Herndon's Informants*, 331. Stoddard, *Inside the White House*, 57. Donald, *We Are Lincoln Men*, 200, 209. Burlingame, *An Oral History of Abraham Lincoln*, xiii. Also see Burlingame, *With Lincoln in the White House*, 60; and Burlingame, *Abraham Lincoln*, 2:209–10. Stoddard was the first of those who Nicolay recruited to help with the routine tasks, but he was not the last, nor did he typically work alone. At least three other people who were formally clerks in the Interior Department—Nathaniel Howe, Gustave Matile, and Charles Philbrick—spent their days in Hay's increasingly crowded office. See Holzer, *Dear Mr. Lincoln*, 29–30.

50   David Donald, *Lincoln Reconsidered: Essays on the Civil War Era* (New York: Vintage; second edition, enlarged), 193. On Polk's administrative style, see Sellers, *Polk*, 305; and Charles A. McCoy, *Polk and the Presidency* (Austin: University of Texas Press, 1960), 69–81.

51   *Diary of James K. Polk*, September 23, 1848 (4:130–31); December 29, 1848 (4:261).

52   Edward D. Neill, *Reminiscences of the Last Year of President Lincoln's Life* (St. Paul, MN: Pioneer Press, 1885), 4. Donald, *Lincoln Reconsidered*, 194.

53   G.S. Boritt, *Lincoln and the Economics of the American Dream* (Memphis: Memphis State University Press, 1978), 228. Donald, *Lincoln*, 401, 404. Richard Ellis and Aaron Wildavsky, *Dilemmas of Presidential Leadership: From Washington through Lincoln* (New Brunswick, NJ: Transaction Publishers, 1989), 183–84.

54   Donald, *Lincoln Reconsidered*, 194. Donald, *Lincoln*, 449, 479. Boritt, *Lincoln and the Economics of the American Dream*, 199.

55   Donald, *Lincoln*, 400, 449. Donald, *Lincoln Reconsidered*, 193. On Polk, see McCoy, *Polk and the Presidency*, 62–63, 69–70.

56   Donald, *Lincoln*, 365. Goodwin, *Team of Rivals*, 468.

57   Donald, *Lincoln Reconsidered*, 193.

58   On the evolution of the term "cabinet" in the United States, see Henry Barrett Learned, *The President's Cabinet: Studies in the Origin, Formation, and Structure of an American Institution* (New Haven, CT: Yale University Press, 1912), ch. 6.

59   On the twice-weekly cabinet meetings between Grant and McKinley, see Leonard D. White, *The Republican Era, 1869–1901: A Study in Administrative History* (New York: Macmillan, 1958), 101, 104; Homer Socolofsky and Allan B. Spetter, *The Presidency of Benjamin Harrison* (Lawrence: University Press of Kansas, 1987), 85; and Ari Hoogenboom, *The Presidency of Rutherford B. Hayes* (Lawrence: University Press of Kansas, 1988), 59. For a sampling of complaints about cabinet meetings during the Grant administration, see Allan Nevins, *Hamilton Fish: The Inner History of the Grant Administration* (New York: Dodd, Mead, 1937), 584–85, 589–90, 733. Not until Woodrow Wilson's administration was the ritual of twice-a-week cabinet meetings abandoned, leading Republicans to pillory Wilson for his "one man government." In the 1920 campaign, Warren Harding promised to bring back "plural leadership"—a chief executive flanked by "a Cabinet of the highest capacity, equal to the responsibilities which our system contemplates." Richard F. Fenno, Jr., *The President's Cabinet* (Cambridge, MA: Harvard University Press, 1959), 34–35.

60   Originally christened the Department of Labor and Commerce, it became the Department of Commerce in 1913 when a separate Labor Department was established.

61   Fenno, *President's Cabinet*, 24, 28. Shirley Anne Warshaw, *The Keys to Power: Managing the Presidency* (New York: Pearson Longman, 2005; second edition), 304.

62   William S. McFeely, *Grant: A Biography* (New York: W.W. Norton, 1982), 300–01.

63   The phrase "salvation by staff" was used by George Graham in "The Presidency and the Executive Office of the President," *Journal of Politics* (November 1950), 600. Also see Aaron B.

Wildavsky, "Salvation by Staff: Reform of the Presidential Office," in Wildavsky, ed., *The Presidency* (Boston: Little, Brown, 1969), 694–700.

64   Jean Edward Smith, *Grant* (New York: Simon and Schuster, 2001), 301–02n. McFeely, *Grant*, 302–03.

65   John Y. Simon, ed., *The Papers of Ulysses S. Grant* (Carbondale: Southern Illinois University Press, 1969–2009), 19:142–43n. Hart, *Presidential Branch*, 16. Grant's first assistant private secretary was Robert Douglas (*Papers of Ulysses S. Grant*, 19:143n), the 19-year-old son of storied Illinois senator Stephen Douglas. An outsider to Grant's inner circle, Douglas left the White House in 1872 to be replaced by Babcock's crony Levi Luckey. Hart mistakenly identifies Douglas as Grant's private secretary (rather than assistant private secretary), and makes the same mistake with Luckey. He also errs by having Luckey die in a drowning accident in 1876 (*Presidential Branch*, 17–18). The boating accident was in 1884, and was the same accident that claimed Babcock's life. Hart's errors mirror those made in W.W. Price, "Secretaries to the Presidents," *The Cosmopolitan* (1901), 490, which is presumably Hart's source.

66   "Proceedings of the Court," *New York Times*, February 18, 1876, 1. Nevins, *Hamilton Fish*, 281. Geoffrey Perret, *Ulysses S. Grant: Soldier and President* (New York: Random House, 1997), 402. Smith, *Grant*, 474.

67   John Hay to William Herndon, September 5, 1866, in Wilson and Davis, eds., *Herndon's Informants*, 331. Mark Wahlgren Summers, *The Era of Good Stealings* (New York: Oxford University Press, 1993), 180.

68   "Proceedings of the Court." Medved, *Shadow Presidents*, 44. Josiah Bunting III, *Ulysses S. Grant* (New York: Times Books, 2004), 103. Nevins, *Hamilton Fish*, 588. McFeeely, *Grant*, 338, 362. Perret, *Ulysses S. Grant*, 34.

69   McFeeely, *Grant*, 297. Medved, *Shadow Presidents*, 40–41. *The Papers of Ulysses S. Grant*, 19:151–52.

70   Nevins, *Hamilton Fish*, 731, 734, 738; also see 355–56, 656–57, 729–32, 737–38.

71   Nevins, *Hamilton Fish*, 723, 729–30. McFeeely, *Grant*, 366; also 345. Mark Wahlgren Summers, *The Press Gang; Newspapers and Politics, 1865–1878* (Chapel Hill: University of North Carolina Press, 1994), 177, 272.

72   William B. Hesseltine, *Ulysses S. Grant: Politician* (New York: Dodd, Mead, 1935), 380–81. Nevins, *Hamilton Fish*, 762–63. Medved, *Shadow Presidents*, 45.

73   Medved, *Shadow Presidents*, 44–45. Summers, *The Era of Good Stealings*, 188. Hesseltine, *Ulysses S. Grant*, 381. Nevins, *Hamilton Fish*, 794–97.

74   McFeeely, *Grant*, 408. Nevins, *Hamilton Fish*, 797–99.

75   Hesseltine, *Ulysses S. Grant*, 381.

76   Theodore Clark Smith, ed., *The Life and Letters of James Abraham Garfield* (New Haven, CT: Yale University Press, 1925), 1069–71.

77   White, *The Republican Era*, 103. Hart, *Presidential Branch*, 16, 18–19. "Civil Service Reform," *New York Times*, March 22, 1877. "Major O.L. Pruden Dead," *New York Times*, April 20, 1902. "Col. W.H. Crook Dead," *New York Times*, March 14, 1915.

78   White, *The Republican Era*, 103. Medved, *Shadow Presidents*, 84. Not all late nineteenth-century private secretaries were as weak or ineffectual as Thurber, as Cleveland well knew. During his first term Cleveland was blessed with an astute private secretary, Daniel Lamont, who perfectly complemented the president: while Cleveland "had no equal in provoking men to wrath," observed one congressman, Lamont had "no rival in applying poultices and administering soothing syrup." McKinley, too, formed a highly productive political partnership with his secretary George Cortelyou, who began his White House career as a stenographer in the Cleveland White House. Although Cortelyou was formally an assistant secretary until 1900, he was the de facto private secretary for almost the entire McKinley

presidency on account of the illness, laziness, and ineptitude of McKinley's official private secretary John Addison Porter. A testament to the political acuity and influence of both Lamont and Cortelyou is their subsequent promotion into the cabinet: Cleveland made Lamont secretary of war in his second term and Theodore Roosevelt picked Cortelyou to be the first secretary of commerce and labor and later the secretary of treasury. See Medved, *Shadow Presidents*, 80. Hart, *Presidential Branch*, 19–21. Gould, *Modern American Presidency*, 9–12. During McKinley's presidency, the position of private secretary was renamed secretary to the president, apparently as a way to enhance the "dignity" of the office (Hart, *Presidential Branch*, 20).

79 Table Ea894–903—Federal government employees, by government branch and location relative to the capital: 1816–1992; and Table Ea584–587—Federal government finances—revenue, expenditure, and debt: 1789–1939, in *Historical Statistics of the United States, Millennial Edition Online*. Also see James D. Savage, *Balanced Budgets and American Politics* (Ithaca, NY: Cornell University Press, 1988), 131–35, 288–89.

80 White, *The Republican Era*, 97–98; also 66–67. Also see White, *The Jacksonians*, 77–78; and Peri Arnold, *Making the Managerial Presidency: Comprehensive Reorganization Planning, 1905–1980* (Princeton, NJ: Princeton University Press, 1986), 28.

81 White, *The Republican Era*, 55; also see 60–64. Louis Fisher, *Presidential Spending Power* (Princeton, NJ: Princeton University Press, 1975), 60–61. There were exceptions to this general pattern, most notably President Polk, who insisted on reviewing all budgetary requests before they were submitted to Congress. Anxious to keep tariffs low without compromising the war with Mexico, Polk pressured his department heads to scrutinize budgetary requests closely and to pare any unnecessary expenses. When they faltered he did not hesitate to meet with bureau heads himself, to admonish them, highlight mistakes, and point out where further cuts could be made. McCoy, *Polk and the Presidency*, 74–76.

82 Welch, *The Presidencies of Grover Cleveland*, 49. Summers, *Era of Good Stealings*, 181.

83 White, *The Republican Era*, 52.

84 Arnold, *Making the Managerial Presidency*, 27.

85 Arnold, *Making the Managerial Presidency*, 29–32.

86 Arnold, *Making the Managerial Presidency*, 33, 35–37, 43–44 (quotation at 43).

87 Arnold, *Making the Managerial Presidency*, 37–41, 44, 48.

88 Arnold, *Making the Managerial Presidency*, 44–46. Charles Beatty Alexander, "The Need for a Budget System in the United States," *Annals of the American Academy of Political and Social Science* (July 1918), 144. Fisher, *Presidential Spending Power*, 30–31.

89 Arnold, *Making the Managerial Presidency*, 49, 53. Fisher, *Presidential Spending Power*, 32. Savage, *Balanced Budgets and American Politics*, 289–90.

90 Fisher, *Presidential Spending Power*, 33–34. Larry Berman, *The Office of Management and Budget and the Presidency, 1921–1979* (Princeton, NJ: Princeton University Press, 1979), 3–4.

91 Berman, *The Office of Management and Budget and the Presidency*, 4. Arnold, *Making the Managerial Presidency*, 54–55. Fisher, *Presidential Spending Power*, 39.

92 Berman, *The Office of Management and Budget and the Presidency*, 7.

93 Berman, *The Office of Management and Budget and the Presidency*, 8–9.

94 Richard E. Neustadt, "Presidency and Legislation: The Growth of Central Clearance," *American Political Science Review* (September 1954), 648–51.

95 Louis Brownlow, *A Passion for Anonymity: The Autobiography of Louis Brownlow, Second Half* (Chicago: University of Chicago Press, 1958), 392. John P. Burke, *The Institutional Presidency* (Baltimore: Johns Hopkins University Press, 1992), 6.

96 Brownlow, *A Passion for Anonymity*, 323–24. Burke, *The Institutional Presidency*, 8. Fisher, *Presidential Spending Power*, 62–63. Barry Dean Karl, *Executive Reorganization and Reform in*

the New Deal: The Genesis of Administrative Management, 1900–1939 (Chicago: University of Chicago Press, 1963), 197. Matthew J. Dickinson, Bitter Harvest: FDR, Presidential Power and the Growth of the Presidential Branch (New York: Cambridge University Press, 1997), 75.

97   Richard Polenberg, Reorganizing Roosevelt's Government: The Controversy over Executive Reorganization, 1936–1939 (Cambridge, MA: Harvard University Press, 1966), 9. Dickinson, Bitter Harvest, 77. Burke, The Institutional Presidency, 8. Arthur M. Schlesinger, Jr., The Coming of the New Deal (Boston: Houghton Mifflin, 1959), 270–71. William E. Leuchtenburg, Franklin D. Roosevelt and the New Deal, 1932–1940 (New York: Harper & Row, 1963), 122–23.

98   Arnold, Making the Managerial Presidency, 89. Schlesinger, Coming of the New Deal, 527–28.

99   Arnold, Making the Managerial Presidency, 89–90. Dickinson, Bitter Harvest, 52–57. Schlesinger, Coming of the New Deal, 545–49. Franklin D. Roosevelt, Executive Order 6202A, Appointing the Executive Council, July 11, 1933; Executive Order 6433A, Creation of the National Emergency Council, November 17, 1933; Executive Order 6770, Creating the Industrial Emergency Committee, June 30, 1934.

100   Dickinson, Bitter Harvest, 56–58 (quotation at 58). Schlesinger, Coming of the New Deal, 546–47. Franklin D. Roosevelt, Executive Order 6889A, Consolidating the National Emergency Council, the Executive Council and the Industrial Emergency Committee, October 31, 1934.

101   Dickinson, Bitter Harvest, 77. Table Ea894–903—Federal government employees, by government branch and location relative to the capital: 1816–1992, in Historical Statistics of the United States, Millennial Edition Online.

102   Polenberg, Reorganizing Roosevelt's Government, 8, 15. Burke, Institutional Presidency, 9.

103   The President's Committee on Administrative Management, Administrative Management in the Government of the United States (Washington, DC: US Government Printing Office, 1937), 2, 3, 47. The report is reprinted in Frederick C. Mosher, ed., Basic Documents of American Public Administration, 1776–1950 (New York: Holmes & Meier, 1976), 110–38. On Roosevelt's workload, see Dickinson, Bitter Harvest, 80–81; and Schlesinger, Coming of the New Deal, 523.

104   President's Committee, Administrative Management, 5.

105   Polenberg, Reorganizing Roosevelt's Government, 21, 28. Dickinson, Bitter Harvest, 87 n8. Arnold, Making the Managerial Presidency, 110. Roosevelt was the first to poke fun at Brownlow's "passion for anonymity" phrase, alerting reporters at a January 1937 press conference to this "purple patch, one you will never forget" (Hart, Presidential Branch, 28). On Roosevelt's role in shaping the committee report, see Dickinson, Bitter Harvest, 91–94, 99–104.

106   President's Committee, Administrative Management, 36. Arnold, Making the Managerial Presidency, 105. Polenberg, Reorganizing Roosevelt's Government, 29–30. Burke, Institutional Presidency, 10.

107   Burke, Institutional Presidency, 10–11. Arnold, Making the Managerial Presidency, 105, 114.

108   Dickinson, Bitter Harvest, 64, 68, 87. During his first term, Roosevelt's three secretaries were FDR's chief advisor and troubleshooter Louis Howe, press secretary Steve Early, and appointments secretary Marvin McIntyre (69–70). Roosevelt actually designated Early and McIntyre as assistant secretaries and paid them $9,500 rather than $10,000, largely as a way of signaling Howe's preeminent position (65) and avoiding the power struggles that hampered the effectiveness of Hoover's three co-equal secretaries (Hart, Presidential Branch, 24).

109   Dickinson, Bitter Harvest, 66–67. Hart, Presidential Branch, 21, 27.

110   President's Committee, Administrative Management, 5. Dickinson, Bitter Harvest, 66–67, 87 (quotation from FDR at 87). Harold C. Relyea, "The White House Office," in Harold C. Relyea, ed., The Executive Office of the President: A Historical, Biographical, and Bibliographical Guide (Westport, CT: Greenwood Press, 1997), 47–48.

111   Dickinson, Bitter Harvest, 78–79. Arnold, Making the Managerial Presidency, 82–83.

112   Burke, Institutional Presidency, 11.

113 Franklin D. Roosevelt, Executive Order 8248: Reorganizing the Executive Office of the President, September 8, 1939. Hart, *Presidential Branch*, 29–30. Dickinson, *Bitter Harvest*, 112 n101. In language that closely mirrored the original Brownlow report—not surprisingly since the final draft of the executive order was written by Brownlow—the executive order mostly specified what these administrative assistants would not do. They would not have "authority over anyone in any department or agency" and they would not be "interposed between the President and the head of any department or agency, or between the President and any one of the divisions in the Executive Office of the President."

114 Hart, *Presidential Branch*, 30. Dickinson, *Bitter Harvest*, 90, 97, 101.

115 Berman, *The Office of Management and Budget*, 12. Hart, *Presidential Branch*, 32. Matthew J. Dickinson and Andrew Rudalevige, "'Worked Out in Fractions': Neutral Competence, FDR, and the Bureau of the Budget," *Congress and the Presidency* (Spring 2007), 13.

116 Matthew J. Dickinson, "The Executive Office of the President: The Paradox of Politicization," in Joel D. Aberbach and Mark A. Peterson, eds., *The Executive Branch* (New York: Oxford University Press, 2005), 143–45. Hart, *Presidential Branch*, 99–101.

117 Another factor was that the increase in presidential staff over the previous two decades remained largely hidden from public view. Government statistics suggested that the White House Office staff was roughly the same size in 1968 as it had been in 1948. Only when scholars subsequently looked more closely at these numbers—counting detailees and staffers funded by special projects—did it become apparent that the White House staff during those two decades had actually grown by a couple hundred personnel. See Hart, *Presidential Branch*, 98–101; Dickinson, "The Executive Office of the President," 143–45; and Hugh Heclo, *Studying the Presidency: A Report to the Ford Foundation* (New York: Ford Foundation Press, 1977), 36–37.

118 Thomas E. Cronin, "The Swelling of the Presidency," *Saturday Review* (February 1973), 30–36; reprinted in Harry A. Bailey, Jr., ed., *Classics of the American Presidency* (Oak Park, IL: Moore Publishing, 1980). Some of the data fueling this alarm was misleading. The doubling of budgeted White House staff between 1970 and 1971, for instance, was an artifact of the Nixon administration's more honest budgeting that counted detailees and many special projects staff. But there was also real growth in the White House staff during Nixon's presidency. Matthew Dickinson has shown that the "real" number of White House staff expanded by about 200 aides during Nixon's first term. At its peak, according to the government's Federal Civilian Work Force statistics, the White House Office under Nixon had about 600 full-time employees, almost 200 more than worked in the White House Office under President George W. Bush. The "real" number of White House staff includes the staffs of the National Security Council staff and variously named domestic policy councils. Although formally part of the EOP, these council staffs have become "for all intents and purposes . . . extensions of the White House staff" (Dickinson, "The Executive Office of the President," 145–46). The Federal Civilian Work Force statistics on White House Office employees are based on estimates by Dickinson, who averaged the monthly figures for each year going back to 1943.

119 Andrew Rudalevige, *The New Imperial Presidency* (Ann Arbor: University of Michigan Press, 2005), 64–65, 73–74.

120 Stanley I. Kutler, *Abuse of Power: The New Nixon Tapes* (New York: Free Press, 1997), 3, 6, 8, 13; also see 10, 17. Rudalevige, *The New Imperial Presidency*, 74. Hart, *Presidential Branch*, 97. The phrase "blind ambition" here comes from the title of Nixon aide John Dean's mea culpa, *Blind Ambition: The White House Years* (New York: Simon & Schuster, 1976). In his memoirs, Nixon's chief of staff H.R. Haldeman reported that to protect Nixon from himself he often needed to ignore presidential directives or at least drag his feet until the president had cooled down. See *The Ends of Power* (New York: Times Books, 1978), 58–59. Haldeman took no action, for instance, when Nixon ordered him to get the CIA to give lie detector tests to every

State Department employee in the world in order to identify the source of foreign policy leaks (Burke, *Institutional Presidency*, 41). Also see Henry Kissinger, *White House Years* (Boston: Little, Brown, 1979), 1168.

121 Arnold, *Making the Managerial Presidency*, 276. Richard P. Nathan, *The Plot That Failed: Nixon and the Administrative Presidency* (New York: John Wiley, 1975), 82. Also see Joel D. Aberbach and Bert A. Rockman, "Clashing Beliefs within the Executive Branch," *American Political Science Review* (July 1976), 456–68.

122 Hess, *Organizing the Presidency*, 92–93. Nathan, *Plot That Failed*, 37. Warshaw, *Powersharing*, 39–40. Nixon's philosophy of empowering department heads was never intended to apply to foreign policy. Foreign policy was too important, in Nixon's view, to be left to those "striped-pants faggots" in the State Department. To ensure that foreign policy would be conducted from the White House, Nixon selected as his secretary of state a little-known but loyal associate, William Rogers, who knew little about foreign policy and who accepted that Nixon wanted the secretary of state to "play a subordinate role." On the most important foreign policy initiatives—opening relations with Communist China, negotiating the end of the Vietnam War, and negotiating the Strategic Arms Limitation Treaty (SALT) with Russia—Nixon relied not on Rogers and the State Department but on National Security Advisor Henry Kissinger and a bulked-up National Security Council staff of more than 50 professional analysts, all housed in the West Wing of the White House. See Elizabeth Drew, *Richard M. Nixon* (New York: Times Books, 2007), 63; Warshaw, *Powersharing*, 50. Nixon saw no contradiction between trusting in his cabinet members to make domestic policy while centralizing control over foreign policy in the White House. Indeed, the two were inextricably linked, since a leading reason for farming out "the humdrum of domestic affairs" to the cabinet was that it would allow the president more time to focus on what mattered most to him, namely foreign affairs. Whereas Lyndon Johnson had striven to make his mark as a great president by building a Great Society at home, Nixon intended to make foreign policy the hallmark of his bid for greatness. Arnold, *Making the Managerial Presidency*, 274–75.

123 Nathan, *Plot That Failed*, 39–40; also see 13–14.

124 Nathan, *Plot That Failed*, 46, 82.

125 Nathan, *Plot That Failed*, 45. Joan Hoff, *Nixon Reconsidered* (New York: Basic Books, 1994), 67. A secret memo prepared for the president's eyes only in October 1972 explained the White House first-term strategy this way: "faced with a bureaucracy we did not control, [that] was not staffed with our people, and with which we did not know how to communicate, we created our own bureaucracy." Matthew J. Dickinson and Andrew Rudalevige, "Institutionalizing Responsiveness: Roosevelt, Nixon, and the Evolution of the Office of Management and Budget," Paper presented at the annual meeting of the American Political Science Association, Chicago, August 30, 2007, 32.

126 Warshaw, *Powersharing*, 47–49, 51–52. Hart, *Presidential Branch*, 123. Dickinson and Rudalevige, "Institutionalizing Responsiveness," 25.

127 Arnold, *Making the Managerial Presidency*, 284.

128 Dickinson and Rudalevige, "Institutionalizing Responsiveness," 22. Arnold, *Making the Managerial Presidency*, 285. Andrew Rudalevige, *Managing the President's Program: Presidential Leadership and Legislative Policy Formulation* (Princeton, NJ: Princeton University Press, 2002), 58, 210 n87. Arnold, *Making the Managerial Presidency*, 294, 298. Dickinson and Rudalevige, "Institutionalizing Responsiveness," 26. Also see Egil Krogh's underappreciated memoir, *Integrity: Good People, Bad Choices, and Life Lessons from the White House* (New York: PublicAffairs, 2007).

129 Nathan, *Plot That Failed*, 51–53, 65. "Topsy" was a slave girl in Harriet Beecher Stowe's 1852 novel *Uncle Tom's Cabin*. Asked who made her, Topsy replies, "Nobody, as I knows on. I spect I grow'd. Don't think nobody never made me." The expression "grew like Topsy" came to be a popular figure of speech denoting growth without an apparent plan or conscious design.

130   Nathan, *Plot That Failed*, 7–8.

131   Nathan, *Plot That Failed*, 62. Also see John H. Kessel, *The Domestic Presidency: Decision-Making in the White House* (North Scituate, MA: Duxbury Press, 1975), 82–84. The logic applied to foreign policy as well. A second-term planning document, prepared in October 1972 for Nixon's eyes only, explained that "if the State Department can be 'retaken' by Nixon loyalists, then it would be possible to shift more of the policy option development function to State and cut down somewhat the size of the National Security Council" (quoted in Dickinson and Rudalevige, "Institutionalizing Responsiveness," 33).

132   Nathan, *Plot That Failed*, 49–50. Also see Andrew Rudalevige and David E. Lewis, "Parsing the Politicized Presidency: Centralization and Politicization as Presidential Strategies for Bureaucratic Control," Paper presented at the annual meeting of the American Political Science Association, Washington, DC, September 1–4, 2005, esp. 7–8.

133   Nathan, *Plot That Failed*, 68, 81. Melvin Small, *The Presidency of Richard Nixon* (Lawrence: University Press of Kansas, 1999), 191. Dickinson and Rudalevige, "Institutionalizing Responsiveness," 33.

134   Berman, *Office of Management and Budget*, 116. Dickinson and Rudalevige, "Institutionalizing Responsiveness," 23–24. Nathan, *Plot That Failed*, 53. Arnold, *Making the Managerial Presidency*, 298 n77.

135   Dickinson and Rudalevige, "Institutionalizing Responsiveness," 32.

136   Dickinson and Rudalevige, "Institutionalizing Responsiveness," 27–28; also see 25. Berman, *Office of Management and Budget*, 119, 126; also see 118–25. Malek was also in charge of the so-called "responsiveness program"—a secret effort in 1972 to get agencies and departments to steer federal funds toward those who could help the president's reelection effort.

137   Dickinson and Rudalevige, "Institutionalizing Responsiveness," 29–30.

138   Nathan, *Plot That Failed*, 76.

139   Dickinson, "The Executive Office of the President," 158–59. Rudalevige, *Imperial Presidency*, 60.

140   Warshaw, *Powersharing*, 65–66. On the evolution of the chief of staff role, see David B. Cohen, Karen M. Hult, and Charles E. Wolcott, "White House Evolution and Institutionalization: The Office of Chief of Staff since Reagan," *Presidential Studies Quarterly* (March 2016), 4–29. Also see Samuel Kernell and Samuel L. Popkin, eds., *Chief of Staff: Twenty-Five Years of Managing the Presidency* (Berkeley: University of California Press, 1986); and Chris Whipple, *The Gatekeepers: How the White House Chiefs of Staff Define Every Presidency* (New York: Crown, 2017).

141   Andrew Rudalevige, "The Administrative Presidency and Bureaucratic Control: Implementing a Research Agenda," *Presidential Studies Quarterly* (March 2009), 13. Richard P. Nathan, *The Administrative Presidency* (New York: John Wiley, 1983), 87. Also see Nathan, *Plot That Failed*, 92.

142   Nathan, *The Administrative Presidency*, 72, 74. Warshaw, *Powersharing*, 134, 139. Bradley H. Patterson, Jr., *The Ring of Power: The White House Staff and Its Expanding Role in Government* (New York: Basic Books, 1988), 241.

143   Patterson, *White House Staff*, 219. Patterson, *The Ring of Power*, 243–44. Nathan, *The Administrative Presidency*, 74–76. Warshaw, *Powersharing*, 134–35.

144   Nathan, *The Administrative Presidency*, 76–78. Patterson, *The Ring of Power*, 236. David E. Lewis, *The Politics of Presidential Appointments: Political Control and Bureaucratic Performance* (Princeton, NJ: Princeton University Press, 2008), 27. Warshaw, *Powersharing*, 131. No SES job is permanently designated a career or noncareer post. Once a post is vacated, it becomes a generic SES position that can be filled with a career person or an appointee. If an SES position is occupied by a careerist, the president, after 120 days, can reassign the careerist to another position, and then fill the position with an appointee of his choice. A lucid explanation of the modern personnel system, including the SES, can be found in Lewis, *The Politics of Presidential Appointments*, 20–26.

145   Patterson, *Ring of Power*, 244. Also see Nathan, *The Administrative Presidency*, 76; Lewis, *The Politics of Presidential Appointments*, 11, 24.

146   Rudalevige and Lewis, "Parsing the Politicized Presidency," 8. Warshaw, *Powersharing*, 137, 160–61. Nathan, *The Administrative Presidency*, 75.

147   Lewis, *The Politics of Presidential Appointments*, 36. Also see Shelley Lynne Tomkin, *Inside OMB: Politics and Process in the President's Budget Office* (Armonk, NY: M.E. Sharpe, 1998), 54, 109. Dickinson, "The Executive Office of the President," 152. Few OMB directors have been as publicly visible as Stockman, but subsequent presidents have tended to follow the Nixon/Reagan model of selecting like-minded politicians or trusted political advisors for the post rather than the sort of professional administrators who had commonly been selected to head the old BOB. George W. Bush, for instance, had four OMB directors, each of whom was a partisan politician: Bush's first OMB director, Mitch Daniels, had been an aide to Senator Richard Lugar and political director in the Reagan White House (and subsequently was elected governor of Indiana); Daniels's successor, Joshua Bolten, had been Bush's deputy chief of staff of policy development (and subsequently became Bush's White House chief of staff); Bush's third pick, Rob Portman, had been an Ohio congressman for more than a decade (and was elected to the Senate in 2010); and Jim Nussle, Bush's last OMB director, was a 16-year veteran of the House of Representatives, who first attracted national attention in 1991 for wearing a paper bag over his head during a speech on the House floor in which he pilloried the Democratic-controlled Congress for bouncing checks at the House "bank." Donald Trump's first OMB director, Mick Mulvaney, was also a veteran of the House of Representatives and was a founding member of the far-right Freedom Caucus. None of Obama's four OMB chiefs had previously held elective office, though all four had worked in the Clinton White House.

148   Melanie Marlowe, "The Unitary Executive and Review of Agency Rulemaking," in Ryan J. Barilleaux and Christopher S. Kelley, eds., *The Unitary Executive and the Modern Presidency* (College Station: Texas A&M University Press, 2010), 85. The idea of making OMB responsible for regulatory review did not begin with Reagan. Once again, Nixon was the pioneer. In fact, in creating OMB, Nixon insisted that program evaluation—that is, evaluating the effectiveness of government programs—must be lodged at the heart of its mission. Consistent with that overarching goal, Nixon required certain agencies to submit draft regulations and an accompanying cost–benefit analysis to OMB. In practice, however, regulatory review under Nixon focused on a relatively small number of regulations, almost all of which were environmental regulations issued by the fledgling Environmental Protection Agency. See Marlowe, "The Unitary Executive and Review of Agency Rulemaking," 81–82.

149   William F. West, "Presidential Leadership and Administrative Coordination: Examining the Theory of a Unified Executive," *Presidential Studies Quarterly* (September 2006), 442–43. Joseph Cooper and William F. West, "Presidential Power and Republican Government: The Theory and Practice of OMB Review," *Journal of Politics* (November 1988), 876.

150   William F. West, "The Institutionalization of Regulatory Review: Organizational Stability and Responsive Competence at OIRA," *Presidential Studies Quarterly* (March 2005), 84. West, "Presidential Leadership and Administrative Coordination," 444.

151   West, "Presidential Leadership and Administrative Coordination," 443–44. West, "The Institutionalization of Regulatory Review," 85–87.

152   Rudalevige, "The Administrative Presidency and Bureaucratic Control," 15. Testimony of Rick Melberth, before the Subcommittee on Commercial and Administrative Law, Committee on the Judiciary, US House of Representatives, May 6, 2008, *OMB Watch*, p. 5. Bush's executive order also included the requirement that no agency regulation could be promulgated without identifying a specific "market failure" that necessitated government action (4).

153 Juliet Eilperin and Darla Cameron, "How Trump Is Rolling Back Obama's Legacy," *Washington Post*, March 24, 2017 (updated June 9, 2017). Christopher S. Kelley, "The Unitary Executive and the Clinton Administration," in Barilleaux and Kelley, *The Unitary Executive and the Modern Presidency*, 110–12.

154 Central to the administration's deconstruction effort was the selection of Neomi Rao to head OIRA. A former law clerk to Clarence Thomas and founder of the Center for the Study of the Administrative State at George Mason University's Antonin Scalia Law School, Rao has been an outspoken critic of the administrative state and has argued for extending OIRA review to independent agencies and limiting Congress's power to delegate rule-making power to administrative agencies.

155 Terry M. Moe, "The Politicized Presidency," in John E. Chubb and Paul E. Peterson, eds., *The New Direction in American Politics* (Washington, DC: Brookings Institution Press, 1985), 235–71.

156 Nathan, *The Administrative Presidency*, 72. Nicholas Thompson, "Dick Cheney's Dick Cheney," *Washington Monthly*, July/August 2001.

157 Lewis, *Politics of Presidential Appointments*, 98. For efforts to specify the causes of—and relationship between—centralization and politicization, see Rudalevige and Lewis, "Parsing the Politicized Presidency." Also see Matthew J. Dickinson and Andrew Rudalevige, "Presidents, Responsiveness, and Competence: Revisiting the 'Golden Age' at the Bureau of the Budget," *Political Science Quarterly* (Winter 2004/2005), 633–54; and Dickinson and Rudalevige, "Institutionalizing Responsiveness."

158 Lewis, *Politics of Presidential Appointments*, ch. 6.

159 Lewis, *Politics of Presidential Appointments*, 159.

160 Al Kamen, "Senators Seek to Slash Number of Presidential Appointees," *Washington Post*, March 8, 2010. Also see Patterson, *The White House Staff*, 237–38; Patterson, *To Serve the President*, 93. Members of Congress from both parties have repeatedly introduced bills to curtail or even abolish Schedule C positions, but presidents have countered that reform should focus not on reducing the number of political appointees but on converting many Senate-confirmed positions into noncareer SES and Schedule C positions, which would allow the administration to fill positions more quickly and without Senate approval.

CHAPTER 8

THE REMOVAL POWER, PARTY PATRONAGE, AND THE UNITARY EXECUTIVE

INTRODUCTORY PUZZLE: THE CURIOUS CASE OF THE IBC COMMISSIONER

The border separating Canada and the United States extends for well over 5,000 miles, "over mountains, down cliffs, along waterways and through prairie grasses." No wall divides the two nations and no troops guard the vast border, but nearly every mile is carefully marked and maintained. Even in the most remote and dense forests, a 20-foot-wide swath of cleared land designates the border. The organization charged with maintaining this boundary is the Canada/United States International Boundary Commission (IBC), established by treaty in 1908.[1]

The IBC consists of two commissioners—one American and one Canadian, each with their own staff and budget. The American commissioner is headquartered in Washington, DC, and reports to the secretary of state; the Canadian commissioner is housed in Ottawa and reports to the minister for foreign affairs. Expenses incurred from clearing brush ten feet on either side of the border line and maintaining and putting up boundary markers are shared equally by the two governments.

The actions of the IBC rarely attract attention. Few Americans or Canadians are even aware that such a commission exists. But the IBC was propelled into the spotlight in 2007 after an elderly American couple, Shirley and Herbert Leu, built a four-foot-high concrete retaining wall that extended two and a half feet into the IBC-controlled boundary vista. When the wall was brought to the attention of the IBC in January 2007, American commissioner Dennis Schornack wrote to the Leus informing them that they were required to take down the wall. The couple refused, even after the commission offered to pay for the wall's removal. Schornack warned the Leus that if they did not take down their wall the commission would do it for them, and that the Leus would have to pay the bill. The couple still refused and vowed to sue the IBC if it did not allow them to keep their wall.

No American had ever sued the IBC before, and so Schornack was in uncharted legal waters. For legal counsel he first approached the State Department's legal office, which refused to help because the IBC was not part of the department. Schornack next contacted the Department of Justice, which consented to defend the commission. The American commissioner also retained an outside lawyer, an expert on international law,

Shirley and Herbert Leu of Blaine, Washington, stand in front of the retaining wall that the International Boundary Commission ordered them to remove.

Courtesy: Brian T. Hedges, Pacific Legal Foundation.

after he was told by the Department of Justice that he would also need "international legal advice." Meanwhile the Leus found a conservative nonprofit legal organization that was willing to take their case for free: the Pacific Legal Foundation, which specialized in cases involving conflicts between property rights and government regulations. The Republican administration of George W. Bush appeared to be on an unlikely collision course with the oldest and best-funded conservative legal foundation in the country.[2]

However, the Bush administration had no stomach for a battle with an ideological ally. Key White House officials were sympathetic to the Leus' property rights claim and were unmoved by Schornack's argument that granting the Leus an exemption would jeopardize the IBC's ability to enforce the 20-foot vista in the future. Two months after the Leus filed suit in federal district court, an assistant attorney general ordered Schornack to terminate the outside counsel. Only lawyers who reported directly to the president could represent IBC, he was now told. After refusing to comply, Schornack was contacted by Luis Reyes, Special Assistant to the President for Presidential Personnel, who upbraided him for his disloyalty to the president and the Republican Party and for his failure to grasp the doctrine of the "unitary executive." Schornack was a member of the executive branch, part of the president's team, and when the president or people representing the president issued an order to subordinates in the executive branch they were duty bound to follow those directives. If Schornack would not dismiss the outside counsel then Reyes would advise the president to ask for the commissioner's resignation. Schornack stood his ground and was terminated the following day and replaced. The administration then orchestrated a deal whereby the Leus kept their retaining wall.[3]

Did the president have the power to dismiss Schornack? Schornack thought not and immediately fired off a letter informing President Bush that he had exceeded his authority. Although the 1925 treaty dictated that the president would appoint the American IBC commissioner, the treaty did not give the president the power to replace the commissioner, except in the event of "death, resignation, or other disability." Schornack complained that officials at the Department of Justice had sacrificed their duty to enforce the laws upon the altar of a political "campaign promoting property rights." He argued that the IBC was an international organization established by international treaty and designed to be "independent of the executive" and insulated from the nation's "political swings." It was unconscionable that he should be dismissed for his fidelity to international treaties that Congress and the president had approved.

The Bush administration saw the situation very differently. The president had appointed Schornack to the IBC because he was a Bush supporter and a reliable Republican who had been a top political aide to Michigan's Republican governor, John Engler. In recent decades the American IBC commissioner had routinely resigned after the election of a new president in order to give the president the opportunity to make the appointment. The commissioner was an "officer of the United States" and was therefore responsible and subordinate to the nation's chief executive. The commissioning document, moreover, clearly stated that Schornack's appointment was "during the pleasure of the President of the United States for the time being." Because neither the treaty nor the United States Congress had ever specified the term's length or placed restrictions on the grounds for removal, the president could fire the commissioner for any reason.

In October 2007, a federal judge sided with the Bush administration, but acknowledged that Schornack's case raised "difficult issues" about the scope of presidential power and that both sides had "strong arguments" in favor of their interpretation. How is it that the profoundly important question of whether or not a president may fire a government official does not have a clear answer and that both sides in this dispute could be convinced that they were right? The answer to this puzzle is rooted in the silences of the United States Constitution as well as in the emergence of new forms of administrative governance in the twentieth century. The fight over the removal power has been central to the development of the American presidency from the earliest days of the republic.[4]

"THE GREAT DEBATE OF 1789"[5]

When the first Congress convened in the spring of 1789, it confronted a glaring omission in the Constitution. Article II, section 2 specified that the president possessed the power to appoint officers of the United States, "by and with the Advice and Consent of the Senate," and that Congress could vest the appointment of "inferior Officers, as they think proper, in the President alone, in the Courts of Law, or in the Heads of

Department." But the Constitution did not reveal who possessed the power to remove an executive officer. The head of a department or any executive branch official could be impeached, of course, but was that the only grounds for removal? Were they to serve "during good behavior," like federal judges? One of the Constitution's most vocal defenders, Tench Coxe, soon to become the nation's first assistant secretary of the treasury, had argued this thesis during the ratification debates in an effort to allay Anti-Federalist concerns about the president's appointment powers. However, precious few members of Congress found this theory plausible. But if department heads and executive officials did not serve during good behavior, then at whose pleasure did they serve? Did they serve at the pleasure of the president, the Senate, or both? The delegates at the Constitutional Convention had avoided the question entirely, but members of Congress did not have that luxury as they strove to establish the first executive departments.[6]

The House Debate

On May 19, 1789, Virginia congressman James Madison introduced a motion to establish a Department of Foreign Affairs, headed by a secretary who would "be removable by the president." Objections to Madison's motion were immediately raised by Representative Theoderick Bland, who argued that since the president and Senate had jointly been granted the power of appointment, it "naturally follows" that the power of removal was also a power conferred on both the president and Senate. Were the president given the unilateral power to remove executive officials it would undo the constraints that the Constitution had placed on the president's appointment power. To prevent the president from becoming "a monarch [with] absolute power of all the great departments of Government," Bland proposed to amend Madison's motion by adding the words "by and with the advice and consent of the Senate."[7]

Madison and his allies pressed the opposing theory that the power of appointment and the power of removal were inherently executive functions. The president only shared his executive powers when the Constitution specified an exception, as it did with appointments. Where the Constitution was silent regarding the exercise of executive power, the power necessarily belonged to the president. As Pennsylvania's George Clymer—one of six Americans to sign both the Declaration of Independence and the Constitution—reminded Bland: "the power of removal was an executive power and as such belonged to the President alone, by the express words of the constitution: 'the executive power shall be vested in a President of the United States of America.'"[8]

However, the success of Madison's motion could not rest on the constitutional argument alone. For if the removal power was inherently an executive power, why include a clause granting the president such a power? Including the removal clause, as even the motion's supporters worried, seemed to concede that the legislature had the constitutional authority to vest the removal power where it pleased. A pivotal block of legislators agreed with New York's John Laurance that the Constitution's silence left it up to the legislature to specify "the conditions upon which [the department head] shall enjoy the office." According to Laurance,

We can say he shall hold it for three years from his appointment, or during good behavior; and we may declare unfitness and incapacity causes of removal, and make the President alone judge of this case. We may authorize the President to remove him for any causes he thinks proper.

For Laurance and many of his colleagues, the real issue facing the House was not "where does the power of removal lie?" but rather "where *should* the power of removal lie?" In Laurance's view, this was "a question of expedience" and boiled down to one query: "could the Legislature safely trust the President with this power?"[9]

Bland's position was that the president could not be trusted with such a power and that the legislature therefore needed to place constraints or conditions on the president's freedom to remove officials. The task that fell to Madison and his supporters was to persuade the House that the president could be safely entrusted with such power and that the government would be better run and the people better served if the removal power was lodged in the president alone. Department heads, Madison noted, are supposed to "aid" the president in carrying out his duties to administer the government. If cabinet officials were not responsible to the president, then the president could not be "responsible to the country." At stake therefore was not only the efficiency and effectiveness of government, but democratic accountability as well. A president who was not responsible for and could not be held accountable for the actions of his administration was, in Madison's view, a far more serious threat to the new nation than the prospect that Bland imagined of a president exercising dictatorial control over the entire government. After all, Madison reminded his fellow members of Congress, even if the president removed a department head, the Senate would still have to approve his successor. Moreover, the "wanton removal of meritorious officers" would surely lead to impeachment by Congress or, failing that, "impeachment before the community, who will have the power of punishment by refusing to reelect him." The people would keep the president honest even if the legislature failed to do so.[10]

Madison's words failed to sway his most determined opponents. Fellow Virginian John Page, a close friend of Thomas Jefferson and a future governor of the state, expressed astonishment that Congress, with one of its first acts, was prepared "to authorize ... a dangerous royal prerogative." Department heads, he conceded, should be responsible to the president, but they should not be made his "abject tools." A free and independent people, Page argued, should prefer an "independent spirit in our officers" to "a prompt servility," a devotion to the laws rather than subjection to the dictates of a ruler. Moreover, placing department heads in the "humiliating" position of submitting to every presidential whim would make it difficult to attract the best and most honorable men to these posts.[11]

After many days of speeches—delivered, as Maryland's Michael Stone observed, not "so much from an expectation of being able to convince as from a desire to assign the reasons upon which our vote is founded"—the House was on the verge of approving Madison's motion to make the secretary of foreign affairs removable by the president. But at the eleventh hour, Congress was pitched an unexpected curve ball by Representative Egbert Benson, a close friend and confidant of Alexander Hamilton. Benson proposed to replace Madison's original language with an amendment to establish a "chief clerk," who would take charge of the Department of Foreign Affairs in the event that the secretary "shall be removed from office by the President of the United States, or in any other case of vacancy." Unlike Madison's original language, Benson's amendment recognized the president's power to remove the department head but cleverly avoided the suggestion that the power had been granted to the president by Congress.[12]

Members such as Page and Bland were as opposed to Benson's amendment as they had been to Madison's original motion, but they could not prevent the amendment's passage. Having secured his amendment by a 30–18 margin, Benson—backed by Madison, who was now convinced that his original language could be construed as conceding that the Constitution gave Congress the power to decide where to vest the power to remove department heads—then moved to strike Madison's original language. This proposal sharply divided the supporters of Benson's amendment. Half of those who had supported Benson's amendment (including three signatories to the Constitution) believed that Madison's original language should be retained because, as Laurance had argued, the legislature possessed the constitutional authority to vest the removal power where it saw fit. However, Benson's motion gave Page and his allies the opportunity to defeat the "to be removable by the president" clause that they had argued so vehemently against for the better part of a month. The clause was struck, on a 31–19 vote, by an unlikely alliance of those who agreed with Benson and Madison that the removal of department heads was inherently an executive power and those who agreed with Page and Bland that the Constitution did not—and that the legislature should not—give the president the sole power of removal.

Having outmaneuvered the opposition, Benson and Madison then secured final approval of the measure by a vote of 29–22, with the support coming from the same alliance that had secured Benson's original amendment. Only 11 House members voted with Benson and Madison on each of the three votes, and thereby endorsed the idea that the president had an inherent, constitutionally based removal power. Although a majority of the House rejected this construction of the Constitution (12 House members, including Laurance, voted not to drop Madison's original language while also voting in favor of the Benson amendment and the final bill, while 16 members, including Page, voted in favor of deleting Madison's original language while also voting against the Benson amendment and the final bill), Benson's legislative maneuver enabled the Benson–Madison coalition to prevail on each of the three votes.[13]

The Senate Debate

The great debate over the removal power now shifted to the Senate. When the Senate took up the clause establishing a chief clerk who would temporarily take over from the secretary of foreign affairs whenever the latter "shall be removed from office by the President of the United States," Pennsylvania's senator William Maclay immediately urged striking out the words "by the President of the United States." Maclay warned his colleagues not to let their judgment be swayed by their trust in the current incumbent, for while Washington might be entrusted with the removal power, "his virtues will depart with him." Future presidents, Maclay predicted, would almost certainly abuse the power. Echoing Page, Maclay also warned that a department head compelled to "consult [the president's] will in every matter" would be reduced to "abject servility."[14]

Maclay's motion triggered a heated debate that predictably reprised most of the arguments that had been voiced in the House of Representatives. More surprising was the broad support Maclay's motion received, even from senators aligned with the Washington administration. Three signers of the Constitution who were supporters of the administration spoke in favor of Maclay's motion: South Carolina's Pierce Butler, the Senate president pro tempore John Langdon, and Connecticut's widely respected William Samuel Johnson, who had been chair of the five-person Committee of Style that molded the Constitution into its final form. Backed also by leading Anti-Federalists such as Virginia's Richard Henry Lee and William Grayson, Maclay's motion appeared to have the votes necessary to pass.

With defeat imminent, the administration's supporters, led by Vice President John Adams, mounted a furious lobbying campaign. "It was all huddling away in small parties," Maclay groused, with Adams, "the great converter," particularly "busy ... running to everyone." By persuading several senators to "recant," the administration managed to engineer a deadlocked vote. Under Article I, section 3 of the Constitution, the vice president, as the Senate's presiding officer, was empowered to cast the deciding vote in the event of a tie, and Adams gleefully did so.[15]

The administration had triumphed. Yet the closeness of the vote and the intensity of the debate suggested that the question of the removal power was far from settled. The opposition could point to the fact that four senators who were signatories to the Constitution—Butler, Langdon, Johnson, as well as Georgia's William Few—did not believe the Constitution gave the president the inherent power to remove a department head.[16] Proceedings in the House, moreover, showed that a majority of representatives believed that it was within Congress's power to limit the president's power of removal if Congress chose to do so. Only two of the eight House members (Madison and Pennsylvania's George Clymer) who had been delegates at the Constitutional Convention embraced the position that the Constitution gave the president the power of removal.[17]

REMOVALS IN THE EARLY REPUBLIC

Although the removal power provoked a historic constitutional debate in the first Congress, removals from office were not a high priority for the nation's first president. When Washington assumed the presidency there was nobody much to remove, only people to appoint. Of course, that quickly changed once the Washington administration had begun to fill the many new offices established by Congress. There was incompetence and malfeasance, then as now. Presidents and department heads were compelled to sift through complaints and grievances, jealousies and rivalries. However, as Leonard White found in his magisterial study of administration in the nation's first decade, the removal power was "used sparingly by the Federalist leaders." Removal in the Washington administration was mostly reserved for cases of "serious delinquency or the failure to account for public funds." Removal "for political reasons," White concluded, was "unknown" during Washington's two terms. The House majority appeared to have been vindicated in the trust it had placed in the president to exercise the removal power judiciously. Even Maclay, however, had conceded that the virtuous Washington could be trusted; the question was what would happen after the first president departed.[18]

The Theory and Practice of John Adams

John Adams had no doubt that the president possessed the constitutional authority to remove executive branch officials. Yet when Adams became president on March 4, 1797, he retained Washington's cabinet intact, despite having an unfavorable impression of Secretary of State Thomas Pickering and knowing little about the other three. Years later, he explained that to remove even one of his predecessor's department heads would have turned "the world upside down." Adams, of course, had political reasons to accent the continuity between his administration and that of the revered Washington, but his concern that removing even a single department head at the outset of his term would be a cataclysmic event is a reminder that there was no tradition that a new president should pick his own cabinet. Nor was there an expectation that cabinet members should offer their resignations at the end of a president's term.[19]

Adams's decision not to pick his own cabinet proved a monumental mistake. Of his four secretaries, three—Pickering, Secretary of War James McHenry, and Secretary of the Treasury Oliver Wolcott—were loyal to former treasury secretary Alexander Hamilton, Adams's chief rival for leadership of the Federalist Party. Despite championing the president's removal power in 1789, Adams as president was extraordinarily reluctant to exercise that power, even in the case of McHenry, whose incompetence was well documented. Not until the spring of Adams's final year did he finally decide to act. Summoning McHenry to the presidential mansion, Adams let loose a volley of insults and complaints. He charged McHenry with having conspired with Hamilton to undermine his presidency and of being "devoid of every moral principle, a bastard [and] a foreigner." McHenry resigned immediately. Pickering, however, refused to resign, so Adams fired him for "diverse causes and considerations, essential to the administration of the government." This was the first time in the nation's history that a president had fired a department head.[20]

The removal of Pickering notwithstanding, Adams continued to subscribe to much the same restrained view of removals as Washington. "When I came into office," Adams explained, "it was my determination to make as few removals as possible [and] not one from personal motives [or] party considerations." His claim that he had "invariably observed" this resolution was not entirely true. In December 1797, for instance, Adams dismissed Commissioner of Revenue Tench Coxe for reasons that were essentially political. Coxe had served as Hamilton's assistant in the Treasury Department before being made revenue commissioner, but had gravitated away from Hamilton's orbit and drawn closer to the emerging Republican Party. Hamilton despised Coxe and, like most Federalists, considered him a traitor to the party, but Washington refused to dismiss him. Adams, though, relented, accepting his cabinet's argument that Coxe lacked the confidence of the treasury secretary and that the conflict between the two men was "utterly incompatible with that harmonious conduct and co-operation in offices so closely connected, which the public interests indispensably require."[21]

Generally, though, Adams did resist calls to remove officials. According to one count, Adams dismissed only 21 executive branch officers whose appointments required Senate approval, and only a "handful" of these dismissals could be classified as political or partisan. The small number of political removals made by Adams is especially notable in view of the intense elite partisanship of the late 1790s, particularly since the Alien and Sedition Act, passed by the Federalist-controlled Congress in 1798, made it relatively easy to confuse partisan differences with lack of loyalty to the nation. Adams's restraint is all the more remarkable in view of his own complaint that he had inherited "a multitude of Jacobins" in federal positions across the nation.[22]

Jefferson and the "Painful Office" of Removals

If Adams felt surrounded by Jacobins, imagine how his successor Thomas Jefferson felt when he assumed the presidency in 1801 after 12 years of uninterrupted Federalist rule. To Jefferson, it seemed a simple matter of fairness that since the Federalist Party had been "in the exclusive possession of all offices from the very first origin of party among us," the president should now appoint Republicans "until something like an equilibrium in office [was] restored." Removals, however, were a different proposition. Jefferson was determined to nullify Adams's so-called "midnight appointments," which in Jefferson's mind included all officials appointed after December 12, 1800, the date it became clear that Adams had lost the election. But beyond undoing Adams's "indecent" late-term appointments, Jefferson envisioned a modest use of the removal power. "Some removals," Jefferson acknowledged, "must be made for misconduct," but he estimated that the total number of these would probably be less than 20. The idea of removing competent government officials "on the ground of political principles alone" was as distasteful to Jefferson as it had been to Adams.[23]

From the outset, however, Jefferson found himself under intense pressure from supporters to act the part of "executioner," "lopping off" unwanted Federalists to make room for Republicans. Reluctant to give up on the possibility of finding a middle ground that would satisfy both his Republican allies and moderate Federalists, Jefferson resisted calls for a "general purgation" of Federalists from office. However, by the summer of 1801 Jefferson was becoming aware that he might need to modify his position. While he was willing to "push the patience of our friends to the utmost it will bear" in order to win over Federalists, he would not, he told his treasury secretary Albert Gallatin, "even for this object, absolutely revolt our tried friends." It would, the Sage of Monticello concluded, be "a poor manoeuvre to exchange them for new converts."[24]

In the heart of New England, in Federalist strongholds such as Connecticut, there was little evidence that Jefferson's policy of conciliation was winning many converts anyway. The Federalist-controlled Connecticut state legislature, Jefferson noted, was "removing every republican even from the commissions of the peace and the lowest officers." A letter signed by 24 of Connecticut's leading Republicans urged the president to rethink his policy and adopt "a very extended system of removals." A policy of conciliating

Federalists might make sense in other states, the letter allowed, but not in Connecticut, where the Republican Party could not survive without breaking the Federalist stranglehold on political offices. It did not matter that Federalists would denounce these removals as "the result of a vindictive spirit, the act of the President of a party," because they would oppose Jefferson's reelection anyway.[25]

Shortly after receiving the letter from Republican leaders in Connecticut, Jefferson received a remonstrance, signed by close to 80 New Haven merchants, protesting Jefferson's removal of Elizur Goodrich as collector of the Port of New Haven. Goodrich was one of those whom Adams had appointed "in the last moments" of his administration, so Jefferson felt Goodrich's removal was fully justified; indeed, in Jefferson's view, it barely qualified as a removal at all, since Goodrich should not have been in the office in the first place. Moreover, Jefferson knew that his own selection, the 77-year-old Samuel Bishop, mayor of New Haven and chief judge of the county court, was widely respected in the community. In replying to the merchants, Jefferson could have merely pointed out both of these facts, but he decided that the time had arrived for a public explanation of his removals policy.[26]

In his reply to the merchants, dated July 12, 1801, Jefferson explained that his declarations "in favor of political tolerance" and his "exhortations to harmony" had been "misconstrued" as an assurance that "the tenure of offices was to be undisturbed." He now announced publicly what heretofore he had only confided privately: his policy would be guided by the desire to ensure that Republicans had "a proportionate share in the direction of the public affairs." There was a clear shift, however, between what he had privately told Republican leaders immediately after his inauguration in March and the policy he now announced to the nation. In March he had explained that appointments would be guided by the goal of giving Republicans a proportionate share of offices but that he would not use removals to achieve that goal. Now, Jefferson was suggesting that removals, too, could be warranted to achieve a proportionate share of federal offices for Republicans.[27]

Jefferson did not define precisely what would count as a proportionate share of offices but he articulated a profoundly democratic rationale for removals: "the will of the nation, manifested by their various elections, calls for an administration of government according with the opinions of those elected." Yet even here, in Jefferson's most expansive defense of the removal power, he was not arguing that his defeat of Adams empowered him to remove any officeholder with Federalist sympathies. The will of the nation was expressed not through his election alone but was instead reflected in all the "various elections" across the country. Jefferson's "duty," as he saw it, was not to color the entire executive branch Republican but instead to ensure that Republicans had a share of federal offices that was roughly proportionate to their political strength in the nation. Had he come into office at a time when the two parties' proportion of offices was more equal, Jefferson said that he would "gladly have left to time and accident to raise them to their just share." The Federalists' virtual monopoly of federal offices, however, meant that he could not wait for death or resignation, or limit removals to the incompetent. The "painful office" that was required of him, he predicted, would be a temporary one. As soon as he had corrected the imbalance, he would "return with joy to that state of things when the only questions concerning a candidate shall be, is he honest? Is he capable? Is he faithful to the Constitution?"[28]

Jefferson promised to carry out removals only after careful "deliberation and inquiry" so as to "injure the best men least." If that vow was meant to reassure nervous Federalists, the subsequent clause must have sent a chill down the spine of every Federalist office-holder. The burden of removals, Jefferson promised, would land "as much as possible, on delinquency, on oppression, on intolerance, on incompetence, on anti-revolutionary adherence to our enemies." Incompetence and delinquency were unobjectionable causes for removal that both sides could agree upon. However, "anti-revolutionary adherence" cloaked political differences of opinion in the protective cover of patriotism and national security, much as John Adams had done in justifying several of his politically motivated removals on the grounds that the officeholders had shown "hostility to the national Constitution and government."[29]

That both Adams and Jefferson used a similar dodge to justify what we would see as plainly partisan removals is evidence of the difficulty both had in accepting the idea that the president should remove subordinate officers for purely partisan reasons. Such partisan removals clashed with their understanding of the president as a leader above party. That nonpartisan image of the presidency also explains Jefferson's insistence that his role was to balance the two parties' fair share of offices and that once he had orchestrated that balance the president could appoint and remove on competence and ethics alone.

Over the next two years Jefferson was remarkably successful in reshaping the political makeup of the federal bureaucracy. He kept close count of the numbers, including the reasons for removal. In July 1803, Jefferson estimated that only 130 of the 316 federal offices that he was empowered to appoint and remove were still held by Federalists. The precise number of politically motivated removals is harder to know, since many removals took the form of resignations offered "to avoid the embarrassment of dismissal" and others lost their jobs when their office was abolished as part of the Republican program of retrenchment. But even by Jefferson's count, only 15 of the approximately 70 office-holders forcibly removed—that is, not counting resignations or offices abolished—during his first 26 months in office were removed solely for reasons of "misconduct or delinquency." The rest of the removals involved political or partisan motives.[30]

Stability in the Executive Branch: The Federalist Argument against Removals

Jefferson's political removals predictably brought howls of protest from Federalists. Connecticut's Oliver Wolcott, secretary of the treasury during the Washington and Adams presidencies, fretted that Jefferson's conduct meant that from now on every time the nation elected a new president there would be a completely new "set of executive officers, down to the most subordinate grades," which would in turn "render peaceable Elections impracticable." Connecticut congressman Simeon Baldwin did not blame Jefferson for wanting his chief "constitutional advisers" to be of the "same political sentiments with him," but he charged Jefferson with "wanton abuse" of the removal power for "removing a host of inferior officers who were honest, faithful and capable, and whose political sentiments had no connexion with the discharge of their official Duties."[31]

It is tempting to dismiss such complaints as sour grapes, but the Federalist position was not entirely unprincipled. Alexander Hamilton, though an unrivaled champion of energy in the executive, had long viewed the removal power with a wary eye. In *Federalist* No. 77, Hamilton had argued that the president did not possess the sole power to remove officers because the Constitution envisioned that the Senate's consent "would be necessary to displace as well as to appoint." Hamilton's interpretation, of course, lost out in the great congressional debate of 1789, and in the 1802 edition of *The Federalist* he acknowledged that "it is now settled practice, that the power of displacing belongs exclusively to the president." Many scholars have interpreted Hamilton's argument in *Federalist* No. 77 as either a disingenuous attempt to sell the new Constitution or a poorly thought-out remark that he quickly repudiated. However, as political scientist Jeremy Bailey has shown, Hamilton's vision of a restrained removal power was consistent with his understanding of executive power.[32]

Hamilton maintained that "unity"—by which he meant a single president rather than a plural executive—was an essential part of "energy" in the executive. Unity was necessary for the executive to act decisively, swiftly, and sometimes secretly. Unity also ensured that the president would be held accountable for his actions. However, Hamilton also valued stability in the executive branch. Frequent turnover in the executive, he feared, would lead to neglect of longer-term projects.[33]

In *Federalist* No. 72, Hamilton favored allowing the president to be eligible for reelection precisely because it would minimize administrative disruption. There was, he stressed, an "intimate connection between the duration of the executive magistrate in office and the stability of the system of administration." If presidents changed constantly, and with them the "men who fill the subordinate stations," then there would be a "ruinous mutability in the administration of the government."

Similarly, in *Federalist* No. 77, Hamilton defended the Senate's involvement in appointments and removals on the grounds that then "a change of the Chief Magistrate . . . would not occasion so violent or so general a revolution in the officers of the government as might be expected, if he were the sole disposer of offices." Requiring the Senate—which "from the greater permanency of its own composition, will in all probability be less subject to inconstancy than any other member of the government"—to consent to removals, in short, would make it more likely that removals would be based on competence and integrity rather than political ideology or personal whim. An unrestrained use of the removal power, in Hamilton's view, thus undermined administrative stability and expertise, which were as central to an energetic executive as was executive unity.

A Quarter-Century of Republican Restraint

Once Jefferson had broken the Federalist monopoly on office, he reverted to a more circumscribed use of the removal power, much as he had promised he would in his reply to New Haven's merchants. During his second term, Jefferson exercised the removal power sparingly, and sometimes retained Federalist officeholders even in the face of intense organized pressure from his own partisans. For instance, Delaware Republicans lobbied fiercely for the removal of the collector of customs at the Port of Wilmington but Jefferson refused. His supporters attributed the president's more cautious second-term approach to "the great noise" that Federalists had made in protesting political removals, but Jefferson's caution also reflected his own discomfort with the idea that the president should remove executive officers purely on account of partisan difference. Increasingly when Jefferson articulated his removal policy it was to emphasize his preference for the "milder measure of waiting till accidental vacancies should furnish opportunity of giving republicans their due proportion of office." Removals would still be made, but only with "sufficient proof" of incompetence, dishonesty, or "open, active, and virulent abuse of official influence."[34]

Jefferson's restraint was emulated by each of his Republican successors. James Madison, champion of the president's removal power in the great debate of 1789, only removed 27 officials during his eight years as president. Madison's successor, James Monroe, was equally cautious in his use of the removal power, leading Monroe's secretary of state, John Quincy Adams, to lament that his boss was too "indulgent and scrupulously regardful of individual feelings" and prone to avert "his eyes from misconduct" rather than confront a subordinate with his faults. However, when it came to Adams's turn to assume the powers of the presidency he showed the same restraint as his predecessors, removing only 12 executive officials in four years.[35]

The small number of removals during John Quincy Adams's presidency is particularly striking because he came under intense pressure from supporters to use the removal power to scrub the government of political opponents. Madison and Monroe had largely escaped such pressures because of the many uninterrupted years of Republican control, but Adams's controversial election had irreparably fractured the Republican Party into warring factions. Secretary of State Henry Clay urged Adams to use the removal power to bolster the coalition that had elected him president. "No officer depending upon the will of the President for his place," Clay told Adams, "should be permitted to [behave] in open and continual disparagement of the Administration and its head." Adams stubbornly refused. Removal simply because "it was the pleasure of the President would be harsh and odious—inconsistent with the principle upon which I have commenced the Administration of removing no person from office but for cause." A strong executive, in Adams's view, required a stable federal bureaucracy, not a politicized one.[36]

In short, presidential removals in the early republic were generally few in number and limited to nonpolitical reasons such as corruption or incompetence. This self-restraint was not on account of constitutional doubts about the president's right to remove subordinate officers. As Attorney General William Wirt expressed it in a formal opinion issued in the final year of Adams's presidency, "the power of the President to dismiss . . . at pleasure, is not disputed." Rather, presidential restraint in exercising the removal power stemmed from a sense that the proper use of such power did not extend beyond ensuring that subordinate officers were executing the law in a competent and honest fashion. The two years between the summer of 1801 and the summer of 1803, during which Jefferson openly wielded the removal power for political ends, stand out as an exception. However, Jefferson did not justify his political removals on the grounds that subordinate officers should follow presidential policies but rather on the grounds that federal offices should reflect the political diversity of the nation. Not the unitary executive but a fair political balance justified Jefferson's temporary departure from the era's general consensus that federal officials should not be removed without good cause.[37]

THE JACKSONIAN DEFENSE OF ROTATION IN OFFICE

When Andrew Jackson assumed the presidency in March 1829, he inherited a remarkably stable executive branch. Allen McLane, the Wilmington customs collector whom Jefferson had refused to dismiss despite persistent pressure from Delaware Republicans, still occupied the same post when Jackson took the oath of office. Even at the cabinet level, there was often significant continuity between administrations. John Quincy Adams retained Monroe's postmaster general and secretary of the navy as well as Attorney General William Wirt, who served for 12 years. Alexander Hamilton would certainly have approved, but many members of Congress as well as local and state officials grew restive about the limited number of vacancies.[38]

The Tenure of Office Act of 1820

In an attempt to promote greater turnover and accountability in the federal bureaucracy, Congress passed a law in 1820 that limited federal officeholders responsible for revenue collection to four-year terms; under the statute, the officeholder's commission ended at the beginning of each president's term. The Tenure of Office Act of 1820 had two, potentially contradictory effects. On the one hand, it enhanced the Senate's power, because if a president wished to retain a person in office beyond four years he needed the Senate's consent. On the other hand, the act facilitated presidential removals since it was easier not to renew an official's commission than to fire the person.[39]

Monroe saw little wrong with the bill when he signed it—his biographer claims that he affixed his signature "without knowing its contents," perhaps because it was one of 34 bills he signed that evening. His predecessors Jefferson and Madison, however, were quick to slam the law. Madison thought it plainly unconstitutional; if a term of office could be limited to four years then what would stop Congress from limiting a term to one year or one day, thereby "annihilat[ing]" the president's power of appointment? Monroe soon accepted that he had made a mistake in signing the bill and blunted its effects by routinely renominating officials. John Quincy Adams pursued the same policy. To do otherwise, Adams believed, would be to "make the Government a perpetual ... scramble for office."[40]

Andrew Jackson, however, viewed the act very differently. Whereas Adams, like Hamilton, associated longevity in office with administrative stability and competence, Jackson associated it with privileged sinecures for "the old, tired, and worn-out." Lack of turnover in federal office, Jackson believed, had created a pervasive culture of corruption in which officeholders used their positions to enrich themselves through graft, bribery, and kickbacks. In running for the presidency in 1828, Jackson made cleaning up government corruption the centerpiece of his campaign. And the Tenure of Office Act made it that much easier for President Jackson to follow through on his campaign promise to cleanse "the Augean stables."[41]

"To the Victor Belong the Spoils"

Jackson's anti-corruption crusade dovetailed with the new president's need to reward his many supporters, who were clamoring for the ouster of "Adams men" and their replacement by reliable "Jackson men." "To the victor belong the spoils of the enemy," Democratic Senator William Marcy famously pronounced on the Senate floor. Adams's insistence on renominating every officer, "friend or foe, against whom no specific charge of misconduct [had] been brought," may have been admirable but it brought him the same political isolation and defeat suffered by his high-minded father. Jackson was not going to make that same mistake.[42]

Jackson's friends and opponents were confident that the president would carry out "a complete overhauling" of the bureaucracy. But the radical overhaul that Jackson seemed poised to embark upon gave even some of his allies pause. Thomas Ritchie, an influential Jackson supporter and editor of the *Richmond Enquirer,* wrote to Secretary of State Van Buren to communicate his grave concern about the president's removal policy. He was all for reform, he said, but was it reform "to turn out of office all those who . . . decently preferred Mr. Adams?" By all means discharge those who "are incapable of discharging their duties, the drunken, the ignorant, the embezzler, [or] the man who has abused his official facilities to keep Gen. Jackson out," but Jackson seemed ready to go well beyond that, turning out people for no reason other than to put his own supporters in office. If the president pursued that course, Ritchie warned, "the contest will be for office and not for principle."[43]

With Ritchie's permission, Van Buren showed the letter to the president. Stung by Ritchie's criticism, Jackson instructed Van Buren to tell Ritchie that the people expected reform and he aimed to give it to them. However, he added, "it must be *judiciously* done and upon *principle.*" Jackson knew he needed a reason for removals that was more compelling than Marcy's maxim about the spoils belonging to the victor. In his first annual message to Congress, delivered on December 8, 1829, Jackson articulated to the country the principle that he believed justified widespread removals.[44]

"Plain and Simple" Duties: Jackson's Theory of Bureaucracy

Jackson began from the premise that there are "few men who can for any great length of time enjoy office and power without being more or less under the influence of feelings unfavorable to the faithful discharge of their public duties." Even those who had too much integrity to use their office to enrich themselves were still "apt to acquire a habit of looking with indifference upon the public interests and of tolerating conduct from which an unpracticed man would revolt." Duration in office was a problem not only because it tended to produce corrupt officials but also, and more disturbingly, because it produced officials who forgot that they were there to serve the people. Bureaucracy, Jackson argued, became "an engine for the support of the few at the expense of the many." Democracy itself demanded rotation in office.

What about the loss of experience and expertise? Jackson's answer was defiant: "The duties of all public officers are, or at least admit of being made, so plain and simple that men of intelligence may readily qualify themselves for their performance." The notion that the business of government was too difficult for the people to understand, Jackson maintained, was profoundly elitist and undemocratic.

Jackson pressed the argument still further. The idea that individuals had a right to a particular office, he maintained, was inconsistent with a democracy:

> In a country where offices are created solely for the benefit of the people no one man has any more intrinsic right to official station than another. Offices were not established to give support to particular men at the public expense. No individual wrong is, therefore, done by removal, since neither appointment to nor continuance in office is a matter of right. The incumbent became an officer with a view to public benefits, and when these require his removal they are not to be sacrificed to private interests.

The people have a right to complain if the president replaces a good officer with a bad one, he said, but they can have no complaint so long as the good man is replaced with another good man. Public office was not the property of an individual, so no harm was committed in taking the office from one person and giving it to another.

Such removals, of course, may create "individual distress," but that was far outweighed by the good that rotation in office served in promoting a healthy democracy. Jackson urged Congress to extend the Tenure of Office Act to encompass all federal offices so as to "destroy the idea," once and for all, that public office was a "species of property." The result, he predicted, would be a government that was more efficient, harder-working, more honest, and better able to carry out the people's will. Bureaucracy's ills could be solved by a fuller democracy.

Jackson's inaugural message provided the theoretical underpinnings for removals on an unprecedented scale. According to a count published in a Jackson paper in September 1830, the administration removed more than 900 federal officials in the first 18 months. To be sure, as the administration was at pains to point out, this was only one-tenth of the total number of federal offices, hardly the "Reign of Terror" that Jackson's enemies alleged. And after 1831, the pace of removals slackened considerably. But the principle and the practice of rotation in office that Jackson put into effect was nonetheless a profound change to established expectations that officeholders should retain their office so long as they carried out their duties conscientiously and effectively.[45]

JACKSON'S REMOVAL OF WILLIAM DUANE

Jackson's critics strongly condemned the president's removal policy as an abuse of power and a violation of the spirit of the Constitution. In Congress, several resolutions were introduced that aimed at restricting Jackson's removal power, including one that called upon the president to provide the Senate with the reasons for each removal.[46] These bitter attacks upon Jackson's partisan removals were mild, however, compared with the calumny heaped upon Jackson for firing Treasury Secretary William Duane after he refused to remove federal deposits from the US National Bank.[47]

The controversy over Duane's removal had its origins in Jackson's veto of legislation to recharter the Second Bank of the United States. The question that then arose was what to do with the federal deposits in the national bank. Jackson wanted the deposits transferred immediately to state banks. But under the 1816 statute that chartered the bank, control over the bank's deposits was vested in the secretary of the treasury, not the president. The problem for Jackson was that his treasury secretary, Louis McLane, a former Federalist and bank supporter, thought the deposits should stay where they were for now, since the bank's charter still had several more years to run. Rather than force a showdown over the issue, Jackson promoted McLane to secretary of state. Jackson then appointed William Duane, about whom he knew little except that he was anti-bank. So confident was Jackson in Duane's anti-bank sentiments that he never asked Duane prior to his appointment whether he would be willing to remove the deposits from the bank.[48]

After Duane's confirmation in May 1833, Jackson explained to his new secretary why he wanted the deposits removed. He assured Duane that he did not intend "to interfere with the independent exercise of the discretion committed to you by law over the subject." Rather, he only wanted to convey his "sentiments upon the subject" so as to "allow them to enter into your decision upon the subject ... as far as you may deem it proper." Duane concluded from this that while Jackson desired the deposits removed from the bank, the president recognized that the ultimate decision, under the terms of the 1816 statute, rested with Duane. Meanwhile, Duane told the president that "when the moment for decision, after inquiry and discussion, shall arrive," he would "concur with you, or retire." Jackson understood this to mean that if Duane concluded that the deposits should not be removed he would resign and allow Jackson to appoint someone who would do what the president wished.[49]

Despite his conciliatory words, Jackson was determined to remove the deposits, and in September 1833 he informed his cabinet that his mind was made up. Although Duane supported Jackson's opposition to rechartering the bank, the treasury secretary wanted to wait until Congress convened in December before making a decision about what should be done with the deposits. The House of Representatives, after all, had overwhelmingly passed a resolution in the previous session declaring that the monies were "safe" in the custody of the national bank. Jackson reminded Duane and the rest of the cabinet that "the Constitution and the suffrages of the American people" had bestowed upon him "the duty of superintending the operation of the Executive Departments of the Government and seeing that the laws are faithfully executed." If Duane had qualms about the president's decision, Jackson told him, he could inform Congress that he had been ordered by the president to remove the deposits. However, Duane did not accept that he could evade responsibility for the act because, as he told the president, "in this particular case, congress confers a discretionary power" on the secretary of the treasury. By law, the president could not compel him to remove the deposits, and so the secretary could hardly blame the president for their removal.[50]

Duane pressed his case, Jackson his. Neither would budge. Jackson reminded Duane about his earlier offer to resign if he could not support Jackson's decisions. Duane said he had changed his mind. Having already offered Duane an appointment as minister to Russia to try to defuse the conflict, Jackson felt he had no option but to fire Duane, which he did, replacing him—through a recess appointment that did not require Senate approval—with the only member of his cabinet who strongly supported the immediate removal of the federal deposits to state banks: Attorney General Roger Taney.

Champions of a strong presidency sometimes point to the firing of Duane as evidence of Jackson's resolute character and forceful leadership. In truth, as Jackson's most sympathetic biographer, Robert Remini, acknowledges, the president's clumsy handling of Duane—including his failure to sound out Duane's views before appointing him—betrayed "poor management and inept executive leadership."[51]

When the Senate reconvened in December 1833, Henry Clay introduced a resolution condemning the removal of Duane as illegal and unconstitutional. Clay insisted that the president, charged by the Constitution with faithfully executing the laws, did not have the constitutional authority to fire an executive official for adhering to the law. Clay also insisted that by law the treasury secretary occupied a distinctive place in the American political system, accountable to Congress as well as the president. He noted that the original 1789 legislation that created the Treasury Department required the secretary to submit reports directly to Congress, not the president. Indeed, Clay went so far as to suggest that the Treasury Department was "not an executive department" at all, for "in all that concerns the public treasury, the Secretary is the agent or representative of Congress."[52]

Other Jackson critics adopted a more moderate position. Daniel Webster conceded that the "established construction of the constitution" gave the president the power to remove a cabinet officer, but insisted that did not give the president "the power to control him, in all or any of his duties, while in office." John Calhoun viewed Duane's removal as an "abuse" of power rather than a "usurpation of power." Jackson's sin, in Calhoun's view, was not in removing Duane but in removing the deposits without sufficient grounds. Whatever the merits of these respective arguments, the opposition had what counted most: the votes to censure Jackson for having "assumed upon himself authority and power not conferred by the constitution and laws." Only after Democrats regained control of the Senate in 1836 was Clay's resolution of censure expunged from the record.[53]

HYPOCRITES ALL: THE "TUMULTUOUS SCRAMBLE FOR PLACE"

After censuring Jackson, the president's critics—who now called themselves Whigs—broadened their attack on the removal power. On behalf of a select committee that had been charged with investigating ways of reducing executive patronage, Calhoun introduced legislation to repeal the Tenure of Office Act's four-year term limits for federal officers, require Senate confirmation of postmasters (which made up more than three-fourths of federal civilian employees), and mandate that the president submit to the Senate his reasons for a removal at the time he nominated the officer's replacement.

Calhoun's bill placed Jackson's supporters in an awkward position, since it was a carbon copy of legislation that had been introduced a decade earlier by Jackson's supporters during the presidency of John Quincy Adams. Calhoun relished reminding Democrats that the committee that reported the original legislation in 1826 had been packed with staunch Jackson allies, including Martin Van Buren, now Jackson's vice president, and Mahlon Dickerson, now Jackson's secretary of the navy. The committee chair, moreover, had been Missouri's Thomas Hart Benton, who during the previous session had defended Jackson's removal power in the most sweeping terms. To rub the point in, Calhoun had copies printed of Benton's accompanying "Report on the Reduction of Executive Patronage," a report that warned of "the dangerous tendency of executive patronage" unless checked by "the vigorous interposition of Congress."[54]

Calhoun found it easy to expose Jacksonian hypocrisy, but the Whigs could not easily paper over their own hypocrisy. As secretary of state, Clay had pressed President Adams, largely without success, to use his removal power to sweep his political opponents out of office. Jackson's allies now scoffed at Clay's born-again discovery of the perils of executive removals. "There seems," noted New Hampshire Democrat Isaac Hill, "to be a sort of hydrophobia-dread of removals from office whenever a certain party is at the bottom of the wheel." The constitutional and legal arguments seemed merely costumes thrown on to disguise the naked struggle for political power.[55]

Whig hypocrisy was most starkly revealed after the party triumphed in the presidential election of 1840. After securing control of the White House, the Whigs immediately set about removing thousands of Jacksonian officeholders. Still ensconced in the Senate, Clay pressed the new administration for removals so his personal friends could be given the positions instead. Postmaster General Francis Granger removed 1,700 postmasters in six months, and boasted that he would have removed 3,000 more had he not left the administration.[56]

By now, there was no going back. With each new presidential administration, partisans of the losing side were thrown out of office and the spoils were doled out instead to the partisans of the winning side. Some regretted that rotation in office had turned elections into "a tumultuous scramble for place," but the development could not be arrested because it was powered by an increasingly well organized and highly competitive two-party system. Rotation in office became institutionalized, as Leonard White observed, "because it was demanded from below, not merely because it was advocated from above." Presidents needed to use the removal power to reward the many state and local partisans without whom the president and his party could not win elections. Constitutional debates about the appropriate powers of the executive and Congress were ultimately less important than the political demands imposed upon the presidency by a party system built upon patronage.[57]

Andrew Johnson and the Tenure of Office Act of 1867

Although the electoral demands of a patronage-based party system induced the Whigs to embrace rotation in office, they nonetheless retained a distrust of presidential power and an expansive conception of congressional power. They continued to believe, as Ohio senator Thomas Ewing put it, that the removal power was "a mere matter of legislative provision, subject to be vested, modified, changed, or taken away by the Legislature at their will." While the coming of the Civil War wrecked the Whig Party, the Republican Party that emerged in its place harbored many of the same Whiggish biases about executive and legislative power, including the removal power.[58]

During the presidency of Republican Abraham Lincoln, the Republican-dominated Congress passed several laws restricting the president's removal power. In 1863, Congress passed and Lincoln signed the National Bank Act, which established a comptroller of the currency, who was to serve a five-year term and could be removed by the president only with the Senate's consent. The following year, Lincoln signed legislation that specified that consular clerks could not be removed "except for cause" and that the president must submit to Congress his reasons for the removal. Despite Lincoln's deserved reputation as a strong president, he never lodged any objection to these restrictions on his power to remove executive branch officials.[59]

Republicans' willingness to regulate the removal power during the Lincoln presidency paled in comparison to the steps they took to restrict the removal power during the presidency of Andrew Johnson. Lincoln and the congressional Republicans had sparred over control of the conduct of the war but ultimately they shared a common objective: winning the war and ending slavery. That agreement, together with Lincoln's considerable political skills, kept their disagreements manageable. Johnson, however, lacked Lincoln's political skills and possessed a radically different vision of post-war Reconstruction policy from most congressional Republicans. Johnson wanted southern states readmitted as quickly as possible, whereas congressional Republicans wanted to reshape southern society and politics before allowing the South's elected representatives back into the halls of Congress. That fundamental political disagreement led directly to the most famous showdown over the removal power in American history.

In an attempt to build political support for his Reconstruction policy, Johnson did what every president since Jackson had done—use the removal power to reward friends, punish enemies, and cow the rest. In many ways, Lincoln had been even more aggressive in ousting officials than Johnson, but Lincoln had removed Democrats. Johnson, in contrast, was throwing out members of his own party who had been appointed by Lincoln.[60] As the conflict between Congress and the president over Reconstruction deepened, Johnson dramatically escalated the pace of removals. Between December 1865 and June 1866, Johnson only removed about 50 postmasters. In contrast, over the subsequent five months, with Congress out of session and a new postmaster general in place, Johnson removed close to 1,700 postmasters. By the time the 39th Congress resumed its work in December 1866, Republicans were desperate to stop Johnson.[61]

The most important step Congress took to rein in Johnson was the Tenure of Office Act of 1867. The act required Senate approval before the president could remove any officer whose appointment required the advice and consent of the Senate. The act applied not only to subordinate officers but to cabinet members as well. Reviving a proposal first made by Henry Clay in 1834, the act allowed the president to suspend an officer for cause while the Senate was not in session, but as soon as the Senate reconvened, the president had to submit "the evidence and reasons" for the suspension. If the Senate did not accept the president's decision, the officer would be reinstated. Johnson vetoed the legislation, but Congress easily overrode the veto.

Although Johnson believed the law unconstitutional, he initially complied with its provisions. In the summer of 1867, with the Senate in recess, the president suspended Secretary of War Edwin Stanton and named Ulysses Grant as the acting secretary of war. When the Senate convened again in December, Johnson sent the Senate a message explaining why he had suspended Stanton and why he thought the Tenure of Office Act unwise and unconstitutional. The president, he told the Senate, "is the responsible head of the Administration, and when the opinions of a head of Department are irreconcilably opposed to those of the President in grave matters of policy and administration there is but one result which can solve the difficulty, and that is a severance of the official relation." By a vote of 35–6, the Senate refused to sanction the removal of Stanton, who then resumed his duties as secretary of war. Six weeks later, Johnson fired Stanton, inducing a dramatic constitutional showdown that would result in impeachment proceedings against the president. The principal charge against Johnson was that his removal of Stanton was illegal because it violated the Tenure of Office Act.

The Senate fell one vote short of impeaching Johnson. Only then did Stanton resign, allowing Johnson to install his replacement. The act, however, had served its purpose of crippling Johnson's presidency, and after the election of Grant in 1868 the Republican-dominated House rushed to repeal it. The Senate, however, balked at relinquishing its new-found authority, voting by a better than two-to-one margin to retain the act. Upon assuming office, Grant urged Congress to reconsider, vowing not to remove any of Johnson's appointees until Congress repealed the act. A compromise was worked out by which the act was retained but amended to relieve the president of the responsibility to report to the Senate the evidence and reasons for suspending an officer. In addition, whereas the original act had required that removals be limited to cases of misconduct, criminal action, disability, or disqualification, the amended act authorized the president to suspend officials at "his discretion."[62]

Party Patronage and Civil Service Reform

Presidents and Congress continued to spar over the removal power in the immediate post-war era, though a succession of Republican presidents meant that the conflict was more muted than it might have been had a Democratic president been elected. Still, Grant's Republican successors Rutherford Hayes and James Garfield were intent on reversing what they considered the Senate's usurpation of the president's power of appointment and removal.

Rutherford B. Hayes's Fight for "Thorough, Radical and Complete" Reform

The highest-profile fight involved Hayes's attempt to remove Chester Arthur as collector of customs for the Port of New York, the port in which a great majority of the nation's customs duties were collected. Arthur was a close ally of the powerful New York senator

Roscoe Conkling and the lucrative port was a linchpin of Conkling's corrupt political machine. Conkling engineered the defeat of Hayes's nominee for the post—Theodore Roosevelt, Sr., the father of future president Theodore Roosevelt—and succeeded in retaining Arthur, at least while the Senate remained in session. After the Senate recessed, however, Hayes replaced Arthur. When the Senate reconvened, Conkling held up confirmation of Arthur's replacement for several months, but the Senate eventually bowed to Hayes's will and confirmed the president's nominee. For Hayes the removal and replacement of Arthur was a key victory in what he viewed as his most important objective: to "break down" the Senate's control of patronage, a control that stemmed not only from the Tenure of Office Act but from the development of legislative norms—such as senatorial courtesy—that enabled the senators of a single state to block presidential nominees.[63]

Hayes did not want to replace the senatorial stranglehold over patronage with presidential control of patronage. Instead he wished to smash the patronage system altogether. A committed civil service reformer, Hayes's aim was to reconstitute the federal bureaucracy so that offices would be filled and retained based not on partisan affiliation but on merit, measured by objective competitive examinations. Hayes forbade federal officers from participating in any political activity beyond voting and public speaking and sought to prevent federal employees from being leveled "assessments" that required them to give a percent of their salary to a party campaign funds. Hayes aimed to return the political system not to the era of Jackson and the Whigs but to the earliest years of the republic.[64]

As a presidential candidate, Hayes made no secret of his reform agenda. In accepting the Republican nomination in 1877 he clearly articulated his position. "More than forty years ago," Hayes lamented, "a system of making appointments to office, grew up, based upon the maxim, 'To the victors belong the spoils.'" That maxim replaced "the old rule, the true rule that honesty, capacity and fidelity constitute the only real qualifications for office." By making federal office a reward for service to a party, Hayes continued,

> the system destroys the independence of the separate Departments of the Government; it tends directly to extravagance and official incapacity; it is a temptation to dishonesty; it hinders and impairs that careful supervision and strict accountability, by which alone faithful and efficient public service can be secured; it obstructs the prompt removal and sure punishment of the unworthy. In every way it degrades the civil service and the character of the Government.

Reform, Hayes insisted, needed to be "thorough, radical and complete." The nation should abolish the patronage-based system that had grown up since Jackson and "return to the principles and practice of the founders of the Government, supplying by legislation when needed, that which was formerly the established custom." The framers, Hayes insisted, intended that an executive officer "should be secure in his tenure as long as his personal character remained untarnished, and the performance, of his duties satisfactory." Hayes promised his party and the nation that if elected he would conduct his administration upon those principles, and that he would use "all the Constitutional powers vested in the Executive" to carry out the needed reform.[65]

Hayes also promised the nation that he would serve only a single term. The reason for taking that vow, Hayes explained, was that "the restoration of the civil service, to the system established by Washington and followed by the early Presidents," required a president who was "under no temptation to use the patronage of his office, to promote his own re-election." The removal and appointment power, Hayes argued, was a corrupting influence on the politicians who wielded it. Only a president without political ambitions could be trusted to destroy it. Or so Hayes thought. But by binding himself to the mast of a single term and resisting the mantle of party leader, Hayes deprived himself of the legislative influence necessary to secure the systemic transformation he so desperately desired.[66]

The patronage-based system that had grown up over the previous half-century was defended by powerful interests and legitimated by a potent ideology. Whereas Hayes and other civil service reformers envisioned a heroic battle between virtuous reformers and corrupt politicians, defenders of party patronage derided "snivel service reform" as antirepublican and elitist. Rotation in office was a fundamental democratic principle because it allowed every citizen "to become for a time a portion of the administrative force of the Government." Critics of civil service reform predicted that party activists at the state and local levels would not "work with the same energy, and zeal, and ability" if there was not "a chance of a change of the offices, with the change of the Executive." What Hayes and his ilk derided as corruption and spoils were the lifeblood of participatory democracy and the guarantee of a democratic executive branch.[67]

James Garfield's Conversion

Attitudes in the country toward party patronage, however, were gradually becoming more skeptical of the Jacksonian orthodoxy about the virtues of rotation in office. James Garfield was one barometer of those changes. In 1869, as a member of Congress, Garfield had strenuously opposed repeal of the Tenure of Office Act. Never, he declared, would he acquiesce in allowing "to any one man, be he an angel from Heaven, the absolute and sole control of appointments and removals from office in this country." But a decade later, the veteran congressman had reconsidered his position. The Tenure of Office Act, he now believed, had "virtually resulted in the usurpation, by the senate" of the president's appointment and removals powers; the result, he lamented, had been not only to "seriously crippl[e] the just powers of the executive" but to place "in the hands of senators and representatives a power most corrupt and dangerous." Like Hayes, Garfield now believed that the solution was to curtail the numbers of political appointees in the federal bureaucracy.

The removal power was key to the patronage-based system, and both Garfield and Hayes believed that removals were not a source of presidential strength but rather a vehicle by which the president was held hostage to the demands of state and local organizations. That was why, in his inaugural address, President Garfield put Congress on notice that he intended to ask them "to fix the tenure of the minor offices of the several Executive Departments and prescribe the grounds upon which removals shall be made during the terms for which incumbents have been appointed." Curtailing the removal power would not only improve the quality of public service, Garfield argued, but would strengthen the presidency because it would protect "those who are intrusted with the appointing power [that is, the president and department heads] against the waste of time and obstruction caused by the inordinate pressure for place."[68]

Garfield never got a chance to send Congress the promised reform; the assassin Charles Guiteau saw to that. However, Garfield's death turned out to be a fortuitous development for civil service reformers. Believing that he had made a vital contribution to Garfield's victory, the deranged Guiteau visited the White House almost daily in the spring of 1881 to press his claim for the public office he thought he deserved. After having his appeals repeatedly rejected and then having been banned from setting foot in the White House, Guiteau determined to kill the ungrateful president. After murdering Garfield, Guiteau proclaimed that he had acted to make Chester Arthur president and to give the "Stalwart" faction of the party led by Roscoe Conkling control of the government. The assassination of a president by a disappointed office-seeker galvanized civil service reformers and enabled them to pass the Civil Service Act of 1883, also known as the Pendleton Act. The act established the Civil Service Commission, whose members were removable by the president, and gave it the authority to regulate open competitive exams for public office. The act also authorized the president to extend civil service protections beyond those named in the original law, a key provision that enabled outgoing presidents to classify political appointees as civil service officers, thereby preventing their successors from removing them.

Grover Cleveland's Defiance of the Senate

Two years after passage of the Pendleton Act, Grover Cleveland became president. Although Cleveland was a strong proponent of civil service reform, he was also the first Democrat to win the presidency in nearly 30 years. Having been largely shut out of federal patronage since before the Civil War, Democrats demanded removals. Cleveland complied by suspending hundreds of Republican officeholders and replacing them with Democrats, whom he hoped the Senate would confirm when it reconvened in December. Republicans, though, controlled the Senate, and they were determined to resist, both to assert Senatorial prerogative over patronage and to embarrass Cleveland by highlighting the hypocrisy of his claim to be a civil service reformer. Although the amended Tenure of Office Act no longer included a requirement that the president provide "the evidence and reasons" for suspension, Republican senators insisted that since Congress created all federal offices they had the right to investigate why officers had been suspended. Cleveland directed his cabinet not to comply with any requests for information relating to suspensions, and Republicans vowed to refuse to act on his temporary appointments until the president complied with their requests.[69]

On January 25, 1886, Senate Republicans passed a resolution directing Attorney General August Garland to hand over "all documents and papers" relating to the "management and conduct" of George M. Duskin as the US attorney for the southern district of Alabama. Duskin, a loyal and able Republican, had been suspended by Cleveland in the summer, and replaced by a loyal and able Democrat, John D. Burnett.

SCENE OF THE ASSASSINATION
GEN. JAMES A. GARFIELD, PRESIDENT OF THE UNITED STATES.

An artist's rendering of the shooting of President James Garfield on July 2, 1881, at the Baltimore and Potomac Railway Depot in Washington, DC. The murder of the president by a disappointed office-seeker helped civil service reformers to secure passage of the Pendleton Act in 1883.

Courtesy: Library of Congress, Prints and Photographs Division, LC-DIG-pga-02118.

Acting on the president's orders, Garland refused the Senate's request. In a message to Congress, Cleveland defended the president's power to remove or suspend an executive officer, a power he said that derived from the Constitution, which "in express terms" provided that the executive power shall be vested in the president and charged the president with faithfully executing the laws. More important, he pointed out that the Senate's demands were inconsistent with the amended Tenure of Office Act, which had explicitly dropped the requirement that the president must submit to the Senate his reasons for suspending an officer. The Senate was free to scrutinize his appointees to the fullest extent but they had neither statutory nor constitutional grounds for demanding that the president explain why he had removed an executive officer.[70]

Cleveland's argument was strong but the Senate was unimpressed. The Senate censured the attorney general and secured a resolution declaring that the Senate would act on no nominations until the requested information was handed over. Few Americans probably paid much heed to the constitutional arguments involved, but most believed that the Senate had gone too far in threatening to leave countless offices across the country unfilled simply because the president refused to comply with a request that was plainly not required by law. The Senate's stubborn insistence on the information was made to look sillier still when it was discovered that Duskin's term of office had in fact already expired, since district attorneys were still covered by the 1820 Tenure of Office

Act, which had never been repealed. Sensing that they were on the wrong side of public opinion and had overplayed their hand, Republicans beat a hasty retreat. They confirmed Duskin, stopped asking department heads for information relating to suspensions, and proceeded to confirm Cleveland's other nominations.

When Congress reconvened in December, Massachusetts Republican George Frisbie Hoar, long a critic of the corrupting effects of patronage, moved to repeal the Tenure of Office Act of 1867. Opposition to the repeal was spearheaded by Vermont Republican George Edmunds, the powerful chairman of the Senate Judiciary Committee who, as a freshman senator, had voted for the Tenure of Office Act and had played a leading role in the effort to remove Andrew Johnson from office. Edmunds argued that repealing the act would set back the cause of civil reform by making removals easier and that it would eliminate a much-needed check on presidential power. The majority of Republicans lined up behind Edmunds, but enough defected or abstained to enable a chastened Senate to pass the repeal, by a vote of 32–22. On March 3, 1887, Cleveland signed the repeal bill into law.[71]

Republican efforts to stem partisan removals were largely unsuccessful. In the first year and a half of his term, Cleveland removed 90 percent of "presidential officers"—that is, those executive branch officials who were appointed by the president with the advice and consent of the Senate. All told, Cleveland removed over 20,000 federal officeholders, including huge numbers of fourth-class postmasters—that is, those postmasters who were appointed by the postmaster general and who did not require Senate approval (in 1884 there were about 2,300 presidentially appointed postmasters—in first- through third-class post offices—and over 47,000 postmasters in smaller, fourth-class post offices). No wonder many civil service reformers felt betrayed. Despite the best efforts of reformers, rotation in office was alive and well. Indeed, Cleveland's successor, Republican Benjamin Harrison, exercised the removal power even more freely, removing close to 36,000 officials in his four years as president.[72]

The Extension of Civil Service Protections

The large number of removals in the 1880s and 1890s was driven by the same dynamic that had fueled removals in the pre-Civil War era: constant turnover in party control of the presidency. Just as the White House changed party hands in every election between 1840 and 1852, so too did party control of the White House change in each election between 1884 and 1896. Unlike in the Jacksonian era, however, party turnover was having an additional effect that worked to restrict rotation in office. Knowing that the opposition was set to take control of the White House, presidents in their last months in office (in the nineteenth century there were four months between election day and inauguration day) used the authority vested in them by the Pendleton Act to classify political appointees as civil service appointees. At first, this tactic did not always protect officials because presidents were slow to accept that civil service employees could not be removed, particularly if they felt that the civil service status had been illegitimately extended to protect political appointees and circumvent civil service exam requirements.

The Civil Service Commission pressed for the adoption of a rule that would require removal of a civil service employee to be accompanied by a statement of cause to be placed on file in the department. However, Congress was reluctant to create rules that would prevent a supervisor from removing an inefficient clerk. Presidents, too, dragged their feet. Not until 1897 were civil service rules amended—through an executive order by William McKinley—to mandate that no civil service employee could be removed without "just cause and upon written charges filed with the head of the department or other appointing officer." The rule also required that the official "shall have full notice and an opportunity to make defense." In 1912, with passage of the Lloyd–LaFollette Act, these and other protections became law.[73]

The number of civil service (sometimes called classified) positions that were filled by competitive examinations and protected by administrative requirements climbed steeply in the last decade of the nineteenth century and the first decades of the twentieth. In 1891 only about 33,000 government jobs were civil service protected; by 1901 the number exceeded 100,000 and by 1913 nearly 300,000 federal workers held classified positions, including all 50,000 fourth-class postmasters, courtesy of an executive order issued by William Howard Taft in the closing months of his presidency.[74]

Despite the extension of civil service protections, presidents still found ways to preserve their power to remove political enemies and reward political friends. When Democrat Woodrow Wilson became president in 1913, for instance, he immediately amended Taft's executive order protecting postmasters. No fourth-class postmaster, Wilson ruled, could be given civil service protection unless that person had been appointed on the basis of a competitive examination—this enabled Wilson to remove thousands of Taft's political appointees. Moreover, civil service regulations typically allowed the government to select from among the top three scorers on a competitive examination—the so-called "rule of three"—which gave the administration some discretion even in filling many civil service jobs. Overall, though, civil service reformers in the late nineteenth and early twentieth centuries had succeeded in dramatically curtailing party patronage in the federal bureaucracy.[75]

ENTER THE COURTS

When it came to appointments that required Senate approval, however, presidents were still besieged by patronage requests from state and local officials and held hostage to the demands of congressmen. Although the 1867 Tenure of Office Act had been repealed, the constitutional requirement that the president gain the consent of the Senate was still in place. Moreover, several statutes that explicitly restricted the president's removal power remained in place. The most important of these was an 1876 statute, signed into law by President Grant in his final year in office, which provided that "Postmasters of the first, second, and third classes shall be appointed and may be removed by the President with the advice and consent of the Senate." Nearly a half-century after its passage, this statute precipitated a landmark legal showdown over the removal power.

Myers v. United States: The Case of the First-Class Postmaster

Frank S. Myers was appointed first-class postmaster in Portland, Oregon, in 1913 as a reward for loyal service to the Democratic Party. The term was for four years, and in 1917, after Woodrow Wilson's reelection, Myers was reappointed. In January 1920, after an internal investigation found that Myers's "autocratic tendencies" had alienated staff and customers, he was asked to resign. Myers refused and was fired by the president. Myers sued, insisting that his firing was illegal because the Senate had not approved of his dismissal. He demanded that the government pay him the $8,000 he would have received had he finished his term.[76]

Up to this point the courts had steered clear of the many fights over the removal power. The courts never offered an opinion on the constitutionality of the controversial 1867 Tenure of Office Act during the 20 years it was in effect. After McKinley's 1897 executive order, a few civil service employees sought judicial remedies for what they felt was wrongful discharge but courts refused to intervene. The court of claims that heard Myers's case continued that pattern of judicial restraint by deciding the case on the narrowest grounds possible. The court dismissed the suit, insisting that Myers—who filed suit 15 months after he had been fired—had waited too long. It declined to find the 1876 statute unconstitutional, noting that "doubts should be resolved . . . in favor of the power of Congress."[77]

Myers appealed and, to the surprise of many, the Supreme Court took the case. By the time the Court heard oral arguments in the spring of 1925, Myers was dead, but his widow continued the case. It took the court almost 18 months—and a second set of oral arguments—before it was ready to render a verdict. Writing for a 5–4 Court was the chief justice and former president William Howard Taft, who issued a sweeping defense of the president's removal power. Not only was the 1876 statute unconstitutional, Taft announced, but so too was the long since repealed 1867 Tenure of Office Act. The Constitution, according to Taft, prohibited any legislation that required the president to obtain the Senate's consent before removing an executive official. Since the Constitution said nothing about removals, Taft relied heavily on the "decision of 1789," which he said had settled the matter in the president's favor.

Champions of the unitary executive have hailed Taft's opinion as "masterful and scholarly,"[78] but the chief justice's reading of the 1789 debates was in fact sloppy and inaccurate. Contrary to Taft's reading, only a minority in Congress in 1789 believed that the Constitution vested the president with the removal power. A sizeable majority believed that the Constitution left it to Congress to decide whether the president should have the power to remove officials. Moreover, the 1789 debate was focused on the removal of a department head and did not address the question of the power to remove lower-level executive branch officials. What Congress decided in 1789 was that it was *prudent* that the president should be the one empowered to remove a *department head*. By the same token, the 1876 statute reflected the judgment of Congress and the president— Grant after all signed the bill into law—that it was prudent to require Senate consent for the removal of postmasters. Contrary to Taft's opinion, then, nothing in the "decision of 1789" conflicted with the 1876 statute.

Taft's misguided judicial activism did not stop at striking down the 1876 statute. He also maintained that Congress could not place *any* restrictions on the president's power of removal. Taft allowed that Congress could specify the length of term that a particular office may be held, but he insisted that the Constitution required that the officer be removable at the president's discretion. Congress could not, for instance, specify that the holder of an office be removable only for cause. Such a regulation, Taft insisted, would abridge the president's executive power and his constitutional duty to take care that the laws are faithfully executed.

Taft's opinion induced vigorous dissents from three justices. The longest of the three, at 62 pages, was authored by Justice James Clark McReynolds, who rejected Taft's doctrine as nothing short of "revolutionary." Briefest of the three dissenters was the 85-year-old Oliver Wendell Holmes, who required only three paragraphs to explain why he believed the Court had got it wrong.[79]

Holmes concisely summed up the essence of the dissenters' case. The office that Myers held, Holmes noted, was created by Congress and could be abolished by Congress. The four-year term was set by Congress, as was the salary attached to the office. Congress had given the president the power to appoint the office of first-class postmaster and could, if it wished, "transfer the power to other hands"; in fact, prior to 1836 Congress had vested the power of appointing postmasters in the postmaster general, not the president. The Constitution, after all, explicitly empowered Congress to vest the appointment of inferior officers, "as they think proper, in the President alone, in the Courts of Law, or in the Heads of Departments." Given these powers, Holmes thought it clear that Congress could if it wished "prescribe a term of life ... free from any interference" or "prolong the tenure of an incumbent until Congress or the Senate shall have assented to his removal."

Louis Brandeis's 56-page dissent developed this argument in painstaking historical detail, demonstrating that Taft's position ran counter to more than a half-century of lawmaking. Brandeis noted that, with the exception of Garfield, every president since 1861 had signed legislation that restricted the president's power of removal, most recently President Warren Harding, who in 1921 signed into law a bill creating the General Accounting Office, which was headed by a comptroller general who served a 15-year term and could be removed only by a joint resolution of Congress. Brandeis argued, moreover, that the chief justice had failed to understand the spirit of the Constitution. Taft's argument rested on the importance of an unfettered removal power in sustaining an efficient executive branch; if the president was not free to remove incompetent, corrupt, or recalcitrant subordinates he could not ensure the efficient workings of the executive branch that he was constitutionally charged with overseeing. Brandeis read the Constitution very differently. The separation of powers, he argued, had been adopted in 1787 "not to promote efficiency but to preclude the exercise of arbitrary power. The purpose was not to avoid friction but, by means of the inevitable friction incident to the distribution of the governmental powers among three departments, to save the people from autocracy."[80]

Taft had desperately wanted all the Court's members to back what he felt was the most important opinion of his career. He was deeply offended that Brandeis and McReynolds had gone to such great lengths to expose the flaws in his reasoning and evidence. Taft groused that Brandeis was "in sympathy with the power of the Senate to prevent the Executive from removing obnoxious persons, because he always sympathizes with the obnoxious person." He also hinted darkly that the dissenters' position played into the hands of the "socialists" who wished to undermine effective administration so that a "small number" of them could "acquire absolute power."[81]

The disappointment Taft felt at not being able to secure a unanimous opinion in *Myers* pales in comparison to the despair he would have experienced had he lived to see the Court's ruling a decade later in *Humphrey's Executor v. United States*, which dramatically repudiated the sweeping language of Taft's opinion.

Humphrey's Executor v. United States: The Case of the FTC Commissioner

Created in 1914, the Federal Trade Commission (FTC) was charged with investigating and prohibiting "unfair methods of competition." It embodied the Progressive idea that a capitalist economy needed an impartial umpire to ensure that powerful corporations did not combine and collude in ways that hurt consumers and small producers. By endowing the commissioners with seven-year terms, Progressives hoped the FTC would rise above partisan bickering and act in the public interest. Congress also stipulated that no more than three of the five commissioners could be of the same party, and that they could be removed by the president for "inefficiency, neglect of duty, or malfeasance in office." Each commissioner was to be appointed by the president with the advice and consent of the Senate.[82]

The effort to insulate the FTC from politics failed. Republican appointments in the 1920s turned the FTC into an ally and protector of corporate interests rather than the regulatory watchdog the Progressives had originally envisioned. Particularly important in the FTC's transformation was Calvin Coolidge's appointment in 1925 of the stridently conservative William Ewart Humphrey, whom Nebraska senator George Norris called "the greatest reactionary of the country." Humphrey made an immediate impact on the commission, both because of his forceful pro-business views and because his appointment gave the pro-business forces on the commission a 3–2 majority. In 1931, President Herbert Hoover nominated Humphrey for a second term, and six months later the Senate confirmed him by a vote of 53–28.

When Franklin Roosevelt became president in 1933 his attention quickly turned to the FTC, which had administrative jurisdiction over several important New Deal programs. Fortunately for Roosevelt, two vacancies had opened up on the FTC, enabling him to forge a commission sympathetic to his administration's aims. But Roosevelt still worried that the cantankerous Humphrey might weaken the resolve or disrupt the workings of the FTC. So in July 1933 he asked Humphrey for his resignation. The work of the commission, FDR explained to Humphrey, "can be carried out most effectively with personnel of my own selection."

Humphrey refused to resign. If FDR wanted rid of Humphrey, he would have to fire him. Roosevelt's advisors assured the president that he had the legal authority to do so, given the Supreme Court's sweeping affirmation of the president's power of removal in

Myers. Taft's opinion, after all, had explicitly declared that the president's removal authority extended to independent commissions. On October 7, the president notified Humphrey of his dismissal.

A furious Humphrey filed suit in the US Court of Claims. Claiming he had been illegally fired, Humphrey demanded restitution and back salary. Six weeks later, Humphrey dropped dead from a stroke, but his executor carried on the legal fight. The court of claims asked the Supreme Court to settle two questions. First, did the act establishing the FTC limit the dismissal of commissioners to the grounds specified in the statute, namely "inefficiency, neglect of duty, or malfeasance in office"? Second, if the act did so limit the president's power of removal, were those limits constitutional? The Supreme Court agreed to take the case and scheduled oral arguments for May 1, 1935.

The Roosevelt administration's legal team believed that the Court's opinion in *Myers* made the case a slam dunk. So confident was the administration that when advised by Attorney General Homer Cummings to be sure to start out on a winning foot, the new solicitor general—whose job it is to argue the government's case before the Court—carefully picked out *Humphrey's Executor* as his maiden assignment. The Court did not appear to find the case a difficult one; less than a month after hearing oral arguments it announced its unanimous verdict: Humphrey's firing was illegal.

Although the statute did not explicitly stipulate that "inefficiency, neglect of duty, or malfeasance in office" were the only reasons a commissioner could be fired, the Court thought it obvious that Congress intended to insulate the commissioners from presidential whims so that they could "exercise the trained judgment of a body of experts." After all, why list the reasons an official could be removed if Congress wanted the president to be free to fire the official for any reason at all? In addition, the Court could find nothing unconstitutional in these limits on the president's removal power. Although acknowledging that Taft's opinion in *Myers* made expansive claims about the president's constitutional removal power that would seem to make the statute's restrictions unconstitutional, the Court found Taft's sweeping claims to be "out of harmony" with its reading of the Constitution.[83]

The *Humphrey's* Court did not say that *Myers* had been incorrectly decided. Instead the Court reconciled the two cases by distinguishing between administrative officials who exercised purely executive powers and those who discharged quasi-judicial or quasi-legislative duties. A postmaster was a "purely executive officer" who could be discharged at the president's pleasure, but agencies such as the Federal Trade Commission and Interstate Commerce Commission could not "in any proper sense be characterized as an arm or an eye of the executive." Because these agency officials had rulemaking and adjudication functions, Congress could place restrictions on the conditions under which the president could remove these officials.

By reconciling the holding in *Myers* with the decision in *Humphrey's*, the Court was able to secure a unanimous judgment that was supported by three justices who had signed Taft's opinion in *Myers*. But while the Court's reasoning in *Humphrey's* was politically savvy, it was substantively flawed. To begin with, it cemented in place *Myers'* mistaken premise that the framers of the Constitution intended to prevent Congress from restricting the president's power to remove "purely executive officers." In addition,

Humphrey's established functional distinctions that were unclear at best (what tasks exactly qualified as quasi-legislative or quasi-judicial?) and advanced the improbable claim that the FTC was not a part of the executive branch (an FTC commissioner, the Court wrote, "occupies no place in the executive department and ... exercises no part of the executive power").

What *Humphrey's* made clear, however, was that a class of administrative agencies existed for which Congress could limit the president's discretion in removing officials. And Congress lost no time in taking advantage of this ruling. Just a few months after the Court's judgment in *Humphrey's*, Congress established the National Labor Relations Board, which was empowered to investigate and adjudicate allegations of unfair labor practices. The board members were given five-year terms and could be removed by the president for "neglect of duty or malfeasance in office, *but for no other cause.*" Similar restrictions on the president's removal power were written into the Merchant Marine Act of 1936, which established a US Maritime Commission, and the Civil Aeronautics Act of 1938, which established the Civil Aeronautics Board. In other cases, however, Congress set up boards or commissions without specifying the conditions under which a member could be removed. The unresolved question in such cases was whether the president could remove an official at his own discretion.[84]

Wiener v. United States: The Case of the War Claims Commissioner

President Dwight Eisenhower thought that if Congress did not limit the grounds for removal, then the president was free to remove an official for whatever reason. Acting on this understanding, he asked for the resignations of all three members of the War Claims Commission, which Congress had set up in 1948 to adjudicate claims filed by prisoners of war who had "suffered personal injury or property damage at the hands of the enemy in connection with World War II." One of the commission members, Myron Wiener, refused to resign and took the Eisenhower administration to court.

The court of claims agreed with the government that the president had the right to dismiss Wiener because Congress had not specified the grounds of removal, but a unanimous Supreme Court disagreed. Since war claims commissioners exercised quasi-judicial functions, the Court held that the president could not ask Wiener to resign simply because he wanted someone of his own party or choice. Even if Congress had not specified grounds for removal, the president needed cause to dismiss an agency official who had adjudication or rulemaking functions.

The Court's ruling in *Wiener v. United States* clarified the legal terrain, but it hardly settled the political contest over the removal power. It did not prevent presidents from asking for resignations, and the president could still dismiss agency officials so long as they were careful about the reasons they gave. Congress, meanwhile, could constrain the president's removal power by endowing an agency official with quasi-legislative or quasi-judicial functions. The continuing political tug-of-war over the power of removal between the president and Congress wound up back in the Supreme Court in the fight over the Office of the Independent Counsel.

Morrison v. Olson: Upholding the Office of the Independent Counsel

The Office of the Independent Counsel was created in 1978 in reaction to executive abuses during Watergate. Born from the belief that the executive branch could not be trusted to investigate its own wrongdoing, the Office of the Independent Counsel was designed to be independent of the president and the attorney general so that the investigation and prosecution of high administration officials could be carried out without fear or favor. Congress stipulated that an independent counsel would be selected by a panel of three federal judges and could only be removed from office by the president for "good cause" (the original law stipulated that an independent counsel could be removed only for "extraordinary impropriety" but that was softened to "good cause" in 1982). The Reagan administration challenged the independent counsel law in court, arguing that prosecution was a purely executive function and that therefore the president should be free to dismiss an independent counsel for any reason. In 1988, the case reached the Supreme Court.

Morrison v. Olson exposed the limitations of the Court's earlier distinction between executive functions and quasi-legislative or quasi-judicial functions. The Court conceded that an independent counsel exercised executive functions "in the sense that they are law enforcement functions that typically have been undertaken by officials within the Executive Branch." However, the Court argued that the real constitutional test should be whether the removal provisions prevented the president from carrying out his constitutionally prescribed duty to see that the laws are faithfully executed. By allowing the executive branch to remove an independent counsel for "good cause," the law preserved the executive's ability to "perform his constitutionally assigned duties," particularly since, unlike a cabinet member or agency head, the independent counsel had a narrow jurisdiction and a negligible impact on government policy. Therefore, the Court concluded, the law's removal provision was constitutional.[85]

The Court's verdict in *Morrison v. Olson* had been nearly unanimous; the majority opinion, crafted by the conservative Chief Justice William Rehnquist, gained the support of the Court's liberals and conservatives. Only one Justice dissented—the Court's newest member Antonin Scalia, who had been named to the Supreme Court by President Reagan in 1986. The issues raised by *Morrison* were particularly close to Scalia's heart. As a law professor at the University of Chicago in the late 1970s and early 1980s, Scalia had been a nationally recognized authority on administrative law. He had served as editor of *Regulation,* a journal published by the American Enterprise Institute, a prominent conservative think tank devoted to the cause of deregulation. Something of Scalia's enthusiasm for deregulation is captured in a 1984 speech in which he hailed the "Age of Deregulation" as the new "Age of the Enlightenment."[86]

In his dissent, Scalia excoriated the Court for declaring "open season upon the President's removal power for all executive officers." Scalia believed that there were prudential reasons to strike down the independent counsel statute. He embraced the opinion expressed by three previous attorneys general—two Republicans and one Democrat—that the statute heightened "all of the occupational hazards of the dedicated prosecutor; the danger of too narrow a focus, of the loss of perspective, of preoccupation with the pursuit of one alleged suspect to the exclusion of other interests." Scalia was prescient, as Democrats conceded after watching Independent Counsel Kenneth Starr's relentless pursuit of the impeachment of President Bill Clinton. In 1999, both parties agreed to terminate the Office of the Independent Counsel.[87]

Scalia's opinion, however, did not rest merely or even mostly on prudential grounds. The independent counsel statute, he argued, was not merely unwise but also unconstitutional. Scalia maintained that the text of the Constitution was unambiguous: all executive powers were vested in the president. The Court, he complained, "replaced the clear constitutional prescription that the executive power belongs to the President with a 'balancing test'" that was utterly subjective, to be decided on a case-by-case basis by "the unfettered wisdom of a majority of this Court." A disgusted Scalia concluded that this was "not only not the government of laws that the Constitution established; it is not a government of laws at all." Faithfulness to the text of the Constitution, Scalia maintained, required the Court to strike down any legislative restriction on the president's power to remove officials exercising executive powers. At stake, Scalia argued, was the "unitary Executive" established by the framers of the Constitution.[88]

Scalia used the phrase "unitary Executive" twice in his dissent, though without ever defining the term. At the time, few people would have recognized the phrase or understood precisely what it meant. Of course, the notion of "unity in the executive" was familiar from Hamilton's famous *Federalist* No. 70. However, when Hamilton defended unity in the executive he was supporting the Constitutional Convention's decision to have a single president rather than a plural executive. For Scalia, it meant that the president had unfettered power to direct and remove all executive branch officers. Any Congressional restrictions on this power were unconstitutional. The unitary executive, in short, was an attempt to revive the sweeping constitutional theory that Taft had introduced in *Myers*.

THE POLITICAL ORIGINS OF THE UNITARY EXECUTIVE: THE REAGAN YEARS

Although the intellectual origins of the unitary executive can be traced to *Myers*, the political crucible for the theory was the Reagan presidency. Government, Reagan famously declared in his first inaugural address, "is not the solution to our problem; government is the problem." Government was the problem not only because high taxes, intrusive regulations, and liberal handouts stifled individual entrepreneurship and retarded economic growth but also because liberal bureaucrats and self-interested agencies obstructed the conservative reform agenda. One of the Reagan administration's priorities was to make the bureaucracy responsive to the president's policy agenda, including regulatory relief for business.

Ed Meese's "Revolutionaries" and the Attack on Independent Agencies

Some in the administration saw the many independent agencies as a serious obstacle to implementing Reagan's deregulatory agenda. Lawyers at the Department of Justice, particularly in the second term under the leadership of Attorney General Edwin Meese III, sought to lay the groundwork for a Supreme Court ruling that, as Solicitor General Charles Fried explained, "would hold that agency commissions served at the pleasure of the President, and that statutory limitations on their removal were unconstitutional." Speaking before the Federal Bar Association in 1985, Meese signaled the administration's intent: "Federal agencies performing executive functions are themselves properly agents of the executive. They are not 'quasi' this or 'independent' that." Meese went further still, suggesting that not only were restrictions on a president's removal power unconstitutional but "the entire system of independent agencies may be unconstitutional."[89]

These views reflected the influence of a cadre of eager, smart, young conservatives whom Meese had assembled at the Justice Department. Many of them belonged to a fledgling organization called the Federalist Society. Founded in 1982 by law students at Yale University and the University of Chicago as a way to bring conservative speakers to campus, the Federalist Society quickly evolved into an important network of conservative legal activists and thinkers. At Yale the club's first campus advisor was Robert Bork, whom Reagan nominated to the Court of Appeals for the DC Circuit in 1982 and the Supreme Court in 1987, and at Chicago the club's first advisor was Scalia, whom Reagan named to the DC circuit in 1982 and the Supreme Court in 1986. Three of the society's co-founders—Steven Calabresi, Lee Liberman Otis, and David McIntosh—served as special assistants to Meese and each also clerked for Scalia after he was appointed to the Supreme Court.[90]

Some of the more traditional conservatives within the Reagan administration were wary of Meese's young assistants. The Czechoslovakian-born Fried, who was nearly twice their age, noted that Meese's aides "thought of themselves as revolutionaries." For Fried, conservatism meant a commitment to "order and law" (the title of his account of his years in the Reagan administration) and he worried that their "revolutionary zeal" made them at times overly eager to overthrow or disrupt well-settled understandings of the law. Others worried that "movement conservatives" were allowing short-term political commitments and contingencies to drive their constitutional theory. An anonymous source in a 1986 Justice Department report expressed the point this way:

> Conservatives traditionally have valued separation of powers because it operates to limit government. However, some conservatives now are also finding separation of powers frustrating because it is sometimes an obstacle to the conservative political agenda, thereby serving to preserve the liberal status quo.

In this view, conservatives' newfound interest in "a very strong President" was adopted "primarily for the practical reason that an activist conservative currently sits in the White House."[91]

The practical contingency most responsible for conservative frustration with the separation of powers was that the House of Representatives was dominated by the Democrats and had been for decades. House Republicans had become a permanent minority. Meese's young advisors had not even been alive in 1954, the last time that House Republicans had been in the majority. Even Reagan's landslide victory over

Mondale in 1984 had barely dented the commanding Democratic majority in the House. In the view of many conservatives, young and otherwise, Congress had become insulated from public pressures, not unlike the federal bureaucracy.

Challenging Gramm–Rudman

When Congress passed the Balanced Budget and Emergency Deficit Act of 1985 (commonly called Gramm–Rudman), Reagan's legal team saw an opportunity to persuade the Supreme Court to reconsider its opinion in *Humphrey's* and perhaps even to rethink the constitutionality of independent agencies. The legislation required the president and Congress to follow a timetable that would eliminate the federal deficit in six years. If they failed, the head of the General Accounting Office—called the comptroller general—was empowered to make the cuts he deemed necessary to meet the prescribed timetable. To many observers, the act vested administrative discretion in the comptroller general that was quintessentially executive power. The constitutional problem was that the comptroller general could only be removed by a joint resolution of Congress, and only then for cause ("inefficiency, neglect; duty or malfeasance; or a felony or conduct involving moral turpitude").[92]

The administration's challenge to Gramm–Rudman (in a case called *Bowsher v. Synar*) came first to a three-judge panel of the Court of Appeals for the DC Circuit; one of the three judges, and the author of the court's opinion, was Antonin Scalia. As an appeals court judge, Scalia had to accept that *Humphrey's* was the law of the land, but he made it clear that he thought the Court's opinion misguided. "It has ... always been difficult," Scalia opined, "to reconcile *Humphrey's Executor*'s 'headless fourth branch' with a constitutional text and tradition establishing three branches of government." In Scalia's view, *Humphrey's* was an outdated relic of a misguided Progressive belief that there could be

> such things as genuinely "independent" regulatory agencies, bodies of impartial experts whose independence from the President does not entail correspondingly greater dependence upon the committees of Congress to which they are then immediately accountable; or, indeed, that the decisions of such agencies so clearly involve scientific judgment rather than political choice that it is even theoretically desirable to insulate them from the democratic process.

Since no agencies could be genuinely impartial or scientific or above partisan politics, there was no justification for insulating them from their political master, the president. Scalia's dicta stated precisely the view that conservative activists in the Reagan Department of Justice hoped the Supreme Court would adopt. A few months later, the Reagan White House nominated Scalia to join the Supreme Court.[93]

Although Scalia clearly believed that *Humphrey's* should be overturned, he did not need to reject *Humphrey's* to strike down Gramm–Rudman. There was no question in Scalia's mind that the 1985 law required the comptroller general to exercise "the sort of power normally conferred upon the executive officer charged with implementing a statute." Moreover, Scalia stressed that *Humphrey's* could be distinguished from *Bowsher* because in the case of the FTC commissioner, Congress had merely placed restrictions on the president's removal power—requiring a removal be made for good cause—whereas only Congress could initiate the removal of the comptroller general. Thus even if *Humphrey's* was good law, Gramm–Rudman violated the separation of powers by allowing Congress to remove an official vested with executive power.[94]

On July 7, 1986, the Supreme Court agreed with Scalia by a 7–2 vote that Gramm–Rudman was unconstitutional. However, the Court did not accept the administration's argument that the law was unconstitutional because it prevented the president from removing an officer who exercised executive power. Instead the Court struck the law down on the narrower grounds that "Congress cannot reserve for itself" the power to remove an official who exercises executive powers. In other words, Congress was still free to place "good cause" restrictions on the president's power to remove those vested with powers deemed executive in nature. The Reagan administration had won its case, but had gained no ground in its struggle to overturn *Humphrey's* or win legal acceptance of an expanded conception of the president's removal power. And at oral argument, the administration actually conceded ground on its most audacious objective. After the opposing counsel suggested that the implications of the government's argument would require the Court to invalidate all independent agencies, Solicitor General Fried rushed to reassure the justices that these charges were just "scare" tactics. To which Justice Sandra Day O'Connor responded, "Well, Mr. Fried, you certainly scared me."[95]

Contra Neustadt: These Powers Are Not for Sharing

One week after Fried's exchange with O'Connor, Attorney General Edwin Meese received a confidential report from the Justice Department's Domestic Policy Committee (DPC), a group stacked with daring young conservatives, including Calabresi, Liberman Otis, and McIntosh. The 80-page report, innocuously titled "Separation of Powers: Legislative–Executive Relations," did not use the term "unitary executive" but it offered a sustained defense of the theory that would soon come to bear that name. In his hugely influential 1960 book *Presidential Power*, Richard Neustadt famously declared that the framers had created "a government of separated institutions sharing powers." The DPC's report rejected this idea that powers were shared. The Constitution, they argued, vested the president with all executive power; neither Congress nor the courts could share that power. Statutes that restricted the president's power to remove or control agents of the executive branch were not textbook instances of "checks and balances" but were instead unconstitutional encroachments on presidential power. In this view, as Charlie Savage has written, the executive branch was "a unitary being with the president as its brain." The report was an effort to arm the administration for a legal assault on *Humphrey's* and the regulatory state in place since the early twentieth century. O'Connor had good reason to be alarmed.[96]

The administration got the opportunity to test this theory when Theodore Olson, who had been the head of the Office of Legal Counsel (OLC) in Reagan's first term, refused to comply with a subpoena from an independent counsel that had been set up to investigate charges that Olson had lied to Congress. The independent counsel's inquiry into Olson's behavior stemmed from a bitter first-term struggle between the president and Congress over environmental regulation. In the fall of 1982, the Democratic House of Representatives had launched an investigation into charges that the Environmental Protection Agency (EPA), under the direction of Anne Gorsuch, had allowed partisan and electoral considerations to influence the cleanup of hazardous waste at Superfund sites. Upon Olson's advice, Gorsuch refused to comply with the House's request for information; the House retaliated by holding her in contempt of Congress. When documents emerged that substantiated the charges of political influence, one of Gorsuch's top assistants, Rita Lavelle, was fired and subsequently convicted of lying to Congress. Shortly thereafter Gorsuch resigned. The House withdrew its contempt citation but the House Judiciary Committee launched a two-year investigation into the episode that focused not only on officials at the EPA but also on top officials in the Department of Justice. When the report was released in December 1985, the Judiciary Committee requested that the attorney general ask a court to appoint an independent counsel to investigate Olson, which Meese reluctantly did in early April 2006.[97]

After a district court held Olson in contempt for refusing to comply with a court order enforcing the independent counsel's subpoena, Olson appealed to the Court of Appeals for the DC Circuit, insisting that the independent counsel statute was unconstitutional. The Department of Justice joined the argument, filing an amicus brief on behalf of Olson that urged the court to strike down the independent counsel statute. The three-judge panel that heard the case included Carter appointee (and future Supreme Court justice) Ruth Bader Ginsburg and two recent Reagan appointees, Stephen Williams and Laurence Silberman. The court divided 2–1, along ideological lines, with the conservative Reagan appointees siding with Olson and the liberal Carter appointee upholding the statute.

Silberman, a veteran of the Nixon, Ford, and Reagan administrations, wrote a sweeping opinion that gave the administration everything it had hoped for. Silberman not only struck down the statute but also advanced the Reagan administration's theory of the unitary executive. By snatching away the president's constitutional power to appoint, supervise, and remove at will officials charged with executing the law, Silberman wrote, Congress had "invade[d] the President's executive prerogatives and responsibilities and so jeopardize[d] individual liberty." Silberman embraced the administration's argument that the independent counsel statute "jettisons traditional adherence to constitutional doctrines of separation of powers and a unitary executive." Over and over again, 12 times in all, Silberman used the phrase "unitary executive." In Silberman's view, "the doctrine of the unitary executive" was "central to the government instituted by the Constitution." The framers, he suggested, had two principal reasons for establishing a unitary executive. The first, as Taft wrote in *Myers*, was to ensure the "unitary and uniform administration of the laws." The second was "to ensure that the branch wielding the power to enforce the law would be accountable to the people." In other words, both the Constitution and democracy required a unitary executive.[98]

The conservatives in the Meese Justice Department who had labored to build up the unitary executive argument were thrilled with Silberman's ruling. That delight, however, quickly turned to disappointment when the Supreme Court, less than six months later, overturned the appeals court decision and upheld the independent counsel statute.

Making the Court's 8–1 ruling in *Morrison v. Olsen* all the more difficult for conservatives to swallow was that the majority opinion was written by Rehnquist, whom Reagan had appointed chief justice in 1986. Fried, who argued the case before the Court, pronounced the unitary executive thesis "dead."[99]

THE UNITARY EXECUTIVE IN THE PRESIDENCY OF GEORGE W. BUSH

Reports of the unitary executive's death proved to be greatly exaggerated. The theory articulated in the 1986 Justice Department report turned out to be not a political dead end so much as an opening gambit in a conservative power play that would extend into the twenty-first century. Silberman's opinion and Scalia's dissent in *Morrison* had been in a losing cause, but they became important touchstones in conservatives' campaign to advance the doctrine of the unitary executive.

"The Gospel according to OLC"

The Federalist Society played a particularly important role in keeping the idea alive. The year after the Supreme Court's decision in *Morrison*, the Federalist Society hosted a debate entitled "After the Independent Counsel Decision: Is Separation of Powers Dead?" Selected to introduce the debate was Samuel Alito, a society member who had been a deputy assistant attorney general between 1985 and 1987 before being picked by Reagan to serve as a federal district attorney. Alito deplored the "congressional pilfering" of presidential power that the Court had sanctioned and he applauded Scalia's "brilliant but very lonely" dissent. A decade later, now a federal court of appeals judge, Alito was again invited to speak to the Federalist Society and reiterated his commitment to the unitary executive thesis, which he described approvingly as "the gospel according to OLC." Five years after this, Alito was George W. Bush's pick to serve on the Supreme Court.[100]

During George W. Bush's presidency, the term "unitary executive" became a mantra. The phrase was routinely slipped into signing statements and executive orders in which the president would direct that a law or order be implemented in a manner consistent with "the President's constitutional authority to supervise the unitary executive branch." In his first term alone, Bush invoked the unitary executive 82 times in signing statements. In contrast, his predecessor Bill Clinton never used the term.[101]

In advancing the unitary executive doctrine, the lawyers in the Bush presidency interpreted *Morrison* as well as *Humphrey's* and *Wiener* in the narrowest possible terms. The tactic of narrowly construing these precedents had been first advanced in 1989 by William P. Barr, head of the OLC (and later attorney general) for the first President Bush. In a memo sent to the general counsels of each executive agency, Barr instructed them to be on the lookout for any legislative attempts to constrain the president's appointment or removal power or to create "hybrid commissions" that combined both executive and legislative functions. The administration, he argued, must construe the *Morrison* case narrowly as applying only to the independent counsels. The executive branch, he emphasized, must speak "with one voice"—that of the president.[102]

The OLC under George W. Bush pursued the same strategy with even more gusto. At the outset of the Bush administration, the White House asked the OLC for an opinion on whether the president could remove the chairperson of the Consumer Product Safety Commission (CPSC). Established in 1972, the CPSC was precisely the type of independent commission that advocates of the unitary executive found so disturbing. Commissioners served seven-year terms and, by statute, could be removed by the president for "neglect of duty or malfeasance in office but for no other cause." The administration did not allege misconduct by the chairperson Ann Brown, a Clinton appointee, but wanted a Republican chair who shared the administration's policy commitments.

The OLC opinion, written by John Yoo, affirmed the president's right to remove the chairperson for any reason. "The power to remove," Yoo underscored, "is the power to control." Yoo read the case law as affirming that if Congress did not explicitly state "its intention to challenge the President's authority to remove subordinate officials," then "a statute should be read to preserve the President's removal power." Since the statute did not explicitly forbid the president from replacing the chairperson, the statute should be read as not encroaching on the president's power to do so. Indeed, Yoo ventured the opinion that even the statute's "for-cause removal for commissioners itself could prove to be unconstitutional," though he also made it clear that the deposed chairperson, under the statute, would remain a commissioner.[103]

With the OLC memo in hand, Bush nominated the only Republican on the three-person commission, Mary Sheila Gall, as chair. The Senate, however, on a party-line vote, rejected Bush's nominee, leaving Brown as chair. Several months later, the impasse was broken when Brown resigned from the commission, leaving Bush free to nominate New Mexico Republican Harold Stratton, who was then chairman of a New Mexico think tank devoted to free-market principles. The White House had finally prevailed.

"Firegate": The Dismissal of Nine Federal District Attorneys

By far the most contentious episode involving the removal power during the Bush administration was triggered by the administration's dismissal of nine federal district attorneys—seven on a single day, December 7, 2006. There are 93 US attorneys, each of whom is the chief federal law enforcement officer within a given jurisdiction. Appointed by the president, with the advice and consent of the Senate, a US attorney serves a four-year term and is removable by the president. However, for most of American history the law included a provision that reduced the incentive for a president to remove a US attorney. Until the law was amended in 1986, the courts were empowered to fill the position on an interim basis for any US attorney who died, resigned, or was fired. In 1986, the law was changed to give the attorney general the power to select an interim replacement, who could serve for 120 days. If, after those 120 days, the president had not appointed and the Senate had not approved a permanent replacement, then a federal judge was empowered to fill the vacancy on an interim basis.

For supporters of the unitary executive, the provision allowing judges to appoint US attorneys, even with the 1986 amendment, was anathema. Law enforcement was a quintessentially executive responsibility and any restraint on the president's power to hire and fire the nation's chief law enforcement officers was a gross violation of the unitary executive doctrine. The reauthorization of the Patriot Act presented the Justice Department with an opportunity to rid the administration of the offending provision. An administration official persuaded a Senate Judiciary Committee aide to slip into the act a provision that removed the 120-day limit on the president's interim appointments. When Bush signed the act on March 9, 2006, the attorney general could thus select an "interim" appointment to serve until the end of the president's term without Senate confirmation. Steven Calabresi and Christopher Yoo have described this change, which removed courts from the interim appointment process, as "a huge victory for the theory of the unitary executive." However, it would turn out to be a pyrrhic victory.[104]

The change in the law emboldened the administration to proceed with its plan to remove "weak U.S. Attorneys who have ... chafed against Administration initiatives"— those who, in the words of the attorney general's chief of staff Kyle Sampson, had not been "loyal Bushies." The day after Bush signed the act into law, the White House secured the resignation of Todd Graves, federal attorney for the Western District of Missouri. The White House was unhappy with Graves because he had resisted a lawsuit that the Justice Department wished to pursue against the state for failing to purge the voter rolls of ineligible voters—voters the administration believed leaned toward the Democratic Party. Missouri was particularly critical to the White House because incumbent senator Jim Talent faced a formidable challenge from Claire McCaskill—who ended up beating the first-term Republican by a few percentage points. In Missouri, a state the Republican presidential nominee John McCain would win in 2008 by a mere 4,000 votes (of nearly 3 million cast), every vote counted.[105]

The next attorney general to get booted was Bud Cummins, a widely respected Arkansas Republican. Like Graves, Cummins had no negative performance job reviews and was told by the director of the Executive Office for US Attorneys, Mike Battle, that his resignation had nothing to do with his performance. He was being asked to step down by the Justice Department solely to give someone else in the party a turn. Cummins was not told that Karl Rove, Bush's chief political advisor, wanted him out in order to open the door for the appointment of Rove's 37-year-old former aide Tim Griffin. A legal neophyte, Griffin would likely never have been confirmed by the Senate, but under the new law the administration didn't need the Senate's approval.[106]

Had the White House stopped at Cummins's removal they might have avoided igniting a national firestorm. But the decision to ask for the resignations of seven more attorneys general, all on the same day, proved to be a major political miscalculation, particularly since the 2006 elections had given Democrats control of both the House and the Senate. Democrats accused the administration of politicizing law enforcement and summoned the administration to explain. Deputy Attorney General Paul McNulty assured the Senate Judiciary Committee that all the dismissals but Cummins's were for "performance-related" issues and downplayed the White House's involvement in instigating the dismissals. Attorney General Alberto Gonzales told the committee that he "would never, ever make a change in a U.S. attorney position for political reasons." The testimony of Gonzales and McNulty outraged the dismissed attorneys, who had never been informed of any performance-related issues when they had been asked to resign. Several went public, telling the media that they had received only positive job evaluations in their performance reviews. Democrats in Congress then invited the district attorneys to give their side of the story.[107]

The testimony of the ousted attorneys as well as subsequent investigations by Congress and the Justice Department laid bare the political motives the White House was trying to conceal. David Iglesias, the US attorney in New Mexico, revealed that Senator Pete Domenici and Representative Heather Wilson called him in the weeks prior to the 2006 election about the timing of an indictment relating to a corruption case against a prominent New Mexico Democrat. They were hoping for a pre-election indictment that could help Wilson, who was locked in a perilously close contest with the Democratic challenger and state attorney general Patricia Madrid. New Mexico's Republicans were also hopping mad that Iglesias had not aggressively pursued voter fraud cases, especially in Albuquerque, the heart of Wilson's district. Domenici contacted top Justice Department officials, including the attorney general, four times between September 2005 and October 2006 to complain about Iglesias. Domenici also took his case directly to Rove and White House Chief of Staff Josh Bolton. Rove also met with Republican Party leaders in New Mexico and called White House Counsel Harriet Miers in an "agitated" state to tell her that Iglesias was "a serious problem and that he wanted something done about it."[108]

A report by the Justice Department's inspector general concluded that at least seven of the nine removals were not undertaken for "performance-related" reasons but rather for reasons of party politics. A subsequent criminal investigation by special prosecutor Nora Dannehy unearthed evidence of the deep involvement of the White House's political arm in many of the firings. Although many of the details were not fleshed out until these inquiries were completed, even in early 2007 more than enough contradictory statements and untruths had been offered by White House officials to create a devastating scandal that dominated the headlines during the spring of 2007. The first to resign was Michael Battle, who, as director of the Executive Office for US Attorneys, had been tasked with informing the attorneys of their dismissal. The following month, a week after the ousted attorneys appeared on Capitol Hill, Gonzales's chief of staff, Kyle Sampson, resigned. In April, another top Gonzales aide implicated in the firings, Monica Goodling, resigned. The month of May brought the resignation of deputy attorney general McNulty, followed in June by McNulty's chief of staff Michael Elton—who at McNulty's direction had called several of the ousted attorneys in February, including Cummins, to warn them against going public with their stories. At the end of June, the head of the Justice Department's Office of Legal Policy resigned. Finally, in August, came the biggest scalps, when both Karl Rove and Alberto Gonzales announced that they were quitting.

Adding insult to injury, the White House watched helplessly as Congress passed the Preserving United States Attorney Independence Act, which restored the 1986 law that limited the attorney general's interim appointments to 120 days. The Senate voted 94–2 in favor and the House passed the bill by a veto-proof 3–1 margin. Bush capitulated and signed the bill.

Six US attorneys are sworn in on March 6, 2007, before testifying to Congress about their firing by the Bush administration. From left to right, they are Carol Lam (Southern California), David Iglesias (New Mexico), Daniel Bogden (Nevada), Paul Charlton (Arizona), Bud Cummins (Eastern Arkansas), and John McKay (Western Washington).
Courtesy: Getty Images.

Gonzales and Rove, among others, insisted that the so-called "Firegate" scandal was contrived by Democrats who wished, in Rove's words, "to make a political stink." The administration's defenders underlined that US district attorneys are political appointees who serve at the pleasure of the president. As Iglesias understood, his initial appointment in 2001 owed almost everything to the political calculations of the White House, which preferred him over other more experienced Republican prosecutors because they wanted to appoint a high-profile Hispanic to boost Republicans' electoral fortunes in a state that Bush had lost to Gore by fewer than 300 votes. Presidents have long dispensed these positions with an eye to building the résumés of promising party politicians. Moreover, Republicans pointed out that President Clinton asked for the resignation of every federal attorney but one when he entered office in 1993. As Bud Cummins conceded, the president is "entitled to make these changes for any reason or no reason or even for an idiotic reason."[109]

In a world of limited resources and time, moreover, prosecutors cannot focus equal attention on all crimes. The president, therefore, has a constitutional obligation to set the legal agenda, to direct prosecutors to focus, for instance, on immigration or white-collar crime or drug smuggling or civil rights violations. Republican presidents may justly direct prosecutors to prevent ineligible voters from voting, while Democratic presidents are within their rights to direct prosecutors to ensure that citizens are not prevented from voting. It is a fool's errand, on this view, to attempt to take the politics out of law enforcement.[110]

THE UNITARY EXECUTIVE RECONSIDERED

Bush's firing of the nine attorneys takes us to the heart of the debate over the unitary executive. For advocates of the unitary executive, there is hardly any such thing as expertise, impartial judgment, or neutral competence. Decisions are inevitably suffused with politics. In a democracy, the appropriate check on improperly politicized decision-making lies in the ballot box. As the only elected executive officer, the president must be accountable for all that his subordinates do and must therefore be able to direct what they do and how they do it. And the president cannot control their actions if he is not empowered to remove them for any reason.

Defenders of the unitary executive argue that Firegate vindicates their thesis. To those who worry that the unitary executive doctrine invites the aggrandizement of presidential power, unitary executive proponents point to the ferocious political backlash that greeted the president's firing of fewer than 10 percent of US attorneys. Calabresi and Yoo argue that these events show that "supporters of the unitary executive are right" that "political safeguards [are] in place" that prevent presidents from abusing their removal power. It is in the president's political self-interest, on this view, to use the removal power wisely and responsibly.[111]

Skeptics of the unitary executive thesis draw different lessons from the scandal. They note that the firings were a dramatic departure from well-established precedents, as the administration knew. In a January 9, 2006, email to Harriet Miers, Sampson acknowledged that "Presidents Reagan and Clinton did not seek to remove and replace U.S. Attorneys they had appointed ... but instead permitted such U.S. Attorneys to serve indefinitely." The removal of district attorneys in the middle of a presidency had been limited to clear cases of prosecutorial misconduct.[112]

Whether the administration's actions broke with precedent was not the crux of the matter, however. The question at the heart of the debate was whether restraints should be placed upon the president's control over federal law enforcement officers. For advocates of the unitary executive the answer is a resounding no. Critics of the unitary executive thesis, in contrast, doubt that the "take care" clause "was intended to establish unbridled authority in the President and his men." "More plausibly," as then-DC circuit judge Ruth Bader Ginsburg wrote in her 1988 dissent, "the words were meant to import a limitation" on the president's power, to ensure that the president did not disregard or suspend laws passed by Congress.[113]

Whereas the unitary executive doctrine privileges political responsiveness, critics of the doctrine place at least equal weight on the value of neutral competence, that is, professional norms of impartiality, codes of best practices, and legal and scientific expertise. On this view, taking care that the laws are faithfully executed requires leaving decisions about whether to proceed with a prosecution in the hands of professional, experienced law enforcement officers who can make informed judgments about whether a suit is warranted or likely to be successful. Allowing those decisions to be influenced by the president's aides, who have likely never tried a case, is unlikely to improve the execution of the laws.

One of the central arguments on behalf of the unitary executive, as articulated by Chief Justice Taft in *Myers*, is that presidential control—which depends on the removal power—is necessary to ensure the "unitary and uniform execution of the laws." In other words, presidential control is required to make sure that the law is enforced in a uniform way in different jurisdictions. However, Firegate suggests the problem with this doctrine. The Bush administration's political interests meant that they were most interested in pursuing voter fraud cases in battleground states in which a small number of votes could make a large electoral difference. If Iglesias had been a US attorney in Oklahoma instead of an attorney in New Mexico, he would not have been under the same pressure to pursue voter fraud cases. Strict adherence to the norms and rules of the legal profession is likely to be the best guarantee of the "unitary and uniform execution of the laws."

The unitary executive, as Charles Fried has written, is an elegant construct with "a beautiful symmetry" and a "perfect logic."[114] Under the Constitution, the president is the chief executive and is explicitly vested with the executive power. The legislature therefore has no business intruding on the executive power. Moreover, since the president is elected and his subordinates are not, principles of democratic accountability require that the president must be able to direct the behavior of his subordinates. Only if the president has the unfettered power of removal can democratic accountability for the vast executive branch be maintained. Not just constitutional government but democracy itself depends on it.

Against this beautiful doctrine stands a much messier one. It is a vision that recognizes that Article II vests executive power in the president, but doubts that powers were intended to be hermetically sealed within the different branches of government. As Madison emphasized in *Federalist* No. 47, "the three great departments of power should be separate and distinct" but that does "not mean that these departments ought to have no partial agency in, or no control over, the acts of each other." On this reading, the Constitution's aim is not an elegant or simple governmental structure but a complex system of checks and balances that are designed to curb the abuse or accumulation of power. As a matter of constitutional law, this interpretation of the American political system envisions a delicate balancing act to determine "the effect of an intrusion into one branch's assigned functions on the overall balance of powers."[115] As a matter of political theory, it insists on the legitimacy and quality of political decisions informed by legal and scientific expertise and experience. As a prudential or strategic matter, it recognizes that presidents are often better off politically when they heed the guidance of subordinates insulated from direct political control.

NOTES

1   The quotation is from the websites of the International Boundary Commission (www. internationalboundarycommission.org/boundary.html) and Natural Resources Canada (http://sgb.nrcan.gc.ca/ibc_e.php).

2   David C. Weiss, "The International Boundary Commission, Treaty Interpretation, and the President's Removal Power," *Loyola University Chicago Law Journal* 41 (Fall 2009–Summer 2010), 56. *Leu v. International Boundary Commission* 523 F. Supp. 2d 1199; all quotations in subsequent paragraphs in this section are from *Leu.*

3   At the same time, the administration fired Schornack from his $145,000-a-year job as chairman of the International Joint Commission, which oversees issues relating to US Canadian water and air quality. Schornack did not receive a government salary for his role as IBC commissioner. Weiss, "International Boundary Commission," 57 n123.

4 Schornack appealed the ruling to the Ninth Circuit Court of Appeals, but in May 2010 a three-judge panel dismissed Schornack's claim on technical grounds while declining to express an opinion on the merits of the administration's termination of Schornack (605 F.3d 693).

5 This phrase was famously used to describe the 1789 debate by Chief Justice William Howard Taft in *Myers v. United States* (1926).

6 Richard J. Ellis, ed., *Founding the American Presidency* (Lanham, MD: Rowman & Littlefield, 1999), 213–14. When South Carolina's William Smith argued that the Constitution did not provide any means for removing an executive officer except impeachment, James Madison immediately objected that such a construction was untenable, for it would make the framers guilty of "a fatal error" that would destroy the new government. See *The Debates and Proceedings in the Congress of the United States* (Washington, DC: Gales & Seaton, 1834), 1st Congress, 1st session, 1:387 (May 18, 1789).

7 *Debates and Proceedings*, 1:397 (May 19, 1789). Bland had voted against the Constitution at the Virginia ratifying convention the previous summer.

8 *Debates and Proceedings*, 1:397 (May 19, 1789).

9 *Debates and Proceedings*, 1:392–93 (May 19, 1789).

10 *Debates and Proceedings*, 1:480, 517 (June 16 and 17, 1789).

11 *Debates and Proceedings*, 1:480, 571–72 (June 18, 1789).

12 *Debates and Proceedings*, 1:585, 600–01 (June 19 and 22, 1789). Benson had been New York's attorney general for the past decade.

13 The three roll-call votes can be found at *Debates and Proceedings*, 1:603, 608, 614 (June 22 and 24, 1789). Charles C. Thach's definitive study *The Creation of the Presidency, 1775–1789* (Baltimore: Johns Hopkins University Press, 1969; originally published 1923) mistakenly counts 15 who "voted aye on all three motions"; his count includes Georgia's Abraham Baldwin, who only voted on the second of the three measures.

14 *Journal of William Maclay* (New York: Appleton, 1890), 110–12, available in digital form on the Library of Congress website at http://memory.loc.gov/ammem/amlaw/lwmj.html.

15 *Journal of William Maclay*, 114–16, 119. Maclay's motion would have failed even had the vice president refrained from voting, since it did not receive support from a majority of senators.

16 Six senators who had been delegates at the Constitutional Convention opposed Maclay's motion.

17 Three House members who had been delegates at the Constitutional Convention (Daniel Carroll, Thomas Fitzsimons, and Nicholas Gilman) endorsed Laurance's position that Congress had the constitutional power to restrict the president's power to remove executive officers but that the political system would be better off if Congress allowed the president to remove department heads for any reason. Two House members who had been convention delegates (Elbridge Gerry and Roger Sherman) agreed with Page that Congress should not give the president the authority to remove department heads. One of the eight convention delegates (Baldwin) only voted on one of the three motions, so his views cannot be determined from the votes.

18 Leonard D. White, *The Federalists: A Study in Administrative History* (New York: Macmillan, 1948), 202, 284, 287; compare Steven G. Calabresi and Christopher S. Yoo's highly selective and misleading reading of White's evidence in *The Unitary Executive: Presidential Power from Washington to Bush* (New Haven, CT: Yale University Press, 2008), 42. A more reliable and balanced treatment of the removal power is the more recent work by J. David Alvis, Jeremy D. Bailey, and F. Flagg Taylor IV, *The Contested Removal Power, 1789–2010* (Lawrence: University Press of Kansas, 2013).

19 Adams to Benjamin Rush, April 22, 1812, in John Schutz and Douglass Adair, eds., *The Spur of Fame: Dialogues of John Adams and Benjamin Rush, 1805–1813* (San Marino, CA: Huntington Library, 1980), 214.

20 White, *The Federalists*, 250, 252; David McCullough, *John Adams* (New York: Simon & Schuster, 2001), 538.

21 White, *The Federalists*, 288–89.

22 White, *The Federalists*, 285, 290. Carl Russell Fish, "Removal of Officials by the Presidents of the United States," *Annual Report of the American Historical Association for the Year 1899* (Washington, DC: Government Printing Office, 1900; 2 vols.), 1:70. The confusion of political differences with insufficient loyalty to the new nation was evident in Adams's dismissal of two federal officials in New Hampshire whose "political conduct," it was reported to the president, "has been disrespectful to the Government and offensive to good men in the extreme." Adams did not believe the removal of these two men contradicted his resolve to avoid partisan removals because their "daily language" expressed such "hostility to the national Constitution and government" that he felt he "could not avoid" dismissing them (White, *The Federalists*, 287–88).

23 Jefferson to Benjamin Rush, March 24, 1801. Jefferson to James Monroe, March 7, 1801. Unless otherwise noted, all the letters from Jefferson quoted in this chapter are from *The Works of Thomas Jefferson* (New York: G.P. Putnam's Sons, 1904–1905; 12 vols.), available at *The Online Library of Liberty* (http://oll.libertyfund.org). Jefferson made an exception "in the case of attorneys and marshals." He reasoned that because the judicial branch was completely controlled by the Federalists and because judges were "irremovable," it was necessary for him to be more aggressive in replacing attorneys and marshals, "being the doors of entrance into the courts." Jefferson to William B. Giles, March 23, 1801.

24 William B. Giles to Jefferson, March 16, 1801, quoted in Noble E. Cunningham, Jr., *The Jeffersonian Republicans in Power: Party Operations, 1801–1809* (Chapel Hill: University of North Carolina Press, 1963), 13. Jefferson to Levi Lincoln, August 26, 1801. Jefferson to Albert Gallatin, August 14, 1801.

25 Jefferson to Wilson Cary Nicholas, June 11, 1801. Cunningham, *Jeffersonian Republicans in Power*, 20–21.

26 Jefferson to Elias Shipman and others, a committee of the merchants of New Haven, July 12, 1801. Cunningham, *Jeffersonian Republicans in Power*, 20, 22–23.

27 Cunningham, *Jeffersonian Republicans in Power*, 23.

28 Cunningham, *Jeffersonian Republicans in Power*, 23–24.

29 Cunningham, *Jeffersonian Republicans in Power*, 24.

30 Cunningham, *Jeffersonian Republicans in Power*, 60–62. Of the removals that Jefferson counted, 22 involved undoing Adams's "midnight appointments."

31 Cunningham, *Jeffersonian Republicans in Power*, 53.

32 Calabresi and Yoo, *The Unitary Executive*, 444 n104. Jeremy D. Bailey, "The New Unitary Executive and Democratic Theory: The Problem of Alexander Hamilton," *American Political Science Review* 102 (November 2008), 453–65.

33 Bailey, "The New Unitary Executive," 459–61.

34 Cunningham, *Jeffersonian Republicans in Power*, 44–49.

35 Leonard D. White, *The Jeffersonians: A Study in Administrative History, 1801–1829* (New York: Free Press, 1951), 379–80.

36 White, *The Jeffersonians*, 380.

37 Wirt, quoted in Calabresi and Yoo, *The Unitary Executive*, 92.

38 Leonard D. White, *The Jacksonians: A Study in Administrative History, 1829–1861* (New York: Macmillan, 1954), 300. Cunningham, *Jeffersonian Republicans in Power*, 48. Strictly speaking, the postmaster general did not officially become a cabinet-level position until the Jackson administration.

39 White, *The Jeffersonians*, 387. Harry Ammon, *James Monroe: The Quest for National Identity* (Charlottesville: University Press of Virginia, 1990), 494–95. *Annals of Congress,*

16th Congress, 1st Session, Appendix, 2597–98. The precise list of offices included in the legislation was: "all district attorneys, collectors of the customs, naval officers, and surveyors of the customs, navy agents, receivers of public moneys for lands, registers of the land offices, paymasters in the Army, the apothecary general, the assistant apothecaries general, and the commissary general of purchases." Although commonly referred to as the Tenure of Office Act of 1820, its actual title was "An Act to limit the term of office of certain officers therein named, and for other purposes."

40 Ammon, *James Monroe*, 494. White, *Jeffersonians*, 388–90. Calabresi and Yoo, *Unitary Executive*, 86–87, 92. Also see Noble E. Cunningham, Jr., *The Presidency of James Monroe* (Lawrence: University Press of Kansas, 1996), 121.

41 Robert V. Remini, *Andrew Jackson: The Course of American Freedom, 1822–1832* (New York: Harper & Row, 1981), 187–88, 199; also see 183–84.

42 Remini, *Andrew Jackson: Course of American Freedom*, 185. John Quincy Adams, *Memoirs*, ed. Charles Francis Adams (Philadelphia: Lippincott, 1874–77), VII:425 (February 7, 1828).

43 Remini, *Andrew Jackson: Course of American Freedom*, 184, 197. White, *Jacksonians*, 307.

44 Remini, *Andrew Jackson: Course of American Freedom*, 189–190. White, *Jacksonians*, 307.

45 White, *Jacksonians*, 308. Remini, *Andrew Jackson: Course of American Freedom*, 193. Fish estimated that Jackson removed 252 "presidential officers"—defined by Fish as those officers appointed by the president with the advice and consent of the Senate—during his two terms, more than double the number removed by Jefferson and more than the first six presidents combined. See Fish, "Removal of Officials by the Presidents of the United States," 1:85. Citing Fish's study, Calabresi and Yoo maintain that "in percentage terms" Jackson made fewer removals of presidential officers than Jefferson (*Unitary Executive*, 100), but Fish's data show the opposite is true. By Fish's count, in 1829—Jackson's first year in office—there were approximately 610 presidential officers (Fish, "Removal of Officials by the Presidents of the United States," 1:74), which means that Jackson removed about four in ten presidential officers. Jefferson, according to Fish's count, removed 109 presidential officers, which is about one-fourth of the 433 presidential officers that Fish estimates to have existed at the beginning of Jefferson's presidency (1:70).

46 *Register of Debates in Congress*, Senate 21st Congress, 1st Session, April 21, 1830, 367–68; April 28, 1830, 384. Also see Calabresi and Yoo, *Unitary Executive*, 100; and White, *Jacksonians*, 40. In January 1832, Ohio senator Thomas Ewing offered a resolution maintaining that "the practice of removing public officers by the President, for any other purpose than that of securing the faithful execution of the laws [was] hostile to the spirit of the constitution [and] never contemplated by its framers[,] a daring extension of Executive influence [,] prejudicial to the public service, and dangerous to the liberties of the people." The resolution called upon the Senate to refuse to confirm any person appointed to fill a vacancy created through removal of an official unless that official had been removed "for sufficient cause." *Register of Debates in Congress*, Senate, 22nd Congress, 1st Session, January 26, 1832, 181–82.

47 Remini, *Andrew Jackson: Course of American Freedom*, 192.

48 Robert V. Remini, *Andrew Jackson: The Course of American Democracy, 1833–1845* (New York: Harper & Row, 1984), 57–58. Duane was the son of Colonel William Duane, who had upheld Jeffersonian orthodoxy as editor of the Philadelphia *Aurora* for nearly three decades.

49 White, *Jacksonians*, 35–36.

50 White, *Jacksonians*, 36–37. Remini, *Andrew Jackson: Course of American Democracy*, ch. 6.

51 Remini, *Andrew Jackson: Course of American Democracy*, 104.

52 *Register of Debates in Congress*, Senate, 23rd Congress, 1st Session, December 26, 1833, 58–59, 65.

53 *Register of Debates in Congress,* Senate, 23rd Congress, 1st Session, January 13, 1834, 216; May 7, 1834, 1664. White, *Jacksonians,* 44. David P. Currie, *The Constitution in Congress: Democrats and Whigs, 1829–1861* (Chicago: University of Chicago Press), 69.

54 *Register of Debates in Congress,* Senate, 23rd Congress, 2nd Session, February 9, 1835, 361; February 13, 1835, 418. White, *Jeffersonians,* 390–93.

55 White, *Jeffersonians,* 380. *Register of Debates in Congress,* Senate, 23rd Congress, 2nd Session, February 20, 1835, 564.

56 White, *Jacksonians,* 310–11.

57 White, *Jacksonians,* 325, 301; also see 320–21.

58 *Register of Debates in Congress,* Senate, 23rd Congress, 2nd Session, February 14, 1835, 447.

59 Leonard D. White, *The Republican Era, 1869–1901: A Study in Administrative History* (New York: Macmillan, 1958), 28. Calabresi and Yoo, *Unitary Executive,* 172, 460. The National Bank Act was modified the following year so as only to require the president to communicate his reasons for the removal of the comptroller (Calabresi and Yoo, *Unitary Executive,* 460 n39).

60 According to Fish's count of removals from "presidential offices"—that is, those appointed by the president with the advice and consent of the Senate—Lincoln removed 1,457 and Johnson 903. See Fish, "Removal of Officials by the Presidents of the United States," 1:85.

61 Michael Les Benedict, *The Impeachment and Trial of Andrew Johnson* (New York: Norton, 1973), 48. Strictly speaking, most of these removals were made by the postmaster general. In 1866, only about 700 of the roughly 24,000 postmasters in the United States were appointed by the president; the power to appoint and remove the rest was vested by statute in the postmaster general. See House Executive Document No. 96, 39th Congress 2nd Session (Letter from the Postmaster General, February 20, 1867), 64. In July 1866, Lincoln's postmaster general William Dennison resigned and Johnson replaced him with Alexander W. Randall.

62 Calabresi and Yoo, *Unitary Executive,* 191–92. White, *Republican Era,* 29.

63 Calabresi and Yoo, *Unitary Executive,* 203. White, *Republican Era,* 34.

64 Calabresi and Yoo, *Unitary Executive,* 199.

65 Rutherford B. Hayes, *Letter Accepting the Republican Party Nomination for Presidency of the United States,* Columbus, Ohio, July 8, 1876, www.rbhayes.org/hayes/president/display.asp?id=514&subj=president.

66 Hayes, *Letter Accepting the Republican Party Nomination.*

67 White, *Republican Era,* 292–93.

68 Calabresi and Yoo, *Unitary Executive,* 203–04. James A. Garfield, Inaugural Address, March 4, 1881.

69 Richard E. Welch, Jr., *The Presidencies of Grover Cleveland* (Lawrence: University Press of Kansas, 1988), 53–55, Calabresi and Yoo, *Unitary Executive,* 210–11. White, *Republican Era,* 30.

70 Grover Cleveland, "On Giving Reasons for Removals for Office," March 1, 1886, *Writings and Speeches of Grover Cleveland,* ed. George F. Parker (New York: Cassell, 1892), 465–66.

71 Carl Russell Fish, *The Civil Service and the Patronage* (New York: Longman, 1905), 206–07. Welch, *The Presidencies of Grover Cleveland,* 55–56. Calabresi and Yoo, *Unitary Executive,* 212. Also see "Civil Service Reform; Views of Hon. George F. Hoar—Congressmen and the Offices," *New York Times,* September 26, 1876, p. 2.

72 Fish, *Civil Service and the Patronage,* 222, 224. White, *Republican Era,* 342. The number of postmasters is derived from the Annual Report of the Postmaster-General of the United States, for the Fiscal Year ended June 30, 1884 (Washington: Government Printing Office, 1884), 9. Post offices were divided into four grades depending upon the office's annual receipts, with first class having the highest receipts and fourth class the lowest.

73 White, *Republican Era,* 343–44.

74 Table Ea894–903—Federal government employees, by government branch and location relative to the capital: 1816–1992, in *Historical Statistics of the United States*, Millennial Edition Online. Taft's order protected about 36,000 fourth-class postmasters. An earlier executive order by Theodore Roosevelt, issued after the 1908 election, had brought about 14,000 fourth-class postmasters into the civil service.

75 National Civil Service Reform League, *Good Government*, June 1913, 58; also see September 1922, 121–26.

76 Saikrishna Prakash, "The Story of *Myers* and its Wayward Successors: Going Postal on the Removal Power," in Christopher H. Schroder and Curtis A. Bradley, eds., *Presidential Power Stories* (New York: Foundation Press, 2009), 165–67. Jonathan L. Entin, "The Pompous Postmaster and Presidential Power: The Story of *Myers v. United States*," November 2005, Case Legal Studies Research Paper No. 05–39. Available at http://ssrn.com/abstract=845026.

77 White, *Republican Era*, 344. Prakash, "The Story of *Myers*," 170.

78 Calabresi and Yoo, *Unitary Executive*, 248.

79 Prakash, "The Story of *Myers*," 185.

80 *Myers v. United States* (1926), 241 n3, 262–64, 293.

81 Prakash, "The Story of *Myers*," 186–87.

82 The description of the *Humphrey's* case and its aftermath is adapted from Richard J. Ellis, ed., *Judging Executive Power: Sixteen Supreme Court Cases That Have Shaped the American Presidency* (Lanham, MD: Rowman & Littlefield, 2009), 17–19, 23–24.

83 *Humphrey's Executor v. United States* (1935), 624, 626.

84 Calabresi, and Yoo, *Unitary Executive*, 287, 477.

85 *Morrison v. Olson* (1988), 670, 696. Also see Kevin M. Stack, "The Story of *Morrison v. Olson*: The Independent Counsel and Independent Agencies in Watergate's Wake," in Schroder and Bradley, eds., *Presidential Power Stories*, 401–46.

86 James B. Staab, *The Political Thought of Justice Antonin Scalia: A Hamiltonian on the Supreme Court* (Lanham, MD: Rowman & Littlefield, 2006), 143.

87 *Morrison v. Olson* (1988), 727, 731.

88 *Morrison v. Olson* (1988), 711–12.

89 Charles Fried, *Order and Law: Arguing the Reagan Revolution—A Firsthand Account* (New York: Simon & Schuster, 1991), 157. Stack, "Story of *Morrison v. Olson*," 413; Calabresi and Yoo, *Unitary Executive*, 380.

90 Charlie Savage, *Takeover: The Return of the Imperial Presidency and the Subversion of American Democracy* (Boston: Little, Brown, 2007), 44–45.

91 Fried, *Order and Law*, 51–52. Savage, *Takeover*, 45.

92 Because a joint resolution requires the president's signature, the comptroller general could not be removed without the president's consent, unless Congress overrode the president's veto.

93 Staab, *Political Thought of Scalia*, 63, 143. The "headless 'fourth branch'" phrase comes originally from the 1937 Report of the President's Committee on Administrative Management, more commonly known as the Brownlow Report.

94 Staab, *Political Thought of Scalia*, 63.

95 Stack, "Story of *Morrison v. Olson*," 414–15. This larger issue was very much on the justices' mind as they discussed the case in private conference. O'Connor wrote to Chief Justice Warren Burger to emphasize that "those who voted to affirm hope to make sure that the opinion not cast doubt on the constitutionality of independent agencies" (415). Bernard Schwartz shows that Burger's first draft—which argued that "the sole power of removal of an officer charged with the execution of the laws . . . resides in the President"—did indeed cast doubt upon the constitutionality of independent agencies. See Bernard Schwartz, *Decision: How the Supreme Court Decides Cases* (New York: Oxford University Press, 1997), 124–34.

96   Savage, *Takeover*, 47–48. Richard E. Neustadt, *Presidential Power: The Politics of Leadership* (New York: Wiley, 1960), 33.

97   Stack, "Story of *Morrison v. Olson*," 416–19.

98   *In re Sealed Case* 838 F.2d 476. In her dissent, Ginsburg wrote, "There is an irony in the majority's holding that the Act is constitutionally infirm, for the measure strives to maintain the structural design that is the genius of our Constitution—the system of mutual checks and balances; the Act's sole purpose is to curb or avert abuses of executive branch power."

99   Fried, *Order and Law*, 167.

100   Savage, *Takeover*, 270–71.

101   Phillip J. Cooper, "George W. Bush, Edgar Allan Poe, and the Use and Abuse of Presidential Signing Statements," *Presidential Studies Quarterly* (September 2005), 531. Jeffrey Rosen, "Power of One," *The New Republic*, July 24, 2006, p. 8.

102   Savage, *Takeover*, 58. The July 27, 1989 memo was titled "Common Legislative Encroachments on Executive Branch Authority."

103   John Yoo, "President's Authority to Remove the Chairman of the Consumer Product Safety Commission," July 31, 2001, Memorandum Opinion for the Counsel to the President, https://biotech.law.lsu.edu/blaw/olc/cpscchairmanremoval.htm.

104   Calabresi and Yoo, *Unitary Executive*, 413.

105   Richard A. Serrano, "Emails Detail White House Plan to Oust US Attorneys," *Los Angeles Times*, March 14, 2007. Dan Eggen and Paul Kane, "Justice Dept. Would Have Kept 'Loyal' Prosecutors," *Washington Post*, March 16, 2007. The White House was also being pressured by Missouri's Republican senator, Kit Bond, who, according to Sampson, "was not happy with Graves and wanted him out." According to a report by the Justice Department's inspector general, Bond, or at least his chief of staff, was "irate" with Graves for refusing to become involved in a personnel dispute that had developed between Bond's staff and the staff of Graves's brother, a Republican member of the House of Representatives. William Freivogel, "Bond 'Pressure' Led to 'Inappropriate' Firing of U.S. Attorney, Report Says," *St. Louis Beacon*, September 29, 2008.

106   Amy Goldstein and Dan Eggen, "Number of Fired Prosecutors Grows: Dismissals Began Earlier than Justice Dept. Has Said," *Washington Post*, May 10, 2007. David Iglesias with David Seay, *In Justice: Inside the Scandal that Rocked the Bush Administration* (Hoboken, NJ: John Wiley and Sons, 2008), 61–65.

107   Office of the Inspector General, "An Investigation into the Removal of Nine U.S. Attorneys in 2006," September 2008, ch. 3, section II. G.1 ("McNulty's February 6, 2007, Testimony before the Senate Judiciary Committee"), www.usdoj.gov/oig/special/s0809a/final.pdf. Dan Eggen, "Prosecutor Firings Not Political, Gonzales Says," *Washington Post*, January 19, 2007.

108   Iglesias, *In Justice*. Interview of Harriet Miers, Unofficial Transcript, Committee on the Judiciary, US House of Representatives, Washington, DC, June 15, 2009, http://judiciary. house.gov/hearings/pdf/MTranscript.pdf. Carrie Johnson, "Miers Told House Panel of 'Agitated' Rove," *Washington Post*, August 12, 2009.

109   Iglesias, *In Justice*, 50, 165, 199.

110   Iglesias, *In Justice*, 72.

111   Calabresi and Yoo, *Unitary Executive*, 414.

112   "Inside the U.S. Attorneys Emails: Major Players and Themes," *Wall Street Journal Online*, http://online.wsj.com/public/resources/documents/info-retro_DOJemails_070319.html.

113   *In re Sealed Case* 838 F.2d 476.

114   Fried, *Order and Law*, 171. Fried concedes that the unitary executive vision, however appealing, "is not literally required by the words of the Constitution. Nor did the framers' intent compel this view" (170).

115   *In re Sealed Case* 838 F.2d 476.

THE PRESIDENT AND THE LAW

PART IV

THE PRESIDENT AND
THE LAW

CHAPTER 9

THE PRESIDENT AND THE JUDICIARY

INTRODUCTORY PUZZLE: HOW EARL WARREN BECAME THE LAST LIBERAL CHIEF JUSTICE

On the morning of June 13, 1968, Chief Justice Earl Warren met with President Lyndon Johnson to inform him that he intended to resign from the Supreme Court. There was nothing wrong with his health, but after 16 years on the job Warren felt it was time to step aside and let a younger man take the reins. That was what the 77-year-old chief justice told the president, but it was only half the story.

A presidential election was less than five months away and it seemed all but certain that the Republican nominee would be Warren's least favorite politician, Richard M. Nixon. The loathing was mutual: Nixon rarely passed up an opportunity during the primary campaign to accuse the Warren Court of coddling criminals and legislating from the bench. The Democratic Party, meanwhile, was in disarray. The unpopular war in Vietnam had prompted Johnson to announce that he would not seek reelection. A week after Johnson's announcement, Martin Luther King Jr. was assassinated, sparking urban riots and heightening the appeal of Nixon's racially charged "law and order" platform. And on June 5, 1968, Democrat presidential candidate Robert Kennedy was assassinated as he celebrated his victory in the California primary, removing the one Democrat that Warren thought could beat Nixon. Warren judged that the only way to stop his archenemy from appointing his successor was to resign immediately.[1]

Johnson knew who he wanted as Warren's replacement: the sitting Justice Abe Fortas. Without consulting anyone, Johnson called Fortas the next day to offer him the position. Johnson later explained that he selected Fortas because of his brilliance as a lawyer and because he would "carry on in the Court's liberal tradition." But Johnson also picked Fortas because he had served for several decades as the president's confidant and legal advisor. Fortas had remained the president's trusted counselor even after Johnson appointed him to the Supreme Court in 1965. Throughout his tenure on the Court, Fortas seemed to spend as much time in the White House as he did in his chambers in the Supreme Court Building.[2]

By selecting Fortas, Johnson created another opening on the Court, which he hoped to fill with his friend and protégé, federal appellate judge Homer Thornberry. Thornberry

President Lyndon Johnson meeting with foreign policy advisors on November 2, 1967. Sitting at the far corner of the table is Supreme Court Justice Abe Fortas. To Fortas's right is General Maxwell Taylor and to his left is Clark Clifford, both of whom served as chairmen of the President's Intelligence Advisory Board during the Johnson administration. President Johnson is second from the right on the near side of the table. To Johnson's right is Secretary of State Dean Rusk and to his left is Secretary of Defense Robert McNamara.

Courtesy: LBJ Library photo by Yoichi Okamoto.

owed his advancement in politics almost entirely to Johnson. When Johnson became a United States senator in 1948, Thornberry took Johnson's seat in the House. Johnson introduced the freshman representative—whom he called "my congressman"—to powerful people who could advance his House career. When Johnson named Thornberry to the appellate court in 1965, he was sworn in on the front porch of the LBJ Ranch, where the two men had played endless games of dominos while Senator Johnson recovered from his heart attack a decade earlier. Picking Thornberry was not only an opportunity for Johnson to place his ideological stamp on the Court and reward a loyal friend. It was also a political stratagem to grease the way for Fortas, since Johnson calculated that southern Democrats would swallow Fortas as the price of securing a spot for Thornberry, a southern good ol' boy and duck-hunting buddy of Georgia's influential Democratic senator, Richard Russell.[3]

Johnson thought he was being clever, but his advisors warned the president that pairing Fortas and Thornberry would look like cronyism. They suggested pairing Fortas instead with a widely respected, moderate Republican, but Johnson wouldn't hear of appointing a "damned Republican" to the Court. Indeed, the president wouldn't hear of any of the alternatives proffered by his advisors.[4]

None of this would probably have mattered if Warren had resigned the year before. But with the election so near and the strong chance of a Republican victory, Republicans were desperate to prevent Johnson from naming Warren's successor. They argued that a "lame duck" president should not make such an important decision. They maintained, too, that the Supreme Court was no place for cronies like Fortas and Thornberry. And they insisted that Fortas had behaved improperly and violated the separation of powers by continuing to advise the president after becoming a justice.[5]

Fortas's defenders tried to deflect these charges by appealing to history. They attacked the lame-duck argument as a "novel and radical" theory that was inconsistent with the Constitution and the nation's past. They pointed to the many presidents who had put their cronies on the bench, including Abraham Lincoln, who named his campaign manager David Davis to the Supreme Court. Fortas defended himself by providing the committee with numerous examples of Supreme Court justices who had served as presidential advisors. The nation's first chief justice, John Jay, for instance, was not only a trusted advisor to President Washington but also acting secretary of state for six months. Franklin Roosevelt, too, received political advice from sitting members of the Court.[6]

Fortas did not seem entirely convinced by his own history lesson. Instead of acknowledging the full extent of his advisory relationship, Fortas minimized and even lied about it in testimony before the Senate Judiciary Committee. His role in White House discussions about Vietnam, he assured the committee, was limited largely to restating and clarifying the arguments advanced by others. In reality, Fortas played a key advocacy role in deliberations about the Vietnam War, consistently pressing Johnson after the spring of 1967 to pursue the war "without explanation or apology." Fortas also denied writing speeches for the president, even though the president frequently solicited Fortas's help in crafting speeches. The committee directly asked Fortas whether he had drafted the president's message ordering federal troops to Detroit in response to riots in July 1967, and Fortas lied that he had not.[7]

Was it wrong for Fortas to have advised and aided the president while serving as a Supreme Court justice? He broke no law. Nor did he violate the Constitution. Fortas was right that Washington, an enduring symbol of rectitude as well as a delegate at the Constitutional Convention, saw nothing wrong with seeking Chief Justice Jay's political and constitutional counsel. Fortas's critics alleged that his close relationship with Johnson violated the separation of powers, but would anyone have lodged a similar complaint if the president had solicited the counsel of a member of Congress? Still, even Fortas's admirers felt that he had transgressed in remaining part of Johnson's inner circle after taking his seat on the Court.

Fortas's behavior made many people uneasy because it violated the notion that justices should be above politics and partisanship. During his confirmation hearing in 2005, Chief Justice John Roberts gave expression to this idea when he likened a Supreme Court justice to an umpire, whose job was only to call balls and strikes. Like an umpire, the justice should not take sides with one team over the other, let alone try to play the game. Using this analogy, then, Fortas should have been rejected because he had failed to remain neutral.

But is a Supreme Court justice really like an umpire, either in practice or in theory? Chief Justice Warren obviously did not believe that justices were like umpires, or he would not have timed his retirement to prevent Nixon from choosing the next chief justice. Neither did President Johnson, who freely admitted that he selected Fortas for his liberal views. Nor did Fortas's Republican opponents, who mounted a successful filibuster against Fortas in order to give a Republican president the opportunity to nominate the next chief justice and to reverse the liberal direction of the Warren Court—an opportunity that Nixon seized in 1969 by appointing Warren Burger, a conservative Republican.[8]

Was there ever a time when justices were more like umpires than players? A time when presidents did not try to pack the Court with like-minded players but picked the best legal minds and judicial talents regardless of party? A time when senators asked not about ideology but competence? Would a return to the framers' original understanding help us to restore the traditional game in which judges were neutral umpires rather than partisan players?

Founding Arguments

Article II states that the president "shall nominate, and by and with the Advice and Consent of the Senate, shall appoint ... Judges of the Supreme Court." But the Constitution says nothing about the qualifications needed for that high office. The president must be a natural-born citizen, at least 35 years old, and a resident of the United States for 14 years. A member of the House of Representatives must be at least 25 years of age and a citizen for a minimum of seven years, and a senator must be at least 30 years of age and a citizen for nine years. All members of Congress must also be inhabitants of the state in which they serve at the time of their election. A Supreme Court justice, in contrast, can be a minor and never have lived in the United States. A justice need not be a United States citizen or even trained in the law. What qualifies a person for the Supreme Court is left entirely to the president and the Senate.[9]

Judicial Selection: A Shared Responsibility

The Constitutional Convention's decision in 1787 to give both the president and the Senate a role in the selection of judges was a compromise between two groups of delegates: one favored giving the president the sole power to appoint judges, the other wanted the Senate to make the selections. The senatorial camp emphasized that senators were drawn from every state, and therefore would be far more knowledgeable than the president about candidates for judicial office. In addition, they thought that the president would be more prone to "intrigues" and favoritism than a collective body that included diverse representatives from across the country. These delegates also warned that granting the president the power to make judicial appointments, a power that the king exercised in England, would not sit well with the American people, who still looked upon executive power "with a jealous eye." The presidential camp countered that decisions reached by a collective body such as the Senate would suffer from "intrigue, partiality, and concealment" of responsibility. Only the president, they argued, would take the broad, national view in choosing fit characters as judges.[10]

Initially, the convention backed the senatorial camp. On June 13, the delegates unanimously agreed to Madison's motion to give the Senate the power to appoint federal judges. However, after July's Great Compromise, which gave each state an equal number of senators, delegates from more populous states began to reconsider the wisdom of senatorial selection of judges. A proposal by Pennsylvania's James Wilson to allow the executive alone to appoint judges was easily defeated, but other compromise proposals attracted greater support, including one by Massachusetts' Nathaniel Gorham that judges "be nominated and appointed by the Executive, by and with the advice and consent" of the Senate. Among those who now backed Gorham's compromise was Madison, who complained that senatorial selection enabled judges to be "appointed by a minority of the people, though by a majority of the States." The least populous states held firm, however, and the convention reaffirmed its support for the original plan of senatorial selection, with only the three most populous states dissenting: Pennsylvania, Massachusetts, and Virginia.[11]

Dissatisfaction remained, however. Toward the end of August, the leaders of the presidential camp, Gouverneur Morris and James Wilson, renewed their attack on senatorial selection of judges. With time running short and the most populous states still unhappy about the earlier rejection of Gorham's compromise, the convention turned the matter over to the Committee on Postponed Matters. On September 4, the 11-member committee endorsed Gorham's original compromise, which was adopted unanimously. The delegates evidently agreed with Morris that "as the President was to nominate, there would be responsibility, and as the Senate was to concur, there would be security." Working together, the president and Senate would select more meritorious judges than either could alone.[12]

Some legal scholars—and some presidents—have argued that the framers intended the Senate's role in the selection process to be the relatively modest one of keeping the president honest. They typically appeal to the words of Alexander Hamilton, who in *Federalist* No. 76 argued that the Senate's check would largely be "a silent operation," one that would discourage the president from nominating "unfit characters," whether out of "State prejudice, from family connection, from personal attachment, or from a view to popularity." Few have put the presidential position quite so baldly as President Richard Nixon, who in the spring of 1970 fired off an angry letter to a Republican senator complaining about the Senate's refusal to confirm his Supreme Court nominee G. Harrold Carswell. At stake, Nixon insisted, was whether the president's judgment "can be frustrated by those who wish to substitute their own philosophy or their own subjective judgment for that of the one person entrusted by the Constitution with the power of appointment."[13]

Of course, the argument that the Constitution gave the power of appointment to the president alone is plainly wrong. Moreover, one would be hard-pressed to find a more "unfit character" nominated for the Supreme Court than Carswell, whom even the president's most loyal aides decided was "a boob" and "a dummy." But what about the core of Nixon's contention: that unless the president nominated a plainly "unfit character" the Senate should defer to the president's pick? On Nixon's reading, the Constitution allows the president to nominate judges on the basis of judicial or political philosophy, but the Senate is not permitted to use those same criteria in judging whether to confirm a nominee.[14]

Nixon's reading of the Constitution assumed that the framers had a single intent in crafting the appointments clause. In reality, the clause was the product of a compromise between starkly different visions of how judges should be selected. That compromise would surely have collapsed had delegates suggested that the president be permitted to use a broader range of criteria in nominating than the Senate could use in considering whether to consent. Delegates from smaller states accepted the compromise precisely because they believed it preserved a robust role for the Senate. Certainly, no delegate on either side of the argument ever suggested that the Senate, in exercising its advice and consent function, must use a narrower set of criteria than the president should employ in nominating a candidate. To the extent that the rival sides in the debate agreed on any proposition, it was that both the president and the Senate should make their judgments based on merit rather than on what Hamilton called "a spirit of favoritism." The philosophical argument at the convention revolved around whether the Senate or the president was most likely to make meritorious choices—and the compromise reflected broad acceptance that merit would most likely be used as the criteria if both president and Senate shared the responsibility of appointing judges.[15]

Judicial Terms: "During Good Behaviour"

On one point the framers were unanimous from the outset: federal judges should "hold their offices during good behaviour." That was the wording in the original Virginia Plan and not once did anyone suggest altering it. Each delegate believed that life terms were indispensable for preserving an impartial and independent judiciary. That principle had been enshrined in English law after the Act of Settlement of 1701, which safeguarded an independent judiciary by preventing the Crown from removing judges. The Act of Settlement did not apply to the colonies, however, where judges served at the pleasure of the Crown and were widely viewed as mere "appendages or extensions of royal authority embodied in the governors." Among the revolutionaries' sharpest grievances against George III was that he subverted the course of justice by making judges, in the words of the Declaration of Independence, "dependent on his Will alone for the tenure of their offices."[16]

The historical context explains why the framers believed that the impartial administration of justice required life tenure. Were they right? Most Americans would unhesitatingly answer "yes." But there seems little reason to think that life terms secure judicial independence better than long, fixed terms. Moreover, fixed terms have an important advantage over life terms: they prevent justices from timing their retirements to coincide with the tenure of a like-minded president, as Earl Warren tried to do in 1968. To be sure, Johnson's political miscalculation foiled Warren's strategy, but other justices have done the same thing, with more success, most recently when John Paul Stevens and David Souter waited until after George W. Bush's presidency to announce their resignations, thereby giving Barack Obama the chance to fill their seats with ideologically compatible justices.[17]

Judicial Power: "The Least Dangerous Branch"

The idea of fixed terms and strategic retirements never occurred to the framers. They could imagine presidents and senators playing politics with appointments, but so long as judges could not be removed—absent an impeachable offense—judges would have no reason to play politics with the law. But what precisely was to be the role of the Supreme Court? Was it to be Roberts's umpire, the final arbiter in a political contest played by presidents and legislators? The Constitution is silent on this all-important question, and the convention debates do not suggest that the framers gave the scope of judicial review— let alone judicial supremacy—sustained thought.

One of the few times that the convention delegates touched upon this question was when Madison proposed a complex plan by which all bills would have to be submitted for approval to the president and the Supreme Court. If both the president and Court objected, then it would take a three-fourths vote in each house of Congress to enact the law. If only the president or only the Court objected, then the supermajority requirement would drop to two-thirds of each house. South Carolina's Charles Pinckney immediately objected to "the interference of the Judges in the Legislative business," which would prejudice their judgment in future cases that might come before them.[18]

Madison's scheme was decisively rejected but several delegates did speak in favor of it. One of those proponents, Maryland's John Mercer, explained that his support owed to his disapproval of the doctrine that "Judges as expositors of the Constitution should have authority to declare a law void." Once a law had been "well and cautiously made," Mercer argued, it should be "uncontroulable" by the judiciary. Mercer's comment resonated with Delaware's John Dickinson, who agreed that judges ought not to be able "to set aside the law," lest "by degrees" they became "the lawgiver." Dickinson conceded, however, that he was "at a loss what expedient to substitute."[19]

If the framers spent little time thinking about the problems of a too powerful judiciary it was because the prospect seemed so far-fetched. When an opponent of the Constitution, signing himself Brutus, raised the specter of a Supreme Court that "would be exalted above all other power in the government, and subject to no controul," Hamilton responded in *Federalist* No. 78 that the judiciary was "beyond comparison the weakest of the three departments of power." The judiciary, Hamilton pointed out, "had no influence over either the sword or the purse; no direction either of the strength or of the wealth of the society." Granted, judges had an obligation to say when "a particular statute contravenes the Constitution," but a court "must ultimately depend upon the aid of the executive arm even for the efficacy of its judgments." The judiciary, Hamilton concluded, was plainly "the least dangerous" branch. Contrary to Brutus's claims, life tenure did not make judges into all-powerful players in the game of politics, but rather ensured that they would be fair and objective umpires, uninfluenced by appeals to party or popularity. That, at least, was the theory.

COURT PACKING IN THE FEDERALIST ERA

The Constitution specified that there should be a Supreme Court and "such inferior Courts as the Congress may from time to time ordain and establish," but did not prescribe the size of the highest court or the number of lower courts. In the Judiciary Act of 1789, Congress provided the missing pieces. The Supreme Court was to have six members: five associate justices and a chief justice. In addition, there were to be 13 district courts—roughly one per state—and three regional circuit courts, which could hear appeals from the district courts.

Washington's First Justices

On the same day that Washington signed the Judiciary Act, he submitted his six Supreme Court nominees to the Senate. Two days later, the Senate confirmed all six by voice vote. Washington said he had picked the "fittest characters to expound the Laws and dispense Justice," and his six picks were certainly a distinguished bunch. But legal talent and judicial temperament were not the only criteria that Washington applied. He also sought geographic diversity—his six nominees hailed from six different states, three southern, three northern. He also picked only from among those who had strongly supported the new Constitution. Indeed, three of the six—Pennsylvania's James Wilson, South Carolina's John Rutledge, and Virginia's John Blair—had an important hand in drafting the Constitution.[20]

The Senate's speedy approval of Washington's six picks was a tribute to the distinguished characters the president selected, but it was also a sign of the Senate's deference to Washington and the absence of organized political parties. If this was the way the framers always hoped it would be, however, those hopes would be shattered with Washington's choice of John Rutledge to succeed Chief Justice John Jay, who had resigned in the summer of 1795 to become governor of New York.

The Senate Says No: The Failed Nomination of John Rutledge

Rutledge himself had quit the Court in 1791 after being elected chief justice of South Carolina's state supreme court. The resignations of both Jay and Rutledge are reminders that federal positions in the early republic were not necessarily seen as more important or desirable than state posts. Service on the Supreme Court was often seen more as an onerous public duty than a position of great power. What made the job especially grueling was the responsibility under the 1789 Judiciary Act for "riding circuit"—that is, Supreme Court justices were responsible not only for hearing cases in the capital but for traveling thousands of miles on often poor roads to hear cases in one of the three circuits (eastern, middle, and southern) to which each Justice was assigned.[21]

Washington received Jay's resignation after Congress had already adjourned for the year. Believing that he could not afford to leave the seat vacant for another six months, Washington used a recess appointment that would allow Rutledge to serve on an interim basis until Congress returned to the capital. Since Rutledge was a distinguished jurist who had been unanimously approved as associate justice by the Senate in 1789, Washington had no reason to expect the Senate would balk at Rutledge's permanent selection. After all, none of his previous nine Supreme Court nominees had met with a single dissenting vote. He did not anticipate that his choice of Rutledge would be enveloped by fierce partisan disagreement over the Jay Treaty—a treaty with Britain that had been negotiated by Chief Justice Jay.

The terms of the treaty were publicly unveiled on July 2, 1795, the day after Washington appointed Rutledge. The treaty sharply divided the country along partisan lines: Federalists urged its ratification while Republicans condemned the treaty for forging closer ties with monarchical England at the expense of America's revolutionary ally, France. At a public meeting in Charleston, South Carolina, Rutledge condemned the treaty, thrusting himself into the center of a raging partisan debate. The author of *Federalist* No. 76, Alexander Hamilton, orchestrated a campaign to keep Rutledge off the bench, but Washington chose to ignore the public controversy and submitted Rutledge's name to the Senate for approval as soon as Congress reconvened in December. Five days later, with Hamilton lobbying feverishly against Rutledge, the Senate voted along party lines to reject Rutledge.[22]

Washington got the message. In place of Rutledge, he nominated a stalwart Federalist, Oliver Ellsworth. Like Rutledge, Ellsworth had served on the Committee of Detail at the Constitutional Convention and been a strong supporter of the Constitution, but unlike Rutledge, Ellsworth was firmly wedded to the Federalist Party. As a United States senator, Ellsworth had not only enthusiastically backed the Jay Treaty but had been, in the words of John Adams, "the firmest pillar" of the Washington administration's policies.[23]

John Adams's Partisan Appointments

As partisanship increased in the 1790s, party became a litmus test for every judicial appointment. Adams filled the courts almost exclusively with adherents of the Federalist persuasion. His three Supreme Court picks were all strong Federalists, including Washington's 36-year-old nephew Bushrod Washington, who remained on the Court until his death in 1829. Adams's most consequential pick was his choice of John Marshall to replace Ellsworth as chief justice.

By resigning on the eve of the 1800 election, Ellsworth gave Adams and the Federalist-controlled Senate the opportunity to keep the chief justiceship in Federalist hands even if Adams lost the election. Adams's first choice to replace Ellsworth was Jay, but Jay detested circuit riding so much that he declined. Adams received Jay's refusal on January 20, 1801, less than six weeks before Jefferson was set to take the oath of office. Unable to afford any further delays, Adams immediately offered the job to his secretary of state, John Marshall, who was confirmed by the Federalist-controlled Senate a week later. On January 31, without giving up his job as secretary of state, Marshall officially became chief justice of the Supreme Court, a position he retained until his death in 1835. During his 35-year reign, Marshall put an indelible Federalist stamp on American politics.

The Judiciary Act of 1801

Marshall's last-minute appointment rankled Republicans, but that was mild compared to their outrage at the Judiciary Act that Adams signed into law on February 13, 1801.

Passed on a purely party-line vote, the act contained a mix of valuable reforms and pure partisan spite. In the latter category, it shrunk the Court from six to five justices, so that two justices would have to retire before Jefferson would be able to name a Supreme Court justice. In the former category, it abolished circuit riding by Supreme Court justices, a reform that had been urged repeatedly over the past decade. Abolishing circuit riding would make it easier to recruit and retain justices as well as eliminate the conflict of having the Supreme Court hearing appeals from circuit court rulings by one of their own.[24]

To retain circuit courts while abolishing circuit riding by the justices required Congress to create a cadre of circuit court judges, but the act went well beyond what was required by creating six new circuit courts and 16 circuit court judgeships. Had Adams left it to Jefferson to fill these new positions, Republicans likely could have reconciled themselves to the act. But instead Adams used his final weeks in office to pack the new courts with Federalists. Gouverneur Morris freely confessed the strategy: bracing for "a heavy gale of adverse wind," the Federalist Party was "casting many anchors to hold their ship through the storm." The federal judiciary was to be the Federalists' anchor in the coming Republican storm.[25]

JEFFERSON'S ASSAULT ON THE "GIBRALTAR OF THE JUDICIARY"

Undoing the Judiciary Act of 1801 was at the top of the Jeffersonian agenda. The question was how far Republicans were prepared to go in assaulting what one Virginia Republican called the Federalist "Gibraltar of the Judiciary Department." Some Republicans pressed for a constitutional amendment that would abolish life tenure for judges and perhaps even do away with the Supreme Court. Others wanted only to trim the act's excesses. Jefferson at first was noncommittal. In his first annual message, he suggested that the expanded federal court system was larger than necessary given its caseload, but beyond that he revealed little.[26]

Repealing the Judiciary Act

If Jefferson was uncertain about whether to press for a total repeal of the act, his doubts evaporated after the Supreme Court decided to hear *Marbury v. Madison*, a case brought by four men who had been commissioned by President Adams to serve as justices of the peace for the newly established District of Columbia. The legislation that created these and a host of other presidentially appointed offices in the district was signed by Adams only four days before he was to relinquish his office to Jefferson. On March 2, 1801, the lame-duck Federalist Senate hurriedly confirmed all of Adams's nominees, leaving the president and Marshall (acting in his capacity as secretary of state rather than chief justice) until midnight the next day to sign, seal, and deliver each of the commissions. They succeeded in signing commissions for all 42 new DC justices of the peace, but Marshall failed to deliver those intended for William Marbury and his three co-petitioners. When President Jefferson discovered the undelivered commissions he refused to deliver them.[27]

On December 17, 1801, Marbury and his fellow petitioners asked the Supreme Court to order the Jefferson administration to deliver their lawfully concluded commissions. The next day, speaking for a Court made up exclusively of Federalists, Chief Justice Marshall agreed to hear oral arguments on the case and commanded the administration to explain its actions. Jefferson was outraged by the impropriety of Marshall presiding over a case that involved his own failure, as Adams's secretary of state, to deliver Marbury's commission. Making Jefferson even more unhappy was the prospect of Federalists securing political influence through the courts that they had been denied at the ballot box. On the day that Marshall announced his ruling, Jefferson vented his anger. The Federalists, he fumed, "have retired into the Judiciary as a stronghold ... and from that battery all the works of Republicanism are to be beaten down and erased." Jefferson now instructed his political lieutenants in Congress to push for a total repeal of the Judiciary Act.[28]

Six weeks after its introduction in Congress, the repeal bill became law on a straight party-line vote. Federalists deplored the repeal, warning that it was the first step in a Republican assault on an independent judiciary. Unable to defeat the repeal in Congress, Federalists looked to the Supreme Court to invalidate the measure. Repeal was unconstitutional, they argued, because Congress had no right to abolish the office of a judge who served during good behavior. Repeal would leave all lower-court judges at the mercy of Congress and vitiate the independence of the judiciary. Republicans countered that the Constitution gave Congress the power to establish all lower courts and so Congress must also have the power to abolish them. They also denied that the Supreme Court had the power to tell Congress what the Constitution meant. If the Court declared the repeal unconstitutional, Republicans warned, Congress would impeach the justices.[29]

Some Republicans itched for a showdown with the Supreme Court. They believed that by goading the Marshall Court into showing its true Federalist colors, they could maneuver Jefferson into backing an overhaul of the federal judiciary that went well beyond the repeal's restoration of the status quo ante. Some Federalists, too, welcomed a confrontation, confident that the Court would embarrass the administration by repudiating the repeal and upholding Marbury's commission. Jefferson, however, wanted no part of such a confrontation. He knew that many moderate Republicans, who were committed to a strong and independent judiciary, had backed repeal with the greatest reluctance. And he feared that a bitter fight with the Court could fracture his fledgling party. Anxious to avoid giving Marshall the opportunity to rule on repeal before it had gone into effect—the Supreme Court was scheduled to meet in June 1802 and the repeal did not take effect until July—Jefferson gave his blessing to a bill that pushed back the opening of the Court's next term until February 1803. This way, the Court would not convene until the new circuit court judges were already out of a job.[30]

Unable to prevent Republicans in Congress from adjourning the Court, Federalists hatched a new strategy. They pressed the justices to refuse to act as circuit court judges, on the grounds that requiring Supreme Court justices to serve as circuit court judges was unconstitutional. Justice Samuel Chase enthusiastically endorsed the plan, and Marshall was tempted by it. However, after polling others on the Court, the chief justice discovered that his other colleagues had no appetite for the proposal. Having ridden circuit for a decade while the Federalists were in power without ever questioning its constitutionality, a majority of the justices concluded that it would be imprudent to refuse now that the Republicans were in power. Unable to marshal a united front, the chief justice backed away from the high-risk strategy of refusing to ride circuit.[31]

The Court's growing concerns about the wisdom of forcing a confrontation with Republicans were magnified by the elections of 1802, which produced massive Republican majorities in Congress. Federalists had made the Judiciary Act's repeal a central campaign issue and Republicans now pointed to the election returns as vindication of their policy. When the Court met in February 1803, Marshall seemed as eager as Jefferson to skirt a constitutional showdown. In *Stuart v. Laird*, the Court unanimously rejected a Federalist challenge to the constitutionality of the repeal act—thus avoiding an all-but-certain Republican push to enact the repeal via constitutional amendment. And in *Marbury v. Madison*, the Court declined the invitation to order Jefferson to reinstate Marbury as justice of the peace.[32]

John Marshall's Strategic Retreat in *Marbury v. Madison*

Marshall's opinion in *Marbury* was a masterful display of brinkmanship. Had he ordered the administration to deliver the commission to Marbury, Jefferson would have refused to comply and Marshall would have been powerless to do anything about it. The challenge for Marshall was how to assert the Court's authority without inviting a Republican counter-attack against which the Court would have been defenseless.

Marshall's solution was ingenious. First, he chastised Jefferson for failing to deliver a lawfully signed commission. Marbury, he declared, had a legal right to the office that no president could take away. However, Marshall then added that there was nothing the Supreme Court could do because the provision of the 1789 Judiciary Act that gave the Court jurisdiction over such matters was unconstitutional. By declaring a minor part of the 1789 act unconstitutional, Marshall achieved two ends. First, he affirmed the Court's right to pass judgment on the constitutionality of federal laws. Second, he criticized Jefferson's action without precipitating an institutional battle with the chief executive that the Court was certain to lose.

Although constitutional law classes give pride of place to the first motive, the latter appears to have been uppermost in Marshall's mind. Marshall loathed Jefferson, whom he thought "totally unfit for the chief magistracy." Had Marshall wanted only to establish judicial review or had he sincerely believed that the 1789 act prevented the Court from ordering Jefferson to deliver Marbury's commission, there would have been no reason for Marshall to pass judgment on the propriety of Jefferson's actions. If the Court did not have jurisdiction over the matter because of the 1789 act's constitutional infirmities, that should have been the end of the inquiry. Marshall took the unusual step of confronting the question of jurisdiction only after dealing with the merits of Marbury's claim because he was determined to scold Jefferson.[33]

Jefferson resented Marshall's gratuitous rebuke, but otherwise paid the opinion little heed. Neither Jefferson nor the great majority of Republicans objected to judicial review. However, he denied that the judiciary had the exclusive right to interpret the Constitution. "Nothing in the Constitution," Jefferson insisted, gave judges "a right to decide for the Executive" any more than it gave "the Executive [a right] to decide for them." To accept the Court as the only or supreme arbiter of constitutional meaning would make the judiciary "a despotic branch." But there was nothing despotic in *Marbury*: it made no claim to judicial supremacy and made no attempt to compel the president to deliver Marbury's commission. Ruling on the constitutionality of a provision of the Judiciary Act was clearly within the judiciary's "sphere of action," and it circumscribed rather than expanded the jurisdiction of the Court. Jefferson correctly judged *Marbury* for what it was: a tactical retreat by Marshall, not the opening salvo in a judicial assault upon the Republican legislative agenda.[34]

The Impeachment of Samuel Chase

The decisions in *Marbury* and *Stuart* might have laid the groundwork for a *modus vivendi* between the Marshall Court and the Jefferson administration had it not been for Samuel Chase, the Court's most unapologetic partisan. Chase was bitterly disappointed with the Court's capitulation over the Republican repeal act, which he insisted violated the constitutional guarantee that federal judges serve during good behavior. Two months after watching Marshall and his fellow justices surrender in *Marbury* and *Stuart*, Chase lashed out against Republicans' perfidy in a charge to a federal grand jury. Chase insisted that by abolishing the offices of 16 circuit court judges, Republicans had "shaken to its foundation ... the independence of the national judiciary." Unless things were reversed soon, he warned, the Constitution would "sink into a mobocracy."[35]

This was too much for Jefferson, who fired off an angry missive to Maryland's Joseph Nicholson, a trusted Republican leader in the House. Chase's "seditious and official attack on the principles of our Constitution," Jefferson suggested, should not "go unpunished." The punishment that Jefferson had in mind was impeachment. However, impeaching a Supreme Court justice, even one as reactionary and impolitic as Chase, was risky business, and Jefferson warned Nicholson that Congress would be on its own. As president, Jefferson explained, "it is better that I should not interfere." Jefferson watched nervously from the sidelines as the unpredictable and irascible John Randolph seized control of the proceedings, submitting eight articles of impeachment, including one that targeted the impropriety of Chase's partisan charge to the grand jury.[36]

From Jefferson's perspective, Randolph was the worst possible person to lead the effort to remove Chase. Randolph had no legal training, a handicap that became all too clear once the impeachment trial began in the Senate. In addition, he had an unrivaled capacity to alienate political allies with intemperate attacks. By the time the Chase trial was underway Randolph had also turned on the administration, accusing it of "all kinds of corrupt motives and private deals." Despite alienating Republican moderates and bungling the prosecution, Randolph came within four votes of securing Chase's removal from office. Of 25 Republican senators, 19 voted to impeach Chase; all nine Federalists supported Chase. Had someone more politic than Randolph been in charge, Jefferson likely would have secured Chase's impeachment.[37]

Next on the Republican agenda might very well have been the chief justice himself. Certainly that was Randolph's hope. Marshall was sufficiently alarmed by the prospect that, prior to the start of the Senate trial, he suggested to Chase that rather than impeach a judge for essentially political differences, it would be better to allow the legislature to reverse "those legal opinions [it] deemed unsound." If the legislature were seen as "the appellate jurisdiction," Marshall explained, then impeachment could be restored to its more limited and intended purpose of removing only those who were guilty of "high crimes and misdemeanors." To save his skin and preserve judicial independence, Marshall seemed prepared to curtail the Court's power of judicial review.[38]

After Chase's acquittal, Marshall never again mentioned the idea of giving the legislature "appellate jurisdiction." Still, the trial had a chastening effect on the Federalist justices. Chase, who had vigorously campaigned for Adams in 1800, steered clear of politics and controversy for the remainder of his time on the Court. The justices recognized that the Court's legitimacy and even survival hinged on forging a clear distinction between law and politics, which required refraining from electioneering and overt partisanship. Over the next 30 years, Marshall not only nurtured this distinction but sought to avoid direct confrontation with Congress and the president. In fact, *Marbury* was the only case in Marshall's 35 years on the bench in which the Court found a federal statute unconstitutional. Not until the notorious 1857 case of *Dred Scott v. Sandford*, in which the Court ruled that Congress did not have authority to prohibit slavery in the federal territories, did the Supreme Court strike down another federal law.[39]

The failed Chase impeachment also took the steam out of the Republican assault on the judiciary. On the day Chase was acquitted, Randolph introduced a constitutional amendment to allow the president, at the request of both houses of Congress, to remove any federal judge. The Republicans had the political muscle to push through such an amendment. They outnumbered the Federalists by nearly 3–1 in both houses. Moreover, Randolph's proposal was not unprecedented; Jefferson had toyed with the same idea in early 1803, when tensions with the judiciary were at their height. But moderate Republicans had tired of Randolph and his war on the judiciary. If Jefferson wanted to remake the Court he would have to do it the way the Constitution intended, by waiting for justices to resign or die.[40]

"DRIVING US INTO CONSOLIDATION": ON THE ROAD TO *McCULLOCH*

Jefferson would have had little difficulty remaking the Court in his image if the rapid turnover of justices of the 1790s had continued into the nineteenth century. Between 1791 and 1800, five justices resigned their seat and another two died in office, but after Jefferson took office the justices clung to their seats. Five years into his presidency, Jefferson had appointed only one Supreme Court justice—a replacement for Alfred Moore, who had been forced to resign due to failing health. The only other member of the Court that Jefferson replaced was William Paterson, who died in the fall of 1806—for which Jefferson had the repeal of the 1801 Judiciary Act to thank, since Paterson's demise was due to an accident he suffered while riding circuit in 1803. Jefferson was able to appoint a third Republican in 1807, when Congress expanded the size of the Court to seven justices in order to extend the circuit courts to the newest states of Kentucky, Tennessee, and Ohio.[41]

Madison's Failure to Remake the Court

By the end of Jefferson's tenure, time was clearly on the Republicans' side. Two more Federalist justices—William Cushing and then Chase—died during Madison's first term, leaving Marshall and Washington as the only Federalist appointees on the bench. Informed of Cushing's death, Jefferson hailed it as a "circumstance of congratulation" because it meant that Madison would have the long-awaited chance of "getting a republican majority on the supreme bench" and thereby completing "that great reformation in our government" that had begun with the 1800 election. Jefferson's hopes were dashed, however, when Madison selected as Cushing's replacement the 32-year-old Joseph Story, whom Jefferson considered a "pseudo-Republican" and "unquestionably a tory." Jefferson's worst fears were confirmed as Story quickly emerged as Marshall's staunchest and most gifted ally on the Court.[42]

Madison's selection of Story demonstrates the constraints that presidents face in trying to pack the Court. In selecting Cushing's replacement, Madison felt compelled to select someone also from New England, the heartland of what remained of the Federalist Party. And the Republican bench of legal talent was much thinner in New England than in the rest of the country—indeed, Jefferson reckoned there were only two men in the whole of New England who possessed "unquestionable republican principles" and great ability. Story was also not Madison's first choice but his fourth.

Two of Madison's previous picks to fill Cushing's seat had been confirmed by the Senate but turned down the arduous honor, including Madison's and Jefferson's first choice, the stalwart Republican Levi Lincoln, who had served as attorney general in Jefferson's presidency. Madison's second choice was Connecticut's Alexander Wolcott, a zealous Republican partisan who, as the federal customs collector, had strictly enforced Jefferson's embargo in a region where it was intensely unpopular. (Story, in contrast, as a Republican member of Congress during Jefferson's final year in office, spearheaded the successful effort to end the embargo—which was why Jefferson disliked him so much.) New England's Federalists, however, were able to capitalize on Wolcott's meager legal experience to defeat his nomination in the Senate. After Wolcott's rejection, Jefferson lobbied for Connecticut's Gideon Granger, another reliable Republican, who for the past decade had dispensed party patronage as the nation's postmaster general. But Granger had many enemies and Madison feared a repeat of the Wolcott fiasco. Finally, after the seat had been vacant for more than a year, Madison reluctantly settled on Story, who was the nephew of an old friend. Story's chief virtue, from Madison's perspective, seemed to be that he was confirmable.[43]

After the confirmation of Story and Gabriel Duvall (who replaced Chase), the window of opportunity for transforming the Court slammed shut. Twelve years would pass before there would be another opening. The new Republican majority did have some immediate effects on the Court's functioning. Marshall wrote almost all the Court's opinions between 1801 and 1811, but the year after the arrival of Duvall and Story one-third of the Court's opinions were assigned to other justices.[44]

Marshall nevertheless continued to exert a remarkable degree of control over the Court's functioning and its ideological direction. Over the next decade, he still wrote more than 40 percent of the Court's opinions—and a higher percentage of the important ones. Many of the rest were written by Story, whose opinions closely mirrored Marshall's. Even when the Court was divided, it typically spoke with a single authoritative voice, its divisions concealed beneath a mask of unanimity. Dissents remained rare. Thomas Todd, the last of Jefferson's three appointees, wrote one five-line dissent in 19 years on the Court. William Johnson was by far the most independent-minded of the Jeffersonian appointees, but he too found—as he later explained to Jefferson—that he needed to "bend to the current" after an early dissent brought stern lectures from Marshall "on the indecency of justices cutting at each other."[45]

The Argument over *McCulloch v. Maryland*

Jefferson remained far from happy at the course the Marshall Court was setting, despite its five Republican appointees. His discontent became particularly acute after the Court's landmark ruling in *McCulloch v. Maryland* (1819), which upheld the constitutionality of the national bank, struck down a Maryland law taxing the bank, and offered an expansive reading of the powers of the national government. The federal government, Marshall explained, is "a government of the people," not a compact of "sovereign and independent states." Moreover, its powers were not limited to those explicitly enumerated in the Constitution. Instead the federal government had "implied powers" under Article I, section 8's "necessary and proper clause." As Marshall read this clause, it meant: "Let the end be legitimate, let it be within the scope of the constitution, and all means which are appropriate, which are plainly adapted to that end, which are not prohibited, but consistent with the letter and spirit of the constitution, are constitutional."

While affirming Congress's broad powers to legislate in the public interest, Marshall also brandished the Court's own power. Only the Supreme Court, Marshall insisted, could definitively and peacefully settle conflicts between the federal and state governments. In the case of the national bank, the Court had sided with the federal government. In future cases, though, if the Court found the federal government had exceeded its constitutional limits, it would be the Court's "painful duty . . . to say that such an act was not the law of the land."[46]

Jefferson could barely contain himself. In several letters to close political associates, the former president slammed Marshall's broad reading of the federal government's powers. "Opinion," Jefferson seethed, "is huddled up in conclave, perhaps by a majority of one, delivered as if unanimous, and with the silent acquiescence of lazy or timid associates, by a crafty chief judge." The Constitution was becoming "a mere thing of wax in the hands of the judiciary, which they may twist and shape into any form they please." To Jefferson, it seemed profoundly undemocratic that after 20 years of Republican rule, the Court seemed to remain as solidly Federalist as ever, still "driving us into consolidation" and impervious to the "voice of the nation, declared through the medium of elections."[47]

Jefferson was particularly upset at Marshall's notion that the Supreme Court was the "ultimate arbiter" of conflicts between state and federal government. Jefferson believed that the only arbiter was the people themselves, acting through the Constitution's amendment process. Madison thought Jefferson's idea was madness. To require a constitutional convention to referee every disagreement between the federal government and the state governments, Madison informed his old friend, would be "too tardy, too troublesome, and too expensive." Madison agreed that Marshall offered a dangerously expansive reading of the powers of the federal government and the Supreme Court. Yet Madison insisted Marshall was right that the federal judiciary was the proper place to decide where the powers of the federal government ended and those of the state government began. However, Madison conceded that if the Court continued on its current course, then a constitutional amendment reforming the Supreme Court might become necessary.[48]

Marshall's opinion in *McCulloch* agitated and divided the nation as no previous Supreme Court decision had done. The Virginia state legislature passed a resolution condemning the opinion and half a dozen legislatures called for a constitutional amendment to outlaw a national bank. So ferocious was the criticism that Marshall, writing under a pseudonym, felt compelled to defend himself in the press. Supporters hailed Marshall's opinion for restoring the Constitution to "its great original principle," but opponents jeered it as a "deadly blow ... struck at the Sovereignty of the States." That blow was felt particularly acutely in the southern states, where there was a growing concern that an expansive reading of the government's "implied powers" could jeopardize slavery.[49]

McCulloch helped to sharpen an ideological divide over government that had become increasingly blurred during James Monroe's presidency—the so-called "era of good feelings." For nearly two decades Marshall had carefully husbanded the Court's political capital, preferring to sidestep broader claims and avoid partisan controversy that might damage the Court's reputation. That Marshall chose this opportunity to throw down the ideological gauntlet was due both to his growing confidence in the security of the Court's place in the political system and to the apparent weakness and divisions within the presidency and Congress. Marshall could not foresee that his sweeping language in *McCulloch* would help to galvanize an opposition movement that would sweep into power in 1828—and that at its head would be a president determined to repudiate *McCulloch* and remake the Court to secure states' rights and slavery.

ANDREW JACKSON CONFRONTS THE COURT

Ever since the Chase impeachment trial Marshall had sworn off voting or any other partisan involvement, but the prospect of Andrew Jackson's election so appalled Marshall that he decided to vote for President John Quincy Adams. Like so many of his social class, Marshall considered the poorly educated Jackson unworthy of the nation's highest office, especially when compared with the glittering talents of the Harvard-educated Adams. Marshall also had good reason to fear that Jackson and his states' rights coalition posed a profound challenge to Marshall's vision of a strong central government.[50]

Challenging Judicial Supremacy

Jackson challenged Marshall on two key fronts: the national bank and Indian removal. Although Jackson had little legal training, he was convinced that the Court had got it horribly wrong in *McCulloch*. When Congress passed a bill renewing the national bank's charter, Jackson vetoed it, not only on the grounds that it was bad policy but also because he considered it unconstitutional. To those who said the Court had already settled the constitutional question, Jackson countered that each branch of government must "be guided by its own opinion of the Constitution. Each public officer who takes an oath to support the Constitution swears that he will support it as he understands it, and not as it is understood by others." The Court's opinion was just that—an opinion, and entitled only "to such influence as the force of [its] reasoning may deserve." Like Jefferson, then, Jackson rejected the idea that the Supreme Court should be the ultimate arbiter of constitutional questions.[51]

Jackson also made it clear that he would not enforce the Supreme Court's efforts to make Georgia comply with treaties made between the United States government and the Cherokee Indians. On Jackson's reading of the Constitution, Georgia had the constitutional authority to enact laws dealing with the Cherokees who resided within Georgia. The Marshall Court was free to come to its own judgment—as it did in *Worcester v. Georgia* (1832)—but the Court could not obligate Jackson to enforce a decision that would require the president to "make war upon the rights of the States." The president, in short, could not be forced by the Court to act in a way that he considered contrary to the Constitution. Jackson's argument was constitutional, but his motives were political and prudential. A showdown with Georgia over Indian policy would have lost Jackson the support of not only Georgia but several other southern states, including his home state of Tennessee, in the upcoming 1832 election. Jackson also knew that even had he wanted to enforce a Court order, the federal government lacked the strength to coerce states whose residents were determined to expel the Indians.[52]

Although Jackson publicly defied the Marshall Court, he did not lend his support to any of the many efforts to restructure the judiciary that were urged by congressional supporters and several of his closest advisors. Among the reform proposals given serious consideration in Jackson's first term were a constitutional amendment limiting judges to seven-year terms, a bill requiring that the Court could not invalidate a law on constitutional grounds unless the decision was unanimous, and a repeal of section 25 of the 1789 Judiciary Act, which gave the Court the authority to hear appeals from state courts. Jackson was hardly averse to conflict, so why did he not declare war on the Marshall Court as he did on the national bank? In many ways, the Court would have made an ideal enemy—an aristocratic and elitist foil for the populist man of the people. Part of the answer may be that Jackson genuinely valued—as he wrote in 1822—"an independent and virtuous judiciary." But more important was Jackson's confidence that he could remake the Court through the appointment power.[53]

The Court's Extreme Makeover

In his first year, Jackson had already filled two vacancies: one at the outset of his term, courtesy of his Senate supporters who had blocked his predecessor John Quincy Adams's nomination of John Crittenden, and the second when Bushrod Washington, who had been on the Court since 1798, finally died. By 1831, moreover, the 76-year-old Marshall was in poor health, and Jackson was convinced that he would soon get the opportunity to name the next chief justice. Marshall doggedly hung on, determined not to quit while Jackson was in office, but he died in 1835, giving Jackson the opportunity to nominate his trusted political and legal advisor Roger Taney to be the next chief justice. That same year Jackson filled two more seats on the Court, bringing the number of Jackson appointees to five, leaving only two survivors from the Court that had been in place when Jackson came to power.

Jackson's stamp on the Court was made more indelible when Congress expanded the Court to nine justices so as to create two new circuit courts that would serve the eight states (Alabama, Louisiana, Mississippi, Missouri, Arkansas, Illinois, Indiana, and Michigan) added to the Union between 1812 and 1837. By expanding the Court, the Democratic-controlled Congress enabled Jackson to put an old Tennessee pal, John Catron, on the bench for the new eighth circuit. Jackson's choice for the other open slot turned down the post, but Jackson's successor, Martin Van Buren, quickly filled it with Alabama's reliably Democratic senator John McKinley. The extreme makeover of the Court that Jefferson had long sought had finally been achieved.

MAKING THE COURT SAFE FOR SLAVERY

In creating two new circuits, the Democratic Congress did more than just add two more Jacksonians to the Court. It also tilted the Court decisively toward the South. Prior to 1837 the seven circuits were evenly balanced between North and South: three circuits encompassed northern states, three consisted of southern slave states, and the seventh circuit, added in 1807, included one free state (Ohio) and two slave states (Tennessee and Kentucky). Had the eight new states been assigned to the two new circuits, the delicate balance between North and South would have been roughly preserved. But instead Congress added the three new free states (Illinois, Indiana, and Michigan) to the existing seventh district, in which Ohio remained. That enabled Congress to create two new southern districts—one made up of Tennessee, Kentucky, and Missouri (the eighth district), and the other of Alabama, Louisiana, Mississippi, and Arkansas (the ninth district). Although Congress reshuffled the southern circuits in 1842, it did not alter the regional imbalance of five circuits representing slave states and four representing free states. From 1837 until the onset of the Civil War, the circuit court system ensured that the Supreme Court would have a majority of southern justices.

Jefferson and his Virginia comrades had complained for decades about the Marshall Court's lack of responsiveness to public opinion. Yet Jefferson's political heirs rigged a reorganization of the judiciary calculated to insulate the Court from population changes. Rapid growth in the free states meant that by 1860 the four northern circuits contained almost 17 million people. In contrast, the five southern circuits in 1860 contained only 11 million people, and almost 4 million of those were slaves. The seventh circuit alone (encompassing Ohio, Illinois, Indiana, and Michigan) included more than 6 million people. In contrast, the fifth circuit, which after 1842 consisted of only Louisiana and Alabama, counted fewer than 1.7 million people, almost half of whom were slaves. And the ninth circuit, as reconfigured in 1842, was made up of 1.2 million people (almost half of whom were again slaves) in Mississippi and Arkansas. The Supreme Court's infamous *Dred Scott* ruling was no accident; it was a logical outcome of a Court packed, by design, with southern slaveholders.

The *Dred Scott* Decision

Dred Scott was a slave by birth but he had lived for a number of years on military bases in the free state of Illinois and in the Wisconsin Territory, where slavery was prohibited by Congress. Upon the death of his owner, Scott sued for his freedom in Missouri state court, arguing that the state's legal precedents prevented him from being reenslaved. A jury agreed with Scott but the Missouri state Supreme Court reversed the jury's decision. Precedents, the court argued, were irrelevant because "times are not now as they were." Scott could not be freed because to do so would "gratify" the abolitionist spirit that aimed at "the overthrow and destruction of our government." Scott persevered, suing next in federal court. The judge, however, determined that this was not a federal matter, and so deferred to the Missouri High Court's interpretation of its own state laws. Scott then appealed to the United States Supreme Court.

The Court could easily have followed the prudent path of judicial restraint, and affirmed the lower court's judgment and reasoning. Indeed, this was precisely the route mapped out in the initial Court opinion written by New York Democrat Samuel Nelson. Instead, Taney and the four other southern justices pressed for the most radical affirmation of the slaveholders' republic that was possible. Writing for the Court, Taney argued that Scott had no right to bring his case because he was not a citizen of the United States. According to Taney, no descendants of slaves could be American citizens because the Constitution recognized blacks as a "subordinate and inferior class of beings" who had "no rights which the white man was bound to respect."[54]

Taney could have stopped there, since nothing more needed to be said to dispose of Scott's case. Instead, Taney thrust the Court into the midst of the fierce national debate about whether slavery should be permitted in the federal territories. In the historic Missouri Compromise of 1820, Congress had banned slavery north of the latitude 36°30'. In 1854, however, Congress opted for a different tack, adopting the Kansas–Nebraska Act, which allowed a territory's residents to decide whether to prohibit slavery. The Kansas–Nebraska Act was immensely unpopular in the North, and Congress was under intense pressure to again impose federal restrictions on the spread of slavery into the territories. Into this enormously complex debate, Taney lobbed his bombshell: the Missouri Compromise had been unconstitutional because Congress had no constitutional power to restrict or regulate slavery in the territories. Congress's only constitutional duty with respect to slavery, Taney insisted, was "protecting the rights of the slave owner," which were guaranteed by the Fifth Amendment.[55]

Why did Taney take the extraordinary step of invalidating the Missouri Compromise given that he had already found that Scott had no business being in federal court in the first place? Apparently the chief justice hoped that the Court's decisive intervention would settle the slavery dispute by taking it out of the realm of contested politics and making it a matter of authoritative law. There was nothing political about his judgment,

Taney insisted. He was not taking a position "upon the justice or injustice, the policy or impolicy of these laws." Instead he was merely interpreting the Constitution "according to the true intent and meaning when it was adopted" by the framers.[56]

Behind the scenes, this strategy was receiving encouragement from president-elect James Buchanan, who desperately wanted the Court to help him quiet anti-slavery agitation by turning the question of slavery in the territories into "a judicial question, which legitimately belongs to the Supreme Court." Buchanan was in close communication with several justices as they deliberated on the case, including fellow Pennsylvanian Robert Grier, whom Buchanan persuaded to side with Taney so that "the line of latitude should [not] mark the line of division in the court." In his inaugural address, Buchanan highlighted the forthcoming Court ruling. Feigning ignorance of what the Court would decide, Buchanan pledged that "in common with all good citizens" he would "cheerfully submit [to] whatever" the Court decided. Political differences of opinion would thus be superseded by the obligation of all citizens to follow the law as laid down by the nation's highest court.[57]

The effort by Buchanan and Taney to cloak their political ends in abstract constitutional law fooled nobody. Far from calming the conflict over slavery, Dred Scott inflamed it, dividing the nation along sectional lines more deeply than ever before. Outrage over the decision fueled the rise of the Republican Party, which attracted not only ex-Whigs but disaffected Democrats. Leading the attack on Dred Scott was an unheralded Illinois congressman, Abraham Lincoln, whose devastating critique of Taney's reasoning in a speech at New York City's Cooper Union helped to make him the nation's sixteenth president.[58]

Lincoln's Defiance

In his inaugural address, Lincoln announced that he had no intention of deferring to Taney's faulty understanding of the Constitution. Lincoln did not deny that the Court's decision was binding "upon the parties to a suit, as to the object of that suit." In other words, the Court legitimately had the final word about whether Dred Scott should be freed. Lincoln allowed too that the Court's judgment was "entitled to very high respect and consideration in all parallel cases by all other Departments of the Government." But that did not mean that the executive and legislature must forfeit their own reading of the Constitution, particularly on an issue as important as the spread of slavery into the territories. For "if the policy of the Government upon the vital questions affecting the whole people is to be irrevocably fixed by the decisions of the Supreme Court, ... the people will have ceased to be their own rulers, having to that extent practically resigned their Government into the hands of that eminent tribunal." At the close of Lincoln's speech, a "much agitated" chief justice swore in the new president.[59]

As president, Lincoln paid little heed to the Court's ruling in Dred Scott. He directly repudiated the Court's constitutional interpretation by signing legislation that abolished slavery in every federal territory and the District of Columbia. In signing the bill ending slavery in DC, Lincoln took the unusual step of including a statement in which he declared that he had "never doubted the constitutional authority of Congress to abolish slavery in this District." Moreover, Lincoln refused to abide by the Court's under-standing of the Constitution as a charter that denied blacks citizenship rights, issuing passports and patents to black Americans.[60]

RIDDING THE COURT OF SOUTHERNERS

Lincoln not only insisted on his independent responsibility to interpret the Constitution, he also took steps to remake the Court so that its constitutional views would more closely correspond with his own. When Lincoln was elected president in 1860, every justice on the Supreme Court was a Democratic appointee. But within two months of his swearing in, Lincoln had three Court vacancies to fill: one due to the death of Ohio's John McLean, the only Democratic justice to dissent in *Dred Scott*; the second due to the Senate's rejection of Buchanan's nominee to succeed the zealously pro-slavery justice Peter Daniel; and the third a result of Alabama's John Campbell leaving the Court to join the Confederate government.

Finding a Republican replacement for McLean was simple enough since his seventh circuit included the Republican strongholds of Ohio, Illinois, and Michigan. But the other two vacant seats were both southern circuits made up entirely of states that had seceded: Louisiana and Alabama in the fifth circuit and Mississippi and Arkansas in the ninth circuit. Custom dictated that a nominee be from the circuit, but instead of scouring the country for loyal Republicans from states that had seceded, Lincoln and Congress capitalized on secession to restructure the circuit court system and eliminate the southern tilt that had produced *Dred Scott* in the first place.

In his first annual message in December 1861, Lincoln proposed several different plans. First, Congress could abolish circuit riding by the justices and instead provide for dedicated circuit court judges, as the repealed Judiciary Act of 1801 would have done. Alternatively, circuit courts could be scrapped altogether. Or, finally, the circuit court system could be maintained as it was, but reconfigured so that each region of the country was more equitably represented. He reminded Congress that eight more states had entered the Union since 1845 and that they were currently excluded altogether from any of the nine circuits. Lincoln left it to Congress to decide which of these three routes was best, though he counseled Congress against simply adding more circuits as it would create a Court too large and unwieldy to operate effectively.[61]

Some radicals pushed for more drastic reforms. New Hampshire senator John Hale proposed abolishing the Taney Court, which was merely a discredited "part of the machinery of the old Democratic party," and replacing it with a new Republican Supreme Court. Horace Greeley's *New York Tribune* pressed for expanding the Court to 13 members, thereby giving Lincoln the chance to fill seven seats and Republicans an instant majority. But most Republicans, including Lincoln, believed that these more radical remedies were imprudent and unnecessary. Taney was in his eighties and illness increasingly kept him from his judicial duties. And two other Jackson appointees, Tennessee's John Catron and Georgia's James Wayne, were in their seventies.[62]

After deliberating for six months, the Republican Congress finally hatched its reor-ganization scheme. Following Lincoln's advice, Congress left the size of the Court untouched. But whereas the old Court had five southern circuits, the new Court would have only three. Rather than southern circuits of two or three states, each of the new southern circuits would be made up of four or five states. Moreover, Congress made sure that the three remaining southern justices—Catron, Wayne, and Taney (Jackson appointees all)—were assigned to the three southern circuits, so that the two vacancies would represent northern circuits. Lincoln picked Samuel Miller—"Iowa's most dedicated campaigner" for Lincoln in 1860—for one spot and his old friend and campaign manager David Davis for the other. Congress's reorganization scheme left California and Oregon outside of the nine circuits but shortly thereafter Congress remedied this by creating a tenth seat, giving Lincoln his fourth appointee in his first two years.[63]

A month before Lincoln's reelection, the 87-year-old Taney finally died. Casting geographic considerations aside, Lincoln named his treasury secretary, Salmon Chase, to be the next chief justice. Chase's appointment not only put a second anti-slavery Ohio justice on the Court but also left the Court with only two southern slaveholders, fewer than at any time in the nation's history. In four years, Lincoln and the Republicans had transformed the Court almost as dramatically as Jackson and the Democrats had in eight years.

The Republicans' transformation of the Court continued during the presidency of Andrew Johnson, this time by neutralizing rather than empowering the president. During the presidencies of Jefferson, Jackson, and Lincoln, a newly ascendant party expanded the Court to give their president the power to reshape a Court packed with defenders of the old regime. Under Johnson, Republicans tore a sheaf out of the Federalists' 1801 playbook: saddled with a president they despised, they shrank the Court.

Johnson had been president only six weeks when the 79-year-old Jackson appointee John Catron died. Johnson took nearly a year to nominate a replacement (Henry Stanbery), by which time the president's relations with congressional Republicans had deteriorated so badly that Johnson had little chance of getting his pick confirmed—particularly not one who was thought (correctly) to have had a hand in drafting Johnson's veto of recent civil rights legislation. To ensure that Johnson would not be able to name a replacement, Republicans in Congress abolished the seat, reducing the Court's membership to nine and the number of Southerners to one, and making Lincoln's appointees a majority on the Court. Congress also rearranged the circuits once more, shrinking the number of entirely southern circuits from three to two. Then, as insurance, Republicans stipulated that upon the next vacancy the Court would be cut to eight members, thereby denying Johnson any chance of nominating a justice. To no one's surprise, the next justice to die was the 77-year-old James Wayne, the last of the long-serving Jackson appointees. With Wayne's death in 1867, Republicans had purged the Court of its last Southerner.[64]

For three decades prior to the Civil War, Jacksonian Democrats had fashioned a southern-dominated Supreme Court that appeared to be an impregnable fortress of states' rights dogma. In just six short years, anti-slavery Republicans had transformed the Court into a radically different body—one dominated by Northerners and deeply skeptical of states' rights. So long as Reconstruction continued, Republicans showed no inclination to remedy the Court's gross geographic imbalance. All four of Ulysses Grant's appointees—three to fill vacancies and one to fill the ninth seat that Congress restored immediately after Grant became president—were northern Republicans, leaving the South shut out of the Court despite two of the nine circuits being composed entirely of southern states. In addition, Republicans pushed through the Judiciary Act of 1869, which significantly curtailed the justice's circuit-riding responsibilities and created one full-time circuit judge for each of the nine circuits, thereby resurrecting something closely akin to the Federalist plan of 1801. The 1869 act not only gave Grant the opportunity to select nine additional Republican judges but also helped to fortify the federal judiciary in the former Confederate states.

THE RISE OF JUDICIAL SUPREMACY

In the 80 years between 1789 and 1869, Congress and the president altered the size of the Supreme Court six times: twice (1801 and 1867) Congress shrank the Court to limit the president's power of appointment, and four times (1807, 1837, 1863, and 1869) Congress expanded the Court to help the president remake the Court. Then a strange thing happened. The Court remained fixed at nine members for the next 150 years and counting. Why?

One factor was the Judiciary Act of 1891, which finally cut the knot between the circuit courts and the Supreme Court. With justices no longer required to ride circuit, legislators could not use the expansion of the Union as justification for expanding the Court. After 1891, the partisan motives for modifying the Court's size would be transparently obvious to all.

But transparent partisanship did not stop the Federalists and Republicans from shrinking the Court in 1801 and 1867, respectively. Moreover, it does not explain why, when six states stretching from South Dakota to Washington were added to the Union in 1889 and 1890, the Republican-controlled Congress passed the 1891 act rather than expanding the Court to give Republican president Benjamin Harrison the opportunity to select an additional justice or two. The underlying causes of the Court's newfound stability lie elsewhere, in the politics of the late nineteenth and early twentieth centuries.

The Court expanded during the presidencies of Jefferson, Jackson, and Lincoln because each president came to power at what political scientist Stephen Skowronek describes as a political moment of reconstruction, a moment in which the old regime stood discredited and the new president and his party could claim a popular warrant for reconstructing the nation's political order. No such reconstructive moments occurred in the late nineteenth century. Between 1869 and 1899, Republicans controlled the Senate in all but six years and the presidency in all but eight. Only once, during the first two years of Grover Cleveland's disastrous second stint as president, did the Democrats command both the Senate and the presidency.[65]

When Cleveland became president for the first time in 1885, the Supreme Court consisted entirely of Republican appointees (although Stephen Field, a Lincoln appointee, was a Democrat). But unlike Jefferson, Jackson, and Lincoln, Cleveland had few complaints with the ideological direction of a conservative Court bent on striking down state laws deemed to impede national economic development. When vacancies opened up on the Court, Cleveland picked conservative Democrats, who reinforced rather than challenged the late nineteenth-century Court's understanding of its role as protector of the economic liberties guaranteed by the Constitution.[66]

Both Cleveland and his Republican successor Benjamin Harrison viewed the judiciary in essentially the same terms: as an essential bulwark against economic radicalism and social disorder. Packed with railroad attorneys and insulated from popular pressures, the Supreme Court seemed ideally suited to protect property rights "against the radical experimentation of social reformers." Both Cleveland and Harrison applauded Court decisions that restricted the states' powers to regulate railroad rates and both looked to the federal judiciary to issue injunctions against striking workers. Whereas Jefferson, Jackson, and Lincoln had vigorously contested judicial supremacy, Cleveland and Harrison championed it, insisting that in a well-ordered constitutional system the courts, rather than the legislature or the president, must have the final word on contested matters. It was during these crucial decades at the end of the nineteenth century, as political scientist Keith Whittington has shown, that the idea of judicial supremacy—that the Constitution means what judges say it means—put down deep roots in American society.[67]

Things might have been different had William Jennings Bryan defeated William McKinley in 1896. The economic and political forces that backed Bryan were as outraged by the Court's pro-business rulings as the anti-slavery forces backing Lincoln had been at the Court's pro-slaveholder rulings. James Weaver, the Populist presidential candidate in 1892, drew the comparison explicitly, reminding his audiences that when judges "not subject to popular control" had sided with the slave power, the nation had "no alternative but the sword." In the 1896 campaign, Bryan's Populist supporters vented their anger at the Court's striking down of a federal income tax (*Pollock v. Farmers' Loan and Trust Co.*). The "judicial oligarchy," they complained, was trying to "rob the people of the powers of self-government," and it was up to the people to decide "whether they will accept the decision of the Supreme Court as being final." To bring the Court to heel, Bryan's backers urged a host of judicial reforms, including judicial elections and empowering Congress to override a federal court's constitutional judgment.[68]

Had Bryan and his insurgent coalition prevailed in 1896, they would likely have challenged judicial supremacy as vigorously as Lincoln, Jackson, and Jefferson. Admittedly, in accepting the Democratic nomination Bryan was careful to disavow any intention "to dispute the authority of the Supreme Court" or "the binding force" of judicial decisions. But Lincoln, too, had been careful to insist that his criticisms were not intended as "any assault upon the court or the judges." And Jackson and Jefferson also challenged judicial supremacy while declaiming any intention of undermining an independent judiciary.[69]

The political pressure on Bryan to contest judicial supremacy or to reform the Court would likely have been even greater than during past reconstructive moments. For not only would a victorious Bryan have faced a conservative Court strongly opposed to his reform ambitions, but, unlike Lincoln and Jackson, he faced the prospect of an entrenched Court with few imminent vacancies; in fact, only one seat—that of Lincoln appointee Stephen Field—opened up during McKinley's presidency.

Bryan's defensiveness, however, provides a clue to two important differences between his circumstances and those that faced Jefferson, Jackson, and Lincoln. First was the increased acceptance of judicial authority in American society. Second was the resilience of the regime being challenged by Bryan and defended by the Court. Both of these factors contributed to the eagerness with which Republicans seized on respect for the law and courts as a defining theme in the 1896 campaign. Even conservative Democrats joined the chorus of condemnation of "all efforts to ... impair the confidence and respect" in which the Court was "deservedly held" by the American public.[70]

The emphatic Republican victory in 1896 was widely viewed as a repudiation of radicalism and a vindication of "the dignity and supremacy of the courts." Emboldened by McKinley's victory, the Court became even more vigilant in its scrutiny of state laws that unreasonably impinged on economic liberties, most famously in *Lochner v. New York* (1905), in which the Court struck down a state law limiting the number of hours that bakers could work in a day (10) and in a week (60). A majority composed of two Cleveland appointees, two Harrison appointees, and a McKinley appointee decided that such a regulation was "an unreasonable, unnecessary arbitrary interference with the right and liberty of the individual to contract."[71]

Animated by the spirit of "Lochnerism," states' courts also became increasingly bold in striking down government regulations. In 1911, for instance, New York's top court relied on *Lochner* in striking down the state's workmen's compensation law—a ruling that so outraged ex-president Theodore Roosevelt that he called for changing state constitutions to allow the people to vote "whether or not they will permit the judges' interpretation of the Constitution to stand."[72]

In his campaign to wrest the Republican nomination from President William Howard Taft in 1912, Roosevelt attacked judicial supremacy as profoundly undemocratic. In the "Charter for Democracy" speech that launched his campaign, Roosevelt thundered: "If the courts have the final say-so on all legislative acts, and if no appeal can lie from them to the people, then they are the irresponsible masters of the people." Although Roosevelt insisted that his call for popular referenda on judicial decisions applied only to state courts, his argument that democracy demanded that the people be the final judges of what was constitutional applied with as much force to federal as to state courts.[73]

By attacking the judiciary in the name of democracy, Roosevelt was branded a radical demagogue. Conservative Republicans rallied around Taft, who made the independence and authority of the courts the centerpiece of his unsuccessful reelection campaign. In fomenting division between the progressive and conservative wings of the party, Roosevelt helped to elect Democrat Woodrow Wilson, who throughout the campaign artfully avoided getting drawn into his opponents' war of words over the judiciary. Fearful of being tarred with the brush of radicalism that had blackened both Bryan and Roosevelt, President Wilson showed little appetite for judicial reform and even less for renewing Roosevelt's assault on judicial supremacy.[74]

Wilson also had few opportunities to remake the Supreme Court in his two terms, largely because his predecessor Taft was gifted six appointments in four years. Of the three picks Wilson did make, one turned out to be a reactionary (James McReynolds) and another (John Clarke) quit after five years. Only Wilson's selection of Louis Brandeis made a lasting progressive mark on the Court. Wilson's presidency, in any event, proved an aberration. After Wilson, Republican hegemony resumed. Twelve uninterrupted years of Republican control of the presidency and Congress solidified the conservative cast of the Court, which under the leadership of Chief Justice William Howard Taft (appointed by Warren Harding in 1921) became increasingly aggressive in striking down both state and federal laws.[75]

FRANKLIN ROOSEVELT V. THE SUPREME COURT

In the 1932 campaign, Democrat Franklin Roosevelt had a simple task: fixing responsibility for the Great Depression on the incumbent Herbert Hoover and the Republican Party. Every campaign speech he gave had the same fundamental purpose: to remind Americans, as he told a crowd in the Baltimore Armory one week before the election, that the economic catastrophe had occurred while "the Republican Party was in complete control of all branches of the federal government." During the campaign, Roosevelt generally stuck closely to his prepared script, but that night in Baltimore he departed from the text just once, to enumerate each branch that the Republicans controlled: "the Executive, the Senate, the House of Representatives and, I might add for good measure, to make it complete, the Supreme Court as well."[76]

Republicans immediately pounced on Roosevelt's slip. They expressed shock that a presidential candidate would describe the Court as Republican. "There never has been and never can be any politics in our Supreme Court," insisted Silas Strawn, a prominent Republican and past president of both the American Bar Association and the Chamber of Commerce. Roosevelt was roundly condemned by Republicans for "dragging the Supreme Court into partisan politics." Hoover slammed Roosevelt for his "atrocious" slander on the Court's integrity and objectivity, and warned Americans against the "deeper," subversive implications of Roosevelt's statement: the "sinister" threat posed by the radical notion that the Court should be made "subservient" to the president and "an instrument of party policy."[77]

Privately, Roosevelt was unapologetic. Writing to Senator James Byrnes (who Roosevelt would later name to the Court), Roosevelt insisted that what he had said the previous evening about the judiciary was true. "Whatever is in a man's heart," Roosevelt explained, "is apt to come to his tongue," and he vowed not to "make any explanations or apology" for it. But if Roosevelt did not apologize for his jab at the Court, he also did not repeat it. His campaign managers made sure of that. They wanted the final week of the campaign focused on the unpopular Hoover, not on the nation's "sacred shrine," as Taft had called the Court. Despite the Republicans' best efforts to fan the flames of outrage against Roosevelt's "slur" against the Court, the controversy quickly receded to the back pages, and Hoover and the Republicans in Congress were resoundingly rejected by voters. Of the old Republican regime, only the Court remained.[78]

At first it appeared that the Court might not be an insurmountable obstacle to Roosevelt's agenda. Just a few days after Roosevelt's swearing in, an excited Felix Frankfurter informed the president that two of the Court's most conservative and oldest justices—Willis Van Devanter and George Sutherland—were likely to step down soon.

Frankfurter, who had close relations with several of the justices, knew that both Van Devanter and Sutherland had wanted to retire in 1932 but had changed their plans when the Republican Congress cut in half the pensions of retired federal judges. Now that the new Democratic Congress had restored the pensions, Frankfurter thought the two vacancies would certainly follow. But in the wake of Roosevelt's election, the two conservative justices had reconsidered, deciding not to quit after all. As it turned out, during Roosevelt's first term not a single vacancy opened up on the Court, something that had not occurred since James Monroe's first term, more than a century before.[79]

Judging the New Deal

The Supreme Court that Roosevelt inherited was conservative but not uniformly so. Four justices—Van Devanter, Sutherland, McReynolds, and Pierce Butler—were conservatives in the *Lochner* mold, demanding that the Court serve as a "shield" against government regulations that impaired economic liberty. The remaining five justices were less doctrinaire. Two were progressive or liberal Democrats—Brandeis and Benjamin Cardozo—who seemed likely to uphold the president's policies. The other three justices were all Republicans—Harlan Fiske Stone, Chief Justice Hughes, and Owen Roberts—but of a more pragmatic bent.[80]

A Coolidge appointee and a close friend of Hoover's, Stone considered Roosevelt "an utterly impossible man for President" but was also committed to judicial restraint and exasperated by his colleagues' dogmatic Lochnerism. Hughes was more conservative than Stone, but had been a two-term progressive governor of New York—as well as Republican presidential nominee and secretary of state—and his political antenna attuned him to shifting currents of public opinion. Of the Republican swing justices, Roberts was the most conservative, but he too seemed ready to abandon the absolutist view of property and contract rights that had prevailed on the Court in the 1920s. In March 1934, for instance, writing for a 5–4 majority, Roberts upheld a New York state law that empowered a board to set the price of milk, explaining that the Constitution did not give "any one the liberty to conduct his business in such fashion as to inflict injury upon the public at large." The power "to promote the general welfare," Roberts concluded, was "inherent in government."[81]

The Court's conservative dissenters railed against the majority's abandonment of fixed constitutional principle while liberal New Dealers hailed the Court's newfound pragmatism. Both sides seemed convinced that the Supreme Court was determined to modify its jurisprudence in order to avoid provoking an institutional showdown with Roosevelt. But the cases that came before the Court in the first year and a half did not involve the New Deal itself, but rather state policies. Not until the end of 1934, in the immediate wake of the Republicans' crushing defeat in the midterm elections, did the first of the cases challenging the New Deal finally make their way to the Supreme Court.

The first case the Court decided involved an obscure section of the National Industrial Recovery Act (NIRA) in which Congress gave the president broad authority to stem the flow of "hot oil," that is, oil that was being illegally produced and transported. States had tried to limit oil production to counter plummeting oil prices—in 1933 a barrel of oil fetched ten cents, the same as a tin of Campbell's Soup—but their regulatory efforts had been undermined by bootleggers transporting oil across state lines. Following passage of the NIRA, the president made the production and transport of hot oil a federal crime, and through aggressive enforcement the government had slowed "the torrent of illegal oil ... to a trickle." In an 8–1 decision (Cardoza was the lone dissenter), the Court struck down the hot oil provision as an excessively broad delegation of legislative power to the executive—even though the president had done pretty much precisely what Congress had wanted him to do.[82]

Publicly, Roosevelt was unruffled. At a press conference, he welcomed the Court's advice on improving the statute. And the administration promptly got Congress to fix the provision so as to meet the Court's approval. But behind the scenes Roosevelt was profoundly concerned. Many parts of the New Deal legislation included broad delegation of authority to the president to combat the economic emergency. And it did not seem inconceivable that the Court would use this elastic legal doctrine to strike down a broad swath of New Deal legislation.[83]

The president's anxiety was heightened by the Court's skeptical questioning during oral arguments in a case that challenged the constitutionality of legislation that voided any contract that guaranteed payment in gold. The measure was part of a complex package of policies through which Congress and the president had sought to stabilize the nation's fragile finances. In oral argument, the attorney general warned the Court that an adverse ruling would result in a "stupendous catastrophe" that would plunge the nation into economic chaos. Alarmed that the Court was angling to do precisely that, Roosevelt prepared an emergency proclamation and a radio address that breathed "outright defiance" of the Court. The Court, he planned to tell the people, had interpreted the case by "the letter of the law as they saw it." But as president he had a higher duty: "to protect the people of the United States" from economic calamity.[84]

The showdown was averted when a divided Court sided with the administration, ruling that Congress had the power to regulate the nation's currency. Roosevelt was elated, but the closeness of the 5–4 decision and the vehemence of the dissenters tempered the celebrations. Roosevelt put aside the defiant speech he had prepared, but not before leaking portions of it to the *New York Times*, which reported the president's comments in a front-page article. Had Roosevelt delivered the speech, announced the *Times*'s Arthur Krock, "it would have marked the most sensational and historic episode in the constitutional history of the United States since Andrew Jackson said of a Supreme Court ruling: 'John Marshall has made this decision; now let him enforce it.'"[85]

Roosevelt wanted to make sure that the Court got the message. But its next ruling, in the spring of 1935, suggested that the Court's conservatives were not listening. The case involved the Railroad Retirement Act of 1934, which established a mandatory pension system for railroad workers. Workers contributed one-third and employers two-thirds of the pension fund. Writing for a 5–4 majority, Roberts struck down the law in sweeping language reminiscent of *Lochner*. Among the law's defects, complained the former railroad attorney, was that it paid no heed to the interests of business and was enacted "solely in the interest of the employee ... purely for social ends." The breadth of the Court's reasoning seemed to imperil the administration's entire social agenda, including the Social Security legislation currently winding its way through Congress.[86]

Three weeks later, on what quickly became known as "Black Monday," the Court announced three more decisions, each unanimous and each ruling against the administration. The Court clamped down on the president's power of removal in *Humphrey's Executor v. United States* (discussed in Chapter 8), struck down the Frazier–Lemke Act limiting the power of banks to repossess bankrupt farms, and in *Schechter Poultry Corp. v. United States* invalidated the National Recovery Administration (NRA) on the grounds that Congress had delegated lawmaking authority to the agency that was so ill-defined as to be "virtually unfettered." Seven judges on the Court seized the opportunity presented in *Schechter* not only to strike down the NRA as an illegal delegation of congressional power but to limit Congress's regulatory powers under the interstate commerce clause. Even had the NRA operated under clear legislative guidelines, the Court ruled, it could not regulate the Schechter brothers' poultry plants because neither the chickens nor the plants' workers were engaged in interstate commerce. Admittedly, the chickens had originated out of state but, Chief Justice Hughes maintained, they "had come to a permanent rest within the state" and therefore could not be regulated by Congress.[87]

Over the next year, the Court showed little mercy to the New Deal. In January 1936, in a 6–3 ruling, the Court invalidated the Agricultural Adjustment Act (AAA). In a bid to arrest the deflationary spiral of agricultural overproduction and falling farm prices, the AAA imposed a tax on textile mills, canneries, meatpackers, and other processors of farm goods and then used that money to pay farmers to plant fewer crops and raise less livestock. Writing for the Court, Roberts conceded that the government had the power to tax and spend for the general welfare, but insisted that the act was still unconstitutional, for two reasons. First, the processing tax wasn't a tax under the meaning of the Constitution. The word "tax," Roberts insisted, "has never been thought to connote expropriation of money from one group for the benefit of another." A tax, under the Constitution, must only be a means of raising revenue. Second, agriculture was "a purely local activity," and under the Tenth Amendment must therefore be left to the states. Roberts hastened to add that the Court neither condemned nor approved of the policy of the legislature. In rendering its judgment, the Court simply "lay the article of the Constitution which is invoked beside the statute which is challenged and ... decide[d] whether the latter squares with the former." The Court, Roberts insisted, was just a constitutional umpire, not a political player.[88]

The umpires struck again in May 1936, this time invalidating the Guffey Coal Act, which established minimum wages, maximum hours, and fair labor practices in the coal industry. Industry compliance was voluntary, but tax refunds were provided to create an incentive to adhere to the regulations. In a 5–4 decision, the Court ruled that Congress had again exceeded its constitutional authority because coal mining was a "local activity." The West Virginia coal company that challenged the law shipped 97 percent of its coal outside of the state, but the Court insisted that while the company's commerce crossed state lines its production process did not. The federal government could not therefore regulate conditions of employment, wages, or labor practices. Under this reasoning, the recently enacted National Labor Relations Act seemed doomed. Indeed, there was little doubt in the president's mind that the Court had determined to make a "clean sweep of all New Deal legislation."[89]

FDR's Court-Packing Plan

The president was under increasing pressure from liberals to do something to halt the Court's "course of destruction," the climax of which came on the final day of the Court's term, when it controversially struck down—again on a 5–4 vote—a New York minimum-wage law for women on the grounds that it violated the liberty of contract. In the year since the *Schechter* decision, countless bills and amendments had been introduced in Congress to curb the Court's powers. Some required the Court to muster seven or even nine votes before it could strike down legislation as unconstitutional. Others gave Congress the power to override a Supreme Court decision after an intervening election. Another route proposed was to amend the Constitution to explicitly give to Congress those powers that the Court said it could not find in Article I. In cabinet meetings and private conversations, Roosevelt discussed all of these options with his advisors, including the "distasteful idea" of "packing the Supreme Court" with new justices.[90]

In public, though, Roosevelt continued to say little. Asked at a press conference about the Court's decision on the New York minimum-wage law—a decision so unpopular that even conservative Republicans like Herbert Hoover condemned it—Roosevelt would acknowledge only that the Court had placed government in "no-man's land." Asked what he planned to do about it, Roosevelt brushed aside the inquiry, saying "I think that is about all there is to say on it." Many liberals urged the president to make the Court and constitutional reform a campaign issue, but Roosevelt refused. Polls showed the election was close, and the president's political instincts told him to run instead on the achievements of the New Deal, the reckless greed of big business, and the failures of Hooverism ("hear-nothing, see-nothing, do-nothing Government").[91]

Roosevelt remembered only too well the glee with which, in 1932, Hoover had pounced on his charge about the Court being Republican. Nor had he forgotten the hammering he took in the press after deriding the *Schechter* Court's "horse-and-buggy definition of interstate commerce." Moreover, as a young New York state legislator in 1912, he had watched the Republican legal establishment pummel his Progressive cousin Theodore for supporting popular recall of judicial decisions. He knew, too, that in the 1924 election, the Progressive Party candidate Robert La Follette had faced devastating attacks from both parties for his support of a constitutional amendment giving Congress the power to overturn Court decisions. And in case Roosevelt was inclined to forget, La Follette's 1924 running mate, Montana Senator Burton Wheeler, was on hand to remind him: "avoid the Court issue at all costs," Wheeler advised, "lest history repeat itself."[92]

Following Wheeler's advice and his own instincts, Roosevelt won reelection in a landslide. Now he was determined to bring the Court to heel. Some advisors counseled patience. His massive victory, they argued, was bound to chasten the Court—as the old saw had it, the Court would follow the election returns. Moreover, the Court was now very old, older than at any time in the nation's history, and the president could thus afford to let nature take its course. Roosevelt was skeptical; he had heard these arguments before. People recited the old saw after the 1934 elections, yet the Court had become more rather than less conservative. And after the 1932 election, he had been assured that two of the elderly conservatives would leave the Court, yet four years later they were all still there.

Roosevelt believed that as long as he was in the White House the conservative justices would not quit, no matter how ill or old they were.[93]

Roosevelt felt he could afford to wait no longer. The Court would soon sit in judgment of some of the most cherished parts of the New Deal, including the Social Security Act and the National Labor Relations Act. Initially, he had been inclined toward a constitutional amendment of some kind, but the more he thought about that remedy the more skeptical he had become. Progressives had been trying for 13 years to get a child-labor amendment and were still nowhere close to success. Moreover, an amendment to expand Congress's powers would seem to concede that the Court had been right to invalidate the New Deal measures as inconsistent with the Constitution. Roosevelt reluctantly reached the conclusion that the only viable option was to put on the Court justices who would support the New Deal.[94]

On February 5, 1937, Roosevelt unveiled his plan, which he said was needed to relieve the burden of overcrowded court dockets on "aged or infirm judges" and inject "younger blood" into the courts. For every federal judge who did not retire upon turning 70, the president would nominate an additional judge to that court. Since two-thirds of the Supreme Court was over 70, Roosevelt would immediately be able to name six new justices.[95]

The plan was audacious. Yes, the Court had been expanded before during the presidencies of Jefferson, Jackson, Lincoln, and Grant. But in each of these cases the proposal for expansion emanated from Congress. Roosevelt, in contrast, had not consulted with anybody in Congress before announcing his plan. Moreover, the total number of seats added during those four presidencies was five, one less than Roosevelt was proposing to add at a single swoop. And it had been seven decades since the Court's size had been altered. Americans may not have believed the number nine was divinely decreed, but most assumed it was an immutable feature of America's constitutional order.

Roosevelt fully expected his plan to provoke a "grand fight." During the 1936 campaign Roosevelt had welcomed the hatred of his enemies and had prevailed in a landslide. Now he seemed to be inviting their hatred again, goading them to attack him, confident that he would prevail again. Roosevelt's conservative enemies followed the script, assailing the president's "revolutionary" plan and dictatorial ambitions. What caught Roosevelt by surprise was the strong opposition among his supporters in Congress. Democratic congressional leaders were upset that the president had not consulted them. Others were angry at the way the president had tried to conceal his true designs. Nobody believed the president's claim that he was merely trying to relieve overcrowded court dockets.[96]

Roosevelt had not banked on needing to rally the country to push a recalcitrant Congress to back his plan. Instead he had been relying on the new congressional math: Democrats now outnumbered Republicans in the Senate by nearly 5–1 and in the House by almost 4–1. After it became clear that the president had miscalculated, he was forced to take his case to the country and to lay out the real reasons for his reform. In a nationally broadcast "fireside chat" on March 9, 1937, Roosevelt explained that his reform was necessary because the Supreme Court "has been acting not as a judicial body, but as a policy-making body." Having "improperly set itself up as a third house of the Congress—a

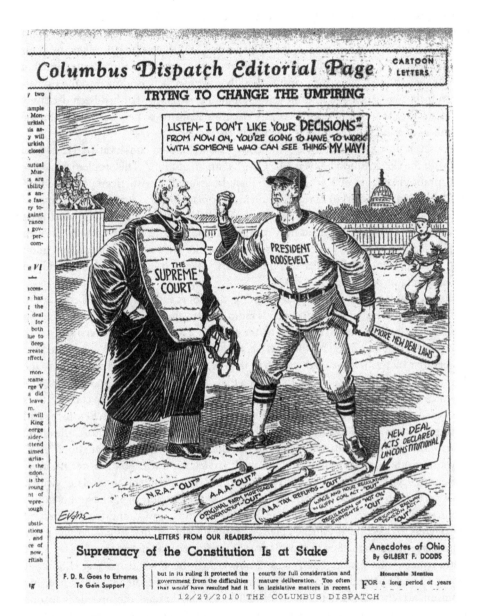

A cartoon from February 10, 1937 showing an unhappy President Roosevelt threatening the umpire, Chief Justice Charles Evans Hughes, for striking down New Deal legislation. The cartoon suggests that in trying to pack the Court and "change the umpiring," Roosevelt was doing violence to the rules of the game.

Courtesy: *The Columbus Dispatch.*

super-legislature," the Court had prevented the country's elected representatives from stabilizing agriculture, improving the conditions of labor, safeguarding business against unfair competition, protecting national resources—in short, "meeting squarely our modern social and economic conditions." Although the conservative majority claimed to be following the dictates of the Constitution, they were in fact "reading into the Constitution their own personal economic" philosophy, a philosophy that had been decisively repudiated by the people in three successive elections. Reform was necessary to prevent the prejudices of a few from thwarting "the will of the people."[97]

Roosevelt portrayed his plan as eminently moderate, even conservative. He had no beef with the Constitution or even "the Court as an institution." The problem was a few recalcitrant ideologues on the bench. His plan, he assured the American people, aimed only "to restore the Court to its rightful and historic place in our system of Constitutional Government." That was precisely why he rejected the many proposals that had been introduced in Congress to amend the Constitution and curb the Court's powers. Instead his plan left it to the Court to correct its own errors, for "the Court itself can best undo what the Court has done." But enabling the Court to take self-correcting action required first changing its personnel.

But then, as if to prove the president wrong, the Court suddenly changed course. On March 29, three weeks after the president's radio address, the Court upheld a Washington minimum-wage law almost identical to the one the Court had controversially struck down the previous spring. The vote was again 5–4 but this time Roberts abandoned the conservative bloc—the so-called "switch in time that saved nine"—and signed on to the chief justice's opinion repudiating the dogma that "liberty of contract" was an "absolute and uncontrollable liberty." Two weeks later Roberts again abandoned the conservatives and joined a 5–4 majority in upholding the National Labor Relations Act. Before the end of its spring term, the Court also upheld the Social Security Act. To cap it off, one of the Court's die-hard conservatives, Willis Van Devanter, announced his resignation.[98]

Van Devanter's resignation and the Court's strategic U-turn took the steam out of Roosevelt's Court-packing plan. Supporters urged the president to declare victory. However, Roosevelt refused to abandon his plan, despite the ebbing of public support and a stinging rebuke from the Democratic-controlled Senate Judiciary Committee, which called on Congress to reject the president's plan "so emphatically ... that its parallel will never again be presented to the free representatives of the free people of America."[99]

Recognizing that his original proposal now lacked the votes for passage, Roosevelt threw his weight behind a compromise plan put together by Senate majority leader Joe Robinson, which increased the age from 70 to 75 and limited the president to one appointment a year. Roosevelt gave up little under this "compromise" since four of the Supreme Court justices were 75 or older. By the end of his term, under this compromise plan, Roosevelt would be guaranteed the opportunity to pick five Supreme Court justices. Passage of the plan seemed within reach until Robinson died of a heart attack, killing any hope Roosevelt had of securing his reform. Six days after Robinson's death, the Senate buried the Court-packing plan by a resounding 70–20 vote.[100]

Roosevelt finally had to concede political defeat, but he felt he had won the constitutional war. The Court had retreated from its "horse and buggy" jurisprudence, saving the New Deal and giving future Congresses broad latitude to legislate in the national interest. But the way in which Roosevelt chose to wage the battle did incalculable harm to his party and his presidency. Squandering his popular mandate, the president plunged the Democratic Party into a debilitating fight that sidetracked important reforms and left lasting scars within the party. The Court fight was the anvil on which was forged an enduring conservative anti-New Deal coalition.[101]

Without rerunning the reel of history, it is impossible to know for certain what the Court or Congress would have done in the absence of Roosevelt's Court-packing plan. Historians have debated this question ever since. But it seems clear that Roosevelt did unnecessary damage to his presidency, the Democratic Party, and the New Deal by stubbornly pressing ahead with the Court-packing plan even after Van Devanter's resignation and the Court's retreat. If Roosevelt won the constitutional war, that war had been well won by the end of May 1937. Robinson's compromise proposal was unnecessary. Even with its defeat, Roosevelt ended up replacing five justices by January 1940: three through deaths, and two (including Van Devanter) through resignations. In the end, Roosevelt packed the Court the old-fashioned way: by winning elections.

A "Reinvigorated, Liberal-Minded Judiciary"

In his March 1937 fireside chat, Roosevelt had called for "a reinvigorated, liberal-minded Judiciary"—which, in practice, meant Democrats who supported the New Deal. Liberals welcomed Roosevelt's liberal judicial appointments, but many had deep misgivings about a president chiding the Court for thwarting the will of the people. In his fireside chat, Roosevelt likened the American government to "a three-horse team." The problem, as Roosevelt explained it, was that two of the horses (the president and Congress) were pulling together to plow the people's furrow while the third (the Supreme Court) was not. The American people were the drivers of the three-horse team, Roosevelt reasoned, and they expected "the third horse to pull in unison with the other two." But many liberals were uneasy with this folksy metaphor, which seemed to leave no role for the Court to protect the rights of unpopular minorities from misguided or oppressive majorities.[102]

Even after the defeat of his Court-packing plan, Roosevelt still ruminated over the appropriate limits of judicial power. In September 1937, speaking at the 150th anniversary of the Constitution's signing, Roosevelt described the Constitution as "a layman's document, not a lawyer's contract." He reminded his audience that the Constitution "says nothing about any power of the Court to declare legislation unconstitutional," and that the convention delegates repeatedly "voted down proposals to give Justices of the Court a veto over legislation." This speech, however, was the last the country would hear from Roosevelt about the dangers of judicial power.[103]

The main thrust of liberal thought was moving in a different direction, one foreshadowed in a famous footnote in a 1938 Supreme Court case, *United States v. Carolene Products*. Writing for a nearly unanimous Court (only McReynolds dissented), Chief Justice Stone announced that in reviewing laws regulating "ordinary commercial transactions" the Court would use a "rational basis" standard. That is, so long as there was a rational basis for the policy, the courts should uphold the statute. But in a footnote, Stone added that "more exacting judicial scrutiny" might be applied when addressing legislation that affected political participation, discrimination against minorities, or rights explicitly conferred by the Constitution. Liberal courts, in short, would give Congress broad power to legislate in the economic sphere while vigilantly protecting civil liberties and civil rights.[104]

A harbinger of this new liberal jurisprudence was a 1944 case involving a legal challenge to the Texas Democratic Party's all-white primary. In 1935, writing for a unanimous Court, Owen Roberts had upheld the all-white primary on the grounds that the Democratic Party was a voluntary association that had a right to exclude blacks. Now, only nine years later, Roosevelt's liberal-minded Court reversed itself, ruling that the all-white primary unconstitutionally infringed on the right to vote. Only one justice dissented, the one that Roosevelt had not nominated: Roberts. The following year, the disgruntled Roberts quit, though not before filing over 50 dissents in his last term.[105]

At the outset of the twentieth century, those on the left had looked on the courts as "the agents of capital," but by the middle of the twentieth century liberals had become the nation's most devoted champions of judicial supremacy. The Court seemed to be the institution most willing to protect minorities—particularly African Americans—from local and state prejudices, intimidation, and violence. When a Court made up of eight Roosevelt and Truman appointees—plus the new Chief Justice Earl Warren, appointed by Dwight Eisenhower—unanimously struck down racial segregation in public schools in *Brown v. Board of Education* (1954), it was liberals who most loudly demanded that the president enforce the Court's edict, by force if necessary.[106]

President Eisenhower was not happy with the *Brown* decision. Politically, he knew enforcement of the decision would endanger Republicans' political prospects in the South. Personally, he felt that it would set back race relations "at least fifteen years." To integrate by force, Eisenhower believed, was "just plain NUTS." But Eisenhower never seriously entertained a Jacksonesque challenge to the Court. Although he never endorsed the Court's decision, he did not defy it either. "The Supreme Court has spoken," Eisenhower announced, "and I am sworn to uphold the constitutional process in this country; and I will obey." His duty was clear, he told his brother, because the Constitution is "what the Supreme Court says it is." In 1957, when Arkansas governor Orval Faubus defied a court order to desegregate Little Rock's Central High School, Eisenhower put aside his political and personal misgivings and sent in federal troops. In an address to the nation, Eisenhower explained that "Our personal opinions about the decision have no bearing on the matter of enforcement; the responsibility and authority of the Supreme Court to interpret the Constitution are very clear." Indeed, the entire "basis of our individual rights and freedoms" rested on the president "carrying out ... the decisions of the Federal Courts."[107]

The reinvigorated, liberal-minded judiciary stirred calls for "massive resistance" in the South, but in the rest of the country judicial supremacy seemed an inviolable principle. Southern complaints about judges substituting their "personal and political and social ideas for the established law of the land" were dismissed as the lawless wheeze of reactionaries and racists. Among liberals especially, judicial supremacy was now an unshakable article of faith. Elected representatives, in the view of liberals, could not be trusted with constitutional interpretation because they were too easily swayed by the prejudices and biases of majorities.[108]

Liberals applauded as the Vinson (1946–1953) and Warren (1953–1969) Courts struck down not only all-white primaries and racially segregated schools but also racially restrictive covenants in property deeds *(Shelley v. Kraemer,* 1948) and prohibitions on inter-racial marriage *(Loving v. Virginia,* 1967). They celebrated Court opinions nullifying legislative malapportionment *(Baker v. Carr,* 1962), religious instruction and prayer in public schools *(McCollum v. Board of Education,* 1948; *Engel v. Vitale,* 1962), and a state prohibition on the use of contraceptives by married people *(Griswold v. Connecticut,* 1965). Other important liberal legal landmarks included the application of the exclusionary rule to the states *(Mapp v. Ohio,* 1961), the right of poor people to a lawyer in all criminal cases *(Gideon v. Wainwright,* 1963), and the right of the accused to be read their rights before police questioning *(Miranda v. Arizona,* 1966).

Between 1963 and 1969, the heyday of judicial liberalism, the Warren Court struck down state and local statutes at a rate unsurpassed by any previous Court, even the activist Taft Court of the 1920s. The 113 state and local laws invalidated by the Warren Court during those seven years were nearly three times the number struck down by the Court in its first 75 years.[109]

TILTING RIGHT

During the presidential campaign of 1968, Richard Nixon blamed the Warren Court's judicial activism for strengthening "the criminal forces" in society and contributing to a breakdown in "law and order." If elected, Nixon promised, he would select judges who would strictly interpret the Constitution, not "make law." Nixon's critique of judicial activism would become a staple of Republican rhetoric over the next half century, but ironically it would be one of Nixon's appointees, Harry Blackmun, who would author the opinion in the case that would become the Republican touchstone of judicial activism: *Roe v. Wade.*[110]

Nixon's Judicial Selections and the Lessons of *Roe v. Wade*

Decided in 1973, *Roe* rested upon the finding that there was a constitutional right to privacy that encompassed a woman's right to choose whether to have an abortion. Blackmun's opinion erected an elaborate trimester scheme, which forbade any state restrictions on a woman's right to choose in the first trimester of a pregnancy, allowed modest restrictions in the second trimester, and granted the state broad scope to legislate in the last trimester. Two other Nixon appointees, Lewis Powell and a reluctant Chief Justice Warren Burger, sided with Blackmun. The only dissenters were William Rehnquist, Nixon's fourth and final Supreme Court appointee, and Kennedy appointee Byron White, who condemned *Roe* as an "exercise of raw judicial power."[111]

Roe polarized American politics between "pro-choice" liberals and "pro-life" conservatives. For liberals, the decision affirmed their faith in the judiciary as the institution best able to protect civil rights and civil liberties. Even a Republican judiciary, it seemed, could be trusted to safeguard individual rights. After all, of the nine justices who decided *Roe*, six had been appointed by Republican presidents, and the seven-person majority included only two Democratic appointees, liberals Thurgood Marshall and William Douglas.

Conservative Republicans drew a different lesson from *Roe*. The problem was that Republican presidents had failed to adequately vet their selections. A slipshod selection process saddled Eisenhower with what he reportedly called the two worst mistakes of his presidency: the appointments of Earl Warren and William Brennan. And the same had happened to Nixon, despite his pledge to appoint only strict constructionists who would leave legislating to the people's elected representatives. In order to weed out the stealth liberals, conservatives argued that Republican presidents needed to be far more systematic in vetting the political ideology and judicial philosophy of judicial candidates.[112]

This conservative critique was not entirely fair to Nixon. Each of Nixon's four Supreme Court selections, including Blackmun, was more conservative than the justice he replaced (the same was not true for Eisenhower's appointments) and collectively they did pull the Court toward the right, especially on matters of criminal justice, the legal issue that Nixon had cared about most. Moreover, Blackmun's leftward evolution was an aberration. Of the other three Nixon appointees, Rehnquist maintained a profoundly conservative voting record throughout his 34 years on the bench, Burger was as reliable a conservative vote when he retired in 1986 as he was on the day he was appointed, and even the more moderate Powell sided with conservatives more often than liberals throughout his 15 years on the Court. Still, conservatives were right that the Burger Court had not initiated a constitutional counter-revolution comparable to that achieved during Franklin Roosevelt's second term. And on issues such as abortion or affirmative action, the Burger Court as well as the lower courts had moved in a liberal rather than a conservative direction.[113]

In making lower-court appointments (district courts and circuit courts of appeals), Nixon picked judges overwhelmingly from within his own party's ranks, as his predecessors also had. Only 7 percent of Nixon's approximately 225 lower-court selections went to Democrats—roughly the same percentage that had gone to Republicans in the Johnson, Kennedy, and Truman administrations. Although most of Nixon's appointees were conservative Republicans, the Nixon White House did not systematically screen lower-court judges for their judicial philosophy or policy views, any more than past Democratic administrations had. Despite Nixon's rhetoric about appointing only "strict constructionists," traditional concerns with party patronage figured more prominently than judicial philosophy in his administration's judicial selections.[114]

Judicial Selection in the Reagan Administration

Ronald Reagan's campaign rhetoric in 1980 was not that different from Nixon's in 1968. Like Nixon, Reagan deplored judges legislating from the bench and promised to appoint judges who would defer to elected representatives and who believed in law and order. But unlike the Nixon administration, the Reagan White House made judicial selection a top priority and rigorously screened nominees for congruence with the administration's conservative ideology and judicial philosophy. Under Reagan, every judicial candidate, even for district court positions, underwent a daylong interview—interviews that took place only after the administration had carefully scrutinized a candidate's paper trail of speeches, law review articles, and judicial opinions. Candidates were asked not just about their general judicial philosophy but also how they would rule on specific issues, most especially abortion.[115]

Critics accused the administration of imposing an ideological "litmus test" on potential judges. Former attorney general Herbert Brownell, who had been responsible for judicial selection in the Eisenhower administration, found the questioning of candidates "shocking." The administration defended its selection process on the grounds that a president who "fails to scrutinize the legal philosophy of federal judicial nominees courts frustration of his own policy agenda." It was Brownell, after all, who had been responsible for vetting Warren, whose appointment conservatives regarded as the mother of all Republican mistakes.[116]

To critics who claimed that the Reagan administration was politicizing the judiciary, the administration responded that its screening was based on judicial philosophy and not policy outcomes. Administration officials were not asking about a judge's personal views on abortion but rather investigating his or her understanding of the judicial role. As President Reagan explained in a 1983 speech to the American Bar Association, "we've sought judicial nominees who support the limited policymaking role for the Federal courts envisioned by the Constitution" and "who understand the danger of shortcircuiting the election process and disenfranchising the people through judicial activism."[117]

The administration's claim that the vetting process was designed to select for judicial decision-making processes rather than policy outcomes was disingenuous. The objective was less to discover judges who believed in judicial restraint than to pick judges who would exercise restraint when confronted with conservative policies and conservative majorities. Attorney General Edwin Meese dropped the pretense when he explained that the administration's fundamental aim in appointing judges was "to institutionalize the Reagan revolution so it can't be set aside *no matter what happens in future presidential elections.*" They sought judges, in short, who would promote and protect the administration's conservative policy agenda long after Reagan left the presidency.[118]

By the time Reagan left office, he had appointed almost half of the nation's federal judges and added three new Supreme Court justices: Sandra Day O'Connor, Antonin Scalia, and Anthony Kennedy. He also elevated Rehnquist to the position of chief justice upon Burger's retirement in 1986. Conservatives were generally happy with Reagan's success in stocking the lower courts with reliable conservatives, but they were much less enthusiastic about his Supreme Court selections, particularly O'Connor, the first woman ever to serve on the Court.

In selecting judges for the lower courts, the Reagan White House paid little heed to racial or gender diversity. What mattered to Reagan's team were candidates' beliefs, not the group to which they belonged. But the Supreme Court was different. During the 1980 campaign, Reagan had promised to appoint a woman to the Supreme Court and he demanded that his aides honor that pledge when Potter Stewart announced his retirement in 1981. O'Connor was a conservative Republican—"the most conservative woman we could find," according to one Reagan official—but she disappointed conservative activists on the issue that mattered most to them: abortion. Whereas O'Connor sought to lead the Court toward a compromise that would narrow *Roe* while preserving a woman's constitutional right to terminate a pregnancy, conservative activists desired the overturning of *Roe*.[119]

Reagan had to wait five more years before he had the opportunity to fill another vacancy on the Supreme Court, but when the occasion arrived in 1986 he thrilled his conservative base by choosing Scalia, a trenchant critic of the "imperial judiciary." Conservatives were equally euphoric the following year when Reagan nominated Robert Bork to replace Powell. Scalia had sailed through the Republican Senate with no opposition, but Bork ran into a buzz saw of liberal opposition in a Senate now controlled by Democrats. The administration's screening process had correctly identified the most conservative judicial candidate available, but it failed to take account of changes in the political environment. Democrats had taken control of the Senate in 1986 and substantially outnumbered Republicans. Moreover, Reagan was now a lame-duck president, whose popularity had plummeted after revelations that the administration had illegally sold arms to Iran to fund rebels trying to overthrow the Nicaraguan government. In addition, whereas Scalia had replaced the reliably conservative Burger, Bork was to take the place of a justice who was a crucial swing vote on the Court.[120]

Reagan tried to stem the criticism by portraying Bork as another Powell. But anyone who read Bork's voluminous writings or watched him spar with the Senate Judiciary Committee could see that Bork was nothing like Powell. Whereas Powell was a conservative with deep respect for legal precedents, Bork's jurisprudence of original intent called for a constitutional revolution that would uproot settled precedents. Ultimately, 58 senators voted to reject Bork, including six Republicans.[121]

Reagan reacted to Bork's defeat precisely as Nixon did to the Senate's rejection of Clement Haynsworth: he resolved to pick a nominee who would upset Democrats "just as much" as his first choice. Nixon's disastrous rebound pick was Carswell; Reagan's was Douglas Ginsburg, whose candidacy flamed out after it was revealed he had smoked marijuana with students while a law professor at Harvard University. Chastened and facing the possibility that, with a presidential election looming, the Senate would stall if the president failed to nominate a broadly acceptable candidate, Reagan nominated Anthony Kennedy. Although Kennedy would more often tip the Court in a conservative than a liberal direction, he angered conservatives by siding with liberals in high-profile cases involving abortion rights (*Casey v. Planned Parenthood*, 1992), gay rights (*Romer v. Evans*, 1996; *Lawrence v. Texas*, 2003; and *Obergefell v. Hodges*, 2015), and prayer in public schools (*Lee v. Weisman*, 1992). It did not take long before conservatives viewed Kennedy as yet another in a long line of Republican mistakes.[122]

An even worse mistake in the eyes of conservatives was George Herbert Walker Bush's selection of David Souter to replace Brennan, one of Eisenhower's original mistakes. Unlike Kennedy and O'Connor, whose voting records were moderately conservative, Souter quickly aligned himself with the Court's liberal wing, which included John Paul

Stevens, a Ford appointee and another one of those mistakes that so upset conservatives, as well as Blackmun, Nixon's great mistake. Bush made amends, however, when he nominated Clarence Thomas to replace the 82-year-old Thurgood Marshall. After a bruising confirmation battle, which featured accusations of sexual harassment by a former employee, Thomas was narrowly confirmed, 52–48. With the Court's most liberal justice replaced by a justice who would prove to be its most conservative, it seemed that at last the conservative constitutional revolution was at hand. Conservative expectations were piqued by Rehnquist's announcement in a 1991 case that the Court would not feel itself bound by precedents that were "unworkable or are badly reasoned."[123]

The Rehnquist Court

Rehnquist believed that at last he had the votes to overturn *Roe*, the case that a quarter-century later still fired conservative anger about judicial activism. When a case challenging Pennsylvania's abortion restrictions came before the Court in 1992, Rehnquist readied what he thought would be the majority opinion. The Court, he proclaimed, "was mistaken in *Roe* when it classified a woman's decision to terminate her pregnancy as a 'fundamental right.'" But Rehnquist had counted wrong. He only had the votes of Thomas, Scalia, and Byron White. O'Connor, Souter, and—most surprisingly—Kennedy fled for the pragmatic middle ground and mounted a conservative defense of *Roe* based on respect for precedent (the legal doctrine of *stare decisis*). "A decision to overrule *Roe*'s essential holding," the three justices wrote, "would address error, if error there was, at the cost of both profound and unnecessary damage to the Court's legitimacy, and to the Nation's commitment to the rule of law." The compromise forged by the three justices substituted O'Connor's preferred "undue burden" standard for *Roe*'s clunky trimesters but it affirmed—with the support of Blackmun and Stevens—"the essential holding" of *Roe*: that women had a fundamental right to choose whether or not to terminate a pregnancy.[124]

Conservative activists again felt betrayed. Every vote to uphold *Roe* came from a Republican-appointed justice—including two of Reagan's three selections. Blame, if blame there was, had to be laid at the doorstep of Republican presidents, who had filled the last ten Supreme Court vacancies dating back to 1969. The sole Democratic president during that period, Jimmy Carter, was the only president in American history apart from William Henry Harrison not to get an opportunity to select a Supreme Court justice—in large part because Republican Potter Stewart, a close friend of Reagan's running mate George Herbert Walker Bush, chose to wait until after the 1980 election to announce his retirement.

The election of Bill Clinton in 1992 gave Democrats their first Supreme Court appointment since 1967, courtesy of the Court's sole Democrat, Byron White, who waited until after the 1992 election to step down. In selecting Ruth Bader Ginsburg to replace White, Clinton not only made *Roe* more secure but, for the first time since Marshall's appointment in 1967, put on the Court a justice who was more liberal than the justice being replaced. White's retirement was followed the next year by that of the 85-year-old Blackmun, who timed his retirement to avoid giving a Republican president the opportunity to nominate another Thomas or Scalia bent on overturning *Roe,* the case that Blackmun regarded as his most enduring and important legacy. Clinton replaced Blackmun with Stephen Breyer. For the next 12 years the composition of the Court remained unchanged, until in 2005 the resignation of O'Connor was followed fast by the death of Rehnquist.

During the Clinton years, conservatives continued to sound the alarm against liberal activist judges who—in the words of both the 1996 and 2000 Republican Party platforms—"make up laws, invent new rights, free vicious criminals, and pamper felons in prison." The problem was that the federal judiciary, including the Supreme Court, had "usurped" the right of the people and their representatives to "decide issues great and small." In the 2000 presidential campaign, Republican nominee George W. Bush promised to appoint justices like Scalia and Thomas, who rejected judicial activism in favor of strict adherence to the Constitution.[125]

Conservatives were right that the Rehnquist Court between 1994 and 2000 was more active in striking down congressional statutes than any previous Court. But the judges most prone to strike down federal legislation were not the liberal Democrats Breyer and Ginsburg but the conservative Republicans Thomas and Scalia. In fact, Breyer and Ginsburg were the *least* likely to overturn federal laws. Moreover, in the half-century between 1953 and 2004, only the liberal lion William Douglas voted to strike down federal laws more frequently than Thomas.[126]

The conservative critique of activist liberal judges is true when it comes to state and local laws. Over the past half-century, liberal justices have been significantly more likely to invalidate state and local laws than conservative justices. But the conservative critique obscures the other half of the story—namely that during the latter half of Rehnquist's reign as chief justice, the Court was less likely to overturn a state and local law than at any other time in the twentieth century. If judicial activism is defined as invalidating state and local laws, then Republican presidents had been successful in creating a Court of judicial restraint.[127]

Perhaps the most damning indictment of liberal jurisprudence is that it leaves judges—in the words of the 1996 Republican Party platform—free to have their "personal preferences masquerade as interpreting the law." If judges should be neutral umpires, as John Roberts insisted at his 2005 confirmation hearing, then the best judges are those who do not allow their own policy preferences to influence their decisions as judges. That is, their level of restraint or activism should be guided by their understanding of the rules of the game rather than the policy result they wish to see achieved.

An empirical study of Supreme Court voting by Stefanie Lindquist and Frank Cross demonstrates that few justices on the Rehnquist Court were even-handed umpires, as likely to strike down a liberal law as a conservative one (see Figure 9.1 and Figure 9.2). Thomas and Scalia, the justices hailed by conservatives as the most faithful to a strict constructionist or original-intent jurisprudence—a jurisprudence that is supposed to minimize the risk of personal bias masquerading as legal interpretation—are in fact the conservatives who were most likely to allow their ideology to dictate their decision whether to invalidate a law. The Court's liberals on the Rehnquist Court also showed an ideological bias in their judicial decision-making, striking down conservative laws

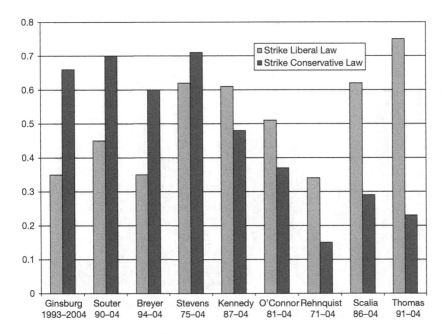

FIGURE 9.1 The Probability of a Justice Invalidating a State or Local Law

Source: Stefanie A. Lindquist and Frank B. Cross, *Measuring Judicial Activism* (New York: Oxford University Press, 2009), 80 (table 6).

significantly more often than they did liberal laws. The only justices on the Rehnquist Court who struck down conservative laws nearly as often as they struck down liberal laws were Kennedy and O'Connor—although when it came to federal laws, O'Connor was almost twice as likely to strike down a liberal law as a conservative law, which explains why the Rehnquist Court tilted right, notwithstanding conservative complaints about O'Connor's apostasy.[128]

The Roberts Court

George W. Bush's selection of John Roberts to replace Rehnquist and, especially, Samuel Alito to replace O'Connor tilted the Court further in the direction of conservative judicial activism. In 2007, for instance, the Roberts Court issued a ruling that essentially invalidated hundreds of local school-integration plans across the nation (*Parents Involved in Community Schools v. Seattle School District No. 1*). In 2008, it uprooted centuries of settled law to declare a DC ban on handguns unconstitutional (*District of Columbia v. Heller*), and two years later struck down a similar ban in Chicago (*McDonald v. Chicago*). In 2010, the Roberts Court overruled longstanding precedents to find that the government could not restrict business corporations from spending on behalf of candidates (*Citizens United v. Federal Election Commission*). Rather than decide the case narrowly—a cardinal tenet of judicial restraint—the Roberts Court offered an expansive

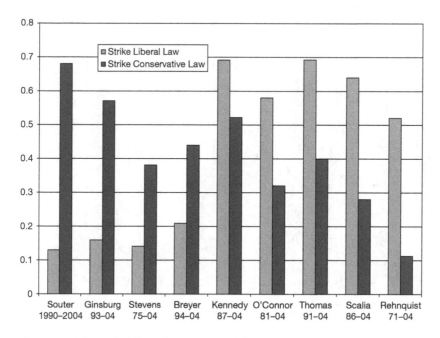

FIGURE 9.2 The Probability of a Justice Invalidating a Federal Law

Source: Stefanie A. Lindquist and Frank B. Cross, *Measuring Judicial Activism* (New York: Oxford University Press, 2009), 61 (table 3).

ruling that went well beyond the facts of the case, which involved not campaign spending by a business corporation but a 90-minute movie on Hillary Clinton that had been produced by a conservative nonprofit corporation. Each of these decisions, like so many of the Roberts Court's most controversial cases, was decided by a 5–4 margin, with Kennedy invariably providing the crucial fifth vote.

By 2017, Kennedy was the lone "mistake" remaining on the Supreme Court, and arguably the closest the Court now had to a neutral umpire—albeit an activist one. To Kennedy's left are four reliably liberal Democrats—Clinton appointees Ginsburg and Breyer and Obama's appointees Sonia Sotomayor and Elena Kagan—and to his right are four consistently conservative Republicans—Thomas, Alito, Roberts, and Neil Gorsuch, who replaced Scalia in 2017. Its moderate-conservative middle largely hollowed out, the Court mirrors the partisan and ideological polarization of contemporary American politics.[129]

PARTISAN POLARIZATION IN THE CONTEMPORARY CONFIRMATION PROCESS

Heightened partisan polarization is evident not only in the Court's voting patterns but in its confirmation process. Clinton's selections of Breyer and Ginsburg were unanimously

A 2010 cartoon by Tom Toles lampoons Chief Justice John Roberts's notion that Supreme Court justices are like umpires who merely call balls and strikes.

Courtesy: TOLES © 2010 *The Washington Post*. Reprinted with permission of UNIVERSAL UCLICK. All rights reserved.

endorsed by the Senate Judiciary Committee, and on the floor of the Senate they were overwhelmingly confirmed (Ginsburg by 96–3 and Breyer by 87–9). In contrast, less than two decades later, only one of seven Republicans on the Judiciary Committee (South Carolina's Lindsay Graham) voted to endorse Obama's nominees, Sotomayor and Kagan. On the Senate floor, 36 out of 41 Republicans voted against Kagan. Sotomayor did marginally better, but still had 31 Republicans vote against her confirmation. The contrast with Clinton's appointees is particularly startling because neither Kagan nor Sotomayor were generally perceived as being more liberal than the Clinton nominees Breyer and Ginsburg, and neither the selection of Sotomayor (who replaced Souter) nor that of Kagan (who replaced Stevens) were expected to alter the ideological balance of the Court.

During George W. Bush's presidency, partisan polarization also shaped the confirmation votes. Every Democrat on the Senate Judiciary Committee voted against confirming Alito and every Republican voted in favor. On the Senate floor, Alito received only four Democratic votes. In Alito's case, the intensity of the opposition stemmed in part from a widely held perception that his appointment would tilt the Court significantly further to the right since he was replacing O'Connor, a moderate conservative. Few observers, however, thought Roberts would be more conservative than the chief justice he had been nominated to replace, yet he was still opposed by a majority of Democrats on the Judiciary Committee, and half of the Senate's 44 Democrats voted not to confirm him, including the then-senator Barack Obama. No Republican voted to oppose either Alito or Roberts, just as no Democrat voted against Sotomayor; one Democrat, Ben Nelson, did oppose Kagan.

Confirmation battles, of course, have long been colored by partisanship. Rehnquist encountered significant partisan opposition when Nixon nominated him in 1971 (26 senators voted against his confirmation, all but two of whom were Democrats) and when Reagan elevated him to chief justice in 1986 (31 Democrats and 2 Republicans voted against his elevation). But the Rehnquist confirmation battles were the exception during the 1970s and 1980s. The other six justices confirmed between 1970 and 1988 were approved either unanimously (Blackmun, Stevens, O'Connor, Scalia, Kennedy) or with only a single dissenting vote (Powell). Even the great confirmation struggles of the late twentieth century—the defeat of Bork in 1987 and the narrow approval of Thomas in 1991—were not entirely partisan affairs. Thomas had solid Republican backing but he also gained crucial support from 11 conservative and moderate Democrats, mostly from the South. Bork was opposed not only by a nearly united front of Democrats but also by six liberal and moderate Republicans.

The shrinking number of liberal Republicans and conservative Democrats has made it far more difficult for presidents to pick up confirmation votes from senators on the other side of the aisle. Confirmation thus depends, now more than ever, on party control of the Senate. Fortunately for Bush and Obama, their opportunity to fill Court vacancies occurred when their party had a majority in the Senate, a luxury that Presidents Nixon, Ford, and George Herbert Walker Bush never had. In fact, between 1969 and 1991, eight of the eleven Court appointments were confirmed under conditions of divided government. In each case, Republicans controlled the presidency and Democrats controlled the Senate, which may help to explain the large number of those "mistakes" that so disappointed conservative Republicans. In other words, many of the alleged mistakes were due to the president's strategic need to mollify the majority party in the Senate.[130]

The greater scarcity of liberal Republicans and conservative Democrats does not alone account for the more partisan confirmation process, for until quite recently even liberal Democrats typically voted to confirm Republican Supreme Court nominees, and conservative Republicans generally voted to confirm Clinton's nominees. Even as the parties became more internally homogeneous, the default condition remained that senators, except in unusual circumstances, would confirm a president's nominee for the Supreme Court. In the twenty-first century, party voting has become the new default. Nor is this necessarily a bad thing. If justices base their legal decisions on political ideology, as the evidence suggests they often do, and if presidents choose Supreme Court justices based on party and ideology—which they certainly do—then there is good reason for the Senate to base their confirmation decisions on the party and ideology of the nominee.[131]

That is exactly the determination that Senate Republicans made when Scalia's sudden death in February 2016 gave President Obama the opportunity to name his third justice to the nation's highest court. Obama's previous two Court picks had replaced liberals but now, for the first time in more than a half-century, Democrats had a chance to replace a conservative Republican-appointed Supreme Court justice with a liberal justice. Not since George Herbert Walker Bush nominated the conservative Clarence Thomas to replace the liberal Thurgood Marshall in 1991 had the ideological and partisan distance between the justice leaving the bench and the president selecting the replacement been so great. But unlike Bush, who nominated a 43-year-old ideologue who had been a judge for all of 16 months, Obama picked a widely respected 64-year-old centrist who had been on the United States Court of Appeals for the DC Circuit for nearly twenty years, including three as chief judge. In both cases, the opposition party controlled the US Senate—Democrats had a 12-seat edge in 1991, Republicans an 8-seat advantage in 2016—but the outcomes were radically different, dramatically illustrating the heightened polarization of the last quarter century.

Thomas's nomination was certainly divisive. The all-male Senate Judiciary Committee deadlocked 7–7 after hearing testimony that alleged Thomas had sexually harassed female employees during his tenure as head of the Equal Employment Opportunity Commission. But despite widespread concerns about Thomas's fitness for office, the Democratic-controlled Senate ultimately voted to confirm him. In contrast, Merrick Garland, Obama's choice to replace Scalia, never received a hearing, let alone a vote in the Republican-controlled Senate. Republicans argued that it would be improper for Obama to pick a justice with a presidential election so close on the horizon (reprising an argument Republicans had made in opposing Fortas in 1968),[132] but the reality is that Senate Majority Leader Mitch McConnell blocked Obama's pick because he could. While many were outraged by the Republicans' refusal to hold hearings, perhaps the outrage is better directed at the Senate Democrats in 1991, who failed to use their control of that coequal branch of government to compel Bush to nominate a more experienced and moderate judge. Given the enormous power of the contemporary Supreme Court—and the length of time justices now typically remain on the Court—the real problem, arguably, is not the Senate rejecting the president's choice but rather the Senate failing to take responsibility for shaping the ideological direction of the Court. From this perspective, blocking Garland was regrettable not because Senate Republicans used ideology as a principal factor but because Garland's nomination was a golden opportunity to begin to steer the Court toward the ideological center—and thus could perhaps have been a step in the direction of making the nomination process less politicized.

Had Hillary Clinton won the presidency in 2016—and had Democrats gained control of the Senate—McConnell's gamble would have backfired spectacularly. Instead of nominating a relatively old and moderate Democrat like Garland, Clinton would have come under intense pressure from fellow partisans to nominate a liberal judge in the mold of Thomas: young and ideologically dependable. Trump's stunning upset—combined, crucially, with Republicans maintaining control over the Senate—saw McConnell's high-stake gamble pay off. Trump appointed the conservative Neil Gorsuch and the Republican-controlled Senate pushed his vote through on a largely party-line vote—every Republican voting in favor and all but three Democrats voting against.

There was nothing particularly novel about the party-line voting—remember, all but four Democrats opposed Alito a decade previously. But the Gorsuch appointment was nonetheless another landmark moment in the escalating partisan polarization of the nomination process, because to get Gorsuch confirmed the Republicans were compelled to abolish the filibuster for Supreme Court justices (Democrats had already done away with the filibuster for the lower courts in 2013). The contrast with the Alito nomination is telling. Neither Alito nor Gorsuch reached the 60-vote threshold it takes to end a filibuster (Alito ended up with 58 votes while Gorsuch received 55) but Alito benefitted from senators who were willing to vote for cloture (thereby ending a filibuster and allowing a vote) even though they opposed the nominee. In Alito's case, 72 senators voted for cloture, including 14 senators who opposed Alito but nonetheless voted to end the filibuster and let the majority rule. In Gorsuch's case, the only senators willing to vote for cloture and end the filibuster were the 55 senators who intended to vote for Gorsuch.[133]

The abolition of the filibuster for Supreme Court justices was a logical culmination of the growing polarization—and the same result could easily have occurred had Democrats won the presidency and secured a Senate majority in 2016. But while abolition of the filibuster was a predictable consequence of polarization, the Senate has done grievous harm to its ability to constrain the president and do the vital work of pushing the Supreme Court toward an ideological middle ground. The power to moderate the Court now depends entirely on which party controls the Senate. To be sure, requiring supermajorities is undemocratic and, in the legislative process, arguably undesirable. After all, marshalling legislation through both houses of Congress and then getting the approval of the White House is already difficult. If the legislation is bad it can be repealed or rewritten, and in any event new elections are never more than two years away. But Supreme Court picks are for life, often a very long life—and there is no real chance of amending or fixing a poor decision once a justice is on the Court. If there is one area in contemporary American politics where a supermajority requirement can be justified, it is in trying to forge a bipartisan consensus around the nine men and women who sit on the Supreme Court.

The "Vacancy Crisis" in the Lower Courts

Partisan polarization has also affected the lower federal courts, particularly the appellate courts. Although the Reagan administration aggressively vetted judicial candidates' ideology, they were still highly successful in getting their nominees confirmed; it helped that Republicans controlled the Senate for six of Reagan's eight years. About 90 percent of Reagan's nominees for the appellate courts were confirmed by the Senate—less than Carter's 93 percent or Nixon's 96 percent, but still impressive. After Reagan's politicization of the judicial section process, however, the Senate began to fight back by holding up nominations. Under George Herbert Walker Bush, the Democratic-controlled Senate approved only three out of every four appellate court nominees. But Democratic resistance to Bush paled in comparison to the obstacles that Republicans put in the way of Clinton's nominees, particularly in his second term.[134]

During the 1992 campaign, Clinton had been critical of the ideological litmus test used by the Reagan and Bush administrations in selecting judges, and promised to appoint more centrist judges. Empirical studies confirm that Clinton's lower-court appointees were less liberal in their judicial decision-making than the judicial appointees made by the previous three Democratic presidents as well as Eisenhower. Yet fewer than six in ten of Clinton's appellate nominees were confirmed by the Senate, and in his second term the number was below 50 percent. Republicans, who controlled the Senate for all but Clinton's first two years, rarely voted down a judge. Instead they stalled. In 1997 and 1998, Republicans took an average of 230 days to schedule a hearing for an appeals court nominee, three times the length it took during Clinton's first term or George Herbert Walker Bush's presidency. Many nominees never received a hearing or vote. So severe was the "vacancy crisis" on the federal bench that Chief Justice Rehnquist issued a report at the end of 1997 calling the Senate's attention to the harm that vacancies were doing to the judiciary's capacity to render justice.[135]

During George W. Bush's presidency, it was the Republicans' turn to sound the alarm of a vacancy crisis. When Democrats controlled the Senate (2001–2002, 2007–2008), they used the same delaying tactics that the Republicans had used in the Clinton era, chiefly refusing to schedule hearings for the president's nominees. And when Democrats were in the minority (2003–2006) and could no longer stop nominees from receiving hearings, they pioneered an unprecedentedly aggressive use of the filibuster to stop Bush nominees, particularly nominees for the appellate courts.[136]

Things got worse in Obama's first term. When Obama took office there were 55 vacancies on the federal bench, but by 2010 that number had ballooned to 100. By the end of Obama's first term there were still 75 vacancies; in contrast, George W. Bush ended his first term with about 40 judicial vacancies, half the number as at the start of his term. In the year after Obama's reelection, there was no sign of improvement: in fact, the median number of vacancies ticked up in 2013.[137]

Obama had particular difficulty getting the Senate to approve his nominees for the crucially important US Court of Appeals for the DC Circuit. In his first term, Obama nominated Caitlin Halligan four times to fill a seat on the court that had been vacant since 2005, and all four times Republicans filibustered to prevent the Senate from voting on her nomination—as Senate Democrats had blocked Bush's effort to fill the same seat. After Obama's reelection, the Republicans consented to the selection of Sri Srinivasan to a different seat on the DC circuit court, one that had been vacant since 2008, but they continued to block Obama's effort to fill the remaining three vacancies on the court. Republicans wheeled out an assortment of specious arguments to justify the filibustering. They said that Obama was trying, FDR-like, to "pack the court"; that the court didn't need more than eight judges; and that Obama's selections would disrupt the ideological "balance" on the court (ignoring that while four of the eight judges were appointed by a Democrat, all but one of the six judges that had taken senior status were appointed by a Republican president, and that they also heard cases).

Frustrated at Republicans' refusal to let Obama put his stamp on arguably the second most important court in the country (three of the current Supreme Court justices— Roberts, Thomas, and Ginsburg—previously served on the DC circuit), Democrats decided to take radical action. Senate Republicans had flirted with the so-called "nuclear option" during the Bush years, but a brokered compromise averted pushing the button.

This time, though, there was no compromise. On November 21, 2013, Senate Democrats ruled that henceforth it would only take a majority vote—rather than 60 votes—to end filibusters of federal judicial (except Supreme Court justices) and executive branch nominations.

The rule change had an immediate effect on the pace of approval of judicial nominations. In the six months before the Democrats triggered the nuclear option, the Senate approved 16 federal judges. In the six months after the rule change, the Senate approved three times that number, including all three of Obama's nominees for the Court of Appeals for the DC Circuit. Once the Republicans regained control of the Senate after 2014, however, confirmations slowed to a crawl. Over the final two years of Obama's presidency, the Republican-controlled Senate only confirmed two appellate court judges and 18 district court judges. In contrast, when Democrats took control of the Senate for the last two years of George W. Bush's presidency, the Senate confirmed ten appellate court judges and nearly 60 district court judges. Not surprisingly, Obama left office with almost a hundred judicial vacancies, nearly twice the number of vacancies that existed at the end of Bush's presidency.

The Republicans' slow walk of Obama's nominees in 2015 and 2016 was a direct result of the Democrats' use of the nuclear option in 2013, which in turn was a response to the Republicans' unprecedented obstructionism during Obama's first five years. Polarization of the parties and politicization of the federal courts have become inextricably linked as federal judgeships, particularly at the appellate level, have become increasingly viewed as crucial outposts in the ideological battle between liberals and conservatives.

THE FUTURE OF JUDICIAL SUPREMACY

If federal courts are the instruments that presidents use to ensure that their policy preferences endure beyond their administration, why should presidents regard judicial pronouncements as anything other than political preferences masquerading as constitutional law? Jefferson, Jackson, Lincoln, and FDR all asked themselves this question about the Supreme Court. It is a question that confronted Obama too. His defining policy achievement, the Affordable Care Act (ACA), narrowly escaped being nullified in 2011 by the five Republican justices on the Supreme Court (*National Federation of Independent Business v. Sebelius*). Of these, four (Alito, Kennedy, Scalia, Thomas) would have struck down the entire law because they said the federal government did not have the power to mandate that individuals buy health insurance; only Roberts' dramatic defection—he said that the individual mandate amounted to a tax, a power that Congress clearly did have under the Constitution—saved the law, or at least most of it (the Court struck down the requirement that states must expand Medicaid eligibility). However, legal challenges to the ACA continued. In 2014, the five Republicans on the Court exempted for-profit corporations with religious objections from the ACA's requirement that employers cover contraceptives for female employees (*Burwell v. Hobby Lobby*). For the first time since the 1930s, liberals began to focus on the dangers of judicial activism and to question judicial supremacy.[138]

Conservatives, of course, have been warning about judicial power and judicial supremacy for the past half-century. The 2000 Republican Party platform, for instance, lamented that "the sound principle of judicial review has turned into an intolerable presumption of judicial supremacy." But while conservatives have railed against unaccountable judges for decades, they have rarely pursued institutional reforms that would curb that power. After his landslide reelection victory in 1972, Nixon flirted with the idea of a constitutional amendment that would require federal judges to be reconfirmed by the Senate every ten years, but any thought he might have had of rewriting Article III was submerged in Watergate. A vague mention of "setting terms for federal judges" resurfaced in the 2000 Republican platform but the idea garnered little attention. Instead, conservatives have relied almost exclusively on extracting promises from Republican presidential candidates that they will only appoint judges who share their conservative beliefs. But pledging to appoint conservative judges, as Donald Trump did in the 2016 campaign, leaves the presumption of judicial supremacy untouched. Indeed, it strengthens judicial supremacy by making it the future guarantor of a president's ideological commitments.[139]

On occasion, President Reagan did challenge judicial supremacy more directly. In 1983, for instance, after the Court struck down a city ordinance that imposed restrictions on women seeking abortions, Reagan called upon Congress to enact a constitutional amendment *or a statute* that would "restore legal protection to the unborn." Implicitly, Reagan was suggesting that the political branches had the power to overturn the Court's decision that abortion was a constitutional right. But Reagan's confrontation with the Court was more rhetorical than real. Democrats controlled the House of Representatives throughout his eight years, giving Reagan no chance of legislatively invalidating *Roe*. Moreover, the Court never stood in the way of Reagan's core legislative agenda—reducing taxes, cutting domestic spending, and increasing military spending. Ultimately, rather than challenge judicial supremacy, Reagan used his appointment power to ensure that his "best legacy" was a conservative judiciary. Subsequent presidents have followed his lead.[140]

Obama was arguably the first president since FDR to face the prospect of a Court invalidating his signature policy achievement, but Obama lacked the overwhelming congressional majorities that made FDR's challenge to judicial power credible. Trump, too, has tangled with the courts, taking to Twitter, for instance, to criticize the "so-called judge" who blocked his travel ban on citizens of seven majority-Muslim nations. But if twentieth-century history is any guide to the twenty-first century, Trump will be no more successful than his predecessors in challenging judicial supremacy. That history shows the only reliable—although hardly infallible—way for a president and his party to get the judicial outcomes they prefer is to win the elections that enable them to pick the so-called umpires.

NOTES

1   Bruce Allen Murphy, *Fortas: The Rise and Ruin of a Supreme Court Justice* (New York: William Morrow, 1988), 270, 286–87.

2   Laura Kalman, *Abe Fortas: A Biography* (New Haven, CT: Yale University Press, 1990), 327. Murphy, *Fortas*, 273.

3   Murphy, *Fortas*, 284–85, 292. Kalman, *Abe Fortas*, 327–28.

4   David Alistair Yalof, *Pursuit of Justices: Presidential Politics and the Selection of Supreme Court Nominees* (Chicago: University of Chicago Press, 1999), 92–93. Kalman, *Abe Fortas*, 356.

5   Kalman, *Abe Fortas*, 331, 335.

6   Kalman, *Abe Fortas*, 334–35, 338–39.

7   Kalman, *Abe Fortas*, 295, 309, 337–38. On Fortas's advisory role on Vietnam, see 295–96, 300, 303–06. On Fortas's role in writing the Detroit message and advising the president on how to respond to the Detroit riots, see 307–09.

8   Through a mix of strategically timed retirements and electoral victories, Republicans capitalized on Johnson's blunder to ensure that the position of chief justice remained in conservative hands for (at least) the next half-century. Burger retired from the Court in the sixth year of Reagan's presidency, though he lived until 1995. William Rehnquist, who Reagan picked to succeed Burger, died of cancer during George W. Bush's second term but it is likely that even had he not been ill he would have retired during Bush's second term so as to give a Republican administration the opportunity to select his replacement.

9   John Anthony Maltese, *The Selling of Supreme Court Nominees* (Baltimore: Johns Hopkins University Press, 1995), 18.

10   Farrand, *Records of the Federal Convention*, 1:119, 2:81. Also see Richard J. Ellis, ed., *Founding the American Presidency* (Lanham, MD: Rowman & Littlefield, 1999), 191–94.

11   Farrand, *Records of the Federal Convention*, 2:81. Also see Michael Comiskey, *Seeking Justices: The Judging of Supreme Court Nominees* (Lawrence: University Press of Kansas, 2004), 21–22.

12   Farrand, *Records of the Federal Convention*, 2:539.

13   Maltese, *Selling of Supreme Court Nominees*, 12. The letter was penned by Nixon aide Chuck Colson, who later explained that he had based it on his "recollection" of Hamilton's argument in *Federalist* No. 76, which he had "done a paper on in law school" (17). Apparently, Colson dashed off the letter as a rough draft and was surprised to find that the White House and president signed off on the letter without revising a word. Colson later acknowledged that he erred in claiming that the Constitution gave the president the sole power of appointment, though he continued to insist that the advice and consent clause was "sort of an afterthought to protect against nepotism" (18).

14   Maltese, *Selling of Supreme Court Nominees*, 16.

15   Comiskey, *Seeking Justices*, 22–23. Henry J. Abraham, *Justices, Presidents, and Senators: A History of U.S. Supreme Court Appointments from Washington to Bush II* (Lanham, MD: Rowman & Littlefield, 2008; fifth edition), 20.

16   Bernard Bailyn, *The Origins of American Politics* (New York: Vintage, 1970), 68. Gordon S. Wood, "Judicial Review in the Era of the Founding," in Robert A. Licht, ed., *Is the Supreme Court the Guardian of the Constitution?* (Washington, DC: AEI Press, 1993), 154. In the colonies, the royal prerogative extended to the creation of courts, a practice which was also condemned in the Declaration of Independence. The framers of the Constitution never wavered in their determination to ensure that Congress rather than the president was given the power to establish all courts below the level of the Supreme Court.

17   The case for fixed terms for Supreme Court justices is made by David Karol in "Pro: Resolved, the Terms of Supreme Court Justices Should Be Limited to Eighteen Years," in Richard J. Ellis and Michael Nelson, eds., *Debating Reform: Conflicting Perspectives on How to Fix the American Political System* (Washington, DC: CQ Press, 2017; third edition), 343–53. Also see Sanford Levinson, *Our Undemocratic Constitution* (New York: Oxford University Press, 2006), 123–40; and Larry J. Sabato, *A More Perfect Constitution* (New York: Walker, 2007), 110–16.

18   Farrand, *Records of the Federal Convention*, 2:298.

19   Farrand, *Records of the Federal Convention*, 2:298.

20 Maltese, *Selling of Supreme Court Nominees*, 24–25.

21 Under the 1789 act, each circuit court consisted of three judges—two Supreme Court justices and the local district court judge. In 1793, Congress eased somewhat the Court's burden by reducing each circuit court to two judges—one Supreme Court justice and a district court judge. Circuit riding by Supreme Court justices continued until 1891. For a history of circuit riding, see David R. Stras, "Why Supreme Court Justices Should Ride Circuit Again," *Minnesota Law Review* 91(June 2007), 1710–51.

22 Maltese, *Selling of Supreme Court Nominees*, 19, 26–31.

23 Adams to James Lloyd, January 1815, in Charles Francis Adams, ed., *The Works of John Adams* (Boston: Little, Brown, 1856), 10:112.

24 Richard E. Ellis, *The Jeffersonian Crisis: Courts and Politics in the Young Republic* (New York: Oxford University Press, 1971), 13–15.

25 Ellis, *Jeffersonian Crisis*, 15.

26 Ellis, *Jeffersonian Crisis*, 40–43. In a draft of the message, Jefferson had fired a provocative shot across the Court's bow, warning that no branch of government had the right to pass judgment on the constitutionality of the acts of another branch of government. But Secretary of State Madison and Secretary of Treasury Albert Gallatin persuaded Jefferson to scrub the passage for fear that it would provide Federalists the opportunity to portray Jefferson as a lawless radical.

27 Ellis, *Jeffersonian Crisis*, 43–44. James MacGregor Burns, *Packing the Court: The Rise of Judicial Power and the Coming Crisis of the Supreme Court* (New York: Penguin Press, 2009), 22. Bruce Ackerman, *The Failure of the Founding Fathers: Jefferson, Marshall, and the Rise of Presidential Democracy* (Cambridge, MA: Harvard University Press, 2005), 136.

28 Ellis, *Jeffersonian Crisis*, 43–45. Ackerman, *The Failure of the Founding Fathers*, 136.

29 Ellis, *Jeffersonian Crisis*, 45, 57–58.

30 Ellis, *Jeffersonian Crisis*, 51, 59.

31 Ellis, *Jeffersonian Crisis*, 60–62. Ackerman, *The Failure of the Founding Fathers*, 164–70.

32 Ackerman, *The Failure of the Founding Fathers*, 176–78. Ellis, *Jeffersonian Crisis*, 68.

33 Gordon S. Wood, *Empire of Liberty: A History of the Early Republic, 1789–1815* (New York: Oxford University Press, 2009), 436, 441.

34 Jefferson to Abigail Adams, September 11, 1804, quoted in Christopher Wolfe, *The Rise of Modern Judicial Review: From Constitutional Interpretation to Judge-Made Law* (Lanham, MD: Rowman & Littlefield, 1994), 94. Wood, *Empire of Liberty*, 442. Ellis, *Jeffersonian Crisis*, 66. Burns, *Packing the Court*, 32.

35 Ellis, *Jeffersonian Crisis*, 69, 79–80. Wood, *Empire of Liberty*, 421.

36 Ellis, *Jeffersonian Crisis*, 80.

37 Ellis, *Jeffersonian Crisis*, 93.

38 Wood, *Empire of Liberty*, 423–24.

39 Ellis, *Jeffersonian Crisis*, 105. Ackerman, *The Failure of the Founding Fathers*, 175, 345 n22. Wood, *Empire of Liberty*, 442.

40 Ellis, *Jeffersonian Crisis*, 106–07.

41 Burns, *Packing the Court*, 34.

42 Maltese, *Selling of Supreme Court Nominees*, 33–34. Ackerman, *The Failure of the Founding Fathers*, 231–33. Ellis, *Jeffersonian Crisis*, 241–42.

43 Jefferson to Madison, October 15, 1810, in James Morton Smith, ed., *The Republic of Letters: The Correspondence between Thomas Jefferson and James Madison, 1776–1826* (New York: Norton, 1995), 1647. Maltese, *Selling of Supreme Court Nominees*, 34. Ackerman, *The Failure of the Founding Fathers*, 232–33.

44 Ackerman, *The Failure of the Founding Fathers*, 234–37.

45   Burns, *Packing the Court*, 35. Ackerman, *The Failure of the Founding Fathers*, 361 n41. Wood, *Empire of Liberty*, 437–38, 455.

46   Burns, *Packing the Court*, 39–40.

47   Burns, *Packing the Court*, 41. The quotations are from Jefferson's letters to Judge Spencer Roane, September 6, 1819, and to Thomas Ritchie, December 25, 1820.

48   Drew R. McCoy, *The Last of the Fathers: James Madison and the Republican Legacy* (New York: Cambridge University Press, 1989), 69–71.

49   Jean Edward Smith, *John Marshall: Definer of a Nation* (New York: Henry Holt, 1996), 447. George Dangerfield, *The Era of Good Feelings* (New York: Harcourt Brace Jovanovich, 1952), 173–74. Daniel Walker Howe, *What Hath God Wrought: The Transformation of America, 1815–1848* (New York: Oxford University Press, 2007), 146, 158–59. Burns, *Packing the Court*, 40.

50   Burns, *Packing the Court*, 43.

51   Keith E. Whittington, *Political Foundations of Judicial Supremacy: The Presidency, the Supreme Court, and Constitutional Leadership in U.S. History* (Princeton, NJ: Princeton University Press, 2007), 33. Robert V. Remini, *Andrew Jackson: The Course of American Freedom, 1822–1832* (New York: Harper & Row, 1981), 367–68.

52   Richard P. Longaker, "Andrew Jackson and the Judiciary," *Political Science Quarterly* (September 1956), 346–49.

53   Longaker, "Andrew Jackson and the Judiciary," 341, 361–64.

54   Burns, *Packing the Court*, 60.

55   Burns, *Packing the Court*, 60.

56   Whittington, *Political Foundations of Judicial Supremacy*, 74.

57   Whittington, *Political Foundations of Judicial Supremacy*, 68–69. Burns, *Packing the Court*, 59, 61. James Buchanan, Inaugural Address, March 4, 1857.

58   Whittington, *Political Foundations of Judicial Supremacy*, 69–70. Brian McGinty, *Lincoln and the Court* (Cambridge, MA: Harvard University Press, 2008), 61–63. On Lincoln's Cooper Union speech, see Harold Holzer, *Lincoln at Cooper Union: The Speech That Made Abraham Lincoln President* (New York: Simon & Schuster, 2004).

59   Abraham Lincoln, Inaugural Address, March 4, 1861. Also see Whittington, *Political Foundations of Judicial Supremacy*, 68–70; and Burns, *Packing the Court*, 63–64. Lincoln articulated the same understanding of constitutional interpretation in his famous debates with Stephen Douglas. Although disavowing any intention "to disturb or resist" the Court's decision as it applied to Dred Scott, Lincoln refused to accept the Court's interpretation of the Constitution as "a rule of political action for the people and all the departments of the government." In defending this position, Lincoln rehearsed the arguments of Jefferson and Jackson, including Jackson's bank veto, which ironically had been drafted by Taney when he was Jackson's attorney general. Whittington, *Foundations of Judicial Supremacy*, 34.

60   Whittington, *Foundations of Judicial Supremacy*, 35.

61   McGinty, *Lincoln and the Court*, 103.

62   McGinty, *Lincoln and the Court*, 104. Burns, *Packing the Court*, 67–68.

63   McGinty, *Lincoln and the Court*, 108–09.

64   Whittington, *Foundations of Judicial Supremacy*, 212–13. Abraham, *Justices, Presidents, and Senators*, 99.

65   Stephen Skowronek, *The Politics Presidents Make: Leadership from John Adams to George Bush* (Cambridge, MA: Harvard University Press, 1993). Also see Whittington, *Political Foundations of Judicial Supremacy*.

66   Whittington, *Political Foundations of Judicial Supremacy*, 115–16, 256. Sheldon Goldman, *Picking Federal Judges: Lower Court Selection from Roosevelt through Reagan* (New Haven: Yale University Press, 1997), 8.

67 Whittington, *Political Foundations of Judicial Supremacy*, 7, 116, 256–57.

68 Whittington, *Political Foundations of Judicial Supremacy*, 258–59.

69 Whittington, *Political Foundations of Judicial Supremacy*, 259. Lincoln, *First Inaugural Address*.

70 Whittington, *Political Foundations of Judicial Supremacy*, 259.

71 Whittington, *Political Foundations of Judicial Supremacy*, 260–61. *Lochner v. New York* 198 U. S. 45 (1905).

72 Sidney M. Milkis, *Theodore Roosevelt, the Progressive Party, and the Transformation of American Democracy* (Lawrence: University Press of Kansas, 2009), 57.

73 Theodore Roosevelt, *A Charter of Democracy* (Washington, DC: US Government Printing Office, 1912), 12. Milkis, *Theodore Roosevelt, the Progressive Party, and the Transformation of American Democracy*, 57, 59.

74 Whittington, *Political Foundations of Judicial Supremacy*, 262–64.

75 Whittington, *Political Foundations of Judicial Supremacy*, 265.

76 Jeff Shesol, *Supreme Power: Franklin Roosevelt vs. the Supreme Court* (New York: Norton, 2010), 9.

77 Shesol, *Supreme Power*, 10–11.

78 Shesol, *Supreme Power*, 11–12, 34.

79 Shesol, *Supreme Power*, 37–41.

80 Shesol, *Supreme Power*, 31.

81 Shesol, *Supreme Power*, 36, 53, 63–65, 71. William E. Leuchtenburg, *The Supreme Court Reborn: The Constitutional Revolution in the Age of Roosevelt* (New York: Oxford University Press, 1995), 84.

82 Shesol, *Supreme Power*, 88–91. The case was *Panama Refining Co. v. Ryan* 293 US 388 (1935).

83 Shesol, *Supreme Power*, 91–92.

84 Shesol, *Supreme Power*, 95, 99. Leuchtenburg, *The Supreme Court Reborn*, 87–88.

85 Shesol, *Supreme Power*, 105. Leuchtenburg, *The Supreme Court Reborn*, 88.

86 Shesol, *Supreme Power*, 116–19. Leuchtenburg, *The Supreme Court Reborn*, 88–89.

87 Shesol, *Supreme Power*, 132, 135. Leuchtenburg, *The Supreme Court Reborn*, 89.

88 Shesol, *Supreme Power*, 184–85.

89 Shesol, *Supreme Power*, 212–13. Leuchtenburg, *The Supreme Court Reborn*, 101, 104. Burns, *Packing the Court*, 142–43.

90 Shesol, *Supreme Power*, 221. Leuchtenburg, *The Supreme Court Reborn*, 95, 102–03.

91 Leuchtenburg, *The Supreme Court Reborn*, 106. Burns, *Packing the Court*, 146. Shesol, *Supreme Power*, 224.

92 Leuchtenburg, *The Supreme Court Reborn*, 90–92. Shesol, *Supreme Power*, 223–24.

93 Leuchtenburg, *The Supreme Court Reborn*, 108–09.

94 Leuchtenburg, *The Supreme Court Reborn*, 108–11.

95 Leuchtenburg, *The Supreme Court Reborn*, 134. Burns, *Packing the Court*, 146–47.

96 Shesol, *Supreme Power*, 301–03, 307. Burns, *Packing the Court*, 146.

97 Franklin D. Roosevelt, Fireside Chat, March 9, 1937.

98 Leuchtenburg, *The Supreme Court Reborn*, 142–44. Burns, *Packing the Court*, 148–50.

99 Leuchtenburg, *The Supreme Court Reborn*, 146.

100 Leuchtenburg, *The Supreme Court Reborn*, 147–52. Shesol, *Supreme Power*, 500.

101 Leuchtenburg, *The Supreme Court Reborn*, 156–61. Shesol, *Supreme Power*, 501–02, 522–24.

102 Roosevelt, Fireside Chat, March 9, 1937. Whittington, *Political Foundations of Judicial Supremacy*, 269.

103 Burns, *Packing the Court*, 155.

104 Whittington, *Political Foundations of Judicial Supremacy*, 270–71.

105 *Smith v. Allright* 321 U.S. 649 (1944). Burns, *Packing the Court*, 157. Although Harlan Stone was put on the Court by Calvin Coolidge, in 1941 Roosevelt nominated him for chief justice, a post he held until his death in 1946.

106 Whittington, *Political Foundations of Judicial Supremacy*, 269.

107 James T. Patterson, *Brown v. Board of Education: A Civil Rights Milestone and Its Troubled Legacy* (New York: Oxford University Press, 2001), 81–82. Whittington, *Political Foundations of Judicial Supremacy*, 146, 148. Yalof, *Pursuit of Justices*, 42.

108 Whittington, *Political Foundations of Judicial Supremacy*, 149.

109 Burns, *Packing the Court*, 193.

110 Burns, *Packing the Court*, 202. Yalof, *Pursuit of Justices*, 97–98.

111 Burns, *Packing the Court*, 208–09.

112 Abraham, *Justices, Presidents, and Senators*, 208.

113 Lee Epstein and Jeffrey A. Segal, *Advice and Consent: The Politics of Judicial Appointments* (New York: Oxford University Press, 2005), 131. Lee Epstein and Jeffrey A. Segal, "Nominating Federal Judges and Justices," in George C. Edwards III and William G. Howell, eds., *The Oxford Handbook of the American Presidency* (New York: Oxford University Press, 2009), 638, 641. Cass R. Sunstein, David Schkade, Lisa M. Ellman, and Andres Sawicki, *Are Judges Political? An Empirical Analysis of the Federal Judiciary* (Washington, DC: Brookings Institution Press, 2006), 114.

114 David M. O'Brien, "The Reagan Judges: His Most Enduring Legacy?" in Charles O. Jones, ed., *The Reagan Legacy: Promise and Performance* (Chatham, NJ: Chatham House, 1988), 62. Goldman, *Picking Federal Judges*, 208. Evidence of the conservative voting records of Nixon's appeals court appointments is reported in Walter F. Murphy, "Reagan's Judicial Strategy," in Larry Berman, ed., *Looking Back on the Reagan Presidency* (Baltimore: Johns Hopkins University Press, 1990), 222–23.

115 O'Brien, "The Reagan Judges," 68. Maltese, *Selling of Supreme Court Nominees*, 122.

116 O'Brien, "The Reagan Judges," 68–69. Abraham, *Justices, Presidents, and Senators*, 200–02.

117 Goldman, *Picking Federal Judges*, 298, 301. The latter quotation is from a speech Reagan gave in 1985 to a group of US attorneys.

118 O'Brien, "The Reagan Judges," 62; emphasis added.

119 Goldman, *Picking Federal Judges*, 290. Burns, *Packing the Court*, 212. Fewer than 8 percent of Reagan's judicial appointments were women, less than half the percentage that Jimmy Carter appointed. For data on the gender and racial diversity of judicial appointments in the Carter and Reagan (as well as Bush and Clinton) presidencies, see David M. O'Brien, "Ironies and Disappointments: Bush and Federal Judgeships," in Colin Campbell and Bert A. Rockman, eds., *The George W. Bush Presidency: Appraisals and Prospects* (Washington, DC: CQ Press, 2004), 147.

120 O'Brien, "The Reagan Judges," 90. Yalof, *Pursuit of Justices*, 161.

121 Burns, *Packing the Court*, 215. O'Brien, "The Reagan Judges," 91.

122 Yalof, *Pursuit of Justices*, 165.

123 Burns, *Packing the Court*, 219. The Rehnquist quotation is from *Payne v. Tennessee*, in which the Court found that a victim impact statement was admissible in the sentencing phase of a criminal trial, overturning a precedent established by the Court in 1987.

124 Burns, *Packing the Court*, 220.

125 Republican Party Platform of 2000, July 31, 2000. Republican Party Platform of 1996, August 12, 1996. O'Brien, "Ironies and Disappointments," 133, 136.

126 Stefanie A. Lindquist and Frank B. Cross, *Measuring Judicial Activism* (New York: Oxford University Press, 2009), 50–51, 55–56. Also see Thomas M. Keck, *The Most Activist Supreme Court in History: The Road to Modern Judicial Conservatism* (Chicago: University of Chicago Press, 2004).

127   Lindquist and Cross, *Measuring Judicial Activism*, 71–72, 76–77.

128   Lindquist and Cross, *Measuring Judicial Activism*, 59–61, 78–80.

129   Updated data (through 2016) provided to the author by Stefanie Lindquist show that Kagan and Sotomayor have invalidated fewer than one-fifth of liberal state laws whereas they have struck down about four out of every five conservative state statutes. The reverse pattern is evident with Alito, who in his first decade on the Court rejected two out of three liberal state statutes and only one quarter of conservative state statutes. Roberts has been far more even-handed, striking down 40 percent of conservative state statutes and slightly more than 50 percent of liberal state statutes.

130   On the impact that the partisan balance of power in the Senate has on a president's strategic choices, see Christine L. Nemachek, *Strategic Selection: Presidential Nomination of Supreme Court Justices from Herbert Hoover through George W. Bush* (Charlottesville: University Press of Virginia, 2007). Also see Keith E. Whittington, "Judicial Checks on the President," in Edwards and Howell, *Oxford Handbook of the American Presidency*, 654.

131   Epstein and Segal, *Advice and Consent*, 122, 125.

132   On the many Supreme Court justices who have been nominated during presidential election years, see Barbara A. Perry, "One-Third of All U.S. Presidents Appointed a Supreme Court Justice in an Election Year," *Washington Post*, February 29, 2016.

133   Harry Enten, "The Gorsuch Vote Shows the Old Senate is Dead," *FiveThirtyEight*, April 4, 2017, https://fivethirtyeight.com/features/the-gorsuch-vote-shows-the-old-senate-is-dead/.

134   David A. Yalof, "In Search of a Means to an End: George W. Bush and the Federal Judiciary," in Colin Campbell, Bert A. Rockman, and Andrew Rudalevige, eds., *The George W. Bush Legacy* (Washington, DC: CQ Press, 2008), 193. Sarah A. Binder and Forrest Maltzman, *Advice and Dissent: The Struggle to Shape the Federal Judiciary* (Washington, DC: Brookings Institution Press, 2009), 80.

135   Sunstein, Schkade, Ellman, and Sawicki, *Are Judges Political?*, 114–15. Nancy Kassop, "Expansion and Contraction: Clinton's Impact on the Scope of Presidential Power," in David Gray Adler and Michael A. Genovese, eds., *The Presidency and the Law: The Clinton Legacy* (Lawrence: University Press of Kansas, 2002), 10. David M. O'Brien, "Judicial Legacies: The Clinton Presidency and the Courts," in Colin Campbell and Bert Rockman, eds., *The Clinton Legacy* (New York: Chatham House, 2000), 113.

136   Binder and Maltzman, *Advice and Dissent*, 80. Yalof, "In Search of a Means to an End," 197–98.

137   Russell Wheeler, "Judicial Nominations and Confirmations in Obama's First Term," *Governance Studies at Brookings*, December 13, 2012.

138   For challenges to judicial supremacy from the left, see Burns, *Packing the Courts*, and Mark Tushnet, *Taking the Constitution Away from the Courts* (Princeton, NJ: Princeton University Press, 1999). Challenges from the right are legion. See, for instance, Robert Bork, *Slouching toward Gomorrah: Modern Liberalism and American Decline* (New York: Regan Books, 1996).

139   Goldman, *Picking Federal Judges*, 207–08. Republican Party Platform, July 31, 2000.

140   Whittington, *Political Foundations of Judicial Supremacy*, 38–39, 68 n154, 274, 286. O'Brien, "The Reagan Judges," 60. Ronald Reagan, Statement on the United States Supreme Court Decision on Abortion, June 16, 1983. Reagan was responding to the Court's ruling the previous day in *City of Akron v. Akron Center for Reproductive Health*.

CHAPTER 10

LAW AND EXECUTIVE POWER

Introductory Puzzle: What Was Nixon Thinking?

"So what in a sense you're saying is that there are certain situations . . . where the president can . . . do something illegal." David Frost seemed incredulous. In the 28 hours—spread over 12 days—that he spent interviewing former president Richard M. Nixon in the spring of 1977, nothing quite matched the drama of this moment. Did Nixon really believe that the president of the United States, charged by the Constitution with taking "Care that the Laws be faithfully executed," was entitled to break the law?[1]

"When the president does it that means that it is not illegal," Nixon answered, astonishing the millions of television viewers who had tuned in to what Frost had promised would be a "cascade of candor" from the former president. Nixon was quick to explain what he meant. "If . . . the president approves . . . an action because of the national security, or . . . because of a threat to internal peace and order . . . then the president's decision . . . enables those who carry it out, to carry it out without violating the law." Nixon was talking specifically about the Huston Plan (named after Deputy White House Counsel Tom Huston), which authorized surveillance of anti-war pro- testers that included burgling, wiretapping, opening mail, and infiltrating groups on college campuses. According to Nixon, his approval of the Huston Plan made legal what would ordinarily be illegal government activity. Otherwise, Nixon reasoned, those charged with carrying out his orders would be "in an impossible position."[2]

Nixon's reply staggered Frost. Did he mean that the president could order the murder of a dissenter and there would be no legal recourse against the murderer or the president? Nixon countered with a question of his own: wouldn't Franklin Roosevelt have been justified to order Hitler's assassination in order to save 6 million Jews from extermina- tion? Frost refused to be put off the scent. He was talking about dissent in the United States. Could the president legally order the murder of dissenters? Nixon shook his head. No president had or ever would order such an action. Certainly the illegal actions he had authorized under the Huston Plan weren't murderous. Still Frost did not give up. He wasn't alleging that Nixon or any other president had ordered the killing of domestic protesters. He was asking: "what's the dividing line between the burglar not being liable to criminal prosecution and the murderer?" Nixon had no definite answer, noting only that "there are degrees, there are nuances" and that "each case has to be considered on its merits." Frost wanted to know if Nixon was saying that "the dividing line is the president's judgment." Nixon paused and then deliberately and firmly answered: "yes."

Nixon quickly offered assurances that this discretionary power wasn't as dangerous as it might seem. "Just so that one does not get the impression that a president can run amok in this country and get away with it," Nixon admonished Frost, he should keep in mind "that a president has to come up before the electorate." The people wouldn't reelect a president who authorized murdering citizens. Remember, too, "that a president has to get appropriations from the Congress," and that the CIA's and FBI's covert operations are disclosed to "trusted members of Congress," albeit on "a very, very limited basis." Of course, as Frost reminded Nixon, the administration never had any intention of revealing the Huston Plan to Congress or the American people.

As the conversation continued, Nixon turned to history and to the president with whom he most closely identified: Abraham Lincoln. What he was trying to say, Nixon told Frost, "was perhaps much better stated by Lincoln." He remembered the quote "almost exactly": "actions which otherwise would be unconstitutional could become lawful if undertaken for the purpose of preserving the Constitution and the Nation." Nixon's rendering was mostly faithful to Lincoln's original, written in April 1864: "measures, otherwise unconstitutional, might become lawful, by becoming indispensable to the preservation of the constitution,

David Frost interviews former president Richard Nixon in 1977. The taping sessions spanned 12 days and 28 hours and were then edited into four 90-minute television shows that were aired on public broadcasting stations in May 1977.

Courtesy: Time & Life Pictures/Getty Images.

through the preservation of the nation." But surely, Frost pointed out, "there was no comparison ... between the situation you faced and the situation Lincoln faced." After all, Lincoln confronted a Civil War that threatened the existence of the nation. Nixon did not flinch. True, there was no North and South fighting each other, but the United States "was torn apart in an ideological way by the war in Vietnam as much as the Civil War tore apart the nation when Lincoln was president."[3]

Exasperated, Frost tried to steer the conversation back to the Constitution. Was there "anything in the Constitution," he asked, that supported Nixon's view that the president is so "far above the law" that he need only authorize an action to make it legal. No, Nixon conceded, "there isn't. There's nothing specific that the Constitution contemplates in that respect." He hadn't "read every word, every jot and every tittle," so he couldn't say for sure. But he did know that it had been "argued ... that in war time, a president does have certain extraordinary powers which would make acts that would otherwise be unlawful, lawful if undertaken for the purpose of preserving the nation and the Constitution." As a wartime president, any actions Nixon took against anti-war protesters were therefore legal so long as they were undertaken for the purpose of preserving the nation and the Constitution.

For Frost, and for many others who watched the interview when it aired on May 19, 1977, Nixon's arguments seemed alien to an American political tradition based on the idea that no individual, no matter how powerful, was above the rule of law. Weren't these the same monarchical principles that the framers had rejected in creating the Constitution? From Nixon's perspective, however, there was nothing un-American or even unusual about his contentions. His actions were in keeping with the finest traditions of the nation's greatest presidents.[4]

Was Nixon right that his actions and principles followed in the footsteps of our nation's great presidents? To answer this question, we first look at the Constitution—not every jot and every tittle, but the specific provisions that can help to reveal the framers' understanding of the president's relationship to the law.

LAW AND THE CONSTITUTION

In November 1787, two months after the delegates at the Constitutional Convention had finished their work, William Symmes, a young lawyer from Andover, Massachusetts, sat down to record his objections to the proposed Constitution. Number 11 on his lengthy list of complaints was the clause that stated that the president "shall take Care that the Laws be faithfully executed." Was there ever "a commission so brief, so general?" Symmes complained. Doubtless it was "a very good thing to have wholesome laws faithfully executed," but what precisely was meant by "faithful" execution? Who would decide whether the president's actions were faithful to the law? The ambiguity of the words "faithfully execute," Symmes fretted, could create an executive that was "to all intents & purposes absolute."[5]

The "Take Care" Clause

What did the framers intend in charging the executive with faithfully executing the laws? The answer is more elusive than one might expect. Although it is much quoted, the "take care" clause was never debated at the Constitutional Convention or at any of the state ratifying conventions. At the outset of the Constitutional Convention, the delegates disagreed about whether to have a single or plural executive, but all agreed with the Virginia Plan's stipulation that the executive should have the authority to "execute the national laws." After all, why else have an executive if not to execute the laws? The Committee of Detail altered the Virginia Plan's wording to read "he shall take care that the laws of the United States be duly and faithfully executed," and the Committee of Style gave the clause its final tweak by dropping the "duly and." But these alterations were neither prompted by nor induced any comment from the convention delegates—at least not a comment that was written down and preserved for posterity.

So where did the wording come from? Like many provisions in Article II, the phrasing seems to have been adapted from New York's 1777 constitution—drafted by John Jay— which made it the duty of the governor "to take care that the laws are faithfully executed to the best of his ability." At least one other state—Vermont—had similar wording in its constitution, but most of the Revolutionary-era state constitutions used language that expressed greater skepticism of executive power. Virginia's 1776 constitution, for instance, stated that the governor "shall exercise the executive powers of government, according to the laws of this Commonwealth; and shall not, under any pretence, exercise any power or prerogative by virtue of any law, statute, or custom of England." And Virginia's bill of rights, drafted by George Mason, insisted that "all power of suspending laws, or the execution of laws, by any authority without consent of the representatives of the people, is injurious to their rights, and ought not to be exercised." The latter was modeled on the English "Bill of Rights" of 1689—actually an act of Parliament—which stated that "the pretended power of suspending of laws, or the execution of laws, by regal authority, without consent of parliament, is illegal."[6]

Nobody at the Constitutional Convention, including Mason, appears to have pressed for a Virginia-style disavowal of what had traditionally been understood in Britain as royal prerogative power—that is, the authority to act "in the absence of law, or in defiance of it." So did the framers intend the "take care" clause to endow the president with something akin to prerogative power? That seems highly doubtful. If the injunction to faithfully execute the laws was intended to include the executive's right to defy laws passed by Congress, then surely Mason or somebody like him, either at the Federal Convention or the state ratifying conventions, would have objected in the most strenuous terms. Yet even the most vocal opponents of presidential power—including those who complained of the resemblance between the president and a monarch—passed over the "take care" clause with barely a mention. Only young William Symmes seems to have recognized the mischief that lurked within those seemingly unobjectionable words.[7]

The Pardon Power: Theory and Practice

The only place in which the framers clearly granted the president the ancient royal prerogative of setting aside the law was in Article II, section 2, which gave the president the power "to grant Reprieves and Pardons for Offences against the United States, except in Cases of Impeachment." In England, according to the influential jurist William

Blackstone, the king possessed the power to pardon on the theory that all criminal offenses were against the Crown. "It is reasonable," Blackstone argued, "that he only who is injured should have the power of forgiving." But for Blackstone, the royal prerogative to pardon was incompatible with a democratic form of government. Only a monarchy was suited to the pardon power because only a monarchical regime acknowledged a person who acts "in a superior sphere" and who could thus act above or outside the law. The convention delegates knew their Blackstone, so why did they give a democratically elected president an almost unrestricted power to pardon?[8]

The answer appears to be that the framers thought of the pardon not, as Blackstone did, as a gift of grace or an act of beneficent mercy, but rather as a necessary tool in the government's arsenal. When convention delegate Luther Martin proposed that pardons only be permitted after conviction—a restriction that applied in many of the state constitutions—he quickly withdrew the motion after James Wilson pointed out that pardon before conviction might be needed "in order to obtain the testimony of accomplices." The "principal argument" for vesting the pardon power in the executive, Hamilton underscored in *Federalist* No. 74, was that "in seasons of insurrection or rebellion, there are often critical moments, when a well timed offer of pardon to the insurgents or rebels may restore the tranquility of the commonwealth." The legislature was not always in session, and so would often be unable to capitalize on these "critical moments." The presidential pardon, in short, was seen primarily as "an instrument of law enforcement" and not, as in England, an act of clemency "opposed to the law."[9]

Several delegates remained unhappy that the president was permitted to pardon treason, a prerogative that no state governor or even colonial governor was granted. In the closing hours of the Constitutional Convention, Virginia's Edmund Randolph moved to amend the pardon clause to make an exception for treason. In cases involving treason, Randolph explained, "the prerogative of pardon ... was too great a trust," especially since "the president may himself be guilty [and] the traitors may be his own instruments." However, the delegates were swayed by the contrary argument that pardons were necessary for dealing with treason and that the executive was a safer repository of this power than the legislature. And, as Wilson reminded the convention, if the president was "a party to the guilt he can be impeached."[10]

The decision to vest the president with a broad pardon power drew the strongest dissent from George Mason, who warned that the president "may frequently pardon crimes which were advised by himself." Mason thought it particularly unwise to allow the president to grant pardons "before indictment or conviction" because by doing so he may "stop inquiry and prevent detection" of his misdeeds or those of his subordinates.[11]

Both sides can point to episodes in American history that vindicate their point of view. On Hamilton's side of the ledger, presidents have made valuable use of pardons during or immediately after major wars or domestic uprisings. After crushing the Whiskey Rebellion in western Pennsylvania in 1794, George Washington issued an amnesty to all those who had violently resisted the government's unpopular whiskey tax. During and immediately following the Civil War, Abraham Lincoln and Andrew Johnson issued amnesties to approximately 200,000 people. And Gerald Ford and Jimmy Carter granted amnesties to more than 10,000 people who evaded the draft during the Vietnam War.[12]

Anti-Federalist critics such as Mason, however, would find their fears confirmed by instances in which presidents have used the pardon power to obstruct inquiries into the misdeeds or crimes of executive branch officials. For instance, after the Iran–Contra affair (the Reagan administration's scheme to gain the release of hostages by selling arms to Iran—in violation of a US arms embargo—and then diverting the proceeds from those arms sales to fund Contra rebels fighting against Nicaragua's Marxist government—in violation of a congressional prohibition against providing military assistance to the Contras), President George Herbert Walker Bush pardoned Reagan's secretary of defense Caspar Weinberger when the latter was indicted for obstructing Independent Counsel Lawrence Walsh's inquiry into the scandal. By pardoning Weinberger, Bush ensured that he would not have to testify under oath at Weinberger's trial about his own role in the Iran–Contra affair, including his own failure to disclose "his own highly relevant contemporaneous notes." Walsh complained that Bush's pardon "undermine[d] the principle that no man is above the law," but the framers of the Constitution must share the blame since they decided to trust one person, the president, with the nearly unrestricted power to set aside the law in the case of pardons.[13]

Mason's alarm at the dangers posed by an almost unlimited pardon power has sounded loudly amid reports that President Donald Trump was considering using the pardon power to undermine a special counsel inquiry into Russian meddling in the 2016 election. Trump evidently looked into not only pardoning family members and political aides who might be targets of the special counsel's inquiry but also exploring whether he could pardon himself. Trump would not, however, be the first president to ask his lawyers about a self-pardon. Before resigning, Nixon asked the same question: the answer he got back from the Office of Legal Counsel (in a memo issued three days before Nixon resigned) was, no, the president could not pardon himself ("under the fundamental rule that no one may be a judge in his own case"). Even Mason, who was ever alert to the dangers of executive misbehavior, never imagined a president pardoning himself.[14]

On balance, up until now at least, history has largely vindicated the framers' conclusion that the president could be safely entrusted with the pardoning power. Unlike many other presidential powers, the pardon power has not expanded over time. In fact, since 1980 presidents have generally used the pardon more sparingly than at any time since the early republic. Among the most reluctant pardoners of all was President George W. Bush, who granted an average of fewer than 25 pardons a year, almost all of them uncontroversial acts of clemency for individuals who had long since served their time. Initially Barack Obama followed this same restrained pattern, but during his final two years he embarked on an ambitious "clemency initiative" aimed at commuting the sentences of nonviolent drug offenders. But while Obama commuted sentences far more frequently than any of his predecessors—indeed, the more than 1,700 sentences he commuted is three times the number of commutations issues by the past ten presidents combined—he rarely pardoned people. Indeed, he issued fewer pardons than Bush or any other two-term president.[15]

Moreover, although the Constitution placed few restrictions on the president's personal discretion to pardon (presidents can only pardon federal offenses and they cannot pardon in cases of impeachment), the pardon process has evolved its own legal bureaucracy. Virtually all pardon requests are routed through the Pardon Attorney's Office in the Department of Justice, and very few people receive a presidential pardon without first receiving a positive recommendation from the pardon attorney. Among the rules established by the Pardon Attorney's Office is that no pardon should be petitioned until five years after the petitioner has been released from prison. So even though the framers explicitly rejected the idea of preventing presidents from pardoning before conviction, in practice presidents have rarely done so. Trump's pardon of ex-sheriff Joe Arpaio in the summer of 2017 was a notable departure from this pattern and from the typical pardon process.[16]

The framers correctly gauged that the president would have powerful incentives not to abuse the pardoning power. Pardons for politicians who have been implicated in wrongdoing are rarely popular. President Ford's pardon of Nixon caused his public approval ratings to plummet and probably cost him reelection in 1976. Of course, concerns with public approval and reelection don't stop a president from issuing controversial pardons in the closing weeks of his administration. George Herbert Walker Bush issued his pardon to Weinberger—which the American people disapproved of by a 2–1 margin—only after he had lost his reelection bid to Clinton.

There have been plenty of presidential scandals in American history, but pardons to cover up misdeeds or obstruct criminal inquiries have been relatively rare. Even Nixon, despite his flagrant disregard for the law, refused to pardon staffers implicated in Watergate, including his chief of staff H.R. Haldeman, who pleaded with his boss to grant him a pardon before he resigned from the presidency. Nixon's restraint stemmed not from a highly developed sense of probity but rather from coldly calculating his own interests. If he had pardoned Haldeman or other co-conspirators early during the congressional inquiry into Watergate, he would have invited certain impeachment. If he pardoned them immediately before resigning, he jeopardized his own chances of receiving a pardon from Ford.

Even presidents who were not angling for a pardon or in fear of impeachment have generally resisted pressure from supporters to pardon presidential aides implicated in wrongdoing. Reagan resisted intense lobbying from conservatives to pardon Oliver North and John Poindexter for their role in the Iran–Contra scandal because he feared it would damage his historical reputation. Similarly, George W. Bush refused to pardon Vice President Cheney's chief of staff, Scooter Libby, after Libby was convicted of lying to a grand jury about his involvement in revealing a CIA agent's name (Valerie Plame) to reporters—a leak that was part of the vice president's campaign to discredit Plame's husband Joseph Wilson, who had accused the administration of lying about Iraq's nuclear program to bolster its case for invading Iraq. Although Bush commuted Libby's 30-month jail sentence, this act of clemency fell far short of the full pardon for which Cheney lobbied unrelentingly in the closing weeks of the administration. Cheney was furious with Bush for leaving a "soldier on the battlefield," while Bush and his allies saw the decision as necessary to protect Bush's reputation and to uphold the principle that no one was above the law.[17] However, the Constitution does little to prevent a president less worried about his own reputation or less committed to upholding the rule of law from making a different calculation.

"So Far Above the Law": Executive Prerogative from Locke to Lincoln

The theory behind the pardon power is that there are extraordinary circumstances in which the president needs to be able to set aside the law in order to serve the national interest or the interests of justice. A president may abuse that power, but the Constitution undoubtedly gives the president that power. A presidential pardon may obstruct the law or be used for corrupt ends but it cannot be illegal or unconstitutional, so long as it is employed "for Offences against the United States, except in Cases of Impeachment."

So to reformulate Frost's question: is there anything in the Constitution apart from the pardon power that suggests that the president is "so far above the law" that he can set the law aside for the good of the country? Even if nowhere mentioned in the Constitution, is such a prerogative implicit in the very idea of executive power? Nixon's answer appealed to the authority of Lincoln, but perhaps a better place to begin is with John Locke, the English political philosopher whose ideas permeated late eighteenth-century American political thought.

John Locke and the "Power to Act according to Discretion"

The central aim of Locke's *Two Treatises of Government* was to refute the notion that monarchs had a hereditary or divine right to absolute rule. Instead, Locke insisted, all political power derived from the consent of the governed. In declaring independence, the American revolutionaries drew upon Locke's argument that the people had a right to take up arms if a ruler violated the people's natural rights to "life, liberty, and estate." And in crafting state constitutions and the federal constitution, Americans were influenced by Locke's insistence that the legislative and executive powers should be placed "in distinct hands." In the well-ordered commonwealth, according to Locke, the executive does not make the laws but rather follows them. The executive "has no will, no power, but that of the law," law that is promulgated by the polity's "supreme power," the legislature.[18]

Locke was not naive. He understood that there were "many things" that the law could not provide for and that "must necessarily be left to the discretion of him that has the executive power in his hands, to be ordered by him as the public good and advantage shall require." Laws articulated general rules and the executive inevitably needed to exercise discretion in applying those rules to specific situations. Moreover, the legislature would frequently not be in session and it was impossible for legislators "to foresee, and so by laws to provide for all accidents and necessities." In some circumstances, Locke conceded, the executive might have to act not only "without the prescription of the law" but "even against it." Indeed, for Locke this was the definition of prerogative: the "power to act according to discretion, for the public good, without the prescription of the law, and sometimes even against it."[19]

In explaining his argument on prerogative, Locke offered the example of a burning house. The law may forbid the destruction of another man's property, but it may be justifiable to destroy the house adjacent to the burning house if it stops the fire spreading to the neighborhood. When "a strict and rigid observation of the laws may do harm" to the community that the executive is pledged to protect, then the "laws themselves" may need to "give way to the executive power, or rather to this fundamental law of nature and government: That as much as may be, all the members of the society are to be preserved."[20]

Does Locke's notion of prerogative vindicate Nixon's claim that "when the President does it, that means it's not illegal"? If executive power is necessarily discretionary, then are the executive's actions inherently legal, at least during emergencies? Not according to Locke, who was well aware of the problem that "a weak and ill prince" might "claim that power which his predecessors exercised without the direction of the law, as a prerogative belonging to him by right of his office, which he may exercise at his pleasure." The prerogative to act outside the law, Locke insisted, was not an inherent power that belonged to the ruler. Instead it was a "right" that belonged to the people, who "whilst it was exercised for their good ... were content" to have it exercised by the executive. The discretionary actions of an executive, in other words, were not inherently legal. Instead the executive had to justify his use of extralegal power to the people and their elected representatives, who retained the right to judge the necessity, wisdom, and legality of the president's discretionary actions.[21]

Jefferson's Louisiana Purchase

The Lockean prerogative was not a warrant for expansive, let alone arbitrary, executive power. It was instead an essential attribute of limited government, a way to check power by not allowing actions taken in an emergency to become a precedent for ordinary politics. This was the view expressed in the first Congress by Alexander White in the debate over the removal power. Fresh from spearheading the fight for the Constitution at the Virginia ratifying convention, White told his congressional colleagues that it was "better for the President to extend his powers on some extraordinary occasion, even where he is not strictly justified by the constitution, than the legislature should grant an improper power to be exercised at all times." White offered the example of Virginia's governor Thomas Nelson, who during the Revolutionary War had been compelled to exercise power "beyond the authority of the law" but was "afterwards indemnified by the legislature" for the actions he had taken to protect the state.[22]

The early republic's most devout Lockean was Thomas Jefferson, who, like Nelson, had been a wartime Virginia governor. Shortly after he left the presidency, Jefferson was asked whether there were occasions on which public officials must "exercise an authority beyond the law." Jefferson acknowledged that "a strict observance of the written laws is doubtless *one* of the high duties of a good citizen," but it was "not *the highest*." The "higher obligation" was adherence to the "the laws of necessity, of self-preservation, of saving our country when in danger. ... To lose our country by a scrupulous adherence to written law, would be to lose the law itself, with life, liberty, property and all those who are enjoying them with us; thus absurdly sacrificing the end to the means." For Jefferson, as for Locke, this duty extended beyond avoiding great harm and encompassed doing a great public good. Jefferson provided a "hypothetical case" to illustrate his point: What if, while the legislature was not in session, there arose the opportunity for the executive to acquire the Floridas "for a reasonable sum," a sum for which the legislature had made no appropriation? Suppose, too, that by waiting for the legislature to convene, the opportunity for the purchase would be lost. "Ought the Executive, in that case, and with that foreknowledge, to have secured the good to his country, and to have trusted to their justice for the transgression of the law?" To Jefferson, the answer was clear: the executive ought to commit the illegal act, trusting that the people would approve it after the fact.[23]

Jefferson did not claim—as Nixon did—that the act became legal because the president did it. Instead, Jefferson conceded the act's illegality and emphasized that it was up to the people and the legislature to decide whether the act was warranted. Jefferson acknowledged that drawing "the line of discrimination" between legitimate and illegitimate uses of discretionary power was not easy, but "the good officer is bound to draw it at his own peril, and throw himself on the justice of his country and the rectitude of his motives." Those entrusted with discretionary power, in other words, must explain why an act not sanctioned by law was necessary to achieve a great purpose. If the executive failed to persuade the people and their representatives of the rectitude of his motives and the necessity of his actions, then he would be exposed as a lawbreaker.

In choosing the Floridas as a hypothetical case, Jefferson was clearly thinking of his own role in the Louisiana Purchase, which transformed the shape of the United States. For about $15 million (about three and a half cents an acre), the French ceded to the United States a massive swath of territory stretching from New Orleans to the Canadian border, including all or most of what is today Arkansas, Missouri, Iowa, Oklahoma, Kansas, Nebraska, North Dakota, and South Dakota, as well as parts of Colorado, Louisiana, Minnesota, Montana, New Mexico, and Wyoming.

As president, Jefferson had not set out to acquire this immense territory. Instead his aim had been merely to buy New Orleans, the strategic port of entry for all shipping trade on the Mississippi River. Jefferson authorized the American envoys to pay France up to $10 million to secure New Orleans and its immediate environs. Much to the Americans' surprise, Napoleon offered to sell not only New Orleans but more than 800,000 square miles of land in the North American interior. Fearing that any delay might prompt Napoleon to withdraw the offer, the American negotiators set aside their official instructions and signed the treaty.

Jefferson was delighted at the purchase and eager for the Senate to ratify the treaty. Yet as a strict constructionist, he also believed that he had committed "an act beyond the Constitution" since the national government lacked the explicit authority to incorporate new territory into the Union or to grant (as the treaty did) the rights of citizenship to the inhabitants of a territory. Writing to Senator John Breckinridge, a close confidant who shared the president's strict constructionist views, he suggested that as "faithful servants," the president and Congress must "throw themselves on their country for doing for them unauthorized what we know they would have done for themselves had they been in a situation to do it." If the people disagreed, they could disavow the act.[24]

That was the Lockean theory, at least. But did Jefferson dare profess it in public? Virginia senator Wilson Cary Nicholas warned the president that if he proclaimed the purchase unconstitutional the Senate would probably reject the treaty. And even if the

Senate did approve it, Nicholas worried that "great use would be made [by the Federalist opposition] with the people of a willful breach of the constitution." Most worrying of all was intelligence from France indicating that Napoleon was having second thoughts about the sale and looking for an excuse to renege on the treaty.[25]

Jefferson had at first thought to publicly declare his transgression of the Constitution and then urge a constitutional amendment that would serve as an "act of indemnity." That way Jefferson could consummate the purchase without relying on the Federalist doctrine of implied powers, which he feared would render the Constitution "a blank paper by construction." But the worrying news from France led Jefferson to change tactics. He now counseled his allies to say nothing that might delay the treaty's approval and give a pretext for its retraction by Napoleon. "The less we say about the constitutional difficulties respecting Louisiana the better," Jefferson counseled. "Congress should act on it without talking." Confessing publicly to having violated the Constitution turned out to be a lot more difficult in practice than it had appeared in Locke's theory.[26]

"All the Laws but One": Lincoln's Suspension of Habeas Corpus

The Constitution made no allowance for the government setting aside the law in emergencies, except in the second clause of Article I, section 9: "The Privilege of the Writ of Habeas Corpus shall not be suspended, unless when in Cases of Rebellion or Invasion the public Safety may require it." A cornerstone of English law and liberty, a writ of habeas corpus required the government to produce a prisoner in a court of law and to give legal reasons justifying the prisoner's detention. Habeas corpus thus protected individuals against arbitrary executive power.

Each president in the early republic confronted a rebellion of some sort. Washington had to deal with the Whiskey Rebellion and John Adams confronted Fries's Rebellion, another armed tax revolt in Pennsylvania. Jefferson and Madison both faced secessionist intrigue in Massachusetts and Connecticut, while Monroe and Jackson wrestled with threats of nullification and possibly secession in South Carolina. In none of these cases was habeas corpus suspended by the federal government. The first time the US government did so was in the spring of 1861, when Abraham Lincoln suspended the writ along the rail line connecting Philadelphia and Washington, DC.

To understand why Lincoln suspended the writ, keep in mind that the only way to get to the nation's capital was through Virginia, which had already seceded, and Maryland, which teetered on the edge of secession. The rail lines connecting Washington, DC, to the northern states ran through Baltimore, a city in which secessionist and anti-Republican sentiments were strong. Lincoln's call for troops to put down the rebellion had been met with violent riots in Baltimore. Mobs of Confederate sympathizers attempted to obstruct the movement of troops through the city, with one clash killing four soldiers from a Massachusetts regiment and 12 Baltimore civilians. Baltimore's mayor urged citizens to resist the "invasion" from the North and persuaded Maryland's governor to order the destruction of railroad bridges to arrest the flow of federal troops into the city. Telegraph lines running through Maryland had also been cut, and rumors of an impending invasion left everybody in the largely defenseless capital in a state of profound anxiety. It was in the immediate aftermath of the Baltimore riot and bridge burnings that Lincoln authorized General Winfield Scott to suspend the writ of habeas corpus.[27]

Among those arrested and imprisoned in Fort McHenry by the Union army for destroying railroad bridges was a prominent Baltimore Democrat, John Merryman. The day after Merryman's arrest, a petition for a writ of habeas corpus was brought to the Washington home of Chief Justice Roger Taney, who immediately dashed off a writ commanding the government to produce Merryman at the federal courthouse in Baltimore the following morning. Taney then rushed to Baltimore to preside at the hearing, in his capacity as chief judge of the fourth circuit, which included his home state of Maryland. A military officer appeared in court Monday morning, sans prisoner, explaining that the president had authorized the suspension of habeas corpus and asking Taney "most respectfully" to postpone the hearing so he could receive instructions from his commander in chief. Taney would brook no delay, however, and he dispatched the court's marshal to Fort McHenry under orders to bring Merryman to court by noon the next day. When the marshal was turned away at the fort gates, Taney was ready with a prepared statement that he read from the bench to a packed Baltimore courtroom.[28]

Less than 60 hours after Merryman's arrest and without giving the administration an opportunity to justify its suspension of habeas corpus, Taney announced his verdict: Merryman's detention was unlawful because only Congress could suspend the writ of habeas corpus. Lacking the power to compel the military to deliver Merryman to the civilian courts, Taney declared his intention to send his judgment along with an expanded opinion to the president and "call upon him to perform his constitutional duty to enforce the laws."[29]

Taney's rush to judgment betrayed his eagerness to rebuke a president he loathed. He blamed Lincoln and his party's antislavery platform for the break-up of the Union, resented Lincoln's attacks on his *Dred Scott* opinion (see Chapter 9), and believed that Lincoln had embarked on an unconstitutional effort to compel the southern states to return to the Union. Although Taney thought that the South did not have the constitutional right to secede, he also believed—as he told former president Franklin Pierce shortly after the Merryman case—that "a peaceful separation" of North and South was much preferable to a civil war followed by a "reign of terror."[30]

If Taney was less than impartial and his haste unseemly, his interpretation of the Constitution in *Ex parte Merryman* nonetheless had a great deal to recommend it. Although the Constitution did not explicitly specify who could suspend habeas corpus, the chief justice was correct that ever since the founding of the Constitution—and even before that in England—it had been an unquestioned axiom that only the legislature could suspend the writ. A clue to the framers' intent lay in the clause's placement in Article I, which specified congressional, not executive, powers.[31]

However persuasive as a reading of the framers' original intent, *Ex parte Merryman* was marred by Taney's unwillingness to acknowledge the conditions that led Lincoln to suspend habeas corpus. A reader of Taney's opinion would not know that 11 states had seceded from the Union or that saboteurs in Maryland threatened the government's existence or that riots in Baltimore had killed federal troops and civilians. Nor did Taney make any effort to recognize Lincoln's dilemma: that without a suspension of habeas corpus the president could not prevent judges sympathetic to the Confederacy (like Taney) from releasing saboteurs as fast as the army arrested them, thereby endangering the army's supply lines and the lives of troops. And as historian Brian McGinty points out, Taney made no effort "to call for calm in Maryland [or] to warn disloyal Marylanders to refrain from attacking federal troops and stop blowing up bridges." The only law-breaker who interested Taney was the president.[32]

It is sometimes said that Lincoln ignored Taney's opinion in *Merryman*.[33] In fact, Lincoln engaged it directly in his July 1861 message to Congress. "The attention of the country," Lincoln began, "has been called to the proposition that one who is sworn to 'take care that the laws be faithfully executed' should not himself violate them." Lincoln denied Taney's charge that in suspending habeas corpus he had violated the law. The Constitution, he pointed out, was "silent" on which branch could suspend habeas cor-pus, but perfectly clear about the conditions under which it could be suspended: "in Cases of Rebellion or Invasion [when] the public Safety may require it." Taney's narrow reading of the clause would make the framers into fools. What sense would there be in writing a clause that was "plainly made for a dangerous emergency" and then only allowing the government to make use of that power on the off chance that Congress was in session when the emergency occurred? "It can not be believed," Lincoln said, that "the framers of the instrument intended that in every case the danger should run its course until Congress could be called together, the very assembling of which might be pre-vented." Taney's interpretation of the habeas corpus clause made the Constitution into a suicide pact.[34]

Even if one conceded Taney's premise that the president had overstepped the law, Lincoln still insisted that his actions were justified by the extraordinary situation he faced. Granted that the president was charged, as the chief justice had pointedly reminded him, to "take care that the laws be faithfully executed," Lincoln nevertheless reminded Taney and all those who thought like him that "the whole of the laws which were required to be faithfully executed were being resisted and failing of execution in nearly one-third of the States." Must they, Lincoln asked, "be allowed to finally fail of execution, even had it been perfectly clear that by the use of the means necessary to their execution some single law [habeas corpus] should to a very limited extent be violated?" To put the question more dramatically: "Are all the laws *but one* to go unexecuted, and the Government itself go to pieces lest that one be violated?"[35]

Lincoln's question echoed Jefferson's Lockean formulation that on occasion fealty to the law must give way to "the laws of necessity, of self-preservation, of saving our country when in danger." But in his next sentence Lincoln signaled his intent to move beyond Jefferson's extra-constitutional laws of necessity or Locke's laws of nature. "Even in such a case," Lincoln asked, "would not the official oath be broken if the Government should be overthrown when it was believed that disregarding the single law would tend to preserve it?" That is, if the president refused to suspend habeas corpus, causing the government to go to pieces, he would be guilty of failing to uphold his constitutional oath to "preserve, protect, and defend the Constitution of the United States." Since his highest consti-tutional duty was to preserve the Constitution, he had a constitutional right to take any actions that were necessary to preserve the Constitution. As historian Arthur Schlesinger Jr. has pointed out, Lincoln was "constitutionalizing the law of necessity."[36]

"Measures, Otherwise Unconstitutional": A Second Look at the Hodges Letter

In his famous 1864 letter to Kentucky editor Albert Hodges, the one Nixon quoted in his interview with Frost, Lincoln returned to his oath of office as a constitutional warrant for actions he had taken during the war—this time to defend not the suspension of habeas corpus but the Emancipation Proclamation and the recruiting of black soldiers. Lincoln wrote:

> My oath to preserve the constitution to the best of my ability imposed upon me the duty of preserving, by every indispensable means, that government—that nation—of which that constitution was the organic law. Was it possible to lose the nation, and yet preserve the constitution? By general law life *and* limb must be protected; yet often a limb must be amputated to save a life; but a life is never wisely given to save a limb. I felt that measures, otherwise unconstitutional, might become lawful, by becoming indispensable to the preservation of the constitution, through the preservation of the nation.

In claiming a constitutional warrant for the otherwise illegal act of freeing and arming slaves, Lincoln did not contend—as Nixon had—that his actions as president were legal by definition. Nor did he contend that the inherent justice of emancipation justified his actions; the oath of office, Lincoln explained, forbade him from indulging his "abstract judgment on the moral question of slavery." Instead his extraordinary actions could only become lawful if they were indispensable to safeguarding the nation and therefore the Constitution.[37]

The sentence recited by Nixon was not the end of Lincoln's argument but its prelude. In the remainder of the letter, Lincoln explained why the actions he had taken in emancipating slaves and then arming them had become indispensable to suppressing the rebellion. After pointing out the gains achieved by the policy over the past year—"with no loss by it in our foreign relations, none in our home popular sentiment, none in our white military force"—Lincoln concluded:

> Let any Union man who complains ... test himself by writing down in one line that he is for subduing the rebellion by force of arms; and in the next, that he is for taking these hundred and thirty thousand [black soldiers, seamen, and laborers] from the Union side, and placing them where they would be but for the measure he condemns. If he can not face his case so stated, it is only because he can not face the truth.

For Lincoln, then, answering the question of the president's constitutional authority did not absolve him of the obligation to offer reasons why the actions he had taken were necessary. Rather than foreclose political debate on the merits of his policy through assertions of inherent executive power, Lincoln tried to persuade border-state skeptics of the need for his policy of enlisting former slaves in the Union army.

Nixon had memorized Lincoln's words but effaced their context and meaning. Words chosen by Lincoln to explain why he had emancipated slaves and enlisted them in a fight for their freedom, Nixon employed to justify burglary and surveillance of student protesters. Even if one ignores the context of the Hodges letter, and reads it instead as a justification for abridging civil liberties, Nixon never comes close to meeting Lincoln's standard of showing that his actions were "indispensable to the preservation of the constitution"—which explains why Nixon rendered Lincoln's words as "for the purpose of preserving the Constitution" rather than the more exacting indispensable necessity standard that Lincoln enunciated. Nor did Nixon have a credible answer to Frost's essential question about the differences in the situations faced by the two presidents. Nixon's assertion that the United States "was torn apart in an ideological way by the war in Vietnam, *as much as* the Civil War tore apart the nation" betrays an impoverished understanding of history. Yes, there were deep divisions within the country about the Vietnam War, but neither the survival of the nation nor the Constitution was ever at stake.

Nixon's attempt to cloak his abuses of power in Lincoln's mantle brings to mind Locke's warning "that the reigns of good princes have been always most dangerous to the liberties of their people." Although the good prince "is mindful of the trust put into his hands, and careful of the good of his people," the danger comes

> when their successors, managing the government with different thoughts ... draw the actions of those good rulers into precedent, and make them the standard of their prerogative, as if what had been done only for the good of the people was a right in them to do, for the harm of the people, if they so pleased.[38]

JUDGING EXECUTIVE POWER

Anxious to reassure Frost that no president is a law unto himself—that he can't simply "run amok"—Nixon had pointed to the electorate and Congress as checks on the president. Notably absent from this calculus were the courts, a striking omission for a president whose political fate was sealed after a unanimous Supreme Court ordered him to relinquish tape recordings the president had made of Watergate-related conversations.

Prior to the Court's ruling, Nixon had defied repeated subpoenas from congressional investigating committees and special prosecutors, arguing that the tapes contained confidential conversations between the president and his aides and were thus protected by executive privilege. The Court acknowledged that Nixon had a constitutional interest in confidential communications—without which the president could not count on receiving candid advice from his aides—but rejected Nixon's argument that he had an absolute right to withhold any information he chose. Instead the president's interest in candid advice had to be balanced against the nation's "historic commitment to the rule of law," specifically the "need to develop all relevant facts" in determining guilt or innocence in a criminal inquiry. In this case, the Court held, Nixon's generalized interest in confidentiality had to yield to "the demonstrated, specific need for evidence in a pending criminal trial."[39]

Among the tapes Nixon was compelled to hand over was one containing the "smoking gun": the president approving a plan to halt the FBI's investigation into the botched break-in at the Democratic National Committee headquarters in the Watergate office complex. The tape conclusively showed that the president had attempted to obstruct justice and prompted even his erstwhile supporters in Congress to abandon him. A few days after the tape was played, Nixon resigned.

Notwithstanding the dramatic outcome of the Court's ruling in *United States v. Nixon*, Nixon may have been right not to count the courts as the first line of defense against a president run amok. To begin with, Nixon's willingness to comply with the Court's ruling was conditioned by the imminent threat of impeachment by a Democratic-controlled House and Senate. Had Nixon had a sufficient number of partisans prepared to acquit him, it is doubtful that he would have given up the incriminating tapes. As it was, he contemplated defying the Court if its decision was divided.

Moreover, the Court was willing to check Nixon's claim of executive privilege because bowing to it would have "gravely impair[ed] the role of the courts under Article III." But the courts have less institutional incentive to be vigilant when the president's assertion of executive power does not directly impair the functioning of the judiciary—as, for instance, when the countervailing value involved is Congress's or the public's right to know what the executive branch is up to. Finally, while the Court dealt Nixon a serious setback, its opinion also explicitly recognized that a president's claim would be far stronger if it involved information related to military or diplomatic secrets.

How much, then, can we count on the Court to check executive power, especially during emergencies and wars when executive claims to power are likely to be at their most expansive? To answer this question, we start by returning to Nixon's favorite president, Abraham Lincoln.

Lincoln and the Copperheads

Two days after issuing the Emancipation Proclamation, Lincoln issued an even more sweeping proclamation. In it, Lincoln took aim at the problem of "disloyal persons" who were "not adequately restrained by the ordinary process of law" from discouraging volunteer enlistments, resisting the draft, or otherwise "affording aid and comfort" to the insurrection. Under Lincoln's order, any person arrested by the military for a "disloyal practice" could be subject to martial law and tried by a military commission.[40]

That was what happened to Ohio Democrat Clement Vallandigham, the North's most vocal critic of the war. As a congressman, Vallandigham frequently denounced Lincoln's despotic rule, warning that the president's war against slavery would result in "the enslavement of the white race, by debt and taxes and arbitrary power." Voted out of Congress in 1862, Vallandigham fixed to run for governor. Appearing before 20,000 people at a Democratic rally in Mount Vernon, Ohio, Vallandigham delivered a two-hour tongue-lashing of "King Lincoln," accusing the president of starting a war "for the purpose of crushing out liberty and erecting a despotism." Four days later, Vallandigham was arrested by order of General Ambrose Burnside. The following day, May 6, 1863, Vallandigham went on trial before a military commission for "declaring disloyal sentiments and opinions, with the object and purpose of weakening the power of the Government in its efforts to suppress the unlawful rebellion." After a two-day trial, the commission found Vallandigham guilty and sentenced him to be imprisoned until the end of the war.[41]

Convinced that the Constitution did not permit the government to try civilians in military court, Vallandigham asked the Supreme Court to hear his case. However, the Court had no appetite for a case that might embarrass Lincoln and damage the war effort. Rather than engage the broader constitutional questions raised by Vallandigham's arrest and trial, the Court sought refuge in the narrower question of jurisdiction. A military commission, the Court held, was outside of its jurisdiction and so there was nothing it could do to aid Vallandigham.[42]

Vallandigham was the most prominent Peace Democrat—or Copperhead, as Republicans called them—to be tried and convicted by military commission, but he was far from the only one. Another was Lambdin Milligan, a prominent, politically ambitious Indiana attorney, who was arrested in October 1864, eight months after the Court's ruling in *Ex parte Vallandigham*. Unlike Vallandigham, Milligan was arrested for more than speaking ill of the administration and the war. He was also active in organizing a secret society that sought, according to government agents who had infiltrated the group, to foment an armed uprising. Milligan and others in the group were also accused of plotting to free Confederate prisoners from Union jails in Indiana, Ohio, and Illinois. Two weeks after his arrest, Milligan and his confederates were found guilty and sentenced to hang. The date of execution was set for May 19, 1865. Fortunately for Milligan, the war ended six weeks before he was to be executed and the new president, Andrew Johnson, commuted his sentence to life imprisonment with hard labor. Milligan then challenged his conviction in court. He argued, as Vallandigham had, that he could not be tried in a military court. His crimes, if crimes they were, must be tried in a civilian court.

It might seem that Milligan's case had little hope of success. After all, only 15 months earlier the Court had declared that it had no jurisdiction over military commissions. And the only change in the composition of the Court in those 15 months had been the replacement of Chief Justice Taney—who had been too ill to participate in *Ex parte Vallandigham*—with Salmon Chase, who was treasury secretary before Lincoln named him to the Court. Moreover, on its face, Milligan's case seemed far weaker than Vallandigham's. Whereas Vallandigham had been tried for exercising constitutionally protected free speech rights, Milligan had been convicted of conspiracy to commit treason.

Nonetheless, the Supreme Court agreed to hear Milligan's case. After six days of oral argument in March 1866, the Court announced its decision: the military commission did not have jurisdiction to try Milligan and he must be freed immediately. Nine months after Milligan's release, the Court explained its reasoning in an opinion penned by David Davis, Lincoln's close friend and campaign manager. The Court now said what it had been afraid to say during the war: civilians could not be tried by military commissions so long as civilian courts were open and functional. Whereas in *Ex parte Vallandigham* the

Court took refuge in technical "legal jargon" about the limits of its jurisdiction, it now used expansive language about "the very framework of the government and the fundamental principles of American liberty." The Constitution, Davis opined,

> is a law for rulers and people, equally in war and in peace, and covers with the shield of its protection all classes of men, at all times, and under all circumstances. No doctrine, involving more pernicious consequences, was ever invented by the wit of man than that any of its provisions can be suspended during any of the great exigencies of government.[43]

The Court's "thunderously quotable" words are hailed today as an historic affirmation of the rule of law. Yet the decision and the words were ventured only after the war was over and "the public safety . . . assured." During the war, Davis conceded, "the temper of the times did not allow that calmness in deliberation and discussion so necessary to a correct conclusion of a purely judicial question." For those looking to the Court to check executive power, *Ex parte Milligan* provides a paradoxical precedent. On the one hand, *Milligan* strongly affirmed the legal limits on presidential and governmental power during emergencies. On the other, the case taught that during an emergency the Court would not insist that the president adhere to those legal limits—a lesson that would be underscored during the greatest crisis of the twentieth century: World War II.[44]

FDR and the Internment of Japanese Americans

On February 19, 1942, two months after the Japanese attack on Pearl Harbor, President Franklin Roosevelt issued an executive order authorizing the secretary of war and army commanders to designate parts of the country as "military areas" from which "any or all persons" could be excluded. The order was necessary, the president maintained, because the government needed to take "every possible protection against espionage and against sabotage." Although the president's order was couched in general terms, it had only one intended target: citizens and residents of Japanese descent who lived on the West Coast of the United States. Pursuant to the president's executive order, the military forcibly removed about 110,000 Japanese resident aliens and Japanese Americans from their homes and relocated them to internment camps in the interior of the country.[45]

The Supreme Court received its first opportunity to pass judgment on the president's exclusion order in the spring of 1943, in *Hirabayashi v. United States*. A Seattle native and student at the University of Washington, Gordon Hirabayashi had marched into an FBI office in May 1942 and announced that he could not obey the exclusion order or the curfew that the military had imposed on all persons of Japanese ancestry. Hirabayashi was promptly arrested and convicted of violating the curfew and of refusing to report to a "relocation center." A Court consisting of eight Roosevelt appointees unanimously ruled that the race-based curfew was a "reasonable" regulation "at a time of threatened Japanese attack upon this country." Having upheld Hirabayashi's conviction for violating the curfew, the Court then sidestepped the more contentious question of whether the government could relocate American citizens based purely on their ancestry. Hirabayashi had been sentenced to serve both three-month prison terms concurrently, so the Court reasoned that there was no need to rule on the constitutionality of the forced evacuations of American citizens, since Hirabayashi's sentence would be three months in federal prison regardless of what the Court decided about the relocation order.[46]

In the case of Fred Korematsu, though, the Court could not avoid ruling on the validity of the exclusion order. Unlike Hirabayashi, who turned himself in to protest the government's actions, Korematsu tried desperately to avoid detection. Hoping not to be separated from his Italian-American girlfriend, he changed his name and even had plastic surgery so he would look less Asian. Korematsu's amateurish attempts to disguise his identity were unsuccessful, and he was arrested and convicted for remaining in his home of San Leandro, California, which was part of the designated military area in which Japanese Americans were no longer allowed to reside.

Korematsu's case deeply divided the Court. The majority followed the same logic it had applied a year and a half earlier in *Hirabayashi*. In excluding persons of Japanese descent from designated areas, military authorities had taken a reasonable step that they deemed necessary to win the war. The courts should not second-guess the military authorities by availing themselves of "the calm perspective of hindsight." Under this logic, the courts had no role to play in checking military directives, at least so long as the executive and the legislature, the "war-making branches," had authorized the actions.[47]

However, three justices offered dissenting opinions. There was a world of difference, the dissenters insisted, between upholding a government order that citizens "stay in their homes during the hours of dark" and a government order that citizens "leave home entirely." Moreover, the government had not simply required Korematsu to leave the West Coast military district—abhorrent though that was—but it also required him to turn himself over to military authorities and be transported to a government detention camp in which he would be held indefinitely. Mass deprivation of fundamental civil liberties, particularly when based on invidious racial distinctions, required the government to produce compelling evidence that its actions really were necessary. Yet the government had produced "no reliable evidence" that American citizens of Japanese descent were disloyal or a threat to the national security.

History has been much kinder to the dissenters than to the *Korematsu* majority, particularly after it was discovered that Roosevelt's solicitor general, who argued the government's case before the Supreme Court, suppressed military intelligence and FBI reports showing that the nation faced no security risk from Japanese Americans at the time Korematsu was arrested. Those few individuals of Japanese descent who were deemed a security threat had already been rounded up before the commanding officer of the Western Defense Command, General John DeWitt, issued his order to relocate all Japanese Americans living on the West Coast of the United States. DeWitt's order was based not on a rational assessment of military necessity but on animus against "the Japanese race," which, Dewitt was convinced, would "turn against this nation when the final test of loyalty comes."[48]

But even if the government had not concealed evidence and the dissenters had prevailed, the Court's decision in *Korematsu* would still have had little or no effect on Roosevelt's actions—just as *Milligan* came too late to affect Lincoln's. Even before the

A posed but poignant photograph of three boys imprisoned in the Manzanar "relocation camp" in California's arid Owens Valley. The photograph was taken by Toyo Miyatake, himself an internee at the camp.

Courtesy: Image by Toyo Miyatake, from the Toyo Miyatake Manzanar Collection.

Court heard oral arguments in October 1944, the Roosevelt administration was already looking to remove the exclusion order as well as to close the internment camps—though FDR insisted on waiting until after the November election for fear of sparking a backlash among whites that might harm his electoral chances, especially in California. By the time the Court announced its judgment in *Korematsu* on December 18, 1944, the War Department had already declared that it was closing the internment camps and that Japanese Americans could once again be "permitted the same freedom of movement throughout the United States as other loyal citizens and law-abiding aliens." Even had the Court done the right thing by Fred Korematsu, it would have been too late to reverse the lasting harm done to the Japanese American community.[49]

FDR and the Nazi Saboteurs

The Court was equally ineffective in checking executive power in the case of eight Nazi saboteurs arrested in June 1942. German submarines had deposited four men near the tip of Long Island and another four in Florida. Their mission was to conduct industrial sabotage at aluminum factories that Americans needed to produce airplanes. They landed undetected, but within 24 hours of their arrival the FBI's New York office received a call from one of the saboteurs, German-born American citizen George John Dasch, who said he was coming to the nation's capital to give FBI director J. Edgar Hoover information vital to America's national security.[50]

The FBI thought the caller was a crank and took no action. Dasch arrived in Washington, DC, five days later and contacted the FBI, asking to speak with Hoover. After being shunted from one receptionist to another, Dasch finally managed to speak with an agent who took his story seriously. Dasch told the agent of the daring plot—code-named Operation Pastorius—that had been hatched at the highest levels of the Nazi regime. Dasch explained that he had gone along with the plot so he could return to the United States—where he had lived for most of the previous two decades and where his wife still lived—and do his part to defeat the Nazi regime by betraying the plot. Using the information that Dasch provided, the FBI quickly rounded up the seven other saboteurs.

FBI agents initially planned to try the saboteurs in civil court, but those higher up in the chain of command had second thoughts. Hoover had been quick to publicize the arrests of the German spies, and the press had run stories lauding the FBI's sleuthing. If Dasch were to tell his story in open court, the FBI's performance would lose its luster. After all, the FBI had been slow to believe Dasch, and without Dasch's help the FBI might not have apprehended the spies at all. Nor was the president eager to publicize how easy it had been for two German submarines to enter American waters undetected. The administration feared that revelation could create panic among the population. Roosevelt and his aides also worried that civilian courts would not serve up sufficiently harsh penalties; the maximum sentence for sabotage was 30 years. The administration was concerned, too, that it might not be able to make a sabotage charge stick in court, since the plotters never got close to carrying out the sabotage they intended. In that case the government might be stuck with pursuing lesser charges. A military tribunal, in contrast, would enable the government to move quickly and secretly and to seek the death penalty—a punishment that FDR told his attorney general was "almost obligatory" in this case.[51]

One week after the last of the saboteurs had been arrested, Roosevelt issued a proclamation that "certain enemies"—those who entered the United States to commit sabotage, espionage, or other hostile or warlike acts—could be denied access to the regular courts if the executive branch so chose. On the same day he issued the proclamation (July 2, 1942), Roosevelt established a military tribunal to hear the saboteurs' case and appointed the tribunal's members as well as the prosecuting and defending attorneys. Six days later, the secret trial commenced. Defense attorneys immediately questioned the constitutionality of the proceedings and persuaded the Supreme Court to hear oral arguments on the case. On July 29 and 30, with the military tribunal still in progress, the Court heard nine hours of oral argument. The government's position was that the decision of how to deal with the saboteurs was the president's alone. The defense team countered that *Ex parte Milligan* had established that the president could not set up a military tribunal when the civil courts were "open and functioning regularly."[52]

The day after hearing oral arguments, Chief Justice Harlan Stone announced the Court's verdict in *Ex parte Quirin*: the military tribunal had jurisdiction to try the case and none of the eight men, including the two American citizens, had a right to file petitions for writs of habeas corpus. The Court did not explain why it had reached this judgment, but promised to issue a full opinion later. The following day, the military tribunal concluded its proceedings and decided that each of the conspirators was guilty and should be put to death. Roosevelt commuted Dasch's sentence to 30 years in federal prison, but six of his co-conspirators were immediately executed.

Drafting the opinion proved more difficult than the quick verdict might have suggested. And the more the justices thought through the case, the more uncomfortable they became. Several members of the Court developed reservations about aspects of Roosevelt's order that departed from the legislatively enacted Articles of War. For instance, FDR's order required a two-thirds vote to convict, whereas the Articles of War required a unanimous vote to sentence an individual to death. The Articles of War also set out a review structure that ensured the tribunal's decision would be reviewed by another military review board, but FDR had directed that it come directly to him for review. The justices, however, found themselves in the position of now having to come up with reasons to justify a decision they had already announced and that had resulted in six men being put to death. Suppressing their doubts and papering over their disagreements, all nine justices signed on to Stone's opinion affirming the legality of the president's military commission to try "unlawful enemy combatants."

Stone had agreed to hear the appeal as a way to assert the Court's relevance during wartime, to show that "in time of war as well as peace" the judiciary's role was to "preserve unimpaired the constitutional safeguards of civil liberty." And many observers at the time hailed the Court's intervention as vindicating the nation's commitment to the rule of law even during the most strenuous emergencies. The justices, however, came to see their intervention as a mistake that compromised the integrity of the Court's deliberative process, a process that depended on the discipline of written opinions. Deciding first and explaining later, Justice Felix Frankfurter conceded, was "not a happy precedent." The enduring lesson of *Ex parte Quirin*, legal scholar David Danelski concluded, is that the Court must be "wary of departing from its established rules and practices, even in times of national crisis, for at such times the Court is especially susceptible to co-optation by the executive."[53]

Truman's Seizure of the Steel Mills

On occasion, the Supreme Court has effectively checked executive power, even in the midst of what the president at least considered an emergency. The most memorable of these occasions was the 1952 case *Youngstown Sheet & Tube Co. v. Sawyer*.[54]

In 1952, the United States was at war in Korea. Since no war could be fought without steel, President Truman was understandably alarmed when United Steelworkers announced that its membership would go on strike. Under existing law (the Taft–Hartley Act, passed in 1947 over Truman's veto), the president had the power to order the steelworkers to return to work for 60 days while federal mediators helped to negotiate a contract acceptable to employers and employees. However, using the Republicans' anti-union legislation was not an attractive option for a Democratic president who relied on the unions' political support. Plus Truman had little reason to think that 60 days would be enough to settle the differences that labor and management had failed to resolve over the previous six months of negotiations.

Facing the prospect that steel factories would shut down and "immediately jeopardize and imperil our national defense," Truman ordered his secretary of commerce to take control of the steel mills until an agreement could be reached between workers and management. The steelworkers would temporarily become government employees. Announcing his nationalization order just two hours before the strike was to take effect, Truman justified his extraordinary actions by appealing to the national emergency that he had proclaimed in December 1950 and to his constitutional powers as president of the United States and commander in chief of the armed forces.

The steel companies immediately took the president to court, arguing that his action was illegal. A district judge agreed with the steel industry, prompting the steelworkers to go out on strike. The government then appealed to the appellate court, which stayed the lower judge's decision so that the government could make its case to the Supreme Court. On May 12, 1952, the Supreme Court heard oral arguments.

Although Truman knew that nationalizing the steel industry by executive order placed him on constitutional thin ice, he expected to prevail. Even if the Court did not accept the more expansive understanding of presidential power peddled by the administration's lawyers, most observers expected the Court to find narrower grounds on which to uphold the government's position. In the past, after all, the Court had shown tremendous deference to the president during wartime. And all nine of the justices had been appointed by either Roosevelt or Truman. Moreover, Chief Justice Vinson had privately encouraged Truman to seize the steel mills, assuring him that such an action had a solid legal grounding.

But Truman was in for a shock. Six justices voted to invalidate Truman's action; only Vinson, Minton, and Reed voted to uphold the president's action. However, the majority did not speak with a single voice. In fact, each of the six justices in the majority wrote separately, and only three endorsed the reasoning in the opinion of the Court penned by Justice Black. In writing for the Court majority in *Korematsu*, Black had upheld the exclusion of Japanese Americans from the West Coast on the grounds that the president's order had been ratified by Congress when it voted to affix criminal penalties to violators of the order. In contrast, Black found no legislative authorization for Truman's seizure of the steel mill. Black rejected Truman's argument that the commander in chief had an inherent constitutional power to do whatever he thought necessary to safeguard the nation during wartime. The president, Black opined, was charged by the Constitution with executing the laws, not making them. And in ordering the seizure of the steel mill, Black insisted, Truman was assuming the power of lawmaker, which the framers had entrusted "to the Congress alone in both good and bad times."

Youngstown's most enduring legacy, however, was not Black's articulation of a strict separation of powers, but Jackson's more flexible standard that held that presidential powers "are not fixed" by the Constitution "but fluctuate, depending upon their disjunction or conjunction with those of Congress." The art of governing, Roosevelt's former attorney general explained, was too complex to "conform to judicial definitions of the power of [the legislature or the executive] branches based on isolated clauses or even single Articles torn from context." Presidential power, Jackson suggested, was "at its maximum" when the executive acted with the expressed or implied support of Congress; in these situations, the courts should afford the "widest latitude" to the president. In contrast, presidential power was at "its lowest ebb" when the executive takes action that is "incompatible with the expressed or implied will of Congress." In between these two polar extremes was a gray area, "a zone of twilight," in which the president acted in the "absence of either a congressional grant or denial of authority." Truman's seizure of the steel mills, Jackson argued, fell into the "lowest ebb" category, and so warranted exacting judicial scrutiny.

Jackson was as adamant as Black in rejecting the administration's claim that the president had inherent constitutional authority to act outside the law during war or other emergencies. Being commander in chief did not give Truman the authority to seize property he deemed "important or even essential" to the war. "No penance," Jackson opined, "would ever expiate the sin against free government of holding that a President can escape control of executive powers by law through assuming his military role." Jackson harshly criticized the administration's "loose and irresponsible" use of terms such as "inherent" powers, "implied" powers, "plenary" powers, "war" powers, and "emergency" powers, terms used "without fixed or ascertainable meanings." Nor was he impressed with the administration's argument that necessity required the seizure of the steel mills. Congress, as it often had in the past, could easily grant emergency powers that were ample to address the current crisis. "With all its defects, delays and inconveniences," Jackson thundered in conclusion, "men have discovered no technique for long preserving free government except that the Executive be under the law, and that the law be made by [legislative] deliberations."

As soon as the Court announced its ruling on June 2, 1952, the steelworkers went out on strike, leaving Truman with two options. He could invoke the Taft–Hartley Act and thereby compel labor to return to work for a period of time while the unions and management searched for an agreement. Alternatively, he could request that Congress pass legislation authorizing him to seize the steel mills temporarily. For political reasons, Truman still refused to invoke Taft–Hartley. Instead he announced that it was "squarely up to Congress" to resolve the standoff by enacting legislation. Congress, in turn, told Truman to invoke the law already on the books, Taft–Hartley. With Congress and the president unable to reach agreement, the strike stretched on for nearly two more months.

In defending his seizure of the steel mills, Truman had pointed to the dire consequences that would result if there was even a temporary halt in the production of steel. In fact, however, there were substantial steel reserves, and the industries that used steel were able to operate essentially at full capacity throughout the nearly two months that the steelworkers were on strike. As the strike continued into its second month, however, the administration became increasingly concerned that the work stoppage was beginning to place the nation's economy and war effort in grave danger. On July 24, the leaders of the two sides were summoned to the White House to negotiate a settlement. By the end of the day the two sides had reached an agreement, and Truman announced the end of the strike. The following day the steelworkers returned to work. For the first time during a wartime emergency, the Court had stood up to the president—and the nation had survived unscathed.

The State Secrets Privilege

Youngstown was not, however, a harbinger of a more aggressive Court posture toward executive power. The very next year, Jackson and Black found themselves in the minority in *United States v. Reynolds*. Little noticed at the time, the case has become the legal foundation for what is known as the "state secrets privilege"—which essentially amounts to an executive privilege to be above the law.[55]

United States v. Reynolds stemmed from the crash of a B-29 bomber that was testing secret military equipment. Five crew members died as well as four civilian engineers involved in the research and development of the equipment. The widows of three of the civilians brought suit against the government for wrongful death. When the widows' lawyer requested that the Air Force provide his clients with its investigative report as well as the statements of the three surviving crew members, the Air Force refused on the grounds that the plane and its crew "were engaged in a highly secret mission" and release of the report "would not be in the public interest." The judge said that he would make his ruling after reviewing the report in private, but the government refused to allow even the judge to see the report. Since the government would not cooperate, the judge found in favor of the widows.

The Air Force could have left matters there, paying out the paltry sum of $225,000 and keeping the report secret. Instead it appealed. A three-judge panel unanimously upheld the position of the lower court judge. The judiciary and not the executive, the appeals court ruled, had the final say in deciding whether a document should be privileged information and thus unavailable to a plaintiff or defendant in a legal proceeding. To allow the government to be judge in its own case was a perversion of the rule of law. The court, moreover, found no danger in allowing federal judges to review classified materials in private (*in camera*); if additional information was necessary for a judge to understand the materials' import, then the government could provide a judge with that information as well.

Again the government appealed, this time to the Supreme Court. The government argued that it was well within its rights to refuse to divulge state secrets. If that meant the three widows could not win their case of wrongful death then that was the price the nation paid for ensuring national security. The lawyer for the widows insisted that justice required the government to offer some evidence to support its claim that the report would compromise the nation's defenses. The Supreme Court agreed with the government. Since military secrets were at stake, the Court ruled, the government did not have to disclose any information in a civil case, even to a judge in secret. Only in 1996, when the accident report was finally declassified, did the world learn that the report did not reveal state secrets that would compromise national security, but rather a pattern of negligence and ineptitude on the part of the Air Force and its crew.[56]

The embarrassing revelations about the misuse of the state secrets privilege in the *Reynolds* case have not affected courts' willingness to adhere to its deferential logic. In both the Bush and Obama administrations, the courts consistently acquiesced to the government whenever the executive branch invoked the state secrets doctrine. For instance, the Bush administration successfully invoked the state secrets privilege to block suits challenging the National Security Agency's program of eavesdropping on Americans' telephone conversations without a court warrant as well as to stymie legal claims brought by individuals who had been abducted by the Central Intelligence Agency (CIA) and sent to other countries to be interrogated and tortured. And the Obama administration relied on the state secrets privilege to dismiss lawsuits brought by individuals who alleged that they were tortured or targeted for killing by the US government.

Bush and the Guantánamo Bay Detainees

The Supreme Court did push back against executive power in several important cases involving individuals detained at Guantánamo Bay by the Bush administration. The most notable of these were the 2006 case *Hamdan v. Rumsfeld* and the 2008 case *Boumediene v. Bush*.[57]

Salim Ahmed Hamdan, a citizen of Yemen, and Lakhdar Boumediene, an Algerian-born Bosnian citizen, were among roughly 770 foreign nationals imprisoned by the Bush administration at Guantánamo Bay. Located at the southern tip of Cuba, the US naval base at Guantánamo Bay was regarded by administration officials as an ideal location for the detention of suspected terrorists. Guantánamo had the virtue of being under the complete control of the United States government while also being officially part of Cuba; the US military indefinitely "leases" the property from Cuba, although the Cuban government has not recognized the lease as valid since the Cuban Revolution in 1959. Since Guantánamo Bay was not technically US territory, the administration's lawyers argued that Guantánamo detainees could not use the US legal system to challenge their incarceration.[58]

The Case of Osama bin Laden's Driver

Salim Ahmed Hamdan was captured in November 2001 by local Afghan warlords and handed over to the American forces for a $5,000 bounty. When the Americans discovered that Hamdan was Osama bin Laden's driver, he was sent to Guantánamo Bay. Hamdan became the first Guantánamo detainee to be tried by the system of military tribunals that Bush established by military order in November 2001—an order that "made the executive the law maker, law enforcer, and law adjudicator." All the rules that were to govern these tribunals—from the standards of evidence to the definition of war crimes—were written by the administration without consulting with Congress. Contested verdicts were to be reviewed not by a federal court of appeals but by a panel selected by the secretary of defense, thereby excluding the judiciary as well.[59]

Hamdan's military trial began in August 2004 before a panel of five government-selected military officers. Hamdan's lawyers filed for a writ of habeas corpus in federal district court, arguing that the presidentially constituted military commissions lacked the authority to try Hamdan. They argued that the procedures governing the military commissions violated fundamental principles of military and international law, including that a defendant had the right to be present at his trial and to see the evidence presented against him.

A federal judge and Clinton appointee agreed with Hamdan's lawyers, bringing the trial to an abrupt halt. The administration appealed, and in July 2005 a three-judge panel of the DC circuit—made up of three Republican appointees, including John Roberts, who six days earlier had been nominated by President Bush to a seat on the Supreme Court—sided with the government and overturned the lower court's ruling. In November 2005, the Supreme Court agreed to hear Hamdan's appeal, and in June 2006 the Court announced its decision.

Writing for a five-justice majority (Roberts recused himself), Justice John Paul Stevens acknowledged that the congressionally enacted Uniform Code of Military Justice (UCMJ) authorized the president to use military commissions to try those determined to be enemy combatants. But the Court rejected the administration's argument that the president had inherent authority as commander in chief to determine the rules and procedures governing military tribunals. Unless military necessity dictated otherwise, the executive was required to conduct military commissions following the accepted legal procedures that Congress had established for regular military courts martial. Nor did the Court accept the administration's contention that the Authorization for Use of Military

A photograph from January 11, 2002 showing orange jumpsuit-clad detainees at a Guantánamo Bay detention facility. Orange jumpsuits were issued to detainees who were deemed non-compliant. Compliant detainees were typically dressed in white.

Courtesy: Getty Images.

Force (AUMF), which Congress passed the week after the September 11 terrorist attacks, gave the executive the authority to conduct military commissions that departed from established legal procedures. Moreover, no emergency existed that prevented the president from seeking legislative authorization. The president, the Court concluded, must either conduct the military commissions consistent with the laws governing regular courts martial or must obtain explicit authorization from Congress to depart from those established legal procedures.[60]

Bush opted for the latter. Four months later, Congress passed the Military Commissions Act (MCA) of 2006, which authorized the president's system of military commissions for unlawful enemy combatants, albeit with a few changes, including the right of defendants to be present at their trial. The following spring, the government put Hamdan back on trial, and charged him with conspiring to commit terrorist acts and with "providing material support for terrorism." In 2008, a jury of six military officers found Hamdan not guilty of conspiracy because he had no role in the planning or execution of terrorist attacks. The jury did find, however, that in driving and fixing bin Laden's vehicles Hamdan was guilty of providing material support for terrorism. The government pressed the jury to sentence this "hardened al-Qaeda member" to at least 30 years and preferably life in prison, so as to "send a message to others that if anyone thinks of providing material support to the sword of terrorism … there will be painful consequences." The defense asked for a sentence of no more than 45 months that took into account Hamdan's cooperation with US officials, his peripheral involvement in al-Qaeda's terrorist activities, and his expressions of regret. The jury settled on 66 months. Since the presiding officer had already given Hamdan credit for the more than five years he had served in Guantánamo since being formally charged in 2003, the jury's verdict meant that Hamdan would have to serve less than six additional months in prison.

Believing the sentence too lenient, the government requested a new sentencing hearing. A Pentagon spokesman defiantly insisted that when Hamdan completed his prison sentence he would still be an "enemy combatant" and could therefore be held by the government indefinitely until such time as a military administrative review board determined he was no longer an enemy combatant. But after the commission's presiding officer refused to reconsider Hamdan's sentence, the administration put Hamdan on a plane to Yemen, where he served the final months of his sentence.

The Case of Lakhdar Boumediene

Hamdan's case was a dramatic chapter in the relationship between the Supreme Court and the executive branch, but Hamdan was not a typical Guantánamo detainee, for he was one of the few to be charged and tried before a military commission during the Bush years. Far more typical was Lakhdar Boumediene, who was held at Guantánamo for more than seven years without being charged with a crime.[61]

Boumediene was arrested by Bosnian police in October 2001 at the request of the United States government, who suspected him of plotting to blow up the American embassy in Sarajevo. The police investigation turned up insufficient evidence to hold Boumediene, and the Bosnian Supreme Court ordered him freed. Upon his release in

January 2002, he and his five alleged confederates were seized by the United States military and flown to Guantánamo Bay.

Lawyers for Boumediene promptly petitioned for a writ of habeas corpus. The federal district court sided with the government, ruling that Boumediene had no grounds to challenge his detention in federal court because he was not a US citizen and was not being held in the United States. The appeals court agreed. However, the Supreme Court disagreed, ruling in June 2004—in *Rasul v. Bush*—that foreign nationals held at Guantánamo Bay, which was under the "complete jurisdiction and control" of the US government, could challenge their detention in US federal court.[62]

The Defense Department responded to the Court's ruling by establishing a system of Combatant Status Review Tribunals (CSRT) in which detainees would, for the first time, be provided an opportunity to challenge their designation as an enemy combatant. However, critics of the CSRT maintained that the new system of tribunals was unfairly stacked against the detainees, who could neither present witnesses nor cross-examine the government's witnesses. Only about 1 in 15 tribunals failed to uphold the government's initial designation of a detainee as an enemy combatant.

While Boumediene (whose designation as an enemy combatant had been upheld by the CSRT) continued to try to challenge his detention in federal court, the Bush administration moved to close off the legal avenue opened up by the Court. For the first time, the administration now sought explicit legislative authorization for its detention policies. Late in 2005, the Republican-controlled Congress passed the Detainee Treatment Act (DTA), which denied any US court from having "jurisdiction to hear or consider ... an application for a writ of habeas corpus filed by or on behalf of an alien detained by the Department of Defense at Guantánamo Bay." Under the DTA, detainees could appeal their status as enemy combatants, but only in the Court of Appeals for the DC Circuit, and the scope of that review was sharply limited. The appeals court was required to defer to the CSRT's findings of fact and the detainee was not allowed to submit new evidence.

In *Hamdan v. Rumsfeld*, the Supreme Court limited the scope of the DTA by ruling that it did not apply to those detainees—like Boumediene—whose habeas petitions were pending at the time the DTA was enacted. When Congress then passed the MCA in 2006, it clarified the law's intent: the privilege of habeas corpus was to be withheld from all Guantánamo detainees who had been designated as enemy combatants, "without exception."

Lawyers for Boumediene went to court again, arguing that the MCA's habeas-stripping provision was unconstitutional. The Court of Appeals for the DC Circuit refused to consider the act's constitutionality, on the grounds that the MCA expressly prohibited federal courts from considering a writ of habeas corpus from any foreign national held at Guantánamo. Boumediene's lawyers then appealed to the Supreme Court, which initially declined to hear the case. A few months later, however, without explanation, the Court reversed course and accepted the case. In June 2008, a bitterly divided 5–4 Court announced its judgment: Guantánamo detainees had a constitutional right to habeas corpus, and the MCA violated that right. Writing for the majority, Anthony Kennedy insisted that "the laws and Constitution are designed to survive, and remain in force, in extraordinary times." Kennedy allowed that the Constitution permitted the government to suspend habeas corpus in cases of rebellion or invasion, but the government had to formally suspend the writ, which it had not done.

The Court's verdict in *Boumediene* was certainly a striking departure from a historical pattern of judicial deference to executive power during wartime, especially when the executive branch's actions had the expressed or implied support of Congress. Under Jackson's *Youngstown* logic, the Court should have afforded the "widest latitude" to executive action in *Boumediene*, since in enacting the MCA Congress had explicitly backed the Bush administration's policy of denying habeas corpus to Guantánamo detainees. In contrast, the Court's judgment in *Hamdan* invalidated presidential power at "its lowest ebb," since the majority deemed that the administration's military commissions were incompatible with the will of Congress expressed in the UCMJ.[63]

The *Boumediene* Court's willingness to depart from past patterns of judicial deference during war-related emergencies can be attributed to the length of time that had elapsed since the administration first seized Boumediene. In explaining its decision, the Court's majority emphasized several times that detainees like Boumediene had already been locked up for more than six years without any judicial oversight. It was one thing to defer to the government during an emergency of limited duration, but it was quite another to defer in the context of an emergency that threatened to stretch out indefinitely into the future—and that could, as Justice Kennedy warned, result in individuals being detained for "a generation or more." The danger was that the exception would come to redefine legal norms. Worried that, by authorizing the executive branch to detain foreign nationals at Guantánamo for as long as it saw fit, the MCA made a mockery of the rule of law, the *Boumediene* Court insisted on its own vision of what the rule of law required, even if it meant second-guessing the judgment of both the executive and the legislative branches in wartime.[64]

The Limits of Judicial Power

In *Rasul, Hamdan,* and *Boumediene,* slim Court majorities provided a robust challenge to executive power. And the Court's rulings undeniably mattered. In November 2008, Boumediene received a habeas hearing that resulted in a federal judge ordering his release, which the Obama administration complied with in May 2009 after France agreed to accept Boumediene. In the three years after *Boumediene,* federal judges granted writs of habeas corpus to almost two-thirds of the roughly 60 detainees whose cases they heard. Moreover, the Court's rulings in *Rasul* and *Hamdan* led the Bush administration to involve Congress in shaping and authorizing its detentions and military tribunals, a step that the administration had previously refused to take. And the changes that were made by the administration and Congress as a result of *Rasul* and *Hamdan* resulted in enhanced legal protections for Guantánamo detainees.[65]

However, the high drama of these few cases should not obscure the limits of the Supreme Court as a check on executive power in the war on terror. First, the Bush administration held Boumediene for seven years without ever charging him with a crime or providing credible evidence that he was connected to al-Qaeda or posed a threat to

United States interests. The same was true for hundreds of others detained at Guantánamo, who turned out to be not even close to "the worst of the worst" that Defense Secretary Donald Rumsfeld promised were the only ones being held at Guantánamo. At the end of the Obama presidency, nine years after *Boumediene* and nearly 16 years after the terrorist attacks of September 11, 2001, 41 detainees were still being held at Guantánamo. As of March 2017, only three detainees had been tried and convicted of a crime.[66]

Second, when federal judges granted writs of habeas corpus to Guantánamo detainees, these decisions were usually appealed by the Obama administration to the Court of Appeals for the DC Circuit, which consistently sided with the executive branch. For instance, when a district court judge in 2010 ruled that the government did not have sufficient evidence to hold Hussain Salem Mohammed Almerfidi, the Obama administration appealed the ruling despite knowing, as one administration official admitted, that the case "was very, very weak." In 2011, a three-judge panel of the DC circuit—consisting of two George W. Bush appointees and Reagan appointee Laurence Silberman—reversed the district court ruling and denied Almerfidi's petition for a writ of habeas corpus.[67]

Third, the appeals court decided that indefinite detention of an individual as an enemy combatant requires the government only to meet a "preponderance of the evidence" standard rather than prove its case beyond a reasonable doubt—as it would have to in a criminal case—or meet the "clear and convincing" evidence often used in civil cases. In addition, the appeals court allowed hearsay evidence to be admissible. The Supreme Court declined to hear several cases brought by detainees that challenged the permissive standard of evidence adhered to by the court of appeals.

Fourth, all the detainees who have been released from Guantánamo were let go at the discretion of the executive branch. Even when habeas petitions were granted by federal judges, no detainee was immediately discharged from Guantánamo. A detainee was freed only after the executive branch found a country willing to accept him. The question of whether federal judges have the authority to order a detainee's release is one the Court has not attempted to answer.

Fifth, the Court never attempted to compel the executive to try detainees in federal court. Instead it insisted only that if the executive branch revived the military commissions, it needed to follow existing standards for military courts martial or receive explicit authority from Congress to depart from those standards. So long as Congress approved, the executive was free to use military commissions that were unfairly stacked against the detainees. Ironically, the impetus for trying Guantánamo detainees in federal court came not from the Supreme Court or from Congress but from the new president, Barack Obama. Adding to the irony, Obama's effort to close the Guantánamo detention facility and try the detainees in federal court, using normal criminal procedures, was blocked by Congress, forcing the president to resume the military tribunals established by the Bush administration.

Finally, the attention showered on the Court's Guantánamo decisions obscures the other areas of the war on terror in which the Court avoided challenging executive authority. In 2007, for instance, the Court refused to hear the case of Khalid el-Masri, whose case against the government for his wrongful imprisonment, interrogation, and torture had been dismissed by the appeals court on state secrets grounds. At no point did the Court try to stop the Bush administration from using torture—what the administration euphemistically called "enhanced interrogation"—to obtain information. And in 2009, the Court refused to let a Pakistani Muslim man proceed in his suit against former attorney general John Ashcroft and FBI director Robert Mueller for discriminatory treatment and abuse that he allegedly suffered at a detention center following his arrest in New York in November 2001. The Court ruled that these high-ranking administration officials had legal immunity against such a suit since there was no evidence that they expressly authorized unconstitutional treatment.[68]

ALL THE PRESIDENT'S LAWYERS

An underlying problem in looking to the Supreme Court to constrain executive power is that the Court decides a relatively small number of cases, whereas the executive branch makes thousands upon thousands of decisions. Moreover, the justices are always in a position of reacting to executive action, often long after the action has been carried out. The government officials in the best position to ensure that executive actions comply with the law are the administration's own lawyers, who routinely advise the president and other executive branch officials about what the law will and will not allow. Indeed, "for the overwhelming majority of administrative decisions," writes law professor Peter Shane, "government lawyering represents the exclusive avenue through which the law is actually brought to bear on decision making." But can the president's lawyers be trusted to give impartial analysis of what the law requires, or are the president's lawyers inevitably advocates for the president's agenda and authority? To address this question, we need to start with a brief history of the evolution of presidential lawyering.[69]

Evolution of the Attorney General's Office

The first bill introduced in the Senate was legislation to establish a federal judiciary. Senate Bill No. 1—what became the Judiciary Act of 1789—included a provision that established the Office of the US Attorney General. The act specified that the attorney general's duties were twofold: to "prosecute and conduct all suits in the Supreme Court" in which the United States government was a party, and "to give his advice and opinion upon questions of law" when required to do so by the president or asked to do so by department heads. The law also stipulated that the attorney general must be "learned in the law"—making it the only top appointed government post with a substantive qualification on who could fill it. The president could nominate any individual to the Supreme Court, but only one "learned in the law" could be made attorney general.[70]

Initially, being attorney general was a part-time job, with no staff support or even office space, and a salary only half of what other cabinet members earned. Only after the Civil War, with the creation of the Department of Justice, did the attorney general become a department head with administrative responsibilities. In the early days of the republic, the attorney general did not even reside in the capital, except during the handful of weeks that the Supreme Court was in session. The first presidents frequently turned to their other cabinet members for legal and constitutional advice. For instance, in the debate over the constitutionality of a national bank, George Washington sought legal opinions from Secretary of State Thomas Jefferson and Secretary of the Treasury Alexander Hamilton, and ultimately ignored Attorney General Edmund Randolph's opinion that the bank was unconstitutional.[71]

When William Wirt became James Monroe's attorney general in 1817, he was shocked to find that none of his eight predecessors had left any record of the advisory opinions they penned. In fact, he found "no books, documents or papers of any kind to inform [him] of what had been done by [his] predecessors." Although precedent was the foundation of Anglo-American law, the government's top lawyer had no way of determining whether his interpretations of the law conflicted with those provided under previous administrations. Wirt established a formal system for recording his official actions—and persuaded Congress finally to give the attorney general a clerk and an office—though not until 1840 were the opinions of the attorney general compiled and published.[72]

Although a more systematic administrator than his predecessors, Wirt shared their view that the attorney general's responsibilities as an officer of the law made the role different from that of other members of the president's cabinet. As attorney general, Wirt explained, he was less like "the advocate of the government" than like "a judge, called to decide a question of law with . . . impartiality and integrity." That Wirt served in his post for 12 consecutive years—a record equaled by no cabinet member before or since—suggests that Wirt's nonpolitical conception of the office was shared by others. In 1828, for instance, Monroe assured Wirt that while Andrew Jackson would rightfully require the resignation of John Quincy Adams's department heads, the attorney general's duties were sufficiently distinct that the new president would likely retain the experienced Wirt since "the President has less connection with, and less responsibility for the performance" of the attorney general's duties.[73]

But Jackson harbored a different understanding of the attorney general's role, one that privileged loyalty to the president and his program. He had no desire to retain the experienced Wirt because he wanted an attorney general who shared his views of the Constitution. Jackson's second attorney general Roger Taney fully embraced the role of advocate for the president's policies and the presidency's power. Taney supplied the legal arguments that Jackson used to justify his veto of the national bank. In fact, Taney wrote Jackson's famous veto message, including the president's defiant assertion that "the authority of the Supreme Court must not . . . be permitted to control the Congress or the Executive when acting in their legislative capacities"—a view from which Taney would later retreat when he became chief justice of the Supreme Court and was trying to induce President Lincoln to obey his order to release John Merryman.[74]

President Lincoln expected the same support for executive authority from his attorney general that President Jackson had expected from his. In his July 4, 1861, message to Congress, Lincoln promised that Attorney General Edward Bates would shortly present a fuller argument that supported the president's constitutional authority to suspend habeas corpus. The following day, Bates dutifully complied with a legal opinion that defended Lincoln's suspension of habeas corpus. Yet while Bates justified Lincoln's actions, he also continued to insist that his office was "not properly political, but strictly legal." In Bates's view, it was the attorney general's "duty, above all other ministers of state, to uphold the law and to resist all encroachments, from whatever quarter, of mere will and power." Yet Bates's opinion justifying Lincoln's suspension of habeas corpus—which included the argument that the suspension of the writ was a political not a judicial question, and therefore could not be reviewed by the courts—compels the question of whether the attorney general could be counted on to resist encroachments when they came from the president. Certainly no attorney general could ignore that he served two masters: the president and the law.[75]

By the time Bates became attorney general in 1861, it had become a full-time job, with a salary equal to that of the other cabinet positions. The attorney general was expected to quit his private practice upon assuming office, often at considerable financial sacrifice. But even working full-time and with the help of an assistant or two, the attorney general could not keep up with the government's rapidly expanding legal needs, especially now that the attorney general had been made responsible for the work of the many US district attorneys scattered across the country. Executive departments increasingly turned to private lawyers for legal counsel and representation. Between 1864 and 1869, the federal government spent at least $750,000 on legal fees. In 1870, in an attempt to reduce the government's reliance on expensive private lawyers and to promote uniformity in the government's interpretation of the laws, Congress established the Department of Justice, headed by the attorney general and supported by a small staff, including the new office of solicitor general.[76]

The attorney general was now a department head responsible for administering a bureaucracy. As that bureaucracy grew, the attorney general increasingly delegated opinion-writing to subordinates, particularly to the solicitor general, whose primary responsibility was arguing cases before the Supreme Court. Although the solicitor general was formally a political appointee just like the attorney general, Congress and presidents recognized the importance of legal professionalism in the job of solicitor general, which the 1870 act required to be an "officer learned in the law" (while dropping that language from the description of the attorney general). Republican presidents Hayes, Garfield, and Arthur each insisted on appointing their own attorney general yet retained Grant's solicitor general, who served for twelve and a half years between 1872 and 1885, during which time there were six attorneys general.[77]

Most of the Justice Department's legal opinion-writing did not involve claims of presidential power. Instead the bulk of the work adjudicated the claims of rival departments and agencies, a job that became increasingly important and onerous as government agencies multiplied in the twentieth century. To relieve the solicitor general's workload, in 1933 Congress created the position of assistant solicitor general, whose duty it was to prepare legal opinions. In 1951, the assistant solicitor general was restyled an assistant attorney general and placed in charge of the Executive Adjudications Division within the Department of Justice. Two years later, the division was renamed the Office of Legal Counsel (OLC), the name it retains today.[78]

OLC's "Capacity to Say No": The Case of Impoundment

The Office of Legal Counsel's ability to adjudicate interagency conflicts over statutory or constitutional interpretation rested on its reputation for impartial legal analysis. After all, government agencies and departments had their own legal counsels, and no statute required that that they seek or follow OLC's legal guidance. During the 1950s and 1960s, OLC's staff of some 20 lawyers built an impressive reputation for objective legal analysis, "free from parochial limitations."[79]

At the same time, however, OLC increasingly assumed responsibilities that made them not only the dispassionate arbiter of interagency feuds but—in the words of the attorney general's 1968 annual report—"the lawyers for the White House." In 1962, for instance, OLC was delegated the job of vetting the president's executive orders and proclamations for "form and legality." And OLC also became increasingly involved during the 1960s with providing legal advice to the White House on its legislative program as well as other issues of pressing concern to the president and his top staff. In mediating between executive agencies, OLC's mission was clear: its job was to provide dispassionate legal opinions that took into account the arguments of the affected parties, almost like a judge would do. But as legal advisor to the president and his staff, the OLC assumed a more complex mission—one that required balancing the "duty to define the legal limits of executive action in a neutral manner and the President's desire to receive legal advice that helps him do what he wants." In other words, OLC increasingly confronted the same dilemma that attorneys general had faced since the early republic.[80]

Helping to offset political pressures from the White House were the experienced, career government lawyers who made up the core of OLC during the 1950s and 1960s. The head of OLC was always a presidential appointee, but his deputies included at least one "career man" and often an appointee who was recruited for specific legal expertise rather than political background. Writing in 1971, Frank Wozencraft, who was head of OLC under President Johnson, acknowledged that the office needed to be "responsive" to the president and the attorney general's leadership, but "they cannot afford to have it staffed by politically oriented lawyers with personal axes or ambitions." Of course, "like any client," the White House prefers "'can do' lawyers who will tell them how to do something legally rather than why they cannot." But "like any good law firm," Wozencraft concluded, OLC must retain "the capacity to say no ... when the law requires that answer."[81]

OLC showed that willingness to say no to the president during the struggle over impoundment during the Nixon years. Nixon felt that the Democratic Congress was spending too much money, and so looked to OLC for legal backing to impound—that is, not spend—money that had been appropriated by Congress. In Nixon's first year, the White House asked OLC head (and future chief justice of the Supreme Court) William Rehnquist for a legal opinion on whether the president had the constitutional power to refuse to spend monies that Congress had appropriated for schools. Rehnquist responded bluntly that the White House's suggestion that the president had such a power under the Constitution was "supported by neither reason nor precedent." Although "it may be argued that the spending of money is inherently an executive function," Rehnquist noted that it seemed "an anomalous proposition that because the Executive branch is bound to execute the laws, it is free to decline to execute them."[82]

Nixon was not the first president to refuse to spend appropriated funds, but most previous instances were uncontroversial. They usually involved cases where the legislative objective could be achieved by spending less than the full appropriation or where changing events had removed the need for the appropriation. For instance, Jefferson impounded $50,000 that Congress appropriated for gunboats on the Mississippi River after the Louisiana Purchase removed the need for them. Nixon, however, sought more than the customary discretionary authority that Congress expected the executive branch to exercise to administer programs flexibly and effectively. Instead he looked to impoundment as a means to nullify legislation by executive fiat, thereby replacing his policy preferences and budget priorities for those enacted into law by Congress.[83]

Although OLC rejected Nixon's claim that he had an inherent constitutional authority to impound any monies appropriated by Congress, it facilitated presidential impoundment by proffering the theory that wherever Congress did not mandate spending, the executive could refuse to spend appropriated monies. When Nixon acted on this legal theory, Congress responded by passing statutes—usually over Nixon's veto—mandating that the executive spend specified amounts in a particular fiscal year. As the conflict between Congress and the president escalated in 1972, the White House wanted OLC to provide legal support for the president's power to disregard these specific legislative mandates. The new OLC head, Roger Cramton, refused: if the law mandated a specific appropriation, Cramton concluded, the president was legally bound to spend the money.[84]

Cramton demonstrated that OLC still had the capacity to say no, at least when claims of presidential authority were clearly fraudulent. But subsequent events also revealed the limits on OLC's ability to check a determined president. Immediately after Nixon's reelection, Cramton was eased out. Disregarding OLC's legal opinions, Nixon announced at a January 1973 press conference that "the constitutional right for the President of the United States to impound funds ... when the spending of money would mean either increasing prices or increasing taxes ... is absolutely clear." The administration then brought in a new deputy attorney general, Joseph Sneed, and dispatched him to Capitol Hill to testify that Congress did not have the power to "legislate against impoundment"—that is, to mandate spending—when it would increase inflation. To allow Congress that power would "convert the Chief Executive into 'Chief Clerk,' a position which he has never held under our Constitution." According to Cramton, Sneed's claim was "greeted with dismay by the career lawyers" in the Justice Department, but that dismay did not stop the president and his aides from continuing to act on their far-fetched theory.[85]

Ultimately, Nixon's theory and practice of impoundment was checked not by the president's lawyers but by the federal courts and Congress. In 1974 Congress enacted the Congressional Budget and Impoundment Control Act, which curbed the president's power to impound funds. And the federal courts consistently ruled against the administration's aggressive use of impoundment, culminating in a unanimous 1975 Supreme Court ruling (in *Train v. City of New York*) that Nixon had acted unlawfully when he impounded funds that Congress had appropriated in 1972 (over Nixon's veto) for controlling water pollution.[86]

The Pressure for Presidential Apologetics

In the four decades that have passed since Cramton's brief tenure, OLC's culture has become even more responsive to the interests of the president and the executive branch. This increase in political responsiveness is both cause and consequence of changes in the staffing of OLC. Whereas during the 1950s and 1960s OLC still resembled the solicitor general's office in that it consisted principally of lawyers who had carved out a career in government service, OLC was transformed in the late 1970s and early 1980s into an institution dominated by talented young lawyers who shared the president's political orientation. The top deputy positions in the office became the monopoly of political appointees—in contrast, all but one of the solicitor general's deputies continued to be career civil servants.[87]

The shift in OLC staffing reflected the growing importance attached to OLC's review of the constitutionality of legislation passed or under consideration by Congress. Whereas adjudicating disputes between executive agencies called for OLC to act akin to a court, reviewing the work of a rival branch of government encouraged OLC to aggressively advocate for the constitutional powers of the executive branch—often, as legal scholar John McGinnis observes, "with little regard for court precedent." Court decisions favorable to presidential authority are usually read broadly while cases adverse to the interests of the executive branch are typically construed narrowly.[88]

OLC's increasing proclivity toward what legal scholar Bruce Ackerman characterizes as presidential "apologetics" has been spurred by increased competition from the Office of the White House Counsel. Although the position of White House counsel can be traced to Franklin Roosevelt's presidency, originally the individual designated as White House counsel was more of an all-purpose advisor than a rival to OLC or the attorney general. Ted Sorenson, for instance, was John Kennedy's White House counsel, but he was principally the president's policy advisor and speechwriter, and lacked the staff, expertise, and time to provide legal analysis that could match that provided by OLC. Beginning in the 1970s, however, the White House counsel's office began to grow. What had been an honorific title for a close presidential advisor morphed during the 1980s and 1990s into the head of an office that housed as many or more lawyers than OLC; during the Clinton administration, for instance, the White House counsel's office had as many as 40 lawyers.[89]

With a band of young, talented lawyers at his or her disposal—lawyers that are almost indistinguishable in background and outlook from the young, talented lawyers installed at OLC—the White House counsel can more easily bypass OLC, especially if an adverse judgment is expected from OLC. Knowledge that the president has a rival legal team prepared to support the president's preferred actions places added pressure on OLC to bend their legal analysis to the president's needs. OLC's leaders know that if they don't serve the president's short-term needs, the White House can simply cut them out of the loop entirely.[90]

White House pressure is exerted throughout OLC's opinion-writing process. OLC never asks the White House to prepare written briefs in defense of its position, as the office routinely does in weighing the legal arguments of rival agencies. Instead, OLC opinions that involve the White House are shaped by myriad informal communications that give the White House counsel's office ample opportunity to shape OLC's final product. When informal give-and-take proves insufficient for the White House to get the opinion it wants, the White House counsel lobbies the head of OLC directly. More often than not, however, the political leadership of OLC and the White House counsel's office are on the same page to begin with—not surprisingly, since the lawyers in both offices see themselves as part of the president's team. And, of course, they have been recruited to their post largely because they are perceived as sharing the president's fundamental assumptions and objectives.[91]

There are, to be sure, countervailing forces that prevent OLC from becoming a mere cipher for the president's wishes. Unlike the White House counsel, the head of OLC has to be approved by the Senate—although between 1995 and 2017 OLC was headed by a Senate-confirmed assistant attorney general less than a quarter of the time, largely because the Senate has refused to act on the president's nominations, itself an indicator of how politicized the office has become in recent decades.[92] Moreover, while the White House can go it alone, it prefers to act with the OLC's seal of approval, precisely because OLC is widely perceived as being more impartial and independent than the White House counsel's office. This gives OLC leverage with the White House and creates an incentive for OLC to protect its reputation for rigorous legal analysis since this is one of the few areas in which it has a competitive advantage over the White House counsel's office.[93]

Nonetheless, the trend over the past four decades has been toward an OLC that is ever more attuned to the needs and desires of the White House. That trend culminated during George W. Bush's administration in the most widely criticized legal opinions in OLC's history: the so-called "torture memos."

The Torture Memos

In the spring of 2002, the US government captured Abu Zubaydah, a man believed—incorrectly—to be one of al-Qaeda's highest-ranking leaders.[94] The administration was convinced that Zubaydah possessed intelligence that could be vital in the war on terror. Perhaps he could even lead them to the elusive Osama bin Laden and his top lieutenant, Ayman al-Zawahiri. After paying the Pakistani intelligence service $10 million for its help in the capture of the administration's first "high-value detainee," the CIA flew Zubaydah to a secret "black site" in Thailand where they could interrogate him. What the CIA needed to know was how far they could go in interrogating Zubaydah.[95]

Tasked with providing an answer to that question were five Bush administration lawyers who styled themselves "The War Council": the vice president's legal counsel, David Addington; White House Counsel Alberto Gonzales and his deputy (and former OLC head under the first Bush), Timothy Flanigan; the Pentagon's general counsel, Jim Haynes; and OLC deputy John Yoo. The White House made clear what it wanted: a legal ruling from OLC that would allow the CIA to use waterboarding on Zabaydah—waterboarding being an interrogation technique that involved partial drowning and asphyxiation and had long been considered torture, both in the United States and abroad. Standing in the administration's way was a 1994 federal law that implemented a global treaty banning and criminalizing torture. Yoo was given the task of finding a way around the law.[96]

The result was an OLC opinion dated August 1, 2002, titled "Standards of Conduct for Interrogation under 18 U.S.C. §§ 2340–2340A." Addressed to White House Counsel Alberto Gonzales and signed by OLC head Jay Bybee, Yoo's memo defined torture so narrowly that almost no interrogation method would qualify. The 1994 federal law defined torture as those acts intended to cause "severe physical or mental pain or suffering." To help determine the meaning of the words "severe pain," Yoo looked to an obscure statute that narrowly defined the emergency medical conditions under which the government would provide federally funded health benefits. Using this definition, Yoo concluded that to qualify as torture, the pain inflicted by interrogators must be "at the level that would ordinarily be associated with a sufficiently serious physical condition or injury such as death, organ failure, or serious impairment of body functions."[97]

The OLC opinion coupled its narrow definition of torture with a broad interpretation of executive power. Even if an interrogation method qualified as torture under the federal statute, OLC opined, "the statute would be unconstitutional if it impermissibly encroached on the President's constitutional power to conduct a military campaign." That is, according to OLC, Congress could not criminalize the torture of battlefield detainees because "any effort by Congress to regulate the interrogation of battlefield combatants would violate the Constitution's sole vesting of the Commander-in-Chief authority in the President."[98]

OLC's opinion gave the administration the legal shield it needed to torture high-level detainees without fear of criminal prosecution. An accompanying OLC opinion issued on the same day, addressed to the CIA's legal counsel John Rizzo, specifically authorized ten interrogation techniques that the CIA had sought permission to use on Zubaydah. These included waterboarding as well as stress positions, sleep deprivation, and confinement in small, coffin-like boxes.[99] Although we do not know precisely what interrogation techniques the CIA used on Zubaydah prior to the OLC opinion, we do know, courtesy of a 2005 OLC opinion released by the Obama administration in 2009, that in the month following these two OLC memos Zubaydah was waterboarded a minimum of 83 times.[100]

Acting on the basis of OLC's still top-secret opinions—and over the strenuous objections of military lawyers—Defense Secretary Donald Rumsfeld approved "enhanced interrogation" techniques for Guantánamo detainees that included stress positions, sleep deprivation, and hooding. In March 2003, Rumsfeld received the OLC seal of approval for the program, in the form of another sweeping Yoo opinion, entitled "Military Interrogation of Alien Unlawful Combatants Held Outside the United States." As in the August 2002 opinion, Yoo concluded that federal laws could not regulate interrogation methods because the president "enjoys complete discretion in the exercise of his Commander-in-Chief authority." What methods the military used to interrogate prisoners at Guantánamo was entirely up to the secretary of defense and the president. The law governing military interrogations, in other words, was essentially whatever Bush and Rumsfeld said it was. Nixon was right after all, at least when it came to wartime.[101]

The existence of OLC memos decriminalizing torture first came to light in June 2004, but ironically not as a result of the CIA's interrogation program, which was still a closely guarded secret, nor as a result of interrogations carried out at Guantánamo. Instead, the memos were brought to the public's attention following the unauthorized release of photographs documenting horrendous interrogation abuses by US military officials at the Abu Ghraib prison in Iraq—presumably whoever leaked the memos was eager to discredit the administration's story that the atrocities at Abu Ghraib were entirely the fault of a few "bad apples." The March 2003 opinion remained secret until 2008 but the August 2002 opinion was leaked in its entirety, and placed on the internet for the entire nation to read.

The public reaction was sharply negative, particularly to OLC's novel theory that only treatment that caused "death, organ failure, or serious impairment of body functions" constituted torture. Within a week of the August memo leaking, OLC chief Jack Goldsmith took the extraordinary step of formally withdrawing it, which meant the administration could no longer rely on its legal analysis. Not until near the end of the Bush presidency, however, did the country learn that the CIA had used waterboarding on several detainees, including Zubaydah and Khalid Sheikh Mohammed, who was subjected to waterboarding 183 times in March 2003.[102]

Although Goldsmith did not withdraw the August memo until after it was leaked to the public, he had decided months earlier that Yoo's legal analysis was flawed and needed to be corrected. In December 2003, just two months after taking over from Bybee as head of OLC, Goldsmith had informed the Pentagon that he was withdrawing the March 2003 interrogation opinion and that they could no longer rely on it. Goldsmith was scathing in his criticisms of both memos. Yoo's argument that Congress could not regulate interrogations, he said, was an "extreme conclusion [with] no foundation in prior OLC opinions, or in judicial decisions, or in any other source of law." The interrogation opinions, he concluded, "seemed more an exercise of sheer power than reasoned analysis," a politically motivated effort to immunize executive branch officials rather than a dispassionate reading of what the law permits.[103]

In the wake of OLC's withdrawal of Yoo's torture memos and the president's public pledge that American personnel would comply with all US laws regarding torture, it was easy to believe that law had won out over politics, albeit belatedly. But Goldsmith's success in disavowing the OLC memos had rested on Attorney General John Ashcroft's willingness to back the legal judgment of his OLC head. In Bush's second term, however, Ashcroft had left the administration, replaced by former White House counsel and Bush's close confidant Alberto Gonzales. Goldsmith was gone, too, having resigned immediately after withdrawing the August torture memo.

In Goldsmith's place, on an interim basis, was Stephen Bradbury. Before the White House would nominate him for the post on a permanent basis, Bradbury had "to prove his chops" and show that he was not another Goldsmith. Knowing that his nomination rested on giving the answers the administration wanted, Bradbury signed three OLC opinions that provided legal immunity for every CIA interrogation method, including waterboarding. Most startling of all, Bradbury's memos concluded that the McCain Amendment of the pending Detainee Treatment Act outlawing "cruel, inhuman, or degrading" treatment of detainees would not require the CIA to change any of its interrogation methods. Straining the bounds of credulity, Bradbury concluded that if interrogators believed the detainee had crucial intelligence, even waterboarding would not "shock the conscience" and would therefore be legal.[104]

Bradbury's OLC memos, none of which came to light until after Bush left office, hint at the problem of singling out Yoo for his part in the justification of torture. Yoo's one-sided jurisprudence was not an aberration, but part of a growing pattern of OLC providing the White House creative legal excuses to justify the actions that it wanted to take. Ashcroft derided Yoo as "Dr. Yes," but Bradbury's equally tendentious analysis suggests that OLC's default judgment is usually "yes" when the question involves presidential power. Only during Goldsmith's nine-month tenure at OLC did the White House get anything other than a green light from OLC in its war on terror. The same was true with another secret part of the administration's war on terror: the warrantless electronic surveillance of Americans.[105]

Warrantless Electronic Surveillance

In December 2005, the *New York Times* reported that the National Security Agency (NSA) was ignoring the Foreign Intelligence Surveillance Act (FISA), which required the government to obtain a warrant from a special court (the Foreign Intelligence Surveillance Court) before conducting electronic surveillance in the United States aimed at gathering foreign intelligence. The NSA program was not a rogue operation: it had been secretly approved by President George W. Bush after the terrorist attacks of September 11, 2001. Public disclosure of what the administration called the Terrorist Surveillance Program (TSP) prompted the Justice Department to launch a criminal investigation into the leak. At the same time, the White House blocked an internal probe by the Justice Department's Office of Professional Responsibility into the question of how the president's lawyers could have signed off on an illegal program of warrantless electronic surveillance.[106]

The program's "chief legal architect" was the vice president's counsel, David Addington, and once Yoo was "read in" to the program he supplied the OLC opinions that justified the president's action. Yoo was instructed to tell nobody about the program, not even his boss at OLC, Jay Bybee. According to Bybee's successor, Jack Goldsmith, Addington, Cheney, Yoo, and Gonzales "dealt with FISA the way they dealt with other laws they didn't like: they blew through them in secret based on flimsy legal opinions that they guarded closely so no one could question the legal basis for the operations." Just how closely guarded? When the NSA inspector general tried in December 2003 to obtain the OLC's analysis of the legal basis for TSP, an incandescent Addington barked that "the president's program" was none of their business. In fact, no NSA lawyer had been permitted to see the OLC's legal analysis of the program the agency had been charged with executing.[107]

The flimsiness of the administration's legal justifications can be judged from the unsigned memo the Justice Department released a month after the appearance of the *Times* story. Titled "Legal Authorities Supporting the Activities of the National Security Agency Described by the President," it advanced two main arguments. First, by passing the AUMF and authorizing the president to use all necessary and appropriate force against those responsible for the September 11 attacks, Congress had given the president the legal authority to conduct surveillance of suspected terrorists. Second, if FISA were construed as preventing the president from engaging in such activities, then FISA was unconstitutional, because the president has inherent authority as commander in chief to take actions he deems necessary "to detect and disrupt armed attacks on the United States."[108]

The first argument, as legal scholar Peter Shane writes, is "plainly wrong." There is no evidence in the legislative record that Congress intended to repeal or relax FISA requirements when it enacted the AUMF. And the language of FISA is unambiguous in making its statutory framework the "exclusive means" through which the government can conduct electronic surveillance for foreign intelligence purposes when one of the parties involved is a person in the United States. Moreover, at the president's request, Congress amended FISA several times after September 11 to enhance the government's surveillance authority—again without any suggestion from Congress or the president that the AUMF overrode FISA's warrant requirements.[109]

The administration's second claim was not so much a legal argument as an assertion of power. Essentially, the administration's claim was virtually identical to the one Nixon made in his interview with Frost: when the president authorizes an act it is by definition legal, at least during wartime. The idea that Congress did not have the constitutional authority to regulate the "means and methods of engaging the enemy"—as the Justice Department memorandum claimed—has no support in history or law.[110]

Doubts about the administration's legal arguments were first expressed by top officials within the Bush Justice Department nearly two years before publication of the *Times* story. After taking over at OLC toward the end of 2003, Goldsmith decided that the warrantless surveillance program was "the biggest legal mess" he'd ever encountered. Goldsmith took his concerns about the program to Attorney General John Ashcroft, who told Goldsmith to fix the problem so that the administration's actions were "being done lawfully." Goldsmith wanted the aid of Ashcroft's deputy attorney general, James Comey, but that required Comey to be read in to the top-secret program. Addington and Gonzales initially ruled that out, but changed their minds after Goldsmith raised the possibility that the attorney general might not recertify the program, which under Bush's secret order had to be reapproved every 45 days by the attorney general.[111]

After intensive study of the program, Goldsmith told the White House that the program was illegal and that the attorney general could not recertify the program unless it was brought into compliance with the law. Addington warned Goldsmith that "the blood of the hundred thousand people who die in the next attack will be on your hands." Goldsmith was unmoved. Two days before recertification was needed, Goldsmith as well as acting attorney general Comey—Ashcroft had been hospitalized just days before with acute gallstone pancreatitis—were summoned to the office of the White House chief of staff to meet with Cheney and Addington, as well as the directors of the NSA, FBI, and CIA. Cheney impressed upon Comey that the program was vital to national security, and wanted to know why the Justice Department was now "reversing course" from its previous legal analysis. Comey explained that the department now believed that analysis had been fundamentally flawed. "No lawyer reading [Yoo's legal analysis] could reasonably rely on it," Comey told Cheney. "Well I'm a lawyer and I did," Addington huffed. "No good lawyer," Comey shot back.[112]

What happened the following evening was straight out of a made-for-television drama. A sedated Ashcroft, "tubes and wires protruding from his body," was in intensive care, recovering from emergency gallbladder surgery, when a call from the president was put through: White House Counsel Gonzales and the president's chief of staff, Andy Card, were on their way to see him. The president didn't say so, but their mission was to get Ashcroft to overrule his deputy and to recertify the surveillance program. By the time Card and Gonzales arrived at the hospital, Comey and Goldsmith were already there, having been tipped off by Ashcroft's wife. Gonzales didn't get far with his entreaty before Ashcroft cut him off. Mustering what little energy he had, he lifted his head from the pillow and, glaring at Gonzales and Card, told the intruders that "they had no business coming." After giving "a lucid account" of why the department could no longer support the program, he announced that if he had known previously what he knew now, he would never have certified the program in the first place. "You drew the circle so tight," he complained, "that I couldn't get the advice that I needed." In any event, Ashcroft said, the decision was not his to make at the moment. "Gesturing at [Comey], Ashcroft said, 'There is the attorney general.'" Then "spent and pale, Ashcroft sank back down," leaving Gonzales and Card to slink from the room.[113]

The next morning, President Bush faced a momentous decision: should he reauthorize the program even though the Justice Department had concluded it was illegal? Gonzales and Card counseled against, while Addington and Cheney urged him to press ahead. Bush sided with his vice president, and Addington drew up a new presidential directive that scrubbed the attorney general's signature line and replaced it with White House Counsel Alberto Gonzales. The document that Addington drew up is still classified, but reportedly it "expressly overrode the Justice Department and any act of Congress or judicial decision that purported to constrain [the president's] power as commander-in-chief." And since it was top secret, neither Congress, the courts, nor the public could challenge it. By lunchtime, Bush had signed the order and Gonzales had countersigned it.[114]

The document that Bush signed asserted that the president alone could decide what was and was not lawful. This was the full-throated Nixonian philosophy: if the president authorized it then by definition it was legal. The theory, however, encountered a practical problem. Upon receiving news that Bush had signed the order, Comey and as many as two dozen other high-ranking Bush appointees readied their resignations. Ready to join them was FBI chief Robert Mueller, who refused to be involved in operations that the Justice Department had decided were criminal activities. When Bush discovered that he faced not just Comey's resignation but a mass exodus of top-tier Justice Department officials, he beat a hasty retreat. With an election looming, Bush knew that he could not afford the firestorm that would be ignited by the simultaneous resignation of virtually every top-tier Justice Department appointee. It could make him a one-term president. Indeed, Bush would be veering, as one Republican operative put it, "into Watergate territory." Moreover, the media frenzy and congressional hearings that would have ensued from the mass resignations would have resulted in the public disclosure of the very program Bush wished to keep secret. Less than 24 hours after signing the original order, Bush reversed course. The Justice Department, he told Comey, should make whatever changes it thought necessary to bring the program into compliance with the law.[115]

In Goldsmith's eyes, the episode was a historic victory for the rule of law—"the first time when the president of the United States *really* wanted something in wartime, and tried to overrule the Department of Justice, and the law held." But the episode was a cautionary tale about presidential power as well. Up until March 2004, the administration operated a secret program that supposedly "no good lawyer" could have believed was legal. By sharply limiting who had access to information about the program and the legal analysis that supported it, Addington insulated OLC's legal reasoning from serious scrutiny for more than two and a half years. And although the president backed down in this instance, he did so only because the prospect of en masse resignations would have been politically crippling. If the law held, it was because politics intruded, not because the president felt obligated to adhere to the law.[116]

The Targeted Killing of an American Citizen

When Barack Obama ran for office in 2008, he did so as a strong critic of what he regarded as the Bush administration's recklessly expansive conceptions of executive power. After he was elected president he tapped two of the legal community's "most vehement critics" of the Bush OLC's overreach in national security for top posts in the Office of Legal Counsel: Harvard law professor David Barron and Georgetown's Martin Lederman. Journalist Glenn Greenwald predicted that in contrast to Bush's OLC, which seemed willing to decree "that anything the President wished to do was legal," Barron and Lederman would "impose real limits when the law or the Constitution dictates." Yet in fact Barron and Lederman, like Bybee, Bradbury, and Yoo, often found themselves crafting legal opinions that stretched executive power and enabled the president to do what he believed was necessary for national security, nowhere more dramatically than in the case of Anwar al-Awlaki.[117]

Al-Awlaki was an American citizen, born to Yemeni parents in Las Cruces, New Mexico. At the time of the 9/11 terrorist attacks, the 30-year-old Awlaki had lived in the US for almost 19 years. He had spent the past decade going to school and working in Colorado and California, before moving to Washington, DC in January of 2001 to start a PhD program at George Washington University and become the imam at a high-profile mosque in a suburb just outside the nation's capital. He supported Bush in the 2000 presidential election (largely on the basis of a shared social conservatism) and even apparently "mused excitedly" that his new job might get him an invitation to the White House. That invitation never came, though Awlaki did get asked to speak at a luncheon at the Pentagon in February 2002 as part of a Defense Department effort to cultivate Muslim leaders seen as moderates. After 9/11 there was a crush of reports and TV crews wanting to meet with Awlaki, whose "Arabic garb and ... American speech" helped them to imagine him as "a new generation of Muslim leader capable of merging East and West." Awlaki's own self-image at the time was similarly as a cultural bridge-builder, who could explain Islam to America and America to the world's Muslims.[118]

Awlaki's ambition to be the bridge between America and Muslims across the globe was short-lived. He abruptly gave up his position as imam six months after 9/11, moved to Britain, and sent his wife and family to Yemen. In the weeks leading up to his departure Awlaki had grown increasingly critical of US policy, especially the government's indiscriminate raids on Islamic organizations, which constituted what Awlaki saw as "a war against Muslims and Islam." But he left his country and his "thriving clerical career" behind not because of growing anger at its government's policy but because he discovered that the FBI had been tailing him for months and had found out about his frequent furtive visits to prostitutes—compromising information that he realized could wreck his life. If made public, his "un-Islamic" behavior could undercut his moral authority and expose him as a hypocrite to his congregation as well as to other Muslims across the country and the world who listened to his increasingly popular CD series on the life of the Prophet Muhammad. Or the FBI might use the information to pressure him to become an informant.[119] His career in the US as a moderate cleric was over and his life as one of the Obama administration's most wanted radical clerics was just beginning.

Whereas in the US Awlaki sought to carve out a role for a himself "as the middleman between America and Islam," in Britain he honed a radically different message that savagely criticized America's "terrorizing of innocents" and stressed an ineradicable clash between Islam and the West. "Never, ever trust a *kuffar*" was Awlaki's message to the Muslim communities in Britain that felt marginalized and alienated. Awlaki's style remained scholarly and "low-key" but his rhetoric became increasingly incendiary in its justification of violence against the enemies of Islam. By the middle of the decade he had gone back to Yemen, where he was soon imprisoned and held in solitary confinement without charges for eighteen months. Upon his release at the end of 2007, he set up a website that would enable him to communicate his message of jihadist violence to a global audience, and soon thereafter joined al-Qaeda in the Arabian Peninsula (AQAP), becoming "deeply involved in plotting attacks on America," including the failed 2009 effort of the "Underwear Bomber" (Umar Farouk Abdulmutallab) to blow up Northwest Flight 253. But for a poorly designed bomb and a few nimble passengers, 290 people would have lost their lives that Christmas morning.[120]

Investigation of the failed Christmas Day bombing—most especially the detailed testimony provided to the FBI by Abdulmutallab—turned up compelling evidence that Awlaki was not just a charismatic AQAP propagandist but had played a pivotal operational role in a terrorist attack specifically aimed at killing Americans. Had he not been an American citizen, that information would have been more than sufficient to place him on the government's "kill-or-capture list" (which in practice was a kill list), but could the government kill an American citizen without a trial or even being charged with a crime? Did Awlaki's actions mean he forfeited his constitutional rights as an American citizen to due process? That was the question put to the Office of Legal Counsel.[121]

Obama made it clear that he regarded Awlaki as one of the nation's most dangerous foes and wanted him "removed from the battlefield." The Christmas Day bombing, following close on the heels of the November mass killing at Fort Hood, Texas, by Nidal Hasan, had exposed the Obama administration to intense public criticism from Republicans that it was soft on terrorism. And Awlaki was the one name to surface in both attacks. Although not involved with plotting the Fort Hood attack, Awlaki's call to violent jihad had inspired Hasan, and after the shootings he used his website to praise his "brother Nidal" as a "hero" who had struck a righteous blow in America's "war against Islam." Obama understood that Awlaki's "bilingual, bicultural charisma" posed "a double menace: stirring alienated Americans like Hasan to attack from inside the country, and dispatching foreign travelers like Abdulmutallab to bring lethal violence from afar." He thus posed a grave threat both to national security and to the administration's political future.[122]

The president's reasons for wanting Awlaki dead were clear enough. Murkier was whether the president had the power to unilaterally order him to be killed. That question was now put to Barron and Lederman in OLC. The legal and constitutional issues were complex and novel. The question cried out for careful deliberation. But the administration wanted an answer quickly. In short order, Barron gave the president the answer he wanted: yes, the president had the legal and constitutional authority to kill Awlaki. As soon as he received OLC's blessing, Obama convened the security cabinet (on February 5), and Awlaki was added to the kill list. Only then did Barron and Lederman begin writing the brief OLC memo (it is dated February 19) that laid out the legal reasoning behind their decision.[123]

As liberal academics Barron and Lederman had been scathingly critical of OLC's results-driven jurisprudence, but now they relied heavily on OLC precedents to get to the result their president wanted. Their first step was to affirm a 2002 OLC opinion that the long-standing executive order banning assassinations by the US government did not apply to targets who posed a "continuing and imminent threat" to the United States. So long as targeted killings were in self-defense they could not be considered assassinations. That conclusion was not difficult for Barron and Lederman to reach by simply following the logic of the precedents established by past executive branch lawyers (and leaving it to the president and his national security advisors to define what counted as an imminent threat).[124]

OLC precedent could not, however, dispose of the question of Awlaki's citizenship and his constitutional rights. The Fifth Amendment states that no person "shall be deprived of life, liberty, or property, without due process of law." Did that prevent the president from killing Awlaki? Barron and Lederman concluded that it did not—due process meant different things in different contexts and here it meant a careful review of his case by the executive branch. Similarly, the Fourth Amendment protection against unreasonable "seizure" was "situation-dependent" and in Awlaki's situation the government's action was reasonable. To bolster their case that Awlaki's citizenship didn't prevent the government from killing him, Barron and Lederman enlisted a medley of Supreme Court cases, including a 2004 case in which the Court ruled that an American captured on the battlefield could be held without trial, and a 1985 case that stemmed from a policeman who shot and killed a fleeing man suspected of burglary.[125]

One might find fault with this constitutional reasoning, but perhaps the bigger problem with the OLC memo was that it paid no heed to a federal statute governing the foreign murder of United States nationals (18 USC 1119). The Constitution's Bill of Rights might be vague and open to interpretation but the statute seemed clear as a bell. It made it illegal for any "person who, being a national of the United States, kills or attempts to kill a national of the United States while such a national is outside the United States but within the jurisdiction of another country." Barron and Lederman's disregard for this statute in authorizing the killing of Awlaki seemed as egregious as the Bush administration's authorizing of torture. In a subsequent and much longer OLC memo (dated July 16, 2010), Barron and Lederman belatedly tried to address the "gaping hole" in the original, rushed opinion. The statute, they argued, was intended to apply to murders committed by individuals, and therefore did not apply to justified killings carried out by "public authority" to protect the nation.[126]

On the last day of September 2011, ten years on from the attacks of 9/11 and 20 months after getting the green light from OLC, Obama finally got his man. A CIA drone missile attack in a desert in northern Yemen incinerated Awlaki as well as his young American protégé Samir Khan (OLC had not approved the targeting and killing of Khan but his death was deemed "acceptable collateral damage"). Perhaps wary of the terrible power they were unleashing, Barron and Lederman tried to limit the scope of their opinion to the particular facts of Awlaki's case. "In reaching this conclusion," Barron and Lederman wrote, "we do not address other cases or circumstances involving different facts." But notwithstanding this hedge, their opinion seems destined to be drawn upon as precedent, just as Barron and Lederman drew upon executive-branch legal precedents to write their brief for the president.[127]

LAW'S LIMITS AND THE POWER OF IMPEACHMENT

In an interview with the *New York Times* two weeks after his election as president, Donald Trump was asked about how he would handle conflicts of interest that could be created by his many real-estate holdings across the globe. His response was that "The law is totally on my side, meaning, the president can't have a conflict of interest." Many saw in this statement echoes of Nixon's claim that "when the president does it that means that it is not illegal." But Trump's claim was nothing like Nixon's. Trump was right that federal conflict-of-interest laws don't apply to the president, but that is because of the way Congress wrote the laws, not because the president is inherently exempt from any conflict-of-interest law that might be written. A president, of course, might challenge the constitutionality of such a law, but there is nothing in the Constitution that suggests that Congress lacks the power to write a conflict-of-interest law that applies to the president.[128]

The question of whether the president is above the law was raised anew a few months later when Trump's Oval Office boasting to Russian diplomats about the "great intel" he receives apparently resulted in the president revealing highly sensitive, codeword-classified intelligence. Had any other person revealed this information to the Russians, they would have been prosecuted and received a lengthy prison sentence. But legal experts agreed that, however damaging the disclosure, Trump had done nothing illegal, since the moment a president discloses the information it thereby ceases to become classified information. In this respect at least, Nixon's claim seems correct: when the president does it, it's not illegal.[129]

But Nixon's resignation arguably reveals more about the scope and limits of presidential power than does his claim that the law does not apply to the president. Ultimately, even where the law cannot touch the president directly, politics still can. That explains why the Trump administration generally responded to the revelation of Trump's "spontaneous" disclosure of classified information not by making the case for unlimited presidential power but by downplaying the importance of the information the president had shared. After all, the same legal experts who agreed that Trump had committed no crime were quick to add that Trump's action could qualify as an impeachable offense.[130]

Of course, the question of what counts as an impeachable offense is highly contested, and the answers have almost invariably been filtered through strongly partisan lenses. Impeachment was the framers' last line of defense against a president run amok, but the language of Article II, section 4 of the Constitution is maddeningly imprecise about what actions warrant impeachment. Treason is clear enough; indeed, Article III, section 3 of the Constitution defines it: "levying war against [the United States], or in adhering to their enemies, giving them aid and comfort." Bribery, too, is a readily understandable offense. But what are "high crimes and misdemeanors"? What did the framers mean by that phrase?

We know that an earlier draft of the Constitution made "treason, bribery, or corruption" impeachable offenses and that "corruption" was subsequently dropped out of concern that the term was too vague. Virginia's George Mason objected that dropping corruption unduly narrowed the scope of impeachment and suggested adding instead "maladministration," a term which was an impeachable offense in a half-dozen state constitutions, including Virginia's. Mason reasoned that bribery and treason "will not reach many great and dangerous offenses," including "attempts to subvert the Constitution." Mason's fellow Virginian James Madison opposed the motion to add "maladministration," arguing that the term was too imprecise and would put the president at the mercy of the legislature. Mason countered by proposing "high crimes & misdemeanors against the State," and the motion quickly carried.[131]

This exchange shows that the language of the impeachment clause, like much else in the Constitution, reflected a compromise between those framers who most feared executive abuses of power (Mason) and those who most feared executive weakness (Madison). The vexing vagueness of the phrase was part of its appeal to framers desperately seeking ways to bridge differences in the convention's closing days. Legal historian Raoul Berger has shown that for the framers the term "high crimes & misdemeanors" retained its traditional meaning in English law denoting "a category of political crimes against the state," and in adding "high crimes and misdemeanors" Mason was striving for impeachment language that would extend to the "great and dangerous offenses" against the state, especially those that undermined the Constitution.

If the framers were imprecise about what counted as an impeachable offense, they were unambiguous as to where the impeachment power would be lodged—and therefore who would get to decide what was an impeachable offense: the House of Representatives was given the sole power to impeach and the Senate the power to try all impeachments. Lawyers and scholars can argue all they want about what counts as an impeachable offense, but ultimately the Constitution leaves the decision not to the lawyers or the courts but to the politicians in Congress. The framers thereby ensured that Congress rather than the legal process would be the ultimate check on presidents who act as if they are above the law.

Not all the framers approved of this decision. Madison objected to the bitter end about placing the impeachment trial in the Senate's hands. He preferred that the Supreme Court try cases of impeachment. The partisan impeachments of Andrew Johnson (discussed in

Chapter 8) and Bill Clinton (for lying to a grand jury about his sexual relationship with a White House intern) vindicate Madison's concerns about the dangers of defining impeachment broadly, but these presidents' acquittals also showcase the effectiveness of the safeguards the framers erected, specifically the two-thirds vote required in the Senate to convict and remove a president.[132] This high hurdle has largely prevented impeachment from becoming the partisan tool that Madison so feared. In our contemporary age of heightened polarization and partisanship, that supermajority requirement must count among the framers' most crucial contributions to an effective presidency.[133]

NOTES

1 All quotations are from the original televised interviews, which are available on DVD as *Frost/Nixon: The Complete Interviews*. Transcripts of this exchange that are available on the web are almost always taken from the heavily edited and sometimes inaccurate transcript that appeared in the *New York Times* on May 20, 1977. The four one-and-a-half-hour segments aired May 4, 12, 19, and 26.

2 On the Huston Plan, see Joan Hoff, *Nixon Reconsidered* (New York: Basic Books, 1994), esp. 292–93. The plan was withdrawn in the face of objections from FBI chief J. Edgar Hoover and Attorney General John Mitchell. The "cascade of candor" quotation is from an interview David Frost gave to Mike Wallace on *60 Minutes*, aired on May 1, 1977.

3 On Nixon's identification with Lincoln, see Michael Paul Rogin, "The King's Two Bodies: Lincoln, Wilson, Nixon, and Presidential Self-Sacrifice," in J. David Greenstone, ed., *Public Values and Private Power in American Politics* (Chicago: University of Chicago Press, 1982), 71–108.

4 Three decades later, in the final year of the presidency of George W. Bush, the critically acclaimed movie *Frost/Nixon* gave Americans the opportunity to revisit this remarkable moment in television history and to ponder again the relationship between the law and executive power. The movie radically condensed the discussion of presidential power—gone were the references to the Huston Plan and to Lincoln—but Nixon's jarring punch line remained: "when the President does it, that means it's not illegal." However, the movie version, watched by more than 400 million people—ten times the number who saw the real interviews—made a crucial departure from the original script. Frost's incredulity is met not with Nixon's steadfast defense of his position's historical pedigree but by virtual capitulation: "That's what I believe. But I realize no one else shares that view." In real life, Nixon's defense rested on the proposition that his views were the same as those of Lincoln and every stalwart president who had faced great crises amid bitter, sometimes violent domestic opposition.

5 William Symmes to Capt. Peter Osgood, November 15, 1787, Massachusetts Volumes of the Documentary History of the Ratification of the Constitution, Wisconsin Historical Society, www.wisconsinhistory.org/ratification/digital/resource/0242.pdf.

6 Charles C. Thach, Jr., *The Creation of the Presidency, 1775–1789: A Study in Constitutional History* (Baltimore: Johns Hopkins University Press, 1923), 110–11. Francis Newton Thorpe, ed., *The Federal and State Constitutions, Colonial Charters, and Other Organic Laws of the States, Territories, and Colonies Now or Heretofore Forming the United States of America*, 7 vols. (Washington, DC: Government Printing Office, 1909), 3813, 3816–17.

7 Donald L. Robinson, "Presidential Prerogative and the Spirit of American Constitutionalism," in David Gray Adler and Larry N. George, eds., *The Constitution and the Conduct of American Foreign Policy* (Lawrence: University Press of Kansas, 1996), 114.

8 David Gray Adler, "The President's Pardon Power," in Thomas E. Cronin, ed., *Inventing the American Presidency* (Lawrence: University Press of Kansas, 1989), 213. William Blackstone,

Commentaries on the Laws of England. Reprint of the ninth edition (New York: Garland Publishing, 1978 [1783]), 4:397.

9   Richard J. Ellis, ed., *Founding the American Presidency* (Lanham, MD: Rowman & Littlefield, 1999), 221, 223, 226–27. Edward S. Corwin, *The President: Office and Powers, 1787–1957* (New York: New York University Press, 1957), 159.

10   Ellis, *Founding the American Presidency*, 219, 223–24, 268.

11   Ellis, *Founding the American Presidency*, 224–25.

12   Ellis, *Founding the American Presidency*, 222. Jeffrey Crouch, *The Presidential Pardon Power* (Lawrence: University Press of Kansas, 2009), 55–56.

13   Crouch, *Presidential Pardon Power*, 102–07. Richard M. Pious, *The Presidency* (Boston: Allyn & Bacon, 1996), 303.

14   Philip Bump, "Can Trump Pardon Anyone? Himself," *Washington Post*, July 21, 2017. Jonathan Turley, "Yes, Trump Can Legally Pardon Himself or His Family. No, He Shouldn't," *Washington Post*, July 21, 2017. Laurence H. Tribe, Richard Painter, and Norman Eisen, "No, Trump Can't Pardon Himself: The Constitution Tells Us So," *Washington Post*, July 21, 2017.

15   Crouch, *Presidential Pardon Power*, 3, 127–28. John Gramlich and Kristen Bialik, "Obama Used Clemency Power More Often than Any President since Truman," Pew Research Center, January 20, 2017, www.pewresearch.org/fact-tank/2017/01/20/obama-used-more-clemency-power/

16   Crouch, *Presidential Pardon Power*, 21–24.

17   Massimo Calabresi and Michael Weisskopf, "Inside Bush and Cheney's Final Days," *Time*, July 24, 2009.

18   John Locke, *Two Treatises of Government.* Quotations are from Book II, ch. 7, § 87; ch. 13, §§ 149, 151; ch. 14, § 159. Also see James P. Pfiffner, *Power Play: The Bush Presidency and the Constitution* (Washington, DC: Brookings Institution Press, 2008), 23–25.

19   Locke, *Two Treatises of Government*, ch. 14, §§ 159–60.

20   Locke, *Two Treatises of Government*, ch. 14, § 159.

21   Locke, *Two Treatises of Government*, ch. 14, § 164. Benjamin A. Kleinerman, *The Discretionary President: The Promise and Peril of Executive Power* (Lawrence: University Press of Kansas, 2009), esp. 4–8.

22   *The Debates and Proceedings in the Congress of the United States* (Washington, DC: Gales and Seaton, 1834), 1st Congress, 1st session, 1:537 (June 18, 1789). Also see Arthur M. Schlesinger, Jr., *The Imperial Presidency* (Boston: Houghton Mifflin, 1973), 9; and Kleinerman, *Discretionary President*, 3.

23   Jefferson to John B. Colvin, September 20, 1810, in volume 11 of *The Works of Thomas Jefferson* (New York: G.P. Putnam's Sons, 1904–1905), accessed from http://oll.libertyfund.org/title/807/88064. For a revealing account of the circumstances surrounding this letter and the uses to which it was put, see Jeremy D. Bailey, *Thomas Jefferson and Executive Power* (New York: Cambridge University Press, 2007), 250–56.

24   Thomas Jefferson to John C. Breckinridge, August 12, 1803, in Lance Banning, ed., *Liberty and Order: The First American Party Struggle* (Indianapolis: Liberty Fund, 2004), accessed from http://oll.libertyfund.org/title/875/64022. Bailey, *Thomas Jefferson and Executive Power*, 177–79.

25   Bailey, *Thomas Jefferson and Executive Power*, 180–81.

26   Jefferson to Breckinridge, August 12, 1803. Bailey, *Thomas Jefferson and Executive Power*, 180, 182. Richard Ellis and Aaron Wildavsky, *Dilemmas of Presidential Leadership: From Washington through Lincoln* (New Brunswick, NJ: Transaction Publishers, 1989), 72–73.

27   William H. Rehnquist, *All the Laws but One: Civil Liberties in Wartime* (New York: Random House, 1998), 18–25.

28 Rehnquist, *All the Laws but One*, 26–34. Brian McGinty, *Lincoln and the Court* (Cambridge, MA: Harvard University Press, 2008), 65–66, 72–74. Phillip Shaw Paludan, *The Presidency of Abraham Lincoln* (Lawrence: University Press of Kansas, 1994), 75–76.

29 Rehnquist, *All the Laws but One*, 34; also see 36, 38, 40–41.

30 McGinty, *Lincoln and the Court*, 195.

31 *Ex parte Merryman* 17 F.Cas. 144 (1861).

32 McGinty, *Lincoln and the Court*, 69, 85, 87. James F. Simon, *Lincoln and Chief Justice Taney: Slavery, Secession, and the President's War Powers* (New York: Simon & Schuster, 2006), 193–94.

33 McGinty, *Lincoln and the Court*, 80; compare Simon, *Lincoln and Chief Justice Taney*, 197. Another frequently neglected part of the story is that 50 days after his arrest, the administration handed Merryman over to a federal marshal. He was then indicted for treason and released on a $40,000 bail. Merryman never came to trial, not because the Lincoln administration suspended habeas corpus but because Taney obstructed legal proceedings against Merryman, whose father Taney had known since his undergraduate days at Dickinson College. Perhaps fearing that a jury—even a Baltimore jury—would convict Merryman, Taney used his poor health as an excuse to repeatedly postpone the trial. Although Taney was ill for much of this time, he could have allowed the district judge who shared responsibilities for the fourth circuit to hear the case, but instead he barred the other judge from hearing Merryman's case (or any other capital cases) in his absence. See Simon, *Lincoln and Chief Justice Taney*, 197–98, and McGinty, *Lincoln and the Court*, 66. Many others, however, were not as fortunate as Merryman, including Baltimore's mayor George Brown, who was arrested shortly after Merryman and spent the remainder of the war incarcerated in Fort McHenry.

34 Message to Congress in Special Session, July 4, 1861, in Roy Basler, ed., *The Collected Works of Abraham Lincoln* (New Brunswick, NJ: Rutgers University Press, 1953), 4:429–31. Also see Richard A. Posner, *Not a Suicide Pact: The Constitution in a Time of National Emergency* (New York: Oxford University Press, 2006).

35 Message to Congress in Special Session, July 4, 1861, in Basler, *Collected Works*, 4:430.

36 Schlesinger, *Imperial Presidency*, 60.

37 Lincoln to Albert T. Hodges, April 4, 1864, in Basler, *Collected Works*, 7:281. The letter summarized—at Hodges' request—"the substance" of what Lincoln had said at a meeting with Hodges, former Kentucky senator Archibald Dixon, and Kentucky governor Thomas E. Bramlette, who came to see the president to object to the enlistment of former slaves as soldiers in Kentucky.

38 Locke, *Two Treatises of Government*, ch. 14, §§ 164, 166.

39 *United States v. Nixon* 418 U.S. 683 (1974).

40 Proclamation Suspending the Writ of Habeas Corpus, September 24, 1862, Basler, *Collected Works*, 5:436–37.

41 McGinty, *Lincoln and the Court*, 185–86. Rehnquist, *All the Laws but One*, 65–66. Lincoln neither authorized nor approved of Vallandigham's arrest and trial by military commission, but he had no wish to undercut Burnside's authority. Despite his misgivings about the wisdom of Vallandigham's "injudicious" arrest, Lincoln stoutly defended it in public, insisting that Vallandigham had not been arrested for criticizing the government but rather for "damaging the army" by undermining its morale and encouraging desertions. "Must I shoot a simple-minded soldier boy who deserts," Lincoln asked, "while I must not touch a hair of a wiley agitator who induces him to desert?" "[T]o silence the agitator, and save the boy," Lincoln reasoned, "is not only constitutional, but ... a great mercy." McGinty, *Lincoln and the Court*, 187–88, 190–92. Lincoln to Erastus Corning and Others, June 12, 1863, Basler, *Collected Works*, 6:266–67. In a bid to defuse the controversy, Lincoln banished Vallandigham to the Confederacy rather than imprison him.

42   McGinty, *Lincoln and the Court*, 189–90.

43   *Ex parte Milligan* 71 U.S. 2 (1866). McGinty, *Lincoln and the Court*, 190.

44   *Ex parte Milligan*. The phrase "thunderously quotable" is from Mark E. Neely, Jr., *The Fate of Liberty: Abraham Lincoln and Civil Liberties* (New York: Oxford University Press, 1991), 176.

45   Scott M. Matheson, Jr., *Presidential Constitutionalism in Perilous Times* (Cambridge, MA: Harvard University Press, 2009), 63–64. Congress enacted legislation imposing criminal penalties for individuals who violated the president's order.

46   *Hirabayashi v. United States* 320 U.S. 81 (1943). Rehnquist, *All the Laws but One*, 198. Peter Irons, *Justice at War: The Story of the Japanese Internment Cases* (New York: Oxford University Press, 1983), 231–34.

47   *Korematsu v. United States* 323 U.S. 214 (1944).

48   Matheson, *Presidential Constitutionalism in Perilous Times*, 64, 69–70. In 1983, the Commission on Wartime Relocation unanimously found that "Executive Order 9066 was not justified by military necessity" but instead stemmed from "racial prejudice, war hysteria and a failure of political leadership" (187–88). Also in 1983, a federal judge in San Francisco erased Korematsu's conviction, and in 1986 a federal judge in Seattle did the same for Gordon Hirabayashi. Evidence of the government's suppression of evidence was discovered in the early 1980s by legal historian Peter Irons, whose research helped to persuade federal judges to overturn the convictions of Korematsu and Hirabayashi. The story of the Japanese internment cases is superbly told in Irons, *Justice at War*.

49   Matheson, *Presidential Constitutionalism in Perilous Times*, 76, 64–65.

50   The account here is adapted from Richard J. Ellis, ed., *Judging Executive Power: Sixteen Supreme Court Cases That Have Shaped the American Presidency* (Lanham, MD: Rowman & Littlefield, 2009), 111–14, which in turn draws on Louis Fisher, *Nazi Saboteurs on Trial: A Military Tribunal and American Law* (Lawrence: University Press of Kansas, 2005; second edition). Also see Michael Dobbs, *Saboteurs: The Nazi Raid on America* (New York: Knopf, 2004).

51   Louis Fisher, *Military Tribunals and Presidential Power: American Revolution to the War on Terrorism* (Lawrence: University Press of Kansas, 2005), 97.

52   Fisher, *Military Tribunals and Presidential Power*, 98–99.

53   Fisher, *Nazi Saboteurs on Trial*, 102, 115. Fisher, *Military Tribunals and Presidential Power*, 124.

54   *Youngstown Sheet and Tube Co. v. Sawyer* 343 U.S. 579 (1952). The account that follows is adapted from Ellis, *Judging Executive Power*, 135–38, 152–53. Also see Maeva Marcus, *Truman and the Steel Seizure Case: The Limits of Presidential Power* (New York: Columbia University Press, 1977).

55   This section is adapted from Ellis, *Judging Executive Power*, 154–60. Also see Louis Fisher, *In the Name of National Security: Unchecked Presidential Power and the Reynolds Case* (Lawrence: University Press of Kansas, 2006); and Robert Pallitto and William G. Weaver, *Presidential Secrecy and the Law* (Baltimore: Johns Hopkins University Press, 2007), esp. ch. 2.

56   The report found that the crew made several crucial errors, including shutting off fuel for the second engine when it was the first engine that was on fire. The report also suggested that the crew were slow to open the bomb bay doors and as a result most of those on board were unable to parachute from the plane. In addition, according to Air Force investigators, the civilian engineers had not been given instructions about emergency procedures, including how to use a parachute. Most important, the investigators concluded that two Air Force orders to modify the exhaust system "for the purpose of eliminating a definite fire hazard" had been ignored; and it was the exhaust system that was at fault for the fire. In addition, the report found that this particular plane had required "more than the normal amount of maintenance." In fact, in the six months prior to the crash the plane had been out of commission more than half of the time.

57   *Hamdan v. Rumsfeld* 548 U.S. 557 (2006). *Boumediene v. Bush* 553 U.S. 723 (2008).

58 Pfiffner, *Power Play*, 99–100.

59 Matheson, *Presidential Constitutionalism in Perilous Times*, 148; also 134. Parts of this section are adapted from Ellis, *Judging Executive Power*, 162–64, 176–79. Also see Jonathan Mahler, *The Challenge: Hamdan v. Rumsfeld and the Fight over Presidential Power* (New York: Farrar, Straus and Giroux, 2008).

60 Matheson, *Presidential Constitutionalism in Perilous Times*, 139–41.

61 Parts of this section are adapted from Ellis, *Judging Executive Power*, 180–82, 209.

62 Pfiffner, *Power Play*, 101. Also see Matheson, *Presidential Constitutionalism in Perilous Times*, 130–31, 138.

63 Matheson, *Presidential Constitutionalism in Perilous Times*, 142, 144.

64 Matheson, *Presidential Constitutionalism in Perilous Times*, 143–44.

65 Linda Greenhouse, "Gitmo Fatigue at the Supreme Court," *Washington Post*, April 6, 2011. Matheson, *Presidential Constitutionalism in Perilous Times*, 146.

66 Pfiffner, *Power Play*, 114–16. Greenhouse, "Gitmo Fatigue at the Supreme Court."

67 Greenhouse, "Gitmo Fatigue at the Supreme Court." For the evidence against Almerfedi, see *Hussain Salem Mohammed Almerfedi v. Obama*, US Court of Appeals for the District of Columbia Circuit, June 20, 2011 (No. 10–5291).

68 Matheson, *Presidential Constitutionalism in Perilous Times*, 145. *Ashcroft v. Iqbal* 490 F. 3d 143 (2009). The four liberal justices dissented in *Ashcroft* and the majority opinion was written by Kennedy, who also authored the majority opinion in *Boumediene v. Bush*.

69 Peter M. Shane, *Madison's Nightmare: How Executive Power Threatens American Democracy* (Chicago: University of Chicago Press, 2009), 83.

70 Nancy V. Baker, *Conflicting Loyalties: Law and Politics in the Attorney General's Office, 1789–1990* (Lawrence: University Press of Kansas, 1992), 46, 48. Harold H. Bruff, *Bad Advice: Bush's Lawyers in the War on Terror* (Lawrence: University Press of Kansas, 2009), 16. An early draft of the legislation gave the Supreme Court the power to appoint the attorney general, though for reasons unknown that idea was abandoned.

71 Baker, *Conflicting Loyalties*, 50, 52, 56. David M. O'Brien, *Storm Center: The Supreme Court in American Politics* (New York: Norton, 2011; ninth edition), 112.

72 Baker, *Conflicting Loyalties*, 55–56. Forrest McDonald, *The American Presidency: An Intellectual History* (Lawrence: University Press of Kansas, 1994), 282.

73 McDonald, *The American Presidency*, 282. Baker, *Conflicting Loyalties*, 129.

74 Baker, *Conflicting Loyalties*, 70.

75 McGinty, *Lincoln and the Court*, 83. Baker, *Conflicting Loyalties*, 3.

76 Baker, *Conflicting Loyalties*, 57–62. Seth P. Waxman, "'Presenting the Case of the United States as It Should Be': The Solicitor General in Historical Context," Address to the Supreme Court Historical Society, June 1, 1998, www.justice.gov/osg/aboutosg/historic-context.html.

77 Waxman, "Presenting the Case of the United States."

78 Frank M. Wozencraft, "OLC: The Unfamiliar Acronym," *American Bar Association Journal* 57 (January 1971), 34. Waxman, "Presenting the Case of the United States." Bruce Ackerman, *The Decline and Fall of the American Republic* (Cambridge, MA: Harvard University Press, 2010), 113–14.

79 Wozencraft, "OLC: The Unfamiliar Acronym," 37.

80 Griffin B. Bell with Ronald J. Ostrow, *Taking Care of the Law* (New York: William Morrow, 1982), 185. Jack Goldsmith, *The Terror Presidency: Law and Judgment inside the Bush Administration* (New York: Norton, 2007), 38.

81 Wozencraft, "OLC: The Unfamiliar Acronym," 36–37. Ackerman, *Decline and Fall of the American Republic*, 114. Also see John O. McGinnis, "Models of the Opinion Function of the

Attorney General: A Normative, Descriptive, and Historical Prolegomenon," *Cardoza Law Review* 15 (October 1993), 425, n186.

82 McGinnis, "Models of the Opinion Function of the Attorney General," 430, n206. Neil M. Soltman, "The Limits of Executive Power: Impoundment of Funds," *Catholic University Law Review* 23 (Winter 1973), 365. Rehnquist's judgment was affirmed by OLC in a 1988 opinion that rejected the Reagan White House's argument that the president had an inherent authority to impound funds regardless of what Congress said. See Op. Off. Legal Counsel 12 (1988), 207–08.

83 Roger C. Cramton, "On the Steadfastness and Courage of Government Lawyers," *John Marshall Law Review* 23 (1990), 174–75. Louis Fisher, *Presidential Spending Power* (Princeton, NJ: Princeton University Press, 1975), 148–50, 177.

84 Cramton, "On the Steadfastness and Courage of Government Lawyers," 175–77. Fisher, *Presidential Spending Power*, 176–77.

85 Cramton, "On the Steadfastness and Courage of Government Lawyers," 177–78. Fisher, *Presidential Spending Power*, 158.

86 Fisher, *Presidential Spending Power*, 175–201. *Train v. City of New York* 420 U.S. 35. In the case considered by the Supreme Court, Congress had appropriated funds "not to exceed" $5 billion for 1973 and $6 billion for 1974, and Nixon ordered the EPA director to allot no more than $2 billion for 1973 and $3 billion for 1974.

87 Ackerman, *Decline and Fall of the American Republic*, 97, 228, n32–33. McGinnis, "Models of the Opinion Function of the Attorney General," 425.

88 McGinnis, "Models of the Opinion Function of the Attorney General," 431. McGinnis offers *Morrison v. Olson* (1988)—in which the Court upheld the independent counsel statute—as a prime example of OLC's narrow reading of Supreme Court cases that have favored Congress over the president (432–33).

89 Ackerman, *Decline and Fall of the American Republic*, 109, 112. Baker, *Conflicting Loyalties*, 14.

90 Ackerman, *Decline and Fall of the American Republic*, 99, 230, n41.

91 Ackerman, *Decline and Fall of the American Republic*, 100–01, 231, n43–44.

92 The only OLC heads during this period who were confirmed were Virginia Seitz (June 2011 to December 2013), Jay Bybee (November 2001 to March 2003), Jack Goldsmith (October 2003 to June 2004), and Randy Moss (December 2000 to January 2001). Moss was acting attorney general for Clinton's final two years but was not confirmed by the Senate until December 15, 2000.

93 Ackerman, *Decline and Fall of the American Republic*, 88, 95–96, 101.

94 In 2006 John Yoo described Zubaydah as "al Qaeda's number three leader ... ranking in importance only behind Osama bin Laden and Ayman al Zawahiri." *War by Other Means: An Insider's Account of the War on Terror* (New York: Atlantic Monthly Press, 2006), 165. In a 2009 habeas filing, however, the government conceded that Zubaydah was not "a member of al-Qaida or otherwise formally identified with al-Qaida," and that he had no "personal involvement in planning or executing" the September 11 attacks. See *Zayn al Abidin Muhammad Husayn v. Robert Gates*, Respondent's Memorandum of Points and Authorities in Opposition to Petitioner's Motion for Discover and Petitioner's Motion for Sanctions. Civil Action No. 08-cv-1360 (RWR), pp. 34, 36, http://archive.truthout.org/files/memorandum.pdf.

95 Jane Mayer, *The Dark Side: The Inside Story of How the War on Terror Turned into a War on American Ideals* (New York: Doubleday, 2008), 140–41, 149.

96 Mayer, *The Dark Side*, 66, 150–51. Supported by memos from OLC and the White House counsel, Bush had already issued an executive order (on February 7, 2002) that al-Qaeda and Taliban detainees were not entitled to protections under the Geneva Convention. The Geneva Conventions, according to White House Counsel Alberto Gonzales, were "quaint" remnants of the past and did not apply to the war on terror.

97 Shane, *Madison's Nightmare*, 101; Goldsmith, *Terror Presidency*, 145.

98 Memorandum from Jay S. Bybee, Assistant Attorney General, to White House Counsel Alberto Gonzales, Re: Standards of Conduct for Interrogation under 18 U.S.C. §§ 2340–2340A, August 1, 2002, pp. 31, 39. This and OLC's other torture memos can be found in David Cole, *Torture Memos: Rationalizing the Unthinkable* (New York: New Press, 2009), quotations at 80, 90.

99 Memorandum from Jay S. Bybee, Assistant Attorney General, to John Rizzo, Acting General Counsel of the Central Intelligence Agency, August 1, 2002. Unlike the memo to Gonzales, this memo remained classified until the Obama administration released it in 2009.

100 The estimate of the number of times Zubaydah was waterboarded is from an internal CIA report, cited in the Memorandum from Steven G. Bradbury, Principal Deputy Assistant Attorney General, to John A. Rizzo, Senior Deputy, General Counsel, Central Intelligence Agency, Re: Application of United States Obligations against Torture to Certain Techniques that May Be Used in the Interrogation of High Value al Qaeda Detainees, May 30, 2005, p. 37; also Cole, *Torture Memos*, 270–71.

101 Goldsmith, *Terror Presidency*, 154. Matheson, *Presidential Constitutionalism in Perilous Times*, 92. Memorandum from Jay S. Bybee, Assistant Attorney General, to William J. Haynes II, General Counsel of the Department of Defense, Re: Military Interrogation of Alien Unlawful Combatants Held outside the United States, March 14, 2003, p. 11. Also see Philippe Sands, *Torture Team: Rumsfeld's Memo and the Betrayal of American Values* (New York: Palgrave Macmillan, 2008).

102 Bruff, *Bad Advice*, 247–48. Matheson, *Presidential Constitutionalism in Perilous Times*, 93. Goldsmith, *Terror Presidency*, 144, 150–51. Memorandum from Steven G. Bradbury to John A. Rizzo, Senior Deputy, General Counsel, Central Intelligence Agency, Re: Application of United States Obligations against Torture to Certain Techniques, May 30, 2005.

103 Goldsmith, *Terror Presidency*, 146, 148–50.

104 Eric Lichtblau, *Bush's Law: The Remaking of American Justice* (New York: Pantheon, 2008), 282–82. Bruff, *Bad Advice*, 255–57. Cole, *Torture Memos*, 4. The three memos can be found in Cole, *Torture Memos*, 152–274.

105 Ackerman, *Decline and Fall of the American Republic*, 95, 105. Mayer, *Dark Side*, 154. The OLC under the Obama administration withdrew each of Bradbury's three opinions.

106 Matheson, *Presidential Constitutionalism in Perilous Times*, 108. Lichtblau, *Bush's Law*, 227–29.

107 Goldsmith, *The Terror Presidency*, 181–82. Barton Gellman, *Angler: The Cheney Vice Presidency* (New York: Penguin Press, 2008), 277–83. Shane, *Madison's Nightmare*, 91.

108 Shane, *Madison's Nightmare*, 92. US Department of Justice, "Legal Authorities Supporting the Activities of the National Security Agency Described by the President," January 19, 2006, news.findlaw.com/hdocs/docs/nsa/dojnsa11906wp.pdf (quotation is from page 1 of the report).

109 Shane, *Madison's Nightmare*, 92. Matheson, *Presidential Constitutionalism in Perilous Times*, 110.

110 Shane, *Madison's Nightmare*, 93–94.

111 Gellman, *Angler*, 287–89.

112 Gellman, *Angler*, 294–96.

113 Gellman, *Angler*, 303–04. Jeffrey Rosen, "Conscience of a Conservative," *New York Times Magazine*, September 9, 2007.

114 Gellman, *Angler*, 309–13.

115 Gellman, *Angler*, 313–23.

116 Gellman, *Angler*, 315, 324–25.

117 Glenn Greenwald, quoted in Chris Edelson, "In Service to Power: Legal Scholars as Executive Branch Lawyers in the Obama Administration," *Presidential Studies Quarterly* (September 2013), 618–19. Also see Charlie Savage, *Power Wars: Inside Obama's Post-9/11 Presidency* (New York: Little, Brown, 2015), 234–35. Obama nominated Dawn Johnson to head OLC but the Senate never voted on her nomination and so Barron became the acting head of OLC. Lederman served as Barron's deputy.

118 Scott Shane, *Objective Troy: A Terrorist, a President, and the Rise of the Drone* (New York: Duggan, 2015), 63–65, 84–86, 111. Scott Shane, "The Lessons of Anwar al-Awlaki," *New York Times Magazine*, August 27, 2015. Laurie Goodstein, "A Nation Challenged: The American Muslims," *New York Times*, October 19, 2001.

119 Shane, *Objective Troy*, 87, 104, 119–21. Shane, "The Lessons of Anwar al-Awlaki."

120 Shane, *Objective Troy*, 146–51. Shane, "The Lessons of Anwar al-Awlaki."

121 Savage, *Power Wars*, 230; Shane, *Objective Troy*, 20–21, 216–17.

122 Savage, *Power Wars*, 230; Shane, *Objective Troy*, 21, 11. Shane, "The Lessons of Anwar al-Awlaki."

123 Shane, *Objective Troy*, 218. Savage, *Power Wars*, 236.

124 Savage, *Power Wars*, 237.

125 Savage, *Power Wars*, 238–39; Shane, *Objective Troy*, 222. Editorial Board, "A Thin Rationale for Drone Killings," *New York Times*, June 23, 2004. Charlie Savage, "Justice Department Memo Approving Targeted Killing of Anwar Al-Awlaki," www.nytimes.com/interactive/2014/06/23/us/23awlaki-memo.html.

126 Shane, *Objective Troy*, 222–23. Barron quit OLC shortly after finishing up the memo. Two years later, Obama nominated Barron to be a federal appeals court judge, a position to which he was confirmed in May 2014.

127 Daniel Klaidman, *Kill or Capture: The War on Terror and the Soul of the Obama Presidency* (Boston: Houghton Mifflin Harcourt, 2012), 264. Shane, *Objective Troy*, 223–24.

128 "Donald Trump's New York Times Interview: Full Transcript," *New York Times*, November 23, 2016. Article I, Section 9 of the Constitution does restrict any member of the government, including the president, from receiving gifts or emolument from a foreign power without Congress's consent.

129 Jack Goldsmith, et al., "Bombshell: Initial Thoughts on the Washington Post's Game-Changing Story," *Lawfare*, May 15, 2017, https://lawfareblog.com/bombshell-initial-thoughts-washington-posts-game-changing-story. "Is a President Sharing Classified Information against the Law?" *NPR Morning Edition*, May 16, 2017, www.npr.org/2017/05/16/528570781/is-a-president-sharing-classified-information-against-the-law.

130 Legal scholars debate whether a president can be indicted. In 1973, the OLC under Nixon determined the answer was no, and that opinion was reaffirmed by the OLC under Clinton in 2000. But the Watergate special prosecutor came to the opposite conclusion, as did a memo written for independent counsel Kenneth Starr, who led the investigation into President Clinton's misdeeds. See Charlie Savage, "Can the President Be Indicted? A Long-Hidden Memo Says Yes," *New York Times*, July 22, 2017.

131 On the origins and meaning of the impeachment clause, see Ellis, *Founding the American Presidency*, 233–53; Peter Charles Hoffer and N.E.H. Hull, *Impeachment in America, 1635–1805* (New Haven: Yale University Press, 1984); John Labovitz, *Presidential Impeachment* (New Haven: Yale University Press, 1978); and Raoul Berger, *Impeachment: The Constitutional Problems* (Cambridge, MA: Harvard University Press, 1973).

132 The two-thirds provision was an American invention. In Great Britain, impeachment was tried in the House of Lords and required only a simple majority for conviction. On the Clinton impeachment, see Richard A. Posner, *An Affair of State: The Investigation, Impeachment, and Trial of President Clinton* (Cambridge, MA: Harvard University Press, 2000); and Nicol C. Rae and Colton C. Campbell, *Impeaching Clinton: Partisan Strife on Capitol Hill* (Lawrence: University Press of Kansas, 2004).

133 The rise of "the age of impeachment" since 1960 is brilliantly illuminated in David E. Kyvig, *The Age of Impeachment: American Constitutional Culture since 1960* (Lawrence: University Press of Kansas, 2008).

PART V

CONCLUSION

CHAPTER 11

EVALUATING PRESIDENTS

The day that Donald Trump delivered his first inaugural address, Gallup was in the field asking citizens its trademark question: do you approve or disapprove of the way Donald Trump is handling his job as President? But how does a citizen answer that question when a president has not even been on the job for a day?

In the not-so-distant past, many Americans would not even have tried. When Gallup came asking whether the public approved of the performance of George Herbert Walker Bush in January 1989, 43 percent said they had no opinion. And 36 percent told Gallup that they had yet to form an opinion about the new president Ronald Reagan—and that was ten days after the inauguration. Evidently in those days even Gallup felt they should give the president a week or so before gauging public evaluations of the president's performance. No longer. Not only was Gallup willing to ask about Trump's performance on his first day in office, but almost all Americans were prepared to render judgment. Of those surveyed in the opening days of the Trump presidency, 90 percent felt that they already had enough information to judge his performance—with half expressing approval and the other half disapproval.[1]

Our rush to judgment on presidents is inevitably clouded by partisanship. At the end of Obama's first hundred days, fewer than three in ten Republicans approved of the president's performance, whereas more than 90 percent of Democrats approved. The same partisan discrepancy was evident in evaluations of President George W. Bush. After Bush's first hundred days, better than nine in ten Republicans approved of the job Bush was doing, while only three in ten Democrats approved. The partisan gap was even greater at the end of Trump's first hundred days, with almost nine in ten Republicans but only one in ten Democrats approving of Trump's performance.[2]

The partisan divide in presidential evaluations is more extreme today than at any time in the past half-century. At the end of Richard Nixon's first hundred days, for instance, his overall job approval was almost identical to Bush's and Obama's, but the gap between Republican and Democratic evaluations was close to half as large as during the Bush and Obama presidencies. As Table 11.1 shows, Bush left office with what was at the time the largest discrepancy between Republican and Democratic evaluations in the history of Gallup polling. As Bush packed his bags, only 6 percent of Democrats said they approved of the president's performance, while three-quarters of Republicans

While running for the presidency, Barack Obama frequently invited comparisons with Abraham Lincoln. He announced his presidential candidacy from the state capitol in Springfield, Illinois, where Lincoln served as a state legislator. Following his victory over Republican John McCain, president-elect Obama rode the train from Philadelphia to Washington, emulating the final leg of president-elect Lincoln's storied rail journey to the nation's capital. Finally, less than 48 hours before taking the oath of office, Obama invoked Lincoln again by kicking off his inaugural celebration with a speech in front of the Lincoln memorial and a crowd of an estimated 400,000 people. Obama chose as the inaugural theme "A New Birth of Freedom," Lincoln's famous phrase from the Gettysburg Address.

Courtesy: Getty Images.

still backed their president. Obama left office a much more popular president than Bush (58 versus 34 percent approval rating), but the discrepancy between Republican and Democratic evaluations was even greater for Obama than it had been for Bush. Obama left office with the approval of 95 percent of Democrats but only 14 percent of Republicans.[3]

But while partisan divisions have sharpened dramatically over the past several decades, Table 11.1 also reminds us that partisanship has always colored citizens' evaluations of presidential performance. When Truman left office, fewer than one in ten Republicans approved of his job performance, yet half of Democrats still reported that he was doing a good job. Eisenhower left office with the approval of about nine in ten Republicans, while a majority of Democrats disapproved of his performance. Indeed, in seven decades of Gallup polling no president has left office with the approval of a majority of citizens from the other party and only Truman, Nixon, and Jimmy Carter have left office without the approval of a large majority of those from their own party.

TABLE 11.1 Gallup Job Approval Rating upon Leaving Office

President	Overall Approval Rating upon Leaving Office	Approval Rating among Partisans of Same Party as President	Approval Rating among Partisans of Opposing Party	Difference between Republican and Democratic Ratings
Truman	32	50	9	41
Eisenhower	59	88	43	45
Kennedy	58	80	31	49
Johnson	49	63	32	29
Nixon	24	50	13	37
Ford	53	80	40	40
Carter	34	49	14	35
Reagan	63	93	38	55
Bush I	56	86	33	53
Clinton	65	91	34	57
Bush II	34	75	6	69
Obama	58	95	14	81

Partisan bias in the evaluation of presidents is even more pronounced among political elites and partisan pundits. Republicans routinely charged that Obama was "the worst president ever."[4] The same tag was frequently used by Democratic elites to describe George W. Bush, though most Democrats today would likely reserve that label for Trump. Nor are scholars immune from the partisan rush to judgment. A 2008 poll of more than one hundred historians—few of whom could have been Republicans—found that more than six in ten said that Bush was the worst president ever: worse than James Buchanan, worse than Warren Harding, and worse than Richard Nixon.[5] The left's loathing of Bush and Trump was more than matched by anti-Obama vitriol on the right. Conservative bookshelves groan under the weight of bestselling diatribes with hyperventilating titles such as *Crimes against Liberty: An Indictment of President Barack Obama*; *Culture of Corruption: Obama and His Team of Tax Cheats, Crooks, and Cronies*; and *Fool Me Twice: Obama's Shocking Plans for the Next Four Years Exposed*. These and scores of other books like them confirm the sage judgment of political scientist John Dilulio that "when it comes to judging presidents and presidencies, partisan or ideological diatribes are a dime a dozen, and not worth the dime."[6]

The problem of fairly evaluating presidents is not only a problem of partisanship, however. For how we ultimately evaluate a presidency may depend as much on what happens after a president leaves office as on what happens during his tenure. The Marshall Plan's success in creating a peaceful and prosperous Europe in the decades after World War II helped to elevate President Harry Truman into the pantheon of near-great presidents, even though he was wildly unpopular during his last years in office. Years or generations may need to pass before we can evaluate the consequences of policies that presidents help to put in place. Perhaps Bush will be judged as harshly by history as he is by historians today. Or perhaps as partisan passions cool and events unfold, Bush's reputation may rise, as happened with Truman as well as Eisenhower and Reagan. Or perhaps, as with Johnson, Nixon, Ford, and Carter, the passage of time will have little impact on the way historians ultimately rate the Bush presidency. One thing is certain: citizens, politicians, and historians will continue to judge presidential performance against the benchmarks of greatness, real and imagined, established by previous occupants of the Oval Office.

The Presidential Ratings Game

The presidential ratings game began in earnest in 1948, when Arthur Schlesinger asked 55 prominent historians to grade the presidents: A signified Great; B, Near Great; C, Average; D, Below Average; and F, Failure. Schlesinger provided no criteria for how to judge presidential greatness or failure. The only instructions provided to the distinguished panel were that "the test in each case is performance in office, omitting anything done before or after." Jefferson, for instance, should not get credit for authoring the Declaration of Independence, nor should Grant be credited for leading the Union armies to victory in the Civil War.[7]

The presidential greats topping the Schlesinger charts were Lincoln, Washington, FDR, Woodrow Wilson, and Jefferson. At the bottom, the two consensus failures were Ulysses Grant and Warren Harding. When Schlesinger administered the survey again in 1962, this time to a panel of 75 experts, he got essentially the same list of presidential greats and presidential failures.

Over the past half-century there have been many efforts to update and improve upon Schlesinger's methodology. Some have employed a much larger sample size. Most impressive were a 1982 survey by Robert Murray and Tim Blessing that polled 846 experts and another by William Ridings and Stuart McIver in 1996 that surveyed 719 authorities. Other surveys have tried to specify the criteria evaluators should use in judging presidents. Both 2000 and 2009 C-SPAN surveys asked experts to rate presidents on ten separate dimensions, including public persuasion, relations with Congress, crisis leadership, and moral authority. Others have tried to correct for the perceived liberal ideological bias of historians by surveying more conservative and Republican scholars, as the Wall Street Journal did in surveys commissioned in 2000 and 2005.[8]

As Table 11.2 and Table 11.3 show, none of these refinements have mattered much in judging presidential success and failure.[9] The wider net cast by the Murray–Blessing and Ridings–McIver surveys yielded much the same list of presidential greats and presidential failures as Schlesinger's smaller sampling of scholars. Factor analysis of the different dimensions used by C-SPAN shows that they are not distinct criteria but instead are all part of an underlying "greatness" construct used by evaluators. This may be because even historians don't know enough about each of these presidents to render separate judgments on each of these criteria. Instead, it seems, evaluators form a global judgment about an individual president's success and failure and then make their rankings on the specific criteria conform to this overall judgment.[10]

Even the inclusion of more Republican and conservative scholars in the greatness surveys had relatively modest effects on the ranking of presidents, particularly at the top

President George W. Bush invited comparisons with the nation's greatest presidents by choosing Mount Rushmore as the backdrop to an August 15, 2002 speech on "the challenge of fighting and winning a war against terrorists." Bush predicted that "out of the evil done to this great land" on September 11, 2001, "is going to come incredible good, because we're the greatest nation on the face of the Earth."

Courtesy: AFP/Getty Images.

and bottom. Lincoln, Washington, and FDR still emerged as the nation's great presidents, and a familiar list of mediocrities—Buchanan, Harding, Pierce, and Andrew Johnson— again brought up the rear.[11] Nor was the result all that surprising. Statistical analyses of past greatness surveys have consistently found that once presidents have passed from the scene there is little relationship between the partisanship of the evaluator and the ranking assigned to a president.[12]

There has, in short, been tremendous stability in these presidential rankings. To be sure, a few presidents have experienced some significant change in their historical reputations. In 1948, for instance, Andrew Johnson rated a place toward the middle of the pack (number 19 out of 29 presidents), but by the 1980s he was consistently ranked among the five worst presidents. Once credited for bravely defying the "vindictive" Radical Republicans and for his unswerving insistence on presidential prerogative, Johnson was widely seen in the aftermath of the 1960s civil rights movement as an inflexible and politically tone-deaf racist who was his own (and the country's) worst enemy. And, of course, presidents who have only recently left office have sometimes experienced dramatic shifts in their historical reputations. In 1996, for instance, Reagan was still ranked in the third quartile of presidents, just below Rutherford Hayes.[13] But by the twenty-first century, as historians increasingly

TABLE 11.2 The Top Five Presidential Greats

1948 Schlesinger	1962 Schlesinger	1982 Murray–Blessing	1996 Schlesinger	1996 Ridings–McIver	2000 Wall Street Journal	2009 C-SPAN	2014 APSA
Lincoln	Lincoln	Lincoln	Lincoln	Lincoln	Washington	Lincoln	Lincoln
Washington	Washington	FDR	Washington	FDR	Lincoln	Washington	Washington
FDR	FDR	Washington	FDR	Washington	FDR	FDR	FDR
Wilson	Wilson	Jefferson	Jefferson	Jefferson	Jefferson	T. Roosevelt	T. Roosevelt
Jefferson	Jefferson	T. Roosevelt	Jackson	T. Roosevelt	T. Roosevelt	Truman	Jefferson

TABLE 11.3 The Top Five Presidential Failures

1948 Schlesinger	1962 Schlesinger	1982 Murray–Blessing	1996 Schlesinger	1996 Ridings–McIver	2000 Wall Street Journal	2009 C-SPAN	2014 APSA
Harding	Harding	Harding	Harding	Harding	Buchanan	Buchanan	Buchanan
Grant	Grant	Grant	Buchanan	Buchanan	Harding	A. Johnson	Harding
Pierce	Buchanan	Nixon	A. Johnson	A. Johnson	Pierce	Pierce	A. Johnson
Buchanan	Pierce	Buchanan	Nixon	Grant	A. Johnson	Harding	Pierce
Taylor	Coolidge	A. Johnson	Hoover	Pierce	Fillmore	G.W. Bush	Hoover

recognized the key role his presidency played in reshaping the Republican Party and the nation's political agenda, Reagan was propelled into the top ten presidents (number eight in the 2000 *Wall Street Journal* survey and number ten in the 2009 C-SPAN survey). Similarly, Eisenhower debuted in the 1962 Schlesinger survey in the bottom third (22nd out of 31), just below Chester Arthur, but over the past quarter-century he has invariably ranked among the top ten presidents—his reputation enhanced by a greater appreciation for what he avoided (war in Vietnam) and the leadership he exercised behind the scenes (what political scientist Fred Greenstein aptly dubbed "the hidden-hand presidency").[14]

Overall, though, the stability of these ratings is what impresses most. Whether we survey Republicans or Democrats, historians, law professors, or political scientists, a broad swath of scholars or only a select few, we continue to get essentially the same cast of great and failed presidencies. But so what? Scholars may agree about who qualifies for the pantheon of presidential greats and who deserves a place in the presidential hall of shame, but does it really make sense to compare a twenty-first-century president with a nineteenth-century president or a wartime presidency with a peacetime presidency? Are the situations faced by presidents simply too diverse for comparative evaluations to be meaningful or helpful?

THE DEAL OF THE CARDS

The basic problem, as political scientist and former Clinton advisor William Galston put it, is how to distinguish "between the deal of the cards and the play of the hand." In other words, some presidents are blessed by history with a favorable hand, while others are saddled with a hand that seems virtually unplayable.[15]

Times That Try Men's Souls

Galston's concern is with a particular variant of the "deal of the cards" problem—namely that "it is impossible to be a great president in times that do not call for greatness." Greatness, according to this view, requires great crises. In Galston's words, only "in the times that try men's souls—war, severe economic downturns, deep social conflict"—can greatness come to the fore. Galston suggests that this was why his former boss Bill Clinton, who presided over a period of relative peace and prosperity, could not hope to join the ranks of the truly great presidents.[16]

A glance at the conventional cast of greats—Washington, Lincoln, and FDR—bolsters Galston's claim about the connection between crisis and presidential greatness. Lincoln was president during the most monumental crisis of the nineteenth century, the Civil War, while Roosevelt was president during the two biggest crises of the twentieth century, the Great Depression and, on its heels, World War II. Although Washington did not face a crisis of these proportions while he was president, as the nation's first president he confronted challenges that were, by definition, unlike those faced by any other president. And, of course, he was the commanding general during the nation's defining crisis of the eighteenth century, the American Revolution—a crisis that not only made him president but also made him a revered national symbol.

But while greatness on the scale of a Washington, Lincoln, or FDR may not be in the cards for other presidents, it is less clear that a place among the supposed near-greats is reserved for those who govern during times of severe crisis. War, in particular, does not seem nearly as important as it is often assumed to be. True, three presidents commonly judged to be near-great presidents presided over major wars: Woodrow Wilson (World War I), Harry Truman (the Korean War), and James Polk (the Mexican War). But the other five often designated near-greats—Jefferson, Jackson, Theodore Roosevelt, Eisenhower, and Reagan—are not typically considered wartime presidents. And certainly none of these five owe their reputations as near-great presidents to war. In fact, Eisenhower's high reputation rests in part on his refusal to get sucked into a war in Vietnam.

Indeed, it is not altogether clear that the near-great reputations of Truman and Polk owe much to the wars in which they enmeshed the country. Truman's stature among presidency raters today owes little to the costly, unpopular stalemate in Korea. Instead it rests on his backing of far-sighted policies such as the Marshall Plan and the creation of NATO that helped to prevent Communist expansion into Europe. Nor did it hurt that he was on the right side of history in ordering the desegregation of the armed forces. Polk's reputation as a near-great president, too, is tied less to fighting a war with Mexico than to his success in achieving the four principal goals he established at the outset of his administration: reestablishing an independent treasury, reducing tariffs, resolving the boundary dispute with Oregon, and acquiring California. The Mexican War was the means Polk used to achieve his final objective, but it was the acquisition of territory, not the fighting of war, that has boosted Polk's reputation.[17]

Recent history confirms that war is more likely to be a drag on a president's historical standing than a boost. The Vietnam War made Lyndon Johnson a deeply unpopular president and did lasting harm to his historical standing. Johnson's record of legislative achievements is unmatched in the annals of presidential history by all except perhaps FDR. And in securing the passage of the Civil Rights Act of 1964 and the Voting Rights Act of 1965, he achieved two of the most important pieces of legislation in American history. Yet despite these achievements and the formidable political skills that helped make them possible, Johnson typically ranks in the second quartile of presidents, those considered merely "above average." But for the Vietnam War, Johnson likely would be remembered as among the nation's greatest presidents, and perhaps would have become the only president other than FDR to serve more than eight years.

Even popular, successful wars do not guarantee a top-tier ranking. Just ask George Herbert Walker Bush. The Persian Gulf War of 1990–1991 was spectacularly successful in liberating Kuwait after Saddam Hussein's invasion. At the end of the seven-month war, about nine in ten Americans approved of the president's job performance. However, the effect was short-lived. As soon as the war was over, Bush's public approval ratings were dragged down by a weak economy, and the once popular president was defeated by Bill Clinton in 1992. The success of the Gulf War was quickly discounted not only by voters but by presidency raters as well. In virtually every greatness survey, Bush is rated as thoroughly average, smack in the middle of the pack.

It is too soon to tell where George W. Bush will end up in the presidential rankings. So far, however, the wars in Afghanistan and Iraq have done little to boost his reputation.

The 2009 C-SPAN poll of presidential historians put him at 36th, sandwiched between John Tyler and Millard Fillmore. By 2017, Bush had inched up to 33rd in the same survey, just behind Rutherford Hayes.[18] As time passes, his rating will likely rise a bit more—Grant and Nixon, after all, are the only reelected presidents to be consistently rated among the failed and below-average presidents. One suspects, however, that despite (or because of) seven years of war, Bush will never be rated alongside the great or near-great presidents.

In sum, apart from the Civil War and World War II—triumphant wars that were universally recognized as just and that involved hundreds of thousands of US casualties—there is little evidence that war, as President Kennedy once speculated, makes "it easier for a president to achieve greatness." And even if Kennedy was right in 1962 that there appeared to be a connection between war and Schlesinger's greatness rankings, the relationship has completely broken down in the half-century since Kennedy's presidency.[19]

If war is not a reliable route to presidential greatness, severe economic downturns are a pretty sure road to ruin. Yes, there is FDR, but he is the exception to an otherwise consistent pattern of presidencies foundering on economic crises. And it is difficult to untangle how much of FDR's standing as one of the three indisputably great presidents rests on his leadership in World War II rather than his leadership during the Great Depression—especially because it was World War II that ultimately lifted the nation out of economic depression and provided the justification for FDR's election to an unprecedented third term.

No other president who presided over an enduring economic downturn is remembered as a great or near great president. The Panic of 1837 and the resulting economic downturn turned an exceptionally talented political strategist, Martin Van Buren, into a one-term president who is consistently ranked average. Rutherford Hayes took office during the "Long Depression" of the 1870s and he, too, is remembered as a distinctly average president. The Panic of 1893 wrecked Cleveland's second term—and while Cleveland is often ranked as above average, that relatively high ranking rests largely on his successful first term rather than his disastrous second one. And Herbert Hoover, of course, is a twentieth-century poster child for the damage that a severe economic downturn can do not only to a president's popularity but to his historical reputation.

There is a simple reason that severe economic downturns rarely enable presidents to be remembered as great presidents. Those who are consistently ranked as great or near-great presidents have one thing in common: they are all presidents who were reelected to a second term (Polk is the sole exception and he had pledged from the outset not to serve a second term). And when the economy is in decline, voters rarely reward the president with a second term, as Jimmy Carter and George Herbert Walker Bush can attest. In this sense, at least, the public's evaluation of presidents has an important indirect effect on how historians rank presidents. An economy in crisis, in short, is usually as damaging for a president's popularity as it is for a president's historical reputation.[20]

In sum, an explanation for presidential greatness that rests on the magnitude of the crisis faced by a president turns out to be more problematic than one might expect. Granted, it may explain why contemporary presidents, no matter how deft or skilled, cannot hope to rival the greatness of an FDR or Lincoln. The Civil War and World War II dealt those two presidents hands that were unlike those seen by any past president—and, it is devoutly to be wished, any future president as well. But if we put the carnage of the Civil War and World War II to one side, crisis does not seem a strong predictor of a president's historical reputation. Part of the problem with the "times that try men's souls" thesis is that all presidents today face perpetual, urgent crises, domestic and foreign. That was precisely political scientist Richard Neustadt's prescient point in 1960, when he argued that all presidents now confronted what he called "mid-century conditions"—namely, a permanent state of emergencies and crisis. The extraordinary had become ordinary. Does this mean, then, that all modern presidents are dealt roughly the same hand and can be compared and evaluated by how they play that hand? Or is there another, better way to think about the "deal of the cards" problem that takes into account the different opportunities that presidents have to achieve greatness?[21]

Political Time

Among the most creative attempts to distinguish the deal of the cards from the play of the hand is political scientist Stephen Skowronek's concept of political time. According to Skowronek, a president's place in political time is structured by two crucial factors: (1) whether a president is affiliated with or opposed to the dominant party regime, and (2) whether that regime is resilient or vulnerable. These two dimensions, as Table 11.4 shows, yield four different kinds of hands that a president may be dealt.[22]

The worst hand is dealt to the president who comes to power affiliated with a vulnerable political regime. These presidents face an almost impossible task. On the one hand, "to affirm established commitments is to stigmatize oneself as a symptom of the nation's problems and the premier symbol of systemic political failure." On the other, to repudiate those commitments "is to become isolated from one's most natural political allies and to be rendered impotent." This was the insoluble dilemma that confronted John Adams (affiliated with a crumbling Federalist Party), John Quincy Adams (affiliated with a fracturing National Republican Party), Franklin Pierce and James Buchanan (affiliated with a Democratic Party coming apart over slavery), Herbert Hoover (affiliated with a discredited Republican Party ideology of competitive individualism), and Jimmy Carter (affiliated with a fraying New Deal coalition). Not surprisingly, none of

TABLE 11.4 Skowronek's Categorization of Political Time

Regime is:	President's Relationship to Regime	
	Opposed	Affiliated
Vulnerable	Politics of reconstruction (e.g., FDR)	Politics of disjunction (e.g., Carter)
Resilient	Politics of preemption (e.g., Eisenhower)	Politics of articulation (e.g., Truman)

these presidents are remembered as great or near-great presidents, and most are commonly ranked as relatively poor presidents.[23]

The strongest hand is dealt to those presidents who take office in opposition to a crumbling party regime. Freed from a discredited politics of the past, these presidents are given the rare opportunity to reconstruct politics, to redefine the nation's political agenda, and to create new alliances that may last for a generation. According to Skowronek, this was the serendipitous hand dealt to Jefferson, Jackson, Lincoln, FDR, and Reagan, each of whom is typically evaluated as a great or near-great president.

The other two positions in political time are less predictive of greatness. What Skowronek calls "the politics of articulation" involves presidents aligned with a resilient regime. Almost half of the nation's 44 presidents fall into this category (including 10 of the 13 presidents between Lincoln and FDR) and, not surprisingly, they are a much more diverse group in terms of achievements and historical reputations. It includes near-great presidents such as Truman and Polk, failures such as Grant and Harding, and a number of average presidents such as Hayes and Taft. But it also includes a disproportionate percentage of the above average presidents—notably, Madison, Monroe, McKinley, Johnson, and Kennedy. These "orthodox-innovators" are committed to continuing the regime's policies and redeeming its unfulfilled pledges while adapting the regime's agenda to meet changing circumstances or shifting cleavages. Generally, the resilience of the regime places these presidents in a strong position to achieve their goals, although they are unlikely to be recognized as achieving the same heights as the path-breaking presidents who remake and reconstruct the nation's politics.

Presidents in Skowronek's final category of "the politics of preemption" are dealt the most unpredictable hand of all—they are, as Skowronek puts it, "the wild cards of presidential history." They often owe their election to a fortuitous but temporary disruption in the dominant party coalition, either because of an unpopular war (Nixon in 1968), an economic downturn (Harrison in 1840 and Clinton in 1992), or a third party candidate (Wilson in 1912). Alternatively, they may come to power through sheer accident (Tyler in 1841 and Johnson in 1865) or by being a popular war hero who transcends partisan appeals (Taylor in 1848 and Eisenhower in 1952). Like the reconstructive presidents, these presidents are unaffiliated with the regime, but unlike the reconstructive presidents they face an established regime that remains politically and ideologically formidable. These presidents, Skowronek explains, "will in effect be probing for reconstructive possibilities without a clear warrant for breaking cleanly with the past." If "they probe too deeply," the empire strikes back, sometimes targeting the president for impeachment (Tyler, Andrew Johnson, Nixon, Clinton) and often leaving him politically isolated. Judging by the greatness surveys, a few presidents have negotiated this predicament well (Eisenhower and Wilson) or passably well (Cleveland in his first term, maybe Clinton), but many have ended up rated among the worst presidents. Five of the nine lowest-ranking presidents in both the 2000 and 2005 *Wall Street Journal* surveys (Andrew Johnson, Fillmore, Tyler, Nixon, and Taylor), for instance, were presidents of preemption.[24]

One of the most perplexing questions about Skowronek's theory is what separates a "disastrous preemption" from "a masterful reconstruction." Could Wilson or Clinton or Nixon, each of whom was unaffiliated with what appeared initially at least to be a regime in disarray, have reconstructed politics? Was the absence of reconstruction a failure of presidential leadership or a result of the underlying resilience of the regime? When is a preemptive president a reconstructive president who failed? And can the resilience of the regime be measured separately from and prior to the reaction that presidential action engenders—or can we only test resilience by the reaction engendered by presidential action?[25]

These questions are particularly important in evaluating Obama's presidential performance. What hand was Obama dealt? Did he misplay the politics of reconstruction or were his struggles the product of the politics of preemption? In 2008, many progressives thought that Obama had the opportunity to reconstruct politics and usher in an enduring Democratic regime. In this scenario, Bush would play Hoover or Carter to Obama's FDR or Reagan. But the ferocious resistance to Obama's ambitious legislative agenda, particularly health care reform and the economic stimulus, together with the president's inability to redefine the terms of political debate, made Obama's political situation appear more akin to Clinton's than Reagan's or FDR's. Despite overwhelming Democratic majorities in Congress for Obama's first two years and the economic meltdown bequeathed by his predecessor, the Republican regime premised upon low taxes and deep suspicion of "big government" seemed anything but vulnerable in the wake of sweeping Republican victories in the 2010 elections.[26]

Should Obama's failure to remake American politics be attributed to the president's individual failings, character flaws, and strategic missteps? Many believe the answer is yes. They say that Obama was too passive or conciliatory, that he engaged the debate too late, that he was too inexperienced in the ways of Washington, and that he allowed his enemies to define him. If only Obama had used the bully pulpit more, twisted more arms, drawn clear lines in the sand, and stuck to his guns, events would have turned out differently. Implicit in this critique is the assumption that Obama's position in political time afforded him a rare opportunity to transform American politics, an opportunity that he squandered.

If it is too soon to evaluate Obama, it is not too late to take a closer look at those past presidential greats that are the standard by which we judge our contemporary presidents. We have already suggested that presidential success and failure often rest as much on the deal of the cards as the play of the hand. So let's look at how the greats actually played the hands they were dealt.

THE PLAY OF THE HAND

Citizens today make exacting demands of a president. They expect the president to set a clear policy agenda, to articulate a vision that citizens will follow, to keep campaign promises and not flip-flop on issues, to do the right thing even if it's unpopular, and to put country above party. They want intrepid statesmen like Lincoln or Washington, not another pliable politician. Perhaps we might evaluate our current presidents more charitably, however, if we kept in view the clever but fallible politicians beneath the heroic garments that have been carefully draped over our greatest presidents.[27]

The Boldness Myth

Although we routinely associate great presidents with bold, uncompromising leadership, each of the indisputably great presidents, Lincoln, Roosevelt, and Washington, usually played their hands cautiously, cards clutched close to the vest. The notion that great presidents are distinguished by the daring with which they played the political game is largely a myth. John Adams took greater risks than Washington, Andrew Johnson was far bolder than Lincoln, and Herbert Hoover was more principled than FDR.

Washington's Prudence

No president is more shrouded in myth-making than the nation's first president, but it is striking how little the real Washington resembles the ideal of presidential greatness we carry around with us in our heads. One of the great canards of the heroic narrative is that the greatest presidents boldly did what was right, regardless of whether it was popular.[28]

Yet no president was more solicitous of his public reputation than the thin-skinned Washington. Almost every action Washington took, including running for president, was made with one eye (or both) on how it would be perceived by his countrymen and how it would affect his reputation as a paragon for virtue.

Nor does Washington's behavior fit the standard storyline about great presidents fearlessly testing the boundaries of presidential power.[29] Instead Washington exercised his powers with great caution and self-restraint. For instance, as we observed in Chapter 4, Washington used the veto sparingly, nixing only two relatively insignificant pieces of legislation. Seeking to conciliate rather than confront Congress, he signed—by his own admission—"many Bills" with which he disagreed. He built presidential authority not through bold defiance of Congress but through building trust in the competence and judgment of the executive branch.

Washington, in fact, was among the most cautious and circumspect of all American presidents. Before making decisions, he consulted broadly and deliberated with excruciating care. Jefferson rightly remarked that "the strongest feature" in Washington's character "was prudence, never acting until every circumstance, every consideration, was maturely weighed." On this one matter, Hamilton was in full agreement with his nemesis. Washington was temperamentally suited to the presidency because, unlike Adams, he "consulted much, pondered much, resolved slowly, resolved surely."[30] What others called bold, Washington regarded as foolishly rash.

Lincoln's "Halting, Shuffling, Backward Policy"

While history remembers Lincoln as the great emancipator, contemporaries were more likely to recognize him as the great equivocator. Prior to issuing the Emancipation Proclamation, Lincoln had rescinded General John C. Fremont's proclamation (issued in August 1861) freeing the slaves of every rebel in the state of Missouri, as well as General David Hunter's order (May 1862) emancipating slaves in Georgia, South Carolina, and Florida. When Lincoln finally got around to issuing his own emancipation proclamation, he justified it not on the grounds of justice but on those of military necessity. In fact, the Emancipation Proclamation contained no indictment of slavery—prompting historian Richard Hofstadter's famous observation that it "had all the moral grandeur of a bill of lading." Moreover, the proclamation did not actually free any slaves because it applied only to those states that were not under the control of the federal government. Lincoln's proclamation left slavery undisturbed in the border states that had remained loyal to the Union, including Maryland, Missouri, and Kentucky. And the administration continued to vigorously enforce the fugitive slave law in the District of Columbia.[31]

In a widely publicized public letter to Horace Greeley, Lincoln declared that his "paramount object" was "to save the Union, and ... not either to save or to destroy slavery." Many historians today are inclined to think that Lincoln did not really mean this, that the public pose was a ploy to keep the border states from defecting. But that is exactly the point. The great emancipator did not fearlessly announce that the nation was fighting a war to end slavery. Rather he carefully concealed his intentions, signaling different and often ambiguous messages to different audiences. Lincoln, noted one newspaperman, "talks as many ways as he has fears, impulses, & fancies." Proceeding with great caution, he waited for public support to develop before taking action.[32]

"My policy," Lincoln liked to say, "is to have no policy"—hardly a credo that we typically associate with presidential greatness. Lincoln did not mean that he had no idea what he wanted to accomplish, but rather that he was not wedded to a particular way of getting there. He was prepared to zig and zag, to experiment and compromise, to be inconsistent if that meant he could be more effective, and to delay if he could thereby avoid needless conflict. Impatient abolitionists derided Lincoln's policies as "muddy" and "vacillating," but Lincoln's genius was not the visionary's talent for articulating a righteous policy but the politician's skill of holding together a diverse political coalition composed of antagonistic parts. The president's "halting, shuffling, backward policy" that William Lloyd Garrison so bitterly assailed was precisely the method that enabled Lincoln to win the Civil War and end slavery—and become the great president we remember today.[33]

FDR's "Engaging Ambiguity"

"Judge me by the enemies I have made," FDR declared during the 1932 campaign against incumbent Herbert Hoover. In the eyes of many, this is the kind of bold, forthright talk that made Roosevelt a great president. In truth, it is not even the kind of rhetoric that made him president, let alone a great one. "From the very beginning of his quest for the presidency in 1931," write Roosevelt biographers James MacGregor Burns and Susan Dunn, Roosevelt "purposefully sought to be elusive, vague and to appear to be all things to all people." Among the few specific campaign promises he made was to balance the budget—a goal he quickly abandoned once he became president. Consistency was never Roosevelt's strong suit.[34]

Those who met with Roosevelt rarely encountered a forthright, let alone confrontational, president. He was a charming, attentive listener, but rarely showed his hand or committed himself to any course of action. He had the useful habit of nodding his head in agreement as visitors talked, which helped to put them at ease as well as leave the impression that the president sympathized with their aims. As Eleanor Roosevelt informed Winston Churchill, "You know, Winston, when Franklin says yes, yes, yes, it doesn't mean he agrees with you. It means he's listening." Some of Roosevelt's advisors were put off by his conflict avoidance. "Perhaps in the long run," reflected one former Roosevelt advisor, "fewer friends would have been lost by bluntness than by the misunderstandings that arose from engaging ambiguity."[35]

Roosevelt's "engaging ambiguity," however, was crucial to his success in holding together the antagonistic elements that made up the Democratic Party—labor leaders and farmers, internationalists and white supremacists, northern liberals and southern states' rights conservatives, not to mention Wall Street financiers. As we saw in Chapter 4, the heroic narrative of FDR as a bold transformational president obscures the real-life experimental and pragmatic politician who forged the New Deal—and who watered down Social Security to make it politically palatable, who resisted FDIC because he feared it would hurt the banks, and who objected to the National Labor Relations Act because he did not want government to take labor's side against business. Almost entirely forgotten, too, are the loud and widespread criticisms from a disillusioned left that felt the president had sold out to powerful conservative interests—particularly bankers—and sacrificed the prospects for meaningful and fundamental reform of the capitalist system.

In short, boldness is overrated as an ingredient in presidential greatness. Great presidents have rarely been far out in front of public opinion—at least not at the moment of their greatest successes. Presidents are not special team players. They are not the ones who bravely race down the field with scant regard for themselves or for what might be in their way. That is the role of the vanguards for social justice, like abolitionists or civil rights activists. Presidents are more like quarterbacks, protected behind their linemen, a position from which they can survey the field and watch the play develop. They lead from behind, not from the front. Their success depends on their elusiveness and their ability to keep the opposition guessing about their intentions, as well as on good decision-making. Bold, dramatic gestures are usually a sign of desperation, an admission that the game is going badly and that options are running out. The Hail Mary pass almost always results in failure, not success.

The Greats' Failures

Our selective memory not only leads us to forget the politician that made the statesman possible, it also makes us overlook or explain away their many mistakes and failures. An exhaustive accounting of the great presidents' failures and miscalculations would require a hefty book of its own, but three telling examples will suffice for now: Jefferson's embargo policy, Wilson's League of Nations, and FDR's party purge. The aim here is not to show that our heroes were fools, but rather to suggest that in judging presidents today we should hold them to a realistic standard of achievement rather than a mythical one of infallibility.

Jefferson's Embargo

Although invariably ranked behind the big three of Washington, Lincoln, and FDR, Jefferson is next on almost everybody's list of presidential greats. And yet few presidents in American history adopted and adhered to a more disastrous and counterproductive policy than the trade embargo Jefferson pursued during the last 15 months of his presidency.

Jefferson imagined the embargo as an alternative to war—a noble goal, no doubt. But the idea was an implausible one from the start. Jefferson hoped that by forbidding Americans to trade with other nations, the young republic could "starve the offending nations" (by which Jefferson chiefly meant the British) into respecting Americans' right to trade with whom they pleased. In other words, America's right to sail the high seas would be vindicated by forbidding all American ships from setting sail for foreign ports.[36]

There may be other presidents who have had worse ideas, but few have stuck with them as stubbornly in the face of overwhelming evidence that the experiment would not work. Britain had little difficulty finding other sources of food and raw materials, but the effects on American commerce were devastating. Exports plummeted, slowing the economy and causing severe economic hardship throughout the northeast, particularly in port cities.[37]

The worse things got, the more determined Jefferson became to ensure full compliance with the embargo. Operating under the delusion that he could bring the British Empire to its knees if only he could stamp out smuggling, he prevailed upon Congress to enact harsher penalties for noncompliance and to give the executive branch progressively greater enforcement powers, including the power to use the army to search and seize any vehicles that were "apparently on their way" toward a foreign country or "toward a place whence such articles are intended to be exported." Ironically, Jefferson's experiment in "peaceable coercion" resulted in enforcement measures that were—in the words of two students of Jefferson's presidency—"more draconian than anything attempted by British authorities throughout the years leading up to the American Revolution."[38]

Making Jefferson's performance all the more abysmal, as we saw in Chapter 3, was that he made few attempts to persuade Americans that the extreme economic sacrifices he was demanding were necessary. Equally bizarre was Jefferson's reluctance to exert leadership behind the scenes during the final few months of his term. Embracing the role of an "unmeddling listener," he sought to foist responsibility for governance onto president-elect (and secretary of state) James Madison. The "hidden-hand" presidency became the "look mom, no hands" presidency—with the predictable smash-up at the end. Two months after signing the fifth and final embargo act—"the most repressive and unconstitutional legislation ever enacted by Congress in time of peace," according to one historian—Jefferson, with only three days left in his term, reluctantly signed a law repealing his failed embargo. The president left office looking foolish and weak—even if that is not the Jefferson we choose to remember.[39]

Wilson's League of Nations

In both the 1948 and 1962 Schlesinger greatness surveys, Wilson ranked as a great president, right behind FDR. Since then, his star has waned some, but he remains ever present among the near-greats. And yet few presidents have failed more utterly and more spectacularly—and unnecessarily—than Wilson in his campaign for the League of Nations.

Admittedly the Constitution, by requiring the approval of two-thirds of the Senate, makes treaty ratification a difficult process. A total of 21 treaties have been rejected by the Senate in American history, including most recently a comprehensive nuclear test ban negotiated by the Clinton administration. At least four times that number have been withdrawn because the Senate failed to take action. So the mere fact that the Senate did not ratify the Versailles Treaty—which would have established a League of Nations—can hardly be considered a defining mark of presidential failure.[40]

It also needs to be acknowledged that a band of Senate Republicans, led by Henry Cabot Lodge, were determined for political reasons to defeat the League at almost any cost. But it is equally true that a large bloc of senators were ready to vote for the League if Wilson would accept minor modifications to the treaty. The president insisted, however, that the other signatories would brook no alterations or reservations to the document—a claim that was patently untrue.[41]

Without ever attempting to find out what (if any) changes would be acceptable to the allies, Wilson continued to insist that there was no room for compromise. One might not fault Wilson if this was his opening gambit. One can even understand Wilson's quixotic speaking tour aimed at pressuring the Senate to accept the treaty without any changes. But Wilson stuck to this position long after it became clear to everybody that the gambit had failed, that the speaking tour had not rallied the nation to his side, and that the only way to rescue his precious League was to accept the reservations that the Senate insisted upon. Even after the British and French governments publicly announced that they had no objections to these reservations, Wilson still refused to budge. His allies in Congress urged him to bend, as did his advisors and even his wife. Yet still he refused. "Better a thousand times to go down fighting than to dip your colors to dishonorable compromise," he told his pleading wife.[42]

Wilson's behavior was so obviously self-defeating that analysts from Sigmund Freud on have sought answers in the president's psyche. Some say he suffered from low self-esteem, probably on account of his exacting, domineering father. Freud thought that Wilson had an unconscious urge for martyrdom, rooted in repressed rage against his father. Others trace the problem to brain damage that Wilson suffered from a succession of small strokes that allegedly dated back a decade or more before he became president.[43]

Whatever the validity of these psychological and neurological explanations for Wilson's bizarre behavior, there is no question that Wilson was responsible for the defeat of the League he so cherished. In the end, had Wilson merely freed Senate Democrats to vote their conscience, the United States would have joined the League of Nations, a goal that Wilson had worked tirelessly to achieve during his second term. Instead he instructed Senate Democrats to oppose the treaty on the preposterous grounds that the

Senate's minor reservations effectively nullified the treaty. A majority of the Senate's 44 Democrats followed their president's instructions and voted "no"—which together with a dozen isolationist Republican "no" votes was enough to kill the treaty and with it the League of Nations. It is not unusual in American politics for a president to fail to achieve his most cherished objective, either because the hand he is dealt is poor or because he misplays his hand. What made Wilson's failure extraordinary is that he had a winning hand and, for reasons unfathomable, chose to throw the game rather than claim victory.[44]

FDR's Party Purge

Ask who was the most skilled politician ever to occupy the White House and the answer you will almost certainly get is FDR. In Richard Neustadt's classic primer *Presidential Power*, he is the very model of a modern major president. He enjoyed the exercise of political power—in fact, wrote Neustadt, his was "a love affair with power." He radiated optimism and cheer. He knew how to persuade and bargain, to charm and wheedle. He knew when to flatter and when to trade, when to press and when to retreat, when to confront and when to evade. He shrewdly calculated his "power stakes"—that is, how decisions he made today would affect his power tomorrow. The payoff for his political skill can be found in the mountains of New Deal legislation, four resounding electoral victories, and his successful leadership during World War II.[45]

Yet we would do well to remember that even a maestro such as Roosevelt was prone to massive miscalculations. His clumsy attempt to pack the Supreme Court, discussed in Chapter 9, ranks among the most egregious of these. An even more glaring mistake was his ill-fated effort, in the 1938 campaign, to "purge" the Democratic Party of conservatives.[46]

The dramatic highlight of Roosevelt's purge campaign came in an appearance before a crowd of 50,000 people in Barnesville, Georgia. With Georgia's widely respected senator Walter George sitting directly behind him, Roosevelt told the crowd that while George was a friend, a "gentleman and a scholar," he lacked the "fighting attitude" and commitment to the New Deal that the nation needed. Instead Roosevelt urged his audience to vote for another man behind him on the stage, Lawrence Camp, an able but relatively unknown attorney whom the administration had cajoled at the last minute into taking on the veteran George. It made for riveting theater but terrible politics. George was chair of the Senate Finance Committee and broadly popular in his home state. Nothing Roosevelt could have said would have resulted in George losing a primary—as Democratic national committee chairman Jim Farley had bluntly told Roosevelt beforehand—particularly not to a candidate like Camp who had never held elective office before. And it could only damage the president's legislative agenda to openly antagonize one of the Senate's most powerful men.[47]

Nor did Roosevelt have any luck unseating his two other principal targets: South Carolina's reactionary "Cotton Ed" Smith and Maryland's Millard Tydings. "It's a bust," Farley admitted to reporters after watching two intensive days of presidential stumping fail to dent Tydings's public support.[48]

Why did a shrewd politician like FDR embark on a crusade that was bound to fail? One answer is that things had been going very badly for Roosevelt. The economy had slid back into recession, his popularity was sagging, and he faced mounting criticism of his heavy-handed tactics in the wake of the failed Court-packing plan. "The old Roosevelt magic" had seemingly "lost its kick." Despite large Democratic majorities in both houses of Congress, Roosevelt found his legislative program blocked at almost every turn by a conservative coalition led by powerful southern Democrats. Growing frustration with those who seemed Democrats in name only—and a desire to punish those who had opposed his Court-packing effort—spurred Roosevelt to launch his improbable purge. It was the proverbial Hail Mary pass—daring and bold no doubt, but a telling sign of FDR's weakness and desperation.[49]

Should we give FDR partial credit, then, for at least trying to break the legislative deadlock and inject fresh life into a paralyzed presidency? But it makes little sense to credit Roosevelt for a strategy that was misguided and counterproductive. He foolishly targeted popular incumbents in southern states, where his political support was relatively weak, rather than focusing his fire on vulnerable conservatives in northern industrial states, where Roosevelt and the New Deal were still popular. In states such as Maryland and Georgia, the best that can be said is that his intervention did not affect the outcome. But in South Carolina, where Smith for once faced a formidable opponent in Governor Olin Johnson, Roosevelt helped secure victory for the very candidate he hoped to defeat. Roosevelt's plan was to transform primary elections into a referendum on New Deal liberalism. Instead Smith easily turned the tables on the president by playing on southern fears of "outside interference" by Yankees. A sign of how badly FDR miscalculated is that Smith won by a greater margin in the 1938 primary than in any of his other six Senate races—despite facing a much better known and popular challenger than in any of his other races.[50]

The purge, in short, was a disaster for Roosevelt. It not only failed to weaken the conservative coalition but emboldened and strengthened it. It fractured the party without clarifying ideological lines. And it exacerbated popular fears that a power-hungry president was trying to make Congress his personal rubber stamp. In the 1938 elections, the Democrats lost 71 House seats, six Senate seats, and a dozen governorships—with the losses greatest among pro-New Deal Democrats. Had World War II not resuscitated Roosevelt's presidency, we would likely remember the purge today as symptomatic of a second term defined by failure and frustration. And many of those failures—most notably, the Court-packing plan and the purge—were self-inflicted wounds brought on by a combination of frustration, revenge, and hubris that prevented the great FDR from thinking clearly about his political interests.[51]

Where Have All the Great (or Even Good) Presidents Gone?

Even if we make liberal allowance for our tendency to romanticize the great presidents of the past—to exaggerate their accomplishments and power and to overlook their limitations and failings—a nagging question remains. Why don't we seem to get great presidents anymore? Even the near-great or above average presidents seem to be in shorter supply than they were a half-century ago.

Consider the following. Between 1932 and 1968, the United States had five presidents: FDR, Truman, Eisenhower, Kennedy, and LBJ. In the 2009 C-SPAN survey, all five were ranked among the top 11 presidents, ranging from FDR at number 3 to LBJ at number 11. In contrast, between 1968 and 2008, the nation had seven presidents: Nixon, Ford, Carter, Reagan, Bush I, Clinton, and Bush II. Of these, only Reagan was ranked in the top 11 (he was number ten) and the average rank was 22 (out of 42 presidents). Even in the *Wall Street Journal* poll, which corrected for Democratic bias, the lowest of the five presidents between 1932 and 1968 were ranked "above average" (Kennedy and Johnson). Eisenhower and Truman were classed as "near-great" and FDR as "great." In contrast, of the seven presidents between 1968 and 2008, only Reagan (near-great) got a rating better than "average." Bush I, Clinton, and Bush II were rated "average" and Ford, Nixon, and Carter "below average."

So what gives? Has the nation's luck run out? Why does a great country keep finding itself ruled by mediocre presidents? This is not the first time in American history that we have heard this question posed. Writing in the late 1880s, the keen British student of American politics James Bryce devoted a famous chapter in his influential treatise, *The American Commonwealth*, to explaining "Why Great Men Are Not Chosen Presidents." The puzzle struck Bryce forcibly because over the previous two decades British politics had been dominated by the towering talents of William Gladstone and Benjamin Disraeli—both brilliant orators, immense intellects, and domineering politicians. Meanwhile, the United States had served up a succession of mediocre presidents: Johnson, Grant, Hayes, Garfield, Arthur, and Cleveland.

Is It the Way We Pick Presidents?

Bryce believed that the key difference was the selection mechanism. In Britain, "the natural selection of the English parliamentary system" tended to raise the "highest gifts to the highest place." In a parliamentary system, the party's standard-bearer was the man judged to be best suited to lead Parliament and the country. With the "more artificial selection" of the United States, in contrast, the choice of nominees was based less on whether a man would be an effective president than on whether he was likely to be a winning candidate. Local party leaders, in whose hands the nominations rested, cared about securing party patronage rather than choosing good, let alone great, presidents.[52]

Some scholars of contemporary American politics have followed Bryce's lead in identifying the presidential selection process as the culprit for poor presidents. On the cover of Nelson Polsby's *The Consequences of Party Reform*, published immediately after Carter's presidency, a cartoon drawing showed a complex contraption, representing the presidential primary system, spitting out two yo-yos. Inside the book, Polsby argued that the post-1960s primary-centered nomination process had displaced state party leaders, who knew candidates personally, in favor of primary voters, who knew only what they saw on television. Candidate-centered campaigns, a politics without party gatekeepers, produced presidents with little or no experience in national politics. Neither Carter nor Reagan—both of whom had been state governors—had held national office before becoming president. Ditto Clinton and George W. Bush. The sum of Obama's national political experience was less than four years in the Senate. Trump had never held elected office of any kind. For a number of these presidents, Congress seemed almost like a foreign country, with unfamiliar customs, language, and inhabitants. No prime minister ever starts with this disadvantage.[53]

It's not clear, however, that national political experience makes for better presidents. Of the eight presidents since 1969, three boasted very impressive political résumés: Nixon had been vice president for eight years as well as a member of the US House and the Senate, Ford a member of Congress for a quarter-century, including nearly a decade as House minority leader, and George Herbert Walker Bush a vice president for eight years as well as director of the CIA, ambassador to the UN, a member of Congress, and chairman of the Republican national committee. Yet none of these three are considered to have been better than average presidents. The rest of American history teaches the same lesson. Few presidents had more political experience than James Buchanan, who before becoming president had been secretary of state, ambassador to Russia, a two-term US senator, and a member of the House of Representatives for a decade. And few presidents assumed office with less political experience than Lincoln, who finished his one term in the House more than a decade before he became president. Their cases were not aberrations from the norm. A recent statistical study found no significant relationship between political experience and a president's greatness rating; in fact, the study found that every two years served in Congress actually lowered a president's ranking by roughly one place in the greatness rankings![54]

Moreover, it is difficult to see how the string of highly rated presidents prior to 1968 can be attributed to a presidential selection process dominated by party notables. Two of the presidents—Truman and Johnson—were accidents, vice presidents who became president only after the death of a president. Kennedy chose Johnson as vice president for electoral reasons, most especially to help him to win Texas. Even the ailing FDR didn't appear to give much thought to whether Truman would make a good president or was prepared to be president. Kennedy was opposed by many party elders who thought him too young and inexperienced—even though he had been a member of Congress and a US senator for more than 13 years. And Eisenhower, who had never held any political office or even voted in his life, was recruited by party leaders principally because they thought the popular general would win. Bryce was right: party leaders want a winning candidate more than they want a great president—and they are usually better judges of who would make a good candidate than of who would make a good president.

Is It an Impossible Job?

Perhaps the real problem isn't the way we select our presidents but the job we ask them to do. Have the demands and responsibilities of the office grown so vast that no individual, no matter how talented or experienced, can hope to do the job effectively? Is the modern presidency, as a 2010 *Newsweek* cover story expressed it, just "too much for one person to handle"?[55]

The growth in presidential responsibilities is rooted in the changing relationship between the citizen and the federal government. At the dawn of the twentieth century, for instance, when a natural disaster struck, citizens looked for help from state and local governments, not the federal government. In the case of a deadly hurricane or killer storm, the president was not expected to do anything. Today a disaster-stricken region immediately looks to the Federal Emergency Management Agency (FEMA) for help. An agency with more than 3,700 full-time employees and a $10 billion budget, FEMA did not even exist prior to the Carter presidency, though piecemeal federal emergency relief efforts dated to the 1930s. When Hurricane Katrina struck in 2005, for instance, the nation's eyes immediately turned to FEMA. And when the agency's response was slow and inadequate, Bush was castigated as incompetent and uncaring, a charge from which his presidency never fully recovered.

Inaction is not an option for presidents. The BP oil spill in 2010 was not only a calamity for the handful of states immediately affected by the oil, but a crisis that demanded Obama's immediate attention. Everyone clamored for the administration to take action—to stop the leak, to clean up the mess, to hold BP accountable, and to revive the local economies. In the first two months after the oil spill, the president made four trips to the gulf states to survey the damage in an effort to communicate the seriousness with which the administration took the matter—making sure not to repeat Bush's public relations disaster of simply flying over the affected areas from the comfort of a couch on Air Force One. To meet the public outcry for stricter federal enforcement of drilling, Obama created three agencies where there had been one (formerly called the Minerals Management Service), including a new Bureau of Safety and Environmental Enforcement, with about two hundred additional government employees.

The growth of the federal government's responsibilities is evident in almost every aspect of American life. Today Americans expect the federal government, among other things, to provide for the old, ensure safe working conditions, regulate pollution of our air and water, protect civil rights, prosecute drug and sex offenders, and provide national education standards. Many of the government agencies that we take for granted did not exist before the 1960s. The Environmental Protection Agency, for instance, was created in 1970, and the Occupational Safety and Health Administration in 1974.

But it's not only the expanded role of government on the domestic side that has escalated demands on the president. On the foreign side, too, the United States' imposing military might has increased demands that the government should act to solve international crises. A government crackdown in Libya in 2011, for example, instantly brought intense national and international pressure on the Obama administration to help the rebels by establishing a no-fly zone, bombing the Libyan regime's strategic installations, and arming and advising the rebels. If the United States government does nothing or too little, the president is criticized for standing by while a brutal dictator massacres his people. If the United States intervenes, the president is criticized for wasting precious American resources and lives in far-off lands.

A president today is buffeted by a cascade of crises and perpetual demands for action or response. The pace of decision-making has quickened. Coolidge and Reagan had time to nap; Lincoln and FDR time to think. A president today seems to have neither luxury. An official who worked in the Reagan and both Bush administrations attested that the

White House had become "a much different place" during the span of a quarter-century. Under George W. Bush, "there was much less time to catch your breath during the day" than there had been under Reagan or even the first Bush. Lamenting the breakneck speed of decision-making, an Obama advisor observed that "sometimes the only way to bring the president important news is to stake out his office and 'walk and talk' through the hall."[56]

Certainly, as we saw in Chapter 7, the number of people in the White House has grown dramatically since FDR's time. Even as late as the Kennedy and Johnson administrations, the White House staff remained small enough for president to manage his senior staff without the aid of a chief of staff. No president since 1969 has been able to do without a chief of staff. In theory, a large staff is supposed to make it easier for the president to meet his increased responsibilities, but in practice it often compounds the problem. As political scientist James Pfiffner points out, "the more people you have in the White House, the more problems are sucked into it." Instead of helping the president manage increased demands, a larger staff may increase the number of problems a president has to deal with and the number of people who want face time with the president.[57]

A tough and demanding job, certainly, but is the contemporary presidency really an impossible one that bars the way to greatness or at least success? Ironically, when Bryce pondered this problem in the age of Cleveland he came to exactly the opposite conclusion: there was so little for the president to do that there was no call for greatness. "Four-fifths of [the president's] work," Bryce wrote, "is the same in kind as that which devolves on the chairman of a commercial company or the manager of a railway, the work of choosing good subordinates, seeing that they attend to their business, and taking a sound practical view of such administrative questions as require his decision." According to Bryce, the job was ordinarily so straightforward that a president needed little more than common sense and honesty to discharge it well. Presidents were rarely great because the job required so little of them.[58]

Are we to believe that the situation now is completely reversed: that the job now rarely allows for greatness because it requires so much of presidents? Perhaps this is true. But the crises and clamor for presidential action that make a twenty-first-century president's life so eventful also provide ample opportunities for a president to shine. For every Hurricane Katrina that humiliates a president there is an Oklahoma City bombing that gives the president a platform on which to stand as a unifying and commanding leader. The same military capacity that made the Libyan uprising a constant headache for the Obama administration also enabled the president to earn plaudits across the political spectrum for his courage and decisiveness in taking out Osama bin Laden.

Are the Media to Blame?

Perhaps it's not so much the sheer number and scope of crises or the pace of decision-making that is responsible for the recent run of troubled presidencies, but rather the way those decisions and crises are portrayed by the media. Some scholars argue that the late 1960s and early 1970s ushered in a dramatically more adversarial media. This was the pivotal period, according to political scientist Aaron Wildavsky, in which "press conferences became battle grounds, reporters exposed rather than excused personal misbehavior, [and] the networks started contradicting presidential addresses as soon as they were made." A more critical media, on this view, has made it more difficult for presidents to get their side of the story across and to sustain the public support needed for success.[59]

Gallup surveys support the idea that presidents since the late 1960s have found it more difficult to maintain public support than did presidents during the preceding decades. The average Gallup approval rating between FDR and LBJ was about 60 percent, whereas between Nixon and Obama the average was around 50 percent. Of course, some of this difference may be the fault of events—especially more failed or inconclusive military ventures and more sluggish economic growth. But that's not the whole story. Even at the height of "the Roosevelt recession" of 1938, with unemployment having jumped to 20 percent (from 14 percent the year before), more than half of the American public consistently approved of the job Roosevelt was doing—and about eight in ten Americans reported liking the president personally. Similarly, during the recession of 1958, when the Democrats picked up nearly 50 seats in the House and 16 seats in the Senate, Eisenhower's popularity remained above 50 percent. No president since Eisenhower has been able to sustain public approval in the face of a comparable economic downturn, not even the supposedly "Teflon" president Reagan, whose approval plummeted to 35 percent during the recession of 1982–1983.[60]

Of course, popularity is no guarantee of greatness, let alone success. George Herbert Walker Bush, after all, had a heady average approval rating of 61 percent, and Truman's 45 percent average approval rating remains the lowest of any president since Gallup began asking about presidential job approval in 1937. However, contrary to conventional wisdom, the evidence suggests that the ability to sustain public support *is* linked to how presidents are evaluated by history. With the exception of Truman, no president with an average Gallup approval rating of less than 50 percent has been judged "above average" or higher in greatness surveys. Reagan is the lowest at 53 percent, followed by Johnson at 55, FDR at 63, Eisenhower at 65, and JFK at 70. And of the presidents rated average or below, only Clinton and George Herbert Walker Bush had average approval ratings above 50 percent—and during the crucial year before his defeat Bush averaged in the low 40s, dipping below 30 at one point. Nixon, Ford, Carter, and George W. Bush all averaged below 50 percent public approval ratings and they are typically the four lowest-rated presidents of the modern post-FDR era.

Perhaps no presidency better illustrates the gulf separating today's media environment from the media environment of 50 years ago than the media coverage of President Kennedy. Shortly after becoming president, Kennedy authorized an invasion of Cuba aimed at the overthrow of Fidel Castro that ended disastrously in a swamp in the Bay of Pigs. Today it would have set off a media feeding frenzy of investigations and recriminations, but in the spring of 1961 the story disappeared almost without a ripple after Kennedy tossed the media a public mea culpa—while privately spinning it as a failure that was really the fault of the CIA—and then announced that he wouldn't talk about it any further.

Even more unimaginable today is the number of Washington reporters who knew or heard rumors about President Kennedy's serial sexual escapades while in the White

House and yet chose to do nothing. Kennedy's sexual partners ranged in age from 19 to 60, and included longtime lovers and virtual strangers, hookers, celebrities, and socialites, as well as a number of White House employees, including his wife's press secretary. Two young staffers, known by their Secret Service code names as Fiddle and Faddle, had no apparent duties beyond frolicking with the president. Although Kennedy's reckless liaisons opened the president up to the possibility of blackmail— especially since one of his lovers was also the lover of a Chicago crime boss—no reporter decided that Kennedy's behavior was news or that the rumors warranted investigation. Had the media disclosed what Kennedy was up to, his presidency would have collapsed in tawdry scandal. Even Kennedy's close friend and admirer Benjamin Bradlee—who was Washington bureau chief for *Newsweek* during Kennedy's presidency and later became executive editor at the *Washington Post*—admitted that had the public found out about Kennedy's "unforgivably reckless behavior," the almost certain result would have been impeachment.[61]

In today's unforgiving media environment, it is hard to imagine that any president could get away with the lies that helped to sustain the Kennedy mystique. When, in 1988, presidential candidate Joe Biden plagiarized from a speech by a British Labour Party leader, a media feeding frenzy quickly drove him out of the race. But in 1960 the media largely refrained from digging into persistent rumors that *Profiles in Courage*, the book that earned Kennedy the Pulitzer Prize in 1955, was written by Theodore Sorenson, not Kennedy. Nor did the media uncover that *Why England Slept*, the book based on Kennedy's undergraduate thesis, had been made into a best seller by Kennedy's millionaire father, who bought upward of 30,000 copies and stored them in his attic. Nor did the media press hard on the lies that Kennedy told about his health, including his denial that he had Addison's disease. And yet, as biographer Richard Reeves points out, his case had been documented in the *Journal of the American Medical Association*, where an enterprising journalist could have readily uncovered the truth.[62]

Although modern presidents typically feel beleaguered by the press, they are hardly defenseless. After all, four of the previous five presidents have been reelected. Presidents know that their words will be reduced on television to sound bites of no more than eight or nine seconds, and so their small army of strategists and speechwriters spend enormous amounts of time crafting the sound bite or message of the day. During the first term of George W. Bush, administration officials openly boasted of their ability to control the media agenda. As a top aide—apparently Karl Rove—put it, "we create our own reality." The media, for instance, uncritically accepted the administration's framing of the response to September 11, 2011 as a "war on terror."[63]

Whether we believe the media are too critical or not critical enough often seems to be determined by how we feel about the current occupant of the White House. In a survey taken in the middle of George W. Bush's administration, 53 percent of journalists who called themselves conservative believed that press coverage of Bush had been too critical and only 17 percent said it had been not critical enough. In contrast, only 3 percent of self-described liberal journalists said media coverage of Bush was too critical and nearly 70 percent said it was not critical enough. During the Obama administration, conservatives complained loudly about a mainstream media being too soft on the president while liberals objected to unfair media criticism of the president, especially on the avowedly partisan Fox News.[64]

Is It the Partisan Polarization?

Perhaps the more fundamental problem facing presidents today is the high levels of partisan polarization. How can presidents be expected to lead a nation that is fiercely divided along ideological and partisan lines? Before the killing of Osama bin Laden in May 2011, only one in ten Republicans approved of Obama's performance (compared to eight in ten Democrats). Even immediately afterwards, only two in ten Republicans approved. Better than 70 percent of Republicans were willing to give former president Bush, who had been out of office for two and a half years, a great deal or a moderate amount of credit for the killing of bin Laden, but fewer than half of Republicans were willing to give Obama, the president who ordered the attack on bin Laden's hideout in Pakistan, the same level of credit.[65]

The partisan and ideological divide, moreover, is greatest among those who pay the closest attention to politics—those most likely to vote in primary elections, write to their members of Congress, and contribute money to campaigns. Among the most politically active and informed segments of the public, there often seems to be little or no middle ground on the important issues facing the country. These ideological differences are reinforced by today's fragmented media environment. Unlike a half-century ago, when television viewers had a choice between three largely indistinguishable network newscasts, in today's more specialized 24-hour news environment Republicans and Democrats gravitate toward media sources that reinforce pre-existing biases.

A deeply polarized electorate creates several problems for the president, as Obama discovered. First, it makes it more difficult for a president to gain the political trust and support of a large segment of the American public. Second, it becomes more difficult for the president to negotiate agreements with Congress, both because there will be fewer moderates in Congress and because even members inclined to moderation, either by temperament or because of the makeup of their district, must pay close heed to the wishes of the primary voters upon which their electoral survival rests.

Particularly in the context of divided government, hyper-polarization spells gridlock and places the president on the horns of a dilemma. With the opposition in Congress unwilling or unable to negotiate, the president may feel he has no option but to break the logjam by going over the heads of Congress and appealing directly to the people. But, as we saw in Chapter 3, going public in today's environment is unlikely to succeed. Partisans of the other party are very unlikely to be persuaded. And the independents and moderates who might be persuaded are disproportionately concentrated among the apolitical and uninformed citizens who are the most difficult to reach in a fragmented media environment that makes it easy to tune out the news and the president. Hence by encouraging presidents to go public, as political scientists Brian Newman and Emerson Siegle write, "polarization may be pushing presidents toward failure."[66]

Even under conditions of unified government, polarization can stymie presidential leadership, because determined minorities in the Senate can use the threat of a filibuster to block all manner of legislative action. In fact, the use of the filibuster has accelerated at precisely the same time as the increase in polarization. During the 1960s, there were never more than a handful of cloture motions—a motion to bring an end to a filibuster or the threat of a filibuster—in a legislative session. As Figure 11.1 shows, that number has grown dramatically over the past half-century. During Obama's presidency, there were an average of nearly 80 cloture motions filed each year, about twice the rate under Clinton and George W. Bush and nearly four times the number under Reagan. The more polarized Congress and the nation have grown, the more uninhibited Senate minorities have become in using the filibuster to thwart the majority—and the president.

In sum, the "disappearing center" undermines the president's ability to negotiate bipartisan compromises with the opposition without putting the president at the head of a responsible party that can—as in a parliamentary system—push through the agenda on which the president and his party campaigned. Does that mean that presidents today are bound to fail or at least never rise beyond the ranks of the mediocre? Politics today is more polarized and partisan than in the 1950s and 1960s, but hard-edged partisanship is hardly a novelty in American politics. Indeed, the bipartisan accommodations of the 1950s and early 1960s may be more the oddity than the standard by which we should measure contemporary politics. With the exception of George Washington, the great and near-great presidents were often unapologetically partisan leaders who endured a constant barrage of partisan attacks. The partisan ridicule and vitriol in the nineteenth century were in fact often far worse than anything contemporary presidents have faced. So is the

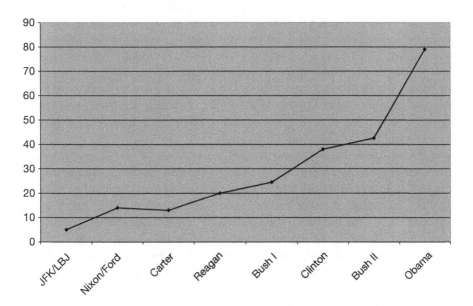

FIGURE 11.1 Number of Cloture Motions in the Senate, 1961–2016

Source: Data from www.senate.gov/pagelayout/reference/cloture_motions/clotureCounts.htm.

next Jefferson or Jackson just around the corner, awaiting the right moment in political time to transform American government and politics for a new century—perhaps by sweeping away barriers to majority rule such as the filibuster, as Trump has urged the Senate to do? Or have we perhaps at last reached the end of political time?

Is It the End of Political Time?

In *The Politics Presidents Make*, published in 1993, Skowronek identifies two developments that have contributed to the "waning of political time." First is the "thickening" of "the institutional universe of political action." That is, "at each stage in the development of the office there are more organizations and authorities to contend with, and they are all more firmly entrenched and independent." The proliferation of interest groups and government agencies makes it increasingly difficult for reconstructive presidents to dismantle the institutional and policy infrastructure of the old order. President Reagan reframed the ideological debate and cemented a powerful new Republican coalition but he was not able to dismantle important New Deal or Great Society programs, let alone stem the growth of the federal government. He was not even able to carry out a campaign pledge to abolish the Education Department, which had been in operation less than a year when he took office. And Reagan the tax-cutter was also the president who saved Social Security by hiking payroll taxes. Reagan's reconstruction, Skowronek concludes, was far "shallower" than that of any previous reconstructive president, "more rhetorical and political than institutional and governmental." And his claim to greatness is consequently far more tenuous than those of any of the other previous reconstructive presidents.[67]

The second important change that Skowronek identifies is the growing power and independence of the presidency. Presidents can increasingly act alone, drawing upon the powers of the executive branch to act independently of their party and the legislature. If institutional thickening means that reconstructive presidents find it progressively more difficult to sweep away the old regime, the growing power of the presidency means that even a president affiliated with a vulnerable regime will have greater capacity to forge an independent path and exert power successfully. If we may see fewer great transformative presidents like FDR or Jackson, so too will we experience fewer weak and ineffectual presidents like Pierce and Buchanan.[68]

Skowronek suggests that with the waning of political time we may be entering what he calls "a state of perpetual preemption" in which all presidents are converging "toward opposition leadership in a relatively resilient regime." In this perpetual politics of preemption, leadership roles are less determined and presidents have "more equal opportunity" to succeed and fail on their own merits. Politics becomes less predictable but, according to Skowronek, evaluating presidents ironically becomes simpler, for a politics less encumbered by political time means "a more equal and exact test of the capacities of the incumbents themselves—their political skills, governing talents, and personal character."[69]

A presidency characterized by perpetual preemption will be one in which every president promises change but none will truly be able to transform politics. For those looking for a great president to overhaul the political system, the result will be disappointment. Reconstruction on a grand scale will elude presidents. That does not mean that presidents cannot bring about important policy changes. Their influence may be at the margins, but modern presidents who size up their opportunities and skillfully build political coalitions can secure lasting policy changes that address, if not solve, important social problems. Judge them by their success in achieving their stated policy goals, and contemporary presidents may fare very well.[70]

But Skowronek's analysis also suggests that a perpetual politics of preemption is likely to be volatile, since established institutions have ample capacity to check and embarrass, if not destroy, a president. Recall that the threat of impeachment has been a recurrent pattern in the politics of preemption. In fact, both of the most recent preemptive presidents—Clinton and Nixon—faced impeachment by the House.[71]

But have we really reached the end of political time? Certainly, the presidency is more powerful now than it was a century ago. A Pierce or Fillmore is, of course, unimaginable today. Interest groups in Washington are certainly better organized and more entrenched. On the other hand, political parties in the early twenty-first century are remarkably cohesive and disciplined, perhaps more so than at any time in the past century. The "waning of political time" thesis was linked, as Skowronek has admitted, to "the secular decline over the course of the twentieth century in the governing role and political strength of the traditional party organizations." In the latter decades of the twentieth century, many scholars thought they were witnessing "dealignment." Citizens no longer seemed to closely identify with parties, candidates no longer seemed so dependent on parties, and parties in government were becoming less cohesive. As parties appeared to become less salient in the electorate, in campaigns, and in governance, it made sense to think that American politics had entered a perpetual politics of preemption, the hallmarks of which would be "the exploitation of ad hoc coalitions" and "the cultivation of independent political identities." Since the recurrent cycles of political time presupposed periodic electoral realignments ushering in new party systems, the end of realignments seemed to signal the end of political time.[72]

But a funny thing happened on the way to the twenty-first century. Parties came roaring back. Scholars and pundits no longer talk about partisan dealignment but rather about intractable partisan polarization—polarization in the electorate, polarization in campaigns, and polarization in governance. Moreover, as Skowronek was quick to recognize, George W. Bush and Bill Clinton proved to be "eerily vivid exemplars" of the political types he had originally sketched. Clinton was a paradigmatic instance of the politics of preemption, right down to the impeachment. And Bush was a fascinating case of the orthodox innovator, right down to the "little wars of dubious provocation, muscle-flexing adventures driven more by ideology and political management than by necessity"—think the Mexican War (Polk), the Spanish–American War (McKinley), and the Vietnam War (Kennedy and Johnson). Bush did capitalize upon and expand independent presidential power but he also tied his presidency to a disciplined party committed to pressing forward with the Reagan agenda, especially on tax cuts.[73]

What, though, are we to make of Obama? Is his failure to reconstruct American politics evidence that political time is in fact waning? The problem with this interpretation is that there are strong reasons to doubt that reconstruction was ever in the cards for Obama. To begin with, as Skowronek points out, "no second-round opposition leader has successfully reconstructed American government and politics": not Zachary Taylor and Millard Fillmore, not Woodrow Wilson, and not Nixon. More telling still is the sharp contrast between Reagan's moment in political time and Obama's. Obama was preceded by a president who remained an unapologetic booster of the Reagan Revolution until the final few months of his presidency, when a financial crisis threatened a historic economic meltdown. Reagan, in contrast, was preceded by a president "who came to power candidly acknowledging the deep-seated problems within the older order and directing his leadership to resolving them." In fact, every reconstructive president has been preceded by a one-term president who spent his entire term trying vainly "to rehabilitate and repair an old order already in deep trouble." Reagan had his Carter, FDR his Hoover, Lincoln his Buchanan, Jackson his Quincy Adams, and Jefferson his Adams. Without disjunction, it seems, there can be no reconstruction. If Obama seems to fit the bill for the politics of preemption, that may be a sign not that political time is waning but that the politics of preemption was Obama's moment in political time.[74]

If Obama is a president of preemption, where does that leave Trump? His backers have cast him as an Andrew Jackson figure who has a popular warrant to take on a corrupt political order that serves the interests not of the American people but of party donors and government bureaucrats. Trump promises to disrupt politics as usual, to "drain the swamp" of Washington, DC. Trump's appeal (and Bernie Sanders's too) speaks to the frustrations Americans have with the current political regime and the hunger for something genuinely different. On this reading, Trump is on the only sure road to presidential greatness: the politics of reconstruction.

But Trump's position in political time may have more in common with Jimmy Carter's than with Andrew Jackson's. Carter, too, came to power as a DC outsider and a scathing critic of the corrupt ways of Washington. From the moment he sought the Democratic nomination in 1976, Carter warred with Democratic party orthodoxy and party leaders. He bragged (and believed) that he owed the presidency to no party and no special interests. He was the "loner-as-leader." And yet Carter remained tethered in practice to the party he disdained—unable to fully repudiate its discredited policy agenda but unwilling to fully embrace it either, stuck in what Skowronek describes as "a political no man's land." Carter's ideological heterodoxy and political ineffectualness led to a crippling primary challenge by Ted Kennedy. Indicted by Kennedy in the primary for abandoning the party's core ideological commitments, he was then lambasted by Reagan in the general election as the personification of the Democratic Party's failed ideology and its crumbling coalition of special interests. Carter disrupted but could not reconstruct American politics.[75]

For Trump, it may matter little whether we have reached the end of political time or whether recurring patterns of political time are still operative. Either way, Trump's efforts to emulate Jackson's success in building a new majority party and reconstructing the American polity seem likely to be frustrated. But for the future of American politics and the American presidency, everything hinges on this question. A politics of perpetual disruption in which presidents tear apart institutions and understandings without the capacity to build and legitimate new ones is a politics likely to magnify popular frustrations with American democracy. The problem is not that a politics of perpetual preemption may spell the end of great reconstructive presidents but rather that presidents intent on being remembered among the pantheon of greats will damage the nation by claiming mandates they do not possess and promising change they cannot deliver. It is imperative that the American people, no less than American presidents, be aware of what (political) time it is.

NOTES

1. That Trump began his presidency with the disapproval of half of those expressing an opinion is unprecedented in the history of public opinion polling. Prior to Trump, those citizens willing to make an early snap judgment of presidential performance overwhelmingly tended to give the president the benefit of the doubt and express their approval. Obama, for instance, began his presidency with the approval of 85 percent of those who were willing to offer an opinion of the president's performance. See Lydia Saad, "Trump Sets New Low Rating for Inaugural Approval Rating," *Gallup*, January 23, 2017, www.gallup.com/poll/202811/trump-sets-new-low-point-inaugural-approval-rating.aspx?g_source=position1&g_medium=relate

2. Data in this and the following two paragraphs are derived from the Gallup Presidential Job Approval Center, www.gallup.com/poll/124922/Presidential-Job-Approval-Center.aspx.

3. The increasingly polarized assessments of presidential performance are documented in Brian Newman and Emerson Siegle, "The Polarized Presidency: Depth and Breadth of Public Partisanship," *Presidential Studies Quarterly* (June 2010), 342–63. Newman and Siegle show that not only has the partisan gap grown but so too has the intensity of feeling. That is, presidents are increasingly likely to be strongly approved by fellow partisans and strongly disapproved by partisans of the other party.

4. Anti-Obama "Worst President Ever" bumper stickers went on sale within months of Obama taking office. Among those who called Obama "the worst president ever" was Donald Trump in 2011. In 2014, Dick Cheney reduced the charge to "the worst president of my lifetime."

5. The "informal survey of 109 professional historians" was carried out by Robert S. McElvaine through the History News Network, and is reported at http://hnn.us/articles/48916.html. Also see Scott Horton, "Worst President Ever," *Harper's Magazine*, April 5, 2008.

6. John J. Dilulio, Jr., "Afterword: Why Judging George W. Bush Is Never as Easy as It Seems," in Robert Maranto, Tom Lansford, and Jeremy Johnson, eds., *Judging Bush* (Stanford, CA: Stanford University Press, 2009), 294. Dilulio was the director of the White House Office of Faith-Based and Community Initiatives in George W. Bush's administration.

7. Thomas A. Bailey, *Presidential Greatness, The Image and the Man from George Washington to the Present* (New York: Appleton-Century-Crofts, 1966), 24.

8. The 1982 survey by Robert K. Murray and Tim H. Blessing is reported in their book *Greatness in the White House: Rating the Presidents, Washington through Carter* (University Park: Pennsylvania State University Press, 1988), 16. On the Ridings–McIver poll, see William J. Ridings, Jr. and Stuart B. McIver, *Rating the Presidents: A Ranking of U.S. Leaders from the Great and Honorable to the Dishonest and Incompetent* (New York: Citadel Press, 2000; revised and updated), xi.

9. The 2014 APSA survey reported in Tables 11.2 and 11.3 was based on the responses of 162 political scientists who were members of the American Political Science Association's Presidents & Executive Politics section. Brandon Rottinghaus and Justin S. Vaughn, "Measuring Obama against the Great Presidents," Brookings, February 13, 2015, www.brookings.edu/blog/fixgov/2015/02/13/measuring-obama-against-the-great-presidents/.

10   Jeffrey E. Cohen, "Presidential Greatness as Seen in the Mass Public: An Extension and Application of the Simonton Model," *Presidential Studies Quarterly* (December 2003), 916. Curt Nichols, "The Presidential Ranking Game: Critical Review and Some New Discoveries," *Presidential Studies Quarterly* (June 2012), 275–99. The Ridings–McIver survey also included five separate dimensions of evaluation (leadership qualities, accomplishments and crisis management, political skill, appointments, and character and integrity). Each of these five dimensions was also found to load onto a single greatness factor, though "character and integrity" was less strongly associated than the other attributes. See Dean Keith Simonton, "Predicting Presidential Performance in the United States: Equation Replication on Recent Survey Results," *Journal of Social Psychology* 141 (June 2001), 296–97.

11   Cohen, "Presidential Greatness as Seen in the Mass Public," 914. Thomas E. Cronin and Michael A. Genovese, *The Paradoxes of the American Presidency* (New York: Oxford University Press, 2004; second edition, 87). The greater number of Republican and conservative scholars in the *Wall Street Journal* survey did pull down the ratings of a few twentieth-century Democratic presidents. Lyndon Johnson, number ten in C-SPAN's 2000 survey, dropped to 17th in the *Wall Street Journal*'s 2000 survey. Woodrow Wilson slid from 6th to 11th and John Kennedy fell furthest of all, from 8th to 18th. Reagan climbed a few spots, from number 11 in C-SPAN's survey to number 8 in the *Wall Street Journal* survey. The biggest gainer, however, in the *Wall Street Journal* survey was Democrat Andrew Jackson, who shot from 13th to 6th. The results of the *Wall Street Journal* survey are reported in James Taranto and Leonard Leo, eds., *Presidential Leadership: Rating the Best and Worst in the White House* (New York: Wall Street Journal Books, 2004), 11–12.

12   This does not apply to presidents still in office or who have only recently left office. In the 2005 *Wall Street Journal* survey, for instance, Republican-leaning scholars placed George W. Bush in the top six, whereas Democratic-leaning scholars put him in the bottom six. These wildly divergent partisan assessments canceled each other out, leaving Bush near the middle of the pack—just below Lyndon Johnson and above William Howard Taft.

13   In the 1996 Schlesinger poll Reagan was rated 25th, and in the 1996 Ridings–McIver poll he was ranked 26th (and near last on "character and integrity").

14   Fred I. Greenstein, *The Hidden-Hand Presidency: Eisenhower as Leader* (New York: Basic Books, 1982). Eisenhower was number 11 in the 1982 Murray–Blessing survey, number 9 in the 1996 Ridings–McIver survey, number 10 in the 1996 Schlesinger poll, number 9 in the 2000 C-SPAN survey and the 2000 *Wall Street Journal* poll, number 8 in the 2005 *Wall Street Journal* poll and the 2009 C-SPAN survey, and number 7 in the 2014 APSA poll. In a recent 2017 C-SPAN survey he reached number 5, behind only TR, FDR, Washington, and Lincoln.

15   William A. Galston, "Between Journalism and History: Evaluating George W. Bush's Presidency," in Maranto, Lansford, and Johnson, eds., *Judging Bush*, 273.

16   Galston, "Between Journalism and History," 273. Also see Clinton Rossiter, *The American Presidency* (New York: Harcourt Brace, 1956), 138 ("A man cannot possibly be judged a great President unless he holds office in great times").

17   David Gray Adler, "Presidential Greatness as an Attribute of Warmaking," *Presidential Studies Quarterly* (September 2003), 476–77.

18   C-SPAN Presidential Historians Survey 2017, www.c-span.org/presidentsurvey2017/?page=overall. The 2014 APSA survey of political scientists ranked Bush 35th of 43 presidents, just ahead of Tyler and right behind Nixon. See Rottinghaus and Vaughn, "Measuring Obama against the Great Presidents."

19   Arthur Schlesinger, Jr., "The Democratic Autocrat," *New York Review of Books*, May 15, 2003, 18–19 (a review of Andrew Burstein's book, *The Passions of Andrew Jackson*). Two earlier

empirical analyses of greatness surveys found a connection between war and greatness rankings: David C. Nice, "The Influence of War and Party System Aging on the Ranking of Presidents," *Western Political Quarterly* 37 (September 1984), 443–55; and Dean Keith Simonton, *Why Presidents Succeed: A Political Psychology of Leadership* (New Haven, CT: Yale University Press, 1987). But if FDR and Lincoln are removed from the equation, the relationship largely disappears. Moreover, a study by Jill Curry and Irwin Morris that analyzes C-SPAN's 2009 greatness survey found that even with FDR and Lincoln included, Simonton's measure of war—based on the length of the war—does not have a statistically significant relationship with greatness. Even more striking, Curry and Morris find that even their own measure, which takes into account the outcome of the war, also fails to predict presidential greatness rankings. See Jill L. Curry and Irwin L. Morris, "Explaining Presidential Greatness: The Roles of Peace and Prosperity," *Presidential Studies Quarterly* (September 2010), 515–30. Another study (Nichols, "The Presidential Ranking Game"), using the same crude dichotomous measure of war (1 = war; 0 = no war) employed by Nice, also found no statistically significant relationship with greatness in either the *Wall Street Journal*'s 2005 survey or C-SPAN's 2009 survey—though a relationship did exist in the earlier 1982 Murray–Blessing survey.

20   In "Explaining Presidential Greatness," Curry and Morris find that economic growth—measured by growth in the per capita real gross domestic product—is positively associated with greatness ratings, even when one controls for length of term in office, which has consistently been found to be a strong predictor of greatness rankings.

21   Richard E. Neustadt, *Presidential Power: The Politics of Leadership from FDR to Carter* (New York: John Wiley, 1980), 5.

22   Stephen Skowronek, *The Politics Presidents Make: Leadership from John Adams to George Bush* (Cambridge, MA: Harvard University Press, 1993). Stephen Skowronek, *Presidential Leadership in Political Time: Reprise and Reappraisal* (Lawrence: University Press of Kansas, 2011; second edition).

23   Skowronek, *The Politics Presidents Make*, 39.

24   Skowronek, *The Politics Presidents Make*, 44.

25   Skowronek, *The Politics Presidents Make*, 45.

26   For Skowronek's analysis of Obama see *Presidential Leadership in Political Time*, ch. 6.

27   On the high (and contradictory) public expectations of presidents, see Cronin and Genovese, *Paradoxes of the American Presidency*, esp. 72–86.

28   See Cronin and Genovese, *Paradoxes of the American Presidency*, 84.

29   See Neil Reedy and Jeremy Johnson, "Evaluating Presidents," in *Judging Bush*, 3.

30   Ron Chernow, *Alexander Hamilton* (New York: Penguin, 2004), 290, 510.

31   Don E. Fehrenbacher, *Lincoln in Text and Context: Collected Essays* (Palo Alto, CA: Stanford University Press, 1987), 207. Richard Ellis and Aaron Wildavsky, *Dilemmas of Presidential Leadership: From Washington through Lincoln* (New Brunswick, NJ: Transaction Publishers, 1989), 190, 194–95.

32   Lincoln to Horace Greeley, August 22, 1862, in Roy P. Basler, ed., *The Collected Works of Abraham Lincoln* (New Brunswick, NJ: Rutgers University Press, 1953), 5: 388–89. Benjamin P. Thomas and Harold M. Hyman, *Stanton: The Life and Times of Lincoln's Secretary of War* (New York: Knopf, 1962), 391.

33   Ellis and Wildavsky, *Dilemmas of Presidential Leadership*, 191, 196–97.

34   Cronin and Genovese, *Paradoxes of the American Presidency*, 78. James MacGregor Burns and Susan Dunn, "It Worked for FDR," *Los Angeles Times*, November 8, 2007, http://articles. latimes.com/2007/nov/08/news/OE-BURNS8.

35   Doris Kearns Goodwin, *No Ordinary Time: Franklin and Eleanor Roosevelt, The Home Front and World War II* (New York: Simon & Schuster, 1994), 311, 78 (quoting Raymond Moley).

36 Leonard D. White, *The Jeffersonians: A Study in Administrative History, 1801–1829* (New York: Free Press, 1951), 424. Ellis and Wildavsky, *Dilemmas of Presidential Leadership*, 74.

37 John M. Murrin et al., *Liberty, Equality, Power: A History of the American People, Volume I: To 1877* (Boston: Thomson Wadsworth, 2008; fifth edition), 242.

38 Leonard W. Levy, *Jefferson and Civil Liberties: The Darker Side* (New York: Quadrangle, 1963), 138–39. Robert W. Tucker and David C. Hendrickson, *Empire of Liberty: The Statecraft of Thomas Jefferson* (New York: Oxford University Press, 1990), 325 n45.

39 Robert M. Johnstone, Jr., *Jefferson and the Presidency: Leadership in the Young Republic* (Ithaca, NY: Cornell University Press, 1978), 286–88. Levy, *Jefferson and Civil Liberties*, 139.

40 A full list of the defeated treaties can be found at www.senate.gov/artandhistory/history/common/briefing/Treaties.htm.

41 James David Barber, *The Presidential Character: Predicting Performance in the White House* (Englewood Cliffs, NJ: Prentice Hall, 1992; fourth edition), 17. Juliette L. George and Alexander L. George, *Woodrow Wilson and Colonel House: A Personality Study* (New York: Dover, 1964), 310.

42 Barber, *The Presidential Character*, 39.

43 Barber, *The Presidential Character*, 57. Juliette L. George and Alexander L. George, "*Woodrow Wilson and Colonel House*: A Reply to Weinstein, Anderson, and Link," *Political Science Quarterly* 96 (Winter 1981–1982), 642. Edward A. Weinstein, J.W. Anderson, and Arthur S. Link, "Woodrow Wilson's Political Personality: A Reappraisal," *Political Science Quarterly* 93 (Winter 1978–1979), 585–98. Peter Gay, *Freud: A Life for Our Time* (New York: Norton, 1988), 558–59.

44 George and George, *Woodrow Wilson and Colonel House*, 310–13.

45 Neustadt, *Presidential Power*, esp. 115–21 (quotation at 119). The 1996 survey by Ridings and McIver evaluated presidents on five different dimensions, including political skill. Although FDR was second in the overall ratings, he was ranked first on political skill (and 15th on character and integrity). See Ridings and McIver, *Rating the Presidents*, 196.

46 Susan Dunn, *Roosevelt's Purge: How FDR Fought to Change the Democratic Party* (Cambridge, MA: Harvard University Press, 2010), 6.

47 Dunn, *Roosevelt's Purge*, 160–63. James MacGregor Burns, *Roosevelt: The Lion and the Fox* (New York: Harcourt, 1956), 362–63.

48 Burns, *Lion and the Fox*, 363. Sidney M. Milkis, *The President and the Parties: The Transformation of the American Party System since the New Deal* (New York: Oxford University Press, 1993), 87.

49 Burns, *Lion and the Fox*, 346. Dunn, *Roosevelt's Purge*, 29.

50 Milkis, *The President and the Parties*, 87, 90–92. Charles M. Price and Joseph Boskin, "The Roosevelt Purge: A Reappraisal," *Journal of Politics* 28 (August, 1966), 660–70.

51 Milkis, *The President and the Parties*, 94–96. Andrew E. Busch, "The New Deal Comes to a Screeching Halt in 1938," May 2006, Ashbrook Center for Public Affairs, www.ashbrook.org/publicat/oped/busch/06/1938.html.

52 James Bryce, *The American Commonwealth* (Indianapolis: Liberty Fund, 1995), 1:75; also see 1:71.

53 Nelson W. Polsby, *The Consequences of Party Reform* (New York: Oxford University Press, 1982).

54 John Balz, "Ready to Lead on Day One: Predicting Presidential Greatness from Political Experience," *PS: Political Science and Politics* 43 (July 2010), 487–92.

55 Daniel Stone, "God of All Things: Why the Modern Presidency May Be Too Much for One Person to Handle," *Newsweek*, November 22, 2010, www.newsweek.com/2010/11/13/is-the-presidency-too-big-a-job.html.

56 Stone, "God of All Things."

57 Stone, "God of All Things."

58 Bryce, *The American Commonwealth*, 1:72.

59 Aaron Wildavsky, *The Beleaguered Presidency* (New Brunswick, NJ: Transaction Publishers, 1992), x.

60 On Truman through Obama, see Gallup Job Approval Center, www.gallup.com/poll/124922/Presidential-Approval-Center.aspx. On FDR, see Franklin D. Roosevelt Presidential Approval, Roper Center for Public Opinion Research, https://presidential.roper.center/. Also see Burns, *Lion and the Fox*, 338.

61 James P. Pfiffner, *The Character Factor: How We Judge America's Presidents* (College Station: Texas A&M University Press, 2004), 74–79 (Bradley quoted at 78–79). Also see James N. Giglio, *The Presidency of John F. Kennedy* (Lawrence: University Press of Kansas, 1991), 267; and Thomas C. Reeves, *A Question of Character: A Life of John F. Kennedy* (New York: Free Press, 1991), 240–42.

62 Reeves, *A Question of Character*, 49–50, 127. Richard Reeves, "John F. Kennedy, 1961–1963," in Robert A. Wilson, ed., *Character above All: Ten Presidents from FDR to George Bush* (New York: Touchstone, 1995), 85–86.

63 Bartholomew Sparrow, "Con: Resolved, the Media Are Too Hard on Presidents," in Richard J. Ellis and Michael Nelson, eds., *Debating the Presidency: Conflicting Perspectives on the American Executive* (Washington, DC: CQ Press, 2006), 68–74.

64 These results are from a 2004 Pew survey of 500 national and local reporters, editors, and executives, available at http://stateofthemedia.org/2006/journalist-survey-intro/survey-findings/section-ii-covering-the-president-and-the-campaign.

65 "Americans Back Bin Laden Mission," www.gallup.com/poll/147395/americans-back-bin-laden-mission-credit-military-cia.aspx.

66 Newman and Siegle, "The Polarized Presidency," 342. Also see Alan I. Abramowitz, *The Disappearing Center: Engaged Citizens, Polarization, and American Democracy* (New Haven, CT: Yale University Press, 2010), 5; and Martin P. Wattenberg, *Is Voting for Young People?* (New York: Pearson Longman, 2007), esp. 43–50.

67 Skowronek, *The Politics Presidents Make*, 55. Skowronek, *Presidential Leadership in Political Time*, 188–89. Also see Marc Landy and Sidney M. Milkis, *Presidential Greatness* (Lawrence: University Press of Kansas, 2000), 219–25.

68 Skowronek, *The Politics Presidents Make*, 56, 443–44.

69 Skowronek, *The Politics Presidents Make*, 56–57, 444–45.

70 Skowronek, *Presidential Leadership in Political Time*, esp. 193–94.

71 Skowronek, *The Politics Presidents Make*, 445.

72 The first quotation is from the preface, written in June 2007, to the first edition of Skowronek, *Presidential Leadership in Political Time*, xii–xiii. Skowronek, *The Politics Presidents Make*, 444. Also see Walter Dean Burnham, *The Current Crisis in American Politics* (New York: Oxford University Press, 1983).

73 Preface to the first edition of Skowronek, *Presidential Leadership in Political Time*, x.

74 Skowronek, *Presidential Leadership in Political Time*, 177–78.

75 Stephen Skowronek, "Is Donald Trump the Great Disrupter? Probably Not," *Washington Post*, April 24, 2017. Also see Julia Azari, "Trump's Presidency Signals the End of the Reagan Era," *Vox*, December 1, 2016.

INDEX

Note: page numbers followed by 'f' refer to figures and photographs, followed by 'n' refer to notes, followed by 't' refer to tables